The Chartered Institute of Marketing

Chartered Graduate Diploma in Marketing

STUDY TEXT

Managing Corporate Reputation

For exams up to and including June 2011

First edition July 2009

ISBN 9780 7517 6819 0

British Library Cataloguing-in-Publication Data
A catalogue record for this book
is available from the British Library

Published by

BPP Learning Media Ltd
Aldine House, Aldine Place
London W12 8AA

www.bpp.com/learningmedia

Printed in Great Britain by
Hobbs the Printers Ltd
Totton
Hampshire

We are grateful to the Chartered Institute of Marketing for
permission to reproduce in this text the syllabus, tutor's
guidance notes and past examination questions. We are also
grateful to Superbrands and The Centre for Brand Analysis for
their support of our online feature 'A Word From...'

Author:
CIM Publishing Manager: Dr Kellie Vincent
Template design: Yolanda Moore
Photography: Terence O'Loughlin

Your learning materials, published by BPP Learning Media Ltd,
are printed on paper sourced from sustainable, managed
forests.

Contents

Introduction

• Aim of the Study Text • Studying for CIM qualifications • The Chartered Postgraduate Diploma Syllabus • CIM Magic Formula • A guide to the features of the Study Text • A note on pronouns • Additional resources • Media • Your personal study plan v

Chapters

1 Aim of the Study Text

This book has been deliberately referred to as a 'Study Text' rather than *text book*, because it is designed to help you through your specific CIM Chartered Postgraduate Diploma in Marketing studies. It covers Unit 4 Managing Corporate Reputation.

So, why is it similar to but not actually a text book? Well, the CIM has identified key texts that you should become familiar with. The purpose of this workbook is not to replace these texts but to pick out the important parts that you will definitely need to know in order to pass, simplify these elements and, to suggest a few areas within the texts that will provide good additional reading but that are not absolutely essential. We will also suggest a few other sources and useful press and CIM publications which are worth reading.

We know some of you will prefer to read text books from cover to cover while others amongst you will prefer to pick out relevant parts or dip in and out of the various topics. This Text will help you to ensure that if you are a 'cover to cover' type, then you will not miss the emphasis of the syllabus. If you are a 'dip in and out' type, then we will make sure that you find the parts which are essential for you to know. Unlike a standard *text book* which will have been written to be used across a range of alternative qualifications, this *Study Text* has been specifically compiled for your CIM course, therefore if a topic appears in this book then it is part of the syllabus and therefore will be a subject the examiners could potentially test you.

Throughout the Study Text you will find real examples of marketing in practice as well as key concepts highlighted. The Study Text also aims to encourage you to not only learn the theory but also provides cues and helps you to plan your own project work. You should use the activities to help you to build a portfolio of your own organisation.

2 Studying for CIM qualifications

There are a few key points to remember as you study for your CIM qualification:

(a)   You are studying for a **professional** qualification. This means that you are required to use professional language and adopt a business approach in your work.

(b)   You are expected to show that you have 'read widely'. Make sure that you read the quality press (and don't skip the business pages), read Marketing, The Marketer, Research and Marketing Week avidly.

(c)   Become aware of the marketing initiatives you come across on a daily basis, for example, when you go shopping look around and think about why the store layout is as it is, consider the messages, channel choice and timings of ads when you are watching TV. It is surprising how much you will learn just by taking an interest in the marketing world around you.

(d)   Get to know the way CIM write its exam papers and assignments. It uses a specific approach which is referred to as The Magic Formula to ensure a consistent approach when designing assessment materials. Make sure you are fully aware of this as it will help you interpret what the examiner is looking for (a full description of the Magic Formula appears later and is heavily featured within the chapters).

(e)   Learn how to use Harvard referencing. This is explained in detail in our CIM Chartered Postgraduate Diploma in Marketing – Stage One Assessment Workbook.

(f)   Ensure that you read very carefully all assessment details sent to you from the CIM. It is very strict with regard to deadlines, eg completing the correct paperwork to accompany your assignment. Failing to meet any assessment entry deadlines or completing written work on time will mean that you will have to wait for the next round of assessment dates and will need to pay the relevant assessment fees again.

3 The Chartered Postgraduate Diploma Syllabus

The Chartered Postgraduate Diploma in Marketing is aimed at Brand Manager, Strategic Marketing, Marketing Manager, Business Development Manager, middle to senior Marketing Managers. If you are a graduate, you will be expected to have covered a minimum of half your credits in marketing subjects. You are therefore expected at this level of the qualification to demonstrate the ability to manage marketing resources and contribute to business decisions from a marketing perspective or senior marketing management and pass Entry test to Level 7.

The aim of the qualification is to provide the knowledge and skills for you to develop an 'ability to do' in relation to marketing planning. CIM qualifications concentrate on applied marketing within real workplaces.

The complete Chartered Postgraduate qualification is split into two stages. Stage 1 compromises with four units. Stage 2 is a work-based project to enable students to gain Chartered Marketer status immediately.

The Stage 1 qualification is made from four units:

- Unit 1 Emerging Themes
- Unit 2 Analysis and Decision
- Unit 3 Marketing Leadership and Planning
- Unit 4 Managing Corporate Reputation

The syllabus as provided by the CIM can be found below with reference to our coverage within this Study Text.

Unit characteristics

The strength and magnitude of an organisation's reputation represents the way in which a complex range of stakeholders perceive an organisation, entity or destination. All too often, a gap develops between the way an organisation intends to be seen and the reality, namely the way stakeholders actually perceive it. This can be due to a range of forces, some slow, foreseeable and manageable, and some sudden, unforeseen and relatively unmanageable. All can result in organisational underperformance, destabilisation, financial difficulties, leadership change, a fall in market valuation, and even difficulty in raising finance or recruiting the right personnel. This unit explores ways in which organisations can minimise the gap and avoid these potentially serious issues.

Overarching learning outcomes

By the end of this unit students should be able to:

- Critically evaluate the way organisations develop their identities and some organisations use these to form images and assign reputational status

- Critically analyse the elements that contribute to the identity that an organisation projects to its stakeholders, sometimes through a corporate brand

- Critically evaluate linkage between how an organisation wants to be seen and how it is seen, namely corporate communications

Students will normally base their learning and development of these issues on an organisation. However, some may choose to use this unit to explore the reputational development of a place. This might involve for example, a tourist destination (eg country or region), a business area (eg seaport or park) or a city or town. The detail specified in this syllabus is based on ideas, practice and the research literature relating to corporate branding, communications and reputation.

Part 1 – Understanding the nature and characteristics of reputational management (weighting 25%)

SECTION 1 – Developing the rationale for managing corporate reputation

		Covered in chapter(s)
1.1.1	Critically evaluate the context and concepts relating to corporate reputation: • Development, evolution and perception • Corporate image versus corporate identity • Context: industrial, not-for-profit, competitive, societal, political • Criteria: credibility, trustworthiness, reliability and responsiveness	1
1.1.2	Justify the importance and significance of managing an organisation's corporate reputation: • Financial performance • Managing shareholder value • Improved competitiveness • Relative ease of recruitment	1
1.1.3	Identify the forces that can influence an organisation's reputation, and develop forecasts concerning their level of current and potential influence: • External forces: environmental, financial, political, social, industry-wide, legal, technological, community-based • Relational: competitive and collaborative strategies, resources, mergers/acquisitions, repositioning • Internal forces: resources, political, strategy, structure, behaviour, communication climate	2

SECTION 2 – Determining the scope of corporate reputation

		Covered in chapter(s)
1.2.1	Critically assess the compatibility of an organisation's corporate strategy, structure, systems and culture with its positioning and reputation: • Vision, mission, values, objectives • Organisational structure and culture • Organisational communication climate • Perception and positioning	3
1.2.2	Develop processes leading to the identification of key external and internal stakeholders, and understand the nature of associated communication programmes: • Investors – investor relations • Customers – marketing communications • Employees – internal communications • Government – public affairs • The public – public relations	9, 10

1.2.3	Propose and justify the use of a portfolio of broad indicators to evaluate the strength of an organisation's reputation:	5

- ROI
- Brand equity
- Shareholder value
- Media comment

Part 2 – Managing the dimensions of an organisation's reputation (weighting 25%)

SECTION 1 – Understanding the current corporate reputation

		Covered in chapter(s)
2.1.1	Critically evaluate the corporate 'character' (personality) of an organisation	3

- Organisation culture
- Strategy; mission, values and positioning, formulation process
- Organisational structure
- Communication climate

2.1.2	Critically assess the strength and potential of the corporate identity and/or brand	3

- Meaning: visual, organisational, corporate, visual identity versus strategic identity
- Identity mix: behaviour, communication and symbolism
- Brand strategy: structure, architecture and promise
- Systems and processes, eg formalistic or organic, developing or established, communication culture
- Measurement of reputation using commercial systems, eg Brand Asset Valuator, BrandZ, Equitrend, Brand Power, USA's Most Admired, Reputation Quotient, RepTrack

SECTION 2 – Developing corporate brands

		Covered in chapter(s)
2.2.1	Critically evaluate the nature of corporate brands and make recommendations concerning any gap between identity and image:	1

- Definitions
- Elements: differentiation, transferability, psychic value, recall, premium
- Typologies: Olins, Kammerer, van Riel
- Drivers: strategy, organisational, employee, value
- Levels of corporate endorsement
- Rebranding

2.2.2	Propose changes to enhance the systems, structure and processes necessary to support the management of corporate reputation:	4

- Communication audits
- Targeting stakeholder groups
- Targeting employees
- Reputation platforms
- Corporate stories and story telling
- Corporate positioning

Part 3 – Developing effective corporate communications (weighting 50%)

SECTION 1 – Determining the dimensions of corporate communications

		Covered in chapter(s)
3.1.1	Critically appraise the nature and characteristics of corporate communications: • Definition • Corporate communications mix: management, organisational, marketing • Principal activities: internal, investor, marketing, public affairs, issues management	6
3.1.2	Critically assess the different reasons for using corporate communication: • Aims and purpose: four visions • Tasks, eg informing, exploring, relating, negotiating and mixed formats • Circumstances, eg periodic reporting, crisis, merger/acquisition, repositioning, strategic change, decline • Stimulating change, eg knowledge, attitudes, behaviour	6
3.1.3	Propose what is to be communicated to particular stakeholders and how to measure the effectiveness of the communications used: • Vision, mission and values • Identity or brand • Ethics, CSR, sustainability and environmental issues • Strategic repositioning • Measuring the effectiveness of corporate communications: eg Kelly Repertory Grids, Natural Grouping, Q-Sort, Photo-Sorting, Attitude Measurement, Card Sorting	6

SECTION 2 – Corporate communication strategies and methods

		Covered in chapter(s)
3.2.1	Critically evaluate the different methods through which corporate communications can be delivered in order to deliver effective messages and enhance reputation: • Tools: corporate advertising, public relations, sponsorships • Media: offline and digital/online • Symbolism: logos, names, signage, music, styling, uniforms, design and architecture • Behaviour: employees, management performance, corporate, brand, communications	7
3.2.2	Formulate approaches to corporate communications that are investor-focused and contextually determined: • Roles of investor relations, eg compliance, relationships, building (reputation) • Purpose: create demand for shares, reduce churn, present past performance, predict future performance, manage perceptions	9

3.2.3	Formulate approaches to corporate communications that are customer-focused and contextually determined:	8
	• Tools: advertising, sales promotion, personal selling, marketing, public relations	
	• Media: offline/online	
	• Messages: informational and emotional dimensions of engagement	
	• Experience marketing	
3.2.4	Formulate approaches to corporate communications that are employee-focused and contextually determined:	10
	• Types: structure, flow, content and climate	
	• Roles: efficiency, shared meaning, connectivity, satisfaction	
	• Intellectual and emotional engagement	
	• Messages: information and emotional dimensions of engagement within the organisation	
3.2.5	Formulate approaches to corporate communications that are government-focused and contextually determined:	9
	• Breadth: regulators, legislators, elected officials and appointed representatives	
	• Public affairs	
	• Lobbying, relationships, timing and objectivity	
3.2.6	Formulate approaches designed to defend an organisation's reputation:	10
	• Nature of issues management: detection, marshalling and strategy	
	• Crisis communications: nature, risk analysis, agenda setting, response and rumour management	

BPP LEARNING MEDIA

4 CIM Magic Formula

The Magic Formula is a tool used by the CIM to help both examiners write exam and assignment questions and you to more easily interpret what you are being asked to write about. It is useful for helping you to check that you are using an appropriate balance between theory and practice for your particular level of qualification.

Contrary to the title, there is nothing mystical about the Magic Formula and simply by knowing it (or even mentioning it in an assessment) will not automatically secure a pass. What it does do, however, is to help you to check that you are presenting your answers in an appropriate format, including enough marketing theory and applying it to a real marketing context or issue. Students working through the range of CIM qualifications, are expected to evaluate to a greater extent and apply a more demanding range of marketing decisions as they progress from the lower to the higher levels. At the Chartered Postgraduate Diploma level, there will be an emphasis on evaluation while at the Introductory Certificate level the emphasis is on developing concepts.

Graphically, the Magic Formula for the Chartered Postgraduate Diploma in Marketing is shown below:

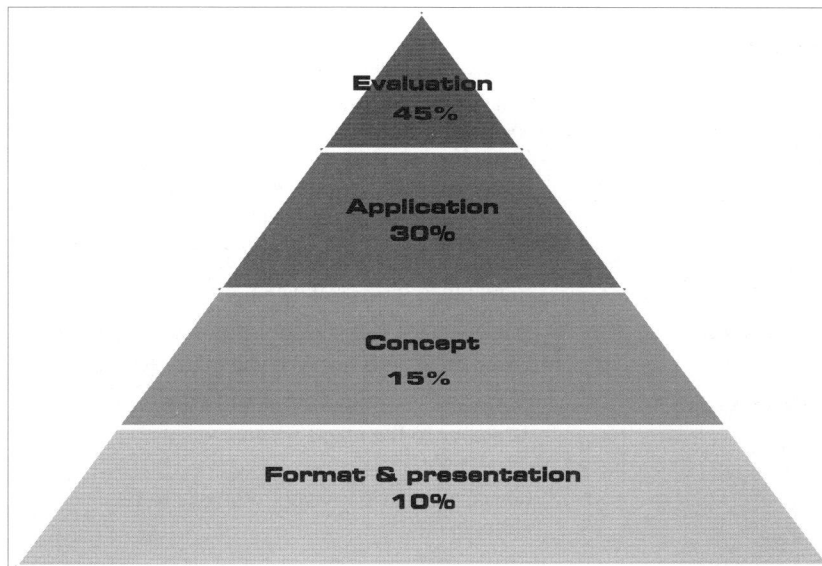

The Magic Formula for the Chartered Postgraduate Diploma in Marketing

You can see from pyramid that for the Chartered Postgraduate Diploma marks are awarded in the following proportions:

- ## Format and Presentation – 10%

  Remember, you are expected to present your work professionally which means that it should ALWAYS be typed and attention should be paid to making it look as visually appealing as possible even in an exam situation. It also means that the CIM will stipulate the format that you should present your work in. The assessment formats you will be given will be varied and can include things like reports to write, slides to prepare, e-mails, memos, formal letters, press releases, discussion documents, briefing papers, agendas, and newsletters.

- ## Concept – 15%

  Concept refers to your ability to state, recall and describe marketing theory. The definition of marketing is a core CIM syllabus topic. If we take this as an example, you would be expected to recognise, recall, and write this definition to a word perfect standard to gain the full marks for concept. Understanding marketing concepts is clearly the main area where marks will be given within your assessment.

- ## Application – 30%

  Application-based marks are given for your ability to apply marketing theories to real-life marketing situations. For example, you may be asked to discuss the definition of marketing, and how it is applied within your own organisation. Within this sort of question 30% of the marks would have been awarded within the 'concept' aspect of the Magic Formula. You will gain the rest of the marks through your ability to evaluate to what extent the concept is applied within your own organisation. Here you are not only using the definition but are applying it in order to consider the market orientation of the company.

- ## Evaluation – 45%

    Evaluation is the ability to asses the value or worth of something sometimes through careful consideration or related advantages and disadvantages or weighing-up of alternatives. Results from your evaluation should enable you to discuss the importance of an issue using evidence to support your opinions.

    Using the example of you being asked whether or not your organisation adopts a marketing approach, if you were asked to 'evaluate' this, it would be expected that you would provide reasons and specific examples why you thought they might take this approach but to also consider issues why they may not be marketing-oriented before coming to a final conclusion.

5 A guide to the features of the Study Text

Each of the chapter features (see below) will help you to break down the content into manageable chunks and ensure that you are developing the skills required for a professional qualification.

Chapter feature	Relevance and how you should use it	Corresponding icon
Chapter topic list	Study the list. Each numbered topic denotes a numbered section in the chapter. Identified as a key concept within the syllabus	–
Introduction	Shows why topics need to be studied and is a route guide through the chapter.	–
Syllabus-linked Learning Objectives	Outlines what you should learn within the chapter based on what is required within the syllabus	–
Format & Presentation	Outlines a key marketing presentation format with reference to the Magic Formula	
Concept	Key concept to learn with reference to the Magic Formula	
Application	An example of applied marketing with reference to the Magic Formula	
Evaluation	An example of evaluation with reference to the Magic Formula	
Activity	An application-based activity for you to complete	
Key text links	Emphasises key parts to read in a range of other texts and other learning resources	
Marketing at work	A short case study to illustrate marketing practice	
Assessment tip	Key advice based on the assessment	
Quick quiz	Use this to check your learning	
Objective check	Review what you have learnt	

6 A note on pronouns

On occasions in this Study Text, 'he' is used for 'he or she', 'him' for 'him or her' and so forth. While we try to avoid this practice it is sometimes necessary for reasons of style. No prejudice or stereotyping accounting to sex is intended or assumed.

7 Additional resources

7.1 The CIM's supplementary reading list

We have already mentioned that the CIM requires you to demonstrate your ability to 'read widely' . The CIM issue an extensive reading list for each unit. For this unit they recommend supplementary reading. Within the Study Text we have highlighted within the wider reading links specific topics where these resources would help. The CIM's supplementary reading list for this unit is:

van Riel, C.B.M. and Fombrum, C.J. (2007) Essentials of corporate communications. Routledge

Davies, G. et al (2003) Corporate reputation and competitiveness. Routledge

Balmer, J.M.T. and Greyser, S.A. (2003) Revealing the corporation. Routledge

Cornelissen, J. (2008) Corporate communications: theory and practice. 2nd edition. London, Sage

Doorley, J. and Garcia, H.F. (2007) Reputation management. Routledge

Elliot, R. and Percy, L. (2007) Strategic brand management. Oxford, Oxford University Press

Griffin, A. (2008) New strategies for reputation management. London, Kogan Page.[ISBN 978-0749450076, £30.99 New edition due September 2009]

Ind, N. (2007) Living brand. 3rd edition. London, Kogan Page

Kapferer, J. (2008) The new strategic brand management. 4th rev edition. London, Kogan Page

Kotler, P. and Pfoertsch, W. (2006) B2B brand management: the success dimensions of business brands. Berlin, Springer-Verlag. [ISBN 978 3540253600, £29.50]

Melewar, T.C. (2007) Facets of corporate identity, communication and reputation. London, Routledge

Oliver, S. (2007) Public relations strategy. London, Kogan Page

van Riel, C.B.M. (1995) Principles of corporate communications. Prentice Hall

Oliver, S. (2004) Handbook of corporate communication and public relations. London, Routledge

7.2 Assessment materials from BPP Learning Media

To help you pass the entire Stage 1 of the Chartered Postgraduate Diploma in Marketing we have created a complete study package. **The Chartered Postgraduate Diploma Assessment Workbook** covers all four units for the Postgraduate Diploma level. Practice question and answers, tips on tackling assignments and work-based projects are written to help you succeed in your assessments.

This unit is assessed by an assignment with a number of compulsory tasks.

Our A6 set of spiral bound **Passcards** are handy revision cards and are ideal to reinforce key topics for the pre-seen case study exam.

7.3 BPP Learning Media's Online Material

To complement this Study Text, our Assessment Workbook and Passcards we have also produced some online materials for both students and tutors. These materials have not been designed to remain static but we will be developing more and adding to the content over time. If you have purchased a product within our CIM range then you will be able to access the online materials for free at:

www.bpp.com/lm/cim

Typical content will include:

- Links to the most useful web-sites for marketers
- Syllabus links to key marketing developments and 'big news' stories
- Proforma's for key marketing documents such as Marketing Plans, Research Proposals etc
- Tutor only content including slides and case studies

We are also pleased to announce an exciting partnerships with Superbrands and The Centre for Brand Analysis to bring you a new online feature titled 'A Word From . . .'. This feature is covered online and from time-to-time will include more material gathered from the Superbrand Marketers.

8   Your personal study plan

Preparing a study plan (and sticking to it) is one of the key elements to learning success.

Think about the number of hours you should dedicate to your studies. Guided learning hours will include time spent in lesson, working on fully prepared distance learning materials, formal workshops and work set by your tutor. We also know that to be successful, students should spend *at least* the same amount of time spent working through guided learning conducting self-study. This means that for the entire qualification with four units you should spend time working in a tutor-guided manner and at least the same time completing recommended reading, working on assignments, and revising for exams. This Study Text will help you to organise this portion of self-study time.

Now think about the exact amount of time you have (don't forget you will still need some leisure time!) and complete the following tables to help you keep to a schedule.

	Date	Duration in weeks
Course start		
Course finish		Total weeks of course:

Assignment deadline	Assignment prep commence	Total weeks to complete assignment:

Content chapter coverage plan

Chapter	To be completed by	Revised ?
1 Managing corporate reputation		
2 Influences on corporate reputation		
3 Organisational character or personality		
4 Corporate identity and branding		
5 Evaluating reputational strength		
6 Corporate communication		
7 Developing corporate communication		
8 Customer, public and media relations		
9 Investor and government relations		
10 Internal communications		
11 Defending reputation		

Chapter 1

Managing corporate reputation

Topic list

Introduction

This chapter sets the scene for the management of corporate reputation, and covers some of the key concepts set out in part 1 of the *Managing Corporate Reputation* syllabus.

We start in sections 1 and 2 by outlining the nature of corporate reputation, image and identity. The terminology in this area varies across the literature, and we attempt to give a clear foundation from which you can discuss and examine these core concepts as you proceed through the module.

In section 3, we explore the rationale for managing corporate reputation, explaining its increasing significance and making the 'business case' for the management of reputation at a strategic level in the organisation.

In section 4, we give an overview of what makes a 'good' reputation: what criteria will an organisation (and its various target audiences) use to gauge reputation? These criteria will be explored further in Chapter 5, where we look in more detail at the measurement and evaluation of reputational strength.

In the phraseology of the guidance notes to the first section of the syllabus, this chapter covers: 'This is what corporate reputation is, and this is why we do it...' Chapter 2 will go on to complete the syllabus summary: '... and this is what affects it.'

Syllabus-linked learning objectives

By the end of the chapter you will be able to:

Learning objectives	Syllabus link
1 Explain the meaning of corporate reputation, image and identity in various contexts	1.1.1
2 Explain key elements considered to constitute corporate reputation	1.1.1
3 Present a rationale for an organisation's directors to support the proactive and overt management of corporate reputation	1.1.2

1 What is corporate reputation management?

Reputation scholar Charles Fombrun offers an initial working definition of reputation as the sum of the images various constituencies (or stakeholders) have of an organisation:

KEY CONCEPT

concept

'Corporate reputation is the **overall estimation** in which a company is held by its constituents. A corporate reputation represents the **'net' affective or emotional reaction** – good-bad, weak or strong – of customers, investors, employees and general public to the company's name' (Fombrun, 1996, p. 9).

We will build on this definition as we proceed through the chapter, but it is worth starting out with the understanding that the reputation of an organisation – and indeed that of a person or a place – is a kind of aggregate of the perceptions built up in the minds of interested parties: how others 'think of you' or your character or standing, as an overall assessment. Varey (2002, p. 193) suggests that: 'Corporate reputation is an all-encompassing term for what employees think about their employer, what customers think about their provider, what investors think about their shareholding and so on.'

As we will see, reputations are built up over time, as people have positive and negative direct experiences of the organisation, and receive positive and negative messages from it or about it – each reinforcing or adjusting their overall evaluation. Reputations are therefore built on both the reality of what an organisation is (or how people experience it), and the messages that are conveyed by and about the organisation, both of which shape the perceptions of its various stakeholders. Doorley & Garcia (2007, p. 4) express this by the simple formula:

Reputation = Sum of Images = (Performance and Behaviour) + Communication

As Varey *(ibid)* argues: 'Reputation does not originate from the corporate communications office, or the marketing plan, or individual behaviour. It is not a fabricatable artefact that can be used to manipulate others' feelings, in the way that advertising can be (mis)used. Reputation springs from experiences, thought processes and values of people who see themselves as stakeholders of a business.'

Throughout this Study Text, we will emphasise that reputation management requires attention to both the reality of performance and behaviour and the messages conveyed by corporate stakeholder communication and stakeholders' communications among themselves. It is not just about marketing-controlled 'spin'!

ACTIVITY 1

application

Quick 'spot check' to start your thinking on corporate reputation. In two or three words, or a short sentence, write down your answers to the following questions.

- What kind of employer is your work organisation?
- What do you think of your banking services provider?
- If you own shares in a company, what is your overall impression of your investment?
- Where would you want to go on your next overseas holiday, and why?
- If you had a significant sum of money to donate to charity, which charity would you choose and why?
- Is there an organisation that you would definitely not do business with? If so, why?

1.1 Corporate reputation management

Reputation has long been recognised as an asset. Shakespeare's Othello conveys something of this value when he says: 'He who steals my purse steals trash... But he that filches from me my good name... makes me poor indeed.'

Broadly speaking, a positive reputation is a key source of distinctiveness for an organisation, which can differentiate it from its competitors; produce support for and trust in the organisation and its products (which in turn may enhance its stability and resilience in times of change and crisis); and help it to attract and retain quality staff, business partners and allies (Fombrun & van Riel, 2004).

Conversely, a negative reputation – or reputational damage – can erode support and trust for the organisation and its products; create negative expectations (which in turn encourage negative perceptions); attract hostile scrutiny from the media and pressure groups; and damage the organisation's relationships with its key stakeholders (which in turn can have negative affects on its productivity, profitability, share price and so on).

Reputation is thus a significant asset, and one that is highly vulnerable to risk: it is often said that reputations are hard won – and easily lost. But for a long time it was thought of as an **intangible or 'soft' asset**: something that could not be measured or quantified – and therefore could not be systematically managed. Until comparatively recently, many corporations made little attempt proactively to manage how they were regarded by their stakeholders, other than customers. Even when reputation-damaging crises arose (such as a product recall, exposure of unethical dealings or an incident of environmental damage), many attempted to 'ride out the storm' by ignoring criticism or making token attempts to put a positive 'spin' on the issue to selected audiences.

'Although CEOs agree that reputation has a value – is an asset – few firms actually treat it as such. Few companies or non-profits take a **rigorous, quantifiable approach** to reputation management – measuring, monitoring and managing reputation assets and liabilities – yet such an approach is intrinsic to the concept of asset management. Most organisations have no idea what their reputations are **worth**, yet reasonable measurements (absolute or relative) can be agreed upon and taken. Most companies do not have a system in place for **regular, periodic accountability** on variations in reputation, yet without such a system opportunities will be missed and problems will become magnified. Measurement, acknowledgement and planning make possible **proactive behaviours and communications** to take advantage of reputational opportunities and minimise problems – thereby building reputational capital.' (Doorley & Garcia, *ibid*, p. 4).

This picture has begun to change, as corporate scandals have demonstrated the importance of building, maintaining and defending reputation; as the public and other secondary stakeholders have demanded greater governance, accountability and responsibility from organisations; and as communications professionals and academic researchers have argued that it is possible – and necessary – to integrate, quantify and manage reputational factors, as an approach to both asset and risk management. The emerging consensus, reflected in the inclusion of this module in your studies, is that corporate reputation management should be a significant part of a **strategic communication** and **stakeholder relationship** management agenda.

The fact is, however, that an organisation will *have* an image and reputation in the public sphere, whether it attempts to manage it or not. An organisation cannot *not* have a reputation: the question is whether it attempts to control, maintain, improve or defend the reputation that it has.

1.2 Development of reputation management as a discipline

The evolution and perception of reputation management as a discipline, over time, can be traced in various ways.

1.2.1 Development via Public Relations (PR)

Academics and practitioners in the discipline of Public Relations see the origins of reputation management in the role of what is variously called public relations, or corporate or public affairs. Davies *et al.* (2003, p. 24) point out that 'reputation management is not new. Organisations, individuals, even informal groups have been concerned about the way others see them from time immemorial. What has changed is the way organisations have approached their management of this area and the importance they give to it.'

The traditional perception of Public Relations within organisations is associated almost entirely with **media relations** (such as the preparation and placing of press releases). PR is often organised as a sub-unit of marketing or a specialism outsourced to agencies: PR managers often have a background in journalism or media. 'PR is a function that is rarely seen as strategic in nature. While there may be an overarching sense of **supporting the corporate image**, much of PR is short-term and tactical in nature.' (Davies *et al.*, *op cit*). PR also has its own reputation problem, often being negatively associated with public suspicion of 'puff' (making exaggerated or misleading claims) and 'spin' (manipulating information and perceptions to make negative incidents and issues reflect well on the organisation) – creating resistance to press and advertising messages.

These factors, together with the enduring importance of the media as a mediator of corporate communication, have created pressure from within public relations to **broaden the scope** of PR activity and increase its **strategic integration**. 'As the term PR becomes ever more closely connected to negative terms such as 'spin doctor' and publicity, practitioners have differentiated themselves to signify a more strategic approach to communications management and management of reputation... Research on behalf of the Corporate Communications Institute in 2004 looked at the primary roles of communications practitioners in the Fortune 1000. The highest figure (18.4%) said managing company reputation was their primary role.' (Franklin *et al.*, 2009, p. 196)

Reputation management is, as we noted earlier, partly about improving what the organisation really *is* and *does* – not just the image it conveys. It therefore embraces part of what used to be called PR, but with a wider scope and at a higher level.

One stage in the evolution of PR into reputation management is the emergence of public relations, public affairs or corporate communication departments in large organisations, the role of which is broadly to **improve the perceptions of the organisation** held by a range of key **stakeholder audiences**. The scope of this activity has been growing, with typical public affairs activities now including: dealing with government and community organisations; pressure and interest groups; issues and crisis management; media relations; public relations; investor relations; employee communications; corporate philanthropy (charitable activity); and research and measurement in these areas.

Key concerns of large corporations seeking to manage their reputation through such activities (Post & Griffin, 1997) include:

- The potential for **gaps** between what the various publics might expect from a large corporation, and the actual or perceived performance of the individual corporation
- The proliferation, speed and reach of **media** (such as the internet), allowing issues to explode quickly and with high impact.

ACTIVITY 2

evaluation

Who is responsible for reputation management in your own organisation, or an organisation you know well (and might focus on in your assignment)? Is there a dedicated function, and if so, what is it called? Or is the function spread across different marketing, communication or legal specialisms? – Public + Internal Affairs

What is the scope of reputation management activity in your organisation? At what level does it operate (strategic, tactical or operational)? Recommendations.

See if you can get hold of a functional job description for whatever unit(s) are responsible for reputation management or corporate communication in the organisation.

1.2.2 Development via the integration of corporate communication

Some commentators (eg van Riel & Fombrun, 2007; Van Bekkum *et al.*, 2008) regard the emergence of reputation management as a bi-product of the integration of corporate communication.

Communication is the key medium through which organisations access the physical resources (capital, labour, raw materials) and symbolic resources (such as legitimacy and reputation) that they need to operate. Organisations have tended to proliferate a range of **specialised groups** with responsibility for communicating with target stakeholder audiences: departments for community relations, government relations, customer relations, employee relations, investor relations and so on.

This specialisation has fostered a **fragmentation of the communication system**, which has progressively limited its effectiveness. 'The presence of multiple specialised senders of information when they are not explicitly and strategically co-ordinated, stands in the way of creating consistency of external and internal corporate communication. Managers in different geographical locations or working for different parts of the same firm find themselves frequently contradicting one another, and therefore conveying **inconsistent impressions** about the company and its products to resource-holders.' (van Riel & Fombrun, *op cit.*, p. 3)

Faced with global competition, wider public access to information and increasing public demand for corporate social responsibility and transparency, organisations have grown increasingly aware of the need to **re-integrate their communication activities**, so that a more coherent and consistent set of messages is given to stakeholder groups.

In addition, there has been a rising understanding of the economic value that can be created by strengthening **corporate brands**.

KEY CONCEPT

concept

A **corporate brand** consists of 'the features of a company that employees, investors, customers and the public associate with the organisation as a whole... The corporate brand is increasingly being used to cast a favourable halo over everything the organisation does or says – and capitalise on its reputation'. (van Riel & Fombrun, *op cit.*, p. 4).

The concept of '**corporate reputation**' has gained attention because it captures the *effects* that brands and images have on the overall evaluations that stakeholders make about organisations and their products: as a multi-stakeholder construct, corporate reputation is a powerful tool for measuring the effectiveness of an organisation's communications with its stakeholders.

The growing interest in corporate reputation analysis has also been supported by *Fortune* magazine's publication, since 1982, of its list of America's Most Admired Companies, and a growing body of academic research, reflected in conferences organised by the Reputation Institute (RI) and its quarterly journal *Corporate Reputation Review.*

1.2.3 Contributions of other disciplines

Fombrun & van Riel (1997) survey a number of disciplines which have contributed concepts and perspectives to the field of corporate reputation.

- **Psychology** has contributed various information processing theories, describing how reputations are built up through perception (the organisation and interpretation of stimuli); awareness; memory; affect (emotion); and evaluation (the attaching of emotional and moral judgements). Reputations are meaning systems which individuals use to organise their impressions, forming a 'short-hand' way of thinking about an organisation which colours their further perceptions and evaluations. For low-involvement decisions, where audiences are not highly motivated to seek out and process information about the organisation or its products, corporate reputations will play a central role in influencing their behaviour, as a kind of decision-making short-cut.

- **Economics** views reputations as character traits or informational signals which are used by organisations to build competitive advantage. Consumers rely on the reputation of an organisation, in the absence of more direct information about the organisation's capabilities or commitment to delivering satisfying products or services. Investors similarly rely on a positive corporate reputation for confidence that management will act in ways that are reputation-consistent. In other words, reputations generate perceptions which stabilise interactions between a firm and its stakeholders, enabling it to gain access to resources and competitive advantage. Investment in reputation-building may also allow a firm to charge premium prices (by signalling the quality of its products and services), and may generate profits from repeat purchase, cross-selling and up-selling.

- **Strategic management** has contributed an understanding of the competitive benefits of acquiring favourable reputations. Reputations can be seen as both assets and 'mobility barriers' (Caves & Porter, 1977). They are difficult for competitors to imitate or duplicate, and are therefore core competitive resources. At the same time, they are difficult to shift, once formed, and they constrain firms' actions (and competitors' reactions) because of the need for consistency with reputation.

- **Organisational sociology** focuses on the relationships that firms have with their stakeholders in a shared institutional environment. Firms have multiple evaluators, each of whom will have different criteria for assessing them – but these evaluators also interact, acquire and exchange information among themselves. Corporate reputations are aggregate assessments of an organisation's performance in relation to the expectations and norms of the social system surrounding firms and industries (Shapiro, 1987): market analysts, the media, the internet and 'blogosphere' and so on. Our society is flooded with 'reputational cues' (Alvesson, 1990): reputations arise out of information which is transmitted via the mass media and through interpersonal communication, which is often haphazard, infrequent and superficial. There is often a discrepancy between the fabricated reputation conveyed by the media and a person's direct experience with the 'real' organisation.

- **Organisational science** focuses on the experience of employees, which shapes organisational cultural and i (self image), which in turn shape the organisation's business practices and stakeholder relationships. By creat shared guiding values about 'how we do things around here', strong cultures contribute to the consistency of performance and messages – and therefore of their reputation with stakeholders (Camerer & Vepsalainen, 1988).

- **Accounting** has contributed approaches to the valuation of intangible assets such as brands and reputations, highlighting the gap between the 'book' value of firms, as reported in financial statements, and their market valuation (when capitalised). Investments in branding, advertising, training and research and development (R & D) build stocks of intangible assets which may not be recorded in financial statements – but which contribute to higher reputational assessments among observers (Rindova & Fombrun, 1999). A company's 'reputational capital' can be estimated using a basic 'market-to-book' ratio: subtracting the market (share) value of a company from its book value (assets minus liabilities). Reputation is an economic asset, which effective reputation management is designed to defend and develop.

If you want to follow-up on these surveys of the evolution of reputation management at source, see:

- *Davies, Chun, Da Silva and Roper,* Corporate Reputation & Competitiveness *(2003: Routledge), Chapter 2: Reputation Management: The Traditional Approach*

- *van Riel & Fombrun,* Essentials of Corporate Communication *(2007: Routledge), Introduction: the Communication System, Chapter 1: What is Corporate Communication? And Chapter 2: From Communication to Reputation.*

1.3 Reputation management in different contexts

Although the syllabus and literature refer to 'corporate reputation' and 'corporate communication', it would be a mistake to think of these processes as relevant only to business corporations: in this context 'corporate' (from the Latin *corpus* or 'body') refers simply to the 'whole organisation' or 'whole body' nature of the discipline.

Ideas about corporate communication are relevant to all kinds of organisation and entity, not just private or public companies. The development and maintenance of a positive image is generally associated with businesses, because it has long been recognised as a necessary source of differentiation, advantage and defence in competitive environments.

However, in recent years, there has been a growing awareness in the **not-for-profit sector** of the need for commercial disciplines, with the recognition that such organisations do, in fact, operate in competitive environments (competing for resources such as funding, support, advocacy, volunteer labour) and do, in fact, need to attract, retain and engage target 'markets' to obtain these resources.

There has been increasing social and legislative pressure on all organisations, including institutions subsidised by public funding and voluntary contributions, to be more transparent and accountable to their audiences. How is our money being used? What does the organisation we support really stand for?

MARKETING AT WORK

application

Oxfam is to continue sourcing anti-poverty wristbands from China, despite concerns about ethical standards. But the charity has stopped supplies from one manufacturer whose staff were found to be working under poor conditions.

The move follows national media reports that some 'Make Poverty History' bands had been manufactured at the Tat Shing Rubber Manufacturing Company, which forced new workers to pay 'financial deposits'. The coverage also reported how employees worked in unsuitable conditions and raised concerns over health and safety. Each of these points breached Oxfam's own Ethical Trading Initiative guidelines.

The charity has stressed that the 'mistake' highlights the importance for buyers to ensure goods are sourced at plants where conditions meet minimum standards.

'This should not mean a blanket rejection of sourcing in China. Instead we can work with the local company or factory to improve conditions. It is important that we engage to have a positive impact.'

Supply Management, 23 June 2005

For reflection: How might the emergence of this 'mistake' affect Oxfam's reputation with different audiences, and why? What aspects of the 'mistake' might be taken up by 'national media reports' and specialist media such as *Supply Management?* What matters would Oxfam have had to consider in the wake of this 'mistake' to re-establish its reputation, and what core messages would it have needed to convey?

Reputation management can thus be applied in a range of settings.

- In **consumer** marketing, a positive image is regarded (as we will see in section 3 below) as a source of brand differentiation, competitive advantage and enhanced earning potential. Reputation often acts as a 'short-cut' to evaluation of products and brands, particularly for relatively low-involvement purchases (low cost, low risk, low significance), for which the consumer is not highly motivated to seek out detailed product information. Positive reputation supports trust and emotional engagement with a brand, facilitating profitability and competitive advantage through customer loyalty. In addition, with increasing public concern for social and environmental responsibility, there has been a growing interest in 'the company behind the product/label'.

- In **industrial** marketing, purchase is often based on longer-term partnership relationships between buyer and supplier, negotiating a more complex total offering of customised requirements, price, service and collaboration on supply chain competitiveness. While information search in support of the purchase decision is likely to be both more objective and more rigorous than in consumer marketing, reputational factors are still influential:

  - In facilitating trust (Is this customer/supplier known as being trustworthy, credible, reliable?).

  - In the perception of compatibility or potential synergy necessary for partnership (What is this organisation 'like'? What will it be like to deal with? Will we 'get on'? Do their values match or compliment ours?).

  - In the assessment of value added by the relationship (eg through association with the reputational strength and status of the other party – or the risk of association with the reputational weakness or vulnerability of the other party).

- For **service** organisations corporate reputation is particularly relevant.

  - With services (unlike products), there is no tangibility or transfer of ownership involved in the purchase, so reputation is a key differentiating factor, and a important part of the overall value package. The customer has no 'sample' of the service to evaluate, and must therefore trust in the service provider's image for trustworthiness, reliability, quality and so on.

  - With services (unlike products) creation and delivery are inseparable. The organisation's employees and customers interact directly in the creation and delivery of the service: the customer experiences (and in many service businesses such as hotels, restaurants, transport and education, temporarily 'enters') the internal ambience or culture of the business. Reputation management in service businesses is therefore more likely to be concerned with positioning the business simultaneously to employees *and* to customers: there is a close interrelationship between organisational culture (what the organisation 'is' and what employees perceive it to be) and organisational image (what customers perceive it to be).

  - Because of the importance of the 'people' element in the service marketing mix, reputational factors (is this a good organisation to work for?) are also important in attracting and retaining quality service staff.

  - Research by Davies *et al.* (*op cit*, p. 52) suggests service businesses are more likely than manufacturing businesses to accept the idea of direct linkage between reputation and financial performance, and to manage cultural and external image as a coherent whole.

- Many **not-for-profit** and **societal** organisations can be seen in a similar light to the services sector, when it comes to the relevance of reputation. Charities, churches, educational institutions, public health and leisure services, clubs and associations tend to have a wider range of key stakeholders than commercial firms (which are focused on shareholders and customers): funds-providers, volunteer labour, customers (for services or products provided), beneficiaries (of activity), regulators, trustees and so on. However, they must still engage, attract and retain these resource-holders, in competition with other organisations and resource users. Reputational factors are likely to be important in:

  - Establishing the credibility of organisations attempting to persuade others of their point of view (eg pressure and interest groups, causal charities)

BPP LEARNING MEDIA

- Establishing the trustworthiness and legitimacy of organisations soliciting public funds or donations

- Establishing the mission, core values and congeniality of organisations soliciting membership, support or volunteer labour

- Managing the extent, focus and tone of regulatory, media and public scrutiny of the organisation's operations and affairs (agenda setting)

- Retaining the legitimacy of the organisation's 'licence to operate', in the face of public expectation that such organisations will uphold ethical and socially responsible values.

- For **political** organisations, institutions and individuals, similarly, reputation is a key currency in establishing legitimacy; garnering and maintaining political, media and public support; conveying core value (platform) messages; building political alliances and coalitions; gaining a voice and influence in public/political debate and policy-making; and so on.

- **Cities**, **regions and countries** also have to market themselves in various circumstances: in competition for government infrastructure funding (eg regional development grants); to attract business development (increasing service provision and contributing to employment, economic activity, infrastructure development and tax revenue); to attract the immigration or relocation of residents, skilled workers and service-providers; and/or to attract tourism revenue, by marketing the city/region/country as an appealing, safe, welcoming destination.

ACTIVITY 3

application/evaluation

[handwritten: PEST]

What core values might a city, region or country want to convey in order to make itself an attractive tourist destination? *[handwritten: openness, flexibility & resources, activities for families]*

What image or reputation does your own city or region have, locally and overseas? *[handwritten: poor (cosmopolitan, historical, wide range of things to see & do.)]*

What does or might it do to (re-)position itself as a tourist destination? What hurdles might it have to overcome? *[handwritten: Bad press, investment, research]*

What risk factors might damage its reputation? *[handwritten: Crime statistics, poor reviews.]*

ASSESSMENT TIP

application

Obviously, there is much more that could be said on the different contexts of reputation, and you may well choose, or be asked, to apply your learning on reputation management and corporate communication to one or more of these non-commercial contexts. We will focus our coverage in this Study Text on commercial companies, although many of the principles will be relevant to other contexts as well, and we will include 'Marketing at Work' examples and 'Activities' from a variety of contexts. You will therefore need to take some responsibility for generalising and transferring concepts to particular contexts of interest to you (or the focus of your assessment, if known).

- As you read through this Text, consider how key points might be applied to different contexts, particularly those of interest to you. *[handwritten: Articles or CR]*

- Use your wider reading in textbooks, the quality press and the internet to scan for examples of reputational messages, strength or damage in service, charity, political, societal and destination marketing contexts. *[handwritten: Articles or CR writes]*

If you are interested in destination marketing (ie managing the reputation of a place as a stimulus to tourism), you might like to check out the website of the Destination Marketing Association: its resource centre has many interesting articles and links.

Link: http://www.destinationmarketing.org/resource_centre/rc_index.asp ■

2 Reputation, image and identity

The use of terminology in this area varies across the literature – as do the explanations of how the various concepts interrelate. We have focused on the concepts as portrayed in the core recommended reading for this module, but you may put forward alternative interpretations in your assessment, where relevant – as long as they are internally consistent, and supported by references.

2.1 Corporate identity

Perhaps the greatest variety comes in the meanings allocated to the concept of '**corporate identity**'.

- In one use of this term, it refers solely to the '**visual identity**' of an organisation, or the 'visible artefacts' of a corporate culture: 'the symbols (such as logos, colour scheme) which an organisation uses to identify itself to people' (Dowling). For clarity, we will refer to this in this Text as 'corporate visual identity'.

- In a slightly broader use of the term, it refers to the various ways in which the organisation chooses to **project, identify or express itself** to stakeholders, via its symbolism, behaviour and communications (sometimes called the '**identity mix**'). This meaning of the term is often also associated with **corporate branding**. You should be familiar with the concept of branding in relation to the perception and market positioning of a product or product range: this concept has more recently been extended to the perception and positioning of an organisation (or destination) as a whole, as we will see in detail in a later chapter. The management of corporate identity or brand conveys key ideas to target audiences about what the organisation is, what is does and how it does it (Olins, 1989) in ways that differentiate the organisation from its competitors.

- In another use of the term, corporate identity refers to **organisational reality**: the distinctive and defining attributes of the organisation; 'what the organisation is, its personality; the sum total of its expertise, history, philosophy, culture, strategy and structure' (*Marketing Business*, February 1994, p. 5); or its 'intrinsic identity… what the organisation stands for above all else' (Doorley & Garcia, 2007, p. 5). '[Corporate identity] constitutes the current attributes of the corporation. It is shaped by a number of elements, including corporate ownership, the leadership style of management, organisational structure, business activities and markets covered, the range and quality of products and services offered and overall business performance. It also encompasses the set of values held by management and employees.' (Balmer & Greyser, 2003).

- The term 'identity' may also be used to refer to the '**self perception**' of the organisation: how it sees itself, or, more correctly, how its members see it.

  - In some models (eg Davies *et al.*, 2003), a distinction is made between '**identity**' (as the *internal* stakeholder view of the company) and '**image**' (as the *external* stakeholder view of the company).

  - In other models (eg Albert & Whetten, 1985), a distinction is made between '**organisational identity**' (self-perception: '(a) what is taken by organisational members to be central to the organisation and (b) what makes the organisation distinctive from other organisations in the eyes of the beholding members, and (c) what is perceived by members to be enduring or continuing') and '**corporate identity**', which is concerned with what the organisation is actually like.

Corporate communication and corporate branding are, as we will see in future chapters, two broad ways in which an organisation projects its **actual** or intrinsic identity and/or its **desired** identity to the outside world, creating a **communicated or projected** identity – which in turn influences its **conceived** identity (image and reputation in the eyes of the world). We will explore these concepts further in a later chapter.

2.2 Corporate image

KEY CONCEPT

concept

The term 'corporate image' is used to describe the **perceptions** of an organisation (or organisational identity) in the minds of its external stakeholders.

There is some potential confusion here, as the phrase 'corporate image' is sometimes used in the same limited sense as 'corporate identity' to mean 'visual identity', or the names, icons and designs which are used to symbolise the organisation. However, the term 'image' as we use it in this Study Text carries the broader meaning of how stakeholders perceive and interpret the ways in which an organisation manifests and expresses its identity: the transmitted or projected corporate identity, *as it is received* by stakeholders.

[handwritten: image = perception]

ACTIVITY 4

evaluation

What do you think are the key implications for corporate reputation management of the fact that corporate image is primarily 'in the eye of the beholder'? *[handwritten: Clear communication of values?]*

Corporate image is created by:

- The **signals** that an organisation broadcasts about itself, both through its actions and through its communicated messages, to stakeholders

- The **conduct** of employees and managers who represent the organisation to stakeholders

- The transmission of **information and rumour** about the organisation among stakeholders (eg via financial analysts, the media, the internet)

- The **interpretation** of all these 'cues' and messages by stakeholders, based on expectation, perception, rationality and emotion, and influenced by contextual conditions.

Communications alone cannot shape image. If an organisation has a poor image, this may be attributed to communication – or reality. 'If the image is false and our performance is good, it's our fault for being bad communicators. If the image is true and reflects our bad performance, it's our fault for being bad managers.' (Bernstein, 1984).

Nevertheless, communication and branding are an important interface between identity (what the organisation is and projects about itself) and image (what stakeholders see, believe and think about the organisation). Fill (2002), for example notes that people's perceptions of an organisation are often based on a small amount of information. 'The strategic credibility of Microsoft may be based largely on the image of Bill Gates rather than the current financial performance of Microsoft and the actual strategies being pursued by the organisation. Stakeholders *extrapolate* that Bill Gates has a high reputation for business success, therefore, anything to do with Bill Gates is positive and likely to be successful.' (Fill, 2002, p. 395)

As we will see, much of reputation management is concerned with identifying and diagnosing mismatches or gaps between identity and image: why aren't stakeholders hearing what we think we're saying?

2.3 Corporate reputation

The term 'corporate reputation', for many commentators, describes the **aggregate effects** of identity/brand and image on stakeholders' **overall evaluation** of an organisation: in other words, the overall **estimation** or **regard** in which the organisation is held by its stakeholders – a good (or bad) employer, a trustworthy (or untrustworthy) service-provider, a socially responsible (or irresponsible) operator, and so on. The precise nature of reputation has not really been pinned down, however, and the following are just some of the definitions that have been put forward in the literature.

- 'Reputations are **overall assessments** of organisations by their stakeholders. They are aggregate perceptions by stakeholders of **an organisation's ability to fulfil their expectations**, whether those stakeholders are interested in buying the company's products, working for the company, or investing in the company.' (van Riel & Fombrun, 2007, p. 43)

- 'Reputation is a **perception of an organisation built over time** (Balmer, 1998). It results from a reflection upon historical accumulated impacts of previously observed identity cues and transactional experiences (Melewar, 2003). In other words, it is evaluative and is **image endowed with judgement** (Simões & Dibb, 2002) on what the organisation has done and how it has behaved (Balmer & Greyser, 2003). Image may be changed relatively quickly while reputation requires consistency of image and nurturing over a relatively **longer time period**.' (Vella & Melewar, 2008, p. 12)

- 'Corporate reputation is the **evaluation** (**respect, esteem, estimation**) in which an organisation's image is held by people... A reputation is the set of meanings by which a company is known and through which people describe, remember and relate to it. It is the net result of the interaction of a person's beliefs, ideas, feelings and impressions about the company. A company will not have a reputation: people hold reputations of the company.' (Dowling)

- 'Reputation refers to a **holistic and vivid impression** held by a particular group towards a corporation, partly as a result of information processing (**sense-making**) carried out by the group's members [image] and partly by the aggregated **communication** of the corporation in question concerning its nature, ie the fabricated and projected picture of itself [identity].' (Alvesson, 1990)

Again, perhaps the most important point to note about these definitions is the joint emphasis on both identity cues (communications) and experience of organisational behaviour. 'Leveraging a positive reputation is not about parading awards, achievements or positive testimonials, although these can certainly help bolster a reputation. It is about living and **demonstrating** the reputation in practice, on a day-to-day basis, over days, weeks and years, gaining trust and respect in the process. The more highly esteemed our reputation becomes, the more it behoves us to ensure it is **justified**. There is no doubt that actions speak louder than words. What we do is more powerful than what we say. The most effective way of positively influencing our reputation is to behave in ways that support and demonstrate it.' (Samuel, 2007, p. 236).

ACTIVITY 5

evaluation

Find your own example, from your reading or experience, of a critical incident representing a mismatch between the claims made by an organisation and its conduct in practice.

What were the consequences of this? What could have been done to prevent the mismatch, or to address it once it emerged?

2.4 How identity, image and reputation relate

Since the terminology of identity, image and reputation are so varied, there are different ways of understanding how they relate or operate on each other. The following is just a brief survey of some of the models set out in the literature, highlighting different ways of conceiving the formation of reputation.

2.4.1 (Internal) identity + (external) image = reputation

Davies *et al.* (*op cit*, p. 61) distinguish the different elements of reputation by **audience**:

- **Identity** is the internal (employee) view of the company

- **Image** is the view of the company held by external stakeholders, especially customers

- **Reputation** is the collective term for *all* stakeholders' views of corporate reputation, including identity and image.

Their '**Corporate Reputation Chain**' model (Figure 1.1) shows how the various elements might tie in together – and how they might impact on staff retention and motivation on the one hand (arising from a positive identity), and business performance on the other (arising from a positive image).

'Reputation management should be concerned with two things: image and identity... It is the role and objective of managers to work to ensure that links are forged such that image and identity **harmonise**, that there are **links from image to sales** or some other objective measure of performance, that there are positive **links from identity to staff retention**, and ultimately that identity can be linked through to performance.' (*ibid*, p. 75).

BPP LEARNING MEDIA

Figure 1.1: The Corporate Reputation Chain

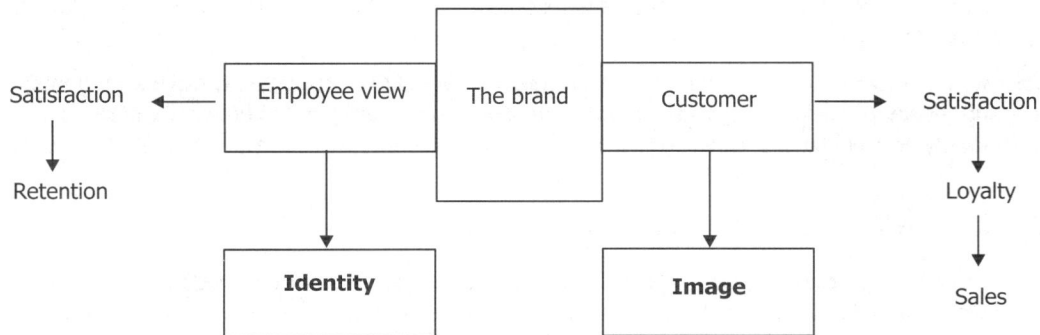

Source: adapted from Davies *et al.* (*ibid* p. 76)

Davies *et al.* argue that identity and image are **causally linked**. The management of (internal) identity influences the attitudes, morale, motivation and commitment of employees – which in turn influences the contacts and experiences they create for customers and other external stakeholders – which in turn shape the organisation's image (in the minds of external stakeholders). This will be an important element of our discussion of organisational identity and employee communications in later chapters.

MARKETING AT WORK

application

Jobber (2007, p. 865) cites the example of software giant **Microsoft**.

'It is very easy for senior management to decide upon a set of values that represent a company's ethos, but much harder to **engage employees' attention**. This was the problem Microsoft faced when trying to **communicate its identity** as a company internally. It expressed its company values in terms of six attributes: passion, respect, accountability, integrity, self-criticism and eagerness.

Its **internal marketing strategy** was to ensure this ethos was communicated to employees in three stages. First, there was a campaign across the UK to generate positive feelings about the project. Second, a series of road-shows was held around the firm's UK offices to discuss the core values in depth. Third, a compulsory education programme was launched to ensure all staff understood the proposition.

The creative element of the programme was centred on the well-known David Brent character from the BBC series *The Office*. Actor Ricky Gervais, who played this character, became involved and a special 15-minute video in the style of the programme was filmed, adding humour to the project and raising its appeal to staff.

The result was that the project achieved high recognition levels of the main message of the campaign about employees, national press coverage and an award for the best internal marketing campaign from the magazine *Marketing*.'

2.5 Expression + promise > impression + evaluation

Dowling (2004) distinguishes and relates the terms in the following ways.

- **Corporate identity** is the attributes, symbol, nomenclature and behaviours used by the company to express and identify itself. The role of corporate identity is to answer the question: *Who are you?*

- **Corporate brand** is the promise made by the company. The corporate brand answers the question: *What is your offer?* (This in turn largely determines if people 'like' you.)

- **Corporate image** is the beliefs and impressions received and held by stakeholders about the company. The corporate image answers the question: *What do people think about you?*

- **Corporate reputation** is the overall evaluation (often expressed as admiration, respect and esteem) in which a company is held. Corporate reputation answers the question: *Are you good or bad?* (This in turn largely determines if people 'trust' you.)

In other words, a company's corporate identity and corporate brand (its **expressed nature and ideals**) drive the corporate images and reputations held by stakeholders (**stakeholder perceptions**), which potentially create positive **outcomes** such as trust, loyalty and reputational capital (the stock of trust and goodwill value attached to the company name).

2.6 Personality > identity > image

In his book *Marketing Communications,* Chris Fill (the CIM's senior assessor for this model) uses the term '**corporate personality**' to describe the reality or significant and distinctive attributes of an organisation: the totality of the characteristics which identify an organisation. (Fill, 2002, p. 390)

In his model (following Abratt & Shee, 1989: Figure 1.2), he argues that organisations, like individuals, *project* their personalities through their '**identity**' (or corporate brand: visible artefacts or cues by which stakeholders can recognise and identify the organisation). The target audience's *perception* of these cues then forms the corporate '**image**' (the perception that different audiences have of the organisation).

Figure 1.2: The basic sequence of corporate image formation

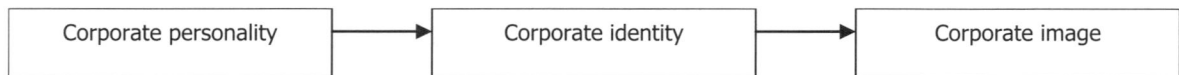

Corporate personality	→	Corporate identity	→	Corporate image

Corporate **reputation** is a 'deeper set of images', based on stakeholders' reflections on the historical and accumulated impacts of **identity cues** or messages, reinforced or adjusted by actual **transactional experiences**. Images may be influenced quite quickly: reputation is more embedded, and takes longer to change.

This is the language used by the syllabus in most cases, and we adopt Fill's terminology of corporate personality, identity and image in this Study Text – although we occasionally also use 'corporate identity' to refer to the internal self-image of the organisation (stating clearly that we are doing so in the text – as you should do in your assessment).

If you are interested in following up the viewpoint of the senior assessor on corporate reputation and identity, you might like to browse one of the following titles:

- *Fill, C: **Marketing Communication: Engagement, Strategies & Practice** (2005: Pearson Education), Chapter 15: Corporate Identity, Reputation and Branding*

- *Fill, C: **Marketing Communication: Interactivity, Communities & Content** (2009: Pearson), Chapter 13: Corporate Reputation: Identity and Branding* ■

2.7 Identity > image > reputation

For Vella & Melewar (2008, p. 8): 'Corporate **identity** is transmitted to various stakeholders who then formulate **images** that, in turn, form the basis of the company's **reputation**'. This is perhaps the most straightforward of the available views. However, the authors also helpfully highlight the implied need for **consistency** between, or 'matching' of, the various elements.

- The (projected) identity should as far as possible be consistent or congruent with the (real) identity of the organisation, otherwise stakeholder expectations will be continually disappointed, eroding trust and leading to negative overall evaluation (reputation).

- The identity projected to external stakeholders should as far as possible be consistent or congruent with the (internal) identity of the organisation, in the perception of its employees, otherwise, again, mixed messages will be broadcast by corporate communications on the one hand and organisational behaviour on the other.

- The image formulated by external stakeholders should be consistent or congruent with the identity projected by the organisation, otherwise there has been a failure of communication, and the organisation is less in control of its image and reputation than it might wish. What is influencing stakeholders' impressions of the organisation, over and above (or contrary to) its behaviour and communications?

We will look further at this 'gap'/'mismatch' view of reputation management in a later chapter.

3   Why manage corporate reputation?

We suggested earlier what you may already believe to be the case intuitively or from anecdotal evidence: that a positive reputation has benefits for an organisation, while a negative reputation – or reputational damage – has costs and drawbacks. The fact is, however, that few organisations as yet make proactive attempts to measure and manage their reputations as a significant asset or source of business risk. A systematic business case for reputation management may need to be made, to justify the resources and changes required to put reputation and corporate communications on the strategic agenda. As Samuel (2007, p. 235) notes: 'Reputation always influences [stakeholder] decisions involving an evaluation of value versus investment or cost. It is therefore important to ensure your reputation will be viewed as desirable by those making the decision where possible.'

ACTIVITY 6   concept

Before we go on, what would you assume to be the benefits of positive reputation, from all that we have said so far?

van Riel & Fombrun (*op cit*, p. 47) summarise the benefits of positive reputation as follows.

'A positive reputation works like a magnet. It strengthens the **attractiveness** of an organisation, simplifying the realisation of a broad range of activities. From the research literature, we know that companies with a positive reputation can more easily attract and retain employees and can ask a higher price for its [sic] products. They more easily attract new sources of financial capital and are less likely to find themselves at risk.'

Doorley & Garcia (*op cit*, p. 4) highlight a wider range of intangible and tangible benefits of a good reputation.

'It is important for audiences, from customers to employees to consumer advocates, to feel good about an organisation, and it is important to build a good reputation to sustain an organisation through the tough times. But a reputation is worth much more than that. Companies with the better reputations attract more and better candidates for employment, pay less for supplies, gain essentially free press coverage that is worth as much if not more than advertising, and accrue other benefits that actually contribute to profits. Reputation adds value to the actual worth of a company – that is, market capitalisation (the number of shares outstanding times the price per share) includes more than just the book value or liquidation value of assets. The reputation component of market capitalisation, reputational capital, is a concept closely related to 'goodwill', and it is worth many billions of dollars in many large corporations. It has a value in not-for-profits, government and universities as well. For instance, a good reputation helps a university attract students and donors.'

Davies *et al.* (*op cit*, p. 70) give their own overview.

'Reputation is about more than just the customer view. It is about attracting and retaining the best employees, finding it easy to be trusted and being well treated by suppliers, being seen as the kind of company able to influence local and national governments. In the key area of customer relationships, a good reputation is likely to reduce transaction costs (because the customer trusts you to offer a fair price and not to hide things). In the labour market, it will reduce labour turnover and attract better quality, more productive employees… '

In more detail, the reputational benefits highlighted by the syllabus are as follows.

3.1 Financial performance

A strong, positive reputation can enhance an organisation's business and financial performance in a number of direct and indirect ways.

- **Attracting and retaining customers**, based on positive promotional and attitudinal effects. A study in the *Journal of Public Relations Research* ('Measuring the economic value of public relations', 2001) found a positive causal relationship between reputation and revenue.

  Customer-attracting effects of positive reputation include:

  - Improved marketing **planning and stakeholder management**. If managers recognise and understand how reputation influences the decision-making processes of customers and other stakeholders, they can use it effectively to add customer and organisational value and manage risk.

  - **Differentiation** from competitors, particularly when there is little difference in their product or service offerings. (According to research, nine out of ten consumers report that when choosing between products that are similar in price and quality, the reputation of the company determines which product or service they purchase: Mackiewicz, 1993). Positive reputation and particular reputational values (such as quality, reliability, ethics or environment-friendliness) may form part of the product's 'bundle of attributes' or the distinctive perceptions identifying the brand. This may be a key strategic resource.

  - **Securing support** during times of turbulence, contributing to organisational **resilience** or ability to bounce back. Positive reputation may create loyalty, and – as a value judgement – may be hard to shift even in the face of contrary information (such as a poor service experience or negative publicity): it causes less psychological dissonance for people to minimise, forgive or explain away the negative information than it would to change their previous judgement. When a company with a strong reputation makes a mistake or suffers a crisis, audiences are more likely to trust their motives and communications (explanations, assurances). A good reputation can thus serve to buffer a corporation from economic loss in certain types of crises such as product recalls.

  - **Brand engagement and loyalty**. Businesses, brands and people with a strong positive reputation are more likely to score highly on un-prompted recall, because of the extent and positive associations of their media and word-of-mouth exposure. They are more likely to be perceived as being trustworthy and providing high-value returns (Samuel, *op cit* p. 235). They are also likely to generate higher profits: customer retention is less cost-intensive than acquiring new customers, generates additional profits through cross-selling and up-selling, and revenue through endorsements, recommendations and referrals (Reichheld, 2001).

  - **Unpaid promotion and endorsement**. A positive reputation increases the likelihood of customer referrals, as it reduces the risk that the recommender's own reputation will be damaged by a misplaced recommendation. In addition, companies with strong reputations tend to gain more positive media coverage, which may be more effective (due to the perception of third-party endorsement) and less expensive than advertising. The Body Shop is just one example of a successful corporate brand that has relied almost exclusively on non-paid (non-advertising) promotion.

- **Brand positioning and price premiums**. Reputation may contribute to the quality positioning of a company's brands and/or to a reduction in price sensitivity (since purchase decisions are more likely to be made on non-price criteria), allowing it to charge premium prices. Research studies have found a positive correlation between reputation and the prices a company can charge.

- **Employer branding**. Firms with a reputation for being a good employer, or a 'great place to work', are more likely to attract and retain highly skilled employees – a strategic resource, particularly in times or areas of skill shortage.

- **Employee satisfaction and loyalty**. Peters & Waterman (1982), among others, have argued that a positive reputation (and the internal cultural values reflected in it) can contribute to the satisfaction, engagement and loyalty of team members: giving jobs meaning and significance beyond the mere performance of tasks. Employee motivation, commitment and retention in turn support continuity, organisational learning, and improved product and service quality. Which in turn leads to more satisfied customers, customer retention, opportunities to develop customer relationships and customer loyalty – and hence opportunities for enhanced profitability and competitive advantage (Grönroos, 2000).

- **Establishing high-quality value networks** (or 'competitive architecture'). A positive reputation makes it easier to attract and retain not only employees and customers, but also suppliers, investors, supporters, business allies and other network partners.

BPP LEARNING MEDIA

- In modern competitive environments, it is not just companies at the same level of the supply chain that compete, but whole **supply chains** and networks, each element of which contributes to customer value. 'The real competitive struggle is not between individual companies, but between their supply chains or networks... What makes a supply chain or network unique is the way the relationships and interfaces in the chain or network are managed. In this sense, a major source of differentiation comes from the quality of relationships that one business enjoys, compared to its competitors.' (Christopher *et al.*, 2002). Quality suppliers may be attracted to high-reputation companies (a) because they trust that such companies will deal fairly with them and (b) because such companies make status-enhancing customers/clients.

- A good reputation supports the organisation's ability to establishe relationships with key **influencers** in the business environment, and therefore potentially to influence them in its favour: local and national government, pressure and interest groups, the media and so on.

It should be noted that claims for the link between reputation and business performance are controversial. They are often supported by rankings such as *America's Most Admired Companies* surveys – but the reputation measure used in such surveys includes an appraisal of the financial performance of the company, so a correlation is hardly surprising. In fact, it may be less a case of reputation leading to financial success, than a case of financial success creating a positive reputation, since this factor is most likely to 'impress' the survey respondents (peer-group managers) and influence their perception of other measures (the 'halo effect').

If you would like to explore a range of reputation factors, and their link to business performance, via the **America's Most Admired Companies** *study, see:*

http://money.cnn.com/magazines/fortune/mostadmired/2009 ▮

Moreover, it is worth noting that in certain market conditions, companies that have what might be regarded as a negative image (being aggressive, being a poor employer, exploiting workforce or suppliers, damaging the environment) – still survive and prosper. Examples might include Wal-Mart in the United States, or the continuing marketing success of companies like McDonalds (in view of reputational damage due to alleged damage to health and the environment), Nike (alleged exploitation of workers in low-cost labour countries), Shell (environmental damage), Perrier (highly publicised contamination fiascos) and Microsoft (trouble with competition regulators).

MARKETING AT WORK

application

Watson & Kitchen (2008) cite the following case vignette of **Johnson & Johnson**, to illustrate how reputation speeds recovery after a crisis.

'The case study of the Johnson & Johnson Company and the pain relief drug Tylenol is one most frequently referred to. Although it happened two decades ago, it illustrates the value of a strong brand image, a strong company reputation, and an ethical core to the business which was immediately operationalised once a problem arose. Note that the managerial response to this case is a response which few firms seem to carry out nowadays.

A few capsules of Tylenol were contaminated with cyanide by an unknown person and the top-selling analgesic was immediately withdrawn from the market. Market research showed a high level of confidence in both the Johnson & Johnson name and the Tylenol brand, and this trust was used as the basis to relaunch the drug after the packing had been redesigned to make it tamper-proof. The company's speed of response and highly effective communications throughout the crisis process – closely allied to its decision to take its best-selling product off the market – has become the management template for product withdrawal and ethically prompt corporate communication.

Jim Burke, then chairman of Johnson & Johnson, said 'the reputation of the corporation, which has been carefully built over 90 years, provided a reservoir of goodwill among the public, the people in the regulatory agencies, and the media, which was of incalculable value in helping to restore the brand' (quoted in Dowling 1994, p. 215). Even now, Johnson & Johnson continually heads the list of most respected corporations in the USA.'

For reflection: What features of Johnson & Johnson's corporate character, practice and communication contributed to its resilience in the face of crisis? (You may like to pick out some key phrases from the account given.)

3.2 Managing shareholder value

Reputation supports shareholder value in various ways.

- It is a significant **intangible asset**. Reputational capital contributes to corporate value or worth, representing the difference between the 'book' value of the organisation (or liquidation value of physical assets) and its market value. Companies with strong brands such as Coca-Cola have stock values that are large multiples of their tangible asset worth, due to the company's ability to earn revenue, supported by its name and attached 'goodwill'.

- It supports strong **financial performance and profitability** (as explained above), which:

  - Enables higher returns on shareholders' investment, in the form of capital growth and dividends.

  - Affects market (including financial media and market analysts') perceptions of the company's future prospects – and so influences its market value.

- Strong reputations (and, conversely, reputational damage) may themselves be reflected in a company's **share price**, and therefore the value of shareholders' holdings. The trust built up by strong reputation may also buffer the company against economic loss, and share price collapse, caused by crises.

3.2.1 The Reputation Value Cycle

van Riel & Fombrun (*op cit*, p. 271) describe how financial value and stakeholder support are dynamically related, in their **Reputation Value Cycle**: Figure 1.3. 'Endorsements build value, and enable a company to expense [*sic*] funds on corporate activities such as advertising, philanthropy and citizenship that generate media endorsements, attract investors, and add financial value. The need effect is a reinforcing loop through which communication, recognition, endorsement and supportive behaviours from stakeholders create equity and financial value.'

Figure 1.3: The Reputation Value Cycle

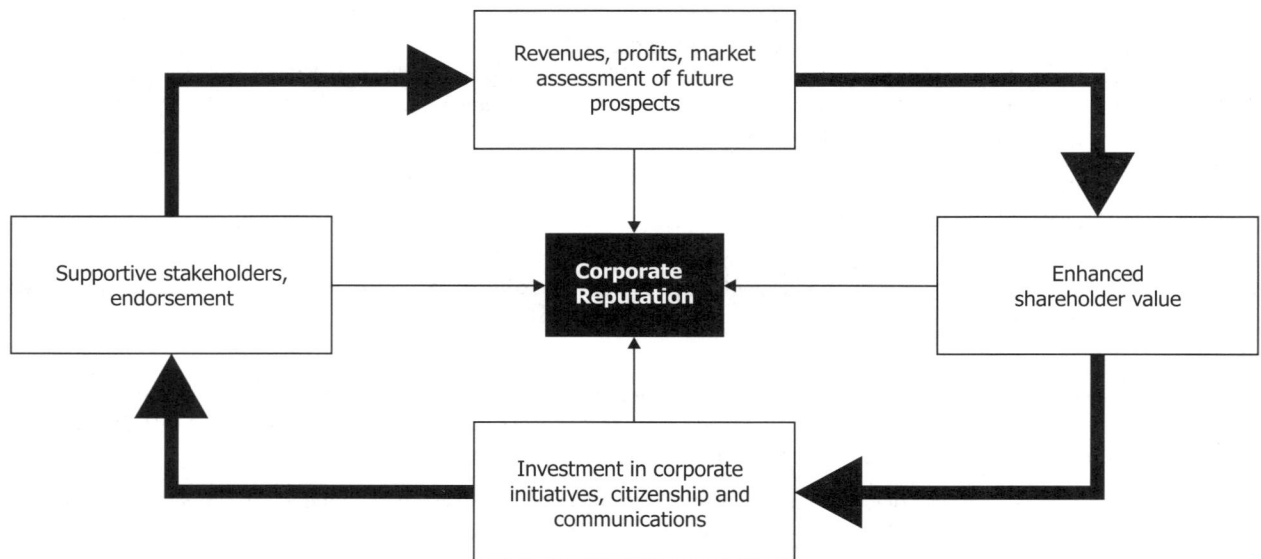

3.3 Improved competitiveness

Good reputation paves the organisational path to acceptance and approval by stakeholders, and underpins competitive advantage by demonstrating distinctive differences from other [similar] organisations (Watson & Kitchen, 2008).

ACTIVITY 7   application

In your role as a stakeholder in (or observer of) various commercial and non-commercial organisations, brainstorm some examples of entities which immediately come to mind as having 'bad' or 'good' reputations.

Body Shop, Virgin   BP, Ryanair,

More specifically, Dowling (1994) argues that a positive reputation can support competitive advantage by:

- Inhibiting the mobility of rival firms (by defining the grounds of competition)
- Acting as a market entry/penetration barrier to new competitors
- Differentiating a firm's products from their competitors
- Signalling the quality (reliability, ethicality etc) of the firm's products to customers and consumers – which may in turn offer competitive advantages, such as allowing the firm to exercise price leadership
- Enhancing the firm's access to capital markets (new sources of financial capital) and investors
- Enhancing the firm's ability to recruit and retain quality employees.

In addition, Davies *et al.* (*op cit*, p. 66) suggest that 'If you have a weak reputation among your competitors or an image for incompetence, you risk being the focus of competitive action more so than a company whose reputation is to respond quickly and aggressively to any challenge.'

MARKETING AT WORK

Fombrun & van Riel (2004, p. 9) cite a case study by McQuire, Schneewis and Branch, illustrating the power of reputation and corporate branding to create differential purchasing decisions.

'The **Toyota Corolla** and the **Chevrolet Prizm** [produced through a joint venture in the US], though built side-by-side from identical components and with only minor trim differences, had quite different fates. Only one-quarter as many Prizms were sold, their trade-in value depreciated more quickly, and the Prizm required up to $750 more in buyer incentives to support its sales. Having Toyota's name on the Corolla attracted customers – while the Prizm was lost among the Chevy dealer's other offerings.'

3.3.1 Predisposing stakeholder decision-making in the organisation's favour

Reputation summarises stakeholders' perceptions of a company in terms of aggregate evaluations (good/bad, strong/weak). Stakeholders often *rely* on these evaluations in making purchase and investment decisions, particularly when:

- The information to make a decision is complex, conflicting or incomplete
- There is too little or too much information to make a purely rational judgement
- They have too little involvement (emotional or financial stake) in the decision to warrant going through complex information analysis
- External conditions pressure them to make a rapid decision.

'Consumers are losing their ability to act as the economists' ideal-type 'rational decision-makers': in judging a product, consumers are not familiar with all available alternatives; they are not aware of all the features of a particular product; they are unable to judge all of those features correctly prior to purchasing the product... Ultimately, reputation reduces the search for information by **simplifying information processing** ... Reputation creates a mental shortcut for stakeholders by providing them a global understanding that they can ascribe to a company and on which they can rely to justify relevant decisions.' (van Riel & Fombrun, *op cit*, p. 48).

3.3.2 Predisposing media comment in the organisation's favour

A good reputation is a form of insurance against the occasions when an organisation is involved in actions or circumstances that could show it in a negative light. If a subject's reputation is positive, journalists are likely to interpret or 'frame' situations in a more positive way: they may be more open to hearing the company's point of view, less likely to sensationalise the issue. They may actively seek out the organisation as a 'spokesperson' and interpreter on issues.

Once a subject's reputation is negative, however, any news will tend to be interpreted negatively, and any input from the organisation regarded with suspicion. Is the closure of an under-performing factor evidence of sound management safeguarding shareholder interests and the future of the company? Or is it evidence of managerial incompetence, lack of foresight and lack of concern for the fate of workers? The company's reputation will create the 'frame' or perspective from which the media – and its audiences – will interpret the situation.

3.4 Employer branding and employee satisfaction

3.4.1 Employer branding

Research findings confirm that companies can leverage their reputations to recruit, retain and motivate high-quality employees (Vella & Melewar, *op cit*, p. 8): 'Employees derive superior value from their organisation from a variety of sources including such extrinsic measures as competitive pay structures and intrinsic means such as challenging and self-actualising jobs. Through internal corporate identity management programmes, managers also communicate these benefits, which form the basis of positive employee images, organisational identity and affinity. Over time, a favourable reputation is created within the labour market.' This reputation within the labour market is known as an employer brand.

KEY CONCEPT

concept

An **employer brand** is the distinctive image carried by an organisation within the labour market: that is, the values associated with it as an employer or potential employer.

Depending on market conditions (eg levels of unemployment, rates of pay, demand for particular skills), reputation may become a key differentiator for an employer, giving it access to better skills – which in turn may allow it to create and sustain competitive advantage, and contribute to profitability and growth.

MARKETING AT WORK

application

The **Great Place to Work Institute** conducts an annual survey identifying the best workplaces in Europe and around the world. The following were some of the top European Firms in the 2004 survey.

- **Danone** (Spain: food and beverages) **Link**: http://www.danone.com
  Pioneering role in corporate responsibility, rapid growth in the number of female managers; development opportunities for young professionals and managers; free summer camp for all staff children.

- **Kanal 5** (Sweden: media)
  Lively atmosphere; employees and managers discuss mutual concerns openly; offers parental leave; contracts with a service company to take care of errands such as shopping.

- **Kraft Foods** (Germany, Greece: food and beverages) **Link**: http://www.kraft.com
  Every year, 15 manual staff are selected for a five-day visit to a Kraft facility in another country; selected young professionals spend 12–18 months seconded to another country; a diversity council encourages promotion and integration of disadvantaged people.

- **Timpson** (UK: service retailing) **Link**: http://www.timpson.co.uk
  'The people who serve our customers run the business – everyone else is there to help'; elaborate training; all managers swap jobs for six weeks; constant internal communications; area managers are expected to praise ten times as much as they criticise!

(Boddy, 2005, p. 485)

You might like to check out **www.greatplacetowork.co.uk** for more recent listings, and follow-up on some of the links to learn more about these best-practice employer brands.

3.4.2 Employee satisfaction

The relationship marketing literature suggests that there is a positive correlation between organisational, employee satisfaction and customer satisfaction. As we noted earlier, strong cultural values associated with positive reputations – such as quality and customer focus, reliability, ethics and corporate social responsibility – are a source of intrinsic job satisfactions for employees. They also enable the organisation to direct and control employees' activities without resorting to close supervision and detailed rules, and this style of control is regarded as satisfying for employees (as well as empowering them to take more flexible initiative to satisfy customers).

A good reputation may **pre-condition** both employees and customers (or other stakeholders) to expect a positive interaction or transaction with an organisation. This leads to a greater likelihood that the actual interaction will be positive (and/or perceived to be positive) – which in turn leads to customer satisfaction and employee motivation – which in turn leads to customer loyalty and employee retention and motivation.

Reichheld (2001) similarly developed a 'loyalty-based cycle of growth', based on a firm's relationships with three core stakeholders: employees, customers and investors. This model shows the linkages between loyalty, value and profits: Figure 1.4.

Figure 1.4: Reichheld's loyalty-based cycle of growth (simplified)

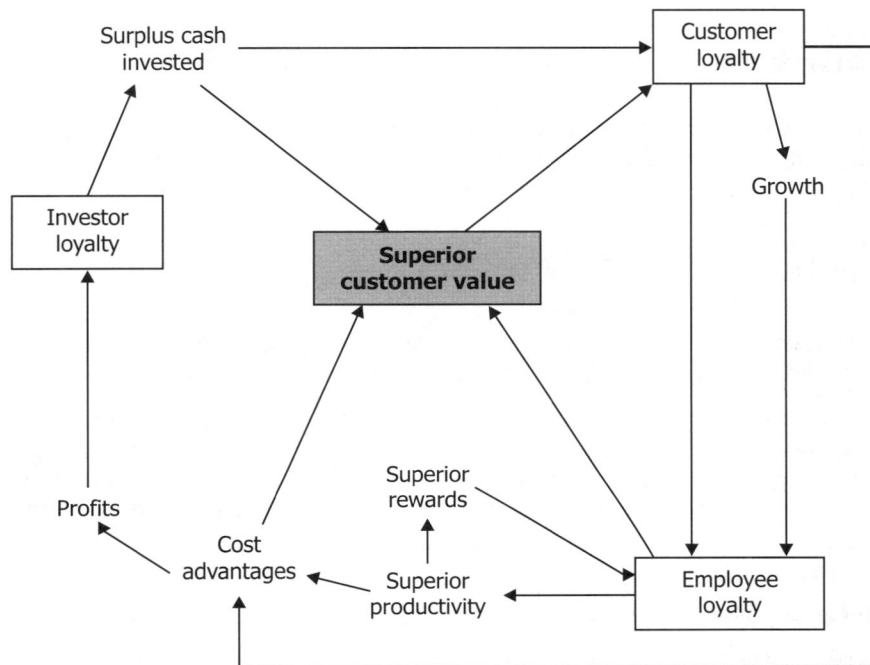

Working through the elements of this model one by one:

- Superior service and value (and positive reputation, which is partly built on sustained superior service and value) creates loyal customers.

- Revenues and market share grow as the best customers are prioritised, building repeat sales and referrals.

- Sustainable growth enables the firm to attract and retain the best employees (supported by a positive employer reputation/brand).

- Consistent delivery of superior value to customers (and resulting high reputation) increases employees' loyalty by giving them pride and satisfaction in their work.

- Long-term employees get to know long-term customers, enabling further service and value enhancement, which in turn further enhances customer and employee loyalty (and reputation).

- Loyal long-term employees generate superior productivity. This surplus can be used to fund superior rewards, tools and training – which further reinforce employee productivity, reward growth and loyalty (and employer brand).

- Increased productivity and the efficiency of dealing with loyal customers generates cost advantages over competitors – and high profits.

- High profits (and a positive reputation for profitability) make it easier for the firm to attract and retain high-quality investors.

- Loyal investors stabilise the system, funding investments that increase the company's value creation potential.

A strong corporate identity is more likely to create identification on the part of employees, with the organisation, its values, aims and objectives.

✏ ACTIVITY 8

concept

What would you anticipate to be the benefits of widespread employee identification with their employing organisation and its goals, which might support positive reputation management?

We will discuss these matters further in Chapter 10 on employee communications.

4 What makes a 'good reputation'?

What makes a good or positive reputation? What qualities earn the positive regard or esteem of stakeholders? In an influential model, Fombrun (1996) argues that in order to build a favourable reputation, an organisation must develop four key attributes: credibility, trustworthiness, reliability and responsibility.

📰 MARKETING AT WORK

application

Fill (*op cit*, p. 396) suggests that Fombrun's criteria for a favourable reputation can be illustrated with reference to a company such as **Nokia**, the Finish mobile phone manufacturer.

'**Credibility** is established through its range of products, which are perceived to be of high quality and branded. **Trustworthiness** has been developed through attention to customer service and support. **Reliability** and **consistency** have been achieved by setting and adhering to particular standards of quality, and **responsibility** is verified through a strong orientation to service and values manifested through the company's strong product development and innovation policy.'

Different stakeholder groups may have different expectations, satisfiers and perspectives in relation to an organisation. Broadly:

- **Employees** may be looking for an employer they can **trust**, to provide an on-going livelihood, to uphold their employment rights, and not to exploit their labour and contribution.

- **Customers** may be looking for a **reliable** provider of quality products and services, reducing their risk in purchase decisions by the consistency with which the company fulfils their needs and expectations.

- **Investors** may be looking for a **credible** company, reducing their investment risk by the confidence inspired by the company's management, track record and market standing.

- The **community** as a whole may be looking for a **responsible** business, which takes into account its potential impacts on people and the environment, and invests in good corporate citizenship.

Davies *et al.* (*op cit*, p. 60) summarise Fombrun's thinking as follows: Figure 1.5 opposite.

4.1 Credibility

🔑 KEY CONCEPT

concept

Credibility is the extent to which corporate statements, promises and claims are believable to investors (and other stakeholders): the belief that the organisation will do what it says it will.

Figure 1.5: A stakeholder perspective on reputation

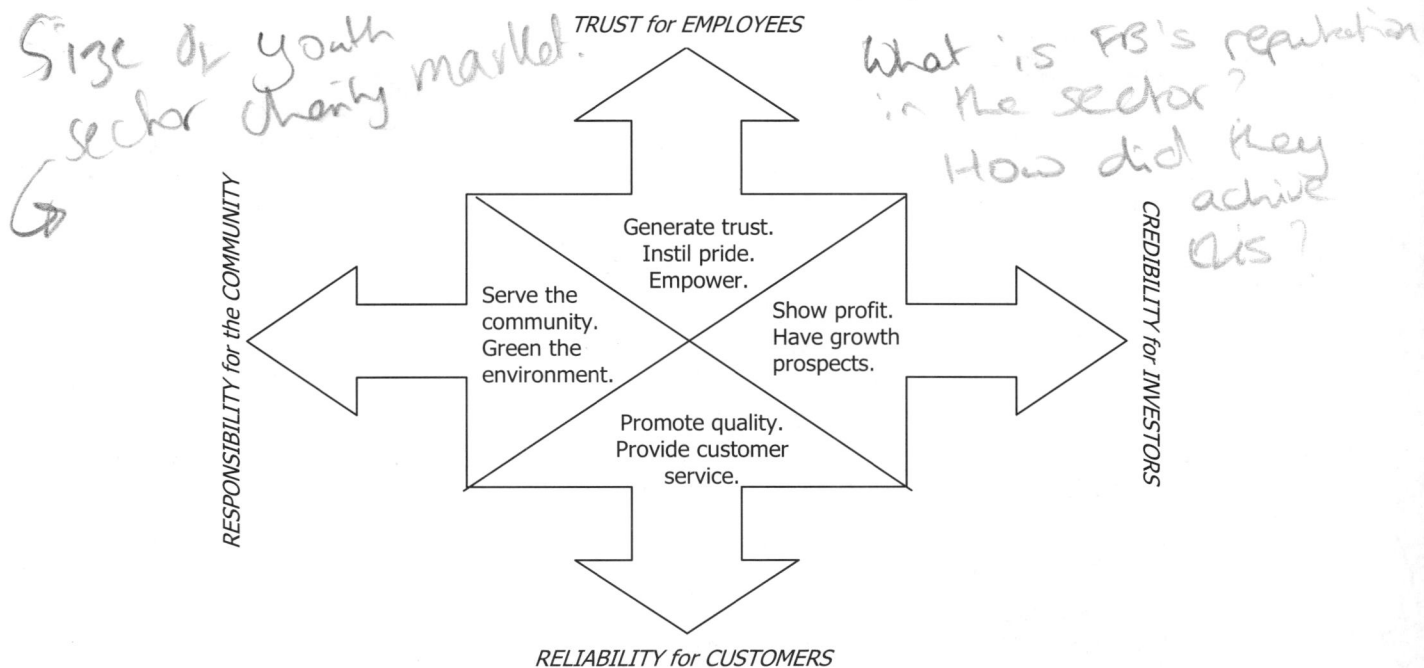

[Handwritten notes: "Size of youth sector charity market.", "define what reputation is.", "What is FB's reputation in the sector? How did they achieve this?"]

An organisation, and by extension its communications, may be credible by virtue of factors such as:

- **Track record and credentials**: proven and consistent performance, attainments, capabilities and capacities; proven and consistent record of following through on claims and promises. *[handwritten: — FB M+E]*

- **Market and industry standing**: reputation among peers; market/industry awards; the quality of suppliers and other business partners associated with the company. *[handwritten: — FB reputation]* *[handwritten: how does FB meet this?]*

- **Character**: demonstrated (or a reputation for) integrity, honesty and good intent. *[handwritten: — how does FB meet this?]*

- **Credible leadership**: visible, expressive, high-status, peer-respected leaders; competent management; strong (innovative, sustainable) strategic management and direction.

- **Credible spokespersons or intermediaries**: eg recognised and respected authorities, co-opted to present or corroborate the organisation's message. (You may recognise this from 'scientific' and celebrity advertising and endorsements, for example.) *[handwritten: — Andrew Purvis.]*

- **Objectivity**: demonstrated consideration of both sides of an issue (or stakeholder conflict) before formulating the organisation's approach or perspective.

- **Coherence and consistency** of messages (from different leaders, business units and brands) and between messages and behaviours/results.

- **Asset backing** for claims and promises requiring investment.

- **Sound risk management** practices, supporting business continuity and stability.

As we will see in Chapter 11, credibility is particularly important in crisis communication, when the organisation has to explain and reassure stakeholders – often against competing (negative) views and interpretations. Who will the target audience choose to believe?

Credibility is also, however, important in all image and reputation building, because it influences the extent to which the organisation's attempts to project its actual and/or desired identity are believed by the target audience. At the same time, reputation (or image) contributes to credibility, by creating the perception of all the above credibility factors in stakeholders' minds.

4.2 Trustworthiness

Trustworthiness is closely allied to credibility, describing how far stakeholders are exposing themselves to risk in dealing or allying themselves with the company: in other words, the likelihood that their expectations will be disappointed or that they will be 'let down' by the company.

An organisation may make itself trustworthy (worthy of trust) by virtue of factors such as:

- **Track record** of consistently delivering on promises or claims made, or expectations raised. (Note that the management of expectations – eg avoiding 'over-claiming' – is just as important as fulfilling expectations in building trust: 'under promise, over deliver' is a good motto...)

- Demonstrated (or strong reputation for) **honesty**, **integrity and fairness**, which would support the belief that the company will 'do the right thing' by its stakeholders.

- **Consistent reliability** of performance, service and brand qualities: building stakeholder confidence that they know what to expect.

- **Credibility of expressed values**, such as customer focus, value for employees, quality or environmental sustainability – which increases the stakeholder's belief that the company will 'do the right thing' if issues in these areas arise.

- **Transparency**: willingness to share information appropriately, in order to support stakeholder decision-making and collaboration. Transparency also *demonstrates* trust, because information can be *misused*: used to the advantage of one party at the other's expense (eg exploiting information on a supplier's costs or problems to strengthen one's bargaining position in price negotiation); or released to unauthorised third parties (eg giving customer data to commercial mailing lists, leaking unfavourable company reports to the press, or divulging plans to competitors).

- **Relationship marketing**: strategies aimed at on-going contact and connection with customers and other stakeholders, rather than one-off transactions. Trust is built up by experience: the more often and consistently stakeholders have positive experiences and encounters with the company, the greater the level of trust will be. (In turn, trust is central to the success of relationship marketing strategies, as it reduces the perception of risk and supports mutual investment in relationship. Without trust, the investment of time, money and commitment in a relationship, on either side, would simply be too risky: there would be no reason to believe that the benefits, promised in exchange, would accrue.)

The requirements for developing trust have been described as Three Cs:

- **Competency**. Does the organisation know what it is talking about? Can it deliver on claims and promises?

- **Caring**. Does the organisation asking for trust really care about the issue and its stakeholders? (If so, it is more likely to be fair and supportive in dealing with them.)

- **Character**. Does the organisation have character and values (eg honesty and integrity), on which it consistently bases its behaviour?

'If there is a vacancy in any of these areas, all is not lost: consider filling in the gaps. It may be a matter of who is chosen as the spokesperson to deliver a message, or it may involve drafting a recognised expert to corroborate the message or appeal. People will respect competence, disregard incompetence, and respect the incompetent when they are honest about their lack of competence. Begin with a firm grip on reality, build small wins, and advance trust one step at a time.' (Davies *et al.*, *op cit*, p. 280)

If you are interested in the trust element of reputation, you may like to dip into a highly accessible book by Stephen MR Covey called The Speed of Trust: The One Thing That Changes Everything *(2006, New York: Simon & Schuster). Covey looks at issues of credibility (self-trust), reliability (relationship trust), alignment (organisational trust), reputation (market trust) and contribution (societal trust).*

4.3 Reliability

Again, reliability is closely related to credibility and trust. Can stakeholders believe in the organisation (credibility)? Is the organisation *worthy* of that trust (trustworthiness)? And can stakeholders therefore *rely* on the organisation: take a risk on purchase or relationship, without having their rights or legitimate expectations disappointed?

For customers, reliability is crucially a matter of consistency of product and service quality. A reputation for reliability depends on the organisation's ability consistently to fulfil customer expectations and to create a positive experience of doing business with it, at every encounter and touch point with the organisation.

Samuel (2007, p. 63) emphasises that 'No matter how much effort we spend on promoting, positioning or profiling ourselves, failing to live up to individual expectations will severely damage our reputation. Everything counts. Every element of every transaction either enhances or damages our reputation. Whatever statements or claims we make, we must deliver on. No excuses. No blame. At all costs we must avoid giving others the opportunity to doubt us, as doubt calls our reputation into question.'

- Modern consumers want instant gratification – and alternative providers and solutions are available if one organisation fails to get it right first time.

- Reputation depends on the 'weakest link': the potential for the organisation to fail to deliver customer expectations at any interaction or touch point.

- Doubt spreads from a single demonstration of unreliability to damage reputation: 'If they don't deliver in this area, what else might they fail to deliver on?'

- People seek reinforcement and confirmation of their expectations. If they believe they have been failed in some way, they are more likely to seek out and focus on information that would tend to confirm this belief: negative experiences of others, negative press coverage and so on.

Service encounters are potentially critical incidents in building, maintaining or losing a reputation for reliability. A single disappointing service encounter – and/or a firm's subsequent poor response to handling the problem may be sufficient to reduce loyalty, make the customer more amenable to switching brands in response to competitor offers, and create reputation-damaging negative word-of-mouth. Customers may tolerate negative critical incidents for a while, but they are taken into account in the long-term evaluation of the organisation's performance.

Nor is this dynamic confined to customers. Think, for example, of the effect on a supplier's willingness to deal with an organisation, if it is unreliable in the payment of its debts or following through on agreed actions.

4.4 Responsibility

KEY CONCEPT

concept

The concept of **corporate social responsibility (CSR)** embodies a range of responsibilities that an organisation might consider it has towards its wider or secondary stakeholders, including the society and natural environment in which it operates.

We will consider this area in detail in Chapter 6, as one of the key messages to be conveyed to stakeholder audiences through corporate communication, and will only give some introductory remarks here.

Carol & Buchholtz (2000, cited in Jobber, 2007) suggest that there are four main 'layers' of corporate social responsibility.

- **Economic responsibilities**. The firm must produce goods and services wanted by the market, profitably – otherwise it cannot survive, and will not be able to fulfil any other obligations to stakeholders. Economic responsibilities include: operating efficiently and effectively, aiming for consistent levels of profitability, and competing effectively in the market.

- **Legal responsibilities**. Economic goals must be pursued within the framework of the laws of the society within which the firm operates. It is sometimes said that 'the law is a floor': it does not define best practice, but does set out the minimum principles and standards that are considered acceptable. The news is full of examples of how business practices can fail to comply with contract, employment, consumer protection, health and safety, competition law and so on – and the consequences of non-compliance.

- **Ethical responsibilities**. Ethical responsibilities comprise the expectations of society, over and above basic economic and legal requirements: honesty in business relationships, for example; not exploiting small suppliers and retailers; or not marketing manipulatively to children. This is a more discretionary area, because there are fewer direct sanctions against unethical behaviour. Ethical principles may be enforced via Codes of Ethics or Practice in an industry, profession or individual firm – but they are often also subject to stakeholder pressure (demands, protests, boycotts and so on).

- **Philanthropic responsibilities**. Above and beyond even ethical dealings, society increasingly expects that marketing organisations be 'good corporate citizens': that is, that they proactively and positively contribute to the society in which they operate. Examples of philanthropy include corporations building community amenities, sponsoring local causes and events, donating money to charity, promoting or campaigning on issues of concern and so on.

Society as a whole, because of its diversity, may have low direct influence on the policies and activities of an organisation. However, society's interests are organised, focused and represented in various ways: by government policy, legislation and regulation; by 'consumerism' or the consumer rights movement; by pressure and interest groups seeking to exert influence on behalf of particular constituencies or on particular issues; and by the fact that wider society is part of the environment within which the organisation operations – and within which it competes for labour, suppliers, customers, support and other key resources.

MARKETING AT WORK

application/contemporary issues

Alcoholic versions of soft-drinks – so-called 'alcopops' – have caused controversy and opposition worldwide, particularly because the brands seem to be directed mainly at young people, in the face of widespread concern at the level of youth alcohol abuse and binge drinking.

The need for tighter controls over the marketing of alcopops has been recognised by the drinks industry itself. A code of practice was introduced by the **Portman Group**, an organisation founded by the major UK drinks producers to promote sensible drinking and to reduce misuse of alcohol.

The code of practice complements and is consistent with all other relevant self-regulatory codes, and it helps to control the industry without the burden of new legislation. The provisions of the code are wide-ranging and cover the naming, packaging and merchandising of drinks.

An example of its operation could be seen in the marketing of Carlsberg-Tetley's 'Thickhead' drink, which was held by the Portman Group to be breach of industry guidelines, and a 'serious misjudgement'. Carlsberg-Tetley responded by agreeing to change the label.

For reflection: what other industries and entities (eg sporting codes) have taken concerted self-regulatory action to change their culture or practices, in order to improve or protect their reputations?

'Better-regarded companies build their reputations by developing practices which integrate social and economic considerations into their competitive strategies. They not only do things right – they do the right things. In doing so, they act like good citizens. They initiate policies that reflect their core values; that consider the joint welfare of investors, customers and employers, that invoke concern for the development of local communities; and that ensure the quality and environmental soundness of their technologies, products and services.' (Fombrun, cited in Watson & Kitchen, *op cit*, p. 126).

4.5 Creating a strong, sustainable and positive reputation

As we will see, strong reputations are partly formed by corporate communications designed to produce favourable perceptions in the minds of the public (by corporate '**expressiveness**'). Research by Fombrun and van Riel (2004) suggests that the expressiveness profile most supportive of a strong, sustainable and positive reputation is made up of five elements.

- **Visibility**. High reputation companies invest in communications.

- **Distinctiveness**. High reputation companies differentiate themselves (via the identity mix) from their competitors.

- **Authenticity**. High reputation companies match their communications to their values and actions, and live up to their promises and commitments.

- **Transparency**. High reputation companies have a culture of openness, having 'nothing to hide'.

- **Consistency**. High reputation companies cultivate consistency and coherency in the messages given by their different business units and brands, and avoid 'mixed messages'.

Learning objectives	Covered	
1	Explain the meaning of corporate reputation, image and identity in various contexts	☑	Introduction to corporate reputation management
		☑	Development of reputation management: from public relations; from the integration of corporate communications; from multi-disciplinary contributions
		☑	Reputation management applied to consumer, industrial, service, not-for-profit, societal, political and destination marketing
2	Explain key elements considered to constitute corporate reputation	☑	Definitions of corporate identity, image and reputation
		☑	Models of how identity, image and reputation relate to each other
		☑	Factors which make a 'good reputation': credibility, trustworthiness, reliability, responsibility (Fombrun)
3	Present a rationale for an organisation's directors to support the proactive and overt management of corporate reputation	☑	Overview of the benefits of positive corporate reputation
		☑	Reputation and financial performance
		☑	Reputation and shareholder value; the Reputation Value Cycle
		☑	Reputation and improved competitiveness
		☑	Reputation and employer branding: employee satisfaction and identification effects

Quick quiz

1   Complete the formula: Reputation = Sum of Images =

2   What are the key contributions of (a) psychology and (b) accounting to the discipline of reputation management?

3   Why is the concept of corporate reputation particularly relevant for (a) service and (b) not-for-profit organisations?

4   Distinguish between corporate identity and corporate image.

5   Outline a basic sequence of corporate image formation.

6   Describe how positive reputation can support financial performance by attracting customers and sales revenue.

7   Outline the Reputation Value Cycle.

8   When are stakeholders more likely to rely on reputation to make a purchase or investment decision?

9   What are the key expectations or satisfiers of employers, customers, investors and the community, which shape the elements of a positive reputation according to Fombrun?

10   What are the Three Cs of developing trust?

1   Your own judgements. This activity is designed to highlight the 'short-hand' nature of aggregative/evaluative assessments of reputation. (If you are interested, you might go further and try to unpack where you 'got' these assessments, or how you developed them. What was the balance of your own direct experience, things you 'heard' from others, and the communications of the entity concerned.)

2   Relevant to your own organisation. These are some key issues in the organisation of corporate communications and reputation management. Writers on the subject now argue the need for integration (or co-ordination) of communication activities; a wide scope (taking in a variety of stakeholder audiences, not just customers); and strategic-level involvement. If this is not the case in your organisation, you may want to flag these issues for further consideration later.

3   In terms of core values and attributes for an attractive destination, you may have thought about amenities and accommodation; entertainment and activities; value for money; ease of access; safety and security; cultural distinctives.

Limiting and risk factors for destination positioning include lack of amenities (etc) plus a wide range of perceptions about the destination itself and its surrounding region and country: expensive, hard to get to, dangerous, uncongenial.

There may also be particular perceptions arising from crisis. Think of the potential effect on tourism of terrorist activity in a region, for example. Or the reputational damage suffered by Mexico, as a tourist destination, in 2009, for example, with the outbreak of – and global media frenzy surrounding – 'Mexican/swine flu'...).

4   An important implication is that, while their images are what most organisations are most interested in, image cannot be directly manipulated by the organisation: it lies 'in the eyes of the beholder'. An organisation can only manage its *identity* and the ways in which it *projects* its identity – in order to *influence* the image stakeholders hold of it (in competition with a variety of other contextual influences). Since different stakeholders will have different experience of an organisation, it may have multiple images – and any of all of these may be quite different from what the organisation's leaders think or assume its image is (based on what it is trying to project or communicate). It is therefore critically important for the organisation to ascertain by research and feedback what stakeholders think – not just what the organisation is trying to portray.

5   Your own examples. (Think, for example, of a bank promoting itself as 'The bank that likes to say Yes' or 'The Listening Bank' turning people down for loans...) In terms of what can be done about mismatches, the basic point is that the entity will have to change *either* its behaviour (and supporting values, systems and processes) *or* its communications (in order to manage stakeholder expectations), or both.

6   According to Varey (2002, p. 205), the reasons managers give for attempting to manage corporate identity and image include the following.

- There is general promotional value.
- It encourages favourable behaviour towards the company.
- There is likely to be an effect on product sales.
- Products can be differentiated.
- Shareholders and employees can be recruited.
- It helps good relations with the community and government.
- It reflects the company more accurately.
- It services corporate objectives
- It operates as a competitive tool.

7   The daily news offers examples of destroyed reputations leading to organisational collapse or damage: names such as Barings Bank, Enron, Arthur Andersen, James Hardie or Merck may come to mind from recent years. Conversely, strong reputation often correlates with the expansion and resilience of companies such as Johnson & Johnson, Philips, The Body Shop, Tesco or Marks & Spencer.

8　Strong employee identification can:

- Foster a supportive attitude toward the company
- Result in behaviour and decisions by employees that are consistent with the company's objectives
- Encourage a unity of purpose between the company's leaders and its employees (vertical alignment)
- Encourage unity, consistency and coherence between different units of the organisation (horizontal alignment)
- Create an 'authenticity' of values and performance which is projected to stakeholders, potentially resulting in stakeholder identification and alignment.

1　Reputation = Sum of Images = (Performance + Behaviour) + Communication

2　Psychology has contributed information processing theories, describing how reputations are built up through perception, awareness, memory, affect and evaluation. Accounting has contributed approaches to the valuation of intangible assets and the recognition of financial benefits (eg price premium) of positive reputation.

3　See section 1.3 for a full explanation.

4　There are two ways of doing this. Identity is what is projected; image is what is perceived. Or (Davies *et al.*) identity is the internal stakeholder view; image is the external stakeholder view.

5　See Figure 1.2.

6　Customers can be attracted by improved marketing planning; differentiation from competitors; securing support in turbulence; securing brand engagement and loyalty; unpaid promotion/endorsement.

7　See Figure 1.3.

8　Stakeholders are more likely to rely on reputation when: information is complex, conflicting or incomplete; there is too little or too much information for rational judgement; there is too little involvement to warrant detailed information search; or there is pressure for a rapid decision.

9　Trust (employees); reliability (customers); credibility (investors); responsibility (community).

10　The three Cs are: Competency, Caring and Character.

Abratt, R and Shee, P S B (1989) 'A new approach to the corporate image management process' in *Journal of Marketing Management* Vol 5 (1): pp 63-76

Albert, S and Whetten, D (1985) 'Organisational identity' in LL Cummings & BM Shaw (eds) *Research in Organisational Behaviour*, pp 263-295. Greenwich, CT: JAI Press

Alvesson, M (1990) 'Organisation: from substance to image?' in *Organisation Studies*, Vol 11 (3): pp 373-394

Balmer, J M T (1998) 'Corporate identity and the advent of corporate marketing' in *Journal of Marketing Management* No 14: pp 963-996

Balmer, J M T and Greyser, S A (2003) 'Managing the multiple identities of the corporation' in J M T Balmer and S A Greyser (eds) *Revealing the Corporation: Perspectives on Identity, Image, Reputation, Corporate Branding and Corporate-Level Marketing*. London: Routledge, pp 15-29

Bekkum T van, Cornelissen J P & Ruler, B van (2008) 'Corporate communications and corporate reputation' in Melewar T C (ed.) *Facets of Corporate Identity, Communication and Reputation*. Abingdon, Oxon: Routledge

Bernstein, D (1984) *Company Image and Reality: A Critique of Corporate Communications*. London: Cassell Educational

Boddy, D (2005) *Management: An Introduction* (3rd ed). Harlow, Essex: FT Prentice Hall

Carroll, A B & Buchholtz, A K (2000) *Business and Society: Ethics and Stakeholder Management*. Cincinnati: South-Western Collage

Camerer, C and Vepsalainen, A (1988) 'The economic efficiency of corporate culture' in *Strategic Management Journal* Vol 9: pp 115 – 126

Caves, R E & Porter, M E (1977) 'From entry barriers to mobility barriers', in *Quarterly Journal of Economics* Vol 91 pp 421-434

Christopher M, Payne A & Ballantyne D (2002) *Relationship Marketing: Creating Stakeholder Value*. Oxford: Elsevier Butterworth-Heinemann

Covey, S M R (2006 *The Speed of Trust: The One Thing That Changes Everything*. New York: Simon & Schuster

Davies G, Chun R, Da Silva R V & Roper S (2003) *Corporate Reputation and Competitiveness*. Abingdon, Oxon: Routledge

Doorley, J & Garcia, H F (2007) *Reputation Management: The Key to Successful Public Relations and Corporate Communications* New York: Routledge

Dowling, G R (1994) *Corporate Reputations: Strategies for Developing the Corporate Brand*. London: Kogan Page

Dowling, G R (2004) 'Corporate Reputations: should you compete on yours?' in *California Management Review*. 46 (3) pp 19-36

Fill, C (2002) Marketing Communications: Contexts, Strategies and Applications (3rd ed). Pearson Education: Harlow, Essex Limited

Fombrun, C J (1996) Reputation: Realizing Value from the Corporate Brand. Harvard Business School Press: Boston

Fombrun, C J & Riel, C B M van (1997) *'The reputational landscape'*, in Corporate Reputation Review, Vol 1 (1 & 2): pp 5-13

Fombrun, C J & Riel, C B M van (2004) Fame and Fortune: How Successful Companies Build Winning Reputations. Upper Saddle River, Pearson Education: NJ

Franklin B, Hogan M, Langley Q, Mosdell N & Pill E (2009) Key Concepts in Public Relations. Sage: London

Grönroos, C (2000) Service Management and Marketing. Wiley: Chichester

Haywood, R (2002) Managing Your Reputation (2nd ed). Kogan: Page London

Mackiewicz, A (1993) The Economist Intelligence Unit Guide to Building a Global Image. McGraw Hill: New York

Melewar, T C (2003) *'Determinants of the corporate identity construct'* in Journal of Marketing Communications No 9: pp 195-220

Olins, W (1989) <u>Marketing</u>, 12 April pp 21-4

Peters, T J and Waterman, R (1982) <u>In Search of Excellence</u>. Harper & Row: New York

Post, J E and Griffin J J (1997) *'Corporate reputation and external affairs management'* in Corporate Reputation review. Vol 1(1): pp 165-171

Reichheld, F (2001) <u>The Loyalty Effect</u>. Boston, Mass: Harvard Business School Press

Riel, C B M van & Fombrun, C J (2007) <u>Essentials of Corporate Communication: Implementing Practices for Effective Reputation Management</u>. Routledge: Abingdon

Rindova, V & Fombrun, C J (1999) *Constructing competitive advantage: the role of firm-constituent interactions* in Strategic Management Journal, Vol 20 (8): pp 691-710

Samuel, H (2007) <u>Reputation Branding</u>. Wellington, NZ: First Edition Ltd

Shapiro, S P (1987) *'The social control of impersonal trust'* in *American Journal of Sociology* Vol 93, pp 623 – 658

Simões, C and Dibb, S (2002) *'Corporate Identity: Defining the Construct'*. Warwick Business School research Papers, Number 350: http://www.wbs.ac.uk

Varey, R J (2002) *Marketing Communication: Principles and Practice*. Abindgon: Routledge

Vella, K J & Melewar, T C (2008) 'Relationship between Identity and Culture' in Melewar T C (ed.) <u>Facets of Corporate Identity, Communication and Reputation</u>. Routledge: Abingdon

Watson, T & Kitchen, P J (2008) *'Corporate Reputation in Action'* in Melewar T C (ed.) <u>Facets of Corporate Identity, Communication and Reputation</u>, Routledge: Abingdon

Chapter 2

Influences on corporate reputation

Topic list

Introduction

This chapter builds on our discussion of reputation and related concepts in Chapter 1, looking in more detail at how reputations form, what influences them, and how they can be managed.

In section 1, we look at some models which describe how reputations form or are developed, as a framework for exploring some of the influences which impact on this process.

In sections 2–4, we consider some of the controllable and uncontrollable forces and factors that can influence an organisation's reputation: external, relational and internal.

In section 5, we set out some further broad precepts and models of reputation management found in the recommended reading, as an orientation to the following chapters. We also introduce a framework for managing corporate reputation based on the identification and reduction of 'reputational gaps': the potential mismatch between what the organisation *is,* how it wishes to be seen (positioning) and how it is actually perceived by its stakeholders (image).

This will create a foundation for our examination of corporate personality and identity in Chapter 3, and corporate image and reputational strength in Chapters 4 and 5, where we give you tools to identify potential gaps or mismatches, as a basis for making recommendations to develop greater consistency and congruence.

Syllabus-linked learning objectives

By the end of the chapter you will be able to:

Learning objectives	Syllabus link
1 Outline the forces that influence reputation, and how they can be assessed as a measure of reputational risk	1.1.3
2 Evaluate the contexts and concepts relating to corporate reputation	1.1.1
3 Identify gaps or mismatches between identity and image, and begin to make recommendations to close those gaps	2.2.1

Fairbridge rely heavily on P.R + lobbying external stakeholders e.g. MP's.

1 How are reputations formed?

In Chapter 1, we suggested that corporate images and reputations are formed by a number of factors.

- What the organisation is, does and values (corporate personality).

- How the organisation projects itself to stakeholders via its visual identity cues, behaviour and controllable communications (the corporate identity mix).

- How the organisation is portrayed by uncontrollable communications (eg rumour, word-of-mouth, media coverage).

- How stakeholders perceive all the above factors, in the light of their own expectations and attitudes, sense- or meaning-making activity (interpretation), and contextual factors.

In section 2 of this chapter, we will look at some of the factors which influence the perceptions of stakeholder audiences. Here, we will review some overarching ideas about how reputations are formed.

1.1 Internal and external influences

Perhaps the most important insight from this chapter is that multiple, complex factors form and influence corporate reputation – and that many (perhaps most) of these factors are *external* to the organisation: that is, they are not directly within the control of management. This is not to minimise the internal actions taken by managers and employees, from the internal development of corporate mission, values and strategy to the outward expression of corporate identity through symbol, behaviour and communication. However, it does reinforce the point that reputation is in the eye of the beholder. Organisations cannot assume that the image they are projecting (or trying to project) is what their target audiences receive and hold in their minds: there are many intervening factors which may create a gap between identity (what is projected) and image (what is perceived).

Nelson & Kanso (2008) offer the following summary (adapted from the work of Gotsi & Wilson) of the various internal and external factors influencing corporate reputation: Figure 2.1.

Figure 2.1: Internal and external influences on corporate reputation

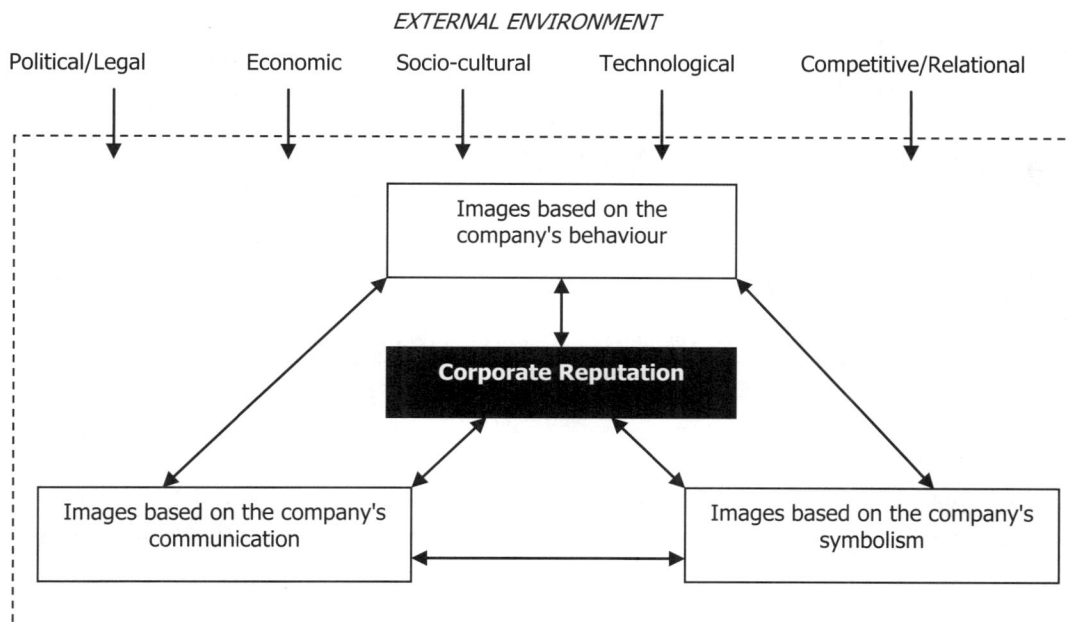

EXTERNAL ENVIRONMENT

| Political/Legal | Economic | Socio-cultural | Technological | Competitive/Relational |

Images based on the company's behaviour

Corporate Reputation

Images based on the company's communication

Images based on the company's symbolism

Bernstein (1984) similarly argues that corporate reputation is created through a complex range of factors: multiple **interactions** and **touch-points** with the organisation (experience with products, service encounters, corporate communications and branding); **preconceptions** and **expectations** based on contact with other similar organisations; **messages** derived from word of mouth and media comment; and so on. In addition, our image of an organisation is **filtered** by stereotypes or relatively fixed public preconceptions about:

- The **industry** in which the organisation operates.
- The organisation's **country of origin**.

ACTIVITY 1

application

Again, in your role as a representative stakeholder in, and observer of, public entities:

- What impressions and messages come to mind when you think of oil companies, banks, logging companies and politicians?

- What impressions and messages might you associate with a company or product that is German, Swedish, Belgian, Argentinian or Chinese?

Bernstein argues that individual organisations may not be able to do much about these preconceptions (given the public belief that 'the exception proves the rule'). To create and modify their own image and reputation, they can only manipulate **controllable factors** such as product/service quality, personal interactions, advertising and other marketing communications, visual identity elements – and (to a lesser extent) media comment and word-of-mouth: Figure 2.2.

Figure 2.2: Reputation filters

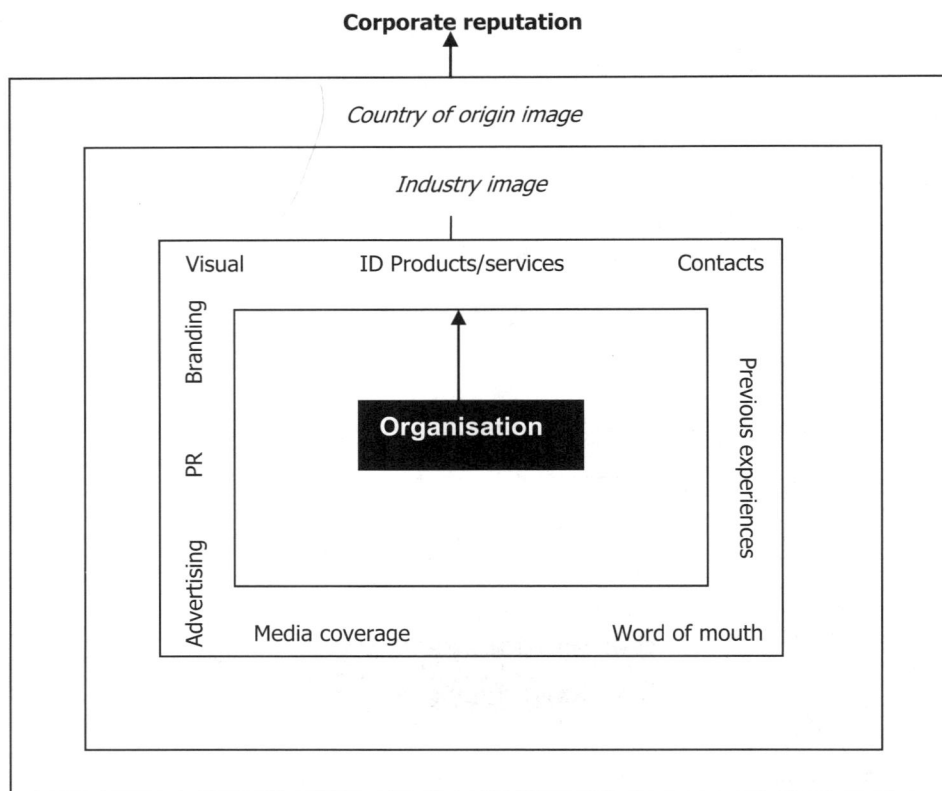

Corporate reputation

Country of origin image

Industry image

| Visual | ID Products/services | Contacts |

Branding

PR

Advertising

Organisation

Previous experiences

Media coverage

Word of mouth

We will look further at industry and country-of-origin effects – and other filters – in section 2 of this chapter.

1.2 From the inside out

Another key point about the formation of reputation is the link between corporate **identity** (defined as how the organisation sees and presents itself) and corporate **image** (how the various stakeholder publics perceive the organisation): Figure 2.3. Ideally, corporate reputation should reflect the authentic self-expression of the organisation, if identity and image are integrated or congruent over time.

Figure 2.3: Reputation as corporate self-expression

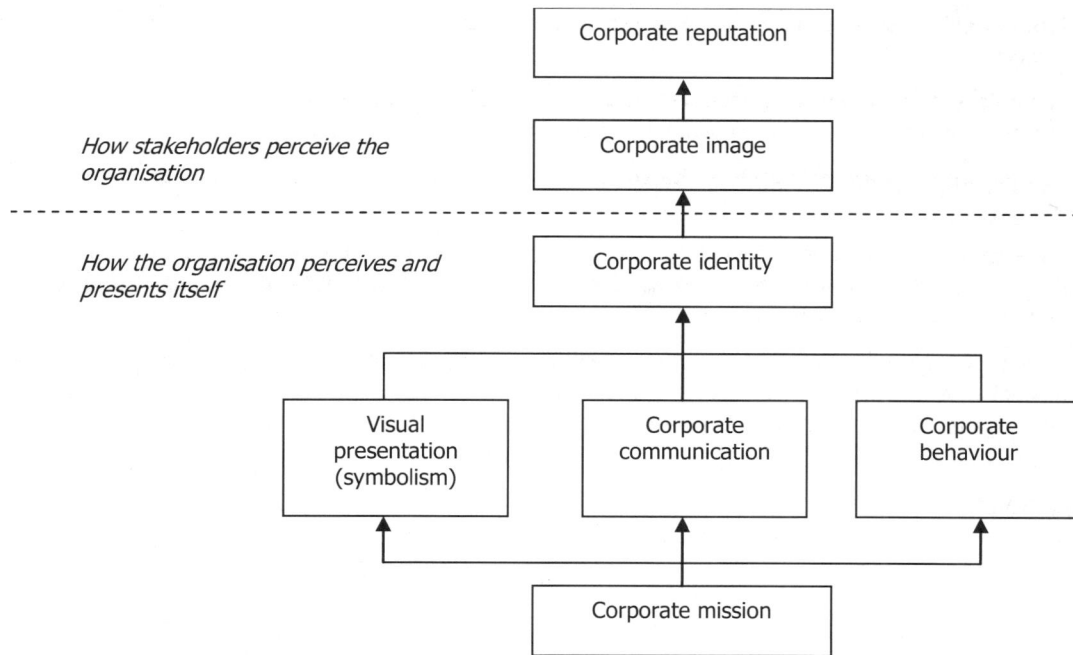

```
                              ┌─────────────────────────┐
                              │  Corporate reputation   │
                              └─────────────────────────┘
                                          ▲
                                          │
  How stakeholders perceive the  ┌─────────────────────────┐
  organisation                   │     Corporate image     │
                                 └─────────────────────────┘
                                          ▲
- - - - - - - - - - - - - - - - - - - - - │ - - - - - - - - - - - - - - - -
                                          │
  How the organisation perceives and ┌─────────────────────────┐
  presents itself                    │   Corporate identity    │
                                     └─────────────────────────┘
                                          ▲
              ┌───────────────────────────┼───────────────────────────┐
   ┌──────────────────┐      ┌──────────────────┐      ┌──────────────────┐
   │      Visual       │      │    Corporate     │      │    Corporate     │
   │   presentation    │      │  communication   │      │    behaviour     │
   │   (symbolism)     │      │                  │      │                  │
   └──────────────────┘      └──────────────────┘      └──────────────────┘
            ▲                         ▲                         ▲
            └─────────────────────────┼─────────────────────────┘
                              ┌──────────────────┐
                              │ Corporate mission│
                              └──────────────────┘
```

In fact, the translation of corporate mission into corporate identity is much more complex than this. Internal aspects of the organisation such as **corporate personality** (philosophy, core values and mission), **corporate strategy** (top management vision, corporate objectives, products and services, organisational structure) and **corporate identity** (behaviour, symbolism and communication) are all relevant to the identity projected to the outside world. For some authors, these are all elements of **corporate culture**, an umbrella term for the distinctive shared beliefs, values and norms of the organisation: 'the way we do things round here.' We will explore this model further in Chapter 3.

Greyser (1999) suggests that the key drivers of corporate reputation are:

- Competitive effectiveness (eg in areas such as innovation)
- Market leadership
- Customer focus
- Familiarity/favourability
- Corporate culture
- Communication

However, as we will see in our discussion of 'reputation gaps' at the end of this chapter, the most important impact on reputation is the relationship between stakeholder **expectation** and organisational **action**. Whether at the corporate or the product level, brand promises must be delivered – otherwise there will be disappointment, loss of trust and reputational damage. If stakeholder expectations can be consistently managed, met and/or exceeded, a positive reputation will (all other things being equal) be developed and maintained. 'A false reputation can be built by convincing publics that the corporation possesses certain desirable characteristics which it does not have. The danger of discovery is that the whole reputation is damaged, not just the attribute that was simulated or hidden.' (Varey, 2002, p. 206)

1.3 In the eye of the beholder

Another branch of reputation and communication theory, based on the contributions of psychology, stresses the **information-processing** and **sense-making activity** of **target audiences**. A reputation (like other forms of awareness and evaluation) develops as a result of the networks of cognitive associations that develop in people's brains, as they are exposed over time to sensory stimuli. The cumulative perceptions and associations come together to create an overall impression and value judgement.

Bromley (2000), suggests that different levels of information-processing affect people's impressions of an organisation.

- **Primary information processing** – based on direct personal experience of the organisation, its representatives or products.

- **Secondary information processing** – based on what reference groups (such as friends, family, colleagues, internet communities) have to say about the organisation and/or its products.

- **Tertiary information processing** – based on mass media information, including paid advertising and unpaid publicity.

Primary information is the most powerful influence on reputation formation; hence the importance of using marketing communication to secure **contact** with the organisation or product **sampling/trial** – and ensuring that all **experiences** and interactions with the organisation live up to stakeholder expectations.

However, people tend to have limited access to direct information about (experiences of) an organisation, compared to the greater amount of second- or third-hand information they receive from word-of-mouth and mass media sources. It is therefore equally important to manage secondary and tertiary communication – where possible.

ACTIVITY 2

application

What, broadly, do you think an organisation might be able to do to manage the secondary and tertiary information received by key stakeholders?

MARKETING AT WORK

application

van Riel and Fombrun (2007, p. 46) cite the example of the Marlboro cigarette brand, and its parent company **Philip Morris**.

'The reputation of Philip Morris is coloured by the direct experience that people have from smoking its Marlboro cigarettes. But they are probably more affected by the ubiquitous cowboy imagery in the brand's secondary marketing communications. Most recently, many people's impressions of the company will also have been heavily coloured by tertiary information revealed during the widely publicised anti-trust and healthcare lawsuits brought by the US federal and state regulators against the tobacco industry in the 1990s (to which Philip Morris was a party).'

'In summary: what is reputation management about?

So what is reputation? If we say someone or something has a clear 'reputation' we are saying that we expect that entity to behave consistently and therefore predictably in certain circumstances. We build this expectation through an accumulation of all of our experience and interactions together with reports of those of others, together with the (filtered) view of others of the entity's reputation. We constantly evolve our expectations as experience accumulates and as we accept some or all of the views of others and the evidence of our own experience. Our first view is likely to be a simply stereotype based upon limited information. We draw upon a library of stereotypes to make an initial judgement (all German companies are efficient; all oil companies damage the environment). This simple starting point can change dramatically but is more likely to evolve. Indeed dramatic change in reputation is the exception rather than the rule. However, highly significant incidents, such as crisis, can trigger a change in our views.

Our perception of reputation can also be shaped in part by the deliberate actions of the entity we are appraising, motivated to mould our perceptions to create a favourable disposition towards it. An individual or organisation can manage our view of their reputation through what it chooses to communicate to us. Formal communication will dominate this process when the entity is something we cannot or do not interact with. Thus a product brand is normally something we cannot interact with, while the image we have of a service organisation we use everyday will be dominated by the informal communication we are involved with, by being with employees or being in a building associated with the entity.

We also form an impression of organisations by working with them or for them. If the organisation is our employer, the experiences we have during the working day, the ways of working, its rules, its culture, the views of others when they discover where we work all influence what we have called 'identity' [internal stakeholders' perceptions of the organisation].'

Davies et al. (2003, p. 74) ▌

2 External influences on corporate reputation

As Figures 2.1 and 2.2 above illustrate, a wide range of external forces may impact on an organisation's identity, image and reputation.

- External factors impact on the **personality** (mission, strategy and culture) of the organisation. In a marketing-oriented organisation, most obviously, the mission and objectives of the organisation will be built around satisfying customer needs and wants, more efficiently and effectively than competitors. More specifically, as we will see in Chapter 3, the traditional 'positioning' approach to strategic planning identifies factors in the external environment which represent opportunities and threats for the organisation, and then seeks to develop strategies which will enable the organisation to position itself in such a way as to exploit the opportunities and counter the threats. An organisation's culture is also shaped by its members – who are also members of 'external' cultural spheres such as national, regional and occupational cultures.

- External factors impact on the organisation's **communicated identity**: for example, by creating opportunities or constraints for the dissemination of marketing messages; or by offering conflicting reputational messages (such as industry and country-of-origin stereotypes, media coverage and word of mouth).

- External factors impact on the organisation's **image and reputation**: for example, by influencing the kinds of values and attributes that are positively regarded by stakeholders; or by creating the potential for reputation-damaging 'crises' (eg compliance, green and ethical issues).

Obviously, we can't cover external factors in detail, because they will depend on the circumstances of each organisation. The point is that managers will need to conduct **environmental scanning** and/or **environmental audits** (such as PESTLE analysis) to identify the factors in their own operational environments that may pose reputational opportunities or risks. We will just give a broad framework for analysis here, with some examples to stimulate your own thinking.

2.1 PESTLE factors

PESTLE analysis is perhaps the most commonly used framework for analysing and classifying external environmental factors. There are various versions of the framework:

Political/Legal	**P**olitical	**S**ocio-cultural
Economic	**E**conomic	**T**echnological
Socio-cultural	**S**ocio-cultural	**E**conomic
Technological	**T**echnological	**E**nvironmental
	Legal	**P**olitical
	Environmental	**L**egal
		Ethical

You should have explored this framework in your early studies of the marketing 'macro' environment, and we will not go into detail here. However, we will look briefly at each of the PESTLE factors, and suggest some examples of potential reputational impact.

2.1.1 Political factors

The political environment embraces factors such as: the policies of local and national government bodies, and supra national institutions such as the EU; state support for industry and industry sectors (eg industry subsidies, or assistance for small firms); the influence of pressure, interest and lobbying groups and public opinion on government policy; and international relations.

ACTIVITY 3

evaluation

How might such political factors affect an organisation's reputation?

Managers will need to monitor the political situation in order to identify potential issues of concern to stakeholders (and potential reputational risk or opportunity). Sources of political information include: published government policy; direct contact with government representatives and lobbyists; media analysis of the political scene; published, online or specially commissioned surveys and reports; and specialist consultancies dealing in political risk analysis.

2.1.2 Economic factors

Macro-economic factors include the general level of activity and growth in the economic system, and the effect of economic 'boom and bust' cycles (such as the present recession) – which in turn are related to more detailed economic factors such as a government's fiscal (tax) and monetary (money supply) policy; interest and foreign exchange rates; inflation; consumer demand and levels of spending; labour costs and unemployment levels; international trade agreements and so on.

Forecasts in relation to all these factors will be crucial in shaping business strategy and operations – but how might they impact on corporate reputation? Some examples include:

- The need for an organisation to make workers redundant, when demand drops due to recession (or other factors). This is almost never regarded positively by the media and general public – let alone internal stakeholders affected by the move – although the economic rationale may be respected by shareholders. Redundancies are a key area of reputational risk, but companies that handle them well (with compassion, consultation, adequate compensation and support for affected staff) have an opportunity to rise in the public's estimation.

- Organisations 'off-shoring' production activities in order to take advantage of economies of specialisation and/or low labour costs (especially in developing countries). This carries reputational risk through (a) taking jobs away from the local and national economy and (b) potentially being seen to exploit low cost labour (which typically carries a stereotype of poor pay and conditions).

- Organisations paying high salaries to their directors in times of economic recession. ('Fat cat salaries' often hit the headlines in times of recession and corporate difficulties.)

- The perception that product prices and/or corporate profits are unreasonably high or rising (exploiting consumer demand, or failing to support consumers in a recession).

- Organisations failing to meet demand for basic or valued goods and services, due to economic rationalisation. This may be an issue of disappointed consumer expectation: in a recent example, the EU imposed quotas on clothing imports from China, leaving UK retailers short of stock to meet demand. It may also be perceived as a social responsibility issue: eg the withdrawal of unprofitable banking, transport or post office services from poor or rural areas.

- The economic performance of the organisation (of particular interest to industry, financial media and share market stakeholders).

Sources of economic data include: published government forecasts, reports and statistics; media analysis; industry projections and reports; and industry conferences and contacts.

'How does a firm that prides itself on its ethical approach to its employees, customers, franchisees, suppliers and shareholders negotiate the process of making redundancies?

At the start of 1999, **The Body Shop** found itself in the potentially embarrassing situation of having to cut jobs in order to press ahead with restructuring and fight off competition from cheap suppliers... An ethical employer cannot be seen to hand out redundancy notices without any thought for the people involved...

The entrepreneurs' club was set up to try and reduce the impact of impending redundancies on the local area. As well as loans, it also provided coaching and mentoring, opportunities for networking and access to an IT business centre... Mark Barrett, Head of HR at Body Shop International says: 'We're a young company. People leaving the Body Shop were well thought of, and so found it easier to get new roles.'

About 40% of the redundancies were voluntary, although Barrett believe some of those who were made compulsorily redundant were also happy to leave. Outplacement support was provided. Special treatment was given to staff aged over 50. This was partly a result of pressure from the consultation and representation committee, made up of employee representatives (the firm is non-unionised). People over 50 who had not found a job by the end of their redundancy period were entitled to an extra 25% on top of their original redundancy payment. Employees leaving the firm were also offered £1000 to spend on training, matched by a further £1000 from Sussex Enterprise, a local training and enterprise council... It was later decided to extend the £1000 offer to people who weren't leaving: 'There was a feeling at the time that people were leaving and being well supported, but that maybe those who were staying were not being given the same backing'...

An employee attitude survey was carried out among 390 staff who stayed at BSI and 220 who left or transferred to other parts of the Body Shop. Sixty one percent of those who took compulsory redundancy were satisfied with the outplacement support... More than two-thirds of all leavers said that they had enjoyed their time at the Body Shop and would consider working for the company again.

People Management (Neil Merrick, 26 October 2000)

2.1.3 Socio-cultural and ethical factors

The socio-cultural environment involves the 'people' aspects of the society in which an organisation operates, and from which it draws its strategic resources (including employees, suppliers and customers). Socio-cultural factors include: the demographic characteristics of the population (age, gender and geographical distribution, population density and movements, educational and occupational trends); the norms, values and customs of the culture; lifestyle and fashion trends; changing social attitudes; and so on.

These factors reflect the needs and expectations of the organisation's target market and customers, and will obviously be taken into account when developing marketing plans. However, they also apply to other stakeholder groups: affecting the availability of skilled employees, say, and the interest and influence of pressure groups.

Within this sphere, you might also include the **ethical environment**, which embraces a range of issues connected with corporate social responsibility and business ethics: what constitutes 'right conduct' for an organisation in its context. This overlaps with legal and environmental factors, since compliance and environmental protection are generally regarded as ethical responsibilities. However, it also includes industry and professional Codes of Practice and stakeholder expectations (and/or pressure) in areas such as: the fair treatment of employees and suppliers; investing in local communities; and environmental and social sustainability.

The potential for reputational risk and opportunity is perhaps more obvious in this area, since it so directly involves the expectations and perceptions of target audiences. Examples include:

- The extent to which an organisation's products are perceived to **promote or damage** human health (eg the perception that fast food chains and their marketing contribute to obesity, particularly in children) or the environment. There is potential for reputational crisis in these areas: a product recall for health and safety reasons, for example (as with global toymaker Mattel's recall of millions of toys contaminated with toxic lead paint) or the exposure of environment-damaging practices (eg Shell's management of the decommissioning of the Brent Spar oil drilling platform).

- The extent to which an organisation is perceived as supporting or promoting **social values** such as diversity and equal opportunity, or 'caring' and catering for the needs of particular social groups or audiences: the 'grey' (mature age) market, for example, women, or minority groups.

- Whether the organisation's visual identity, expressed values and marketing messages fit with prevailing **cultural norms and expectations**. If not, there is potential for the organisation to look foolish, as in the celebrated example of the Vauxhall Nova car's failure as a brand in South America, because in Spanish 'No va' means 'doesn't work'. There may also be potential for outrage, gaining the organisation a reputation for insensitivity or irresponsibility: examples include the use of distasteful or emotionally manipulative images, or insensitive placement of advertisements.

- Whether the organisation is perceived as **ethical and fair** in its employment and trading practices. Charity Oxfam, for example, recently suffered a reputational crisis when a major overseas supplier of its 'Make Poverty History' wristbands was discovered to be exploiting its workforce with poor pay and conditions. Nike has similarly had to work hard to improve its reputation, which was damaged by exposure in the area of labour exploitation.

- Whether the organisation is perceived to be **innovative**, **responsive and 'in touch'** in its product/service development, designs and offerings: Apple (especially through its i-Pod brand) has a strong reputation in this area, for example – while Marks & Spencer has had to rebuild a reputation for quality eroded by the growing perception that its retail outlets and products were 'old fashioned' and 'out of touch' with its core market.

Sources of socio-cultural data include: published demographic surveys and reports; media and specialist analysis of trends; market research programmes and consultancies and/or access to their published research reports; stakeholder feedback; and general 'scanning' of the environment. However, since reputation is in the eye of the beholder, there is arguably no substitute for going direct to stakeholders for their demographic and cultural data – and their perception of how the organisation matches up.

2.1.4 Technological factors

The technological environment embraces the technological sophistication of the organisation's national or international markets; developments in the particular fields that are relevant to the organisation; and development in information and communication technology (ICT).

Technological innovations and developments influence the type of products or services that are made and sold (eg digital cameras and MP3 players); how products are made (eg using computer-assisted design and manufacture) and services are provided (eg online); how market segments and customer needs are identified (eg using database management and data mining); how organisations are managed (eg the emergence of 'virtual' organisations and teams linked wholly or mainly by ICT networks); how organisations communicate with their stakeholders (eg via digital, interactive media, e-mail, SMS text messaging, web marketing and so on); and how stakeholders communicate with each other (eg on online content-sharing and social networks such as YouTube and FaceBook).

Technology can affect an organisation's reputation by, for example:

- Creating a reputation for innovation and/or technology leadership (or their reverse)

- Supporting consistent quality in product manufacture and customer service (eg through 24/7 customer access, or computer-telephony integration and e-CRM systems allowing caller recognition and real-time access to customer and product information)

- Supporting environmental scanning and stakeholder feedback gathering, enabling the monitoring of reputational issues and stakeholder/pubic perceptions (eg using search programmes to monitor online media, the 'blogosphere' and community message boards for comments about the organisation or brand)

- Creating a forum for uncontrollable communications about the organisation or brand by stakeholders. Internet penetration means that reputation-building or reputation-damaging messages can be disseminated very widely, very fast, and largely without any checking or censorship.

This latter point is of particular interest in the sphere of reputation management. Samuel (2007, p. 34) argues that:

'The explosion of blogs, personalised web sites, community and other online interactive forums on the internet has changed the way information is received and processed and how we represent ourselves or find ourselves being represented... Web sites such as Bebo, YouTube and MySpace enable individuals to present whatever content and image they choose to the entire world. They have enabled consumer communities to develop at incredible speed and give anyone with internet access the opportunity to publish whatever content they choose, largely without being censored... Before the internet, if you disagreed with an opinion you might write a letter to the editor of whichever paper you read it in, and your opinion may or may not have been published. Today, literally millions of individuals are expressing their unedited opinions in cyberspace for anyone to see...'

✏️ ACTIVITY 4   application/contemporary issues

What challenges are posed to reputation/communication managers by the existence of the explosion of blogs, websites, community and other online interactive forums?

📰 MARKETING AT WORK   application

This cautionary tale from Samuel (*op cit*, p. 85):

In 2005, **Kryptonite Locks** was approached by a consumer letting it know that its bike locks could be picked using a humble biro pen. Unhappy with the company's lacklustre response, the complainant decided to post a complaint a www.bikeforums.net alerting other bike enthusiasts to the situation. Not only did he post his complaint in writing, he decided to put a video clip on the internet, clearly demonstrating how a Kryptonite bike lock could be picked using a Bic pen.

Within 48 hours, an estimated 180,000 blog readers had watched the video clip. A blog-storm had started. Kryptonite Locks went public and released statements countering the claims in an attempt to reassure consumers its locks were effective – in spite of the fact that the video clip was available online for anyone to view.

The New York Times picked up and publicised the story and within another 48 hours more than 1.8 million blog readers were aware of the claim. Sales slumped and just three days later the company conceded its position and announced a free product exchange that was estimated to cost the company US$10 million. Within just 10 days, Kryptonite Locks' reputation had gone from trusted to doubted and US$10 million had been wiped off its bottom line.

The story doesn't end there however. Ten months later, in July 2006, the blog-storm and on-line aftermath continued to damage Kryptonite's reputation. A Google search for 'Kryptonite' came up with its product recall pages at number one and two. Their official web site sat below these – and just below that sat Engadget.com's pages about the whole debacle, including the original video clip. The ongoing damage continued long after the initial incident.

The crucial element of this was the company's failure, at the outset, to take the allegation seriously and to respond swiftly *in the medium in which the allegation was made*: the blogosphere.

2.1.5 Legal factors

There is a wide range of national and transnational (eg EU) law and regulation on issues such as: the rights of employees; health and safety at work; consumer rights; product safety/quality; environmental protection; data protection; the protection of intellectual property (designs, patents and copyrights); the legitimacy of competitive practices; and so on. As well as the law, there is an increasing amount of quasi-law which affects marketers, based on voluntary codes (eg advertising standards) which do not normally have the full sanction of legal punishment, but are self-enforcing due to the negative reputational effect of non-compliance.

Compliance with relevant legal and regulatory provisions is essential both to demonstrate ethical behaviour (an important reputational factor) – and to avoid penalties and sanctions for *not* doing so, including reputational damage. You should be able to think of plenty of examples, from the news media, of organisations whose reputations have been damaged by high-profile law suits, or allegations of illegal activity. In May 2009, for example, pharmaceutical giant Merck faced on going legal action in Australia over claims that its arthritis drug, Vioxx, increases the risk of heart attack – and that it continued to promote the product despite knowing the risk: the company has been in the courts – and in the press – worldwide over this issue since 2004, with damaging exposure of its corporate culture and practices.

2.1.6 Environmental (green) factors

The natural environment embraces factors such as: legislation, international obligations (such as the Kyoto agreement on climate change) and government targets in regard to environmental protection and sustainability; consumer and pressure-group demand for eco-friendly products and business processes; issues of pollution, waste management, disposal and recycling; the depletion of non-renewable natural resources; the protection of habitats and biodiversity from urbanisation and industry; pressure for the reduction of greenhouse gas (GHG) emissions and carbon footprints; and so on.

All these factors will influence the reputation of organisations: positively (eg in the case of Marks & Spencer, with its industry-leading 'Plan A' programme for sustainability) or negatively (eg in the case of polluters and energy-consumers). Many organisations are developing strategies, capabilities and communication strategies in this area. The UK construction industry, for example, is making a concerted effort to change its image, by promoting 'Sustainable Construction' (including initiatives to reduce energy consumption, materials waste and environmental pollution). Similarly, reputation-aware airlines like Virgin are investing heavily in research into renewable, clean energy sources (to counter the negative perceptions arising from air travel's high carbon footprint).

Specific industries and organisations will also have particular concerns: you might like to think what 'green' issues might be a priority for a car manufacturer, a brand of canned tuna, a retail chain and a tourist destination, say.

MARKETING AT WORK
application/contemporary issues

The natural environment also poses other reputational hazards. Examples include:

- Natural disasters, which may be well or poorly handled by entities. The current 'text book' example is the reputational damage suffered by the US government and other agencies, due to their poor handling of the aftermath of hurricane Katrina in New Orleans.

- Resource scarcity or disruption to supply (arising from weather or other natural factors), creating reputational risk in areas such as pricing and reliability.

- Diseases such as BSE or foot and mouth disease – and more recently the 'Mexican' or 'swine' flu, affecting the reputation of countries/regions (as tourist destinations), products (as unsafe) and agencies handling the crisis.

ACTIVITY 5
application

What PESTLE factors are most likely to impact on your own organisation and its sector? Brainstorm a quick PESTLE analysis.

2.2 Country-of-origin effects

The country-of-origin of an organisation or brand strongly colours stakeholder perceptions: a phenomenon known as Country-of-origin (COO) effects. This is particularly important for international marketing organisations.

KEY CONCEPT
concept

The **country-of-origin (COO) effect** is 'the picture, the reputation, the stereotype that businessmen and consumers attach to products of a specific country' (Nagashima, 1977).

People tend to develop generalised images, stereotypes or preconceptions about the products of different countries, based on factors such as:

- The level of industrialisation or technological development of the country, which tends to be associated with a perception of reliability and quality

- Representative products of the country, or identified with the country

- Historical events, traditions and international relations, creating positive or negative associations with a particular country

- Stereotyped perceptions of national characteristics and image, based on limited information available through the media, travel, passed-down stories and jokes and so on. These perceptions may be specifically related to product attributes. For example, German products (notably cars) are viewed as high on prestige and engineering quality, but low on economy. Latin countries are seen as relaxed, 'laid back' and low on time-consciousness – a positive for holidays, but a negative in business evaluations.

According to Davies *et al.'s* survey of available research (*op cit*, p. 96), some consumers appear to be indifferent to the country-of-origin effect, while others search for country-of-origin information. While COO effects are more influential for some products than for others, COO stereotypes generally tend to be more influential when little information about product attributes is available. Perceptions of quality are particularly susceptible to the COO effect.

It should be noted that COO effects work both ways: a positive national image can be exploited to advantage (as with French perfumes and German and Italian cars), while a negative national image may act as a drag on corporate brand and reputation.

It should also be noted that COO effects may reflect reality. Competition guru Michael Porter (1980) suggested that a country may indeed have an economic advantage (comparative advantage) in supplying a particular type of product or service, due to the concentrated availability of skills, infrastructure, natural resources, specialism, accumulated learning and so on. In other cases, however, the perceptions associated with a country may have little foundation in reality.

2.3 Industry-wide factors

The influence of industry image or reputation is similar to that of the country-of-origin. People develop generalised pre-conceptions about different industry sectors, as reflected in popular culture – and 'most trusted company' surveys.

Oil companies, for example, generally suffer from an image problem. They are seen as large and powerful, and their products and policies are associated with a number of negative attributes: the high price of petrol at the pump; global warming; oil pollution and so on. Companies such as Shell and BP have to work extra hard to create and maintain positive, 'green', corporate-citizen identities.

Other industries subject to generalised reputational damage include: the armaments industry; the tobacco and alcohol industry (perception of making profit from addiction and damage to health); pharmaceutical companies (perception of undue influence on the medical profession, maximisation of profit by prohibiting the development of generic drugs for poorer markets, recurring health scares); fast food providers (perception of manipulative advertising to children, contribution to obesity); the fashion and cosmetics industries (perception of negative influence on body image, testing of products on animals etc); and the construction industry (perception of poor quality from 'cowboy' builders, exploitation of casual labour, poor health and safety record, environmental waste and damage).

Such industries argue that they create employment and generate tax revenue, and that consumers are free to choose their products or not – but there are strong and public counter-arguments from pressure groups and regulators, including individual and class action law suits for compensation for damage caused by the continuing promotion of potentially harmful products and practices.

Davies *et al.* (*op cit*, p. 98) argue that the stereotyping of an industry can, with sustained effort, be avoided.

'The **Body Shop** is a part of the cosmetics industry. It is a multinational. It trades with the Third World. Founder Anita Roddick emphasised that her products were not tested on animals, a feature of most cosmetics; that they were not over packaged (originally you could refill the basic containers); and that she aimed personally to support Third World initiatives, particularly those associated with women. In doing so, she positioned her own company, repositioned her competition and created a strong corporate reputation – and all within a market, cosmetics, that would not have been everyone's first choice of a sector in which to launch an ethical positioning.'

Note from this example that an organisation will be subject to different **levels of reputational effects**. The Body Shop has its own corporate reputation, which is partly filtered through the sector reputation of the cosmetics industry and the COO effect of being a British company.

2.4 Community-based factors

Organisations may also develop 'local' reputations within the community within which they operate, according to factors such as:

- Whether they invest in the local community and community projects: using local suppliers and local labour; contributing finance or skills to infrastructure projects; contributing volunteers, finance or publicity to local charities and community group projects

- How willingly they comply with local government policies and the requests of local bodies such as town planners, police and traffic authorities

- How co-operatively they deal (and/or how fairly they compete) with other local businesses

- How considerate and responsive they are to the needs of other residents and land-holders: ie whether they are a 'good neighbour' in terms of noise, traffic congestion, building works, pollution etc

- How proactively and openly they communicate and consult on plans which will affect their neighbours and the local community.

ACTIVITY 6 application

What country-of-origin and industry effects are likely to filter stakeholder perceptions of your own organisation, or another organisation of your choice (as a possible focus of your assessment)? You may like to do a quick 'poll' of friends and colleagues, to determine the kinds of stereotypes and preconceptions people have about the country (or region) and sector with which the organisation is associated.

3 Relational influences on corporate reputation

Relational influences on corporate reputation imply a number of factors:

- Factors that influence an organisation's reputation **within a relationship** – that is, the perceptions and evaluations of the other party to the relationship, based on that party's specific knowledge and experience of the organisation

- Factors that influence an organisation's reputation by virtue of the way in which it **conceives and conducts relationships** – that is, whether it competes fairly, uses its power and influence ethically, collaborates constructively and so on

- Factors that influence an organisation's reputation by virtue of **particular relationships** – that is, by association with another party (whose reputation may 'rub off' on a relational partner)

3.1 Competitive and collaborative strategies

An organisation is more likely to have a position reputation with its stakeholders (both those involved in relationship and outside observers) if it conducts both its competitive and collaborative strategies ethically and positively.

Competitive strategies pose **compliance and ethical issues** – as well as reputational issues. Competition and fair trading law recognises a difference between legitimate (even if aggressive) competition and **unfair competition**. Head-to-head advertising comparisons and price wars are legitimate (if not, in the long run, sources of sustainable competitive advantage): 'dirty tricks' campaigns, misleading advertising claims and restraint of competition (eg by exploitation of a dominant market position) are not. Witness the damage caused to the reputation of Microsoft by its attempts to squeeze out software competitors by bundling applications and creating compatibility issues for competitor software. This caused negative publicity (particularly once it became the subject of repeated legal action under EU competition law) and negative word-of-mouth among IT-user communities.

MARKETING AT WORK

application

Consider the reputational implications of the following prominent news story in the *Wall Street Journal* (April 18, 2009).

Hotel giants' legal battle of the brands

Starwood Hotels & Resorts Worldwide have sued Hilton Hotels, accusing its rival of using stolen confidential Starwood documents to develop a new luxury hotel chain. The lawsuit ... alleges that former Starwood executives who joined Hilton last summer, stole more than 100,000 electronic and paper documents containing 'Starwood's most competitively sensitive information.'

'This is the clearest imaginable case of corporate espionage, theft of trade secrets, unfair competition and computer fraud,' the complaint alleges. In addition to monetary damages, Starwood is seeking a court order that could, in effect, force Hilton to cancel the rollout of the Denizen Hotels chain, which it unveiled last month.

The former employees named in Starwood's suit allegedly played key roles managing the image of its luxury W Hotels. The lawsuit could imperil Hilton's global ambitions for the Denizen brand, which is aimed at travellers drawn to upscale accommodations with a modern flair...

Starwood's allegations set the stage for a battle between two of the world's largest hotel companies and comes as both are struggling to weather a global recession that has driven down room rates and revenue.

The case opens a window into the inner workings of the hotel business, where companies spend years studying consumers, analysing fashion and social trends, fabrics, room lighting, building costs and food choices. Thousands of discrete decisions on these matters go into creating a 'brand profile'. Such profiles, which hoteliers regard as trade secrets, are especially prized in the market for luxury hotels, the industry's most lucrative and competitive segment... The allegedly stolen information, it is claimed, has allowed Hilton to exploit the time and tens of millions of dollars invested by Starwood to bring a 'competitive hotel chain to market expeditiously', avoiding the 'inevitable and costly trials and errors along the way'...

The organisation's **choice of competitive strategy** (as we will see in Chapter 3) will shape the corporate identity and image.

- A strategy of **cost leadership**, for example, may position a brand at the 'economy' end of a market (potentially lowering its positioning on quality): it may also create a negative image for squeezing smaller, higher-cost players out of a market, or squeezing the profit margins of suppliers to unsustainable levels (an accusation currently levelled at major supermarkets), or off-shoring production or downsizing to cut labour costs.

- Any strategy of **differentiation** (eg on the basis of customer service, innovation or corporate social responsibility) will inevitably flow through to corporate identity and reputation management, since both – by definition – reflect the distinctive attributes by which the organisation differentiates itself from competitors.

Collaborative strategies are also designed to create competitive architecture, in the form of networks of supply, support and synergy which *together* deliver competitive customer value. In modern competitive environments, it is not just companies at the same level of the value chain that compete, but whole **value networks** (Porter, *op cit*). 'The real competitive struggle is not between individual companies, but between their supply chains or networks... What makes a supply chain or network unique is the way the relationships and interfaces in the chain or network are managed. In this sense, a major source of differentiation comes from the quality of relationships that one business enjoys, compared to its competitors.' (Christopher *et al.*, 2002).

It should be noted that an organisation's reputation can be enhanced or damaged by **association** with network partners and collaborators. Potential partners should therefore be carefully evaluated for reputational strength, congruence of identity and image with corporate reality, track record of delivering on claims, and potential reputational risk factors – before any close relationship is entered into. 'One of the most beneficial aspects of collaborating is being able to leverage and benefit from each other's reputation. Collaboration and association are essentially a form of **endorsement**. Being associated with someone or something held in high esteem results in the positive reputation the person or item has being transferred to a greater or lesser degree to the other party. Of course, the same is true if the person or item you are associated with has a negative reputation. You will acquire some or all of the negative reputation by association.' (Samuel, *op cit*, p. 160)

- An organisation may want to form a joint venture, strategic alliance, supply partnership or co-promotion with a high-status, high-reputation partner, in order to be covered by the 'halo' of its reputation: in other words, positive reputation 'rubs off' by association. (You might argue, for example, that Nike, which had suffered reputational damage in regard to the use of 'sweat-shop' labour, has gained strong reputational attributes by its co-branding with the Apple i-Pod.)

- Organisations may be reputationally damaged by association with suppliers or partners whose ethical, environmental, commercial or governance practices were publically called into question. (The example of Oxfam and its 'Make Poverty History' wristband suppliers again comes to mind.)

- **Advertising placements and sponsorships** are often based on reputational association and (direct or implied) endorsement: think of the value of a brand being associated with a popular TV programme, say, or a major sporting or cultural event, or a worthwhile charity. Similarly, think of the value to a charity of a well-know patron, spokesperson or advocate with a strong positive reputation.

- **Cause-related marketing** may be used to leverage reputation through association with socially-responsible organisations and messages. This is a branch of **affinity marketing**, by which a marketing organisation attempts to 'leverage the felt affinity, goodwill or brand name strength of a partner' (in this case, a charity or cause) to transfer interest, commitment and loyalty to its own corporate brand (Swaminathan & Reddy, 2000, p. 382). This may take the form of companies sponsoring charity, community or arts events; raising funds (through staff, customer and supply networks) on behalf of charities; providing resources (eg computers) for schools; or offering funding for initiatives tackling social or environmental problems. Many large corporations now have major cause-related marketing programmes.

🔑 KEY CONCEPT   concept

Cause-related marketing refers to marketing activities in which a business forms a partnership or association with a charity or cause, in order to jointly promote a product, brand or issue, for mutual benefit.

✏️ ACTIVITY 7   concept

What, broadly, would you see as the aims of causal marketing for reputation management?

Apple i-Pod and Nike

Apple has developed a unique partnership with sportswear giant Nike, on the basis that many walkers and runners like to listen to music using their i-Pods. The partnership includes various aspects including:

- A jointly-engineered and co-branded Nike+i-Pod Sport Kit.

- Nike Sport Music content, available from Apple's i-Tunes music store, including playlists put together by top athletes, and special workout mixes.

- Nike+ clothing designed to hold the i-Pod Nano during the run.

- The facility to synchronise workout data from the i-Pod to a computer, either via i-Tunes or nikeplus.com.

Check out the attractive co-branding proposition: http://www.apple.com/ipod/nike or http://www.nikeplus.nike.com.

Ledingham & Bruning (2000) draw links between the disciplines of public relations (or reputation management) and **relationship marketing**, both of which are built on the negotiation of mutually-satisfying relationships between organisations and their various publics.

- Reputation is based on a network of relationships with internal and external stakeholders, reflecting the orientation of relationship marketing. Relationship marketing is based on an understanding of the range of legitimate stakeholder audiences or 'markets' with which an organisation may seek to develop ongoing supportive relationships. It embraces many of the disciplines used in corporate issues management, such as media, community and pressure group relations, corporate social responsibility and consultative processes.

- Organisations which develop relationship marketing programmes, aimed at mutually satisfying value exchange, embrace relationship values such as trust, transparency, product/service quality, responsibility, sustainability, mutual commitment and corporate ethics – all of which correlate positively with a strong, positive corporate reputation.

- Relationship marketing involves two-way dialogue with stakeholders, and management of all their interactions and touch-points with the organisation (rather than just marketing messages) – with the aim of creating genuine engagement (rather than just sales transactions), leveraging the potential and minimising the risk inherent in stakeholder relationships. Again, this matches the orientation of reputation management.

You should be familiar with the concepts of relationship and stakeholder marketing from your studies in *Stakeholder Marketing*.

If you want to follow-up on the links between reputation management and relationship marketing, an influential starting point would be:

- *Peck, Payne, Christopher and Clark:* **Relationship Marketing: Strategy and Implementation** *(1999: Elsevier Butterworth-Heinemann). Chapter 1 'Relationship marketing: the six markets model' gives a good overview.* ∎

3.2 Mergers and acquisitions

Mergers and acquisitions may be seen as a stronger, more permanent form of association.

- A **merger** is where two companies voluntarily pool the ownership interests of their respective shareholders.
- An **acquisition** is where one firm buys the equity stake or assets of another company.

Inter-organisational integration of this type may influence corporate reputation in a number of ways.

- The way in which a merger or acquisition is **handled and communicated** may reflect on the reputation of one or both of the firms concerned. A hostile take-over, for example, may result in negative press coverage, negative messages by the two parties about each other. Redundancies and relocations as a result of the move, if not well handled, may also cause reputational damage. The acquisition itself may result from the negative market perceptions and prospects of a firm, affecting its share price and making it vulnerable to takeover. Conversely, a positively communicated proposal, stressing the synergy and mutual benefits of the move, may inspire confidence in market analysts and shareholders and add to the firms' combined market value.

- A merged company may take on some of the corporate reputation and standing of each partner, and/or of their industry or country of origin (if different), offering **reputational synergy** (2 + 2 = 5). As we noted above, however, this effect can also be negative, and a company will need to be careful to avoid reputational risk or damage 'rubbing off' as a result of a merger or acquisition.

- Mergers and acquisitions may create a temporary **identity and/or image crisis**, as the organisation's internal and external stakeholders lose certainty about what the new organisation is and stands for. Any or all elements of the identity mix (symbolism, communication and behaviour) may shift. 'Mergers create gaps in organisational images and identities. It is possible that the image, culture and identity of the two organisations merging together will have been significantly different. It is possible that external stakeholders will have seen significant gaps between the two companies in the past and will be confused as to the reputation of the merged entity. There will be a gap between what existed before and what is perceived now.' (Davies *et al.*, *op cit*, p. 218).

- Strategic decisions will have to be made as to whether the two corporate brands will be kept intact and separate, or whether they will be merged into some new brand (with a new visual identity and nomenclature), or whether the subsidiary brand will remain intact but be explicitly labelled and included as within the umbrella of the main corporate brand. These are known as different levels of **brand endorsement**, and will be discussed in detail in Chapter 5.

- Employees in each of the two companies are likely to have an affinity to, or identification with, their old organisation, and this may create resistance to the creation of a new **identity**. This should be assessed prior to the merger. If the two cultures are similar, it will be supportive to emphasise this to employees. If they are divergent (or clashing), it will be useful to understand the underpinning values and work practices of each identity, so that they can be integrated, or so that the replacement of the one by the other can be justified. Mergers tend not to result in amalgamated cultures: one culture will come to predominate, as key culture-drivers reach top positions, and others leave because they do not like the new way of doing things (Fill, *op cit*).

3.3 Re-positioning

Positioning and re-positioning may be seen in two different lights, in the context of corporate identity and reputation management.

3.3.1 Brand positioning

As you should be aware from earlier marketing studies, positioning refers to 'the place the product [or organisation] occupies in consumers' minds relative to competing products' or 'the way the product [or organisation] is defined by consumers on important attributes' (Kotler and Armstrong, 2000).

Corporate brand positioning may be based on factors such as: product/service scope and quality, business performance, leadership, innovation, customer focus, responsibility/citizenship, trustworthiness, congeniality and so on. (We will look at corporate branding in Chapter 4.)

Perceptual maps are often used to plot competing product or corporate brands on two or more dimensions (eg quality and price; or innovation and trustworthiness). By plotting competing brands on these dimensions, it is possible visually to identity 'gaps' (eg for a highly innovative company that is also perceived as highly trustworthy), into which a brand may try to re-position itself, in order to differentiate itself from its competitors on dimensions valued by stakeholders.

Positioning and re-positioning strategies may thus be seen as a relational issue, because they involve changing the perceptions of stakeholders (and therefore, arguably, their 'relationship' with the corporate brand) in relation to other organisations or corporate brands (and therefore, the perceptual map of the market).

Wineries make name change palatable

A tiny, family-owned winery in the rich Rutherglen region [of Victoria in Australia] has become the first in the nation to take the plunge and change the names of its wines, under an agreement forced upon vignerons by the European Union. **Pfeiffer Wines** has changed its tokay to 'topaque', releasing the freshly-labelled bottles several weeks ago, and is about to market its sherry range as 'apera'.

'A lot of people won't drink sherry because they associate it with being three-foot in the grave... To get anyone under 25 to have one, you have to use the new name. It invigorates the category.'

The Australian Fortified Sustainability Project said the sherry descriptors fino, oloroso and amontillado would soon make way for the simple terms dry, medium dry, medium sweet, sweet and cream. Port will be dropped from Labels, rebadged as vintage and tawny, and vermouth and marsala will become Australian Flavoured Fortified Wine...

With wholesale name changes expected to be phased in by companies in coming months, it could cost wineries significant amounts of money to market the new names and change labels. But Mr Pfeiffer said people were relating to the new names. 'It's created a lot of interest (in Topaque) and people like the association with the colour, rather than the gemstone,' he said. 'We've learned a lot about the people who drink it.'

Verity Edwards, *The Australian*, 18 May 2009-05-21

For reflection: what are the positives and negatives of the enforced rebranding for wine producers?

We saw earlier how The Body Shop deliberately positioned itself as an ethical, responsible, 'green' cosmetics firm, contrary to the industry brand. By stressing its product-class disassociation (stand-out attributes), the company simultaneously repositioned its competitors (on the basis that they were still doing all the things The Body Shop disassociated itself from: testing on animals, exploiting Third World suppliers, over-packaging and so on).

3.3.2 Strategic positioning

In strategic management terms, positioning refers to how an organisation 'places' itself in relation to its environment, or how it 'fits' its strategic capabilities and resources to its environment. Essentially, the organisation identifies opportunities and threats presented by its environment, and then positions itself by developing and deploying organisational resources and competences to enable it to exploit those opportunities, or minimise those threats. As new opportunities and threats emerge, it may need to **re-position** itself in order to survive and thrive: for example, by moving into new technology, or by adopting a differentiating capability (such as innovation or corporate social responsibility).

A strategic re-positioning will alter what the organisation does, what it sees as its core competences, where its priorities lie, and how it perceives the nature of its business. This will therefore have an influence on how it presents itself to the world. In addition, the particular attributes on which it repositions itself may help to support a positive reputation, in areas important to stakeholder audiences, such as corporate social responsibility, 'green' manufacturing and marketing, ethical business and so on.

4 Internal influences on corporate reputation

As we have continually emphasised so far, corporate reputation arises from what the organisation is and does – as well as its strategies for corporation communication, positioning and reputation management. The whole of Chapter 3 will be devoted to internal factors in corporate reputation (reflecting considerable overlap in the syllabus content at this point), but to complete our overview of influences on reputation, briefly, internal influences include the following.

4.1 Corporate resources

This refers not just to financial assets (which may enhance the perception of financial soundness and stability of the firm, and enable it to allocate more expenditure to reputation management) but also to:

- The **physical assets** of the firm, including plant and machinery (the age, quality and maintenance of which may contribute to reputation in areas such as product quality, delivery reliability, environmental responsibility or health and safety); facilities (the space, décor and maintenance of which may contribute to reputation by reflecting corporate values and symbols); transport fleets (ditto); and so on.

- The **human resources** of the firm (management and employees), who contribute crucially to reputation via their behaviour and interactions with stakeholders.

- The **network resources** of the firm, or competitive architecture: the strength of its relationships with suppliers, distributors and other partners and allies in delivering value to the customer. The performance of the whole value network may be evaluated by stakeholders to form the corporate reputation.

- The **strategic intellectual assets** of the firm (eg patents, designs and copyrights on proprietary processes or brands), which support distinctive brand attributes and identities.

- The **core competences** of the firm: the distinctive value-creating skills, capabilities and resources which (Hamel & Prahalad, 1994) add value in the eyes of the customer; are scarce and difficult for competitors to imitate; and are flexible for future needs. Organisations often build reputations on core competences with which they strongly identify: eg 3M or Dyson UK, with their reputations for innovation.

4.2 Vision, mission and strategy

KEY CONCEPT

concept

Vision may be defined as 'strategic intent, or the desired future state of the organisation... an aspiration around which a strategist, perhaps a chief executive, might seek to focus the attention and energies of members of the organisation.' (Johnson, Scholes & Whittington, 2005)

Corporate mission statements are concise general statements, answering questions such as: who are we, what are we trying to do, whom do we serve or who or what determines our success? Vision statements are usually longer statements, describing where the organisation sees itself in the future.

Corporate vision, mission and values are the highest level expressions of corporate personality and identity: what the organisation stands for above all else. Vision may be seen as a crucial element in expressing the desired identity of the organisation: what it most wants to be and to project to the world.

KEY CONCEPT

concept

Strategy is 'the direction and scope of an organisation over the long-term: ideally, which matches its resources to its changing environment, and in particular its markets, customers or clients so as to meet stakeholder expectations.' (Johnson, Scholes & Whittington, 2005)

Strategic goals and objectives translate the corporate mission into targets or aims which the organisation will pursue. The reputation of the organisation will be influenced by factors such as:

- The expressed **strategic objectives** of the business, and the extent to which these fit the expectations of key stakeholders. The primary objective for business organisations is profitability or return on stakeholder investment, and the extent to which it pursues this objective effectively will shape its reputation with shareholders. The reputation may be shaped by particular strategic objectives such as technology leadership, innovation, or leadership in human resource management. The overall reputation of the organisation is increasingly likely to be affected by whether it sets and pursues non-economic objectives such as social and environmental sustainability.

BPP LEARNING MEDIA

- The particular **business strategies** pursued by the organisation: what markets it will compete in, what products/service it will offer, how it will compete, how it will pursue growth, how it will treat its employees and so on. Strategy shapes what the organisation does – and this in turn, as we saw in Chapter 1, shapes how it is perceived by stakeholders who encounter or observe its behaviour.

- The **corporate communication strategies** pursued by the organisation: how it chooses to present itself in its advertising and public relations activities; whether these activities are integrated (for consistent/coherent image-making) or devolved to specialists or different business units; whether it chooses to adopt a corporate brand or to allow the 'company behind the product' to remain invisible; how effectively it plans for and responds to reputational threats; and so on.

- How strategy is **formulated**: whether top-down (strong co-ordination and coherence) or bottom-up (strong responsiveness to local conditions and stakeholder demands); whether deliberately and intentionally (allowing for planned positioning) or as a result of the organisation's response to changing demands and emerging ideas over time (allowing for responsiveness and consensus-building).

4.2.1 Organisation structure and culture

KEY CONCEPT

concept

Organisation structure may be defined as 'the pattern of relationships among positions in the organisation and among members of the organisation. Structure makes possible the application of the process of management and creates a framework of order and command through which the activities of the organisation can be planned, organised, directed and controlled.' (Mullins, 1999)

Organisation structure influences corporate reputation by shaping its behaviour (what it does), style (how it does things) and communications – and therefore how it presents itself to the world.

ACTIVITY 8

concept

From your earlier studies of marketing management, or your own experience, identify some ways in which structural elements may influence corporate identity and image. What image-damaging corporate practices, for example, might be caused or exacerbated by structural factors?

KEY CONCEPT

concept

Organisation culture may be defined as: 'The collection of traditions, values, policies, beliefs and attitudes that constitute a pervasive context for everything we do and think in an organisation' (Mullins, 1999) – or, more popularly, 'the way we do things round here' (Schein, 1985).

Cultural assumptions, values and beliefs influence the behaviour of individuals, groups and organisations, creating a shared 'style' of operating or behaviour. For many commentators, culture is synonymous with the 'personality' of an organisation: the reality of what it is, what it stands for, what it is 'like' – and therefore how it presents itself in communication and interaction with the world.

One aspect of corporate culture is the **communication climate**: the structures, norms and values surrounding communication in and by the organisation. The culture of an organisation may support or hinder communication. Gibb (1961) suggested that the 'communication climate' of an organisation may be open (supporting collaborative working and the multi-directional flow of information) or closed (discouraging it).

4.3 Summary

To summarise – and to introduce the model we will explore in detail in Chapter 3 – the following is a more comprehensive model of the corporate identity and reputational management process, taking into account a range of internal and external influences: Figure 2.4.

Figure 2.4: Internal and external influences on identity and reputation management

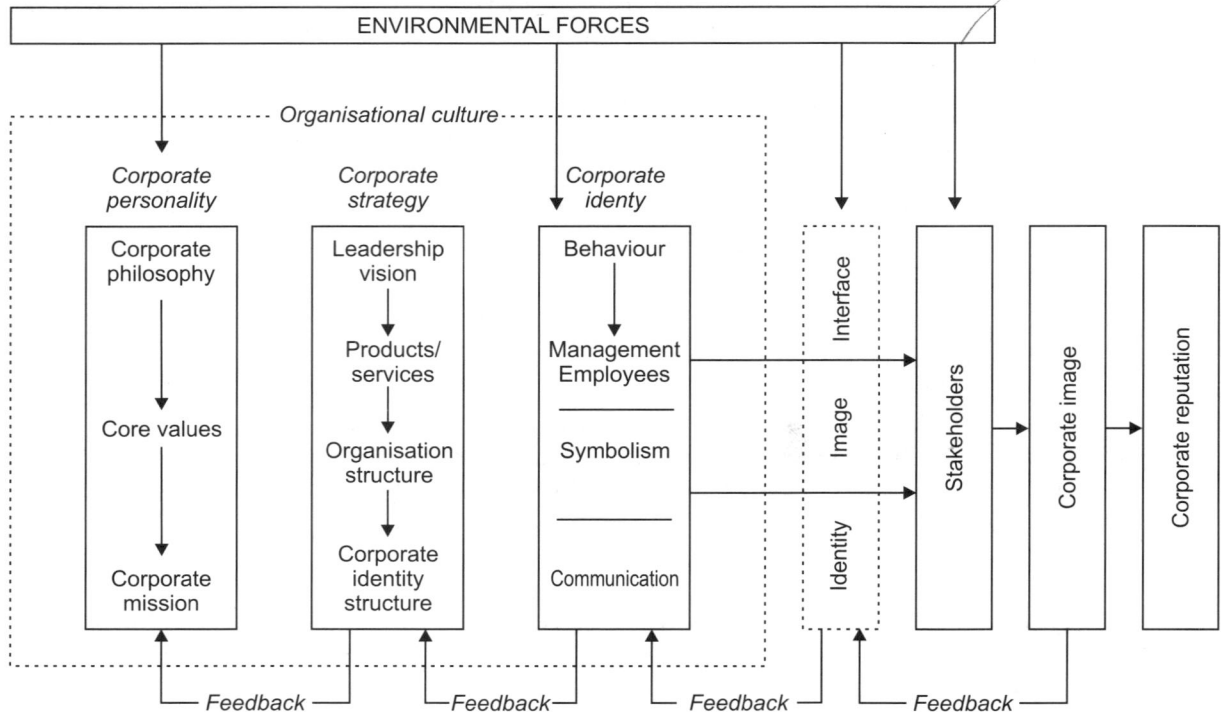

Source: Nelson & Kanso (op cit, p 145)

5 Overviews of corporate reputation management

5.1 The reputation paradigm

Davies *et al.* (*op cit.*, pp. 58–74) enumerate what they take to be the central beliefs and approaches within the study of corporate reputation as follows.

Tenet 1 **Multiple stakeholders need to be considered**

Reputation management requires attention to the potentially differing expectations, needs and perceptions of a range of internal and external stakeholders: customers, shareholders, employees, supply chain partners, government, competitors, media and pressure groups, the wider community and so on. (We discuss how an organisation can identify and prioritise its stakeholder audiences in Chapter 6.)

Tenet 2 **The main elements of reputation are linked**

As we saw in Chapter 1, there is a need to integrate interrelated elements such as corporate personality (what the organisation is), identity (how the organisation projects itself or how employees see it), image (how external stakeholders perceive it) and reputation (how external stakeholders evaluate it overall).

Tenet 3 **Reputation is created through multiple interactions**

Reputations form through multiple encounters with organisational communications, behaviour, representatives and so on, using multiple tangible and intangible, rational and emotional cues and impressions, including pre-conceptions about the organisation's industry and country of origin.

Tenet 4 **Reputations are valuable and have value**

Reputation is a significant, though intangible, asset, because of its demonstrated link to financial performance and competitive advantage. Quantitative valuation is a more contentious area, but methods and tools have been developed, allowing organisations to account for reputational assets.

Tenet 5 **Reputations can be managed**

Despite the fact that reputation 'lies in the eye of the beholder', and that many influences on reputation are not within the direct control of the organisation (eg industry and country-of-origin effects, uncontrollable communications such as word-of-mouth and media coverage), it is possible to manipulate the corporate identity mix (behaviour, symbols and corporate communication) to manage corporate image and reputation.

Tenet 6 **Reputation and financial performance are linked**

As we saw in Chapter 1, a strong positive reputation positively impacts on business performance, through dynamics such as staff retention and motivation, competitive differentiation, the building of customer loyalty, and support for premium pricing.

Tenet 7 **Relative reputation (ranking) drives financial performance**

This relates to the use of rankings (such as *Fortune* Magazine's list of America's Most Admired Companies) as an indicator of reputational value: Davies *et al.* challenge their effectiveness, for reasons we will examine in Chapter 5.

Tenet 8 **Reputation can be measured**

Despite their complexity and intangibility, reputations can be meaningfully measured. Several commercial ranking and survey instruments are available. (These will be discussed in Chapter 5.)

Tenet 9 **Reputation can be lost more easily than it can be created**

'A reputation takes time to create and develop but it can be lost in minutes through an unfortunate action, indeed a single word.' Positive reputations, once developed, need to be defended by proactive issues and crisis management. (This is the subject of Chapter 11.)

Tenet 10 **Reputation can best be studied using an interdisciplinary approach**

Insights and contributions to reputation management come from diverse disciplines: marketing, strategy, economics, psychology and so on.

5.2 The corporate marketing mix

Balmer (2008, p. 47–51) argues that marketing is currently undergoing a paradigm shift, and is increasingly characterised by (a) a corporate (rather than product/brand) focus, (b) recognition of audiences and publics beyond the customer and (c) recognition of the relevance of tools and concerns beyond communications.

He further argues that **corporate marketing** requires a broader paradigm than the traditional 'marketing mix' (the 4 Ps: product, price, place, promotion) applied to products and product brands. His alternative corporate-level marketing mix consists of six Cs: Character, Culture, Constituencies, Covenant, Communication and Conceptualisation.

Element	Comment
Character	
(Corporate identity or personality)	The factors that, in their totality, make one entity distinct from another: consisting of tangible and intangible assets, markets served, strategies, corporate structure and culture, history and so on.
'What we are'	
Key question: 'What are the distinctive and defining characteristics of our organisation?'	*the staff, the way ... engage yp*
Culture	
(Organisational identity or culture)	The perceptions and feelings of the employees about the organisation; the values and norms which define the collective identity of the members.
'What we feel we are'	
Key question: 'What are the collective feelings of employees about the organisation?'	*Pride, worthiness*
Constituencies	
(Marketing and stakeholder management)	Mutually beneficial relationships developed with the range of internal and external stakeholders whose support and engagement secures the organisation's licence to operate.
'Whom we seek to serve'	
Key question: 'Which stakeholders are of critical importance and why?'	*yp ... they use ... staff ... they need FB going*
Communication	
(Corporate communication)	Channels deployed by the organisation to communicate with stakeholders + the communication effects of management, employee and product behaviour + uncontrollable communications (eg word of mouth and media commentary)
'What we say we are'	
Key question: 'Who do we say we are and to whom do we say this?'	*leading youth charity ... (create)*
Conceptualisation	
(Corporate image and reputation)	The perceptions held of the corporate identity and/or brand by stakeholders, affecting their view of and behaviour towards the organisation.
'What we are seen to be'	
Key question: 'How are we seen by our key stakeholders?'	*Vibrant organisation*
Covenant	
(Corporate brand management)	The values and associations associated with a corporate brand (if any), and the expectations aroused in stakeholders by the brand promise (what it offers).
'What is promised and expected'	
Key Question: 'What are the distinct components that underpin our corporate brand promise?'	*) envie to yp ... strive to do better*

ACTIVITY 9

evaluation

Use the key questions set out in the table above to evaluate your own organisation's corporate marketing mix. You might use them as a starting point for your own brainstorming and mind-mapping. Alternatively, you might use them as a simple survey questionnaire for use with selected colleagues or other suitable interview subjects.

5.3 Reputational gaps

Many models advocate a **gap analysis** approach to reputation management. Because there are so many perspectives on corporate reputation, gaps or mismatches may be identified in a number of areas. For example, there may be:

- A mismatch between what the organisation actually is – and how it wishes to be seen (ie behaviour not supportive of desired positioning).

- A mismatch between how the organisation wishes to be seen – and what it says about itself (ie corporate communication not supportive of desired positioning).

- A mismatch between what the organisation says about itself – and what audiences perceive (ie corporate communication failing to get the desired message across).

- A mismatch between what the organisation says about itself – and what it is actually like (ie behaviour failing to live up to the claims made by communication).

Gaps and mismatches create tensions which are potentially damaging to reputation, and this particularly true of the gap between image and reality. 'How long can a company hold itself up to outsiders in ways that do not match its own employees' sense of self? At a time when companies perform in the harsh glare of the media, how long can a company say one thing while being another, without losing credibility and reputation internally and externally? How long can it do so before it loses credibility, authenticity and trustworthiness to its own employees and other stakeholders?' (van Riel & Fombrun, *op cit*, p. 61).

MARKETING AT WORK   application

Consider the following values statement of a large US company (reproduced in Nelson & Kanso, *op cit*, p. 155):

- **Communication**: We have an obligation to communicate. Here, we take the time to talk with one another... and to listen. We believe that information is meant to move and that information moves people.

- **Respect**: We treat others as we would like to be treated ourselves. We do not tolerate abusive or disrespectful treatment.

- **Integrity**: We work with customers and prospects openly, honestly and sincerely. When we say we will do something, we will do it; when we say we cannot or will not do something, then we won't do it.

- **Excellence**: We are satisfied with nothing less than the very best in everything we do. We will continue to raise the bar for everyone. The great fun here will be for all of us to discover just how good we can really be.

Now consider that the company whose values statement this is is giant (former) energy reseller: **Enron**. At the end of 2001 (ten years after the values statement was released), the company suffered a dramatic, public collapse, following revelations that its executives had committed systematic accounting fraud ...

5.3.1 The AC²ID Test of corporate identity

The 'AC²ID Test' model (Balmer & Soenen, 1999) highlights the different dimensions of corporate identity, and therefore the multiple identities possessed by organisations.

- **A**ctual identity: the reality of the organisation, what the organisation is, or its intrinsic identity: the products and services offered; the values, attitudes and behaviours of staff; the performance of the company.

- **C**ommunicated identity: the identity projected by 'controllable' corporate communication programmes (eg advertising, PR, sponsorship and corporate visual identity or branding) and 'non-controllable' communications such as media coverage, word of mouth, pressure group communications, internet communities and the 'blogosphere' and so on.

- **C**onceived identity: perceptions of the organisation held by relevant stakeholders, and therefore reflecting 'corporate image' and/or 'corporate reputation'.

- **Ideal identity**: the optimum or best positioning for the organisation with given strategic capabilities, in a given micro-(industry) and macro-environment.

- **Desired identity**: the leaders' vision for how they want the organisation to be seen (which may not be the same as a rational assessment of ideal identity).

This classification offers a clear vocabulary for describing the kinds of identity mismatches identified earlier. Corporate communications (communicated identity) may fail to reflect the reality of performance and behaviour (actual identity), risking exposure and loss of credibility. Corporate performance and behaviour (actual identity) may fail to match the expectations of stakeholders (conceived identity), causing disappointment and negative evaluation. What stakeholder audiences think about the organisation (conceived identity) may not reflect what it is trying to convey (communicated identity). And none of these identities may match how the leaders *want* the organisation to be seen and positioned (desired identity)!

Balmer and Greyser (2003) developed a model for auditing and resolving the gaps between the various identity dimensions, which they called the **REDS^2 AC^{2}ID Test Process**: Figure 2.5.

The process practically focuses management attention on five key questions:

- What is our current corporate identity (actual identity)?

- What image is communicated by formal and informal communications (communicated identity)?

- What would be the ideal identity for an organisation with our strategic capabilities, in our micro-and-macro environment?

- What corporate identity do our senior managers wish us to have?

- How can the required corporate identity be achieved?

Figure 2.5: REDS^2 AC2^{1}D Test Process

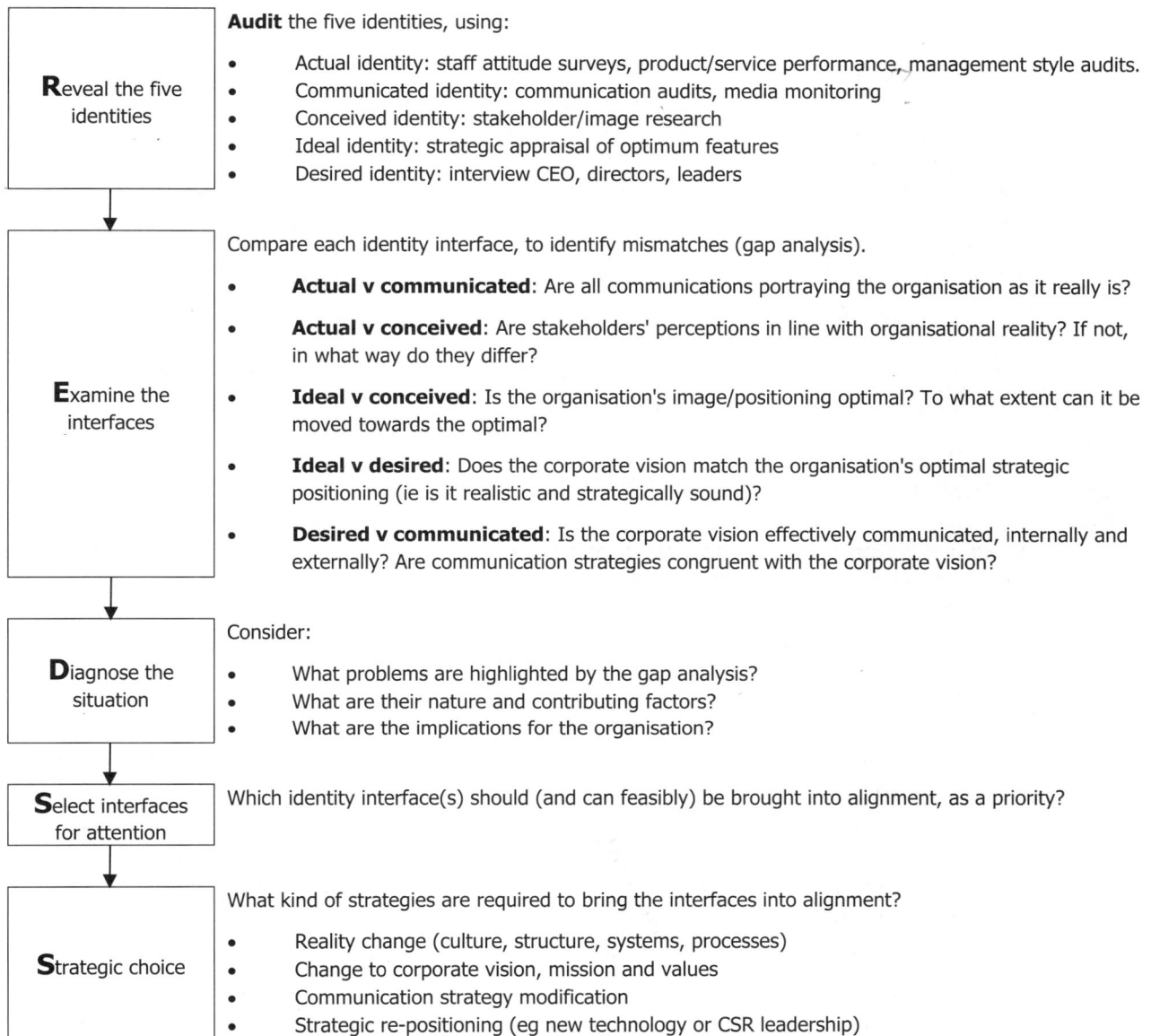

Reveal the five identities	**Audit** the five identities, using: • Actual identity: staff attitude surveys, product/service performance, management style audits. • Communicated identity: communication audits, media monitoring • Conceived identity: stakeholder/image research • Ideal identity: strategic appraisal of optimum features • Desired identity: interview CEO, directors, leaders
Examine the interfaces	Compare each identity interface, to identify mismatches (gap analysis). • **Actual v communicated**: Are all communications portraying the organisation as it really is? • **Actual v conceived**: Are stakeholders' perceptions in line with organisational reality? If not, in what way do they differ? • **Ideal v conceived**: Is the organisation's image/positioning optimal? To what extent can it be moved towards the optimal? • **Ideal v desired**: Does the corporate vision match the organisation's optimal strategic positioning (ie is it realistic and strategically sound)? • **Desired v communicated**: Is the corporate vision effectively communicated, internally and externally? Are communication strategies congruent with the corporate vision?
Diagnose the situation	Consider: • What problems are highlighted by the gap analysis? • What are their nature and contributing factors? • What are the implications for the organisation?
Select interfaces for attention	Which identity interface(s) should (and can feasibly) be brought into alignment, as a priority?
Strategic choice	What kind of strategies are required to bring the interfaces into alignment? • Reality change (culture, structure, systems, processes) • Change to corporate vision, mission and values • Communication strategy modification • Strategic re-positioning (eg new technology or CSR leadership)

You might want to note that in your core reading text, van Riel & Fombrun (op cit., pp. 70–78) use a different version of this model. They refer to it as the AC^{2}ID model, but actually use the terms:

• *Perceived identity: the attributes seen as significant (representing continuity, centrality and uniqueness) for the organisation in the eyes of its members.*

• *Projected identity: organisational characteristics being presented to internal and external target audiences through communication and symbols.*

• *Applied identity: organisational attributes revealed to internal and external target audiences through behaviour.*

• *Desired identity (undistinguished from 'ideal' identity): leaders' vision for the organisation.*

Their version of the gap analysis model is therefore:

Step 1:   *Determine projected identity: testing for continuity (are projected characteristics enduring over time?), centrality (are projected characteristics widely shared throughout the organisation?) and distinctiveness (do projected characteristics differentiate the organisation from other similar organisations?).*

Step 2:   *Analyse desired identity (top management) and perceived identity (employees).*

Step 3:   *Identify gaps between desired, projected, perceived and applied identity (behaviour).*

Step 4:   *Select an identity mix (behaviour, symbolism, communication) and/or implement extra research to analyse the organisation's strengths and weaknesses in these areas.*

Step 5:   *Implement action plans to close the gaps between the desired, projected and 'realised' (or actual) identities of the organisation.* ∎

ACTIVITY 10

application/evaluation

Use either of the gap analysis models outlined above to do some introductory brainstorming about the different identities of your own organisation, or any organisation that might be the focus of your assessment. What potential gaps or mismatches can you identify, for later follow-up?

5.3.2 Comprehensive reputation management

Another gap analysis framework you might like to consider is presented by Doorley & Garcia (*op cit.*, pp. 9–11).

*   **Reputation template**, setting out the attributes by which the organisation will measure and monitor its reputation. A basic template (which can be customised to suit the needs of the organisation) includes: innovation, quality of management, employee talent, financial performance, social responsibility, product quality, communicativeness (transparency); governance, and integrity (responsibility, reliability, credibility, trustworthiness).

*   **Reputation audits** of internal and external stakeholder groups.
    *   Comparison of employee and senior leadership views of the organisation's identity (what it stands for).
    *   Comparison between identity and image (how external constituencies view the organisation).

    The aim of the exercise will be to bring about convergence (close the gaps) in these areas.

*   **Reputational capital goals**, setting out what the organisation wants to achieve within its industry or in relation to competitors (eg improved valuation, enhanced ranking).

*   **Accountability profile**: allocated responsibilities for correcting slippages against reputation template attributes (eg public relations accountability for communicativeness).

*   **Reputation management plan**: a strategic performance (behaviour) and communication plan to move the images that various stakeholders hold about the organisation closer to the intrinsic identity. This includes:
    *   A summary of the reputation audits
    *   Measures of reputational capital
    *   Analysis of reputational challenges and risk areas
    *   Identified goals and opportunities
    *   Communications strategies (including contingency planning for known threats)

*   **Annual follow-up audit and assessment**.

BPP
LEARNING MEDIA

You can follow up any of the models referred to in this chapter, in the books cited, should you wish to apply any of the models in your assessment. ■

Learning objectives		Covered	
1	Outline the forces that influence reputation, and how they can be assessed as a measure of reputational risk	☑	Overarching ideas about how reputations are formed: a mix of internal and external influence; formation from the inside (employee perceptions) out (external stakeholder perceptions); in the eye of the beholder (primary, secondary and tertiary information processing)
		☑	PESTLE factors in the external environment: political, economic, socio-cultural (and ethical), technological, legal and environmental (natural)
		☑	Country of origin (COO) and industry filters
		☑	Relational influences: competitive and collaborative strategies; affinity and relationship marketing; merger and acquisition; brand and strategic re-positioning
		☑	Internal influences on reputation: organisational resources; vision, mission and strategy; structure; culture and communication climate
2	Evaluate the contexts and concepts relating to corporate reputation	☑	The reputation paradigm (Davies *et al.*)
		☑	The corporate marketing mix (Balmer)
3	Identify gaps or mismatches between identity and image, and begin to make recommendations to close those gaps	☑	The concept of reputational/identity gaps
		☑	The AC²ID Text model: Actual, Communicated, Conceived, Ideal and Desired identities
		☑	The REDS² Process for managing AC²ID identities
		☑	A comprehensive reputation management approach (Dourley & Garcia)

[Handwritten note at top: Country of origin image, industry image, image Products/services]

1 Identify three filters through which public images of an organisation are mediated.

2 Distinguish, with examples, between primary, secondary and tertiary information processing by stakeholders.

3 What classifications of external environmental factors are covered by the acronym STEEPLE? *[Handwritten: Social, Technological, Environmental, Ethical, Economic, Political, Legal]*

4 Give two examples each of economic, social and technological influences on organisational reputation. *[Handwritten: Recession, government, poverty, internet, globalised ...]*

5 What factors contribute to pre-conceptions about the products of different countries of origin?

6 Give examples of different forms of 'association' or endorsement which may impact on corporate reputation.

7 Outline some of the issues posed for corporate identity and reputation by a merger.

8 How does corporate strategy influence reputation?

9 What are the six Cs of the corporate-level marketing mix (Balmer)? *[Handwritten: Character, Communication, Culture, coherent, conceptualisation, consistency, constituencies]*

10 Identify the five identities of the AC^{2}ID Test model and explain the key identity interfaces that should be examined to identify gaps.

---

1 Your own impressions and pre-conceptions – but you might like to see what other people say about the same industries/sections and countries. Note how little actual knowledge you need to go on, to form these impressions. Some may come from actual experience – but others may be a mixture of legends, traditions and stereotypes. As an additional exercise, see if you can identify counter-stereotypical examples (the exceptions that 'prove' the rule): how far would these go to change your pre-conceptions?

2 Organisations might manage secondary and tertiary information by: monitoring what is being said about the organisation (eg on the internet); motivating recommendation and referral (eg through relationship and viral marketing); developing corporate communications and media relations; monitoring and managing emerging 'issues'; and so on.

3 Some examples of political influences on reputation include:

- Negative stereotypes about the organisation's country of origin being promoted as a result of poor political relations between two or more nations

- Government championing of the country of origin, industry and/or particular firms as 'national champions' for an industry

- Positive or negative statements about an organisation by pressure, interest and lobbying groups, where the organisation is a 'test case' or exemplar of a political issue (eg labour relations, environmental protection, health promotion)

- Positive or negative evaluation by the public of an organisation's position in complying with – or acting contrary to – government policy (which may be popular or unpopular on a given issue)

- Perceptions of political risk and/or actual war, terrorist acts or civil unrest affecting the image of a tourist destination or location for business operations.

4 The challenges posed by the 'blogosphere' and similar forums for rumour and comment include:

- The need to monitor what is being said on message boards and in the 'blogosphere'

- The need to maximise positive 'share of voice', by encouraging (and deserving) positive user comment, viral marketing, product reviews and so on

- The need to counter, refute or respond to negative comment, where possible

- The need to establish an official on-line presence, which may help to counter unofficial comments

- The need to ensure that the corporate web site is highly ranked on internet search engines, so that when a user types in your company's name, (s)he is directed to that web site – and not to a negative news article, blog or spoof site about the company!

5/6 Your own organisation. Note that this will be useful preparatory thinking for your assessment, where PESTLE factors and COO/industry effects may well be relevant. This brainstorming exercise may at least highlight some points to follow up with more systematic research later.

7   Causal or affinity marketing may be used for two basic purposes.

- Brands may gain reputational 'rub-off' from associating with charities or causes, particularly when they have synergistic messages or common target audiences (for example, health food brands promoting community sports).

- Brands may also use affiliations to counteract opposite messages: for example, Virgin Airlines (which may be accused of having a fairly high carbon footprint) partnering with environmental groups to fund alternative fuel and carbon capture research.

8   Structural elements may influence corporate identity and image, for example, by the extent to which they:

- Facilitate, hinder or slow multi-directional internal communication, which impacts on performance, employee job satisfaction and external stakeholder satisfaction.

- Slow the speed of decision-making, stifle initiative and reduce responsiveness to customer demands, feedback, reputational risk events (eg crises) and environmental changes.

- Facilitate or create barriers to the alignment of corporate mission, values and behaviours across the organisation (eg via cross-functional communication and collaboration) and hence the development of an integrated corporate identity.

- Foster rigidity of behaviour and culture (eg in large, formal bureaucratic structures) or encourage flexibility and responsiveness (eg via cross-functional team-working and flexible structures).

- Offer sufficient job interest and empowerment to satisfy and retain the employees who build corporate identity and operate at the interface with customers and other external stakeholders.

- Position and integrate corporate communication responsibilities to facilitate strategic reputation management.

9/10   Your own organisation. Note that this will be useful preparatory thinking for your assessment. This brainstorming exercise may at least highlight some points to follow up with more systematic research later.

1   Filters include: communication, industry image and country-of-origin effects.

2   Primary information processing is based on direct personal experience of the organisation, its representatives or products. Secondary information processing is based on what reference groups (friends, family, internet communities etc) have to say about the organisation and/or its products. Tertiary information processing is based on mass media information, including advertising and publicity.

3   STEEPLE stands for: socio-cultural, technological, economic, ethical, political, legal and environmental (natural environment)

4   See section 2.1 for a full selection – or add your own.

5   Factors contributing to COO effects include: industrialisation or technological development; representative products; historical events and international relations; stereotypes of national characteristics; and genuine comparative advantage.

6   Different forms of association or endorsement include: formal association with network partners; advertising placements and sponsorships; causal or affinity marketing; merger or acquisition; and endorsement/recommendation.

7   See section 3.2 for a full discussion.

8   See section 4.2 for a full discussion.

9   The six Cs are: Character, Culture, Constituencies, Covenant, Communication and Conceptualisation.

10 The five identities are: Actual, Communicated, Conceived, Ideal and Desired. For interfaces, see Figure 2.5.

References

Balmer, M J T (2008) 'Corporate identity, brand and marketing' in Melewar T C (ed.) *Facets of Corporate Identity, Communication and Reputation*. Abingdon, Oxon: Routledge

Balmer, J M T and Greyser, S A (2003) 'Managing the multiple identities of the corporation' in J M T Balmer and S A Greyser (eds) *Revealing the Corporation: Perspectives on Identity, Image, Reputation, Corporate Branding and Corporate-Level Marketing*. London: Routledge, pp 15-29

Balmer, J M T and Soenen, B G (1999): 'The Acid Test of corporate identity management', in *Journal of Marketing Management*, No 15, pp 69-92

Bernstein, D (1984) *Company Image and Reality: A Critique of Corporate Communications*. London: Cassell Educational

Bromley, D B (2000) 'Psychological aspects of corporate identity, image and reputation' in *Corporate Reputation Review* Vol 3 (3): pp 240-252

Christopher M, Payne A & Ballantyne D (2002) *Relationship Marketing: Creating Stakeholder Value*. Oxford: Elsevier Butterworth-Heinemann

Davies G, Chun R, Da Silva R V & Roper S (2003) *Corporate Reputation and Competitiveness*. Abingdon, Oxon: Routledge

Doorley, J & Garcia, H F (2007) *Reputation Management: The Key to Successful Public Relations and Corporate Communications*. New York: Routledge

Fill, C (2002) *Marketing Communications: Contexts, Strategies and Applications* (3rd ed). Harlow, Essex: Pearson Education Limited

Gibb, J R (1961) 'Defensive Communication' in *Journal of Communication*. 11 (3) pp 141-148

Gotsi, M & Wilson, A M (2001) 'Corporate Reputation: seeking a definition' in *Corporate Communications: An International Journal* 6 (1) pp 24-30

Greyser, SA (1999) 'Advancing and enhancing corporate reputation' in *Corporate Communications: An International Journal* 4 (4) pp 177-187

Hamel, G & Prahalad, C K (1994) *Competing for the Future*. Boston: Harvard Business School Press

Johnson G, Scholes K & Whittington R (2005) *Exploring Corporate Strategy: Text & Cases* (7th ed) Harlow, Essex: FT Prentice Hall

Kotler, P and Armstrong, M (2000) *Principles of Marketing* (9th ed) Englewood Cliffs, New Jersey: Prentice Hall

Ledingham, J A & Bruning, S D (2000) 'Background and current trends in the study of relationship management" in J A Ledingham & S D Bruning (eds) *Public Relations As Relationship Management: A Relational Approach to Public Relations*. Mahwah, N J: Lawrence Erlbaum Associates

Mullins, L (1999) *Management and Organisational Behaviour* (5th ed). Harlow, Essex: FT Prentice Hall

Nagashima, A (1977) 'A comparative 'made in' product image survey among Japanese businessmen' in *Journal of Marketing* 41 (3) pp 95-100

Nelson, R A & Kanso, A M (2008) 'Effective leadership in a crisis' in Melewar T C (ed.) *Facets of Corporate Identity, Communication and Reputation*. Abingdon, Oxon: Routledge

Porter, M (1980) *Competitive Strategy*. New York: Free Press

Riel, C B M van & Fombrun, C J (2007) *Essentials of Corporate Communication: Implementing Practices for Effective Reputation Management*. Abingdon, Oxon: Routledge

Samuel, H (2007) *Reputation Branding*. Wellington, NZ: First Edition Ltd

Schein, E (1985) *Organisational Culture and Leadership*. San Francisco: Jossey-Bass

Swaminathan, V & Reddy, S K (2000) 'Affinity partnering: conceptualisation and issues' in Sheth, J N & Parvatiyar, A (eds) *Handbook of Relationship Marketing*. Thousand Oaks, CA: Sage

Varey, R J (2002) *Marketing Communication: Principles and Practice*. Abindgon, Oxon: Routledge

Chapter 3

Organisational character or personality

Topic list

Introduction

This chapter builds on the concepts discussed in Chapters 1 and 2, and gives you the tools to begin to focus your attention on the specific reputational dynamics associated with a particular organisation, which might be the focus of your assessment.

We start in section 1 by looking at the concept of organisational character or personality: what the organisation is actually like, which you might also identify as its 'actual' or 'intrinsic' identity. The argument of this chapter is that the personality of an organisation is a key factor in shaping the identity that it projects to the world: it influences how the personnel of the organisation perceive the organisation, how they behave, what values they communicate, what symbols and artefacts they value and so on – all of which projects itself to external stakeholders. An organisation cannot *not* communicate: its personality 'speaks' – potentially louder than its planned stakeholder communications! Is what the organisation projects of itself, through its personality, compatible with what it deliberately seeks to communicate about itself? And is the face it presents to the world compatible with how it *wants* to be seen?

In sections 2–4, we explore the application of this concept: the assessment of how far the organisation's corporate strategy, structure, systems and culture (which make up organisational personality) are compatible with its desired positioning and reputation. As the syllabus notes, 'Very often these elements [organisational character] can be disconnected from the intended market positioning and the way an organisation wants to be seen. The result can be confusion, weak positioning and underperformance.'

Finally, in section 5, we return briefly to the concept of organisational identity (introduced in Chapter 1), highlighting the links between personality, organisational self-perception and employee identification. We will return to the concept of identity in its various meanings and manifestations, in more detail, in Chapter 4.

In the terminology of the guidance notes summarising this part of the syllabus, this chapter addresses the themes: 'This is who we are and this is how we want to be seen.'

Syllabus-linked learning objectives

By the end of the chapter you will be able to:

Learning objectives	Syllabus link
1 Critically evaluate the corporate 'character' (personality) of an organisation	2.1.1
2 Critically assess the compatibility of an organisation's corporate strategy, structure, systems and culture with its positioning and reputation	1.2.1
3 Explain the various meanings of corporate 'identity'	

1 Organisational character (personality)

1.1 The analogy of personality

KEY CONCEPT

concept

The term '**personality**', as it applies to individuals, refers to the total pattern of characteristic ways of thinking, feeling and behaving that constitute the individual's distinctive method of relating to the environment: 'the psychological qualities that influence an individual's characteristic behaviour patterns, in a distinctive and consistent manner, across different situations and over time' (Huczynski & Buchanan, 2001, p. 143).

By analogy, the concept of personality can be applied to organisations. **Corporate personality** thus describes the significant characteristics which constitute the organisation's distinctive and consistent method of relating to its environment.

Personality is a useful concept in describing and comparing organisations, because:

- It focuses on consistent and stable factors: those that are 'characteristic' of an organisation in different contexts and at different times

- It focuses on distinctive factors: those which vary from organisation to organisation.

Characteristics which are both stable and distinctive can be used in general comparisons between organisations – and are thus likely to be part of the image of the organisation formed in the minds of stakeholder audiences.

There are two main approaches to the study of human personality in psychology.

- The nomothetic ('law setting') approach *generalises* in order to emphasise regularities in behaviour, isolating elements in personality which operate in the same way from individual to individual: personality traits or types. This is reflected in some of the approaches used to track and measure corporate identity, image and reputation: evaluating organisations on personality traits such as agreeableness, enterprise, competence, chic, ruthlessness, machismo and informality (Davies *et al.*, 2003)

- The ideographic ('portraying individuals') approach *individualises*, bringing out the uniqueness of each person. Personality is assumed to be shaped by the individual's unique experiences, and the way (s)he interprets and learns from them: it changes as the individual refines his or her sense of 'self'. The methodology of this approach is aimed at building up a detailed, complex picture of the specific individual – and this is reflected in approaches to researching corporate identity and image via stakeholder interviews, feedback and self-analysis.

1.2 Components of corporate personality

Corporate personalities are considered to be derived from two core factors (Markwick & Fill, 1997):

- The **organisation culture**: the core assumptions, values and beliefs of an organisation (or corporate philosophy) which manifest themselves in expressions, artefacts, symbols, rituals, structures and norms of behaviour. Culture leads to the formation of particular characteristics or traits: 'the way we do things round here'.

- The **strategic purpose** and **strategic processes** adopted by the organisation: how the organisation pursues its mission via strategic objectives; how strategy is formulated (by formal long-range planning, incremental adjustments, emergence or opportunism); how vision and objectives 'flow down' through the organisation; and how the organisation defines its desired relationships with its various stakeholders.

'Personality is embodied in the way the organisation carries out its business, the logic of its activities, the degree of persistence and aggression it displays in the markets in which it operates and the standards that are expected of all stakeholders... Corporate personality is what an organisation actually is.' (Fill, 2002, p. 390–391)

ACTIVITY 1   evaluation

Again, just as a thought-provoker: what kind of a 'person' would your organisation be if it were a person? Describe him or her, briefly.

One important point about this is that – unlike image and reputation – organisational personality or character is within the organisation's direct control. Organisations that behave and express themselves in line with character attributes that they, their employees and their external stakeholders value are more likely to benefit from: improved individual and team morale; improved productivity; enhanced profitability; improved service quality; lower staff absenteeism and turnover; and supportive, long-term customer (and other stakeholder) relationships (Samuel, 2007, p. 172).

1.3 From personality to reputation

As we saw in Chapter 1, organisations, like individuals, may be said to project their **personality** as an **'identity'** (or persona): Abratt & Shee (1989). The corporate identity mix can be seen as the outer expression of an organisation, crystallising its underlying personality (van Riel & Fombrun, 2007). Corporate identity is shaped by the spirit and commitment with which all members of an organisation embody and articulate the corporate personality (Topalian, 1984). The target audience's perception of all the various identity cues then forms the corporate **'image'**.

van Riel & Balmer (1997) picture the link as follows (although they do not give the term 'corporate personality' to the factors of culture and strategy): Figure 3.1.

Figure 3.1: Culture, strategy, identity and reputation

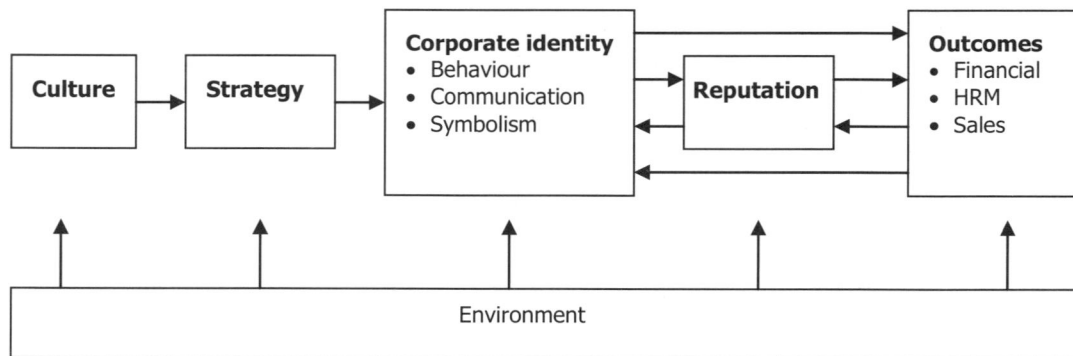

We will look further at the specific contributions of culture, strategy (and related issues such as structure) to identity in the following sections.

1.4 Personality profiling

We will look at the elements of personality (culture, strategy and structure) in detail in the following sections of this chapter. However, it might be worth drawing your attention to some general tools for compiling a 'personality profile' of an organisation.

1.4.1 The Corporate Personality Scale

Davies *et al.'s* classification of character traits in corporate personality, using seven core dimensions, is shown in the following table. These traits are used as part of a measuring instrument (the Corporate Personality Scale) to map various stakeholder images of an organisation: Davies *et al.* (2003, p. 152).

Dimensions and traits of corporate personality						
Agreeableness	**Enterprise**	**Competence**	**Chic**	**Ruthlessness**	**Machismo**	**Informality**
Warmth	**Modernity**	**Conscientious-ness**	**Elegance**	**Egotism**	**Masculine**	**Casual**
Friendly	Cool		Charming	Arrogant	Tough	Simple
Pleasant	Trendy	Reliable	Stylish	Aggressive	Rugged	Easy going
Open		Secure	Elegant	Selfish		
Straightforward		Hardworking				
Empathy	**Adventure**	**Drive**	**Prestige**	**Dominance**		
Concerned	Imaginative	Ambitious	Prestigious	Inward-		
Reassuring	Up-to-date	Achievement-	Exclusive	looking		
Supportive	Exciting	oriented	Refined	Authoritarian		
Agreeable	Innovative	Leading		Controlling		

Dimensions and traits of corporate personality						
Agreeableness	**Enterprise**	**Competence**	**Chic**	**Ruthlessness**	**Machismo**	**Informality**
Integrity	**Boldness**	**Technocracy**	**Snobbery**			
Honest	Extravert	Technical	Snobby			
Sincere	Daring	Corporate	Elitist			
Trustworthy						
Socially responsible						

One way of presenting and using the findings from a personality survey is to score the organisation on each dimension for each respondent group, and to plot identity (employee scores) and image (customer and other external stakeholder scores) on a cobweb diagram: Figure 3.2.

Figure 3.2: Cobweb diagram of an organisation's personality profile

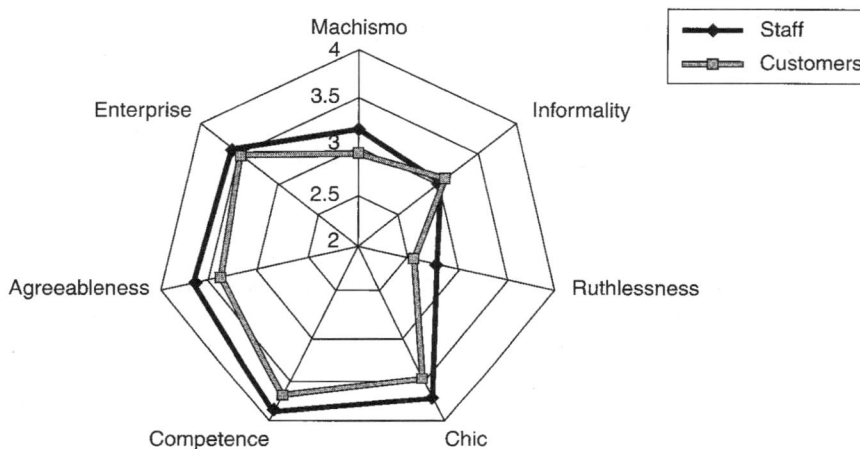

Source: Davies et al. (*op cit,* p. 157)

The use of such profiling techniques and cobweb diagrams can:

- Stimulate management discussion about particular dimensions and traits; whether the current profile is compatible with the organisation's desired image and positioning; and what traits the organisation should seek to develop.

- Indicate any mismatch between identity (employee view) and image (customer view): if the employee view is more positive, it may improve the customer view over time – or there may be a communication problem in failing to translate corporate identity into positive image.

1.4.2 Consensus Profile

A similar cobweb-diagram approach may be used to plot **actual and desired** personality traits or characteristics (Bernstein, 1984). This is known as a Consensus Profile, since it can be used to build management consensus about an organisation's desired identity and positioning.

- Senior leaders in the organisation are asked individually to brainstorm attributes which they think have played a decisive role in the organisation's development, and those which are likely to be important for its future development.

- A small number of commonly-identified key attributes is selected for further consideration, and participants are asked to score each of them on the degree to which the organisation (a) is actually and (b) should be defined by these characteristics.

- The responses can be then be plotted on a cobweb diagram (similar to the above, but showing the selected key attributes, and with the two plotted lines showing actual and desired scores).

The process and diagrams can be used as the basis for managerial discussion: bringing out areas of conflict within the management team, and working towards consensus about desired corporate personality and identity (which may in itself strengthen the focus and coherence of identity within the organisation).

ACTIVITY 2

format

Have a go at using the Corporate Personality Scale or Consensus Profiling method to develop a cobweb diagram of your organisation, or one that you might use as a focus of your assessment.

You might use your own brainstorming and evaluation (scoring each attribute on a scale of 1–5, say, according to how strongly you agree that it applies to your organisation). Alternatively, you might involve colleagues, using the Personality Scale as a survey, or attempting a Consensus Profiling exercise.

If the Corporate Personality Scale and cobweb diagramming interest you as a research methodology, you might follow-up with more in-depth reading in:

- *Davies, Chun, Da Silver and Roper: Corporate Reputation & Competitiveness (2003: Routledge). Chapters 7 to 11 illustrate and apply the methodology in various ways.* ■

1.4.3 Personality Profile

Another approach, suggested by van Riel & Fombrun (*op cit*) is the Personality Profile created by Lux (1986), which allows managers to organise personality data from employee interviews, archival material, stakeholder feedback and personal brainstorming. They can then mind-map the personality of the organisation to stimulate discussion about future direction and positioning.

Lux's core personality dimensions are as follows.

- **Needs**: the basic motivation for the organisation's actions (eg growth, security, competition) – and therefore central to the profile. (Other dimensions should ideally contribute to the fulfilment of the identified needs.)

- **Competences**: special skills, resources and sources of competitive advantage.

- **Attitude**: core organisational philosophy or cultural values.

- **Constitution**: the physical, structural and legal context for operations (eg core business, structure, locations, position in the value chain).

- **Temperament**: how the company operates (eg in terms of strength, intensity, emotional tone).

- **Origin** (or heritage): attributes which have shaped the organisation in the past.

- **Interests** (or goal orientation): the future (medium and long-term) objectives of the company.

The following example is given by Lux (reproduced in van Riel & Fombrun, *op cit*, p. 85): Figure 3.3.

Figure 3.3: A personality profile mind-map

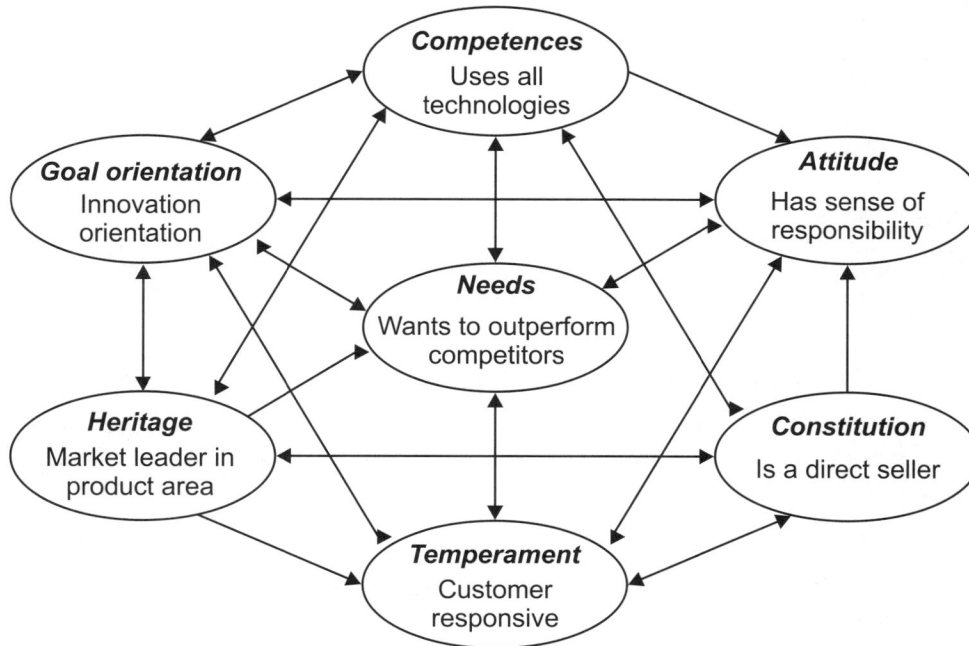

MARKETING AT WORK   application

Concepts like 'trustworthiness', 'credibility', 'reliability' and 'responsibility' may give a rather dull impression of corporate personality and reputation – but remember that 'boldness' and 'extraversion' also appear on the corporate personality scale.

Consider the following comments in the *Weekend Australian* (April 18/19, 2009):

There is one Australian automotive company that has been growing at a compound rate of more than 50% a year, is expanding internationally, employs naked Swedish backpackers and decorates its products with deliberately offensive slogans such as: 'Better to be born black than gay because then you don't have to tell your parents'.

The company is run by John Webb, a former mechanic. Webb tells me he has just started reading a book on how to make a profit and believes that worrying about corporate image screws creativity. Web's company is the Brisbane-based **Wicked Campers** ...

Clearly, [Webb] believes in the Richard Branson strategy that the more outrageous you are, the more free advertising you get, and the more you attract your target younger market. At the moment, Wicked is offering a free day's van rental for people who turn up at the rental office naked. However, the offer says if you're over 60, you get an extra day for free only if you leave your clothes on ...

Talking to [Webb] about Wicked is like talking to a Southern Baptist minister about God ... He talks about working with people who are 'passionate about certain things and giving them the means to do it. It's very inspiring.'

2 Corporate strategy

2.1 Perspectives on strategy

KEY CONCEPT

concept

Strategy is 'the direction and scope of an organisation over the long-term: ideally, which matches its resources to its changing environment, and in particular its markets, customers or clients so as to meet stakeholder expectations.' (Johnson, Scholes & Whittington, 2005)

This definition highlights several aspects of strategic decisions, relevant to reputation management.

- They relate to the 'scope' of the organisation: the range of activities it will pursue ('what business are we in?' or 'what market(s) should we compete in?'), its geographical boundaries, and the kind of human/economic entity it should be (its corporate identity).

- They are likely to influence the direction (and reflect the desired identity) of the organisation in the long-term.

- They attempt to position the organisation in such a way as to match its resources and capabilities to the demands and opportunities of its environment (and may therefore reflect the 'ideal identity' of the organisation).

- They flow down into operational decisions: notably, at the *business* level, decisions about 'How (on what basis) do we compete?' and 'How do we optimise what we do in pursuit of our goals?' It is at this level of business strategy that identity, image and reputation management finds its place.

Influential Japanese strategist Kenichi Ohmae (1983) argued that: 'What business strategy is all about is, in a word, **competitive advantage**. The sole purpose of strategic planning is to enable a company to gain, as efficiently as possible, a sustainable edge over its competitors. Corporate strategy thus implies an attempt to alter a company's strength relative to that of its competitors in the most efficient way.' Ohmae developed what he called the 'strategic triangle', suggesting that three key stakeholders must be taken into account in developing strategy: the Corporation, the Customer and the Competition. The strategist 'must be sure that his [*sic*] strategy matches the strengths of the Corporation with the needs of a clearly defined market (Customers)' in such a way as to 'achieve superior performance, relative to the Competition, in the key factors for success in the business'. You should immediately be able to see the relevance of this to corporate reputation and brand positioning.

Henry Mintzberg (1987) points out that strategy can be seen from a number of different perspectives (helpfully classified as Five Ps):

- **Plan**. Strategy is the output of a systematic planning process: setting objectives; analysing external threats and opportunities, and internal strengths and weaknesses; developing and evaluating options; and selecting preferred options for implementation.

- **Ploy**. Strategy is developed in the process of out-manoeuvring competitors: responding to competitor initiatives, strengths and weaknesses with offensive/ defensive moves, with a view to gaining or maintaining advantage.

- **Pattern**. Strategy is developed from the stream of actions that an organisation adopts consistently over time. A pattern of action emerges by retaining approaches that appear to be working and discarding approaches that don't.

- **Position**. Strategy is a means of identifying an organisation's position in a given environment, and of shaping its response to the opportunities and threats presented by external forces.

- **Perspective**. Strategy reflects an organisation's 'ingrained way of perceiving the world': the corporate personality or culture which influences how it defines its purpose and goals, and chooses how to go about things.

Strategy is the subject of vast amounts of research and writing, and it is impossible to give more than a very brief overview of some key issues here, as a framework for your analysis of the impact of your own organisation's strategy and strategy formulation processes on its identity and reputation. For more detail on strategy, you could:

- *Read Chapter 1 ('Strategic thought: a brief history') in Davies et al.: **Corporate Reputation and Competitiveness** (2003, Routledge).*

- *Browse through specific areas that interest you in the authoritative work by Johnson, Scholes and Whittington: **Exploring Corporate Strategy** (7th ed: 2005: Pearson Education).* ∎

2.2 Vision, mission and values

Corporate vision, mission and values are the highest level expressions of corporate personality and identity: what the organisation stands for above all else. In a study of 100 global brands (cited by Davies *et al. op cit*, p. 20), the biggest internal obstacles to realising corporate brand potential emerged as a lack of clarity in what the organisation/brand stood for. 'The most successfully positioned companies and brands in terms of growth, financial performance, visibility and market share are those that have linked a powerful brand positioning to an inspiring, overarching vision'.

2.2.1 Vision or strategic intent

KEY CONCEPT   concept

Vision may be defined as 'strategic intent, or the desired future state of the organisation... an aspiration around which a strategist, perhaps a chief executive, might seek to focus the attention and energies of members of the organisation.' (Johnson, Scholes & Whittington, 2005)

Hamel & Prahalad (1989) define strategic intent as 'an ambitious and compelling dream that energises; which provides the emotional and intellectual energy for the journey to the future'. They see it as having three elements:

- A **sense of direction**: a unifying and personalising view of the future; a point of view about the long-term market, competitive or reputational position that a firm hopes to build over the coming decade

- A **sense of discovery**: a differentiating, or competitively unique, point of view about the future; the promise of exploring new competitive territory

- A **sense of destiny**: an emotionally-laden goal which employees perceive as inherently valuable.

Johnson & Scholes argue that vision, as an overarching sense of what the organisation is about or is seeking to achieve, allows clarity in the communication of strategic intent to employees and external stakeholders. It offers coherence (or focus), by creating a sense of direction and simple rules for action. At the same time, it is highly flexible, leaving room for diversity and the exploration of different options and pathways. Vision may be seen as a crucial element in expressing the desired identity of the organisation: what it most wants to be and to project to the world.

2.2.2 Mission and values

Mission answers questions such as: who are we, what are we trying to do, whom do we serve or who or what determines our success? It generally comprises four elements (Campbell & Tawaday, 1990):

- **Purpose**: why does the organisation exist, and for whom (shareholders and other stakeholders)?
- **Strategy**: what business are we in? what do we do? how do we do it?
- **Values**: what do we value and believe to be important? what do we stand for?
- **Standards and behaviour**: what are the policies and norms that guide how we operate?

A mission statement is a concise 'word picture' of the organisation: vision statements are often longer, describing the company's view of itself into the future.

The following are some examples of famous mission statements (Garner, 2005).

- **Reebok**: 'Our purpose is to ignite a passion for winning, to do the extraordinary, and to capture the customer's heart and mind.'

- **Walt Disney**: 'To make people happy.'

- **Wal-Mart**: 'To give ordinary folk the chance to buy the same things as rich people.'

- **The Body Shop**: 'Tirelessly work to narrow the gap between principle and practice whilst making fun, passion and care part of our daily lives.'

- **Marks and Spencer**: 'Our mission is to make aspirational quality accessible to all.'

- **Sony**: 'Our mission is to experience the joy of advancing and applying technology for the benefit of the public.'

- **Coca Cola**: 'The basic proposition of our business is simple, solid and timeless. When we bring refreshment, value, joy and fun to our stakeholders, then we successfully nurture and protect our brands.'

- **3M**: 'To solve unsolved problems innovatively.'

- **Glaxo**: 'We are an integrated, research-based group of companies whose corporate purpose is to create, discover, develop, manufacture, and market safe effective medicines throughout the world.'

ACTIVITY 3

evaluation   45%

Evaluate the mission statements above: what makes them effective?

Identify and evaluate the mission and vision statements of your own organisation, or an organisation that may form the focus of your assessment. To what audiences are they primarily directed?

(If no such statements exist, you might like to try drafting them ...)

One of the key elements in the corporate identity mix is behaviour. The management of corporate identity therefore depends (Simões & Dibb, 2007, p. 69) on 'the **endorsement of consistent behaviour** through the **diffusion of a company's mission, values and goals**'. Note that having a mission statement is not enough: the organisation must *live* the values implied by the words.

To support corporate identity, therefore, there is a need for a strong sense of mission, and consistent and congruent guiding values, to be (a) clearly defined, (b) communicated to all employees and (c) implemented in practice (eg through the HR systems of the organisation: selection, training and development, appraisal and reward).

'The rationale is that corporate identity is strategically driven by each organisation's unique corporate philosophy, which is reflected in its mission, values and goals. This dimension, which is a key element of corporate identity, internally diffuses the sense of purpose and singularity of the company, motivating commitment to organisational goals ... And this creates a basis for developing consistent behaviours among employees, emphasising their role in conveying the right business messages.' (Simões *et al.*, 2005, p. 162).

For a highly distinctive presentation of mission, vision and values, see the **Kellogg Company's** web site:

Link: http://www.kelloggcompany.com/company

Follow the links to 'Mission and Vision' and 'Values'.

Evaluation checklist

☐ Does the organisation have clearly and compellingly expressed vision, mission and value statements?

☐ Are the expressed vision, mission and values compatible with the organisation's desired identity, reputation and corporate brand positioning?

☐ Do the expressed vision, mission and values reflect attributes that are valued by key stakeholders (especially employees and customers)?

☐ Do the expressed vision, mission and values reflect attributes that are distinctive and positive in relation to the organisation's competitors?

☐ Have the vision, mission and values been clearly and compellingly communicated to key internal stakeholders (in order to inform corporate identity) and external stakeholders (in order to inform corporate image and reputation)?

☐ Are the vision, mission and core values currently reflected in the corporate identity mix: visual identity/symbolism, communications *and* (most importantly) the behaviour of managers and employees?

☐ Do key stakeholders (especially employees and customers) *perceive* the organisation as embodying the expressed vision, mission and values?

2.3 Strategic objectives

Goals and objectives translate the mission into targets or aims which the organisation will pursue. The terms are often used interchangeably, but it may be helpful to think of goals as statements of a desired future state ('where we want to get to') and objectives as more specific, time-assigned, quantified targets to pursue in order to achieve goals ('what we need to do to get there').

2.3.1 Levels of objectives

Management guru Peter Drucker (1955) argued that 'objectives are needed in every area where performance and results directly and vitally affect the survival and prosperity of the business'. Effectively formulated and communicated objectives promote unity of direction, aiding co-ordination and efficient organisation. They enable the intentional allocation of limited resources to optimise overall corporate performance (and reputation). They provide an objective measure against which performance can be measured and accountability maintained. And they support flexibility, by focusing on desired outputs and results rather than inputs.

- **Corporate strategies** apply to the whole organisation. They focus on the broad, general direction of the organisation, how value will be added, and how and where the organisation will compete, over the long-term.

- **Tactical or business level strategies** apply to particular divisions, functions or strategic business units. They focus on the tasks and objectives required to pursue the chosen corporate strategies and compete successfully in particular markets, over the medium-term.

- **Operational strategies and plans** apply to functions and departments, focusing on the specific detail of tasks, targets, resources and actions needed to deliver the corporate and business level strategies, over the short-term.

All these various objectives and strategies must be aligned or dovetailed with one another, in order to maintain coherence and unity of direction.

How do strategic objectives need to be aligned and dovetailed, in order to maintain unity of direction (everybody pursuing the same goals) and to present a coherent and consistent image to the world?

2.3.2 A balanced scorecard

The **primary objective** of a business organisation is generally financial: eg profitability or return on capital employed. However, a range of **secondary objectives** will be formulated to support the primary goal. These may include: market position or market share; product development and innovation; technology leverage; human resource development; and/or corporate social responsibility and sustainability.

As we will see in Chapter 6, non-economic goals are of increasing importance to business organisations as well as not-for-profit entities (driven by their stakeholders), and corporate strategies are increasingly likely to include such objectives and related performance measures. The Balanced Scorecard approach (Kaplan and Norton, 1996) sets objectives and performance measures using four perspectives, which the authors argued were long-term 'enablers' of success:

- **Financial**: financial performance and the creation of value for shareholders

- **Customers**: delivering value to the customer, and developing mutually beneficial relationships with customers and other stakeholders

- **Internal processes**: developing and implementing effective value-adding processes throughout the business process ('What must we excel at?')

- **Innovation and learning**: developing distinctive competences for future competitive advantage and growth.

The 'balance' of the scorecard is thus between: financial and non-financial performance measures, short-term and long-term perspectives, and internal and external focus – all of which are necessary for the management of corporate identity and image.

2.3.3 Specific business strategies

Obviously, an organisation may adopt a range of strategic approaches according to its offerings, markets, resources and competences – or its SWOT (internal strengths and weaknesses, external opportunities and threats) and other forms of positioning analysis.

From your earlier studies in marketing, you should be familiar with generic competitive strategies such as cost leadership, differentiation and focus (Porter); and generic directional strategies such as market penetration, market development, product development and diversification (Ansoff matrix).

In order to assess the compatibility of an organisation's strategy with its desired positioning, you will have to look at the specific strategic objectives and approaches formulated by whatever organisation is the focus of your assessment.

Evaluation checklist

☐ Does the organisation have clearly expressed strategic objectives at all levels?

☐ Are they vertically and horizontally aligned? If not, what is the likely effect on the consistency and coherence of corporate identity and image?

☐ What are the specific strategic objectives of the organisation?

☐ Are they compatible with the organisation's desired identity, reputation and corporate brand positioning? (Are they responsible, innovative, contributing to strong financial performance etc?)

☐ Do the strategic objectives take into account the needs, concerns and interests of key stakeholders: employees, customers and wider constituencies?

☐ Do the strategic objectives offer the organisation differentiation or other forms of competitive advantage in relation to its competitors?

☐ Have the organisation's strategic objectives been clearly and compellingly communicated to key internal stakeholders?

☐ Are strategic objectives currently reflected in (and supported by) the corporate identity mix (symbolism, communication, behaviour)?

MARKETING AT WORK

application

Balmer (2008, p. 37) presents the following 'case vignette' showing the influence of strategy on corporate branding.

Intel has embarked on a major strategic shift of organisational emphasis and purpose, by embracing new lines of activity such as consumer electronics, wireless communications, and healthcare. Superficially, the change was about tweaking the company's logo but, more substantively, it was fundamentally concerned with a *change in strategy*. As such, the tweaking of the company logo represented the trappings rather than the substantive aspects of the identity change. The substantive change relates to a broadening of Intel's core competences beyond the manufacture of microprocessors. As such, the change of logo and the accompanying corporate advertising had the aim of articulating this change to external audiences (both new and old) in the medium-term.

> **Link**: http://www.intel.com (and follow the 'for everyone' link for vision, mission and value statements, and an interesting tour of the company's online Intel Museum)

2.4 The strategy formulation process

There are a number of approaches to strategy formulation, which can be briefly summarised as follows. As you read, think of some of the advantages and limitations of each approach for the strategic management of reputation.

2.4.1 Planned or deliberate strategy

Traditional strategic planning takes a rational, structured and formal approach. A basic framework for this kind of approach may be as follows: Figure 3.4.

Figure 3.4: The rational strategic planning model

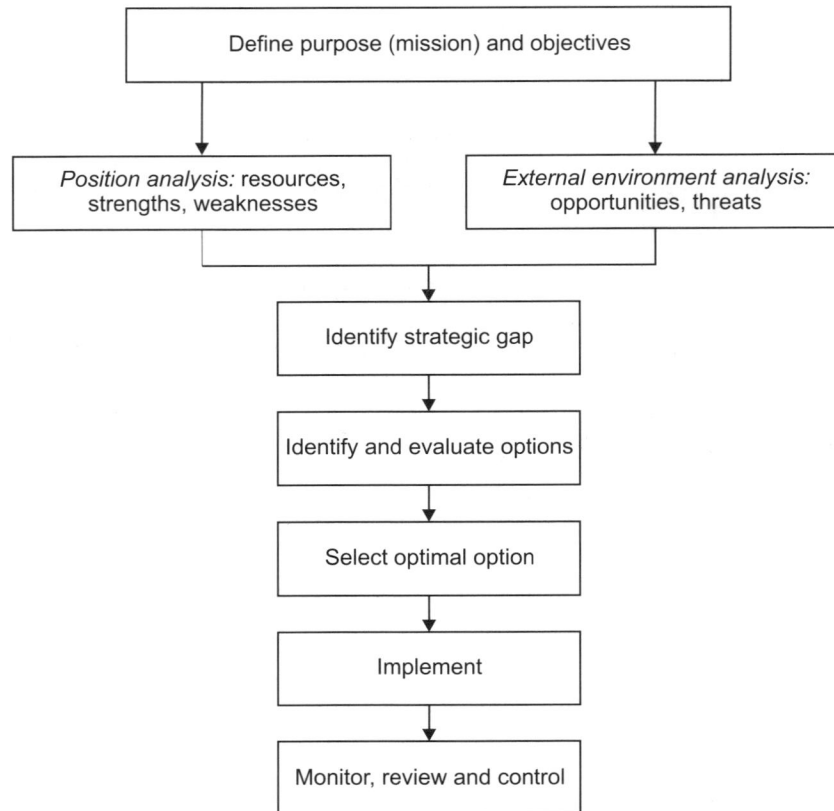

```
          ┌─────────────────────────────────────────┐
          │   Define purpose (mission) and objectives │
          └─────────────────────────────────────────┘
             │                               │
             ▼                               ▼
  ┌──────────────────────┐       ┌──────────────────────┐
  │ Position analysis:    │       │ External environment  │
  │ resources, strengths, │       │ analysis:             │
  │ weaknesses            │       │ opportunities, threats│
  └──────────────────────┘       └──────────────────────┘
             │                               │
             └───────────────┬───────────────┘
                             ▼
                  ┌────────────────────────┐
                  │ Identify strategic gap  │
                  └────────────────────────┘
                             │
                             ▼
                  ┌────────────────────────┐
                  │ Identify and evaluate   │
                  │ options                 │
                  └────────────────────────┘
                             │
                             ▼
                  ┌────────────────────────┐
                  │ Select optimal option   │
                  └────────────────────────┘
                             │
                             ▼
                  ┌────────────────────────┐
                  │ Implement               │
                  └────────────────────────┘
                             │
                             ▼
                  ┌────────────────────────┐
                  │ Monitor, review and     │
                  │ control                 │
                  └────────────────────────┘
```

Note that this model is a **positioning** approach. It utilises strategy to 'fit' the strengths, resources and capabilities of the organisation to the demands of its external environment – using techniques such as PESTLE analysis (external environmental analysis) and SWOT analysis (strengths, weaknesses, opportunities and threats analysis). An identity and reputation management strategy can be seen as one approach by which the organisation can match itself to the changing needs and views of its stakeholders, as an important part of the external environment (Davies *et al.*, *op cit*, p. 4).

The rational model assumes that corporate objectives or outcomes are deliberately chosen; that sufficient, accurate data can be gathered to identity the best possible means of obtaining desired outcomes; and that those means can be pursued and controlled until the intended strategy is realised.

ACTIVITY 5

evaluation

How realistic do you think the rational model is in practice? In what ways might it represent an idealised picture of strategic planning?

2.4.2 Alternative strategy models

Mintzberg (among others) has disputed the idea that strategy necessarily emerges from a formal planning process as a deliberate strategy.

- Strategy may be **opportunistic**: taking advantage of changes in the environment or emerging gaps in the market, or recognising the potential of new skills or technology. Strategy development of this style is dominated by the active search for new opportunities and is characterised by bold decisions in the face of uncertainty. (This is often a feature of young organisations with a dominant, entrepreneurial leader or leadership team.)

- Strategy may be **imposed**, if choice is constrained by environmental pressures and imperatives – such as economic recession, technological development or legislation.

- Strategy may be **emergent**: 'formed' rather than deliberately 'formulated'. 'One idea leads to another until a new pattern forms. Action has driven thinking and a new strategy has emerged. *Ad hoc* choices are made at lower levels of the organisation, and the ones which work spread and stimulate other ideas. Existing patterns of behaviour influence how strategies are implemented. The routines by which resources are allocated, and the political processes by which influence is exerted in the organisation, favour some plans over others. Emergent strategies evolve in response to learning, changes, opportunity, luck (unintended positive results), crises and so on.

Quinn (1995) suggested that there is a strong argument for managers to build on strategies already in place, making only limited small-step changes. Purely deliberate strategies may hinder learning and flexibility, because management becomes attached to implementing a chosen strategy regardless of feedback and change. At the same time, purely emergent strategies may defy control – and may lead to a piecemeal approach to strategy which fragments organisational direction and identity. Managers need to be both responsive to the realities of organisational life and constant environmental change and rational and deliberate in their decision-making. Quinn therefore advocated an approach which he called **logical incrementalism**.

KEY CONCEPT

concept

Logical incrementalism may be defined this as: 'the deliberate development of strategy by experimentation and learning from partial commitments'. Johnson & Scholes (*op cit*)

Logical incrementalism is a deliberate policy of small-step (incremental) strategic changes, within the guiding framework of an overall sense of strategic direction. A series of short-range plans (as opposed to one long-range plan) allows constant adjustments of direction in response to testing, performance and stakeholder feedback and learning. It also gives managers space to gather more information, build stakeholder support and develop resources for change – and to co-ordinate changes across the organisation. Such an approach allows the firm to be flexible and opportunistic – minimising the risks of getting 'locked-in' to a long-term strategy which might turn out to be dysfunctional. At the same time, it retains a supportive and coherent sense of vision and direction. It encourages participation in strategy formation at all levels, with the change-reinforcing sense of 'small wins' (as each short-range plan comes to fruition).

ASSESSMENT TIP

evaluation

Evaluation checklist: **strategy**

☐ Is strategy formation top-down or participative? How might this influence corporate identity – and is it compatible with the organisation's desired positioning (eg as a company that values the input of all its people)?

☐ Is strategy formation formal/deliberate or opportunistic, imposed or emergent? How might this influence the clarity of the organisation's sense of direction and the consistency and coherence of its identity? How might it influence the responsiveness of the organisation to internal and external stakeholder input and other factors? Is this compatible with the organisation's desired positioning?

☐ Is strategy formation long-range or short-range/incremental? How might this influence the organisation's sense of direction and the consistency and coherence of its identity? How might it influence the responsiveness of the organisation? Is this compatible with the organisation's desired positioning?

☐ Are conflicting objectives, priorities and viewpoints (within the management team or between business units or brands) taken into account in strategy formation? How might this influence the clarity of the organisation's sense of direction and the consistency and coherence of its identity?

Are corporate communication and branding issues considered during strategy formation? How might this influence the effectiveness of reputation management? How might it influence the consistency and coherence of corporate identity and image?

3 Organisational structure

concept

Organisational structure may be defined as 'the pattern of relationships among positions in the organisation and among members of the organisation. Structure makes possible the application of the process of management and creates a framework of order and command through which the activities of the organisation can be planned, organised, directed and controlled.' (Mullins, 1999)

Mintzberg (1983) defines an organisation's structure as: 'The sum total of the ways in which it divides its labour into distinct tasks and then achieves co-ordination among them'. Organisational structure implies a formal framework intended to:

- Define **work roles and relationships**, so that areas and flows of authority and responsibility are clearly established

- Define **work tasks and responsibilities**, grouping and allocating them to suitable individuals and groups

- Channel **information flows** (communication) efficiently through the organisation

- **Co-ordinate** the objectives and activities of different units, so that overall aims are achieved without gaps or overlaps in the flow of work.

- Control the **flow of work**, information and resources, through the organisation

- Support **flexibility** and **adaptability** to changing internal and external demands

- Support the **commitment**, **involvement and satisfaction** of the people who work for the organisation, by offering opportunities for participation, responsibility, team-working etc.

- Support **value-adding**, **customer-focused business processes**

- Support and improve **organisational performance** through all of the above.

3.1 Aspects of organisational structure

Some of the decisions that will have to be made in designing (or evaluating) an organisational structure (Huczyinski & Buchanan, 2001) include:

- **Specialisation**: how should the work of the organisation be divided up? Should tasks be grouped to allow units to specialise (allowing efficient focusing of training, equipment and management) – or should specialisation be minimised (to simplify communication and allow units and individuals to be versatile and flexible)?

- **Hierarchy**: should the overall structure be 'tall' (with many levels or tiers of management) or 'flat' (fewer tiers – meaning that each manager has to control more people: a wider 'span of control')? Tall organisations allow closer managerial control (due to narrower spans of control), while flat organisations save on managerial costs and empower and satisfy workers (who are given more authority and discretion).

- **Grouping**: how should jobs and departments be grouped together? Options include departmentation or divisionalisation by the specialist expertise and resources required (function), or the services/products offered (product/market/brand), or the geographical area being targeted (territory).

- **Process alignment and co-ordination**: how can the organisation foster integration between its different units, in order to maximise the 'horizontal' flow of business processes from one to the other? This will involve mechanisms such as rules and policies, carefully aligned goals and plans, liaison/co-ordinator roles, cross-functional team- or project-working and so on.

- **Control**: should decisions be mainly 'centralised' (taken at the top) or 'decentralised' (delegated to lower levels) – or a mixture of both? Centralisation allows swift, decisive control and co-ordination, while decentralisation empowers and satisfies workers, and can support organisational responsiveness by having decisions taken closer to the customer or local market.

3.2 Organisation charts

Organisation charts act as a guide to explain how different task roles and positions related to each other, and how they are co-ordinated and integrated. They typically show:

- **'Shape'**: whether the organisation perceives itself as hierarchical (top-down), or in some other way (an important aspect of identity). A chart may take the form of concentric circles radiating out from a central leader, for example; or a 'web' or network of interrelationships and communication; or an upside-down pyramid with the pointy (senior management) end at the bottom (showing that management sees its role as supporting operational staff in serving the customer, rather than imposing its wishes on them): Figure 3.5.

Figure 3.6: Organisation chart showing an empowerment culture

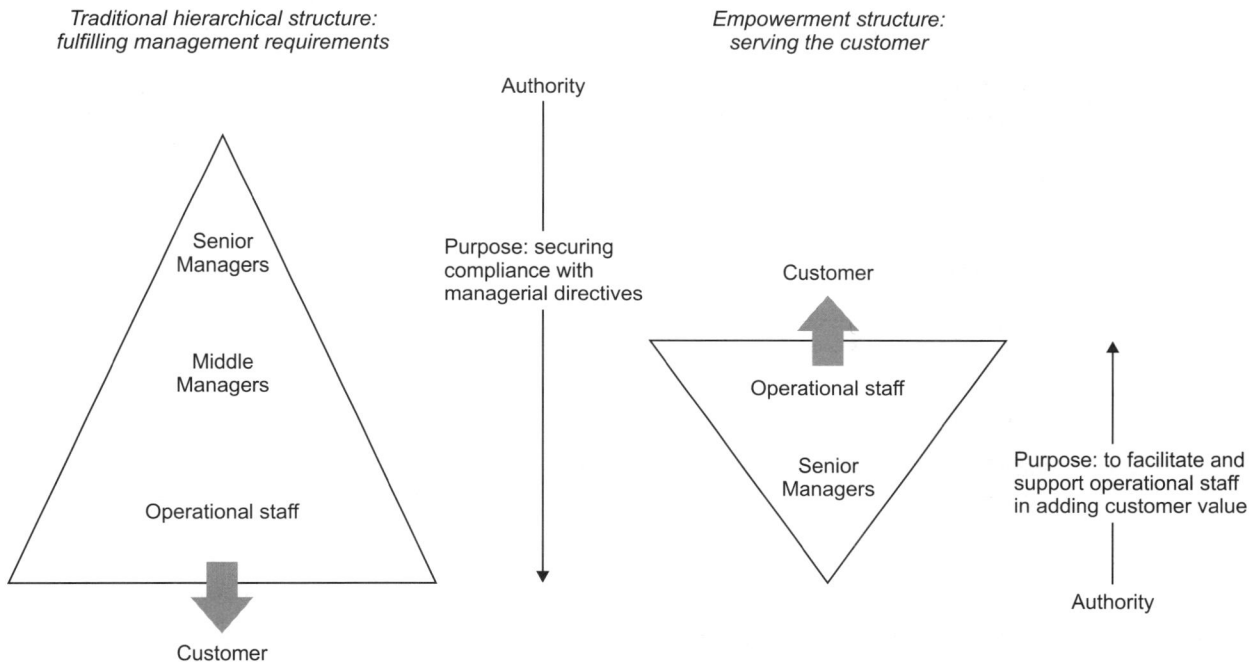

- **Hierarchy**: the number of tiers (or circles) of authority in the organisation – and so, the speed of decision-making and the degree of decentralisation or empowerment of lower levels of staff.

- **Formal communication channels**: the lines connecting different levels (vertical) and units (horizontal) in the organisation, through which information flows in all directions. Horizontal lines are particularly important, as they reflect cross-functional or inter-group communication: a crucial mechanism of co-ordination and identity development.

Note that an organisation chart is only a static 'snapshot' of the planned formal structure of an organisation at a moment in time. It cannot express the *quality* of management or relationships, or whether information flows *effectively* via formal channels. It does not attempt to show the true, complex pattern of relationships and communication in the organisation, taking into account *informal* contacts through 'grapevine'. It can show authority relationships, but not power, influence or leadership relationships. It can show formally designated job roles – but not what people actually do, especially if jobs are loosely defined to allow for initiative, growth and flexible contribution.

Nevertheless, drawing an organisation chart may be a helpful way of:

- **Clarifying basic features** of the organisational structure and self-perception

- **Highlighting potential inefficiencies and dysfunctions**, such as: long lines of communication, lack of cross-functional communication, duplications of activity, unclear boundaries of authority or unclear authority relationships.

ACTIVITY 6

evaluation

Draw an organisation chart for your own organisation, in any way that expresses, for you, both the structure and the self-perception (shape) of the organisation.

Get hold of the formal organisation chart (if any) of your organisation.

Compare the two versions, perhaps in discussion with a colleague or fellow student. Evaluate:

- How far the formal organisation chart expresses the self-image and nature of the organisation.

- The effectiveness of the organisation structure: what potential strengths and weaknesses are highlighted by the chart for effective identity and reputation management.

3.3 Evaluating organisation structures for reputation management

Drucker (1955) argued that: '**good organisation structure** does not by itself produce good performance. But a **poor organisation structure** makes good performance impossible, no matter how good the individual managers may be. To improve organisation structure... will therefore always improve performance.' Signs that a structure may be **ineffective or dysfunctional** include problems such as:

- Slow decision/response times, due to the need to refer decisions via overly lengthy formal communication channels

- Inter-departmental conflicts, due to ambiguities or overlaps of responsibility

- Excessive layers of management (often in the middle line), which slows communication, increases overheads, and often requires work creation (or initiative-stifling micro-management) to justify the positions

- Lack of co-ordination between units, seen in customer complaints, production bottlenecks, inconsistent communications and the proliferation of special co-ordinating mechanisms (liaison officers, committees etc)

- High labour turnover among skilled junior staff, suggesting lack of delegation, challenge and/or development opportunities

- Lack of identifiable accountabilities for key tasks or results.

These kinds of dysfunctions may create particular problems for identity and image management, where they:

- Inhibit or slow down internal communication, which (as we will see in Chapter 10) is an essential element in building corporate identity and identification, and facilitating external stakeholder satisfaction. 'Internal communication is heavily influenced by the official channels that are given life by the organisation's formal structure of reporting relationships. The greater the number of levels in the hierarchy and the more distinct groups that were created for task purposes, the higher the probability of distortion and misinformation across the company, and the lower the likelihood of the company developing shared understandings among employees' (van Riel & Fombrun, *op cit*, p. 190).

- Create barriers to the alignment of corporate mission, values and behaviours, inhibiting the development of an integrated corporate identity, and increasing the risk that inconsistent or incoherent messages will be given out by conflicting units or unconnected departmental or brand 'silos'.

- Slow the speed of decision-making, stifle initiative and reduce responsiveness to customer demands, feedback, reputational risk events (eg crises) and environmental changes.

- Foster rigidity of behaviour and culture. Large, formal organisations (bureaucracies) already have a poor reputation for: being slow to respond to customer demands; failing to learn from external feedback; discouraging individual initiative; being preoccupied by rules and procedures; getting bogged down in 'red tape'; and being slow to adapt to changing demands and conditions.

- Fail to satisfy and retain the employees who build corporate identity and operate at the interface with customers and other external stakeholders.

From the above discussion, suggest how the management of identity and image might be positively supported by structural elements and attributes.

Lancaster & Withey (2005, p. 68) argue that 'There is no one method of organising the implementation of marketing plans which is always and inevitably superior... It is impossible and downright dangerous to be prescriptive about the form which management and organisational structures should take. Having said that... they should be selected and designed ideally so as to provide:

- Company-wide customer orientation
- Organisational flexibility and speed of response
- Innovation
- Co-ordination and integration between different functional areas of the business and outside the organisation
- Effective communication
- Motivation and leadership.'

3.4 Organisational flexibility

The terms 'mechanistic' and 'organic' were coined by Burns and Stalker (1961) to describe forms of organisation which are:

- Stable, efficient and suitable for slow-changing operating environments (mechanistic or '**machine-like**' organisations: also called '**bureaucracies**'), and

- Flexible, adaptive and suitable for fast-changing or dynamic operating environments (organic or '**organism-like**' organisations).

Bureaucracy is a form of organisation characterised by: hierarchical organisation; formalisation of communication channels; impersonality; reliance on job descriptions, rules and procedures; a preoccupation with technical proficiency and internal processes rather than outputs; a high degree of *esprit de corps* and discipline (based on conformity); and continuity (since individuals are replaceable).

Burns and Stalker argue that while such a structure/culture can be highly efficient in stable, slow-change environments, which do not require sensitivity to customer or external environmental demands, **organic structures** are better suited to conditions of change – particularly where there is a need for continuous innovation and creativity. They are typified by:

- A 'contributive' culture of information and skill-sharing, encouraging versatility (rather than specialisation) and team working (rather than functional departmentation)

- A 'network' structure of authority and communication, allowing decentralisation and a range of lateral relationships (crossing functional boundaries) for co-ordination and self-control

- Focus on goals and outputs rather than processes

- Job design that allows flexible definition of tasks according to the needs of the team and changing demands.

Some recent trends have emerged from the focus on **responsiveness and flexibility** as key organisational values.

- **Flat structures**. The flattening of hierarchies removes levels of organisation which lengthened lines of communication and decision-making and encouraged ever-increasing specialisation. Flat structures are more responsive, because there is a more direct relationship between the organisation's strategic centre and the operational units serving the customer.

- **Horizontal structures**. What Peters (1994) calls 'going horizontal' is a recognition that functional versatility (through multi-functional project teams and multi-skilling, for example) is the key to flexibility. In the words (quoted by Peters) of a Motorola executive: 'The traditional job descriptions were barriers. We needed an organisation soft enough between the organisational disciplines so that ... people would run freely across functional barriers or organisational barriers with the common goal of getting the job done, rather than just making certain that their specific part of the job was completed.'

- **'Chunked'** and **'unglued'** structures. So far, this has meant team-working and decentralisation, or empowerment, creating smaller and more flexible units within the overall structure. Charles Handy's 'shamrock organisation' (with a three-leafed structure of core, subcontractor and flexible part-time labour) is also gaining ground as a workable model for a leaner and more flexible workforce, within a controlled framework (Handy, 1989).

- **Output-focused structures**. The key to all the above trends is the focus on results, and on the customer, instead of internal processes and functions for their own sake. A **project management** orientation and structure, for example, is being applied to the supply of services within the organisation (to internal customers) as well as to the external market, in order to facilitate listening and responding to customer demands.

- **Boundaryless structures** (Milkovich & Boudreau, 1996; Welsh, 2005). Horizontal (status) barriers are removed or softened by de-layering and participative decision-making, and vertical (functional) barriers by empowered cross-functional team working – in order to align business processes. The boundaries of the organisation are also softened, by co-opting suppliers, distributors, business allies and customers as collaborators in the value-adding process, creating an 'extended' or 'networked' enterprise.

You might like to consider how these principles could enhance corporate identity and image management, and how elements of such structures could fruitfully be built into your own organisation.

3.5 The informal organisation

An informal organisation always exists alongside the formal one. Unlike the formal organisation, the informal organisation is loosely structured, flexible and spontaneous. It embraces such mechanisms as:

- Social relationships and groupings (eg cliques) within – or across – formal structures

- The 'grapevine' or informal communication which by-passes the formal reporting channels and routes

- Behavioural norms and ways of doing things, both social and work-related, which may circumvent formal procedures and systems (for good or ill)

- Power/influence structures, irrespective of organisational authority: informal leaders are those who are trusted and looked to for advice.

The informal organisation can be beneficial for organisational personality and identity, in some ways. The meeting of employees' social needs may contribute to morale, job satisfaction and identification with the organisation. The availability of information through informal networks can help to meet employees' information needs, giving them a 'big picture' view of the firm and their own role within it: the self-perception of the organisation is often expressed through the grapevine, via news, rumour and opinion swapping. Informal networks and methods may sometimes be more efficient in meeting stakeholder expectations (closing the gap between identity and image) than a formal structure of rigid procedures or lengthy communication channels. The development of interpersonal networks can facilitate team-working and integration of identity across organisational boundaries.

On the other hand, each of these positive attributes could be detrimental if the power of the informal organisation is directed towards goals unrelated to, or at odds with, those of the formal organisation. If employees have a negative perception of the organisation, this will communicate itself in organisational identity through behaviours and messages carried by the informal organisation. Rumours may undermine formal corporate communication.

What do you think managers could do to minimise the potential problems of the informal organisation?

Evaluation checklist: structure

☐ Does the organisational structure support the integration of corporate communication and reputation management, or are messages and strategies fragmented among different specialist communicators and business managers?

☐ Does the structure support multi-directional internal communication?

☐ Does the structure reflect the organisation's orientation towards the customer? Does it facilitate 'horizontal' flow of work, information and value through business processes towards the customer – or place vertical barriers in the way of customer value and service?

☐ Does the structure reflect and support the mission, strategy and priorities of the organisation? (Eg is it organised by brand or customer group, to optimise research and marketing expertise – or by territory, to maximise 'local' adaptation, knowledge and contacts?)

☐ Does the structure reflect and support specific desired/expressed values and cultural attributes of the organisation. Does it support innovation and creativity (by encouraging flexibility and cross-functional project-working), say, or reflect the stated importance of employee contribution and initiative (by flattening structures and empowering teams)?

☐ Is the organisational structure flexible and responsive enough to learn and adapt as a result of image research, stakeholder feedback and environmental change?

☐ Does the informal organisation support or undermine the formal organisation (and the desired identity of the organisation)?

---

4 Organisational culture

Organisational culture may be defined as: 'The collection of traditions, values, policies, beliefs and attitudes that constitute a pervasive context for everything we do and think in an organisation' (Mullins, 1999) – or, more popularly, 'the way we do things round here' (Schein, 1985).

Schwartz & Davies (1981) define organisational culture as: 'A pattern of beliefs and expectations shared by the organisation's members, and which produce norms which powerfully shape the behaviour of individuals and groups in the organisation'.

Culture researcher Fons Trompenaars (1993) suggested that there are different manifestations of culture: Figure 3.6.

Figure 3.6: The cultural 'iceberg'

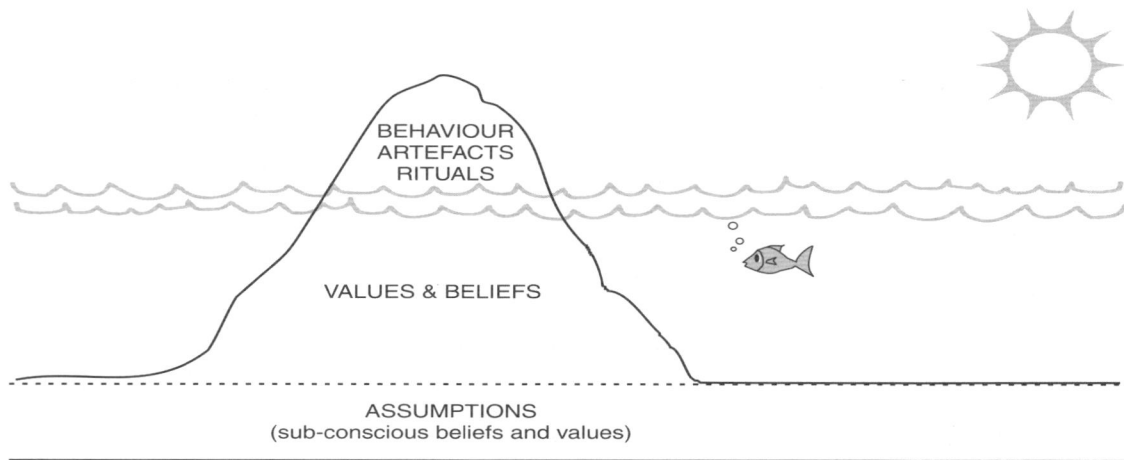

The **observable**, expressed or 'explicit' elements of culture include:

- **Behaviour**: norms of personal and interpersonal behaviour; customs and rules about behaviours that are 'acceptable' or unacceptable.

- **Artefacts**: concrete expressions such as art and literature, architecture and interior design (eg of office premises), dress codes, symbols and 'heroes' or role models.

- **Rituals**: patterns of collective behaviour which have traditional or symbolic value, such as greeting styles, business formalities, social courtesies and ceremonies.

Beneath these observable phenomena lie **values and beliefs** which give the behaviours, artefacts and rituals their special meaning and significance. For example, the design of office space (artefact) may imply status and honour, or reflect the importance of privacy, or reflect spiritual beliefs (as in *feng shui*) within a culture: it 'means' more than the observable features. Values and beliefs may be overtly expressed in sayings, mottos and slogans.

Beneath values and beliefs again lie **assumptions**: foundational ideas that are no longer consciously recognised or questioned by the culture, but which 'programme' its ways of thinking and behaving. Examples include the importance of the individual in many Western cultures: this is taken for granted in designing HR (human resources) policies, for example.

Cultural assumptions, values and beliefs influence the behaviour of individuals, groups and organisations. They create a shared 'style' of operating within a given culture.

4.1 The cultural web

Strategy gurus Johnson, Scholes & Whittington (2005) introduced the concept of the **cultural web**, as a way of representing 'the taken-for-granted assumptions, or paradigm, of an organisation, and the behavioural manifestations of organisational and culture'. The elements of the web can be used as a framework to analyse organisational culture in a wide range of settings.

- The **paradigm** is the set of basic assumptions held by the organisation: eg about the importance of the customer satisfaction, quality, risk, values such as integrity, empowerment or teamwork. It reflects how the organisation sees itself in general, and what it 'stands for': the core of corporate identity.

- **Stories** form the 'mythology' of the organisation: how things came to be the way they were, tales of past successes or failures, heroes and adversaries and so on. Organisations 'see' themselves in terms of these stories.

- **Routines** include formal procedures; 'short-cuts' developed in practice; behavioural norms (such as familiarity or formality); and customs (such as 'pizza Fridays'). **Rituals** are more symbolic behaviours, including business formalities, ceremonies (eg staff awards) and rites of passage (eg celebrating project completions).

- **Organisational structure** is an expression of organisational values about control or empowerment, formality or informality, stability or flexibility, collaboration or competition etc.

- **Control systems** refer to how control is exercised. A culture believing in individual responsibility and initiative, for example, will facilitate self-control and reporting by exception, while a paradigm based on managerial control (or worker resistance) will rely on close supervision and monitoring, rules and sanctions.

- **Power structures** refer to how power is distributed; whether it is based on formal authority, charismatic leadership, democratic consensus or respect for expertise; and who the influential individuals and groups are.

- **Symbols** include formal logos and corporate visual identity, as well as things which take on symbolic value – reflecting status (like office size) or recognition (such as team badges).

Since all these elements are interrelated, any one of them can, theoretically, be changed in order to support a shift of culture (and therefore behaviour and identity).

MARKETING AT WORK

application/evaluation

Since 2000, pharmaceutical giant **Merck** has been the subject of a series of performance and public relations crises. In October 2004, the company 'decided' to recall its arthritis painkiller brand Vioxx, because of cardiovascular side-effects in some patients. Amidst a global storm of product liability law suits, the company is still fighting for its reputation against charges of side-effect cover-up, indifference and internal dysfunction. Merck has already settled thousands of lawsuits in the US for $US 4.85 billion – but has made no admission of guilt.

In October 2004, under legal advice, the company refused to discuss the Vioxx allegations with *The Wall Street Journal* – and a front-page article (November 1, 2004) exposed the company to a media frenzy. In 2005, having suffered enormous reputational damage, the company launched a multimillion-dollar advertising campaign. But here are some of the stories breaking in the Australian media in 2009, as a result of on-going court proceedings:

- **'Lure of lucre drove Vioxx marketeers'**: An Australian sales team boasted that 'money!' was its main motivation in a team profile in the internal company newsletter. (*Australian*, April 28, 2009)

- **'Doctors feted by Merck over Vioxx'**: Merck sales representatives 'wined and dined' scores of doctors at some of the country's most expensive venues in 2001 to promote Vioxx. Meanwhile, managers in Asia and Australia were told 'not to proactively communicate' the preliminary results of the 2000 VIGOR study which revealed the increased cardiovascular risks. 'Widespread communication/promotion of the preliminary results should not be undertaken at this time', an internal instruction said. If the topic of the research was brought up, 'the emphasis' should be turned to positive findings on gastro-intestinal safety. (*Australian*, April 29, 2009)

- **'Sales arsenal'**: Some of the tactics the plaintiff alleges Merck used to protect and boost Vioxx market share include: drawing up a hit list of doctors who had to be 'neutralised' or discredited because they weren't supportive of Vioxx; hinting that it would stop funding for institutions where researchers were critical of Vioxx; publishing Merck's own research in medical journals as 'independent studies'; creating its own journal which looked like a peer-reviewed journal but was produced by Merck; training sales representatives to reassure concerned doctors that the link between the drug and identified risks were 'non-existent'; giving sales staff a motivational CD to play in the car, including a Ricky Martin-style 'Go Vioxx' song. (*Australian*, May 4, 2009)

- **'Science unproven on Vioxx: drug firm'**. Merck maintained in court that there was not enough scientific proof to link the drug to heart attacks – despite having withdrawn it from the market almost five years ago. ('It was the responsible course to take.' The company could have continued selling the drug with new warning labels, but instead took the course of action that 'best serves the interests of their patients'). (*Australian*, May 5, 2009)

- **'Merck staff in comedy skit on Vioxx'**: Merck sales staff were revealed to have spoofed journal articles discussing Vioxx's cardiovascular risks, in a skit presented at an end-of-year celebration. 'The attitude inside Merck marketing and sales was to mock the idea that Vioxx increased CV risks', one lawyer alleged. A Merck employee admitted in 'today's climate' such a mock presentation would be considered an 'unfortunate' approach, but only because it had been seen outside the company and taken out of context. (*Australian*, May 20, 2009)

For reflection: What do these stories say (a) about the underlying culture at Merck and (b) about the role of the media in shaping corporate reputation?

4.2 What shapes organisation culture?

Handy (1995) noted that 'Organisations are as different and varied as nations and societies of the world. They have differing cultures... affected by events of the past and climate of the present, by the technology of the type of work, by their aims and type of people who work in them'. Influences on organisational culture include:

- The organisation's **founder** or strong leader (eg a Henry Ford or Richard Branson). A strong set of values and assumptions is set up by such individuals, and these have their own momentum: an organisation might find it hard to shake off its original culture.

- The organisation's **history**. Culture reflects the era when the organisation was founded, and also the shared history of successes and failures, changes, great leaders and so on. (Think about the traditions built up in a long-established company such as Marks & Spencer, for example.)

- **Leadership and management style**. An organisation with a strong culture recruits and develops managers who naturally conform to – and perpetuate – it. Intentional leadership can, however, shape and change the culture.

- The **organisation's environment**. Nations, regions, occupations and business types have their own distinctive cultures, and these will affect the organisation's style.

4.3 Value of a strong positive culture

In their influential book In Search of Excellence, Peters & Waterman (1981) found that a defining feature of excellent (responsive and innovative) companies was their use of **cultural values** to guide business processes and motivate employees. Deal & Kennedy (1982) likewise argued that **cultural strength** is a powerful tool for shaping the behaviour and success of an organisation. Not all organisation cultures are 'strong' – but those that are contribute to improved business performance.

This school of thought defines 'strong' cultures as those in which key values are widely shared and intensely held, and in which employees allow themselves to be guided by them. In other words, as summarised by Huczynski and Buchanan (*op cit*): 'Strength refers to the degree to which employees share a commitment to a range of goals and values espoused by management, and have a high level of motivation to achieve them.'

It is argued that strong culture can improve business performance in various ways.

- Strong cultural norms can **replace rules**, **guidelines and close supervision**, focusing employees' attention on values such as quality and customer service, and empowering them to make more flexible decisions in pursuit of those values.

- Strong culture can increase **employee loyalty and commitment**. People need both to feel part of something meaningful and to 'shine' as stars in their own right: strong culture can satisfy both needs, by emphasising the 'family' nature of the enterprise, by building myths to reinforce the 'heroic' nature of the enterprise and by using value-laden symbols as rewards and incentives.

- Cultural values can be used to **drive organisational change**, on the basis that if values change, behaviour will follow.

For different (and more detailed) conceptual and practical perspectives on corporate culture and personality, and their relationship to corporate identity, you might like to look at:

- *Davies, Chun, Da Silva and Roper,* Corporate Reputation and Competitiveness *(2003, Routledge): Chapter 11: Managing the personality of the organisation.*

- *Melewar (ed),* Facets of Corporate Identity, Communication and Reputation *(2008, Routledge): Chapter 1: Explicating the relationship between identity and culture (by Vella & Melewar). There is a particularly interesting application of the cultural web analysis of the National Health Service at the end of the chapter.*

For more on culture and the use of the cultural web as a tool of corporate appraisal, see:

- *Johnson, Scholes & Whittington,* Exploring Corporate Strategy: Text and Cases *(7th edition, 2005: FT Prentice Hall) Chapter 4: Expectations and Purposes.* ■

4.4 Communication climate

KEY CONCEPT

concept

Communication climate is a sub-set of the broader organisational climate (culture), embracing the context of internal communications within the organisation and employee perceptions about their nature.

The culture of an organisation may support or hinder communication. Gibb (1961) suggested that the 'communication climate' of an organisation may be open (or supportive) or closed (defensive).

- In an **open climate**, communication is open and honest. Information exchange is positive and directed at solving problems (rather than criticising, judging or scoring points). Everyone's input is valued, regardless of role or status: suggestions and feedback are welcomed, and occasional mistakes are regarded as learning experiences – taking the risk out of contributing new ideas, asking questions and challenging the *status quo*. In such a climate, there is a free, multi-directional exchange of information and views, supported by a sense of confidence and security.

- In a **closed climate**, information is used for competition and political advantage: there is a tendency towards secrecy, insincerity and manipulation. There is little willingness to discuss or question the *status quo*, or to volunteer new ideas, because of the risk judgement or reprisals: the input of 'lower level' team members is not highly valued. In such a climate, communication, learning and creativity are inhibited.

Redding (1972) distinguishes five dimensions of an ideal communication climate:

- Supportiveness
- Participative decision-making
- Trust, confidence and credibility
- Openness and candour
- High performance goals

MARKETING AT WORK

application

Parcelforce

'The results of a national employee opinion attitude survey, conducted in May 1995, showed that morale was low in the company. Perhaps indicative of the communication climate in the North East business unit was the participation rate of their own employee opinion survey: just 32%. Many people aspired to an excellent service culture, but many felt unable to deliver due to obstacles in the way that the business unit operated and was managed.

One of the transformation projects, an integrated communications programme, branded 'Understanding the Business', was being launched as part of a programme of improvement in communication activities, aimed at increasing the knowledge of employees at all levels, especially in the areas of: products and services for external customers; commercial awareness; competitor activity; important customers; and advertising plans and campaigns.

Other developments at that time were in response to a growing recognition that what was needed was a much more open and dynamic communication climate and system. The internal marketing approach offered an integrating system of interactive communication that focused working practices and decisions on customer service in a competitive marketplace.'

Varey (2002, p. 224)

The strength or weakness of an organisation's communication climate can be researched using techniques such as the analysis of **critical incidents** (eg breakdowns in internal communication, occasions when the organisation 'shot the messenger' bringing important information, or operational problems caused by employees lacking information) and **communication attitude surveys**. Dennis (2006) suggests that a broad indication of communication climate can be gauged by asking employees to rate the organisation on a scale of 1 (not at all) to 10 (almost always) on five basic questions:

- To what extent do you think what management has to say is believable? [Credibility]

- To what extent is management a trustworthy source of important information? [Trust]

- To what extent do you feel comfortable sharing your true feelings and opinions at work? [Openness]

- To what extent does management place a high priority on good communication practices in your company? [Priority]

- To what extent do you believe the grapevine should be ignored for important company information? [Rumour management]

An average total score of 40 or more indicates an excellent, supportive communication climate.

More rigorous approaches to climate survey (communication audit) are discussed in Chapter 5.

There are plenty of accessible web resources on communication climate. See, for example:

- *'Open Communication Climate' by William Buchholz, posted at:*

  http://atc.bentley.edu/faculty/wb/printables/opencomm.pdf

- *'Communication Climate' by Harry S Dennis, posted at:*

  http://www.biztimes.com/news/2006/10/12/communication-climate

- *A Communication Climate Inventory (James Costigan and Martha Schmeidler): a survey tool for*

  measuring communication climate in your own organisation, posted at:

  http://www.cps.usfca.edu/ob/studenthandbooks/321handbook/climate.htm

ACTIVITY 9

application   30%

How might an organisation go about fostering a more open climate – or tackling the challenge of turning a closed climate into a more open one?

As an additional exercise, you may like to try using the simple Communication Climate survey outlined above to get an idea of your own organisation's communication climate.

ASSESSMENT TIP

evaluation   45%

Evaluation checklist: culture

☐ What are the basic paradigm, beliefs and values of the culture? Are these compatible with the corporate mission and value statements? Are they compatible with the organisation's desired identity and image? Do they offer a source of differentiation from competitors?

☐ What do each of the elements of the cultural web (rituals, stories, symbols, power structures, organisation structures and control systems) express about the culture? Are they consistent and coherent – or conflicting? Are they compatible with the organisation's desired identity and image? Do they reflect the attributes valued or considered important by employees, customers and other key stakeholders?

☐ Are desired cultural values and norms expressed and modelled (compellingly and consistently) by top management and influential leaders? Are they disseminated (compellingly and consistently) by internal communications? Are they reinforced by HR mechanisms such as recruitment and selection, training and development, appraisal and reward?

☐ What do employees, customers and other key stakeholders perceive to be the cultural attributes of the organisation? Is there a gap between identity and image?

☐ Do the systems, norms and values of the organisation encourage a positive or open communication climate? Do they, in particular, support upward communication (for employee involvement and empowerment, and enhanced responsiveness to the environment) and lateral communication (for cross-functional ideas sharing, co-ordination and integration)?

4.5 How do you change a culture?

Cultures which foster a negative identity and image, are unsuited to changing requirements or are otherwise failing or dysfunctional can be changed. Any element of the cultural web can be manipulated to support cultural change, but three key areas of leverage are:

- Consistent **expression and modelling** of the new values by management (from the top down), leaders and influencers (who may need to be co-opted to a guiding coalition by those in authority).

- Changing **underlying values and beliefs**, through communication, education and involvement of employees in discussing the need for new ideas and behaviours: spreading new values and beliefs and encouraging employees to 'own' them (through incentives, co-opting people to teach others and so on); and reinforcing the change (through implementation, recognition and rewards).

- Use of **human resource management mechanisms** to reinforce the changes: making the new values and behaviours criteria for recruitment and selection, appraisal and reward; including them in competency profiles and learning needs assessments for training and development planning; and so on. (These mechanisms are important because the organisation may need to bring in new people who will 'fit' the new culture – and squeeze out those who don't 'fit'.)

ACTIVITY 10   evaluation

Select any one (or more) of our evaluation checklists and take them for a 'test drive', using them to guide your own brainstorming about your organisation, or any organisation that may be the focus of your assessment.

5 Organisational identity

As we noted in Chapter 1, there is some confusion around the use of the term 'identity' in the literature on corporate communication and corporate reputation. In Chapter 4, we will look at what is often referred to as **corporate identity**: 'the set of meanings by which a company allows itself to be known and through which it allows people to describe, remember and relate to it' (Topalian, 1984) or the ways an organisation identifies itself to its various publics. (As we will see, this may or may not be expressed through a corporate brand.)

In the context of this chapter, however, it is worth noting the use of the term '**organisational identity**' (Vella & Melewar, 2008) to refer to how members perceive, think and feel about their organisation: 'who we are' and 'what we stand for'. In this usage, organisational identity is 'assumed to be a collective, commonly-shared understanding of the organisation's distinctive values and characteristics' (Hatch & Schultz, 1997, p. 357) and this is much closer to what we have discussed as organisational culture.

'Corporate identity' reflects management decisions about the desired identity to be projected by the organisation – while 'organisational identity' reflects **employee perceptions and understandings** of the organisation. In the recommended reading for this module, van Riel & Fombrun call this 'perceived identity' (see our discussion of the ACID Test model in Chapter 2), while Davies *et al*. call it, simply, 'identity'.

'We have our own traditions and history. We may have our own language, the jargon and acronyms that we use to communicate with each other. Our sense of identity is reinforced by having our own sports teams, a works band, an annual outing, a Christmas party and a uniform.... There will be darker sides to our organisation and what it stands for that we are uncomfortable in facing. If we work for a tobacco company, or one marketing alcohol or armaments we will tend to rationalise what others may find unacceptable... We learn about the company identity and culture formally through formal training and informally by working there...' (Davies *et al*., *op cit*, p. 196).

Organisational identity is a key factor in **identification**: the extent to which employees have an affinity with the organisation and identify with the organisation (ie define themselves by the same characteristics, values and goals they see in the organisation). This is important in securing employee engagement, loyalty and commitment to the goals and values of the organisation – which in turn is important in maintaining coherent and positive customer-facing behaviours: contributing directly to *corporate* identity (as the behaviour component of the identity mix).

At the same time, *corporate* identity management helps to shape *organisational* identity (and identification), through internal communication, and the ways that management seeks to create favourable perceptions of the organisation in the minds of employees: employees are a key internal stakeholder audience for corporate identity management.

ASSESSMENT TIP

concept

Don't worry about the potential confusion of terminology around identity, image and reputation: 'diversity of definitions' is clearly acknowledged in the literature. The important point will be:

- To establish (where relevant) how terms are being used in the assessment brief, from the context (and by discussion with your tutor).

- To state clearly (and justify) any assumptions you are forced to make about how terms are being used in the assessment brief.

- To define and reference your own use of terms in your assessment.

An interesting and comprehensive case study of corporate personality, and how it is projected via corporate identity and branding, is given in 'Projecting corporate character in the branding of business schools' (Gary Davies and Rosa Chun), in Melewar (ed) Facets of Corporate Identity, Communication and Reputation (2008, Routledge). This case study looks at aspects such as culture, vision and mission, use of the corporate reputation (personality) scale and cobweb diagrams to measure identity and image, and – introducing topics which we will cover in future chapters – change of visual identity to reinforce desired corporate brand positioning. ■

Learning objectives	Covered
1 Critically evaluate the corporate 'character' (personality) of an organisation	☑ Corporate strategy: different perspectives on strategy; vision, mission and values
	☑ Strategic objectives and specific business strategies
	☑ Strategy formulation: deliberate, opportunistic, imposed, emergent and logical incrementalism approaches
	☑ Organisational structure: structural elements; organisation charts; the identification of dysfunctional elements impacting on corporate identity and image; organisational flexibility; the informal organisation
	☑ Organisational culture: definitions; levels of culture; the cultural web; influences on culture; the value of strong positive culture
	☑ Communicate climate
2 Critically assess the compatibility of an organisation's corporate strategy, structure, systems and culture with its positioning and reputation	☑ Evaluation checklists for all the above elements
3 Explain the various meanings of corporate 'identity'	☑ Organisational identity: employee perceptions; employee identification
	☑ Differences from and links with corporate identity (followed up in Chapter 4).

1   Define corporate personality.

2   What are the dimensions of the Corporate Personality Scale (Davies *et al.*)?

3   Explain the various perspectives on strategy put forward by Henry Mintzberg.

4   What are (a) the four elements of corporate mission and (b) the four elements of a balanced scorecard approach?

5   Distinguish between (a) deliberate strategy, (b) emergent strategy and (c) logical incrementalism, as approaches to strategy formation.

6   Give three examples of structural dysfunction and how they may impact on corporate image.

7   Describe the features of 'organic' (as opposed to 'mechanistic') organisation.

8   Identify the components of the cultural web.

9   What is 'communication climate'?

10 Why is organisational (as opposed to corporate) identity important?

1 Your own research. However, note that this is a legitimate projective technique, used to elicit stakeholder characterisations of organisations and brands – as we will see in Chapter 7.

2 Your own research. Note, however, that this will be useful preparatory material for your assessment.

3 The mission statements given are generally: broad enough to allow for flexibility; concise and 'punchy'; emotion/value laden in their expression; focused on beneficiaries and stakeholder benefits (for internal 'feel good' factor as well as outward marketing); or expressive of what the organisation sees as its core competences. They are designed to be outwardly descriptive – and inwardly inspiring.

4 You should have spotted from the question, if you didn't know, that alignment needs to take place in two directions.

- **Vertical** alignment is about ensuring that the goal of each activity contributes towards the overall or higher objectives of the organisation: so, for example, a firm with the objective of innovation leadership (or, in corporate identity terms, desiring to position itself as a innovative firm) may formulate business level objectives for product development or technology leverage.

- **Horizontal** alignment is about ensuring that the goals of every unit in an organisation are co-ordinated with those of others, so that they work effectively together – and present a consistent, coherent face to the world. Note that strategic alignment is itself a key task of corporate communication: getting all employees and units to understand, buy into and enact the overall corporate strategy and present an integrated corporate identity.

5 A number of writers have argued that the rational model represents an ideal: in practice, decision-making is constrained by lack of information, lack of time, uncertainty about future events, the need to negotiate objectives with stakeholders; and so on. Moreover, not all intended strategies are in fact realised: underlying assumptions turn out to be invalid; environmental factors and competitor actions derail plans; and strategies are resisted and undermined by stakeholders. There is a strong need for compromise, review and flexibility in any strategy formulated.

6 Your own research. Once again, however, note that this will be useful preparatory material for later follow-up, if relevant for your assessment.

7 Organisation structure may be a positive influence on reputation where its effect is:

- **Positioning** the corporate communication or reputation management function centrally, at a strategic level, so that an integrated organisation-wide communication strategy flows down through the organisation. We will discuss the organisation of corporate communication specifically in Chapter 6.

- Establishing mechanisms for **cross-functional collaboration**, such as multi-functional project working, to establish 'horizontal' work and communication flow across the vertical barriers often put up by departmental 'silos'

- Encouraging effective channels and mechanisms for **multi-directional communication** (particularly lateral and upward) for information- and ideas-sharing. This is commonly achieved through cross-functional team-working, meetings and data-sharing networks.

- Encouraging **flexibility**, by removing rigid controls in the form of tight job descriptions, detailed rules and procedures, close supervision, status barriers between managers and staff and so on. Structural flexibility supports cultural flexibility, or flexible thinking. Temporary project or task force teams may be formed as and when required for particular tasks, taking advantage of available expertise and ideas. All structures and arrangements should ideally be regarded as subject to alteration in response to changing conditions, since their purpose is to facilitate learning, innovation and performance.

- Encouraging **initiative, experimentation and risk-taking**, by devolving genuine authority to lower levels of staff: removing layers of control, supervision and upward referral. This will have to be supported by actual managerial behaviours as well: for example, not 'punishing' mistakes made while learning or taking initiative, but regarding them as 'learning opportunities'.

- **Softening boundaries** – not just within the organisation (status boundaries between levels in the hierarchy, and boundaries between functions) but between the organisation and the environment. 'Boundary workers' who have contacts outside the organisation should be encouraged to gather and share information to broaden the knowledge base. Opportunities should be sought to learn from other organisations (including customers and competitors) eg by benchmarking and imitation.

8   Managers can minimise problems of the informal organisation by:

- Meeting employees' needs as far as possible via the formal organisation: providing information, encouragement, social interaction and so on

- Harnessing the dynamics of the informal organisation – for example, by co-opting informal leaders to reinforce desired values and behaviours and shape the organisation's desired identity

- Involving managers themselves in the informal structure, so that they can support information sharing, counter destructive rumours, help break down unhelpful rules and rigidities and so on.

9   Turning round a communication climate may require the coaching/training (or, in extreme cases, replacement) of team leaders, so that they become facilitators and encouragers: modelling, praising and rewarding open communication behaviours; treating 'bad ideas' or 'wrong answers' as learning opportunities; inviting and valuing input from all team members; and so on. These kinds of behaviours will have to be reinforced by senior management and the stated values, policies and practices of the organisation as a whole, however, if they are to become successfully embedded over time.

10   Your own research. Just do it – even if it's only a five minute personal brainstorming session. You might still highlight some useful areas for later diagnosis and follow-up.

Answers to quick quiz

1   Corporate personality consists of the significant characteristics which constitute an organisation's distinctive and consistent method of relating to its environment.

2   The dimensions of the scale are:; agreeableness, enterprise, competence, chic, ruthlessness, machismo and informality.

3   Mintzberg's perspectives on strategy are: plan, ploy, pattern, position and perspective.

4   The elements of mission are purpose, strategy, values and standards/behaviour. The elements of the balanced scorecard are: financial, customer, internal (process) and innovation/learning perspectives.

5   See Figure 3.4 and section 2.4.2 for a full answer.

6   See section 3.3 for a range of examples.

7   Organic organisations tend to have a contributive culture of information and skill sharing; network (rather than hierarchical) structure of authority and communication; focus on goals and outputs (rather than processes); and flexible job design.

8   The cultural web consists of: the paradigm (basic assumptions) and its manifestations in symbols, stories, routines and rituals, control systems, organisation structures and power structures.

9   Communication climate is a sub-set of organisational culture, embracing the context of internal communications within the organisation, and employee perceptions about them.

10   Organisational identity is a key factor in employee identification, which impacts on engagement, loyalty and commitment, which impact on coherent and positive customer-facing behaviour, which impact on corporate image and reputation.

References

Abratt, R and Shee, P S B (1989) 'A new approach to the corporate image management process' in *Journal of Marketing Management* 5 (1): pp 63-76

Bernstein, D (1984) *Company Image and Reality: A Critique of Corporate Communications*. London: Cassell Educational

Burns, S T and Stalker, G M (1961) *The Management of Innovation*. London: Tavistock

Campbell, A & Tawaday, K (1990) *Mission & Business Philosophy: Winning Employee Commitment*. Oxford: Heinemann

Davies G, Chun R, Da Silva R V & Roper S (2003) *Corporate Reputation and Competitiveness*. Abingdon, Oxon: Routledge

Deal, T E and Kennedy, A A (1982) *Organisation Cultures: The Rites and Rituals of Organisational Life*. Reading, MA; Addison Wesley

Dennis, H S (2006) 'Communication Climate' posted at http://www.biztimes.com/news on 10/12/2006

Doorley, J & Garcia, H F (2007) *Reputation Management: The Key to Successful Public Relations and Corporate Communications*. New York: Routledge

Drucker, P (1955) *The Practice of Management*. London: Heinemann

Fill, C (2002) *Marketing Communications: Contexts, Strategies and Applications* (3rd ed). Harlow, Essex: Pearson Education Limited

Garner (2005) 'Mission: how leaders create the greatest version of what you can be': http://www.buzzle.com/editorials , 9/11/2005

Gibb, J R (1961) 'Defensive communication', in *Journal of Communication*, 11 (3) pp 141-148

Hamel, G & Prahalad, C K (1989) 'Strategic Intent' in *Harvard Business Review*. March-April

Handy, C B (1989) *The Age of Unreason*. Harmondsworth: Penguin

Handy, C B (1995) *Gods of management: The Changing Work of Organisations*. Random House

Hatch, M J & Schultz, M (2000) 'Scaling the tower of Babel' in Schultz, Hatch & Larsen (eds) *The Expressive Organisation*. New York: OUP pp 11-35

Huzcynski, A & Buchanan, D (2001) *Organisational Behaviour: An Introductory Text*. Harlow, Essex: FT Prentice Hall

Johnson, G, Scholes K & Whittington (2005) *Exploring Corporate Strategy: Text and Cases* (7th ed). Harlow, Essex: FT Prentice Hall

Kaplan, R S & Norton, D P (1996) *The Balanced Scorecard: Translating Strategy into Action*. Boston: Harvard Business School Press

Lancaster, G & Withey, F (2005) *Marketing Fundamentals*. Oxford: Elsevier Butterworth-Heinemann

Lux, P G C (1986) 'Zur Durchführung von Corporate Identity Programen' in Birkigt & Stadler (eds) *Corporate Identity*. Ladnsberg/Lech

Markwick, N & Fill, C (1997) 'Towards a framework for managing corporate identity' in *European Journal of Marketing*. Vol 31 (5/6) pp 396 – 409

Milkovich, G T & Boudreau, J W (1996) *Human Resource Management* (9th ed) . New York: McGraw Hill

Mintzberg, H (1987) 'The Strategy Concept 1: Five Ps for Strategy.' in *California Management Review*. Vol 30, No 1

Mintzberg, H (1983) *Structures in Fives: Designing Effective Organisations*. New Jersey: FT, Prentice Hall

Ohmae, K (1983) *The Mind of the Strategist*. Harmondsworth: Penguin

Mullins, L (1999) *Management & Organisational Behaviour* (5th ed). Harlow, Essex: FT Prentice Hall

Peters, T J (1994) *Liberation Management*. New York: Harper & Row

Quinn, J B (1995) *Strategies for Change: The Strategy Process*. New Jersey: FT, Prentice Hall

Redding, W C (1972) *Communication within the organisation: an interpretive review of theory and research*. New York: Industrial Communication Council

Riel, C B M van & Balmer, J M T (1997) 'Corporate identity: the concept, its measurement and management' in *European Journal of Marketing* 31 (5/6): pp 240-255

Riel, C B M van & Fombrun, CJ (2007) *Essentials of Corporate Communication: Implementing Practices for Effective Reputation Management*. Abingdon, Oxon: Routledge

Samuel, H (2007) *Reputation Branding*. Wellington, NZ: First Edition Ltd

Schein, E (1985) *Organisational Culture & Leadership*. San Francisco: Jossey-Bass

Schwartz, H & Davies, SM (1981) 'Matching corporate culture and business strategy' in *Organisational Dynamics*.

Simões, C and Dibb, S (2002) *Corporate Identity: Defining the Construct*. Warwick Business School research Papers, Number 350: http://www.wbs.ac.uk

Simões C, Dibb S & Fisk R P (2005) 'Managing corporate identity: an internal perspective' in *Journal of the Academy of Marketing Science* 33 (2)

Topalian, A (1984) 'Corporate identity: beyond the visual overstatements' in *International Journal of Advertising*, 3 pp 55-62

Trompenaars, F (1993) *Riding the Waves of Culture*. London: Nicholas Brealey

Varey, R J (2002) *Marketing Communication: Principles and Practice*. Abindgon, Oxon: Routledge

Vella, K J & Melewar, T C (2008) 'Relationship between Identity and Culture' in Melewar T C (ed.) *Facets of Corporate Identity, Communication and Reputation*. Abingdon, Oxon: Routledge

Welch, J (2005) *Winning*. New York: Harper & Row

Chapter 4
Corporate identity and branding

Topic list

Introduction

The focus of this chapter is on developing knowledge of the nature of corporate brands, and fostering insight into the various ways in which organisations can develop their brands to effectively project their desired identity to stakeholder audiences.

We start in section 1 by revisiting the topic of corporate identity, introduced in earlier chapters, to draw the link between corporate identity and branding.

In section 2, we explore the nature of corporate brands, using various models of brand elements (or assets) and typologies specified by the syllabus.

In section 3, we identify some of the key drivers that have moved organisations towards creating corporate brands – which should additionally provide a business case for encouraging their proactive development and management.

In sections 4 and 5, we explore a range of practical ways of developing, shaping and positioning corporate brands. We look at a range of brand strategies, including re-branding, and at how brands are formed. We explore the concept of 'reputational platforms', as a strategic foundation for the development of corporate stories, which in turn shape the way the brand is positioned.

In the words of the syllabus, this chapter addresses the theme: 'This is a corporate brand and this is how it is developed'.

Syllabus-linked learning objectives

By the end of the chapter you will be able to:

Learning objectives	Syllabus link
1 Explain the various meanings of corporate identity and the importance of strategic identity for reputation management	2.1.2
2 Critically evaluate the nature of corporate brands and make recommendations concerning any gap between identity and image	2.2.1
3 Explain the nature of reputational platforms and corporate stories, and how these assist corporate positioning	2.2.2

BPP LEARNING MEDIA

1 Corporate identity

1.1 Different types of identity

There are various meanings given to the concept of '**corporate identity**'. These can be divided into three major schools of thought:

- Visual identity
- Organisational identity or stakeholder identification
- Corporate identity or strategic identity

1.1.1 Visual identity

KEY CONCEPT   concept

The **visual identity** of an organisation may be defined as: 'a desired image acquired and communicated by the company to the public through consistent visual communications' (Napoles, 1988, p. 93).

Visual identity refers to the various visual communications and manifestations which can be used to project the desired identity of the organisation: 'the symbols (such as logos, colour scheme) which an organisation uses to identify itself to people' (Dowling, 1986, p. 8).

This perspective on corporate identity, growing mainly from the discipline of graphic design, argues that management can significantly influence the images held of the organisation by its stakeholders, and that the devices such as logos, names, designs and other visual cues ('house style', uniforms, fleet livery etc) are effective vehicles for doing this: they can represent and project the 'essence' of the organisation, if compellingly designed and consistently used.

Many organisations have detailed visual identity (or graphic design) manuals, setting out how logos should be used, what design features, typefaces and colours schemes must be used on corporate communications (letter heads, web sites, product packaging, advertisements and so on). The aim of these guidelines is to ensure that all visual cues are used consistently, in order to facilitate recognition, association and engagement.

Visual identity is not, however, purely a graphic design consideration. Practitioners such as Olins emphasise that it is merely the expression of the organisation's underlying identity and self-perception. The design of logos and house styles is the result of a process of internal exploration and enquiry into the core attributes, values and aspirations of the organisation.

ACTIVITY 1   application

Name ten corporate logos that come immediately to mind. Briefly describe the distinctive visual features of the logo (eg colour, typeface, imagery) and the associations they have for you.

The visual identity is not confined to logos, symbols and the house style of printed communications. The **visual** 'style' of an organisation comprises a wide **range of expressions**: the architecture, layout, décor and decoration of its premises; the use of uniforms (including formal or informal 'dress codes'); the use of signage; and the corporate transport fleet (where relevant). A distinctive style may also be expressed in non-visual, **auditory** terms through the use of language (eg special terminology, mottos and slogans) and/or music (eg associated with corporate advertising campaigns).

We will explore some of the visual and auditory (symbolic) elements of corporate identity and branding in Chapter 7, on developing corporate communications.

1.1.2 Organisational identity or corporate identification

As we saw at the end of Chapter 3, the term organisational identity is often used to refer to the collective self-perception of the organisation.

KEY CONCEPT

concept

Organisational identity may be defined as: 'a collective, commonly-shared understanding of the organisation's distinctive values and characteristics' (Hatch & Schultz, 1997, p. 357).

Albert and Whetten (1985) described organisational identity as consisting of three key attributes:

- **Centrality** (or 'claimed central character'): 'what is taken by organisational members to be central to the organisation': that is, attributes that are widely shared by, and important to, the members

- **Distinctiveness** (or 'claimed distinctiveness): 'what makes the organisation distinctive from other organisations in the eyes of the beholding members'

- **Continuity** ('claimed temporal continuity' or 'sense of continuity over time'): 'what is perceived by members to be enduring or continuing': that is, attributes that can be seen to link the organisation's past, present and future.

The concept of **identification** is added by some authors, to emphasise one of the important effects of strong organisational and corporate identity. Positive identification occurs when stakeholders come to internalise or 'own' the values and activities of the organisation. Balmer (2008, p. 42) argues that while the concept of organisational identity focuses on employee identification, other stakeholders (notably customers) can also be brought to identify themselves with aspects of the organisation: to include an organisation or brand within their definition of themselves. (Think about the extent to which particular brands shape your sense of self and your lifestyle: brands which are 'you' or not...)

This view emphasises that corporate positioning or repositioning requires more than manipulating visual identity expressions: it involves shaping the beliefs and values of organisation members; their morale, identification with and commitment to the organisation; and the behavioural expression of that organisational identity in interaction with stakeholders.

MARKETING AT WORK

application

'[Airline] **Virgin Atlantic** has long recognised the critical role internal marketing plays in its success. One of the secrets of the airline's success has been enthusiastic, empowered, motivated employees. Sir Richard Branson has said: 'I want employees in the airline to feel that it is they who can make the difference, and influence what passengers get'.

'We aren't interested in having just happy employees. We want employees who feel involved and prepared to express dissatisfaction when necessary. In fact, we think that the constructively dissatisfied employee is an asset we should encourage and we need an organisation [communication climate and culture] that allows us to do this – and that encourages employees to take responsibility, since I don't believe it is enough for us simply to give it.'

Virgin Atlantic's philosophy has been to stimulate the individual, to encourage staff to take initiatives and to empower them to do so.'

Christopher *et al.* (2002, p. 111)

Link: http://www.virgin-atlanti.com/en/gb – and follow the link to 'Working for Us'.

1.1.3 Corporate or strategic identity

concept

Corporate identity may be defined as: 'the set of meanings by which a company allows itself to be known and through which it allows people to describe, remember and relate to it' (Topalian, 1984) or 'the reality and uniqueness of an organisation, which is integrally related to its external and internal image and reputation through corporate communication.' (Gray & Balmer, 1998).

Corporate identity is thus a more strategic concept, referring to the various ways in which the organisation deliberately **projects, identifies or expresses** itself to stakeholders (visually, verbally and by its behaviour), in order to position and differentiate itself in their perceptions. 'The aim of corporate identity management is to acquire a favourable corporate image among key internal and external stakeholders so that, in the long-run, this image can result in the acquisition of a favourable corporate reputation, which leads to key stakeholders having a favourable disposition towards the organisation.' (Vella & Melewar, 2008, p. 11).

Corporate identity is often identified with **corporate branding**, since an organisation may also choose to create a distinctive name, visual identity and set of associations (as for product brands) for the organisation itself, as a distilled expression of core corporate identity values. 'Corporate identity provides the platform upon which corporate brands emerge' (Balmer, *op cit*, p. 44).

The management of corporate identity or brand **conveys key ideas to target audiences** about what the organisation is, what is does and how it does it (Olins, 1990) in ways that differentiate the organisation from its competitors. It is rooted in a communication model, based on the belief that selected core identity traits of an organisation can be formulated into effective corporate stories and messages, and conveyed to stakeholder audiences via various forms of communication: symbolic, verbal (eg through advertising and public relations) and behavioural.

We will examine how an organisation can (a) discover and define what its core identity elements are and (b) utilise them in corporate communication programmes, later in this chapter.

1.2 The identity mix

As we noted above, visual symbolism (eg logos) is inadequate by itself to communicate the full range of corporate identity elements effectively to stakeholders. People form impressions of an organisation through multiple interactions with the organisation, its representatives, its communications and the shared experiences and opinions of others.

All self-expressions of an organisation can be classified into one of the following three forms, which together form the **'identity mix'**:

- **Symbolism**: the use of a variety of visual and auditory cues to express aspects of the corporate identity; create compelling symbolic 'identifiers' of core identity attributes; and elicit associations and emotional resonances supportive of recognition, engagement and positioning.

- **Communication**: the use of verbal cues and messages to project corporate identity to target audiences. This is a more tactical tool for identity management, involving targeted campaigns and specific issue- or crisis-related messages, using methods such as advertising, sponsorships, public relations, events and exhibitions and so on.

- **Behaviour**: the expression of identity through individual, group and corporate action: the strategies that are pursued, the initiatives that are supported and their implementation or enactment in practice. The most powerful influence on stakeholders' evaluation of a product, service or organisation is their own direct experience, followed by the testimony of other people (also based on experience): actions speak louder than words, particularly in social environments increasingly characterised by risk perception and lack of trust (Regester & Larkin, 2008). It is easy for organisations to make symbolic and verbal claims about quality, service, trust, innovation or responsibility: it is less easy to develop and demonstrate these attributes consistently over time.

The **identity mix** classifies the various elements through which, together, corporate identity is expressed: symbolism, communication and behaviour. Like the 'marketing mix', these elements must be co-ordinated for integrated corporate identity management.

Like any of the various 'mix' models (marketing mix, promotional mix), the emphasis is on the need to integrate and co-ordinate the various elements for overall effect. Mixed messages, or inconsistency in any one element, can let down the whole.

Davies *et al.*(2003, p. 216) suggest that a total '**reputation toolkit**' might therefore include any or all of the following elements (and more):

- **Tangibles** (building design, refurbishment, colour schemes, furniture, signage, uniforms, fleet)

- **Mood** (lighting, sound, smell, heating)

- **Training** (especially for customer-facing employees)

- **Communicating corporate values** (induction training, mission and vision, internal communication, external communication)

- **Corporate visual identity** (logo, letterhead, signage, designs)

- **Culture management** (training for managers to express and model values and behaviours, use of HR systems to reinforce desired values and behaviours)

- **Recruitment** (defining requirements, selecting and rewarding in such a way as to attract staff who are likely to express the desired values)

'In one department store we have worked with the company had spent £20 million on refurbishment only to find that its identity and image were not as good as they expected from this level of investment in tangibles. One shopper captured what had happened brilliantly with the words, 'a facelift with the spirit unchanged'. The company had forgotten to spend money on its staff.' (*ibid*, p. 216).

Perhaps the most important and difficult aspect of the identity mix is to ensure that **behaviours** or actions are **identity-consistent**: that is, that they are congruent:

- With the core values of the organisation (a challenge of securing employee buy-in to mission and values, and managing consistency) and

- With the claims made by corporate symbols and communications, or the total 'brand promise' (a challenge of managing stakeholder expectations, ensuring that the brand promise is realistic and/or making sure that performance lives up to the expectations created by the brand promise).

The following extract from *The Guardian* (13 April, 2002), illustrates how lack of transparency can damage customer relations.

'Watch your plastic closely. A number of credit card companies have recently been changing their customer loyalty schemes – often making them less generous – or fiddling around with their fees... And what has really riled some cardholders is the way these changes are being communicated.

[One holder of several cards issued by **HBC Bank**] says he objects to what he claims is the 'sneaky' way the fee is being introduced. As a result he says he will be cancelling his cards. In each case, he was sent a letter headed, 'Important changes to your terms and conditions', which alerted him to an increase in the handling fee on cash advances. The letter ends: 'please also see the enclosed leaflet for further changes to your terms and conditions'. [The customer] says it would be all too easy to ignore this sentence, and the leaflet accompanying the letter. 'But only if you read the small print do you find out about their new condition which imposes a £10 charge if the card is not used in each six-month period. This seems to me a really underhand way of imposing a new charge which many cardholders may not have any idea about until it's imposed.'

A spokesperson for HBC Bank ... says it costs money to run a credit card account and it believes that when people do not use their card, it is 'only fair' to levy a £10 fee to offset some of these costs...

Meanwhile [another customer] couldn't believe his eyes when he received a letter from Alliance & Leicester relating to his MoneyBack credit card. The letter states: 'At Alliance & Leicester, we are continually looking to improve the products and services that we provide for our customers' – then goes on to say, in a very oblique and easily overlooked way, that it is actually cutting the loyalty perks that some customers enjoy.'

Follow-up: As an exercise, you may like to draft some point-form notes for a presentation to a banking industry meeting, in which you highlight the reputation management issues raised by this extract.

ACTIVITY 2

evaluation

Select a **critical incident** in your experience of your own organisation, which resulted in significant stakeholder (employee, customer, investor) dissatisfaction or withdrawal, negative media exposure or pressure group attack.

Describe the incident and its consequences briefly. Diagnose the extent to which the problem arose due to:

- Inconsistency of the organisation's performance or behaviour with its own stated values

- Inconsistency of the organisation's performance or behaviour with the claims made by its organisational communications or brand promises.

We will look at how each element of the identity mix can be developed in Chapter 7.

1.3 Multiple and hybrid identities

It is worth remembering that organisations inevitably have multiple identities, according to *whose perceptions* you are looking at (eg the 'perceived identity' as seen by the members, the 'desired identity' as seen by management, the 'conceived identity' in the eyes of external stakeholders).

In addition, as organisations develop multiple products/services, brands and markets, or grow by merger or acquisition, they are likely to develop a range of sub-identities, expressing different specialisms, brands, regions, stakeholder groups, divisions and strategic business units. These may or may not be consistent or clearly identified with the 'umbrella' identity (if any) of the organisation as a whole, or of the parent company or 'head office'. If management asks the question 'Who are we as an organisation?', it may get a multiplicity of answers!

Pratt and Foreman (2000) classify the possible responses to this scenario.

- In some cases, the organisation may wish to create a single globally coherent identity out of the various multiple identities (integration strategy), in order to avoid confusion, mixed messages to stakeholders and the pressure of conflicting expectations and demands, arising from 'too many identities'. Alternatively, it may seek to weed out one or more identities which are inconsistent or dysfunctional (deletion strategy).

- In other cases, the organisation may be content to allow individual brand or regional identities to co-exist (compartmentalisation strategy), capitalising on the strength of their targeted appeal and their ability to fulfil the diverse expectations of member and stakeholder groups.

- There may be an attempt to retain individual brand or regional identities, but to exploit the potential synergies between them, by varying degrees of 'endorsement' by, or identification with, the parent company or brand (aggregation strategy).

We will consider these various options in relation to corporate brand strategies, later in this chapter.

It may be worth noting that the example often used of the harmonisation and integration of corporate identities following a merger is that of DaimlerChrysler. Daimler-Benz (Germany) and Chrysler (US) merged in 2000 and an extensive corporate advertising campaign was used to emphasise the shared identity. However, the hoped-for synergies did not, in fact, ensue. In 2007, Chrysler was sold to a US private equity firm, and the company was renamed Daimler AG. ▇

1.4 The importance of identity

Corporate identity management has merged as an important strategic activity for a variety of reasons, including:

- The need to establish an internal sense of unity and external coherent (or reshaped) identity in companies which have grown through mergers, acquisitions and alliances.

- The need to reflect strategic repositioning (eg a move into new technology or a focus on environmental or social responsibility) in 're-imaging' to stakeholders.

- The need to establish distinctive identities in the face of increasing global competition, as a source of competitive differentiation.

- The need to establish coherent identities (and member identification) in 'virtual' organisations, which may be geographically dispersed and loosely connected by ICT links, without a strong physical corporate presence

- The benefits of strong, positive identity for stakeholder recognition and engagement (customer, employee, investor retention etc) and financial performance.

MARKETING AT WORK

application

Melbourne [Australia] is poised to reap the benefits of a series of government initiatives that will promote the city as a centre for books, writing and ideas...

Elliot Perlman recently served on the Melbourne United Nations Educational, Scientific and Cultural Organisation City of Literature advisory committee. Last August, when the word came through from UNESCO that the bid had been successful, Perlman was chuffed for his home town, but reflected: 'The Melbourne I know could go one of two ways with this. It could embrace the designation enthusiastically and with pride, or it could cynically deride the whole concept if it smells of pompous self-importance, cloaking a vacuum where the people and the books should be.'

Few people outside book publishing and state government circles know about the City of Literature title. But the Victorian Government is planning a strong marketing push to coincide with the opening of its $20 million Centre for Books, Writing and Ideas, later this year. It will brand Melbourne as a books and writing capital and hope that tourism, cultural and economic opportunities follow.

A UNESCO City of Literature: what does it mean? In recent years UNESCO has developed a Creative Cities Network to promote cultural diversity and activities in various member cities. Membership is decided by UNESCO and is based on cities meeting specific criteria, including activities, infrastructure, government support and marketing. Once a city gets the nod, it can use the UNESCO name and logo, and is required to maintain its specific cultural activities.

There are two Cities of Craft and Folk Art (Aswan and Santa Fe), six Cities of Design (Berlin, Buenos Aires, Montreal, Nagoya, Kobe and Shenzhen), one City of Gastronomy (Popayan), three Cities of Literature (Edinburgh, Melbourne and Iowa City), three Cities of Music (Bologna, Seville and Glasgow) and one City of Media Arts (Lyon)...

[One public relations advisor] says: 'I actually think Melbourne is more a city of sporting venues and events...But the City of Literature branding will be an interesting work in progress.'

Corrie Perkin, *The Australian*, (May 4, 2009)

For reflection: What potential branding opportunities and challenges are reflected in this story?

BPP
LEARNING MEDIA

2 Corporate brands

2.1 What are brands?

KEY CONCEPT

concept

A **brand** is 'a name, term, sign, symbol or design or combination of them, intended to identify the goods or services of one seller or group of sellers, and to differentiate them from those of competitors [in the perceptions of target audiences].' (Kotler *et al.*, 1999)

Brands have an **identity**, which may begin with a name – such as 'Kleenex' or 'Coca Cola' – but extends to a range of features which assist in reinforcing recognition and attachment: logos (such as the Nike 'swoosh'), product and packaging design, slogans and tag lines ('Gillette: the Best a Man Can Get'), people (like Richard Branson as a visible part of the Virgin brand) and values (like the Body Shop's ethical and environmental commitments).

ACTIVITY 3

concept

What is the key purpose of developing an individualised identity for a brand?

Davies *et al.* (2003, p. 77) argue that: 'Anything can be a brand: anything that has **associations** that are not apparent from an objective assessment of the entity that is purchased can be regarded as a brand. These associations are intangible and emotional in nature…. We associate the word 'brand' with products, particularly those that are heavily advertised. But company names can be brand names too and this is very much the case in the services sector… Product marketers are often changing the way they approach markets and emphasising their corporate names as well as their product names… Any name can also be a brand name if it presents to the observer more than just the word itself.'

In the case of a corporate brand, brand identity is often regarded as synonymous with (or a more up-to-date expression for) corporate identity – although Balmer (2007, p. 45) points out that corporate identity (as the distinctive and defining characteristics of an organisation and/or as a distinct organisational name and visual identification system) is applicable to every identity, while *not* every organisation develops a corporate brand. Many holding or parent companies of successful product brands do not. As we will see later in the chapter, corporate branding is not an appropriate strategy for all organisations.

Corporate branding may, however, be used as part of a company's communication strategy intended to generate positive stakeholder associations with the corporate identity. Corporate identity provides the **platform** upon which corporate brands emerge. (Balmer & Greyser, 2003): 'Corporate identities give life to corporate brands, with the latter being a **distillation of corporate identity values**… Customers and stakeholders associate such values with the brand, and this, in effect, serves as an informal contract or what, in colloquial terms, is know as a 'corporate brand promise'.'

KEY CONCEPT

concept

A **corporate brand** may be defined as: 'a visual representation of a company that unites a group of products or businesses, and makes it known to the world through the use of a single name, a shared visual identity, and a common set of symbols. The process of **corporate branding** consists of the set of activities undertaken by the company to build favourable associations and positive reputation with both internal and external stakeholders…' (van Riel & Fombrun, 2007, p. 107).

'Corporate brands are the features of a company that employees, investors, customers and the public associate with an organisation as a whole. The purpose of a corporate brand is to **personalise** the company as a whole in order to **create value** from the company's strategic position, institutional activities, organisation, employees, and portfolio of products and services. The corporate brand is increasingly being used to cast a **favourable halo** over everything the organisation does or says – and capitalise on its reputation.' (*ibid*, p. 4)

2.1.1 Product branding and corporate branding

Although some of the concepts raised by the syllabus are drawn from the marketing literature on **product branding**, Balmer (2001) argues that there are major differences between product and corporate branding, summarised as follows (sourced from Balmer, 2008, p. 47). You may want to assess the strength and potential of your organisation's product brands, as a key element of its marketing communication, but it will be worth keeping clear in your mind what you mean by a strategic or corporate brand (ie the branding of corporate identity).

Dimension	Corporate brands	Product brands
Underpinnings	Multi-disciplinary	Marketing
Formation	Medium-/long-term	Short
Source	Corporate identity	Product identity
Values	Corporate ('real values')	Synthetic ('created values')
Brand custodian	The CEO	Brand manager(s)
Commitment/responsibility	All personnel	Brand manager(s)
Relevant stakeholders	All/many	Customers
Communication platform	Corporate communications	Marketing communication
Legal ownership	One or more entities	One or more entities
Emotional ownership	Stakeholder communities	Customer communities
Appropriating brands to create a sense of self	Customers, employees, suppliers, shareholders, local community etc	Customers

2.2 Brand elements or assets

So what exactly is a brand? The syllabus content apparently refers (without attribution) to a model by Davies (1992), summarising the various elements, roles or 'assets' represented by a brand: Figure 4.1.

Figure 4.1: Six brand assets or elements

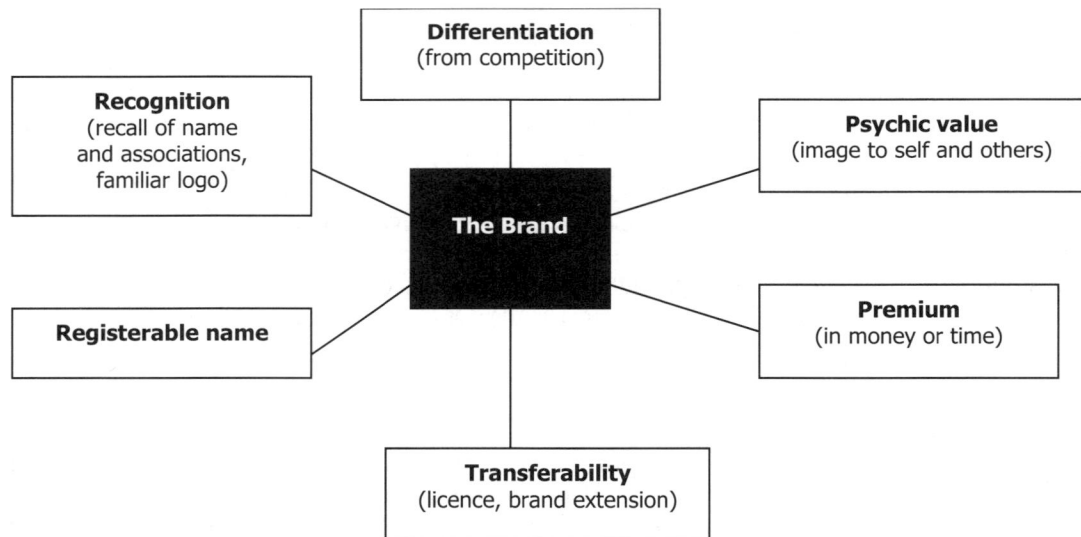

Source: Davies *et al.* (*op cit,* p. 78)

2.2.1 Differentiation

Differentiation is a key role for a brand name and other brand features: in the original meaning of the word, a brand was a device to indicate who owned livestock – and throughout history, items have been marked with distinctive signs to identify their owners or makers.

Branding helps customers to readily identify a product/service or organisation, potentially reinforcing their bias or preference for it over competing offerings. Similarly, an 'employer brand' (as we saw in Chapter 1) distinguishes one employer from another, by creating a distinctive set of associations about what kind of organisation it is to work for.

In blind tests of similar products (Coke & Pepsi colas, Cadbury and Mars chocolates), customer preferences have been shown to be equally divided – but when the brands are identified, respondents show a significant preference from one brand over another (Davies, *op cit*, p. 79). The only conclusion is that the name, and the associations it evokes, is more powerful as a driver of preference than the 'core' product itself.

2.2.2 Transferability

If a brand is, as research suggests, independent from the product or service it is used to label, it can be transferred from one product to another, or used to apply to more than one product or entity – taking some or all of its associations with it. One clear example is the Virgin brand, which started as a record label, but has been successfully applied to airlines, financial services, mobile telecommunications, health and fitness clubs, soft drinks and so on. How far can a brand 'stretch' without its associations being diluted by too much diversity? It depends on the strength of the brand, and its associations: the key attributes of the Virgin brand (innovation, value, individuality, humour, Branson) are not tied to the original product, but are highly transferable.

2.2.3 Psychic value

Stakeholders do value brands on rational attributes of the products or entities concerned: eg the speed, fuel efficiency and performance of a car; the taste and healthiness of food and drink products; the financial performance or service attributes of an organisation. However, many of the associations audiences make with brands are psychological, rather than objective or specification-driven. Brands are often given symbolic and emotional meaning (encouraged by the way they are promoted): they become desirable by association with youth and trendiness, or social/financial success, or attractiveness, or friendship and belonging. Such psychic dimensions are hard to measure, because consumers may not be aware – or may not wish to admit – that they influence purchase decisions to the extent that they do, but the symbolic and emotional influence of brands is central to their value.

'Why do we spend so much on designer clothes compared with the equally good functional quality and design available in a retailer's own brand merchandise? One answer is that when we put on an item marked Calvin Klein or Gucci, we put on more than the article itself. At least for that first moment we put on the **imagery** that the brand owner has carefully crafted to provide us with an additional reason for buying the product.' (*ibid*, p. 80).

2.2.4 Recall and recognition

Branding aids 'front of mind awareness' (recall) and prompted recall (or recognition) of a product or entity.

Brand strength is generally assessed by measuring first **unaided recall** ('Can you name a leading brand of bank?') and then **aided recall** or **recognition** ('Have you heard of Lloyds TSB?') of the brand name. These measures are often used as the basis for brand rankings, although they do not fairly take into account the other assets that contribute to brand strength. (Virgin might underscore on recall in the context of soft drinks, for example, although this would significantly understate its brand strength. This is an example of the trade-off between transferability – or 'stretching' – and recall: recall within a product type may be low if the brand has been transferred widely.)

Davies *et al.* argue that recall of the brand name is less important than whether actual or potential stakeholders recall or recognise the **desired associations** of the brand. ('Can you name a bank that offers 'better banking'?... 'Which banks use the following advertising themes?').

2.2.5 Premium

Leading brands tend to sustain a **price premium** over unbranded items: in other words, you can charge more for branded goods than for unbranded or retailer own-branded items.

It is argued that brand owners are *forced* to charge a premium price for branded items, in order to reflect their investment in branding: the costs of design, packaging and high-profile advertising required to promote recognition and recall of the name and associations. The costs of raw materials to produce different products may be similar, and retailers' overheads and profit takings may be similar: the price differential comes through advertising cost, borne entirely by the brand owner.

Given that brand owners are forced to charge premium prices to reflect their investment in branding, what makes customers willing to pay those premiums for branded goods?

Davies *et al.* note that: 'Money is not the only resource that we are willing and able to exchange for a brand. We will often travel further to visit a more attractive restaurant or leisure centre. We will spend longer somewhere that the 'branded experience' is more satisfying... We exchange time to acquire the brand and time is as valuable if not more valuable than money... Creating and managing a superior experience can be more cost effective than using advertising.'

2.2.6 Registration

A brand's strength depends on the owner's ability to secure control over, and sole use of, the brand name: in other words, to register the brand name so that no-one else can use it.

The rules differ between international jurisdictions, but basically you cannot register a name if someone has already claimed it, or if the name you choose is a word in common use. (You can register a distinctive design or logo using the word, but you can't reserve the use of the word itself.)

The syllabus content in this area is specifically drawn from:

- *Davies, Chun, Da Silver and Roper:* **Corporate Reputation and Effectiveness** *(2003: Routledge),*
  Chapter 4: The Company As A Brand.

The chapter also includes interesting discussion of brand metaphors, brand value and the use of advertising in branding: worth reading in full. ∎

3 Drivers for corporate branding

The syllabus headings in this area are drawn from the core text by van Riel & Fombrun, so our coverage draws heavily on this source.

There are a number of general trends driving the increased importance and visibility of corporate brands (van Riel & Fombrun, *op cit*, p. 6).

- The **proliferation of information sources** (eg via the internet) has eroded trust in products, services and marketing messages. Potential customers, investors and employees seek a better understanding of the organisation 'behind' the product.

- The **media spotlight** is increasingly on companies and their top executives, making corporate brands a source of distinctiveness and value.

- Society is increasingly **saturated with advertising messages**, leading both to audience overload and to media sophistication (and distrust of paid advertising messages). Broader brand-building strategies (eg using public relations, sponsorship and corporate citizenship initiatives) help to cut through advertising clutter.

- Products have become increasingly **homogenised** (commoditised) as a result of global marketing and franchising. Corporate brands may be the only source of distinctiveness.

- Corporate brands strengthen **new entrants** to international markets in securing beneficial relationships with suppliers, distributors and regulators.

- There has been significant pressure on corporations, from governments, investors, public and pressure groups, to become more **transparent and accountable** in regard to their governance processes, financial activities and social and environmental sustainability. Since they are being forced to open themselves up to increasing regulator, investor and public scrutiny, companies have a strong interest in presenting themselves attractively to wider stakeholder audiences. The demand for transparency and openness may be most effectively addressed through coherent communication of corporate identity through a corporate brand.

Nevertheless, some business unit managers will support overall corporate branding – and others will not.

Consider the position of business unit or subsidiary brand managers in an organisation. What arguments might be presented in support of, and against, corporate branding.

In order for corporate branding to be successfully implemented, there needs to be internal support among senior managers and employees. van Riel developed a model to assess the willingness of business unit managers to use the corporate brand in their communications: Figure 4.2.

Figure 4.2: Drivers of corporate branding

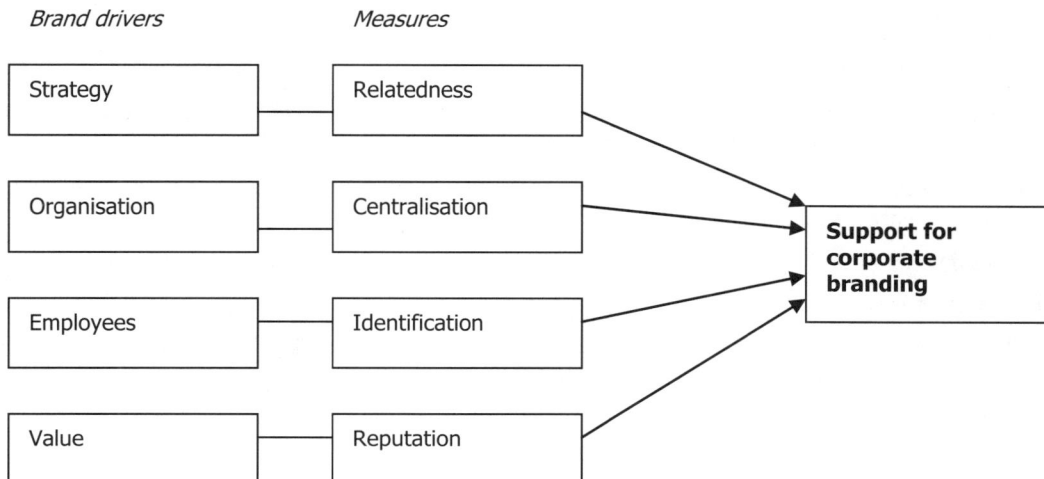

```
Brand drivers              Measures

┌──────────────┐     ┌──────────────┐
│  Strategy    │─────│  Relatedness │──────┐
└──────────────┘     └──────────────┘      │
                                            │
┌──────────────┐     ┌──────────────┐      ▼
│ Organisation │─────│ Centralisation│──┐  ┌──────────────┐
└──────────────┘     └──────────────┘   └─▶│ Support for  │
                                           │ corporate    │
┌──────────────┐     ┌──────────────┐   ┌─▶│ branding     │
│  Employees   │─────│ Identification│──┘  └──────────────┘
└──────────────┘     └──────────────┘      ▲
                                            │
┌──────────────┐     ┌──────────────┐      │
│    Value     │─────│  Reputation  │──────┘
└──────────────┘     └──────────────┘
```

3.1 Strategy drivers

KEY CONCEPT

concept

The term '**relatedness**' is used to describe the extent to which different business units complement or add to the parent company's strategic objectives and overall corporate positioning.

A consolidation of brands and businesses within a corporate brand enables a parent company more effectively to exploit relatedness, capitalise on potential synergies and/or leverage its investment in maintaining multiple product brands.

- Business consolidations tend to stimulate corporate branding (van Riel & Fombrun, *op cit*, p. 107), not least because the corporate brand is important in helping employees understand the value created by the merger.

- There may be cost savings from building a single corporate name which is applied to all products (eg Nestlé and Philips), reducing the burden of multiple brand advertising.

- There may be positioning advantages for subsidiaries in being identified with strong corporate brands: courier DHL positioned in Europe as a member of Deutsche Post.

For parent companies encompassing a diverse set of businesses, operating in multiple industries, corporate brands may also be a useful tool for creating a **unified**, **coherent identity** with consumers and investors. Examples of parent companies developing distinct corporate brands include General Electric (GE) and Unilever.

Companies that can identify with a particular competitive idea or **core competency** (such as innovation or CSR) also tend to support corporate branding initiatives, because the core competency represents a strong internal self-definition or corporate identity. Companies such as Dyson UK and 3M have positioned themselves strongly as corporate brands founded on invention and innovation, for example.

Excerpt from advertisement by the **Altria Group**, 2006 (reproduced in van Riel & Fombrun, *op cit*, p. 108):

The value of seeing the whole forest

By the parent company of Kraft Foods, Philip Morris International and Philip Morris USA.

As a company that is the parent of both tobacco and food companies we know what it is like to make the news – and not only in the financial reports. But what may not always make news is the long-term performance of a company like Altria Group, Inc.

We're not only one of the 30 companies that make up the Dow Jones Industrial Average, we're also one of the most profitable companies in the world. And we've had 39 dividend increases in the last 37 years. The family of brands made by our operating companies includes household names like Maxwell House, Marlboro, Velveeta, Virginia Slims, Philadelphia, Kraft, Nabisco. And many more.

We also know that in order for our companies to continue to be in business they need to strive to meet the expectations of Altria's shareholders, their consumers, regulators and society. It is simply the only path to the future.

For a company as newsworthy as ours, at times it can be hard to see the forest for the trees. But to look beyond immediate challenges and position our company for long-term success, we have to keep the whole forest squarely in sight.

And that's a vision we feel is worth sharing.

Our name is Altria Group.

PS. Altria has since divested itself of the Philip Morris International and Kraft brands. For an insight into corporate brand management and corporate communications, check out:

Link: http://www.altria.com.

3.2 Organisational drivers

A corporate branding strategy is most likely to be supported by organisations with:

- **Centralised control structures**. If the central or 'head' office (or strategic apex) directs and controls the strategy and performance of business units, it will be easier to gain consensus on corporate branding and to implement branding strategies. If the business is decentralised, and business units are relatively autonomous, there may be resistance to corporate branding. Since unit managers are accountable for business/brand performance, they may perceive corporate branding as a loss of control. They may be attached to their own brands, and fear that brand strengths will be diluted by association with a parent brand (and/or other weaker brands in the portfolio).

- **Centralised communications functions**, and related functions such as marketing and IT. Having a central unit or manager responsible for all communications, designs or IT activities (rather than devolving responsibility to regional or brand teams) supports the implementation of an integrated corporate branding initiative.

3.3 Employee drivers

A corporate branding strategy is likely to be more successful if supported by employees who strongly identify with the company as a whole. However, people tend to identify more strongly with whatever working unit is closest to them and is most instrumental in meeting their needs (Ashforth and Mael, 1989) – and this is more likely to be a sub-group such as a business unit or a functional area.

- If employees have low identification with both the company and the sub-group, there is little that can be done without first securing some form of employee engagement! The organisation will need to carry out attitude research and conduct a sustained motivational campaign to secure employee 'buy in' to any further plans.

- If employees have low identification with the company, but high identification with the sub-group (as often occurs in a strongly performing, autonomous business unit), there is likely to be limited support for corporate branding. The best approach may be one of 'weak endorsement', with low parent visibility (see van Riel's brand typology of corporate branding strategies, in section 2 above).

- If employees have low identification with the business unit (eg because of negative developments), they may 'seek shelter' by identifying strongly with the parent company. If the troubled business unit is to be divested, there is no point developing a visible link with the corporate brand. If not, a 'weak endorsement' approach may be pursued.

- If employees have a strong identification with both the business unit and the company, this is an ideal platform for developing a well-supported corporate branding strategy.

3.4 Value drivers

Support for the corporate brand depends on unit managers' perception that it will add value to their own activities, eg by enhancing product sales or by creating a stronger image or reputation in the market.

'The purpose of a corporate branding initiative is to use the corporate brand to cast a positive halo over the products and businesses of the company, and thereby generate more favourable impressions of those products and businesses than they would have on their own' (van Riel & Fombrun, *op cit*, p. 117). Using a corporate brand can:

- Extend the positive associations audiences have with that brand to other entities brought within the brand: there is an 'image spillover effect'. A corporate brand with strong organisational associations (size, culture, employer brand, management, financial performance) can more easily stretch to endorse a broad range of product brands than one dominated by product associations.

- Decrease stakeholders' perception of risk in dealing with the company's products: a corporate brand (like corporate reputation) provides a 'short-hand' assessment that simplifies purchase and investment decisions.

- Increase stakeholder confidence by emphasising the size, standing and asset backing of the whole concern.

ACTIVITY 6

evaluation

Assess your own organisation's suitability and support for corporate branding (whether or not it currently brands itself at the corporate level), on the basis of the drivers discussed above.

3.5 When is corporate branding appropriate?

A survey of academic research by van Riel & Fombrun (*op cit*, p. 109) suggests that corporate branding is an appropriate strategy for companies to adopt when:

- There is significant 'information asymmetry' between a company and its customers: that is, when customers are much less informed about a company's products than the company is (eg highly technical products)

- Customers perceive a high degree of risk in purchasing the products or services of the company, and require the reassurance of 'endorsement' by a strong corporate brand

- Features of the 'company behind the brand' are relevant to the purchase decision

- The corporate brand has a sufficiently high level of awareness with key stakeholders

- The corporate brand transfers added economic value to individual product brands

- The associations with the corporate brand and product brands are broadly consistent: if they are inconsistent, corporate endorsement may only erode the existing product brand.

The syllabus content for many of the topics on corporate branding is specifically drawn from:

• *van Riel & Fombrun:* Essentials of Corporate Communication *(2007, Routledge); Chapter 5, Communicating with the Corporate Brand.*

You should read this chapter in full. ■

4 Corporate branding strategy

4.1 Typologies of branding strategy

4.1.1 Olins

Olins (1990) proposed an influential typology of corporate branding strategies.

- **Monolithic strategy**: the whole company uses one visual style and symbols, for instant recognition. This suits companies which have developed as integrated entities within a relatively narrow field (eg Shell, Philips, BMW).

- **Endorsed strategy**: different subsidiaries or divisions have their own style, but the parent company is clearly identified and recognisable. This suits diversified companies whose divisions have distinctive culture and brands (eg General Motors, L'Oréal, Altria, Kelloggs).

- **Branded strategy**: different subsidiaries or divisions have their own style, without visible relationship to each other or to the parent, which is a company more or less invisible (eg Unilever).

Monolithic and endorsed strategies enable (positive or negative) 'image spillover' or 'halo' effects to different degrees. A branded strategy does not allow the brand to benefit from the parent company's positive reputation – but it also limits the risk to the corporate brand of product failure or reputational damage.

KEY CONCEPT   concept

Endorsement (in the context of corporate branding strategy) is the extent to which a subsidiary brand is associated with, or given approval or sanction by, a parent brand: in other words, the degree of parent company visibility in the management and visual identity of the subsidiary brand.

4.1.2 Kammerer

Kammerer (1988) categorises the internal implementation of corporate branding strategies by four 'action types':

- **Financial orientation**. Subsidiaries are purely financial participants in the overall concern: they are more or less autonomous of the parent company, and manage their own identities.

- **Organisation-oriented corporate branding**. The parent company exercises influence over the culture and strategy of the subsidiaries (eg by setting policy and rules), but this is a form of internal corporate branding – not directly visible to the outside world.

- **Communication-oriented corporate branding**. Advertising and visual identity clearly express the fact that the subsidiaries are part of the parent company – supporting added value from endorsement (as discussed earlier).

- **Single company corporate branding**: similar to monolithic branding, with integration of action, messages and symbols across the whole concern.

4.1.3 van Riel

The model developed by van Riel and van Bruggen (2002) takes into account two key factors in the corporate branding decision, which explicitly acknowledge the influence of business unit managers on the successful implementation of corporate brands:

- **Agreement on parent visibility**: the extent to which business unit managers are willing to communicate that they are part of a larger group of companies

- **Agreement on starting points**: the extent to which there is consensus about the starting points of the corporate branding strategy (what the parent company really stands for, what its values are, and how they can be used to communicate with target audiences).

These two dimensions create four basic choices: Figure 4.3.

Figure 4.3: van Riel and van Bruggen's corporate branding typology

Agreement on parent visibility		Agree on starting points	
		Low	High
	High	Medium endorsement	Strong endorsement
	Low	No endorsement (stand alone)	Weak endorsement

Examining each quadrant in turn:

- **No endorsement** (stand alone). There is a high degree of autonomy in business units, and a low degree of parent visibility, in order to avoid image spillover effects. Visualisation: affiliate/subsidiary name (eg Lipton).

- **Weak endorsement**. Usually a transitional phase, allowing low parent visibility while consensus and support is built for a more integrated market approach. Visualisation: affiliate name + 'member of' parent company name + parent company logo (eg Lipton a member of Unilever[logo]).

- **Medium endorsement**. There is a high degree of parent visibility, but no consistent integration with corporate message. Visualisation: parent company name (logo) + affiliate/subsidiary name (eg Unilever [logo] Lipton). Designed to bolster the strength of the affiliate brand.

- **Strong endorsement**. There is a high degree of parent visibility and corporate identification, transparency, co-ordination of communication strategies: designed to show the strength of the group as a whole. Visualisation: parent company name (logo) + specialisation (eg Unilever [logo] Food and Beverage).

(If you are interested in how Unilever actually approaches this, see: http://www.unilver.com.)

A business unit should only move towards a stronger degree of endorsement as:

- The corporate brand grows more well-known and valued in the local market
- The local brand loses strength in its local market, as the importance of the corporate brand grows.

In practice, this may mean that different business units should be assessed on a case by case basis.

MARKETING AT WORK

application

The **Ford Motor Company** is a strong 'family of brands'. The Ford name is a brand family name for a number of separately branded models (Falcon, Fiesta and so on). It has also been stretched to cover other activities: for example, the Ford Motor Credit Co (offering automotive finance for dealers and customers of other Ford corporate brands).

However, after a series of acquisitions, Ford Motor Company also controls a range of corporate names – strongly branded in their own right – such as Volvo, Mercury and Lincoln. In the dealership environment, Ford may locate their different marques on the same, or adjacent sites, but they keep the experience separate: Volvo drivers are, looking for a different product and service experience than that expected by a Ford customer. Similarly, while the Ford Motor Company web site and advertising emphasises the 'Family of Brands' and features Ford, Mercury, Volvo and Lincoln side by side, each subsidiary brand has its own distinctive visual identity and corporate brand. (The Volvo web site does not identify it as a member of Ford, for example.)

Link: http://www.ford.com/about-ford/company-information
http://www.volvocars.com

4.2 The branding process

This syllabus should build on your existing knowledge of product branding processes and strategies, and we will not cover them in detail here. Some key decisions and activities in corporate or strategic branding will include:

- **Whether or not to brand**. As we saw above, not all parent companies or manufacturers of product brands will want to be branded in their own right. If synergies are not available from linking sub-brands, or associating them with a central corporate identity, the parent company may not be separately branded. (If you have never heard of Yum! Brands Inc, look up its web site: http://www.yum.com/company. You might be surprised to hear that it is the world's largest restaurant company, and even more surprised by its globally familiar, high-profile brands. Then click through to any of the brand sites, and see whether the Yum name or identity features on any of them...)

- **Selection and protection of brand name**. (if not already determined as the company name). Desirable qualities for a brand name are (a) ease of pronunciation, recognition and recall and (b) resonance or suggestiveness (expressing something about the corporate identity).

- **Brand strategy**. Extent of integration or endorsement in the corporate brand in relation to subsidiary brands; and extent to which brand identity is internally and/or externally expressed (as in Kammerer's typology, discussed above).

- **Brand architecture**. The dimensions of stakeholder engagement with the brand: corporate activities (analogous to the features of a product brand); benefits or value added (analogous to the functional benefits of a product brand); and emotional benefits and associations (analogous to the emotional benefits of a product brand). Brand architecture provides a framework for which themes generate the greatest stakeholder engagement with the brand, and acts as a strategic communication framework for expressing the brand to target audiences. This may also be called the brand's 'reputational platform', and will be discussed later in this chapter.

- **Brand promise**. What the brand stands for or offers in the minds of stakeholders. A psychological 'contract' is formed between stakeholders and the brand, based on the values and benefits the brand holds out to its audience: the claims made and expectations raised by brand identity and associations. 'In the case of a bug killer, that means dead bugs when used. Easy to understand, easy to communicate. One famous branded bug killer, Raid® still used 'Kills bugs dead' as its advertising slogan. While it is easier to consider the branding challenge of a tangible product with hard and fast features, functions and benefits, the greater challenge is how does one communicate a corporate brand, especially if the corporate brand is really a holding company that owns many other brands?' (Doorley & Garcia, 2007, p. 283). What real, emotional or symbolic benefits can corporate brands offer or promise to stakeholders? This is again part of the brand's reputational platform, and will be discussed below.

- **Brand fingerprint** (Vyse, 1999). A document that summarises the essential character of the brand for everyone involved with the brand development process, to help ensure continuity and consistency of brand management. This may include:

  - **Target audience(s)**: description of the attitudes and values of the target audiences, in whose perception the corporate brand will be positioned. What attributes and values are relevant and important to them?

  - **Insight**: a description of the elements of stakeholder's perspectives and needs which will form a starting point for brand development

  - **Competition**: a picture of the market as seen by stakeholders, and the relative values the brand offers in the market

  - **Benefits**: the functional and emotional/symbolic benefits offered by the brand (brand promise)

  - **Proposition**: the single most compelling and competitive statement the target stakeholder would make for engaging with the brand (purchase, investment, employment etc)

- **Values**: what the brand stands for and believes in

- **Reasons to believe**: the proof points offered to substantiate positioning

- **Essence**: the distillation of the brand identity into one clear thought (perhaps used as a corporate tagline or motto)

- **Properties**: the tangible and symbolic elements which will immediately evoke the brand.

You will recognise elements of the 'brand fingerprint' when we come to discuss reputational platforms and corporate stories, later in the chapter.

ACTIVITY 7
application

Try drafting a brand fingerprint statement for the corporate brand of your organisation (if any), or for one of its product brands (if any). If this does not apply, you might draft a fingerprint statement for the desired/potential brand of the organisation – or for any brand that you know well. The purpose of the exercise is simply to get you to look at a brand from a variety of perspectives and across a variety of expressions.

4.3 Brand positioning

KEY CONCEPT
concept

Positioning is defined as 'the place the product [or organisation] occupies in consumer's minds relative to competing products [or organisations]' or 'the way the product [or organisation] is defined by consumers on important attributes' (Kotler & Armstrong, 2000).

An organisation will seek to determine how its corporate image (and/or brand, if relevant) is perceived by stakeholder audiences in relation to its competitors. For example, consider Diageo's positioning statement: 'Diageo is the world's leading premium drinks business' (www.diageo.com). This has the virtue of clarity, consistency (over several years' use), credibility (because it is backed by brand performance) and competitiveness (positioning the brand as superior to its rivals).

You should be familiar with the use of perceptual maps or positioning charts to plot competing brands against two or more dimensions (perceived attributes). The same techniques can be used to position company reputations or images, or corporate brands: Figure 4.4.

Figure 4.4: Corporate brand/image positioning map

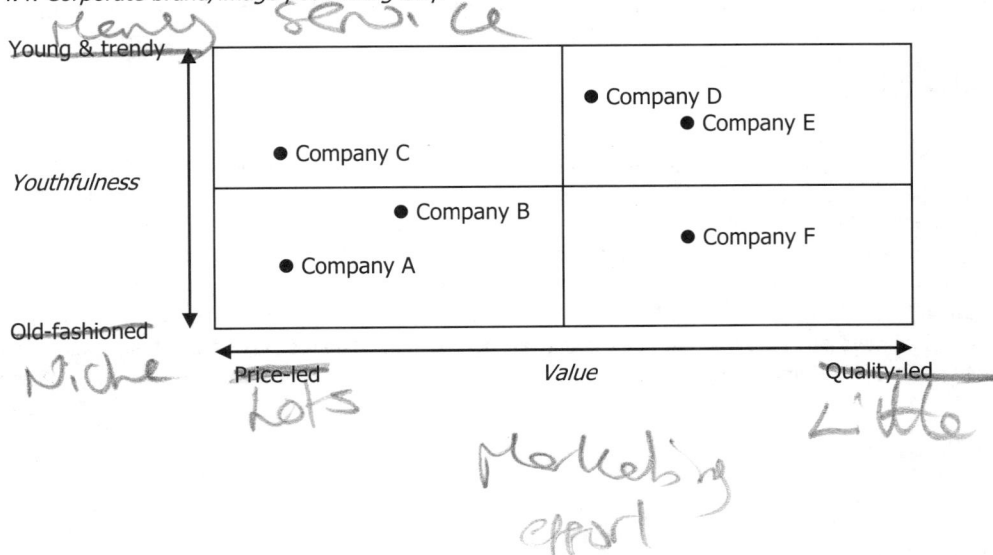

In this generalised example, Company A may have a valuable reputational niche among older, price-conscious consumers. On the other hand, it may note that there is a gap in the market to engage older, or more conservative but more affluent, quality-seeking consumers.

The strength of a brand's positioning in the marketplace is based on elements (Jobber, 2007) such as:

- **Brand heritage**: the background 'story' to the brand and its culture (eg the long retail history of Marks & Spencer).

- **Brand values**: the core values and characteristics of the brand (eg The Body Shop's ethical values, Audi's sophistication and progress, Virgin's entrepreneurship and fun).

- **Brand assets**: what makes the brand distinctive from other competing brands: symbols (eg the Nike 'swoosh'), attributes (eg 3M or Dyson UK's innovation) and relationships (eg Dell Computers' late customisation and direct selling network).

- **Brand personality**: the 'character' of the brand, often described in terms of other entities, such as people, animals or objects. (Eg 'If Organisation X were a person, what kind of person would it be?')

- **Brand reflection and identification**: how the brand relates to stakeholder self-identity, or how stakeholders perceive themselves as a result of engaging with the brand (eg as an Apple user, a John Lewis employee or a Shell investor).

- **Brand awareness**: developing credibility and raising visibility are important tasks in brand management. Brand awareness objectives will depend on the industry and markets, and the organisation's position within them (Aaker, 1991).

    - **Top of mind** awareness requires establishing the brand as one people know without reference to an industry or a prompt (eg Virgin, BBC, Greenpeace)

    - **Brand recall** awareness requires a context prompt (eg industry or category)

    - **Brand recognition** awareness requires the brand being recognised when mentioned.

As environments and stakeholders change and/or the organisation changes, the brand may need to be repositioned. Nokia, for example, repositioned itself from being a paper manufacturer to a market leader in mobile phones.

Brand consultancy Interbrand offers a range of interesting brand-related articles, free to download, on subjects such as the impact of sustainability on corporate brand value, and the kinds of corporate messaging required in an economic downturn.

Link: http://www.interbrand.com   (Follow the link > Knowledge > Papers and articles.) ∎

4.4 Re-branding

There may be occasions when an organisation needs to reposition itself in its market, and a radical change of identity is required to throw off old associations and perceptions in stakeholders' minds. This may involve a change of identity and communications (eg McDonalds highlighting sweeping changes with its global 'I'm Lovin' It' campaign).

MARKETING AT WORK   application

Global brand **McDonalds** was losing ground to competitors by 2001, due to the perception of poor service, boring food – and bad publicity arising form the obesity 'epidemic' associated with fast food. It launched a 'Plan to Win' **total rebranding campaign**, designed to woo back core customers: mothers, kids and 20-somethings. McDonalds recognised that the brand was losing relevance, because it had focused on opening new outlets – rather than maximising sales at existing outlets. The worldwide 'I'm Lovin' It' campaign, featuring celebrities like Justin Timberlake, Destiny's Child and Yao Ming, has **repositioned** McDonalds as an energetic lifestyle brand. Service and outlet décor have been revamped. New health-conscious menus have been introduced – at a profit-raising premium. The results? Same-store results up 7% worldwide. Complaints down 11%. Compliments up 18%.

(Business, Jan/Feb 2005)

However, since the brand name is the encapsulation of the brand image – and all the associations that go with it – rebranding is often identified with **change of name**: if the imagery is changed but the brand name remains the same, customers may become confused and alienated.

Change of name may also be helpful or necessary:

- In overcoming identity crisis following **merger or restructuring**, especially if there are internal political/power issues over 'ownership' of the merged or newly autonomous brand. When a merger or acquisition takes place, for example, the corporate name may reflect the dual identity: as when Glaxo Wellcome and SmithKline Beecham merged to become GlaxoSmithKline (GSK). Or it may be a completely new name, to avoid the difficulties of aggregation (eg when drinks companies GrandMet and Guinness became Diageo). Another interesting example is Andersen Consulting's change of name to Accenture, as a result of a rift with parent accounting firm (Arthur Andersen) in the 1990s. (An interesting exercise in reputational risk management, since Arthur Andersen was dissolved in 2002 following its involvement in the Enron scandal...)

- In disassociating the corporate brand from **negative or old-fashioned images**. BT Wireless, for example, changed its name to O2: away from an old-fashioned, bureaucratic image, and towards a youthful image (based on focus group statements that they saw their mobile phones as essential to life, like oxygen). Similarly, Kentucky Fried Chicken rebranded to KFC because of the negative connotations of fried food.

- In disassociating the corporate brand from negative perceptions of an **industry or country of origin** (where used in the name) or associations with the name itself. An example would be the Philip Morris tobacco companies adopting the name Altria Group to disassociate their (at the time) food business (Kraft) from the negative perceptions of tobacco companies.

- In reflecting corporate **diversification** out of its original product or business category, making the original name limiting or inaccurate. For example, Esso (Standard Oil) changed its name to Exxon, as its portfolio extended beyond oil.

- In taking advantage of **subsidiary brand strength**. For example, Consolidated Foods discarded its unfamiliar name and adopted the name of its leading brand: Sara Lee.

- In creating **global brands**, by harmonising brand names across international markets. For example, the UK One2One brand to T-mobile (as used by its parent company Deutsche Telecom in Germany).

ACTIVITY 8
application

Who will be the primary audiences for a re-branding communication programme, and how might they be reached?

---

van Riel and Fombrun (*op cit*, p. 129) offer the following general points about re-branding programmes.

- Corporate branding initiatives usually develop as a result stakeholder pressure for increased clarity and transparency of corporate communication – which may be resisted by managers.

- Strong and assertive leadership is required to develop and implement corporate branding.

- The (re)launch of a corporate brand must be supported with strong symbolic support, internal and external communication and 'hoopla'!

- (Re)branding generates resistance. Care must be taken to develop and agree rules for business units to follow (eg in regard to visual identity), and to monitor their implementation.

Rebranding presents considerable risks and challenges, where stakeholders have built up powerful engagement with an old brand. The Post Office's attempt to re-brand as Consignia, for example, was short-lived, due to objections from consumers, employees and the media: the decision was reversed and the corporate name 'Royal Mail Group' selected, forming a closer association with the former brand.

For more detail on the branding and re-branding process, if this is relevant to your organisation and assessment tasks, you may want to browse through some of the supplementary readings in this area. See:

- *Elliot and Percy Strategic Brand Management (2007: OUP), especially Chapter 10: Branding services and managing the corporate brand.*

- *Ind Living The Brand: how to transform every member of your organisation into a brand champion (3rd edition, 2007: Kogan Page – note that the title is wrongly written in some versions of the CIM reading list). This title is particularly strong on the internal or 'employee-centric' aspects of developing brands: corporate mission and values, stories and myths, employee participation and empowerment for service quality and so on. See also the short Chapter 9: Managing the brand.*

- *Kapferer The New Strategic Brand Management (4th ed: 2008: Kogan Page). This is good all round on the subject, but see particularly Chapter 5: Brand diversity: the types of brands, which explores countries, towns, universities, celebrities and other non-corporate entities as brands; and Chapter 13: Brand architecture.* ■

5 Developing corporate identity and/or brand

Once again, the syllabus content in this area is based on a specific model put forward by van Riel & Fombrun (2007), and we have drawn substantially on their work in covering this topic.

5.1 Reputation platforms

KEY CONCEPT

concept

A **reputation platform** is the root positioning that a company adopts when it presents itself to internal and external observers (van Riel & Fombrun, 2007, p. 136). Using a musical analogy (Hatch, 2003), it is the melodic 'riff' around which business unit managers improvise, interpreting and adapting the core message for the needs of different audiences.

A reputation platform creates a 'starting point' for the communication system: for all descriptions, discussions and expressions of organisational identity. Strong identities (and corporate brands) are built when logos, taglines, creative concepts and stories recognisably reflect an underlying reputation platform.

The core positioning themes that serve as reputation platforms may be:

- **What the organisation does**: the key activities or business areas it is involved in: eg DHL is in the logistics business; Shell is in the energy business. An activity theme emphasises focus, dedication, expertise and credibility in a given activity.

- **What the organisation offers**: the benefits or attractive outcomes offered by or through the organisation's activities. So Coles supermarkets are about 'everyday low pricing'; IBM is about 'working smarter, not harder'; 3M is about 'innovative and practical solutions from a diversified company'; Marks & Spencer is about 'trust, quality and service'. A benefits theme emphasises value, advantage and desirability, in order to inspire allegiance.

- **What the organisation represents**: the values and emotions the organisation stands for. So, for example, Reebok is about 'a passion for winning'; Volvo focuses on 'safety'; Johnson & Johnson on 'nurturing'; L'Oréal on 'you're worth it'; Intel on 'Today is so yesterday' (note the difference in tone from 3M's innovation theme, for example). An emotional theme seeks to establish a personal connection or emotional bond with target audiences, through empathy and identification.

5.2 Corporate stories and story-telling

KEY CONCEPT

concept

A **corporate story** is 'a structured textual description that communicates the essence of the company to all stakeholders, helps strengthen the bonds that bind employees to the company, and successfully positions the company against rivals. It is built up by identifying the **unique elements** of the company, creating a plot that weaves them together, and **presenting** them in an appealing fashion' (van Riel & Fombrun, *op cit*, p. 144).

van Riel & Fombrun suggest that a good corporate story should be no longer than 400–600 words: a short but distinctive narrative about the organisation that (a) helps stakeholder audiences to understand it better and (b) distinguishes it from other entities in the reputation marketplace (*ibid*, p. 146). It will not necessarily be used for all audiences, or in its totality: it is intended primarily to guide corporate communication, as a briefing for media, marketing agencies, market analysts and other audiences who need to have an 'executive summary' of the essence of the organisation. Expansions, interpretations and versions of the story may, however, be used widely within and beyond the firm.

Unique corporate features may not be easy to identify, given the fairly narrow range of values likely to appeal to stakeholder audiences. (Doesn't every company want to represent customer focus, innovation, quality, value, responsibility, trustworthiness etc?) However, the attributes identified as central, consistent and distinctive, as part of corporate identity analysis, will provide a good starting point. In addition, each organisation will have unique historical roots and key personnel, which may form part of its identity.

MARKETING AT WORK

application

There is no substitute for browsing corporate web sites (especially those which reflect major corporate brands) to appreciate the power of reputation platforms and corporate stories. For example, check out:

- 'Finding Better Ways' (A Brief Introduction to **3M**), downloadable from:
  Link: http://solutions.3m.co.uk/wps/portal/3M/en_GB/about2/Our-Company

  See also the fascinating historical narrative at:
  Link: http://solutions.3m.co.uk/wps/portal/3M/en_GB/about-3M/information/more-info/history

- The timeline of **Marks & Spencer's** history at:
  Link: http://corporate.marksandspencer.com

  See also the material offered on the 'Student Information' link, and the new reputation platform represented by **Plan A** (M & S's CSR platform):
  Link: http://plana.marksandspencer.com

- The corporate responsibility platform of **McDonalds**:
  Link: http://www.mcdonalds.com/usa/good/welcome

- The 'Company overview' of **Nike**:
  Link: http://www.nikebiz.com/company_overview

- The '**Ford Story**' ('See where we are. Be part of where we're going' – including blogs and social networking site links)
  Link: http://www.ford.com/about-ford/company-information

Even if features are not particularly unique, they can be giving distinctive meaning when they are connected and expressed in a **narrative** or **plot**. A story may be a simple narrative history, or statement of what the company stands for and believes in; what it is trying to do; or how it sees its future. However, it can also be made more vivid, in order to create powerful resonances with archetypal narrative themes. In his book *Seven Basic Plots*, Christopher Booker (2004) argues that there are seven basic plot lines: Comedy (confusion resolved in a happy ending), Tragedy (forces driving towards an unhappy ending), Rags to Riches, Journey and Return, The Hero's Quest (searching for something of great value), Overcoming the Monster, and Rebirth. You may be able to imagine how these stories would play out for an organisation: fighting off takeover, natural disaster or recession (overcoming the monster); persevering through obstacles to arrive at an innovative breakthrough (quest); starting small and becoming a global corporation (rags to riches); diversifying and then returning to its roots (journey and return); or undergoing a paradigm shift and turning the business around (rebirth).

If this seems fanciful, consider the 'years of struggle' of 3M before it found its innovation breakthrough. Or the 'rise and fall and rise' of Marks & Spencer in the last few decades – and now its heroic mission to save the planet ('Plan A will see us working with our customers and our suppliers to combat climate change, reduce waste, safeguard natural resources, trade ethically and build a healthier nation. We're doing this because it's what you want us to do. It's also the right thing to do. We're calling it Plan A because we believe it's now the only way to do business. There is no Plan B.'). Consider the rags to riches story of Virgin 'beginning in the 1970s with a student magazine and small mail order record company' (www.virgin.com).

Effective corporate stories (van Riel & Fombrun, *op cit.* p. 146):

- Introduce **unique words** to describe the organisation
- Refer to the organisation's **unique history**
- Describe the organisation's **core strengths**
- **Personalise and humanise** the organisation
- Provide a **plot line**
- Address the concerns of **multiple stakeholders**

ACTIVITY 9   evaluation

Consider the following statement of strategy from global financial group ING (www.ing.com):

'ING's overall mission is to help customers manage their financial future. Capitalising on changing customer preferences and building on our solid business capabilities, ING's strategic focus is on banking, investments, life insurance and retirement services. We want to provide retail customers with the products they need during their lives to grow savings, manage investments and prepare for retirement with confidence. With our wide range of products, innovative distribution models and strong footprints in both mature and developing markets, we have the long-run economic, technological and demographic trends on our side. We align our business strategy around a universal customer ideal: saving and investing for the future should be easier. While steering the business through turbulent times, we will execute efforts across all our business lines to strengthen customer confidence and meet their needs, preserve a strong capital position, further mitigate risks and bring our costs in line with revenue expectations.'

And the following corporate history on the Work@Macdonalds (careers) page of the McDonald's website (www.mcdonalds.com):

'From day one, McDonald's believed in forging new opportunities. The same holds true today, and it's this kind of philosophy that will launch your career. For starters, Ray Kroc, our founder and inspiration, parlayed exclusive distribution rights of an innovative milkshake maker into the first-ever franchise in Des Plaines, Illinois.'

'Later, Ronald McDonald proved another huge idea from a set of wonderful folks. Introduced in his first TV appearance, Ronald became recognised as 'the smile known around the world.' Today, he is as recognised as Santa Claus.'

'In yet another example of empowered big-thinking, franchisee Jim Delligatti invented the Big Mac and changed hamburgers forever. As you can see, broad vision, big ideas, and a family of great people fuel our success. It's true, new employees today are our leaders tomorrow. Will you be among them? You certainly could be.'

What elements of these statements can you identify as (a) reputational platform and (b) corporate story, and how effectively is the story tailored to the targeted stakeholder audience?

Unique presentation in telling a corporate story is also difficult to achieve, given the comparatively narrow range of tools and images available, and the large number of organisations using them! However, consider the diverse ways in which the Disney corporation, for example, uses its logo, music and characters, in retail settings, on film, in theme parks and so on to express its reputational platform: 'Since its founding in 1923, The Walt Disney Company and its affiliated companies have remained faithful to their commitment to produce unparalleled entertainment experiences based on the rich legacy of quality creative content and exceptional storytelling.' (corporate.disney.go.com). Consider McDonald's use of the 'I'm lovin' it' tagline, the golden arches and Ronald McDonald to reinforce its platform as a family food provider. Or Nike's co-branding and sponsorship strategies, expressing its platform of crystallising athletic potential.

MARKETING AT WORK

application

The **Virgin Group** has a strong reputation platform built around several corporate brand values: 'Value for Money, Good Quality, Brilliant Customer Service, Innovative, Competitively Challenging and Fun.' These themes are starting points for the content and style of corporate communication throughout the diverse group. For example, the personality of Sir Richard Branson is highly identified with Virgin's corporate communication, reflecting the reputation platform with a combination of entrepreneurial savvy and adventurous publicity stunts.

The website (www.virgin.com) tells the corporate story, entitled 'What we're about': how the organisation began, what it believes in, what it has achieved, how it operates and why it has succeeded.

'We believe in making a difference. In our customers' eyes, Virgin stands for value for money, quality, innovation, fun and a sense of competitive challenge. We deliver a quality service by empowering our employees and we facilitate and monitor customer feedback to continually improve the customer's experience through innovation.

'When we start a new venture, we base it on hard research and analysis. Typically, we review the industry and put ourselves in the customer's shoes to see what could make it better. We ask fundamental questions: is this an opportunity for restructuring a market and creating competitive advantage? What are the competitors doing? Is the customer confused or badly served? Is this an opportunity for building the Virgin brand? Can we add value? Will it interact with our other businesses? Is there an appropriate trade-off between risk and reward?

'Contrary to what some people may think, our constantly expanding and eclectic empire is neither random nor reckless. Each successive venture demonstrates our skill in picking the right market and the right opportunity.

'Once a Virgin company is up and running, several factors contribute to making it a success. The power of the Virgin name, Richard Branson's personal reputation; our unrivalled network of friends, contacts and partners; the Virgin management style the way talent is empowered to flourish within the group. To some traditionalists, these may not seem hard headed enough. To them, the fact that Virgin has minimal management layers, no bureaucracy and no massive global HQ is an anathema.

'Our companies are part of a family rather than a hierarchy. They are empowered to run their own affairs, yet other companies help one another, and solutions to problems come from all kinds of sources. In a sense we are a community, with shared ideas, valued, interest and goals. The proof of our success is real and tangible.

'Exploring the activities of our companies through this web site demonstrates that success, and that it is not about having a strong business promise, it is about keeping it!...

'Value for Money, Good Quality, Brilliant Customer Service, Innovative, Competitively Challenging and Fun.

'Richard Branson set out with these principles in mind in the 1970s and they still really define what Virgin is all about. Most companies in the world have a set of brand values, which in a lot of cases can be completely meaningless. Virgin believes that the most important thing is the way those values are delivered and brought to life.

Here's some examples of the ways that Virgin delivers its brand values:

Value for money

Simple, honest & transparent pricing – not necessarily the cheapest on the market.
eg Virgin Blue Australia – low cost airlines with transparent pricing.

Good quality

High standards, attention to detail, being honest and delivering on promises.
eg Virgin Atlantic Upper Class Suite – limousine service, lounge, large flat bed on board, freedom menu etc.

Innovation

Challenging convention with big and little product / service ideas; innovative, modern and stylish design.
eg Virgin Trains new pendolino – fast tilting train with shop, radio, digital seat reservations & new sleek design.

Brilliant customer service

Friendly, human & relaxed; professional but uncorporate.
eg Virgin Mobile UK which has won awards for its customer service, treats its customers as individuals, and pays out staff bonuses according to customer satisfaction survey results.

Competitively challenging

Sticking two fingers up to the establishment and fighting the big boys – usually with a bit of humour.
eg Virgin Atlantic successfully captured the public spirit by taking on BA's dirty tricks openly – and winning. Later, advertising messages such as BA Don't Give A Shiatsu both mocked BA and delivered a positive message about the airline's service.

Fun

Every company in the world takes itself seriously so we think it's important that we provide the public and our customers with a bit of entertainment.
eg VAA erected a sign over the BA-sponsored, late finishing London Eye saying: BA Can't Get It Up.

Virgin Cola's launch in USA saw Richard drive a tank down 5th Avenue and then 'blow up' the Coke sign in Times Square, mocking the 'cola wars'.'

Link: http://www.virgin.com/AboutVirgin/WhatWeAreAbout

For reflection: How does this story reflect the reputation platform? What techniques does it use to reinforce a strong sense of identity ('us' versus 'them')?

5.2.1 Creating corporate stories

van Riel & Fombrun (*op cit*, p. 149–158) set out a process for arriving at a sustainable corporate story, which they summarise as follows: Figure 4.5.

Figure 4.5: Creating a corporate story

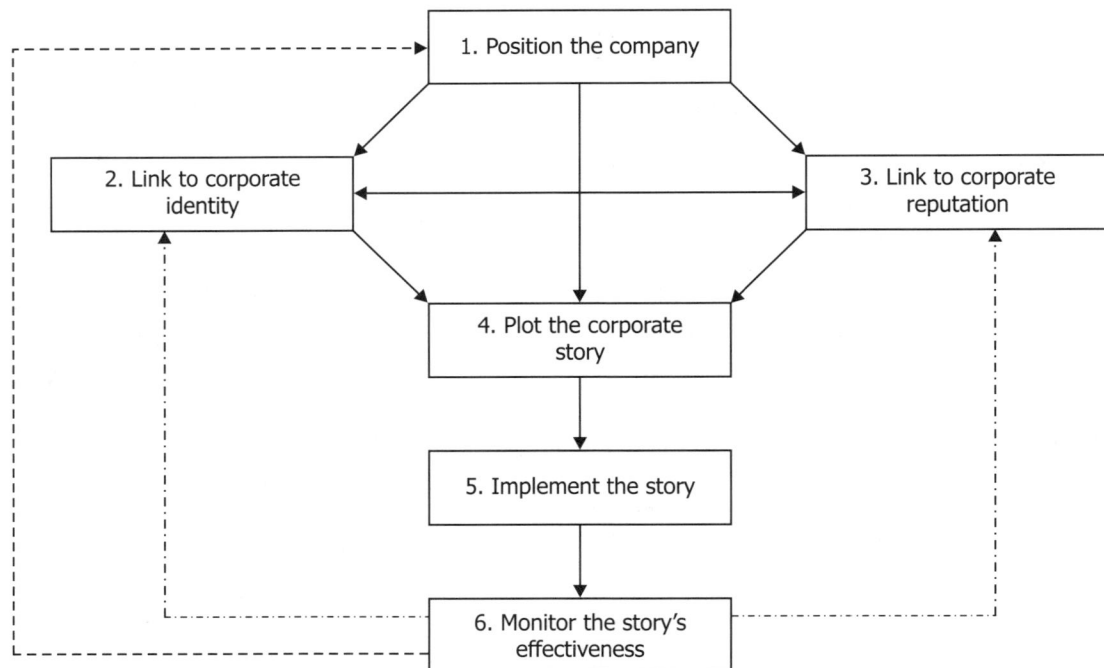

Adapted from van Riel (2001), cited in van Riel & Fombrun (*op cit*, p. 149).

Working through the stages of the model, very briefly:

Step 1   **Position the company**

As a first starting point for the corporate story, position the organisation:

- Against its rivals in the market: this may require research into its sources of competitive advantage, or gaps in the market (as portrayed in perceptual maps or positioning charts of the market).

- In relation to the interests and concerns of its stakeholders: this may require the prioritisation of key stakeholder audiences and stakeholder research.

Step 2   **Link to corporate identity**

A second starting point is offered by the distinctive, continuous and central 'facts' about the organisation, in the perception of its employees and managers. These elements may be determined via internal interviews, focus groups and surveys, or personality profiling (as discussed in Chapter 3).

Step 3   **Link to corporate reputation**

As a third starting point, determine the underlying drivers of external perceptions of the company (which can be picked-up on or emphasised in the story). This may require reputation or image research: what attributes cause stakeholders to perceive and evaluate the organisation positively? (Trustworthiness, social responsibility, value-for-money, good management, innovation, strong financial performance?)

Step 4   **Plot the story**

Given these starting points, a story can be drafted, using:

- A PPT framework:

    - **Promise** (or Positioning Statement): what the company sees as its distinctive strengths. (Check with stakeholders for (a) relevance and (b) realism.)

    - **Proof points**: evidence for each of the starting points selected. (Eg if CSR is a starting point, a proof point might be: 'The company headed the 'Top Brands with a Conscience' ranking last year'.)

    - **Tone of voice**: humour, modesty, excitement, youthfulness etc. How does the organisation 'come across' in telling the story?

- A suitable logical outline: eg chronological (time line), contrast (eg ordinary firms v us), or cause and effect (eg Abilities > Activities > Accomplishments).

Step 5   **Implement the story**

Test external support for the draft, by conducting a survey of key stakeholders: are the starting point claims perceived to be **important** or motivating to stakeholders, **deliverable** by the organisation/ brand, and **unique** to the organisation/brand? (The IDU model: Rossiter & Percy, 1987).

Once a final version has been developed, relevant elements of the story can be incorporated into various communication media. (Internal media may emphasise value for employees; the annual report, financial performance and CSR; corporate advertising and exhibitions, quality and innovation; sponsorship, CSR; and the web site, a range of themes. These can be plotted on a media/message grid.)

Step 6   **Monitor the story's effectiveness**

As the organisation, the environment and stakeholder expectations and interests change, the story must adapt. Stakeholder research, feedback seeking and dialogue (eg on web site message boards) should be used to monitor the story's ongoing impact and currency, public perceptions, and stakeholder suggestions for story improvement.

The syllabus content for this area is specifically drawn from:

- *van Riel & Fombrun: Essentials of Corporate Communication (2007, Routledge); Chapter 6, Developing a Reputational Platform.*

We have summarised some key points, but you should read this chapter in full. ■

ACTIVITY 10

application

Try and draft a corporate story (of 400–600 words) for your own organisation, or any organisation that might form the focus of your assessment, using the processes outlined above. (Compare your version w th existing corporate story expressions, if any.)

5.3 Communication programmes

The next step in van Riel & Fombrun's corporate communication model is 'expressing the company': that is, turning the corporate story into targeted communication campaigns to relevant stakeholder audiences. We will cover this topic separately, in Chapters 6 and 7 (and, as applied to specific stakeholder audiences, in Chapters 8 to 10).

Learning objectives		Covered	
1	Explain the various meanings of corporate identity and the importance of strategic identity for reputation management	☑	Different types of identity: visual identity, organisational identity (or corporate identification); and corporate identity (or strategic identity)
		☑	The identity mix: symbolism, communication, behaviour
		☑	Multiple and hybrid identities
		☑	The importance of strategic identity
2	Critically evaluate the nature of corporate brands and make recommendations concerning any gap between identity and image	☑	Definition and nature of brands: nomenclature and associations
		☑	Corporate brands versus product brands
		☑	Brand elements or assets: differentiation; transferability; psychic value; recall and recognition; premium; registration
		☑	Drivers for corporate branding: strategic, organisational, employee and value drivers
		☑	Branding strategy typologies (degrees of endorsement): Olins, Kammerer, van Riel
		☑	The branding process
		☑	Brand positioning
		☑	Re-branding
3	Explain the nature of reputational platforms and corporate stories, and how these assist corporate positioning	☑	Reputational platforms or 'starting points'
		☑	Corporate stories: unique elements, plots and presentation
		☑	How to create a corporate story: starting points (positioning, identity and reputation); plotting the story; implementing the story
		☑	Communication programmes (followed-up in Chapter 6)

1   Identify the three elements of the identity mix.

2   Why is corporate identity management important?

3   Distinguish between product branding and corporate branding.

4   Identify Davies *et al.'s* six brand assets or elements.

5   Explain three general trends driving the increased visibility and importance of corporate brands.

6   List, with example, Olins' typology of corporate brand strategy.

7   What is (a) brand architecture, (b) brand promise, (c) brand heritage and (d) brand personality?

8   In what circumstances might an organisation wish to rebrand by changing its name?

9   Suggest three core themes that may serve as reputational platforms.

10   What is a 'PPT' framework for telling the corporate story?

1   Your own recall. We will follow this up in Chapter 7. Note that associations may have to do with the symbolism of the logo (eg Apple apple) or your knowledge of corporate philosophy, values and style (eg Nike's 'swoosh'), or your experiences with a particular organisation.

2   Your own analysis. Evaluation of critical incidents is an important technique of organisational analysis, enabling the identification and diagnosis of positive and negative underlying factors. You should start 'collecting' critical incidents in your focal organisation for ongoing analysis.

3   By developing an individualised identity, branding allows customers (and other stakeholder audiences) to develop associations with the brand (eg prestige, quality, friendliness) which – like corporate reputation – supports purchase decisions by providing a 'shorthand' evaluation. The marketing task is to ensure that the associations made with the product – or organisation – are positive, attractive, and in line with the chosen positioning objectives (how the product or organisation wants to be seen in relation to its competitors).

4   The price premium that leading brands have to charge to reflect their investment can only be justified if customers perceive that they are getting something extra for that premium. Many of the associations made with brands in customers' minds are to do with quality: a brand is often preferred to an unbranded item due to its implied promise of consistent quality (precisely because of the owner's investment in the brand). The link between branding, price and quality may be made explicit in brand promotions ('Stella Artois: reassuringly expensive.')

5   Typical arguments can be summarised as follows.

Arguments in support of corporate branding	Arguments against corporate branding
Creating a sense of internal coherence	Implication of wasted resource on sub-brands
Simplifying internal co-operation	Loss of strong 'local' branding advantage
Demonstrating strength and size of the organisation to external publics	Size appeals to financial audiences, but has no appeal to local consumers
Cost saving, compared to multiple branding	Reduced influence for business unit managers

6   This will be your own analysis.

7   Your own choice of subject and analysis. As usual with these kinds of activities, your outputs will form useful material for subsequent follow-up, if required in the assessment.

8   Change of name and symbolism, projected through strong corporate advertising, will be used to convey the new identity to external audiences. However, the change must also be communicated carefully to employees, in order to maintain identification with, and commitment to, the 'new' entity. The full range of cultural mechanisms (belief and value statements, symbols, rituals, stories etc) must be used to confirm and celebrate what the 'new' entity standards for.

9   ING. The reputational platform is a combination of activity, benefit and emotion: helping customers manage their financial future (security, confidence etc). The corporate story is based on this starting point, plus core competence (wide range, innovative distribution). The plot is about the uncertainty of the future – and ING's ability to steer customers, and the business itself, 'through turbulent times'. The style is fairly formal, focused on competences and financial strengths that will appeal to investors and customers.

McDonalds. This portion of the reputational platform is about 'Forging opportunities', empowerment and big thinking (benefits/emotions). The resulting version of the corporate story, specially tailored to a prospective employee audience, is about the founder's 'big idea' and seizing of opportunity, following a thread through other big ideas (Ronald McDonald, reflecting the company's other reputational platform starting point of social responsibility and philanthropy) – and joining the dots to opportunities for the prospective recruit. This is a clear example of selection of elements and varied re-telling of an overall corporate story for a particular audience and purpose.

10 Your own organisation. This would make a very good assessment task, so it is well worth attempting.

---

1   The identity mix is: symbolism, communication and behaviour.

2   See section 1.4 for a range of points.

3   See the table in section 2.1.1 for a full answer.

4   The brand assets are: differentiation, psychic value, premium (price or time), transferability, recall/recognition and registerable name.

5   See the beginning of section 3.1 for a full range of points.

6   Olins' typologies are: monolithic (eg Shell, Philips, BMW); endorsed (GM, Kellogg's); branded (Unilever).

7   Brand architecture is the dimensions of stakeholder engagement with the brand: activities, benefits or valued added and emotional benefits and associations. Brand promise is what the brand stands for or offers in the minds of stakeholders. Brand heritage is the background story to the brand and its culture. Brand personality is the 'character' of the brand, often described in terms of people.

8   An organisation may want to rebrand following merger or restructuring; to disassociate the brand from negative or old-fashioned images, or industry or country of origin effects; to reflect corporate diversification; to take advantage of subsidiary brand strength/familiarity; or to harmonise brands across international markets.

9   Core themes for a reputational framework include: activity (what the organisation does); benefits (value offered to stakeholders); and emotion (what the organisation represents).

10 PPT stands for Promise (or Positioning statement), Proof points and Tone of voice.

Albert, S & Whetten, O (1985) 'Organisational Identity' in L L Cummings & B M Shaw (eds) *Research in Organisational Behaviour*. Greenwich, CT: JAI Press

Ashforth, B E & Mael, F (1989) 'Social identity and the organisation' in *Academy of Management Review*. 14 (1) pp 20-39

Balmer, J M T (2001) 'Corporate identity, corporate branding and corporate marketing: seeing through the fog' in *European Journal of Marketing* 35 (3/4) p 248

Balmer, J M T (2008) 'Corporate identity, brand and marketing' in Melewar T C (ed.) *Facets of Corporate Identity, Communication and Reputation*. Abingdon, Oxon: Routledge

Balmer, J M T and Greyser, S A (2003) 'Managing the multiple identities of the corporation' in J M T Balmer and S A Greyser (eds) *Revealing the Corporation: Perspectives on Identity, Image, Reputation, Corporate Branding and Corporate-Level Marketing*. London: Routledge, pp 15-29

Booker, C (2004) *Seven Basic Plots: Why we tell stories*. Continuum International Publishing Group

Davies, G (1992) 'The two ways in which retailers can be brands' in *International Journal of retail and Distribution Management*, Vol 20 (2): pp 24-31

Davies G, Chun R, Da Silva R V & Roper S (2003) *Corporate Reputation and Competitiveness*. Abingdon, Oxon: Routledge

Doorley, J & Garcia, H F (2007) *Reputation Management: The Key to Successful Public Relations and Corporate Communications*. New York: Routledge

Dowling, G R (1986) *Corporate Reputations: Strategies for Developing the Corporate Brand*. London: Kogan Page

Elliott, R & Percy, L (2007) *Strategic Brand Management*. Oxford: OUP

Gray, E R & Balmer, J M T (1998) *Managing Corporate Image and Corporate Responsibility*. London: Long Range Planning

Hatch, M J & Schultz, M (2000) 'Scaling the tower of Babel' in Schultz, Hatch & Larsen (eds) *The Expressive Organisation*. New York: OUP pp 11-35

Ind, N (2007) *The Living Brand* (3rd ed): London: Kogan Page

Jobber, D (2007) *Principles & Practice of Marketing* (5th ed) Maidenhead: McGraw Hill

Kammerer, J (1988) *Beitrag der Produktpolitik zur Corporate Identity*. Munich: GBI-Verlag

Kapferer, J (2008) *The New Strategic brand Management*. (4th ed). London: Kogan Page

Kotler, P & Armstrong, G (2000) *Principles of Marketing* (9th ed). Englewood Cliffs, N J: Prentice Hall

Kotler P, Armstrong G, Meggs D, Bradbury E & Grech J (1999) *Marketing: An introduction*. Melbourne: Prentice Hall Australia

Napoles, V (1988) *Corporate Identity Design*. New York: John Wiley

Olins, W (1990) *The Wolff Olins Guide to Corporate Identity*. London: The Design Council

Pratt, M G & Foreman, P O (2000) 'Classifying managerial responses to multiple organisational identities', in *Academy of Management Review*, vol 25 (1): pp 18-42

Regester, M & Larkin, J (2008) *Risk Issues & Crisis Management in Public Relations: A Casebook of Best Practice* (4th ed) London: Kogan Page

Riel, C B M van & Bruggen, G H van (2002) 'Incorporating business unit managers' perspectives in corporate branding strategy decision making' in *Corporate Reputation Review* Vol 5 (2/3) pp 241-251

Riel, C B M van & Fombrun, C J (2007) *Essentials of Corporate Communication: Implementing Practices for Effective Reputation Management*. Abingdon, Oxon: Routledge

Rossiter, J R & Percy, L (1997) *Advancing Communications and Promotion Management*. New York: McGraw Hill

Topalian, A (1984) 'Corporate identity: beyond the visual overstatements' in *International Journal of Advertising*, 3 pp 55-62

Vella, K J & Melewar, T C (2008) 'Relationship between Identity and Culture' in Melewar T C (ed) *Facets of Corporate Identity, Communication and Reputation*. Abingdon, Oxon: Routledge

Vyse, K (1999) 'Fingerprint clues identify the brand' in *Marketing*, 9 March, p 19

Chapter 5

Evaluating reputational strength

Topic list

Introduction

One of the 'tenets' or principles of reputation management is that reputation is *measurable* in a meaningful and systematic way. In this chapter, we draw together various syllabus references to this measurement, covering the various frameworks and tools to enable you to analyse the strength and potential of the organisation's corporate identity and/or brand and reputation.

As the syllabus says: 'Having undertaken an analysis of the organisation's character, the student's next task is to critically evaluate the form and strength of the current identity or brand...In undertaking the analysis, students should be able to provide an assessment of the organisation, its brand and communication performance, and the issues and challenges it faces in enhancing its reputation.' This will be the foundation for making recommendations to support the management of corporate reputation, and to close the gap between identity and image, using corporate communication.

In section 1, we look at some general indicators used to evaluate the strength of an organisation's reputation: return on investment, brand equity, shareholder value and media comment. These should be seen as ways of expressing the broad impact of reputation on the organisation.

In section 2 we look at how the strength and potential of an organisation's identity and identity mix can be assessed and measured, highlighting potential challenges for corporate reputation management. This includes the important topic of communication audits, the foundation for planning corporate communications.

Finally, in section 3, we identify and evaluate various commercial systems available for measuring reputation. The syllabus guidance suggests that you do not need deep knowledge of these systems, but you do need sufficient understanding to distinguish between them in terms of their key attributes and issues associated with their implementation.

Syllabus-linked learning objectives

By the end of the chapter you will be able to:

Learning objectives	Syllabus link
1 Propose and justify the use of a portfolio of broad indicators to evaluate the strength of an organisation's reputation	1.2.3
2 Critically assess the strength and potential of an organisation's corporate identity and/or brand, and areas of reputational risk or challenge	2.1.2
3 Undertake a communication audit as a foundation for targeting communications to key stakeholder groups	2.2.2
4 Differentiate between various commercial systems for measuring reputation	2.1.2

1 General indicators of reputational strength

1.1 ROI

Return On Investment (ROI) is one of the basic financial objectives (and performance measures) of any activity in a business organisation. It measures the profits gained by the activity, as a percentage of the capital invested in it.

One of the key measures of success of corporate communication and reputation management activity is that it **pays for itself** – and, better yet, gives **return on investment**, or profit.

For corporations, ROI reflects a return on the value of shareholders' investment of capital in the business. In more general terms, however, it reflects the balance between the costs and benefits of an activity: whether and how far it repays the investment of finance, time and other resources. (Charities and not-for-profit organisations do not have shareholders, but they do still have stakeholders to whom they are accountable for the use of funds.)

As an accounting measure, ROI is normally applied to strategic business units which are viewed as investment centres or profit centres. It shows how much profit in accounting terms has been made in relation to the amount of capital invested (or the value of the assets generating income):

$$\text{ROI (\%)} = \frac{\text{Profit (before interest and tax)} \times 100}{\text{Capital employed}}$$

For example, suppose that a company has two investment centres A and B, which show results for the year as follows:

	A	B
Profit (before tax and interest)	£60,000	£30,000
Assets generating income	£400,000	£120,000
ROI	15%	25%

Investment centre A has made double the profits of investment centre B, and in terms of profits alone has therefore been more 'successful'. However, B has earned a much higher ROI. This suggests that B has been a more successful investment than A.

The basic question here is: does corporate communication or reputation management pay? All business organisations continuously measure return on financial capital (shareholder investment) and assets. Is it also possible to gauge the return on identity, image, relationships and interactions?

As we saw in Chapter 1, enhanced financial performance (increased revenues, decreased costs, increased profitability, growth in share price and ability to raise investment capital) is one of the key business case arguments for reputation management.

1.1.1 Valuing corporate reputation assets

Tangible assets such as land or buildings can be valued because there is a market for them. It is more difficult to ascribe quantitative value to intangible assets such as research and development, technology, employees, brands and reputation. However, an International Financial Reporting Standard (IFRS 3) now allows the inclusion of valuations for **intangible assets** within the corporate balance sheet, and this has driven concerted attempts to value brand and reputational assets.

- Reputational and brand assets are often valued by comparing the 'book' value of the company (tangible assets as shown in the balance sheet) and its 'market' value (or share price). The company may have a stock value well above the value of its tangible asset worth, due to the 'goodwill' provided by its reputation – which represents its ability to earn future revenues.

- Various proprietary methods are also marketed to provide a valuation for a corporate brand name. A widely cited list of the top 100 global brands by financial value is produced by the Interbrand Corporation (www.interbrand.com), which values brands by:

- Estimating the percentage of revenue that can be credited to a brand

- Projecting brand profits over five years

- Applying a discount rate (based on profit risk) to derive a net present value for the brand – much in the same way that organisations value other investments.

- Companies often licence the use of their names to other organisations in exchange for a percentage of revenue: usually from 5–15%. Using an average figure of 10% for a licensing agreement of ten years, the net present value of the reputational assets would be about the equivalent of one year's turnover. (Davies G, Chun R, Da Silva R V & Roper S, 2003).

1.1.2 Return on relationship (ROR)

Since corporate communication and reputation management is primarily about developing beneficial relationships with stakeholders, it is worth noting that the term **return on relationship (ROR)** may be used to describe the long-term net financial outcome caused by the establishment of an organisation's network of relationships (Gummesson, 2002). The measurement of ROR is based on premises such as:

- A link between customer retention and profitability: increased revenue (through cross-selling and up-selling), decreased cost of sales (due to established contact and trust) and increased lifetime value of customers (revenue earned over the total duration of the relationship with the customer)

- A link between the loyalty of employees, customers and investors (the loyalty based cycle of growth: Reichheld, 2001 – discussed in Chapter 1).

1.2 Financial analysis of reputation management activity

The technical details of financial analysis are beyond the scope of the syllabus. However, you should be aware at a basic level that financial analysis may be carried out at the corporate and/or business unit level, to indicate whether reputation management and communications activity has been profitable, economical and cost-effective.

- Has communications activity been carried out within relevant **expenditure budget** constraints? *=yes*

- Has there been a **measurable economic contribution** attributable to the activity (ie increased profit) – and has this outweighed the costs of the activity (ie a positive return on investment)? *No*

- Has the development of the corporate identity, reputation or brand **reduced costs**? *No*

- Have the costs and/or contribution attributable to corporate communications and reputation management **gone up or down** in the past year? Is this a one-off effect or a worrying (or beneficial) trend? How can it be corrected (or maintained)? *down* *Recession*

ACTIVITY 1 *Now focused activity.*   evaluation

How might the development of the corporate identity, reputation or brand reduce costs? (You don't have to be an accountant to find an answer! Think about the costs of poor reputation or lack of employee identification for a start...)

Invalue stakeholder (investor ror, increase fundraising → better management of resources

1.3 Brand equity

KEY CONCEPT   concept

Brand equity is 'a measure of the strength of a brand in the marketplace by adding tangible value to a company through the resulting sales and profits.' (Jobber, 2007, p. 331)

Another of the key measures of communications and reputation management success is that they result in an **overall increase in the valuation of the brand**.

Customer-based brand equity is the differential effect that brand knowledge has on consumer response to the marketing of that brand (Keller, 2002). Positive brand equity is the extent to which customers react more favourably to a product when the brand is identified than when it is not. (Note that brand equity can also be negative!) Customer-based equity arises from:

FB does not have this

- **Brand awareness**. Audiences must be aware of the brand before it can influence their decisions. Brand awareness may be influential in low-involvement purchase situations, where consumers are not motivated to seek more detailed product/service information before making a decision.

- **Brand image**: the extent to which a brand generates strong, favourable and distinctive associations in the minds of consumers. A strong, positive brand image increases the likelihood of purchase. *FB has this with its stakeholders*

Positive brand awareness and image are likely to result in higher sales, higher customer loyalty and lower price sensitivity, lower selling costs, and the ability to charge a brand premium – all of which may lead to greater profitability. In addition, positive brand equity offers a strong base for brand extensions, offering additional revenue from cross-selling and up-selling.

Proprietary-based brand equity is value added to the brand by company attributes. Proprietary-based equity mainly arises from:

- **Designs and patents**, which protect a brand from theft or copying by competitors – and therefore protect the future revenue stream (and therefore value) of the brand.

- **Channel relationships**, since supply and distribution are core competitive competences which enhance the value of the brand by supporting quality and reach.

'The brand is a special intangible that in many businesses is the most important asset. This is because of the economic impact that brands have. They influence the choices of customers, employees, investors and government authorities. In a world of abundant choices, such influence is crucial for commercial success and creation of shareholder value. Even non-profit organisations have started embracing the brand as a key asset for obtaining donations, sponsorships and volunteers.' (Interbrand, 2004).

We will be looking at some of the commercial systems used to measure brand equity, later in this chapter.

If you want to pursue the concept of brand equity and brand valuation in detail for an assessment, from the supplementary reading list, you might start with:

- **Elliot & Percy *Strategic Brand Management* (2007: Oxford University Press). See Chapters 4: Brand Equity and 5: Auditing and Measuring Brand Equity.**

- **Kapferer *The New Strategic Brand Management* (4th ed: 2008: Kogan Page). See Chapter 1: Brand equity in question.** ■

1.4 Shareholder value

As we have already noted, for corporations, the primary aim of securing return on investment and enhancing brand equity through corporate reputation management is to **create and enhance shareholder value**.

In other words, reputation management activity should generate a return on the value of shareholders' investment of capital in the business, in the form of:

- **Profits**, which may be distributed to shareholders in the form of **dividends**

- **Capital growth** of shareholders' investment, through:

  - Retained profits reinvested in the business

  - The rising market value of shares (due to positive market perceptions of the company's future prospects)

  - The increasing value of reputational capital and brand assets, which increases the overall corporate value or worth.

Best Global Brands and Most Admired Companies league tables indicate that companies with strong brands and reputations outperform the market on several indices. The following table indicates the estimated contribution that consumer and corporate brands potentially make to shareholder value:

Company	Brand value 2002 ($bn)	Brand contribution to market capitalisation of parent company (%)
Coca Cola	69.6	51
Microsoft	64.1	21
IBM	51.2	39
GE	41.3	14
Intel	30.9	22
Nokia	30.0	51
Disney	29.3	68
McDonald's	26.4	71
Marlboro	24.2	20
Mercedes-Benz	21.0	47

Source: Business Week, *Interbrand/JP Morgan league table, 2002*

For more in-depth analysis, we can highly recommend a free-to-download article posted at Brand Channel on brand valuation and shareholder value (an excerpt from Brands and Branding, an Economist book):

Link: http://www.brandchannel.com/images/papers/financial_value.pdf ■

1.5 Media comment

A final measure of the success of corporate communication and reputation management success is the **amount and favourability of media coverage** or 'mentions' of the organisation or brand.

Media comment is an effective method for evaluating the effectiveness of media relations, public relations, financial relations, publicity and other corporate communications activity, in the sense that it measures how far the corporate message is getting 'out there' – and what journalists and other commentators think about the organisation: what its reputation is in the pubic domain. 'Product endorsement in the media can be worth more than its weight in gold. A good review by a fashion writer can make or break a designer. A good review in the literary section of a Sunday newspaper can make or break a new novel. The mention of a particular wine on a cookery programme on the television can see sales rocket the following day.' (Davies *et al.*, *op cit*, p. 33).

Media comment has traditionally been monitored by the publicity department of organisations, often using media monitoring (or 'cuttings') agencies, which scan the press for mentions of the organisation or brand, and prepare analysis reports. With the increasing penetration of the internet, and the explosion of community networking sites, discussion groups, message boards and 'blogs' (individual online commentary), this has become a more complex task: many more people may be 'talking about' the organisation or brand. Fortunately, the technology also supports web searches to enable the monitoring of these messages.

Why might you consider media comment/exposure to be a limited measure of reputational strength? What factors might need to be further researched and how?

1.5.1 Total media exposure: Share of Voice

KEY CONCEPT   concept

The term **'Share of Voice' (SOV)** is now often used for a brand's **total communications presence** or 'advertising weight', measured as a percentage of a defined total market or market segment in a given time period.

Communications presence may be expressed as communications expenditure, circulation or audience ratings of media, the amount of media exposure (number of pages, radio spots, posters), and the number of mentions in editorial media, online discussion boards and the 'blogosphere'. Online SOV measuring agency 'Go Global!' explains the concept and importance of online SOV as follows.

'It's the exact number of online mentions, total impressions, and percentage of impressions your brand receives when people search for and read articles about you and your competitor's products or services. Knowing it is key to understanding the effectiveness of your advertising, public relations (PR) and overall online marketing efforts in generating coverage, mindshare, and the attributes you want you target to associate with your brand. Most importantly, it's about driving awareness and sales.' (www.goglobalinteractive.com/share-of-voice).

2 Evaluating corporate identity

2.1 Measuring different identities

As we saw in our discussion of the REDS[2] AC[2]ID Test Model, in Chapter 2, there are a number of ways of auditing and evaluating the strength and potential of the corporate identity or brand.

2.1.1 Actual identity

The actual identity of the organisation (what it is really 'like') can be measured in various ways, by appraising various operational, behavioural and cultural aspects of the organisation:

- Staff attitude surveys may elicit information about how the organisation treats its people, what it is like to work for, and how employees perceive and approach their interactions with external stakeholders.

- Product and service performance, in terms of sales and market share, but also in terms of quality measurements (internal quality control measures, ratings, awards, returns/complaints record, customer feedback)

- Management style audits, via interviews with managers and feedback surveys of subordinates

- Analysis of the components of corporate culture: structure, artefacts, expressed values, underlying assumptions

- Models and measurement instruments for analysing organisational culture and climate: eg the cultural web (Johnson & Scholes), the Social Organisational Climate Index for Profit Organisations (SOCIPO), the Corporate Personality Scale (Davies *et al.*)

- Analysis of positive and negative 'critical incidents' which indicate significant underlying strengths or weaknesses.

For an interesting and influential example of organisation culture research, see the article 'Measuring organisational culture: a qualitative and quantitative study across twenty cases' in Administrative Science Quarterly (June 1990) by Hofstede, Neuijen, Ohayv and Sanders. It is available free at:

Link: http://findarticles.com/p/articles/mi_m4035/is_n2_v35/ai_8620940 ▪

2.1.2 Communicated identity

Communicated identity can be measured by:

- Compiling all the formal communications and messaging vehicles used by the organisation (financial statements and reports, web presentation, corporate advertisements, sponsorships, brochures, newsletters, press releases, managerial speeches and so on)

- Conducting **visual identity analysis**, to determine the meanings and associations conveyed by the use of designs and symbols: what does the visual content 'say' about the organisation?

- Conducting **content analysis** of verbal communications, to determine the themes and values conveyed in the use of words and stories: what does the content 'say' about the organisation? This may involve word/phrase counts, to identify the themes and expression most used (perhaps unconsciously) by the organisation: what does it mostly 'say' about itself? What attributes and values, which the organisation regards as important, are not being expressed or leveraged by its messages?

- Profiling the organisation's '**expressiveness**' (Fombrun & van Riel, 2004), in terms of:
    - Distinctiveness
    - Authenticity
    - Transparency
    - Consistency
    - Visibility and
    - Responsiveness

- Conducting periodic, comprehensive audits of the communication function in the organisation (see section 2.2 below).

2.1.3 Conceived identity

Conceived identity (or image) can be measured by various kinds of stakeholder image research, aimed at establishing:

- Which attributes are important to, or valued by, key stakeholder groups
- Which attributes key stakeholder groups perceive the organisation as possessing, and to what degree

This data may be gathered using research method such as individual depth interviews, focus groups and/or survey questionnaires. Within these method, particular tools – such as projective techniques and attitude scales – may be used to elicit stakeholder associations and opinions in regard to the organisation or corporate brand. A number of these techniques will be discussed in Chapter 7 on Developing Corporate Communications.

2.1.4 Ideal identity

The ideal identity of the organisation will be arrived at by:

- Analysing the strategic capabilities and resources of the organisation: core competences, distinguishing values and attributes, sources of competitive advantage

- Analysing the opportunities and threats represented by the organisation's macro and micro (industry, market) environments

- Determining positioning strategies by which the organisation can express its strategic capabilities and resources in such a way as to exploit opportunities and minimise threats.

This information may well be elicited by the ongoing strategic planning processes of the organisation, and periodic SWOT (strengths, weaknesses, opportunities and threats) analysis or corporate appraisal.

2.1.5 Desired identity

The organisation's desired identity can be measured by researching the vision of the CEO, directors, senior managers and other leaders. This may be elicited using tools such as:

- **Individual depth interviews** with leaders — *A P interview.*

- **Consensus profiling** (discussed in Chapter 3):

  - Individual brainstorming by the leadership team to identify attributes considered most important in the past and future development of the organisation

  - Selection of a small number of attributes on which there is consensus

  - Individual rating of these attributes

  - Compilation of responses in the form of a cobweb diagram showing actual and desired profiles

  - Group discussion of the profiles and identified 'gaps' between actual and desired profiles, bringing leaders' thinking into the open, highlighting areas of disagreement within the leadership team – and ideally arriving at a clear consensus understanding or statement of desired corporate identity.

- **Personality profiling** (discussed in Chapter 3):

  - Classifying leaders' personal observations about the organisation into core personality dimensions (needs, competences, attitude, constitution, temperament, heritage and goal orientation)

  - Mind-mapping leaders' perceptions in each core personality dimension, and the relationship between them

  - Group discussion about potential directions in which the company's identity has potential or need to develop.

In addition to measuring 'identity' overall, in its various manifestations, the organisation may seek to evaluate the strength and potential of its identity mix: communication, symbols and behaviour.

ACTIVITY 3   *The biggest charity you've never heard of!*   evaluation

If you get the opportunity, conduct an interview with a marketing manager in your organisation about its desired identity. What is the managerial vision for how the organisation wants to portray itself? → *Business Plan*

How far is this consistent with (a) the communications being transmitted to the outside world (communicated identity), (b) the image actually held by external stakeholders (conceived identity) and (c) the reality of the organisation (actual identity)? ➤ *Not communicating with outside world (other than those who are already involved with FB) → no one new knows → still a market player.*

2.2 Communication audit

Since communications are a key element of the corporate identity mix, an organisation will wish to ascertain at the outset the nature and effectiveness of its current communication activities. This will be the basis of any recommendations and plans as to initiatives or improvements.

KEY CONCEPT   concept

A **communication audit** is 'a systematic assessment, either formal or informal, of an organisation's capacity for, or performance of, essential communication practices. It determines what is working well, what is not, and what might work better if adjustments are made.' (Coffman, 2004)

A communication audit gives a 'snapshot' (at a given moment in time) of the organisation's strategies, activities and programmes. It assesses the effectiveness and credibility of current communication vehicles and media (publications, advertisements, web site, corporate intranet, face-to-face communication and so on).

Depending on its scope and thoroughness, an effective communication audit may:

- Demonstrate commitment to improving communication (which may be valued by stakeholders)
- Demonstrate willingness to listen and respond to stakeholders' views and information needs (helping to build relationship, trust and credibility)
- Build grassroots support (via consultation) and managerial support (via business case) for communication and identity management initiatives
- Elicit practical recommendations for improving communication and identity
- Form the basis for strategic integrated communication planning
- Offer efficiency gains, by indicating where communication investment can best be focused.

2.2.1 The communication audit process

Different research processes may be used, including: observations and monitoring (eg of meetings, service encounters and phone calls); analysis and evaluation of outputs (eg existing advertisements and publications); and the use of focus groups, survey questionnaires and/or interviews with employees and other key audiences.

A typical audit process would include the following steps, depending on the organisation's needs and approach: Figure 5.1.

Figure 5.1: Typical communication audit approach

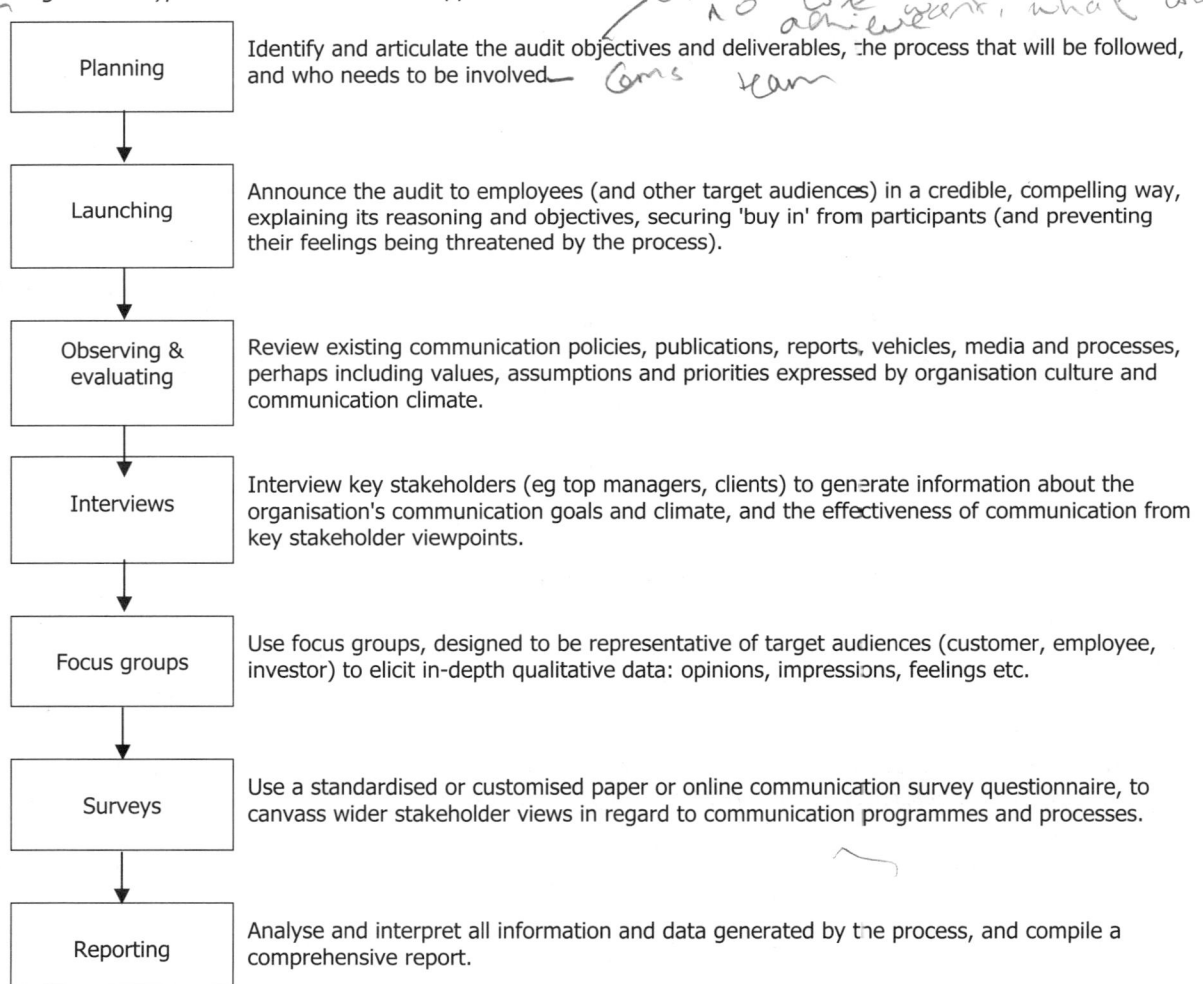

Planning	Identify and articulate the audit objectives and deliverables, the process that will be followed, and who needs to be involved.
Launching	Announce the audit to employees (and other target audiences) in a credible, compelling way, explaining its reasoning and objectives, securing 'buy in' from participants (and preventing their feelings being threatened by the process).
Observing & evaluating	Review existing communication policies, publications, reports, vehicles, media and processes, perhaps including values, assumptions and priorities expressed by organisation culture and communication climate.
Interviews	Interview key stakeholders (eg top managers, clients) to generate information about the organisation's communication goals and climate, and the effectiveness of communication from key stakeholder viewpoints.
Focus groups	Use focus groups, designed to be representative of target audiences (customer, employee, investor) to elicit in-depth qualitative data: opinions, impressions, feelings etc.
Surveys	Use a standardised or customised paper or online communication survey questionnaire, to canvass wider stakeholder views in regard to communication programmes and processes.
Reporting	Analyse and interpret all information and data generated by the process, and compile a comprehensive report.

Depending on the goals and design of the audit, evaluation of some or all of the following factors may be involved:

- Face-to-face communications: processes, effectiveness and management skills

- Information flow: patterns of communication between individuals, departments, business units

- Vehicle use and mix: appropriateness of the vehicles being used to reach different audiences

- Management/leadership communication: trustworthiness, accessibility etc

- Information accessibility: user-friendliness of processes for retrieving information at need

- Feedback-seeking systems: stakeholder surveys, focus groups, suggestion programmes etc

- Listening skills: organisational (eg environmental monitoring) and individual

- Clarity of communication content: readability, meaningfulness, alignment to corporate story and/or organisational goals and values

- Audience factors: knowledge, understanding and perception of messages; issues and concerns; needs and preferences; media consumption; relevant behaviours

- Communication costs and return on investment.

ACTIVITY 4

evaluation

Use the bullet points above to conduct a 'thumbnail' communication audit of your own organisation, brainstorming points under each heading yourself – or asking others. This is just designed to give you a preparatory feel for the process – as well as some groundwork for further analysis. If your organisation has conducted a formal communication audit, see if you can access the audit report, to compare with your own impressions.

The **audit report** output from such a process may include:

- Reports from employee (or other stakeholder) survey results

- Summary of the comments made during focus groups and interviews

- An evaluative review of existing communication climate, policies, publications and vehicles, indicating the strengths and weaknesses of each

- Recommendations for strengthening communication climate, strategies and programmes.

2.2.2 Communication audit survey instruments

There are various approaches to communications audit, at different levels of complexity.

- The organisation may simply review its existing communication activities and outputs (brochures, advertisements, sponsorships, press releases, visual identity etc) and make a more or less subjective evaluation of their **clarity** (do they express core messages and themes clearly); **consistency/coherence** (do they express broadly the same core values and themes, or, if various, do they at least avoid giving mixed or contradictory messages that would confuse a target audience?); and **impact** (do they get core themes across effectively and compellingly)?

- The organisation may review the underlying conditions in which communication is carried out in the organisation, by evaluating its **communication climate**.

- The organisation may use attitude surveys to measure the satisfaction of employees (and/or other key stakeholders) with corporate communications.

A number of standard survey instruments has been developed to audit and measure communication effectiveness (surveyed and compared by Greenbaum *et al.*, 1988), in addition to proprietary instruments developed by communication consultancies.

internal comms

Organisational communication (OC) scale **Roberts & O'Reilly (1973)**	Uses seven-point scales to measure key variables, including: • **Non-communication variables** (considered to be related to attitudes to communication): trust of subordinate for supervisor, influence of supervisor and importance of upward mobility to subordinate • **Desire for interaction** *Sample question:* How desirable do you feel it is in your organisation to be in contact frequently with others at the same job level? (Scale: not important to very important) • **Accuracy** (of information received from different sources) • **Summarisation** (of information provided to different users) • **Gatekeeping** (information received and passed on to different users) • **Overload** *Question:* Do you ever feel that you receive more information than you can efficiently use?' (Scale: never to always) • **Satisfaction** with communication in general Plus additional dimensions asking respondents to indicate what proportion of their time they spend in named communication activity: • **Directionality upward** (contact/communication with superiors) • **Directionality downward** (contact/communication with subordinates) • **Directionality lateral** (contact/communication with peers) • **Modalities of communication** (written, face-to-face, telephone and other methods used)
Communication satisfaction questionnaire (CSQ) **Downs & Hazen (1977)**	Measures employee satisfaction with corporate communication, on a range of communication variables which correlate most highly with job satisfaction, including: • **Communication climate**: how far communication motivates employees and helps them identify with organisational goals; how far attitudes to communication are generally 'healthy' • **Supervisory communication**: upward/downward contact with immediate superior (whether superior is open to ideas, listens, pays attention, offers guidance when required) • **Organisation integration**: information about the immediate work environment (plans, work requirements, personnel) • **Media quality**: eg adequacy of information, well-run meetings, clear written instructions etc • **Co-worker communication**: whether horizontal information is accurate and free-flowing, grapevine is active • **Corporate information**: about organisation-wide issues: strategy, performance, changes • **Personal feedback**: whether supervisors understand the challenge of the job and evaluate subordinates' performance fairly • **Relationships with subordinates** (where relevant): openness of subordinates to downward information, willingness to communicate upward

Communication audit survey – formerly the International Communication Association (ICA) Audit Goldhaber & Rogers (1979)	Compares the *perceived* communication environment with the *desired* situation, on aspects such as: • Information received from others • Information sent to others • Feedback received on the information sent. Survey items examine the quantity of information received/sent, the timeliness of information, the communication climate (eg trust in co-workers), communication channels used, follow-up or response to information sent to superiors; and so on. Databases of audit results are available from the International Communication Association (ICA) for inter-firm comparison and benchmarking.
Organisational Communication Audit (OCA) Questionnaire Wiio & Helsila (1974)	Uses five-point scales (from Very Little to Very Much) to measure: • Amount of information received (from ten named sources and media) • Amount of information the respondent would like to receive (from same sources and media) • Amount of information received relevant to eight categories • Amount of information the respondent would like to receive (on same eight categories) • Degree to which the respondent would like to see improvement in communication in eight dyadic/intergroup relations (plus 'somewhere else' to be specified) In addition, there are questions about: • Overall communication satisfaction and job satisfaction • The respondent's general communication behaviour • Worst communication defects in the organisation (selected from a list).
Organisational communication profile Pace & Peterson (1988)	Gathers data on eight features of organisational communication: • Organisational satisfaction • Communication climate • Information accessibility • Information load • Message fidelity (trustworthiness) • Information dispersion • Media quality • Organisational culture.

✏️ **ACTIVITY 5** ·· evaluation 🃏 `45%`

How would you characterise the differences between these instruments?

📚 *There is a large amount of detailed information about communication audit to support your studies (and guide you in conducting – or briefing an agency to conduct – an audit, if required).*

• *A summary of a range of survey instruments, with further reading references, is provided on the University of Wisconsin web site by Professor W Robert Sampson at:*
   http://www.uwec.edu/sampsow/Measures.htm

• *An interesting white paper by Julia Coffman (2004) is posted online at:*
   www.mediaevaluationproject.org/WorkingPaper1.pdf, discussing the aims and method of strategic communication audit specifically for non-profit organisations.

recommendation.

- *An example of an internal communication audit report (Executive Summary) for the University of Sheffield is posted online at:*
  http://www.shef.ac.uk/content/1/c6/03/03/10/Internal_Communication_Audit_FindingsEXEC SUMMARY.doc

If an audit-related task comes up in your assessment, a simple Google search under 'communication audit' presents a wealth of resources and contacts. ∎

2.3 Symbols audits

A symbol or graphics audit involves the inventory and evaluation of all the symbols used in an organisation (including logos, designs and the objects that carry them such as architecture, décor, vehicles and equipment), and how they are used through corporate communication to convey the visual identity of the organisation.

- How effective are corporate logos and designs in stimulating unaided recall and aided recognition in target audiences?

- What associations are built up in audiences' minds by logos, designs and other symbols? (Do positive associations need to be strengthened or negative associations reduced?)

- Do the associations built up by logos, designs and other symbols match the intended identity that the organisation is seeking to express?

- How effectively are space, architecture, décor and symbols used in all company locations and on all company artefacts (uniforms, transport fleets etc) to express the desired identity?

2.4 Behaviour audits

Assessment of organisational behaviours may involve a wider range of methods, including:

- Observation of managerial and employee behaviours (especially in interaction with other stakeholders)

- Self-assessment by managers and employees (eg diarising and assessing behaviour, or journaling of critical incidents – perhaps as part of ongoing personal development planning or self-managed learning)

- Individual and team performance appraisal reports, compiled in the course of ongoing performance measurement and management

- Individual, team and organisation-wide learning/training needs analyses and competence assessments (compiled in the course of ongoing performance management and human resource development)

- Analysis of work outputs

- Measurement of product and service quality/performance (internal quality control measures, ratings, awards, returns/complaints records, customer feedback, sales and market share measures)

- Employee and management attitude surveys and/or other instruments for measuring culture and climate

- Analysis of the components of corporate culture (eg using cultural web elements).

3 Commercial systems for measuring reputation

An organisation may undertake or commission its own customised research programmes to evaluate the effectiveness of its corporate communication activities – and we will discuss some of the methods used in Chapter 7. The advantage of this is that the criteria for measurement are tailored to the specific circumstances, target audiences and aims of the organisation. The disadvantage is that such research is *not* standardised, and is often not carried out on a periodic basis, so that the tracking of changes, and making benchmark comparisons, is difficult.

A number of commercial research programmes designed to measure corporate reputation and brand value have been developed by research firms and media organisations. The surveys and tests are conducted periodically, large databases are developed over time (so that trends and variables in corporate reputation can be analysed), and rankings and ratings can be published. Organisations can exploit the public relations and advertising value of being ranked 'No 1' on a given attribute by a highly-regarded ranking scheme (such as 'Most Trusted Brands'), award programme (such as 'Top Brands with a Conscience') or consumer rating survey (such as JD Power).

MARKETING AT WORK

application

The **Medinge Group**, an international think-tank on branding and business, annually releases a **Top Brands with a Conscience** list. The international collective of brand practitioners meets in August in Sweden to develop the list, evaluating brands on criteria including expressed values of humanity, ethics and sustainability; evidence of consideration of the human implications of the brand; whether the brand takes risks in line with its beliefs; and positive transformations being made to improve the brand's humanity, responsibility or sustainability.

'The list indicates that it is possible for corporations to maintain their goal of producing shareholder returns, while helping the planet... It also shows that there are plenty of companies operating on the cutting edge of developments. All too often, those who lead by example don't get properly exposed. We attempt to change that.'

'As more and more companies realise that they have a duty to those with whom they share our world, the Brands with a Conscience awards are not only gaining strength of entry, but also honouring those companies that genuinely care and try to give something back.'

You can find the latest list (a great source of short case studies on the impact of ethics, CSR and sustainability on brand reputation) at: http://www.medinge.org.

The syllabus mentions seven proprietary measurement systems identified by the US-based Council of PR Firms as most used by companies to assess or benchmark their corporate reputations (or product brands). We will look at each of these in turn. The choice of which system to use depends on what kinds of information managers require. Access to many of the databases are restricted to clients of the research agency or sponsor: only the Fortune 'Most Admired' scores are publically released in detail.

3.1 America's Most Admired

Compiled by *Fortune* Magazine since 1982, the annual ranking of the 'Most Admired Companies in America' (AMAC) is – as the only publically accessible source of data – the most commonly used monitoring and benchmarking system for corporate reputation. The companies evaluated are the ten largest (by revenue) from each industry.

10,000 executives, directors and securities analysts are asked to select the five companies they admire most, regardless of industry. Respondents are then asked to rank the ten largest companies in their own industry on eight Key Reputation Attributes on a scale from 0 – 10:

- Long-term investment value
- Financial soundness
- Wise use of corporate assets
- Quality of management
- Quality of products or services
- Innovativeness
- Ability to attract and retain talented people
- Social responsibility to the community and the environment

A ninth attribute (effectiveness in doing business globally) is added for global companies (with large US subsidiaries).

Despite the widespread use of these rankings in reputation research, a number of criticisms have been put forward of this survey, and the ranking method in general.

- The criteria are heavily weighted in favour of commercial performance, begging the question whether high reputation leads to good financial performance – or whether good financial performance leads to high reputation. Factor analysis shows that, with the exception of the social responsibility question, the reply to all the questions are influenced by respondents' perceptions of the financial potential of the firm (Fryxell and Wang, 1994).

- The fact that respondents are all executives and analysts further increases the bias towards commercial performance. It also means that the ranking only reflects the rated companies' image among one group of stakeholders, potentially misrepresenting the views of employees, customers and communities.

- The scope of the survey is in any case fairly narrow and restricted to large commercial organisations: the data is not useful to small companies or not-for-profits looking to determine meaningful measures on which to improve their reputation management.

Fortune also produces a ranking of the 'Top 100 companies to work for', based on employee attitude survey (evaluating factors such as trust in management, pride in work and the company, and camaraderie) and explanation by the company of its philosophy and practices (including supporting materials such as employee handbooks and company newsletters).

Other 'Most Admired' rankings are published, including Britain's Most Admired Companies (BMAC) survey, conducted since 1994 by Nottingham Business School and published by *Management Today*. The methodology is similar to the Fortune ranking, using broadly the same criteria.

MARKETING AT WORK

application

In the Britain's Most Admired Companies ranking 2008, the top ten were:

1.	2.	3.	4.	5.
DIAGEO	Johnson Matthey	Unilever	SKY	TESCO
6.	7.	8.	9.	10.
Stagecoach	Rolls-Royce	ManGroup plc	Kingspan Group plc	3i

Previous winners include: Marks & Spencer (2007); Tesco (2003, 2005, 2006); Cadbury Schweppes (2004); BP (2002); Shell Transport & Trading (2001) and GlaxoSmithKline (2000).

Link: http://bmac.managementtoday.com/BMAC_2008.htm

While you have them in front of you, critically evaluate the nomenclature (names and logos) of these ten 'most admired' corporations. How familiar and evocative are these logos? What kinds of associations (if any) do they evoke? Which would you identify as strong corporate brands?

Follow-up any of the companies you are interested in via their web sites, and evaluate their reputation management as expressed in this aspect of their corporate communication.

The consensus is that, despite their wide availability, popularity – and publicity value to high-ranked companies – these kinds of rankings cannot be relied on as a comprehensive measure of corporate reputation.

3.2 Brand Power

Specialist brand development and management consultancy CoreBrand (www.corebrand.com) offers a number of proprietary measurement tools, including:

- **Brand Power Analysis**, determining the size and quality of a company's brand compared with its peers

- **Brand Equity Valuation**, determining the value of the brand (expressed as the brand's contribution to market capitalisation)

- **Brand Return-on-Investment Analysis**, determining the sensitivity of market capitalisation or revenue to changes in communications investment.

Brand Power specifically tracks the **corporate brands** of 1,200 companies in 47 industries, using:

- Survey data measuring **familiarity** with the company (the extent to which an audience feels they know the company) and **favourability** (the percentage of those familiar with the company who are favourably disposed towards it on the basis of its management effectiveness, investment potential and overall reputation), combined into a single 'brand power' score. Familiarity indicates that corporate communication has good 'reach'. Favourability indicates how far the corporate story is effective.

- **Communications expenditure data**. Core Brand analysis suggests that advertising investment is the most significant driver of higher brand power (McNaughton, 2004).

- **Financial performance data**. Core Brand also suggests that high brand power has a positive influence on a company's share price by an average of 5–7% (*ibid*).

You have to be a registered user to access the ranking data on the CoreBrand website, but top brands in previous years have included Coca-Cola, Johnson & Johnson, UPS, FedEx, PepsiCo, Hallmark Cards, Harley Davidson, Microsoft, General Electric, IBM, Disney, Sony, Toyota and Colgate-Palmolive.

3.3 Brand Asset Valuator (BAV)

Developed by marketing agency Young & Rubicam's Brand Asset Consulting division, and available only to clients, the BAV database is based on 260 studies in 51 countries over 16 years (updated quarterly), covering almost 640,000 consumers and 42,700 brands.

The BAV model is based on four key 'pillars' that measure consumer sentiment and usage.

Core brand drivers	Pillars
Brand strength (66%) Leading indicator: future growth value	**Energised differentiation** '...is about innovation, ability to stand out in the marketplace, and pricing power. It reflects a brand's potential to create sustainable competitive advantage. It is the most important brand component in growing intangible value.'
	Relevance '... corresponds to a brand's ability to be personally meaningful. It leads to serious consideration and trial and is highly correlated to household penetration.'
Brand stature (33%) Current indicator: current operating value	**Esteem** '... measures the extent to which consumers like and respect the brand. It captures loyalty and how well a brand fulfils its promise.'
	Knowledge '... measures the level of intimacy a consumer has with the brand. Knowledge is highly correlated with top of mind awareness and brand saliency.'

Young & Rubicam claim that these four attributes are consistently linked to a brand's ability to deliver sustainable revenue and profit across different industries and regions. A brand will have greater brand strength (growth potential) if it is both differentiated and relevant. Similarly, a brand's stature will be greater when it is both esteemed and firmly planted in consumers' minds.

Brands can be plotted on a 'Power Grid', showing strength and stature: Figure 5.2.

Figure 5.2: BAV power grid

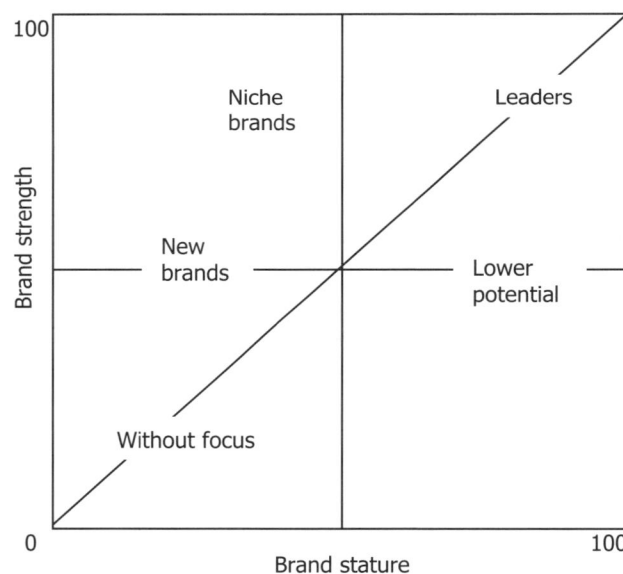

Adapted from Alhers (1996, cited in Van Riel & Fombrun, *op cit,* p. 234)

Brands tend to start out in the bottom left quadrant and move to the upper left, by increasing their strength (differentiation and relevance). The next challenge is to convert strength into stature. New brands in the upper left quadrant are potentially challengers of more established brands that rise in the top right quadrant. Over time, brands may lose strength, and move to the bottom right quadrant: they will have to be 're-energised' (injected with new differentiation and relevance).

Once a given brand is placed on the grid, researchers use Reputation Factor Analysis to identify the factors that are important for the product category, and measure the subject brand against its competitors on those factors.

The power grid has also been adapted to show estimates of contribution to value creation and profitability in each of the segments: Figure 5.3.

Figure 5.3: The power grid and intangible asset values

Intangible Value ÷ Sales

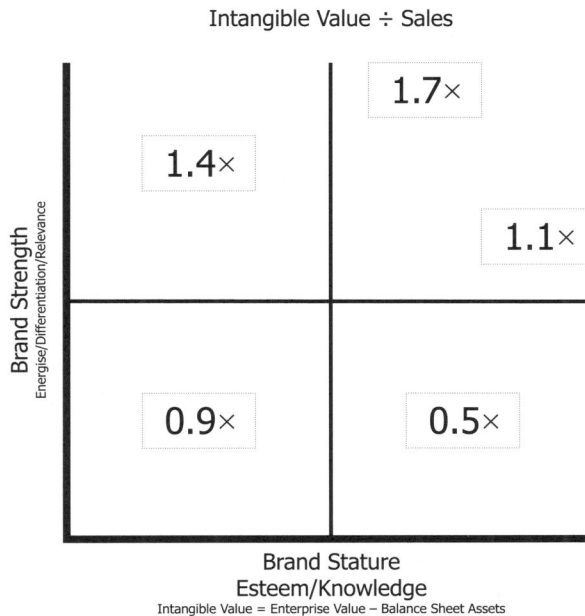

Brand Strength
Energise/Differentiation/Relevance

1.4×   1.7×

1.1×

0.9×   0.5×

Brand Stature
Esteem/Knowledge
Intangible Value = Enterprise Value – Balance Sheet Assets

Source: www.brandassetaccounting.com

The strength of the BAV is its international scope and cross-comparisons with rival brands. Its main limitation is arguably the complexity of the model, and its restricted accessibility as a proprietary tool.

If you are interested in the BAV model, it might be worth browsing the interactive information presented on the web site:

Link: http://www.brandassetconsulting.com ■

3.4 BrandZ

Commissioned by marketing communications agency WPP and published annually by research agency Millward Brown Optimor, the BrandZ Top 100 Most Valuable Global Brands ranking has been published since 2005. It is based on a large research database called BrandZ, which claims to be the world's largest brand equity study (with over one million consumers interviewed globally).

The ranking identifies the **dollar value** (brand equity) of thousands of global consumer and B2B brands, by combining financial data (from Bloomberg) and market and product data (from Datamonitor), together with consumer and B2B user research. Respondents evaluate brands in categories they actually consume: in other words, they know the category and use assessment criteria that are important to them.

The ranking is calculated using a method called '**economic use**': looking at the role that brand plays in the purchase decision, and identifying what proportion of the business value can therefore be attributed directly to the brand. The ranking also offers breakdowns by region and by category (apparel, beer, bottled water, cars, coffee, fast food, financial institutions, gaming, insurance, luxury, mobile operators, motor fuel, personal care, retail, soft drinks, spirits and technology).

BrandZ analysis (www.brandz.com) uses the concept of the Brand Dynamics Pyramid to assign survey respondents to a particular 'level' of attachment with the brand: Figure 5.4.

Figure 5.4: The Brand Dynamics Pyramid

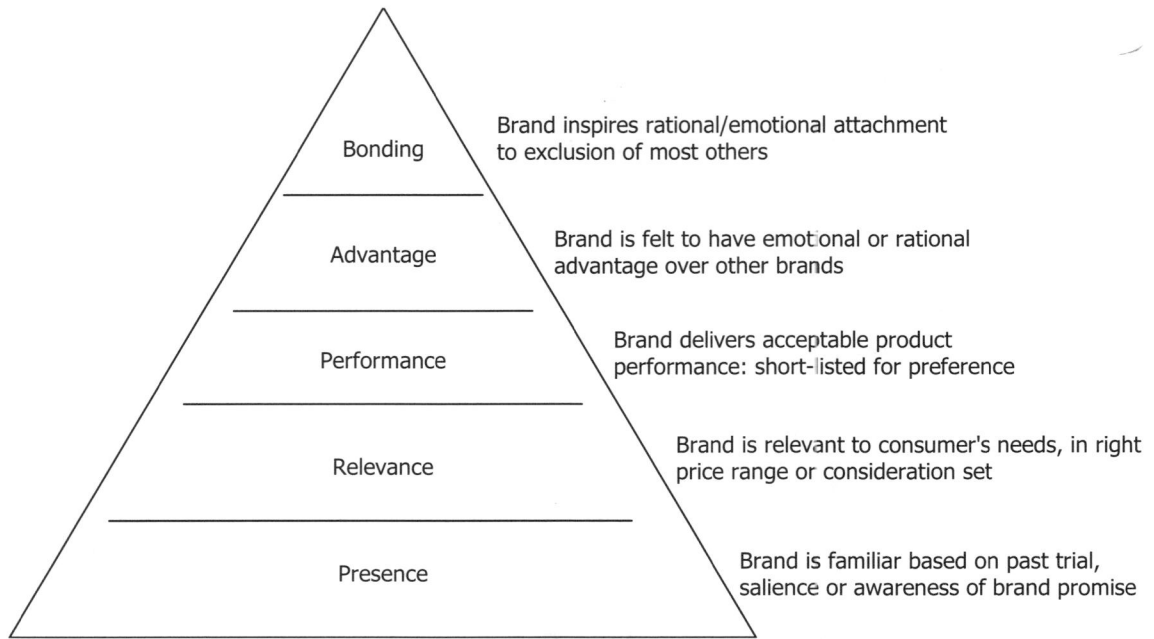

The pyramid suggests that customers' purchasing loyalty, share of spend ('share of wallet') and advocacy increases at higher levels. The relative strength or weakness of a brand, relative to other brands in its category (regardless of size) is measured by the rate at which each brand converts people from one level to the next, compared to what one would expect from the brand's size.

Every brand has a 'signature' that captures its strength (relative to what one would expect) in Presence, Relevance, Performance, Advantage and Bonding on a horizontal bar chart showing negative and positive scores on each level. Negative bars (to the left of the vertical axis) indicate that the brand converts fewer people than expected. Positive bars (to the right of the vertical axis) indicate that the brand converts more people than expected.

Brands are classified within eight typologies (the signature graphs of which can be viewed at www.brandz.com, if you are interested):

- **Clean Slate** (unknown to most consumers)
- **Little Tiger** (relatively unknown but with a strong core following)
- **Cult** (not widely known, and not for everyone, but with a fanatical core following)
- **Aspirational** (relatively well known, but not suitable for a mass audience)
- **Classic** (well known and well loved)
- **Olympic** (well known and well loved, and part of popular culture: 'a household name')
- **Defenders** (good balance of performance and price, but no real emotional/rational advantages)
- **Fading Stars** (previously well known and liked, but has lost appeal)

ACTIVITY 7

application

What risks – and attendant branding strategies – might be raised by the profile of Little Tiger or Cult brands, Aspirational brands, Classic brands and Fading Stars respectively?

Brand Voltage™ is a one-number summary of the growth potential of a brand, taking into account how many people are very loyal to the brand (its 'bonding' score) and purchasing data for the category. A brand with a positive voltage score has potential to gain share from its own marketing actions and resist the actions of competitors. A brand with a negative voltage score will have to work harder, and will be more vulnerable to the actions of other brands.

BrandZ Maps are used to plot a brand's ubiquity (presence within its category) against its voltage, to depict its overall position: the brand's growth potential given its current size in the market. Areas on the map correspond to typical brand signatures – but once you put real brand names on the map, you can compare a brand's health with benchmark brands within country and category, as well as globally and across categories.

The BrandZ published rankings provide data on:

- **Brand value**: expressed in dollars

- **Brand contribution**: a measure of the brand's contribution to business earnings, expressed as an index from 1 (low) to 10 (high)

- **Brand momentum**: a measure of forecast short-term brand growth, expressed as an index from 1 (low) to 5 (high).

MARKETING AT WORK

application

BrandZ Top 100 Brands 2009

'The value of the top 100 brands has held its value at $1.95 tn (a marginal increase of 1.7%). Google is number one with a value of $100 bn, Microsoft is number two at $76.2 bn and Coca-Cola enters the top three for the first time at $67.6 bn.'

'In the current environment, where the value of many businesses has fallen, brand has become even more important because it can help to sustain companies in tough times,' said Joanna Seddon, CEO Millward Brown Optimor. 'Those who continue to invest in their brand will be better positioned for business growth as the economic situation starts to improve than those who have cut spend.'

There are a total of 15 new brands entering the ranking this year. Pampers is the highest entrant at No. 31, followed by Nintendo (No. 32) and VISA (No. 36). Trends that can be identified from this year's rankings are:

- **Value**. Brands that represent good value for money have done well, this is about quality as much as price, for example Wal-Mart (+19%), ALDI (+49%) and Auchan (+48%). H&M (+8%) is now the number one apparel brand.

- **Vice**. People still reward themselves with little treats when money is tight. Brands such as McDonald's (+34%), Marlboro (+33%) and Budweiser (+23%) have all done well.

- **At home**. Brands that can be experienced at home have shown strong growth. This includes home shopping: Amazon (+85%) and eBay (+16%); coffee that can be prepared at home: Nespresso (+27%) and Nescafe (+23%); and gaming — Nintendo jumped into the ranking for the first time at No. 32.

- **Wireless**. The increased popularity of using the internet on the move through devices such as the iPhone and BlackBerry has led to huge increases for the mobile operators category as a whole, driven by demand for data services. Vodafone enters the top 10 for the first time this year (+45%).

Commenting on the ranking, Eileen Campbell, Global CEO of Millward Brown said:

'It is a fantastic achievement to be one of the most valuable brands in the world, and we congratulate all brands that are featured in this ranking. At a time when marketing spend is under greater scrutiny than ever, this ranking is a way for marketers to identify the value that their brand is creating for the business.'

(Press release posted at wpp.com, 29 April 2009)

Our information for this section has been drawn from www.brandz.com. If you would like to browse for more information on the model (including sample voltage scores and graphs) and current rankings, see:

- http:// www.brandz.com.

- http://www.millwardbrown.com/brandz

(And speaking of strong brands, the rankings are also available as a free iPhone application from these sites and from the iTunes store...).

3.5 EquiTrend

The annual EquiTrend tracking survey was developed by the Brand & Strategy Consulting Practice at market research firm Harris Interactive. The data is only available to Harris clients.

The study measures and compares brand equity for over 1,000 brands in 35 categories. It claims to be unique in providing a big-picture perspective: 'an understanding of a brand's widest appeal among the general population, and its status within the universe of brands at large' (www.harrisinteractive.com).

EquiTrend was designed to focus on measurements that reflect fundamental characteristics used by consumers to evaluate and compare brands on a daily basis.

- **Familiarity**: the more people know the brand, the more likely they are to buy it if they like it.

- **Quality** (perceived quality): a benchmark of consumers' general opinion about a brand (perceived as being 'upscale' or 'downscale'), correlated with brand liking, trust, pride and willingness to recommend.

- **Purchase intent**: likelihood of purchase (regardless of price) – a measure of whether the brand is perceived as relevant and appropriate to consumers' needs.

- **Brand expectations**: after consumers used the brand, did it live up to its promise and their expectations?

- **Distinctiveness**: extent to which the brand stands out or is perceived as unique.

- **Trust**: a source of brand differentiation that is enduring and resistant to the competition.

- **Equity**: a score used to rank brands overall, based on a calculation of Familiarity, Perceived Quality and Purchase intent. Research conducted on the database indicates a strong positive association between brand equity and share market returns (Aaker & Joachimsthaler, 2002).

3.6 Reputation Quotient (RQ)

Developed by Charles Fombrun and market research firm Harris Interactive, and sponsored by the Reputation Institute, the Reputation Quotient (RQ) is calculated from a list of twenty attributes representing six dimensions: Figure 5.5.

Figure 5.5: Reputation Quotient

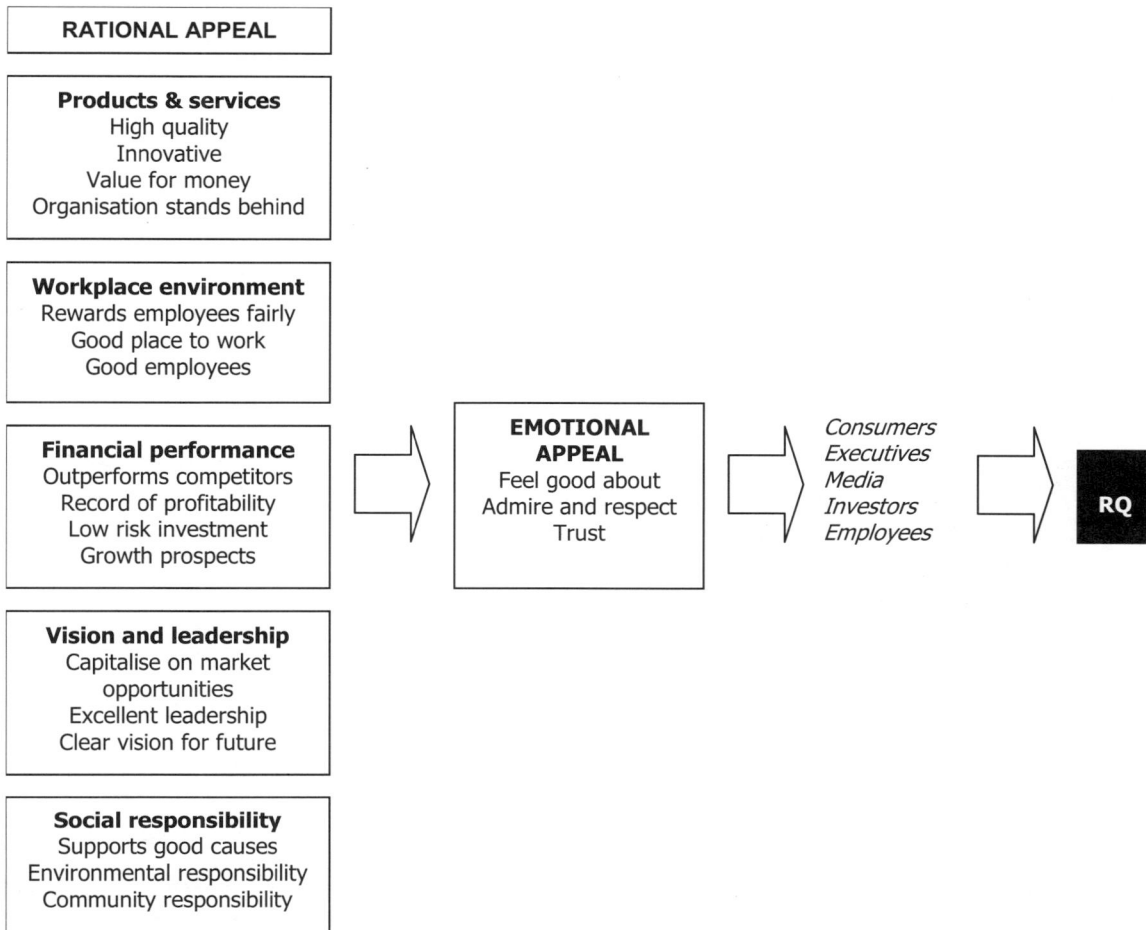

RATIONAL APPEAL

Products & services
High quality
Innovative
Value for money
Organisation stands behind

Workplace environment
Rewards employees fairly
Good place to work
Good employees

Financial performance
Outperforms competitors
Record of profitability
Low risk investment
Growth prospects

→ **EMOTIONAL APPEAL**
Feel good about
Admire and respect
Trust

→ *Consumers*
Executives
Media
Investors
Employees

→ **RQ**

Vision and leadership
Capitalise on market opportunities
Excellent leadership
Clear vision for future

Social responsibility
Supports good causes
Environmental responsibility
Community responsibility

The RQ model intentionally overcomes some of the weaknesses of the 'Most Admired' rankings, by using a broader and more multi-faceted range of criteria, and involving a wider range of stakeholders. It also examines the interrelationships between the attributes and dimensions and the overall or aggregate rating of corporate reputation, aiding research into reputation drivers. In most countries, the products and services dimension has proven the most powerful predictor of RQ, followed by social responsibility and workplace environment – reinforcing the stakeholder interpretation of reputation (van Riel & Fombrun, *op cit*).

Analyses of stakeholder responses on particular attributes can also help managers to identify leverage points for improving reputation with target audiences: some sub-groups may esteem the company more or less than others, and the company may be less favourably rated on some attributes than others – suggesting targeted communication strategies and messages to improve their reputation performance.

However, a number of statistical weaknesses were identified in the RQ model (by its originators, among others): the validity and weighting of the attributes; the relationship between the dimensions; and the validity of the scale internationally.

3.7 RepTrak®

The RepTrak® system is a successor to RQ (from 2005), building on the cumulative research on RQ, and aiming to address some of its weaknesses. It is now used as a proprietary tool by the Reputation Institute to measure the corporate reputation across stakeholders, countries and industries, with over 1,000 of the world's largest companies rated in 27 countries as part of the Global Pulse Project in 2008 (www.reputationinstitute.com). Companies can work with the Reputation Institute in customised or syndicated studies, providing analyses of corporate reputations, with comparative benchmarks and access to online analysis tools.

RepTrak® is designed to track and analyse corporation reputations using the RepTrak® Scorecard instrument, which measures 23 key performance indicators (attributes) grouped around seven core dimensions.

Dimensions	Attributes	
Products/services	High quality Value for money Stands behind Meets customer needs	**Feeling**
Innovation	Innovative First to market Adapts quickly to change	
Workplace	Rewards employees fairly Employee well-being Offers equal opportunities	**Esteem**
Governance	Open and transparent Behaves ethically Fair in the way it does business	'PULSE'
Citizenship	Environmentally responsible Supports good causes Positive influence on society	**Admire**
Leadership	Well organised Appealing leader Excellent management Clear vision for the future	
Performance	Profitable High-performing Strong growth prospects	**Trust**

Like RQ, RepTrack dimensions and attributes can be used both to analyse the factors that drive or influence reputation *and* to analyse the effectiveness of communication strategies in leveraging key reputation drivers (www.reputationinstitute.com). The outputs of RepTrak analysis specifically indicate:

- Which dimensions are the most important drivers of the company's overall reputation

- Which attributes are well leveraged by the company's media relations (eg by comparison of press releases distributed and media coverage obtained)

- Which attributes are well received by the media (ratios of favourable to unfavourable coverage).

Unlike RQ, however, the RepTrak dimensions are statistically independent of each other, reducing problems in data analysis, and strengthening conclusions about the relative impact that specific attributes and dimension have on the company's overall reputation (van Riel & Fombrun, *op cit*).

If you want to find out more about RepTrak (and other measurement and analysis tools offered by the Reputation Institute), see:

- *http://www.reputationinstitute.com/advisory-services*

For an example of a corporate analysis carried out using RepTrak, see van Riel & Fombrun (op cit) pp. 258–259. ■

Learning objectives	Covered	
1 Propose and justify the use of a portfolio of broad indicators to evaluate the strength of an organisation's reputation	☑	Return of investment: valuing corporate reputation assets; return on relationship (ROR); financial analysis of reputation management activity
	☑	Brand equity: customer-based, proprietary-based
	☑	Shareholder value
	☑	Media comment and share of voice (SOV)
2 Critically assess the strength and potential of an organisation's corporate identity and/or brand, and areas of reputational risk or challenge	☑	Measuring Actual, Communicated, Conceived, Ideal and Desired identity
	☑	Measuring the identity mix: communication audits, symbols audits, behaviour audits
3 Undertake a communication audit as a foundation for targeting communications to key stakeholder groups	☑	Communication audits: the audit process
	☑	Audit survey instruments: the organisational communication (OC) scale; communication satisfaction questionnaire (CSQ); communication audit survey (CAS) and organisation communication audit (OCA)
4 Differentiate between various commercial systems for measuring reputation	☑	America's Most Admired and Britain's Most Admired: limitations of the ranking approach
	☑	Brand Power
	☑	Brand Asset Valuator
	☑	BranZ
	☑	Equitrend
	☑	Reputation Quotient (RQ)
	☑	RepTrak ®

Quick quiz

1 Explain the assumptions behind a Return on Relationship (ROR) measurement. — *Investment client activity*

2 What are the four main elements of brand equity? — *share price*

3 Define 'Share of Voice'. *Media coverage exposure*

4 How can (a) communicated and (b) conceived identity be measured? *ROI + ROR*

5 Outline the communication audit process. *Planning, doing, collecting*

6 What variables are measured by the Communication Satisfaction Questionnaire? *Internal*

7 What are the identified limitations of the 'America's Most Admired' rankings as a measure of corporate reputation? *Only relevant to sectors*

8 What are the two core brand 'drivers' and four brand 'pillars' of the Brand Asset Valuator?

9 Explain the BrandZ 'Brand Dynamics Pyramid'. *Familarity.*

10 Identify the seven dimensions used in the RepTrak system. *Product services, innovation, workplace Governance, citizenship, leadership Performance*

1   The following are some straightforward examples of how positive identity, reputation and branding may reduce costs.

    • Productivity may rise through improved employee communications

    • The costs of disputes, absenteeism and labour turnover may be reduced by improved employee relations and identification with a strong corporate identity

    • The costs of supply may be reduced by attracting and retaining co-operative and trusting suppliers, allowing procurement discounts, cost transparency and collaborative cost reduction initiatives

    • The costs of poor public relations (eg in lost sales and reactive PR responses) may be reduced by improved pressure group, media and public relations.

2   Media comment and exposure is a limited measure of reputational strength in that it does not take into account factors such as whether a significant proportion of the organisation's target audience is actually consuming the media concerned, and whether they are noticing, understanding, being attracted to or being influenced by the views expressed. These factors may have to be further researched via recall and recognition tests ('do you recall hearing a comment that...?'), customer media analysis ('where did you hear that...?'), periodic customer (and other stakeholder) perception and attitude surveys – and, ultimately, results-based measures such as the volume of responses, enquiries and sales. The monitoring of sales may be particularly important when media coverage is known to be negative (eg in the case of crisis) and following crisis communication (since effective communication should correlate with sales recovery).

3/4 Your own research and analysis. Once again, this will offer useful preparatory groundwork for your assessment. Don't underestimate brainstorming as an important first tool for highlighting areas for further research.

5   The OC scale focuses on user attitudes and communication practices (the amount of communication etc). The CSQ focuses on employee satisfaction with organisational communication, and how it correlates with job satisfaction. The CAS focuses on identifying gaps between the actual and desired situation in regard to communication. The OCA combines several of these features, being both task-related (rating information sources and task categories) on actual versus desired performance.

6   Your own impressions. At least some of these logos should have been instantly familiar. You might, however, be less familiar with the Man Group (alternative investment management business: see www.mangroupplc.com) – and you might have associations with Rolls Royce (if you thought about cars) that have little to do with the current corporate brand (see www.rollsroyce.com).

7   The risk with Little Tiger and Cult brands is that if you market to a wider audience, you might alienate the core fans. There is a similar risk with Aspirational brands (making them less aspirational as they grow more popular): there is also a risk of pricing them too high (aspirational premium) to stimulate growth. The risk of Classic brands is that they will grow stale: the strategy will be to maintain them through constant re-investment in product and image. The risk for Fading Stars is their fading appeal: the core brand promise will have to be boosted.

1   ROR assumes: a link between customer retention and profitability; and a link between the loyalty of employees, customers and investors.

2   The main elements of brand equity are: customer-based brand equity (brand awareness and brand image); and proprietary-based brand equity (designs/patents and channel relationships).

3   Share of voice is a brand's total communication presence or advertising weight, expressed as a percentage of a defined total market or market segment in a given time period.

4   See sections 2.1.2 and 2.1.3 for a full range of points.

5   See Figure 5.1 for a full explanation.

6   The CSQ measures: communication climate; supervisory communication; organisational integration; media quality; co-worker communication; corporate information; personal feedback; and relationships with subordinates (where relevant).

7   The limitation of the ranking method is the weighting in favour of commercial performance (by attributes measured and by the nature of stakeholder respondents); limited stakeholder relevance; and narrow scope of organisations surveyed (large, commercial).

8   The elements of the Brand Asset Valuator are Brand Strength (Energised differentiation and Relevance) and Brand Stature (Esteem and Knowledge).

9   See Figure 5.4 for a full explanation.

10   The RepTrak System measures product/services, innovation, workplace, governance, citizenship, leadership and performance.

References

Aaker, D A & Joachimsthaler, E (2002) *Brand Leadership*. New York: Free Press

Coffman, J (2004) 'Strategic Communications Audits': http://www.mediaevaluationproject.org/WorkingPaper1, consulted 13 May 2009

Davies G, Chun R, Da Silva R V & Roper S (2003) *Corporate Reputation and Competitiveness*. Abingdon, Oxon: Routledge

Downs, C W & Hazen, M D (1977) 'A factor analysis study of communication satisfaction' in *Journal of Business Communication* 14(3) pp 63-64

Elliott, R & Percy, L (2007) *Strategic Brand Management*. Oxford: OUP

Fombrun, C J & Riel, C B M van (2004) *Fame and Fortune: How Successful Companies Build Winning Reputations.* Upper Saddle River, N J: Pearson Education

Goldhaber, G & Rogers, V (1979) *Auditing Organisational Communication Systems: the ICA Communication Audit.* Brown

Greenbaum H H, Clampitt, P & Willihnganz, S (1988) 'Organisational communication: an examination of four instruments' in *Management Communication Quarterly* 2 (2) pp 245-252

Gummesson, E (2002) *Total Relationship Marketing* (2nd ed) Oxford: Elsevier Butterworth Heinemann

Interbrand (2004) 'Brand Valuation', http://www.brandchannel.com/images/papers/financial_value.pdf, accessed May 2009

Jobber, D (2007) *Principles & Practice of Marketing* (5th ed) Maidenhead: McGraw Hill

Kapferer, J (2008) *The New Strategic brand Management*. (4th ed). London: Kogan Page

Keller, K L (2002) *Strategic Brand Management*. Englewood Cliffs, N J: Pearson

Pace, R W & Peterson, B D (1988) *Analysis in Human Resource Training and Organisation Development*. Reading MA: Addison-Wesley

Reichheld, F (2001) *The Loyalty Effect*. Boston, Mass: Harvard Business School Press

Riel, C B M van & Fombrun, C J (2007) *Essentials of Corporate Communication: Implementing Practices for Effective Reputation Management*. Abingdon, Oxon: Routledge

Roberts, K H & O'Reilly, C A (1973) 'Some problems in measuring organisational communication'. US Department of Commerce

Chapter 6
Corporate communication

Topic list

1   Introducing corporate communication
2   Why and when corporate communication is used
3   Identifying stakeholder audiences
4   Key messages of corporate communication
5   Ethics, CSR and sustainability

Introduction

Corporate communication is one of the key tools by which an organisation can begin to close the gap between how it *wants* to be seen and how it *is* seen by its key stakeholders: part of the process that translates corporate identity into corporate image. In this chapter, we introduce some of the key aims, target audiences and activities of corporate communication: the 'nuts and bolts' of delivering effective communications (and measuring their effectiveness) will be explored further in Chapter 7.

We start in section 1 by explaining the nature and characteristics of corporate communication, and the corporate communication 'mix': management communication, organisational communication and marketing communication.

In section 2, we assess the different reasons for using corporate communication: its aims, purposes and tasks – and some of the circumstances in which communicating effectively with internal and external stakeholders is particularly important for organisations.

In section 3, we build on your studies in *Stakeholder Marketing*, to suggest how an organisation can identify and prioritise its key stakeholders, and the communication needs of each. We briefly survey the communication programmes and activities associated with each stakeholder group: these themes will be picked up in detail in Chapters 8 to 10.

In section 4, we explore some of the key messages to be communicated to particular stakeholder groups, including 'hot' issues such as corporate ethics and corporate social responsibility – which we look at in more detail in section 5. The essence of corporate communication is, in the words of the syllabus, 'developing communication strategies designed to provide points of sustainable differentiation that are of value to stakeholders'.

As summarised in the guidance notes to this part of the syllabus, this chapter covers: 'This is corporate communication, this is why it is used and this is what can be communicated.' We will cover the final element of this formula '... and this is how we can measure its effectiveness' in Chapter 7.

Syllabus-linked learning objectives

By the end of the chapter you will be able to:

Learning objectives	Syllabus link
1 Critically appraise the nature and characteristics of corporate communication	3.1.1
2 Critically assess the different reasons for using corporate communication	3.1.2
3 Develop processes leading to the identification of key external and internal stakeholders, and understand the nature of associated communication programmes	1.2.2
4 Propose what is to be communicated to particular stakeholders	3.1.3

1 Introducing corporate communication

1.1 What is 'corporate communication'?

KEY CONCEPT   concept

Corporate communication is an umbrella term for all the ways in which an organisation 'talks to itself and to the outside world' (Franklin et al., 2009, p. 61). It is part of the process that translates corporate identity into corporate image (Fill, 2002, p 386). It is 'a management function that offers a framework for the effective co-ordination of all internal and external communication with the overall purpose of establishing and maintaining favourable reputations with stakeaholder groups upon which the organisation is dependent' (Cornelissen, 2008, p. 5).

An article in *Marketing Business* ('About face for corporate image', February, 1994: p. 5) defined corporate communication as 'the way in which an organisation projects its identity (or what it would like its identity to be) to the **outside world** via the **media**'.

We would argue that this definition is too narrow: perhaps seen through the lens of a traditional public relations department. The management of corporate reputation, as we have seen, requires that **external communication** be seen in the broadest sense, including every interaction with stakeholders (eg via personal contacts, telephone calls and e-mails) as well paid and unpaid mass media messaging. It also requires **internal communication** (to shape the perceptions, understanding and engagement of the organisation's employees with its desired identity) – which in turn shapes the **behaviour** of the organisation towards its stakeholders: another key element of the identity mix.

According to Balmer (2008), corporate communication is an answer to the question: **who do we say we are, and to whom do we say this**? 'Corporate communication relates to the various communication channels deployed by organisations to communicate with customers and other constituencies... At its most comprehensive, it also takes into account the communications effects of management, employee and product behaviour, and of word-of-mouth and media/competitor commentary.' (*ibid*, p. 51)

Cornelissen (*op cit*) notes that until the 1970s, the term 'public relations' was used to describe stakeholder communications, but that this function was largely tactical (rather than strategic) and focused on communication with the media. When other internal and external stakeholders began to demand greater transparency, the concept – and function – of corporate communication emerged, encompassing a range of specialised disciplines including corporate design, corporate advertising, internal communication, issues and crisis management, media relations, investor relations, change communication and public affairs. 'An important characteristic of the new function is that it focuses on the organisation as a whole and on the important task of how an organisation presents itself to all its key stakeholders, both internal and external...' (*ibid*, p. 5).

Three main categories of formal task-related communication are deployed by organisations in relation to their key internal and external stakeholders, and these are often described as the corporate communication mix (van Riel, 1995).

1.2 The corporate communication mix

1.2.1 Management communication

KEY CONCEPT   concept

Management communication involves communications between representatives of the managerial levels of the organisation and (internal and external) stakeholder audiences.

As you may remember from your studies in *Managing Marketing* at Level 6, communication is a key task (and skill set) of management and leadership. For example, in Mintzberg's categorisation of managerial roles (Mintzberg, 1989) each of the nine roles has a strong communication component, especially in the manager's role as:

- Figurehead (representing the organisation to external audiences)

- Leader (directing and motivating team members)

- Liaison (making contacts outside the vertical chain of command, for cross-functional co-ordination and 'horizontal' flow of work and information)

- Monitoring (networking and information gathering to support strategic decision-making)

- Spokesperson (providing information on behalf of the organisation or business unit to interested internal and external parties)

- Disseminator (conveying relevant information to team members) *- internal / external*

- Negotiator (harmonising different interests and goals). *- internal*

ACTIVITY 1   *- sharing, guidance, communicating, integrating   common goal*   concept

Looking at Mintzberg's managerial roles, what can you see to be the importance of managerial communication (a) to internal stakeholder audiences and (b) to external stakeholder audiences?

Members of senior management have a key communicational (and symbolic) role as figureheads to both internal and external audiences. Think of the publicity, image and reputational value of a highly visible CEO such as Richard Branson, say. Think of the difference made in a public relations or internal crisis if the CEO makes a strong personal statement, or personal appearance to address affected stakeholders.

van Riel & Fombrun (2007, p. 16) argue that communication is too important to be left solely to managerial discretion, so that communications specialists are needed to support management communication: 'preparing the ground' by increasing the engagement and positive perceptions of internal and external stakeholder audiences, through organisational and marketing communication.

MARKETING AT WORK   application

If evidence were needed that CEO communications are highly influential (or that reputation can be lost through an unfortunate single incident or word), consider the notorious case of **Gerald Ratner**.

When the successful jewellery retailer gave a speech to the Institute of Directors in 1991, he added a self-deprecating joke about being able to sell his product for such a low price 'because it's total crap'.

The joke was appreciated by the business people in the audience – and by the tabloid press, who picked it up (and set a rather different agenda) with headlines such as: 'You 22 carat mugs'. The share price rose, as investors appeared to appreciate the CEO's pragmatism.

Unfortunately, customers didn't find the joke very funny. Sales volumes collapsed, recent purchases were returned – and when recession hit, the business had no consumer loyalty to fall back on... Ratner himself did not last long...

Start collecting examples from the media – and your own organisation – of CEO statements which (a) cause problems for the organisation, and (b) show strong vision and leadership (especially in crisis situations). You might also include in this category speeches by church leaders and political figureheads.

1.2.2 Marketing communication

Marketing communication (as, again, you should be aware from your earlier marketing studies) is what used to be called 'promotion' or customer communication. While concepts such as relationship marketing have emphasised the range of internal and external constituency audiences (or markets) with whom beneficial relationships can be built through communication (eg the Six Markets Model: Peck *et al.*, 2003), marketing communication consists primarily of messages sent to potential customer and/or intermediary audiences, supporting the promotion and sale of products, services and brands.

The marketing communication (or promotional) mix consists of tools such as:

- **Personal selling** (particularly for B2B and high-involvement purchases)

- 'Above the line' promotional activity: advertising placed in paid-for media such as the print media, radio, TV, cinema and outdoor/transport poster sites. (The 'line' is the one in advertising agency accounts, above which are shown its earnings on a commission basis, from the buying of media space for clients.)

- **'Below the line'** promotional activity: a blanket term for a range of non-commissionable marketing communication activities. (Agencies' earnings on a fee basis are shown below the 'line' in their accounts.) More specifically, it refers to activities such as direct marketing, sales promotions, sponsorship, exhibitions and trade shows, and marketing-oriented public relations activity (eg publicity).

These kinds of activity occupy by far the largest share of most organisations' communication budgets and efforts, and you should be familiar with them through your studies in *Delivering Customer Value through Marketing* at Level 6. We will survey some of the main tools of corporate marketing communication in Chapter 7, and go on to consider their application in Chapter 8.

1.2.3 Organisational communication

KEY CONCEPT

concept

Organisational communication is communication on behalf of the organisation as whole. It includes activities such as corporate advertising and sponsorship, corporate public relations, public affairs (government relations), investor relations, community relations, corporate philanthropy (charitable contribution), environmental and CSR communication, and employee communications.

Organisational communication is distinguished from marketing communication in two main ways.

- It is aimed at **corporate audiences**, such as shareholders, the financial media and market analysts, regulators and government bodies, employees, pressure and interest groups, and the community as a whole. (This often leads to a more measured and formal communication style than marketing communications.)

- It has a **long-term perspective**, with the aim of enhancing organisational image, influence, relationships and strategic positioning – rather than merely generating sales.

Grunig (1992) also argues that, unlike marketing communication (in which the organisation chooses its target audiences and what it will say to them), organisational communication is to a large extent initiated by **demand** for information from external stakeholders.

Organisational communication may be the responsibility of a public relations, external affairs or public affairs department. In contrast to the marketing communication mix, however, which is generally the responsibility of a marketing director, there has been increasing specialisation and fragmentation of the organisational communication mix: when a need arises for a particular functional area to address specific stakeholders, a new communication department is introduced. This creates the risk of inconsistent and incoherent messages; lack of strategic integration; and failure to link communications activities to common outcome measures, which may make it difficult to resolve turf wars between specialist units.

ACTIVITY 2

application

How is organisational communication activity structured in your own organisation, or the organisation that may form the focus of your assessment? Locate or draw an organisation chart showing the lines of responsibility and communication which link the different units responsible for communication with various stakeholder groups.

How (if at all) is the activity of different communicating units co-ordinated or integrated? How (if at all) does the organisation ensure that they 'talk to each other' about campaigns and messages?

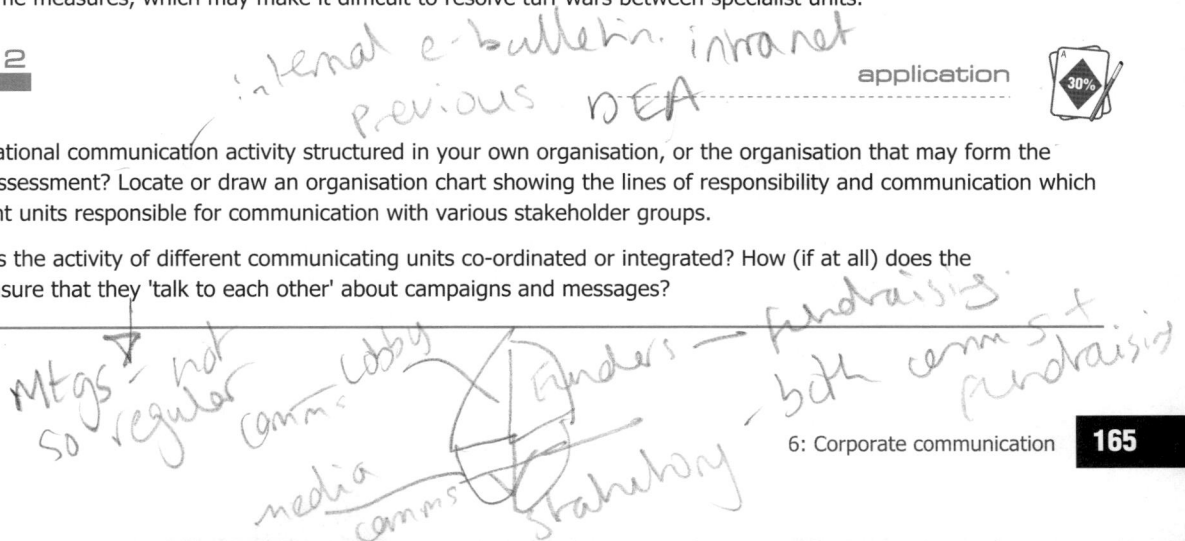

We will look at organisational communication, as it is applied to key stakeholder audiences, in Chapters 8 (media and community), 9 (investors and government), 10 (employees) and 11 (pressure and interest groups).

1.2.4 Integrated corporate communication

'Corporate communication' thus encompasses all three elements of the mix: management, marketing and organisational communication.

'By 'corporate communication', we mean a **coherent approach** to the development of communications in organisations, one that communication specialists can adopt to streamline their own communications activity by working from a centrally-co-ordinated strategic framework. Corporate communication adopts a 'corporate' point of view. Derived from the Latin *corpus*, meaning 'body' or 'the whole', it invites the communication specialist to focus, first and foremost, on the problems of the organisation as a whole. Corporate communication therefore addresses the fulfilment of organisational objectives.' (van Riel & Fombrun, 2007, p. 22)

One of the reasons for the formation of the Reputation Institute (RI) in 1999 was to foster integration and synergy across the various disciplines of corporate communication. A corporate communication perspective is associated with integrated communication policies, corporate image campaigns and corporate branding.

Strategy guru Grant (1996) suggests that four basic mechanisms can be used to integrate knowledge resources which are dispersed in separate functional areas of an organisation. These can be applied to the integration of different communication specialisms, in order to support integrated corporate communication, as follows.

- **Rules and directives**: procedures, rules, guidelines, standardised information and communication systems. These can be used to harmonise expressions of the organisation, eg via: visual identity and house style documents; shared content briefs (eg corporate story statement, corporate brand fingerprint document, or other statements of agreed 'starting points' for communication); guidelines for the briefing of external agencies; clear allocation of task and budget responsibilities.

- **Sequencing or process design**: organising and documenting business processes so that specialist input can be gathered, fed in and linked in a logical and integrated way (eg in planning and implementing corporate communication campaigns, or in gathering multi-functional input to communication strategy formulation).

- **Organisational routines**: establishing and reinforcing (eg by documentation, education, training and coaching) routines or 'protocols' for handling a range of situations. In a communications context, these may include protocols for: making media contacts and issuing media releases; campaign planning, authorisation and implementation; investor reports; issues management; crisis communication and so on.

- **Group problem-solving**: establishing mechanisms for formal and informal cross-disciplinary communication and collaboration. In a communication setting, this may mean: the use of a steering committee (or 'image group' or 'brand committee') to co-ordinate activity and formulate communication policy; periodic or *ad hoc* brainstorming, planning, review or problem-solving meetings; the use of cross-disciplinary teams for issues management and crisis communication.

The structuring of the corporate communications function (with an emphasis on integration and strategic-level involvement) is an important issue, although it is not explicitly mentioned in the syllabus. If integration, status or budgetary issues are relevant to your organisation, or raised by assessment tasks, you might like to look at:

- *Van Riel & Fombrun, Essentials of Corporate Communication: Chapter 11 'Organising Corporate Communication'.*

- *Joep Cornelissen, Corporate Communication: A guide to theory and practice (2nd edition, 2008: Sage), Chapter 6: The organisation of corporate communication. The introductory Chapters 1 (Introduction to corporate communication) and 2 (Corporate communication in historical perspective) are also very accessible. (Note that the title of this book is cited inaccurately in some versions of the CIM recommended reading list.)*

1.3 Corporate communications and identity management

Marwick & Fill (1997) have developed an integrated framework for understanding the link between the corporate identity management process (personality, identity and image: Abratt & Shee, 1989) and the corporate communications mix (management, marketing and organisational communication: van Riel, 1995). Their **Corporate Identity Management Process (CIMP)** model, which draws together a range of the models discussed in this Study Text so far, can be illustrated as follows: Figure 6.1.

Figure 6.1: The corporate identity management process

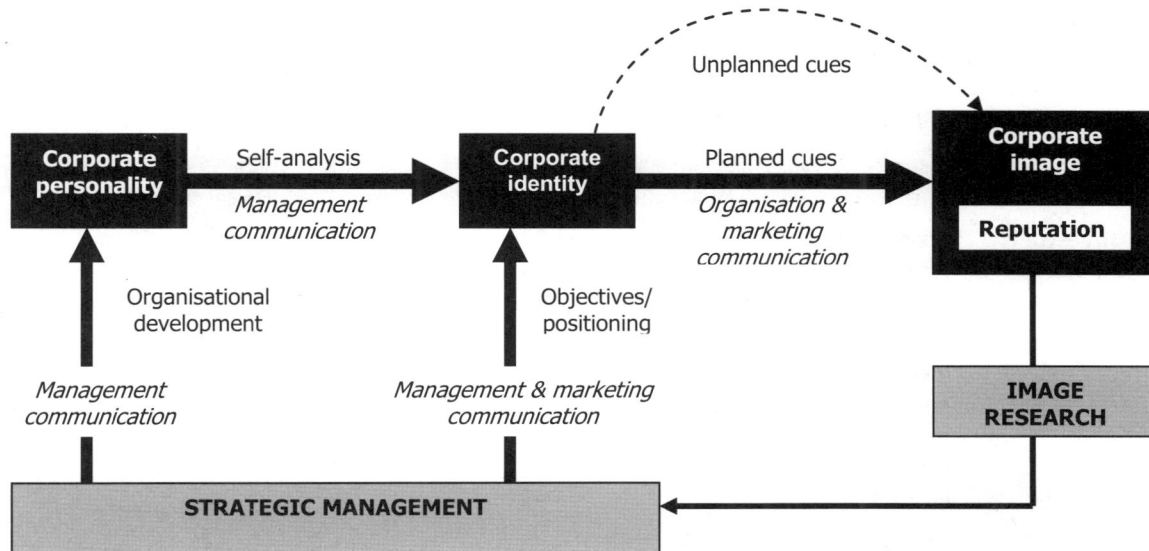

Adapted from Fill (2002, p. 298)

- Managers and corporate identity specialists analyse and interpret the corporate personality (using management corporation) to arrive at a desired – and ideally, realistic – corporate identity and/or brand.

- The organisation projects its desired identity and/or brand (using marketing and organisational communication) to stakeholders, to form a corporate image. These corporate identity cues will involve both planned communications and unplanned communications (eg media and 'blogosphere' comment, product failures, word-of-mouth) – across the whole identity mix.

- The organisation monitors or periodically audits the perceptions of different stakeholder audiences over time, providing feedback for corporate strategy formation. In order to improve its image and positioning, organisation may need to adjust:

  - Its personality, via organisational change and development (mediated through management communication)

  - Its identity, articulating a different identity mix or brand positioning objectives (mediated through management and marketing communications).

1.4 Principle activities of corporate communication

The principle activities of corporate communication include:

- Internal communications
- Investor relations
- Marketing communications
- Public affairs
- Issues management

We will give a very brief overview of these activities, here, as an orientation to the scope of corporate communication and its target audiences. Each will be focused on in detail in Chapters 8 to 11 of this Study Text.

Activity	Key audience(s)	Main strategic task(s)	Main mechanisms
Internal communication	*Employees* Need to be motivated, involved, empowered, equipped and informed to perform tasks at a high level. Key interface with external stakeholders, at organisational 'touch points': providing external identity cues. Key source of internal communication and word-of-mouth image formation.	Formulating direction and policy re the style, channels and methods of employee communication. Establishing KPIs and measuring communication success.	In-house magazines and employee newsletters Formal employee communication networks and feedback channels Recruitment exhibitions/conferences Speech writing and briefings for executives Company notice boards and intranet site Corporate conferences and briefings ~ *national seminar* House style guidelines
Investor relations	*Shareholders/investors* *Financial analysts* *Financial media* *Annual review* Shareholders need info to maintain confidence. Analysts/media need up-to-date info to advise and inform shareholders and investments. Important in: ensuring that organisational performance and potential is reflected in share price; maintaining confidence and share value; shaping reputation.	Formulating direction and policy re the style, content, channels and frequency of investor communication. Establishing KPIs and measuring communication success.	Financial media relations (press releases, press conferences) Design of annual/interim financial and social reports CEO speeches and web cast statements Investor areas of web site Visits by analysts, brokers and large shareholders Shareholder meetings Informal briefings/discussions with analysts Standard investor relations presentations Added value 'partner' benefit schemes for shareholders
Marketing communication	*Consumer, B2B and intermediary customers* *Public and local community (potential customers)* Key source of corporate licence to operate, profitability, performance. Potential to support or resist strategic plans. Key influence on image and reputation via word-of-mouth (C2C) communication. Key source of feedback on success of corporate communication mix.	Formulating direction and policy re positioning of product/brand and corporate brand communication. Establishing KPIs and measuring communication success.	Consumer/trade press releases and review samples Media relations Marketing publicity Product/service literature Produce placement (TV etc) Events (eg launches) Consumer/trade exhibitions and shows Magazines or newsletters Sponsorships Corporate hospitality Briefing and managing advertising/promotion agencies

Activity	Key audience(s)	Main strategic task(s)	Main mechanisms
Government relations or **Public affairs**	*Local and national government bodies* *Legislators/policy-makers* *Regulatory bodies* *Lobby groups* Local authorities need info re strategic intentions. Regulators need info re compliance. Influencing market is important in securing policy support for business.	Formulating direction and policy for government relations. Determining objectives and responsibilities. Establishing KPIs and measuring communication success.	Corporate literature Issues tracking/management Local/central government lobbying Industrial (trade/professional) lobbying Monitoring of compliance Media relations Site visits and corporate hospitality Writing speeches Briefing/advising top management Commissioning research Informal briefings/discussions with legislators, representatives
Public relations **Media relations** **Issues management**	*General public* *Media* *Any or all stakeholder audiences, depending on the issue arising* Potential to support or resist strategic plans. Media 'mediate' much corporate communication. Media depend on info for own audiences: potential for (+ve/-ve) publicity. Key influence on image and reputation via word-of-mouth communication (public) and agenda setting (media).	Formulating plans for identification and monitoring of stakeholder sensitivities and potential issues. Formulating policies and contingency plans for handling issues arising. Determining responsibilities for issues and crisis management. Developing KPIs and measuring communication success.	Discussion/research to determine stakeholder issues Risk analysis and contingency planning Media relations (press releases, relationships with journalists, agenda setting) Dialogue with pressure groups Monitoring media coverage and issues development Writing speeches Community involvement, fundraising

2   Why and when corporate communication is used

2.1 Aims and purposes of corporate communications

Some of the key purposes of corporate communication are:

- To give substance and transparency to the profile of the 'company behind the product or brand' (in other words, corporate identity and/or branding)

- To communicate corporate identity and brand features in a way that actively supports the projection of the organisation's ideal or desired identity

- To mobilise internal and external support for the organisation's mission and strategic objectives

- To manage risk to the organisation's licence to operate and/or particular strategic plans, which may arise from withdrawal of internal/external support as a result of issues or crises impacting on the organisation's image and reputation.

Grunig & Hunt (1984) put forward an influential model to describe the diversity of audiences, circumstances, objectives and relationship styles in what they called 'public relations' (referring to the various 'publics' or stakeholder audiences of the organisation). The model classifies corporate communication approaches according to whether they are:

- **One-way or two-way**: information transfer or information exchange

- **Symmetrical or asymmetrical**: whether power is evenly or unevenly distributed between the organisation and its stakeholders, and therefore the extent to which the organisation is prepared or forced to reveal the complete and accurate truth about its operations and objectives.

The four perspectives on communication which result can be mapped as follows: Figure 6.2.

Figure 6.2: Four visions of communication

Truth important	Public information	Two-way symmetrical communication
Complete truth not essential	Press Agentry (publicity)	Two-way asymmetrical communication
	One-way communication	*Two-way communication*

- In the **Press Agentry/Publicity** model, the purpose of communication is **propaganda**: spreading the organisation's position, through incomplete, half-true or distorted information if necessary. Communication is one-way: essentially, the organisation only gives stakeholders the information it wants them to hear. This is common in sports, theatre and product promotion.

- In the **Public Information** model, the purpose of communication is <u>**dissemination of information**</u>. 'The public relations person functions essentially as a journalist in residence, whose job it is to report objectively information about his [*sic*] organisation to the public' (*ibid*). Communication is still one-way, but because of the balance of power, truth is important: the organisation feels obliged to present a complete and accurate picture of their operations and intentions. This is common in government, not-for-profit and business communications. A specific example might be instructions given to employees about health and safety procedures, say.

- In the **Two-way Asymmetric model**, the purpose of communication is **scientific persuasion**, using social science theory and stakeholder attitude research to attempt to persuade audiences to accept the organisation's point of view and to behave in a way that supports its aims. Communication is two-way (allowing feedback from the audience), but the flow is asymmetric (imbalanced in its effects) because the feedback is used to improve the effectiveness of further outgoing communication, rather than to respond to the issues raised: audiences are not expected to raise arguments that could change the message. This is common in competitive business and PR agencies. A specific example might be the use of scientific research to endorse product benefits, say.

- In the **Two-way Symmetric** model (Grunig & Hunt's ideal type of communication), the purpose of communication is to mediate between the organisation and its publics with the aim of facilitating **mutual understanding**. Communication is two-way (dialogue) and symmetrical (balanced in its effects) because both parties are open and truthful in stating their positions and stakeholders are as likely to persuade the organisation to change its attitude as *vice versa*. This is common in regulated businesses and more enlightened PR agencies. A specific example might be a company dialoguing with pressure groups with a view to mutual endorsement, say.

ACTIVITY 3

evaluation

The following press release (excerpted) was posted on the News Room area of the **Merck & Co** web site (www.merck.com/newsroom/press_releases):

Merck Statement in Response to the FDA's Update Regarding a Safety Review of SINGULAIR® (montelukast)

WHITEHOUSE STATION, N.J., Jan. 13, 2009 – Merck & Co., Inc. issued the following statement in response to the U.S. Food & Drug Administration's (FDA's) update on its safety review of SINGULAIR® (montelukast).

Merck stands by the proven efficacy and safety of SINGULAIR, a medicine that has been prescribed to tens of millions of patients with asthma and allergic rhinitis for more than ten years. Nothing is more important to Merck than the safety of its medicines and vaccines.

Since distribution of the 'FDA Early Communication of an Ongoing Safety Review of Montelukast' on March 27, 2008, the FDA requested that Merck conduct additional evaluations of the data from clinical trials of SINGULAIR for reports of behaviour and mood changes, and for reports of suicidality and suicide. Merck has submitted the information requested by the Agency and is preparing to publish the data in a peer-reviewed medical journal.

Merck also continually reviews post-marketing reports as part of its ongoing commitment to monitor the safety profile of its medications.

After a thorough review of the data from the controlled clinical trials of SINGULAIR, and a careful assessment of post-marketing adverse events, Merck believes that the data support the continued use of SINGULAIR in appropriate patients with asthma and allergic rhinitis.

What model/purpose of corporate communication does this reflect? *Scientific Persuasion*

2.2 Tasks of corporate communications

Like any type of communication, corporate communication may fulfil different functions, depending on the target audience, context and the aims of the organisation. In practice, a given corporate communication programme is likely to be a mix or hybrid of various communication styles: informational, information-seeking, persuasive, relational and so on.

2.2.1 Informing

In some contexts, the role of communication will be primarily to convey or exchange information, to meet the information needs or demands of a given stakeholder group. For example:

- Employees require information about policies, plans and targets, and feedback on performance results, in order to conduct their work.

- Customers require information to support the purchase decision, and this is a key feature of marketing communications for high-involvement purchases, for which consumers seek strong informational support.

- Investors are legally entitled to information about the financial position and future prospects of the company.

- Government and regulatory bodies are likewise entitled to certain reports and returns, for the calculation of corporate tax liabilities, for the monitoring and regulation of corporate activities and for the preparation of statistics on health and safety, equal opportunity and so on.

- The media requires information (in the form of media releases) in order to be aware of, and follow-up on, newsworthy events.

More generally, there has been an increase in pressure for organisations to be more accountable and transparent about their ownership, objectives, policies and performance, particularly in areas touching corporate governance and corporate social responsibility. All stakeholder groups want to know more about 'the company behind the brand'.

While some corporate information will be purely objective (facts and statistics), some will be more subjective (opinions and beliefs) and emotion- or value-laden in its expression. We will discuss the rational and emotional bases of audience engagement in later chapters.

The following press release from toymaker Mattel Inc (excerpted) was posted at http://investor.shareholder.com/mattel:

Mattel Named Among the 2009 'World's Most Ethical Companies'

Company Recognised for Ongoing Commitment to Social, Environmental and Governance Leadership

EL SEGUNDO, Calif., Apr 15, 2009 (BUSINESS WIRE) -- Mattel, Inc. (NYSE: MAT) announced today it has been named one of the 'World's Most Ethical Companies' in 2009 by the Ethisphere Institute. The selection process included a rigorous, multi-step evaluation process that reviewed the ethical and legal performance of more than 10,000 global companies from more than 100 countries and 35 industries, from which 99 were recognised.

'At Mattel, playing fair is one of our company's core values and the cornerstone of our ethical compliance program,' said Robert A. Eckert, chairman and chief executive officer of Mattel. 'We know that how we achieve success is just as important as the success itself, and this recognition underscores our commitment to conduct our business with the highest level of integrity.'

Earlier this year, Mattel also was recognised among Fortune Magazine's '100 Best Companies to Work For,' ranking at #48, as well as CRO Magazine's '100 Best Corporate Citizens,' ranking at #7. Mattel joins honorees such as Nike, Toyota, Target, HP, Best Buy, McDonalds and Starbucks on Ethisphere's 2009 honor roll.

'Mattel has proven to be one of the world leaders in upholding high ethical standards, making it a true standout in its industry,' said Alex Brigham, executive director of the Ethisphere Institute. 'The competition for this year's World's Most Ethical Companies was very strong and we applaud Mattel for rising to the top.'

The methodology for the World's Most Ethical ranking includes reviewing codes of ethics, litigation and regulatory infraction histories; evaluating the investment in innovation and sustainable business practices; looking at activities designed to improve corporate citizenship; studying nominations from senior executives, industry peers, suppliers and customers; and working with consumer action groups for feedback. The 2009 World's Most Ethical Companies methodology committee, comprised of leading attorneys, government officials, professors and organisation leaders, were consulted early on in the 2009 WME process and had the opportunity to review and comment on the methodology used to rate this year's nominees. Ethisphere researchers further analyse information provided by the companies through questionnaires.

To view the complete list of the 2009 World's Most Ethical Companies, visit: http://ethisphere.com/wme2009

2.2.2 Exploring

Corporate communication is <u>designed to elicit information</u>, ideas and feedback from (or in co-operation with) stakeholders, as well as a 'one-way' informing process. Communication programmes may be designed to:

- Elicit the views and perceptions of stakeholder audiences, eg via customer research and feedback-seeking, supplier/intermediary feedback surveys, employee attitude surveys, stakeholder general meetings and so on.

- Co-opt key stakeholders in exploring ideas or issues of potential risk or opportunity for the organisation, eg via employee or customer suggestion schemes, issues management, consultation with pressure and interest groups.

- Co-opt key stakeholders to joint problem-solving or conflict resolution initiatives, designed to generate better problem/need definitions and more solution options – with the potential to move towards a 'win-win' or mutually satisfying solution. This may be the case in negotiations with business allies, pressure groups, government agencies or employee representatives, for example.

2.2.3 Influencing

Influencing is the process of applying some form of pressure in order to change stakeholders' attitudes or behaviours: to secure their compliance (with requests), obedience (to instructions), conformity (to norms or expectations) or commitment (to a shared vision or initiative).

Persuasive corporate communication is designed to achieve understanding between the organisation and its stakeholders, or to influence stakeholder audiences to share, adopt or engage with the organisation's goals or perspectives on an issue. As part of corporate reputation management, the organisation is always seeking to influence audience perceptions of itself and its products and services. There may also be more specific influencing tasks, such as:

- Motivating employees or gaining their co-operation for strategic change

- Persuading consumers to trial or support the organisation's products (particularly following crisis such as a product safety recall, say)

- Persuading legislators and government agencies (eg through lobbying) to support policies favourable to the organisation's interests

- Persuading shareholders to support the plans of the board of directors

- Persuading local community members and activists to support (or not resist) the plans of the organisation which may impact on the community or environment.

2.2.4 Relating

Communication is the basis of relationship. The emerging discipline of **relationship management** places a high emphasis on the frequency and quality of contact with customers and other key stakeholder groups, in order to develop continually deepening relationship, engagement and commitment/loyalty.

- **Multiple on-going communications**, from multiple (co-ordinated) sources and touch-points within the organisation (eg in the case of customers, sales or direct marketing, customer research and feedback-seeking, customer service, after-sales service, the web site, loyalty programmes, newsletter, product up-dates, maintenance reminders, invitations to events, notification of special offers – and so on).

- **Two-way dialogue**: not just marketing messages (eg business-to-customer or B2B) but customer-to-business (C2B) and customer-to-customer (C2C) communication – and their equivalents for other stakeholder groups.

- **Personalised and customised contacts**, where possible: making stakeholders feel recognised and valued, and that their particular needs and concerns are being taken into account.

Relationship marketing models emphasise the importance of forming mutually beneficial relationships with a range of stakeholder audiences: employees; investors; the 'influencing market' of government, media and pressure groups; suppliers; customers and intermediaries; and potential business allies and partners. All require strong communication links.

ACTIVITY 4   application

What tools and mechanisms might an organisation use to establish C2B and C2C communication about the organisation?

2.2.5 Negotiating

KEY CONCEPT   concept

Negotiation is a form of mutual influencing: a process whereby two parties come together to confer, in a situation in which there is some conflict of interests between them, with a view to concluding a jointly acceptable agreement.

Gennard & Judge (2003) describe the negotiation process as one of:

- Purposeful persuasion: whereby each party tries to persuade the other to accept its case or see its viewpoint

- Constructive compromise: whereby both parties accept the need to move closer to each other's position, identifying the areas of common ground, where there is room for concessions to be made.

Negotiation can be seen as a problem-solving technique in stakeholder relations, enabling parties to meet their own needs (as far as possible) in a conflict of interests, without damaging ongoing relations between them. This will be an important communication tool in the management of workforces and teams (eg negotiations on productivity, pay and conditions with employee representatives) as well as in the formulation of commercial contracts (eg B2B sales and purchase contracts), and other stakeholder agreements (eg alliances, co-promotions, sponsorships or causal marketing associations) and conflict resolution settings (eg problem-solving negotiations with community groups negatively affected by corporate plans, or with large institutional shareholders).

2.3 Stimulating change

The objectives of corporate communication are often defined as stimulating change in one or more of three areas: **knowledge**, **attitude** and **behaviour**: KAB. According to the '**domino effect**' model (Grunig & Hunt, 1984), change in behaviour is generated by: creating an effective message (message); getting the target audience to pay attention to the informational content of the message (knowledge); getting them to respond favourably to what they know (attitude); and hence getting them to adopt a supportive behaviour, such as purchase, investment or compliance (behaviour).

Behavioural models of consumer decision-making such as the AIDA model or the buyer readiness model (Lavidge & Steiner, 1961) often portray a sequential link between cognition (thinking), affect (feeling) and conation (will to action), but the relationship between the phases is not so clear cut.

In employee motivation, for example, it is often possible to influence employees to change their behaviour (eg via rules, sanctions or incentives) before they have in-depth understanding of the need to change, or positive perceptions about it. Having changed their behaviour, however, they may experience cognitive dissonance or discomfort because their behaviour is now 'out of line' with their knowledge and/or attitudes: they will be motivated to reduce this dissonance by seeking information which confirms or validates their decision to change their behaviour, and by changing their attitude to the issue. Similar dynamics can be seen in consumer purchase decisions. Studies show that some customers only become aware of key features of a product after product trial or purchase (change of behaviour): they subsequently seek out information about the product, to confirm the validity of their choice.

Different communication approaches might therefore be used, according to the organisation's assumptions about the extent to which knowledge (focus on informational communication) needs to precede attitude change (persuasive and/or emotional communication) and/or behavioural change (incentives or coercion to act).

2.4 Circumstances requiring corporate communications

Corporate communication is therefore, in the widest sense, about the management of an organisation's image and reputation with its publics or stakeholder constituencies. However, there are a number of circumstances in which corporate communication campaigns are likely to be particularly important.

2.4.1 Periodic reporting

An organisation may have a number of periodic reporting responsibilities to key stakeholder groups, requiring the preparation of corporate communications. Examples include: the preparation of statistical reports and returns required by government agencies (eg equal opportunities reports, health and safety reports); the preparation of statutory financial statements and corporate reports for shareholders and the public (eg the annual report and accounts and Annual General Meetings of shareholders); the issuing of financial forecasts to the financial community (eg profit and dividend forecasts); and periodic consultations with employee representatives to discuss issues of concern.

MARKETING AT WORK

application

Increasingly, the stakeholders of **charities** are being given rights to be consulted, and trustees must report on contacts with stakeholders. Recently, the Charity Commission in the UK emphasised that trustees must state whether they have consulted stakeholders (major funders, members, beneficiaries and donors), specifically about payments to trustees. They must also disclose the results of the consultation.

BPP
LEARNING MEDIA

Many charities are, of course, proactive in communicating with stakeholders and have made efforts to explore a number of channels of communication. The anxiety disorder charity No Panic, for example, runs its support and recovery groups by teleconferencing.

The Annual Report of a charity should include an explanation of the charity's strategy, policies and performance, demonstrating how resources are used, outlining successes and setbacks and giving a balanced message. Good means of demonstrating what the charity does include case studies, comments from stakeholders and users, and statistics presented in a reader-friendly way (eg through charts and graphs).

[handwritten note: FB are good at this.]

2.4.2 Crisis situations

As we will see in Chapter 11, a wide range of situations may arise (within or outside the organisation's control) with the potential to cause significant operational, financial or reputational damage. A crisis might include: the recall of a product due to safety defects; an ecological disaster such as an oil spill; product tampering or contamination; the discovery of unethical dealing, fraud or mismanagement (by the organisation or its supply chain); consumer boycotts; a significant restatement of a company's financial position or profit forecasts; industrial accidents; and technical failure or human error causing service/delivery failure or disasters (eg factory explosions or fires).

In any such situation, the organisation may attract negative media, public and regulatory scrutiny, and damaging rumour – in addition to the human, operational and financial costs of the problem itself. Corporate communication (specifically, crisis communication) has a vital role in setting the agenda for media coverage, controlling rumours, minimising damage to corporate image, and repairing relationships with stakeholders.

'Whether a company survives a crisis with its reputation, operations, and financial condition intact is determined less by the severity of the crisis – the underlying event – than by the timeliness and quality of its response to the crisis... Effective crisis response – including both what a company does and what it says – provides companies with a competitive advantage and can even enhance reputation. Ineffective crisis response can cause significant harm to a company's operations, reputation and competitive position.' (Doorley & Garcia, *op cit*, p. 327).

2.4.3 Merger or acquisition

As we saw in Chapter 4, a merger or acquisition can cause significant 'identity crisis' in an organisation, both for internal and external stakeholders.

- Corporate communication will have an important role in strategic decisions of how to brand or re-brand the merged entity to reflect aggregation or integration, or to delete the weaker corporate brand.

- Internal communication will have a vital role in expressing the integrated or selected identity to employees and securing employee identification: particularly where a weaker identity is being 'deleted', necessitating members' socialisation into a new culture (perhaps against resistance created by loyalty to the previous culture).

- Meanwhile, external communication will have an equally important role in justifying the merger/acquisition to key stakeholders (eg employees and investors), and building audience awareness of, and engagement with, the new merged identity.

2.4.4 Re-branding or brand re-positioning

Again, as we saw in Chapter 4, the re-branding of a corporate brand (eg change of name, symbolism and/or core identity values) will have to be communicated clearly and compellingly to target audiences, in order to:

- Accomplish the aims of the re-branding (eg disassociating the brand from negative perceptions and associating it with new, more positive attributes and values)

- Avoid confusion about who the 'new' organisation is (eg by establishing continuity with the old brand for loyal stakeholders) and what it stands for.

- Overcome stakeholder resistance to the new brand, eg in the case of the Post Office trying to re-brand as Consignia.

Corporate communication will also support brand re-positioning, by expressing and prioritising the new values and attributes the organisation wishes stakeholders to associate with the brand.

2.4.5 Strategic change or re-positioning

Examples of strategic change or re-positioning on the part of the organisation may include: restructuring; the adoption of new technologies; the adoption of new business models (eg direct sales or e-commerce); or a focus on different core competences (eg innovation) or competitive attributes (eg environmental responsibility).

Such intentions and plans will have to be carefully communicated to internal stakeholders (ideally using a two-way symmetrical consultation model) to secure formative input and buy-in, and to support the effective implementation of the strategy.

They will also have to be communicated to external stakeholders, in order to:

- Secure formal approval where required (eg from shareholders and/or government and regulatory bodies)
- Reap the intended competitive and reputational benefits of the strategy (by expressing the new reputational platform and corporate story).

MARKETING AT WORK

application

'Yes, Global US retailer **Wal-Mart** provides critical savings for low and middle-income families. Yes, we can thank the company for contributing to today's low inflation and growing productivity. But the darker side of the story is how Wal-Mart achieves its fabled low prices in part by taking unfair advantage of employees and communities...

'Recent pools... show that public awareness of Wal-Mart's labor [*sic*] practices is growing. A company that ignores its workers and its communities will surely have trouble succeeding in today's brand-conscious world. In addition, employees and citizens are consumers too; if they are treated badly, then purchasing power will either erode or be directed elsewhere.'

Garten (2004)

You might like to check out Wal-Mart's web site to see how publicly aware of environmental, community and employment issues it has become in the years since these concerns began to impact on the popularity of the brand.

Link: http://www.walmartstores.com/Sustainability

2.4.6 Organisational decline

Corporate communication is not all about 'good news'! If an organisation's reputation, status or performance is in decline, or in trouble, corporate communication will have an important role in:

- Reassuring internal and external stakeholders of managerial efforts to address the situation, in order to maintain employee morale and investor confidence.

- Informing and/or consulting with stakeholders affected by the decline: managing their expectations and acting responsibly in regard to keeping them informed in areas of concern. Shareholders and financial analysts will be warned if a company has to downgrade its profit and dividend forecasts, or restate its financial position. Employees and their representatives must, by law, by informed and consulted in advance of the possibility of redundancies and so on.

- Researching stakeholder attitudes and perceptions in order to diagnose the roots of a reputational decline (eg that of Marks & Spencer in the 1980s and 1990s)

- Re-energising the corporate brand, or re-branding, to regain reputational strength and re-position the organisation.

For a fascinating case study into the gradual 'fading away' of corporate reputation, and what can be done about it, see:

- *Davies, Chun, Da Silva and Roper, Corporate Reputation and Competitiveness (2003: Routledge): Chapter 3 Defending a Reputation – pp 122–134 ('Reputation isn't built in a day... but it can be [sic] also fade away'), which tells the 'rise and fall and rise' story of Marks & Spencer.*

3 Identifying stakeholder audiences

3.1 Who are your stakeholders?

We have been using the term 'stakeholders' throughout this Text to refer to the various constituency audiences with which an organisation interacts. As we noted above, another term for these target audiences is 'publics': hence the general use of the term 'public relations' to refer to corporate communication. Much of the literature now prefers the term 'stakeholders' (and reserves the term 'public relations' for a sub-set of corporate communication dealing with community and advocacy groups). Let's go back a step and look at the concept of the stakeholder.

KEY CONCEPT

concept

'**Stakeholders** are those individuals or groups who **depend** on the organisation to fulfil their own goals and on whom, in turn, the organisation depends.' (Johnson, Scholes & Whittington, 2005, p. 179)

'Stakeholders are individuals and/or groups who are **affected by or affect** the performance of the organisation in which they have an interest. Typically they would include employees, managers, creditors, suppliers, shareholders (if appropriate) and society at large.' (Worthington & Britton, 2006, p. 220)

'A stakeholder of a company is an individual or group that either is harmed by, or benefits from, the company *or* whose **rights** can be violated, or have to be respected, by the company. Other groups, besides shareholders, who typically would be considered stakeholders are communities associated with the company, employees, customers of the company's products, and suppliers.' (Jobber, 2007, p. 201)

The definitions of stakeholders quoted above come from influential textbooks on corporate strategy and management. In this context, stakeholders are regarded as having an interest in, and the potential to seek influence over, the broad purposes and plans of an organisation: managers are urged to take account of their expectations, concerns and possible positive or negative responses – or even to involve them in decision-making – when developing and communicating strategic changes. However, there are also stakeholders in particular decisions, plans and projects. Huczynski & Buchanan (2001, p. 601) define a stakeholder as 'anyone likely to be affected, directly or indirectly, by an organisational change or programme of changes'.

There are three broad categories of stakeholder in an organisation, as you may remember from your earlier studies.

- **Internal** stakeholders, who are members of the organisation. Key examples include the directors, managers and employees of a company – or the members of a club or association, or the volunteer workers in a charity. They may also include other functions or business units of the organisation which have a stake in a proposed decision or change programme.

- **Connected** stakeholders (or primary stakeholders), who have an economic or contractual relationship with the organisation. Key examples include the shareholders in a business; the customers of a business or beneficiaries of a charity; distributors and intermediaries; suppliers of goods and services; and financiers/funders of the organisation.

- **External** stakeholders (or secondary stakeholders), who are not directly connected to the organisation, but who have an interest in its activities, or are impacted by them in some way. Examples include the government, pressure and interest groups (including professional bodies and trade unions), the news media, the local community and wider society.

Here is a quick visual snapshot of the total stakeholder environment: Figure 6.3

Figure 6.3: Stakeholders in the organisation

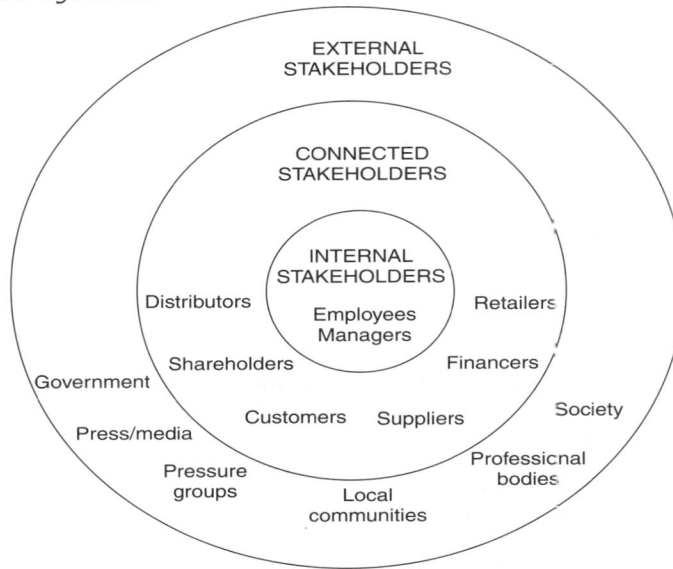

While it is useful to categorise stakeholders in this way, it would be a mistake to think of them as entirely separate groups. Customers are also members of the wider community, and may be shareholders in the company and/or members of a consumer or environmental protection group, for example. Employees of the organisation may also be customers, shareholders and perhaps members of a trade union which can bring influence to bear on their behalf with the management of the organisation. So there are always areas in which membership and interests intertwine.

The key point of stakeholder theory is that an organisation affects its environment and is affected by its environment. The boundaries of the organisation are highly permeable: influence flows from internal stakeholders outwards (eg through corporate communication) and from external stakeholders inwards (eg if a major customer pressures sales staff to represent its interests within the organisation, or more generally if a marketing-oriented organisation seeks to listen to its customers and meet their needs).

MARKETING AT WORK   application

Cadbury Schweppes is an international confectionery and beverages company, selling chocolate, sweets, gum and beverages around the world. It uses different ways to communicate with different stakeholder groups.

Shareholders – Cadbury Schweppes has over 60,000 registered shareholders. These include private individuals as well as large institutional investors, such as pension funds and banks. All shareholders are entitled to attend the Annual General Meeting, at which they have the opportunity to ask questions, discuss the company's performance and vote on certain issues.

Consumers – Consumers can contact the company by various means and Cadbury Schweppes deals with consumer enquiries on a daily basis. It performs market research to track changing consumer trends. Many parts of the business also use survey and market research panels to find out what consumers think of products.

Customers – The company has ongoing discussions with its customers. Wholesalers and retailers (intermediaries) provide the vital link to consumers and it is they who make Cadbury Schweppes' brands widely available.

Employees – Managers hold regular individual and team meetings to inform colleagues about the business and hear their views. The company also conducts surveys to check how its employees feel about working at Cadbury Schweppes. Internal newsletters, a group web site and many local web sites help employees keep up-to-date with what is going on.

Society – The company enters into regular dialogue with organisations such as national governments and international bodies such as the World Health Organisation (WHO), to discuss issues that affect the company. These issues can be anything from agricultural policy to education and skills.

It is worth bearing in mind that entities in the public and not-for-profit and voluntary sectors have similar stakeholder groups to private sector commercial firms – even if their 'customers' are more difficult to define. Consider the cases of:

- A local council which provides services and amenities to the surrounding area
- A charitable organisation which raises funds and volunteer support for environmental 'clean up' activities nationwide
- A tourist destination.

Who are the customers of these entities? To what other stakeholder groups will they need to address corporate communications?

3.2 Prioritising stakeholder groups

As you can see from the above, organisations have way too many stakeholders to target them all with communication programmes. In any case, not all of them will have sufficient interest in the organisation's affairs to be motivated to exercise influence over it – and even if they did, not all of them would be able to exercise sufficient influence to constitute a risk for the organisation.

The stakeholder view argues that it is important for the legitimate interests and information needs of stakeholder groups to be taken into account, but debate still rages about how many such interests are really relevant and which are more important than others. Campbell (1997) argues that organisations need to gain the loyalty of all 'active' stakeholders – shareholders, customers, employees and suppliers – because this is essential to the organisation's ability to compete in the markets for finance, customers, labour and materials/services.

In order to target corporate messages effectively and efficiently, stakeholder audiences will have to be **prioritised**: which are more important and which are less? This can be done in various ways.

3.2.1 Dependency relationships

Grunig & Hunt (1984) advocate prioritisation according to the importance of the linkage (or dependency relationship) with the stakeholder group: the ability of the group to control or influence resources that are required by the organisation to varying degrees.

- **Normative groups** provide the authority for an organisation to function, and the guidelines within which it functions (eg regulatory bodies, professional bodies, the board of directors).

- **Enabling groups** (including shareholders and financiers) supply vital resources required for the organisation to operate.

- **Functional groups** are important as providers of organisational inputs (eg employees and suppliers) or as consumers of organisational outputs (eg customers).

- **Diffused groups** are not identified by membership in any formal organisation (eg the general public, the 'blogosphere', the media).

3.2.2 Interest and influence

Another long-established method of prioritising stakeholder audiences and relationships is **stakeholder mapping**. Mendelow (1985) developed a simple matrix to plot two factors for each stakeholder group:

- How *interested* it is in influencing the organisation to get its needs met or interests protected (or in opposing or supporting a particular decision); and

- Whether it has the *power* to do so.

On the basis of these two factors, the matrix recommends the most appropriate type of relationship to establish with each 'quadrant' of stakeholder group: Figure 6.4.

Figure 6.4: Mendelow's power/interest matrix

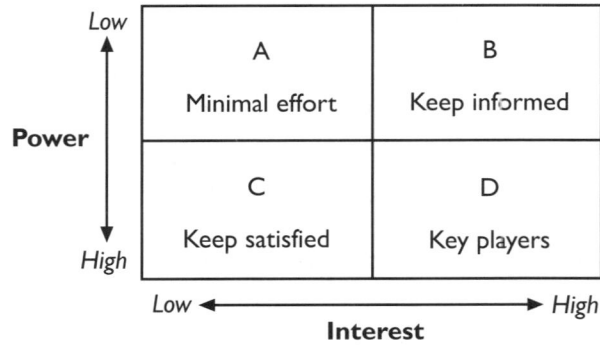

Working through each of the segments in turn:

- Stakeholders in **Quadrant A** have neither interest in influencing the organisation/decision (because it doesn't impact on them greatly) nor the power to do so. They are a low-priority group: it will not be worth investing significant resources in communicating with them – although they will need to be monitored in case their status changes.

- Stakeholders in **Quadrant B** are more important because of their high interest in influencing the organisation/decision. They may have low power to do anything about it, but unless they feel they are being kept 'in the loop' and understand the need for a strategy or decision, their concerns may lead them to seek additional power by lobbying or banding together against it. Community, small supplier and employee groups may be in this category, in relation to decisions which impact significantly on their interests. The appropriate approach is to keep them informed, and monitor and manage any issues that may arise.

- Stakeholders in **Quadrant C** are important because of their high power. They currently have little interest in using that power to influence the organisation, but if they become impacted, dissatisfied or concerned, their interest may be aroused and their power mobilised. A large institutional shareholder may be in this category, as may government agencies and regulatory bodies (in relation to organisations which are currently broadly compliant). The appropriate approach is to keep such stakeholders satisfied, by ensuring that their needs are met and any concerns they may have are anticipated and addressed before they become 'issues' – without irritating them with excessive communication, which they may not see the need for.

- Stakeholders in **Quadrant D** are known as 'key players': they have high power and are highly motivated to use it in their own interests. Major customers, key suppliers and intermediaries, internal senior managers and strategic external allies/partners may be in this category. The appropriate strategy is to manage the relationship closely. This may include early involvement, consultation and negotiation, so that the key players' goals can be integrated with the organisation's goals as far as possible. Plans must at least be acceptable to key players – and ideally, they can be encouraged to co-operate with the organisation, to mutual benefit.

ACTIVITY 6

evaluation

Draw up a blank power/interest matrix, and place each of the stakeholders of your own organisation (or the organisation that is the focus of your assessment) in the appropriate quadrant. For each, add a [+] or [-], according to whether they are supporters or opponents.

A similar, communication-based model (Mitchell *et al.*, 1997) uses the dimensions of:

- **Power**: ability to influence or impose its will on the organisation

- **Legitimacy**: extent to which the stakeholder's claims are perceived as legitimate (proper or appropriate in the social context)

- **Urgency**: the stakeholder's claims are time sensitive and critical.

The concept of 'interest' or 'legitimacy' is important, because groups that are highly motivated and/or widely perceived as deserving of organisational consideration can be important target audiences, even if they have low direct influence on organisational inputs or outputs. van Riel & Fombrun (*op cit*, p. 163) note that: 'Stakeholder groups that are not directly commercially relevant are often the groups most likely to seek contact with the organisation – and to seek contact that the company seldom welcomes but cannot be ignored. NGOs are generally not among a company's target groups and are often treated as irrelevant [or worse]. But ask Nike about NGOs opposing child labour: they regularly complain about Nike's lack of responsible management of sub-contractors in developing nations and make the company a target of its actions and communications. Clearly they have become an important group for Nike to target or consider in its communications.'

MARKETING AT WORK   application

The following are just a few of the high-profile examples in which consumers, mobilised by pressure group action, have been successful in applying pressure to seek changes in business practices.

- Large-scale boycotts of **Shell** filling stations led the company to reverse its policy on the at-sea disposal of the Brent Spar oil drilling platform.

- Pressure was applied to change **Nestlé's** practice of exploiting the market for processed milk in developing countries

- Media campaigns have targeted Nike (alleged exploitation of overseas garment-trade workers in 'sweat shops') and McDonalds (alleged contribution to obesity and related illnesses).

Both Nike and McDonalds have transformed their practices and promotions as a result of these pressures. Check them out – and evaluate the success of their response to negative public relations – on the following web sites.

- http://www.nikebiz.com (follow the links under 'Responsibility' – and also note the pages targeted for communication with other stakeholder groups.)

- http://www.nikeresponsibility.com (a specially targeted CSR site which sets out Nike's CSR values and goals: 'improve conditions in our contract factories', 'design for a better world', 'become carbon neutral' and 'unleash potential through sport'.)

- http://www.mcdonalds.co.uk (Follow the links to 'eat smart', for example, to see how seriously McDonalds has taken pressures from health promotion groups. You might also check out the global home site: www.mcdonalds.com and follow links to other regions/markets.)

3.2.3 Stakeholders in a change

Egan (1994) divides stakeholders in a change into nine distinct groups, in relation to a leader or agent of change (eg the communicating organisation).

Stakeholder	Position
Partners	Support the change agent
Allies	Will support the change agent, given encouragement
Fellow travellers	Passive supporters, who are committed to the agenda or need for change, but not to the change agent in particular
Bedfellows	Those who support the agenda or need for change, but do not know or trust the change agent
Fence sitters	Those whose allegiances are not year clear
Loose cannons	Those who may vote either way on agendas in which they have no direct stake
Opponents	Those who oppose the agenda, but not the change agent in particular
Adversaries	Those who oppose the change agent and the agenda
The voiceless	'Silent' stakeholders who are affected by the agenda, but lack advocates or power to influence decisions (eg future generations, the environment)

Like Mendelow, Egan suggests that these groups require different communication strategies.

- **Supporters** (in various groups) must be encouraged and kept 'on side':

    - **Partners** may require little interaction, but the organisation cannot afford to be complacent: if dissatisfied, they may downgrade to less committed support

    - **Allies** require some encouragement, but infrequent contact (a 'light touch') is usually all that is required to maintain support

    - **Passive supporters** (fellow travellers and bedfellows) require more intense rapport- and relationship-building contacts in order to mobilise commitment to the change agent.

- **Fence sitters** may or may not have the potential to become valuable supporters or harmful opponents. The change agent will need to assess what value can be gained from gaining their allegiance, and this will determine the level and type of interaction invested in the attempt.

- **Opponents** need to be 'converted': persuaded of the merits of the agenda and have their reasons for resistance addressed. This will often require a formal, structured approach to persuasion, eg using a meeting or series meetings for negotiation and conflict resolution.

- **Adversaries** may be too costly and difficult to 'win over': they may have to be marginalised or discredited, to reduce their potential to use their influence to mobilise opposition to the plan.

- The needs of the **voiceless** must also receive attention, despite their relative powerlessness, since they may be co-opted by opponents or adversaries to join the resistance coalition. Again a 'light touch', low-frequency-contact approach is all that is necessary to monitor stakeholders' responses and allow them to feel heard.

3.3 Stakeholder management

Once key stakeholders have been identified, it is possible to plan a management strategy for each. Key issues might include:

- **Stakeholder analysis**. What are the goals, drivers or desired outcomes of these stakeholders? What fears or issues might your plans raise for them? Where might they support you – and where might they oppose you? What aspects of the corporate story are most likely to appeal to them? What are their current perceptions of and attitudes towards the organisation?

- **Desired outcomes**. What do you want or need from these stakeholders? What levels of support do you want from them? What role(s) (if any) would you want them to play in your plans?

- **Communication**. What methods of communication will be most effective for these stakeholders? Who influences their opinions? What messages will you need to convey to them?

- **Issues management**. How will you identify and manage potential issues and problems, where stakeholders' goals may differ from yours? How will you gain stakeholders' early involvement, and collaborate with them in minimising or managing the impacts? What kinds of behaviour or responses might indicate resistance or lack of commitment/ support from your key stakeholders?

From the recommended reading list, lively and accessible coverage of stakeholder issues is available in:

- *Joep Cornelissen,* **Corporate Communication: A guide to theory and practice** *(2nd edition, 2008: Sage), see Chapter 3: Stakeholder Management and Communication. (Note that the title of this book is cited inaccurately in some versions of the CIM recommended reading list.)* ∎

4 Key messages of corporate communication

In Chapter 5, we saw how an organisation can formulate the 'core message' or 'story' of its corporate identity and/or brand, and in Chapter 7, we will examine how this can be developed via integrated communication campaigns. However, different *dimensions* or *themes* within the corporate story may be relevant to particular stakeholder groups. We have already looked at three of the four core messages mentioned in the syllabus (vision, mission and values; identity or brand; and strategic re-positioning) elsewhere, and will only give a brief round-up here. We will explore the fourth message cluster (ethics, CSR, sustainability and environmental issues) in more detail in section 5.

4.1 Vision, mission and values

As we saw in Chapter 3, the vision, mission and values of the organisation are the highest level expressions of corporate personality and identity: what the organisation stands for above all else. Vision may be seen as a crucial element in expressing the desired identity of the organisation: what it most wants to be and to project to the world.

- Mission, vision and values must be communicated among the top management of the organisation, in order to articulate and establish consensus about the desired identity and direction of the organisation, and to provide guidelines for strategy and policy formation. Strategic intent has an important role in focusing the attention and energies of the management and members of the organisation.

- They must be communicated among the employees of the organisation, in order to secure 'buy-in' to, or identification with, organisational goals, objectives and values, and as a guide to what behaviours are acceptable and what are not.

- They must be communicated to external audiences in order to create and position the corporate brand. Vision, mission and values are key components of the reputational platform and corporate story. The most successfully positioned companies and brands are those that have linked a powerful brand positioning to an inspiring, overarching vision. Investors want to know that the organisation is 'going somewhere' – and where. Customers need to know what the organisation 'stands for' in order to engage and identify themselves with a compelling corporate brand.

4.2 Identity or brand

As we saw in Chapter 4, identity and brand messages are the core of corporate communication to both internal and external audiences. 'The aim of corporate identity management is to acquire a favourable corporate image among key internal and external stakeholders so that, in the long run, this image can result in the acquisition of a favourable corporate reputation, which leads to key stakeholders having a favourable disposition towards the organisation.' (Vella & Melewar, 2008, p. 11)

- Employees need a clear, collective understanding of the organisation's distinctive values and characteristics in order to identify themselves with the organisation – and in order to implement desired identity/brand values in their communications and behaviours at touch points with external stakeholders.

- External audiences need a clear and consistent understanding of the organisation's distinctive values and characteristics (as mediated by the corporate identity mix) in order to identify the organisation, engage with the organisation and develop a preferential bias towards the organisation in investment, purchase and support/advocacy decisions.

We hope, after all these chapters, that no more needs to be said about this here.

4.3 Strategic repositioning

Again, as we have seen repeatedly throughout this Text, changes of strategy or strategic re-positioning on the part of the organisation must be communicated to key stakeholder audiences:

- To the top management of the organisation, to secure unity of purpose and direction, and secure 'buy-in' by the people who will have to act as change agents and champions

- To the management and employees of the organisation who will be responsible for implementing the strategic changes, and who will be affected by the change (eg restructuring), and to secure employee buy-in, commitment and retention (particularly in the face of difficult or resisted changes)

- To external stakeholders who may have to approve the decision or resource allocation (eg shareholders and regulatory bodies) or whose support may be required (eg trade unions or supply chain partners)

- To external stakeholders who will be positively or negatively affected by the change (eg customers and local communities) and to general audiences whose image of the organisation will be shaped by re-positioning messages

- To the internal and external stakeholders through whom information about the change will be disseminated (eg customer-facing staff, communicators and communication agencies, media and perhaps pressure or advocacy groups, eg in an affinity or causal marketing relationship).

5 Ethics, CSR and sustainability

The view of what constitutes a legitimate stakeholder has broadened from a focus on groups involved directly with the organisation, or contributing to its operations, to a wider range of groups which are affected by its behaviour and outputs. Secondary stakeholders are likely to have quite diverse objectives, but pressure has increasingly been brought to bear in the areas of corporate ethics, and social and environmental responsibility. CSR and sustainability are now key corporate brand differentiators for industry leaders in these areas (such as The Body Shop with its ethical corporate brand or Marks & Spencer with its high-profile Plan A sustainability programme). They are also a key source of reputational risk for organisations perceived to be non-compliant or uncaring in these areas.

5.1 Corporate ethics

Ethics are a set of moral principles or values about what constitutes 'right' and 'wrong' behaviour. They are shaped by social (and sometimes religious) assumptions and beliefs, and – more deliberately – by public and professional bodies, in the form of agreed principles and guidelines (ethical codes or codes of practice) which are designed to protect society's best interests.

KEY CONCEPT

concept

Marketing ethics are 'the moral principles and values that guide behaviour within the field of marketing, and cover issues such as product safety, truthfulness in marketing communications, honesty in relationships with customers and distributors, pricing issues and the impact of marketing decisions on the environment and society.' (Jobber, 2007, p. 191)

At the macro level, business itself has been subject to criticism from consumer, environmental and anti-globalisation groups for its harmful impacts: generating manufacturing activity and waste products which impact on the environment; encouraging over-consumption of scarce resources; encouraging consumption of harmful products (such as alcohol, tobacco and junk foods); invasion of privacy (eg through direct marketing and customer data collection); erosion of national cultures through globalisation; exploitation of workers and consumers in less developed markets; and so on.

At the corporate level, ethical issues face an organisation as it formulates policies about how it interacts with its various stakeholders. Some of these matters are covered by legislative requirements (eg in regard to product safety, truth in advertising or basic rights of employees). Others are subject to rules laid down by industry regulators, such as Ofcom for the communications industry, the Competition Commission (regulating merger and acquisition activity) and the Advertising Standards Authority (regulating media advertising).

An organisation may have a 'compliance-based' approach to ethics which strives merely to uphold these minimal requirements. Alternatively, it may pursue a more proactive 'integrity-based' approach, which pursues high ethical standards – whether or not they are illegal. (It is not currently illegal in the UK, for example, to promote extreme dieting among teenage girls, or to put genetically modified ingredients in food products – but both have been argued to be unethical, and leading brands have altered their policies accordingly.)

5.2 Corporate social responsibility (CSR)

KEY CONCEPT

concept

The term **Corporate Social Responsibility (CSR)** is used to describe a wide range of obligations that an organisation may feel it has towards its secondary or external stakeholders, including the society in which it operates.

Caroll & Buchholtz (2000, cited in Jobber, 2007) argue that there are four main 'layers' of corporate social responsibility:

- **Economic responsibilities**. The firm must produce goods and services wanted by the market, profitably – otherwise it cannot survive, and will not be able to fulfil any other obligations to stakeholders. Economic responsibilities include: operating efficiently and effectively, aiming for consistent levels of profitability, and competing effectively in the market.

- **Legal responsibilities**. Economic goals must be pursued within the framework of the laws of the society within which the firm operates. It is sometimes said that 'the law is a floor': it does not define best practice, but does set out the minimum principles and standards that are considered acceptable. The news is full of examples of how business practices can fail to comply with contract, employment, consumer protection, health and safety, competition law, human rights law and so on. Law and regulation may affect marketing practices (eg advertising claims), business practices (eg trading, employment, environmental protection, financial management and so on) and its products and services (eg quality, safety, packaging).

- **Ethical responsibilities**. Ethical responsibilities comprise the expectations of society, over and above basic economic and legal requirements: honesty in business relationships, for example; not exploiting small suppliers and retailers; or not marketing manipulatively to children. This is a more discretionary area, because there are fewer direct sanctions against unethical behaviour. Ethical principles may be enforced via Codes of Ethics or Codes of Practice in an industry, profession or individual firm – but they are often also subject to stakeholder pressure (demands, protests, boycotts and so on).

- **Philanthropic responsibilities**. Above and beyond even ethical dealings, society increasingly expects that marketing organisations be 'good corporate citizens': that is, that they proactively and positively contribute to the society in which they operate. Examples of philanthropy include corporations building community amenities, sponsoring local causes and events, donating money to charity, supporting local schools, promoting or campaigning on issues of concern, or offering grants and prizes for research/innovation of benefit to society. (As an example of the latter, the Virgin Group has launched 'Earth Challenge', offering a large monetary prize for a viable solution to carbon emissions.)

MARKETING AT WORK

application

In June 2007, **Nike** unveiled an updated range of CSR goals.

'The firm, once famously criticised for poor conditions at supplier factories, says it wants to improve working conditions for the 800,000 people who manufacture its branded products. It hopes to eliminate the problem of excessive overtime by 2011.

'The company is also keen to increase the transparency of its supply chain operations by posting a list of the 700 factories it uses on the internet. The site will also explain the auditing tools it uses to examine its suppliers.

'It also intended to make its factories, shops and business travel climate neutral by 2011.

'[In May 2007], Nike signed a deal with a new supplier in Pakistan to make Nike footballs after problems with a different supplier last year. The contract has imposed strict guarantees on [the supplier] which is expected to meet nine workplace conditions, including making sure that employees are registered, paid hourly rates and eligible for social benefits, such as healthcare.'

Supply Management, 7 June 2007

ACTIVITY 7

application

How does your work or other selected organisation fulfil its economic, legal, ethical and philanthropic responsibilities? Give at least two specific examples of responsibilities recognised by the organisation in each area, and at least one specific example of measures taken to meet those responsibilities.

How (and how well) are these responsibilities communicated to staff of the organisation, and to other stakeholders? What kinds of mission, ethical or CSR statements does the organisation make? Where, and for what audience(s)?

What is the general attitude of the organisation's culture to these responsibilities? Are they taken seriously – or are 'corners cut' on some issues? What measures might be taken to get them taken more seriously, more consistently?

5.2.1 Why should commercial organisations pursue CSR objectives?

Economist Milton Friedman took the view that 'the social responsibility of business is profit maximisation': that is, to give shareholders a return on their investment. He argued that spending funds on objectives *not* related to shareholder expectations is simply irresponsible: regard for shareholder wealth is a healthy discipline for management, providing accountability for decisions. The public interest is, in any case, already served by profit maximisation, because the State levies taxes on corporate profits. 'Consequently,' argued Friedman, 'the only justification for social responsibility is **enlightened self-interest**' on the part of a business organisation.

So *does* CSR service the interest of the firm? It can be argued that pursuing CSR policies is expensive – and that this represents an opportunity cost: the funds could have been spent on more directly value-adding (and profitable) priorities. It can also be argued that CSR has become so fashionable that it no longer has any credibility with consumers: they see it as a public relations exercise without real substance – and this robs it of any public relations value it may have had.

The consensus, however, is that CSR has many potential benefits for a business.

- **Law, regulation and Codes of Practice** impose certain social responsibilities on organisations, and there are financial and operational penalties for failure to comply (eg 'polluter pays' taxes and compensation claims). Meanwhile, voluntary ethical and philanthropic measures may head off stricter legal and regulatory requirements.

- Increasing **consumer awareness** of social responsibility issues creates market demand for CSR – and risks for irresponsible firms. Failure to meet ethical expectations can cause reputational damage, negative media exposure, consumer boycotts and so on. The risk of reputational damage extends to 'responsibility by association' in supply chains: organisations are increasingly being held responsible for poor labour conditions or environmental damage by their suppliers, for example. Positive CSR can be regarded as a form of reputational and financial risk management.

- Positive CSR may positively **enhance corporate reputation and brand image**. A commonly cited example is The Body Shop, which has positioned itself strongly as an ethical and responsible brand.

- CSR creates **opportunities to add value** to products and services, or to develop new ones. Examples include recyclable packaging, environmental impact consultancy, and products specifically targeted at 'green' and health-conscious consumers (from low-energy light bulbs to low-GI foods).

- CSR can **offset or reduce costs** eg by increasing energy efficiency, creating markets for recycled products, or (as in the case of the Body Shop) reducing the need for expenditure on advertising.

- CSR maintains the **sustainability** of business dealings. Above-minimum standards for the treatment of employees, suppliers and other business partners may be necessary for the business to attract, retain and motivate them to provide quality service and commitment – particularly in competition with other firms. Ethical and responsible business activity helps to create a climate in which mutually-beneficial long-term trading relationships can be preserved.

5.3 Sustainability: the Triple Bottom Line

The term 'sustainability' is often used as synonymous with corporate social responsibility and/or environmental responsibility. More accurately, the term is designed to describe strategies and operations which do not compromise the wellbeing of future generations.

Modern use of the term sustainability reflects three dimensions, embodied in the Triple Bottom Line ('People, Profit, Planet'): a concept which recognises the need for businesses to measure their performance not just by how well they further the interests of their primary stakeholders (shareholders) through profitability (the 'economic bottom line'), but also by how well they further or protect the interests of their secondary stakeholders (including wider society), in relation to three dimensions.

- **Economic sustainability**: profitability, sustainable economic performance – and its beneficial effects on stakeholders (employment, continuing access to goods and services, tax revenue, community investment and so on).

- **Social sustainability**: fair and beneficial business practices toward labour and the society in which the business operates. For example: ethical treatment of labour; support for small and local businesses; support for diversity and equal opportunity in employment; development of skills; promoting (or not jeopardising) public health; and 'giving back' to communities.

- **Environmental sustainability**: sustainable environmental practices, which either benefit the natural environment or minimise harmful impacts upon it. This may involve: reducing pollution and waste; minimising or repairing environmental damage; using renewable or recyclable materials and designs; reducing greenhouse gas (GHG) emissions and 'carbon footprint'; educating supply chains and customers to support environmental practices; investing in 'green' projects such as renewable energy, land reclamation and reforestation; and so on.

5.4 Environmental issues

Consumer choice is increasingly exercised according to environmentally-related criteria (a trend reflected in the term 'green consumption'). High profile environmental issues at the moment include:

- Global warming (embracing the issues of climate change, the 'carbon footprint' of business activities, and the UK's commitments to emissions reduction under the Kyoto Protocol)

- Environmental decline and degradation (eg deforestation), and loss of biodiversity through species extinction

- Over-consumption and waste of non-renewable natural resources, and the need to develop alternative energy sources

- The effects of pollution on air, waterways and ecosystems

- The disposal of waste products (especially those which contain harmful substances, eg chemical and electrical waste)

- Pressure to increase industrial and household recycling.

Marketing organisations need both to manage the risk associated with poor environmental practices (or crises, such as an oil spill) and to capitalise on opportunities presented by green consumption: many brands are now marketed on their green, organic, energy-saving or recycling credentials.

Green marketing programmes may embrace measures such as:

- Conducting market research into demand for green products, potential green market niches and key environmental concerns of consumers

- Driving product modification and development: reducing packaging waste, increasing recyclability, developing 'green' products or product lines

- Developing positive relationships with environmental research and pressure groups

- Using corporate communications to emphasise the green credentials of the organisation or brand

- Using issues and crisis management to control negative public relations effects of environmental problems

MARKETING AT WORK
application

Some creative marketing communication on environmental issues in the last few years include:

- **Genesis Energy** (New Zealand). In response to soaring energy costs, Genesis launched a direct marketing campaign emphasising to customers that the company was there to help them save money on energy bills. They sent out a leaflet of energy-saving tips printed in fluorescent ink (so they could be read with the lights off!)

- **Oroverde** (Tropical Rainforest foundation) sent out a package to potential donors reminding them of the threat to tropical rainforests from land clearing by burning. The package included a 'paint by numbers' picture of the rainforest – but only one colour ink: black.

Gummesson (2002) argues that marketing organisations can use corporate communication to establish relationships with customers and other stakeholders specifically through or on environmental issues: green issues are not just costs or threats, but opportunities for relationship, value and revenue enhancement. 'Building coalitions with all stakeholders keeps the company abreast of environmental regulations, issues, debates, technology and attitudes.' (p. 123).

In 2007, **Marks & Spencer** launched a new CSR programme called 'Plan A' (so called because 'There is no Plan B'), built on five CSR 'pillars':

- *Climate change:* eg reducing energy-related CO^2 emissions from stores and offices; supporting farmers who are investing in small-scale renewable energy production; piloting 'eco-stores'; monitoring the carbon footprint of the food business; and encouraging consumers in more eco-friendly washing of clothing products.

- *Waste:* eg engaging customers in reducing carrier bag usage and recycling clothing; reducing use of packaging, increasing use of recycled materials; improving recycling rates for construction waste and coat hangers. (The target is to send zero waste to landfill from M & S operations.)

- *Sustainable raw materials:* eg promoting animal welfare in fashion and food production (eg implementing lower stocking densities for chicken); increasing use of Fairtrade and organic cotton and recycled polyester; and increasing sales of organic foods.

- *Fair partner:* eg extended use of Fairtrade certified products; supporting local farmers; creating a Supplier Exchange to involve suppliers in Plan A; raising money in the community (for Breakthrough Breast Cancer and Save the Children); updating commitments on labour standards; and working with overseas suppliers to help them develop 'ethical model factories' to identify and share best practice.

- *Health:* eg removing artificial colourings and flavourings from 99% of food products; reducing salt levels; introducing front-of-pack FSA 'traffic lights'; and training shop floor staff as 'healthy eating assistants'.

M & S is involving stakeholders, including employees, suppliers and customers (asking them to sign 'pledges' of commitment to each of the five pillars). Its web site gives case studies for the various pillars, and updates on progress. Benchmark for proactive reputation management based on CSR!

Link: http://plana.marksandspencer.com

5.5 Communication strategies

The following may be a helpful overview, drawn from Jobber (2007).

Dimension of CSR	Key issues	Marketing response
Physical environment	Combating global warming (GHG emissions)	**Sustainability marketing**: positioning product and corporate brands on the platform of environmental sustainability ('green' marketing)
	Pollution control	
	Conservation of energy and other scarce resources	
	Use of environmentally friendly ingredients and components	
	Recycling and non-wasteful packaging	
Social (community involvement)	Support for the local community	**Societal marketing**: developing and positioning products and brands on the basis of concern for consumers' and society's health and well-being.
	Support for the wider community	**Cause-related marketing**: forming association with a cause or charity to co-promote a product, brand or issue, to mutual benefit

Dimension of CSR	Key issues	Marketing response
Consumer	Product safety (including the avoidance of harmful long-term effects)	Societal marketing
	Avoidance of price fixing	
	Honesty in communications	
	Respecting privacy	
Supply chain	Fair trading	**Fairtrade marketing**: developing and promoting Fairtrade brands and positioning the organisation on its fair trade ethos
	Standard setting for suppliers (eg human rights, labour standards and environmental responsibility)	
Employee relations	Fair pay	**Internal marketing**: programmes for developing, motivating, informing and involving employees in such a way as to enhance their ability to provide customer service, satisfaction and value
	Equal opportunities	
	Training and motivation	
	Employee involvement, consultation and information provision	

Source: Jobber (2007, p. 204)

ACTIVITY 8

evaluation

Using the above table as a template, for each dimension of CSR, list the key issues facing your organisation. These may include some of those identified by Jobber and/or others.

Identify specific communication responses your organisation has used or is using to manage audience perceptions of each of the key issues you identify.

Highlight any areas in which the organisation does not appear to be addressing the issue, and consider what responses you might recommend.

Learning objectives	Covered
1 Critically appraise the nature and characteristics of corporate communications	☑ Definition of corporate communications
	☑ The corporate communication mix: management, marketing and organisational communication
	☑ The Corporate Identity Management Process (Markwick & Fill)
	☑ Principle activities of corporate communication: internal communication, investor relations. marketing communication, public affairs, issues management
2 Critically assess the different reasons for using corporate communication	☑ Aims and purposes of corporate communication: Grunig & Hunt's four visions of public relations
	☑ Tasks of corporate communication: informing, exploring, influencing, relating and negotiating
	☑ Stimulating change: KAB – knowledge, attitude and behaviour
	☑ Circumstances requiring corporate communication: periodic reporting; crisis situations; merger or acquisition; re-branding or brand re-positioning; strategic change or re-positioning; and organisational decline
3 Develop processes leading to the identification of key external and internal stakeholders, and understand the nature of associated communication programmes	☑ Definition of stakeholders: internal, connected and external
	☑ Prioritising stakeholder groups on the basis of: dependency relationship (Grunig & Hunt); interest and influence (Mendelow); stake in change (Egan)
	☑ Stakeholder management
4 Propose what is to be communicated to particular stakeholders	☑ Vision, mission and values
	☑ Identity or brand
	☑ Strategic re-positioning
	☑ Ethics, CSR and sustainability; why should organisations pursue CSR?; the Triple Bottom Line (economic, social and environmental sustainability); environmental issues
	☑ Communication strategies for CSR

1   What mechanisms can be used to integrate corporate communication specialisms dispersed among different functional departments?

2   List some of the mechanisms used for (a) investor relations and (b) public affairs.

3   Outline Grunig and Hunt's ideal (two-way symmetrical) form of communication.

4   Outline the key information needs of key stakeholder groups.

5   Explain the 'domino effect' of knowledge, attitude, behaviour (KAB) change.

6   Give three examples of corporate communication's role in periodic reporting.

7   Explain the four quadrants of the Mendelow matrix.

8   Identify the four main layers of CSR and the three dimensions of sustainability.

1   Internal communication by managers is the foundation of key processes such as vision articulation and 'buy-in'; initiating and managing change; employee identification with the organisation; corporate identity (self-perception) building; employee motivation and team-building; cross-functional or 'horizontal' business process flow; and organisational learning.

    Communication by managers in their role as figureheads and spokespersons also has a key influence on the image of the organisation projected to external audiences: eg via executive speeches at shareholder meetings, conferences or press conferences; written statements made in reports and accounts; lobbying of legislators; meetings with representatives of stakeholder groups; and so on.

2   Your answer will be based on your own organisation and research. If the information is difficult to find, or the results inconclusive, make a note: there may be potential for improvement in establishing greater integration.

3   We would probably class this as 'scientific persuasion' (a two-way asymmetric model): the organisation has invited feedback and upheld the principle of transparency, but there is no fundamental change in the message as a result of the feedback received.

4   This may involve mechanisms such as feedback and suggestion seeking, the creation of stakeholder communities (online discussion groups, message boards), networking events, stakeholder-generated web content and so on. Uncontrolled networking communication happens anyway, so it makes sense for the organisation to sponsor and monitor the exchanges; create a sense of belonging or affiliation (adding a social benefit to the total corporate offering); and offer social value which draws people repeatedly to the web site and other mechanisms (where they can be targeted with marketing and organisational messages).

5   *Local authority.* The customers are the people who receive the services or use the amenities, especially if they also pay for them (for example, through local tax charges). Other stakeholder audiences include employees, suppliers and subcontractors, local business and not-for-profit organisations (who may benefit from or compete with local government initiatives for funds and provision of services), the Press (especially local media) and local interest and lobbying groups.

    Charity. The customers are, arguably, the beneficiaries of the services: in this case, local communities and environmental groups. However, key stakeholder audiences will include current and potential funders and volunteers (without whom the charity's activities would cease). Others will include the press and government, whom the charity will attempt to persuade of the importance of local environment issues, and other pressure groups, who may support them in this attempt.

    Tourist destination. The customers are the tourists/visitors, but also, potentially tourism and travel agencies. Other important audiences will include the residents of the destination, who may be beneficiaries of increased tourism – or may resist on grounds of impact on their culture and amenities.

6   Answer will depend on your own organisation's power/interest matrix. Note the 'key players': these are likely to be key target audiences for corporate communication – especially if there is currently a 'minus sign' against them, signalling opposition or negative evaluation of the organisation's reputation.

7   Answer will depend on your own organisation.

8   Your own organisation. You can use some of the ideas covered in the summary table, but it would be good learning to review actual organisational practices, scan the web site – or even ask a colleague, manager or mentor: 'What are we doing to respond to these issues for our firm?'

1   Integrating mechanisms include: rules and procedures, sequencing (process design), organisational routines and group problem-solving.

2   See the table in section 1.4 for a range of points.

3   The two-way symmetric model aims to facilitate mutual understanding between the organisation and its publics. Communication is two-way and symmetrical (balanced in its effects): both parties are open and amenable to persuasion.

4   See section 2.2.1 for some ideas.

5   The domino effect model suggests that change in behaviour is generated by: creating an effective message (message); getting the target audience to pay attention to the information content (knowledge); getting them to respond favourably to what they know (attitude); and hence getting them to adopt a supportive behaviour (behaviour).

6   Examples of periodic reporting include: the preparation of statistical reports and returns for government agencies; the preparation of statutory financial statements and reports; the issuing of financial forecasts to the financial community; and consultations with employee representatives.

7   See Figure 6.4 and following text for a full explanation.

8   The layers of CSR are economic, legal, ethical and philanthropic. The three dimensions of sustainability (as in the Triple Bottom Line) are economic, social and environmental (Profit, People, Planet).

Abratt, R and Shee, P S B (1989) 'A new approach to the corporate image management process' in *Journal of Marketing Management* Vol 5 (1): pp 63-76

Balmer, J M T (2008) 'Corporate identity, brand and marketing' in T C Melewar (ed) *Factors of Corporate Identity, Communication and Reputation*. Abingdon, Oxon: Routledge

Campbell, A (1997) 'Stakeholders: the case in favour' in *Long Range Planning* 30 (3) pp 446-449

Cornelissen, J (2008) *Corporate Communication: A guide to theory and practice* (2nd ed). London: Sage

Davies G, Chun R, Da Silva R V & Roper S (2003) *Corporate Reputation and Competitiveness*. Abingdon, Oxon: Routledge

Doorley, J & Garcia, H F (2007) *Reputation Management: The Key to Successful Public Relations and Corporate Communications*. New York: Routledge

Egan, G (1994) *Working the Shadow Side: A Guide to Positive Behind-the-Scenes Management*. San Francisco: Jossey-Bass

Fill, C (2002) *Marketing Communications: Contexts, Strategies and Applications* (3rd ed). Harlow, Essex: Pearson Education Limited

Grunig, J E (ed) (1992) *Excellence in Public Relations and Communication Management*. New Jersey: Lawrence Erlbaum Associates

Grunig, J E & Hunt, T (1984) *Managing Public Relations*. New York: Holt, Reinhart & Winston

Franklin B, Hogan M, Langley Q, Mosdell N & Pill E (2009) *Key Concepts in Public Relations*. London: Sage

Gennard, J & Judge, G (2003) *Employee Relations* (3rd ed). London: CIPD

Grant, R M (1996) 'Towards a knowledge-based theory of the firm' in *Strategic Management Journal*, no 17, pp 109-122

Gummesson, E (2002) *Total Relationship Marketing* (2nd ed) Oxford: Elsevier Butterworth Heinemann

Huczynski, A & Buchanan, D (2001) *Organizational Behaviour: An Introductory Text* (4th edition). Harlow, Essex: FT Prentice Hall

Jobber, D (2007) *Principles & Practice of Marketing* (5th ed) Maidenhead: McGraw Hill

Johnson, G, Scholes K & Whittington (2005) *Exploring Corporate Strategy: Text and Cases* (7th ed). Harlow, Essex: Ft Prentice Hall

Lavidge, R J & Steiner, G A (1961) 'A model for predictive effects of advertising effectiveness' in *Journal of Marketing*.

Markwick, N & Fill, C (1997) 'Towards a framework for management corporate identity' in *European Journal of Marketing*, Vol 31 (5/6), pp 396-409

Mendelow, A (1985) 'Stakeholder Analysis for Strategic Planning & Implementation' in *Strategic Planning & Management Handbook*, King & Cleland (eds). NY: Van Nostrand Reinhold

Mitchell R K, Agle B R & Wood DJ (1997) 'Towards a theory of stakeholder identification and salience', in *Academy of Management Review* 22(4) pp 853-886

Peck H L, Payne A, Christopher M & Clark M (1999) *Relationship Marketing: Strategy and Implementation*. Oxford: Elsevier Butterworth-Heinemann

Riel, C B M van (1995) *Principles of Corporate Communication*. Hemel Hempstead: Prentice Hall

Riel, C B M van & Fombrun, C J (2007) *Essentials of Corporate Communication: Implementing Practices for Effective Reputation Management*. Abingdon, Oxon: Routledge

Worthington I & Britton C (2006) *The Business Environment*. 5th edition. Harlow, Essex: Pearson Education

Chapter 7

Developing corporate communication

Topic list

Introduction

In Chapter 6, we introduced the concept of corporate communication: when and why it is used, and what is typically communicated to whom.

The focus of this chapter is on evaluating the different methods through which corporate communication can be planned, delivered and measured, in order (a) to deliver effective messages and (b) to enhance corporation reputation.

We start in section 1 by exploring some of the tools and models used to plan corporate communication, linking back to our discussion of the 'telling of corporate stories' in Chapter 4.

In sections 2–4, we explore and evaluate different methods or tools through which corporate communications can be delivered: the corporate communications mix (corporate advertising, public relations and sponsorships); the use of symbolism; and the communication effects of behaviour. This framework should be familiar from our discussion of the 'identity mix' in Chapter 4. The various media and tools of corporate communication will be discussed in more detail in the context of different target audiences in Chapters 8 to 10.

Finally, in section 5, we work through a number of methods by which the effectiveness of corporate communication can be measured and evaluated. As with the reputation measurement tools discussed in Chapter 5, you are not expected to become research experts, but you are expected to be broadly familiar with the terminology and approaches of the tools available – if only so that you can discuss the matter intelligently with research agencies and identity consultancies in your professional work.

Syllabus-linked learning objectives

By the end of the chapter you will be able to:

Learning objectives	Syllabus link
1 Critically evaluate the different methods through which corporate communications can be delivered	3.2.1
2 Propose changes to enhance the systems, structure and processes necessary to support corporate communication	2.2.2
3 Propose methods of measuring the effectiveness of corporate communications	3.1.3

BPP LEARNING MEDIA

1 Planning corporate communication

1.1 Image research

Fill (2002) suggests various models for the use of image or perceptions research in managing corporate identity and communication. He argues that research should be used to determine two key factors: the attributes of corporate identity that stakeholders perceive as **important**; and how stakeholders perceive organisational **performance** on these attributes. This can be plotted on a matrix as follows: Figure 7.1.

Figure 7.1: Attribute perception matrix

		Problem area (Reality or communication?)	Ideal situation (Exploit and maintain)
Importance of attribute to stakeholder	*High*		
	Low	Is this really a problem?	Is this misdirected (wasted) effort and investment?
		Low	*High*

Perceived performance

Adapted from Fill (*op cit*, p. 401, who cites Markwick (1993)).

A third dimension can also be added: namely, how stakeholders perceive organisational performance on these attributes, relative to its competitors.

- The organisation has a severe problem if (a) its customer rating is poor and (b) competitor ratings are high on (c) a factor that is important to stakeholders. Effort should be focused on changing strategy to enhance reality or communication (or both) in this area.

- The ideal position is where its customer rating is high and higher than competitors on a factor that is important to stakeholders.

- If the attribute is not important to stakeholders, the question is whether the organisation is wasting resources developing this image. It should consider changing the attributes on which its image is based (to ones more important to stakeholders) or (if the attribute is central to the organisation's personality) seeking markets where this attribute is more highly valued.

ACTIVITY 1   application

The following extract from *The Guardian* (13 April, 2002), illustrates how behaviours an organisation sees as 'unimportant' can damage corporate image and reputation.

'Watch your plastic closely. A number of credit card companies have recently been changing their customer loyalty schemes – often making them less generous – or fiddling around with their fees... And what has really riled some cardholders is the way these changes are being communicated.

[One holder of several cards issued by HBC Bank] says he objects to what he claims is the 'sneaky' way the fee is being introduced. As a result he says he will be cancelling his cards. In each case, he was sent a letter headed, 'Important changes to your terms and conditions', which alerted him to an increase in the handling fee on cash advances. The letter ends: 'please also see the enclosed leaflet for further changes to your terms and conditions'. [The customer] says it would be all too easy to ignore this sentence, and the leaflet accompanying the letter. 'But only if you read the small print do you find out about their new condition which imposes a £10 charge if the card is not used in each six-month period. This seems to me a really underhand way of imposing a new charge which many cardholders may not have any idea about until it's imposed.'

A spokesperson for HBC Bank... says it costs money to run a credit card account and it believes that when people do not use their card, it is 'only fair' to levy a £10 fee to offset some of these costs...

Meanwhile [another customer] couldn't believe his eyes when he received a letter from Alliance & Leicester relating to his MoneyBack credit card. The letter states: 'At Alliance & Leicester, we are continually looking to improve the products and services that we provide for our customers' – then goes on to say, in a very oblique and easily overlooked way, that it is actually cutting the loyalty perks that some customers enjoy.'

Draft some point-form notes for a presentation to a banking industry meeting, in which you highlight the relationship marketing issues raised by this extract.

1.2 Expressing the company

In Chapter 4, following the syllabus, we looked at van Riel & Fombrun's (2007) model of the identification of reputational platforms and the building of sustainable corporate stories. The same authors also put forward a seven-step model for designing effective communication campaigns, taking the corporate story as a starting point (*ibid*, p. 161), so it is worth mentioning this here: Figure 7.1 In many ways, this is a fairly standard advertising planning model: you may choose to use different versions, which you may have come across in your reading.

Figure 7.1: van Riel & Fombrun's *seven-step model for implementing corporate communication*

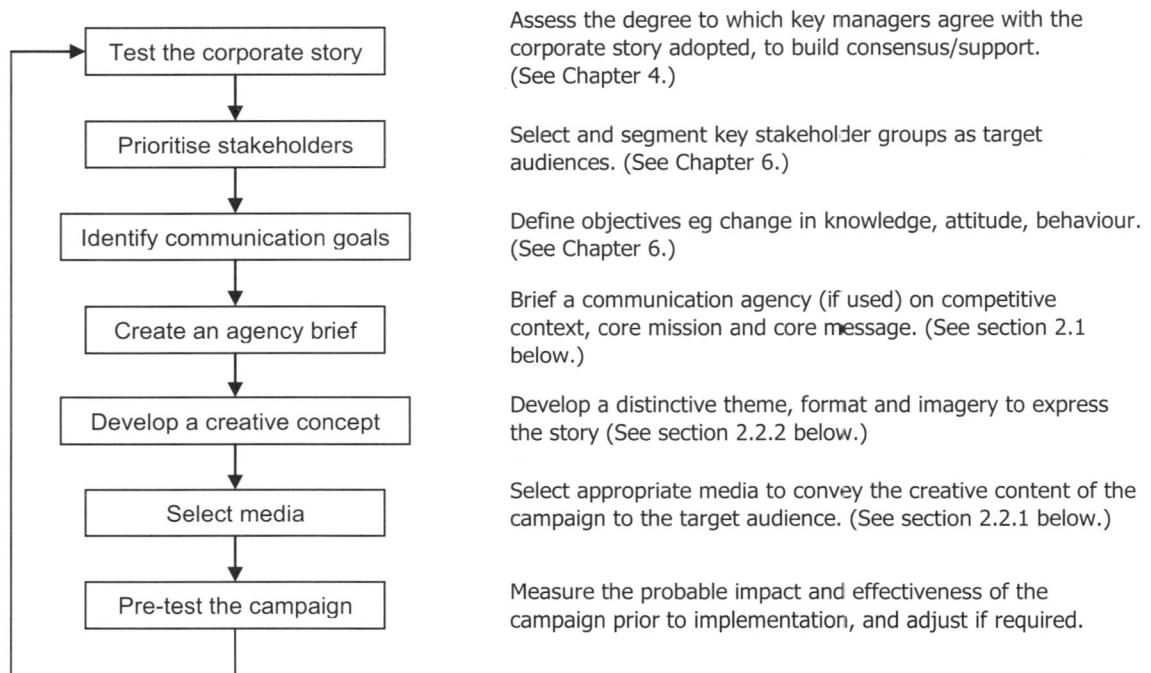

Test the corporate story	Assess the degree to which key managers agree with the corporate story adopted, to build consensus/support. (See Chapter 4.)
Prioritise stakeholders	Select and segment key stakeholder groups as target audiences. (See Chapter 6.)
Identify communication goals	Define objectives eg change in knowledge, attitude, behaviour. (See Chapter 6.)
Create an agency brief	Brief a communication agency (if used) on competitive context, core mission and core message. (See section 2.1 below.)
Develop a creative concept	Develop a distinctive theme, format and imagery to express the story (See section 2.2.2 below.)
Select media	Select appropriate media to convey the creative content of the campaign to the target audience. (See section 2.2.1 below.)
Pre-test the campaign	Measure the probable impact and effectiveness of the campaign prior to implementation, and adjust if required.

From the recommended reading list, lively and accessible coverage of the planning of corporate communication is available in:

* *Joep Cornelissen, Corporate Communication: A guide to theory and practice (2nd edition, 2008: Sage), see Chapter 5: Communication Strategy & Planning. (Note that the title of this book is cited inaccurately in some versions of the CIM recommended reading list.)* ∎

1.3 Outline communication plan

The following is by no means a standard or compulsory model: it is just a suggested framework for thinking about the planning of corporate communications campaigns. (We have, for example, left out more operational aspects such as media scheduling, budgeting, agency briefings and so on.) If asked to compile a communications plan, you should feel free to use whatever other templates you are used to from your work, or prefer from your wider reading or study course.

COMMUNICATIONS PLAN

FOR [IDENTIFIED STAKEHOLDER if relevant]

1	**Communication objectives**	• What problem/need the communication plan is designed to address • What the communications plan is intended to achieve (SMART objectives if possible) • Co-ordinated corporate communication strategies within which the plan has been developed
2	**Target audience(s)**	• Stakeholder group(s) targeted by the plan • Key needs, concerns, interests and drivers of the group • Information needs of the group (either in general or in relation to the specific problem/situation) • Media and communication tools most used by, and influential for, the stakeholder group
3	**Core themes and message(s)**	• Purpose of the message: desired stakeholder response • Content: key points of the message, and how best conveyed (eg text, multimedia) • Style: informative, persuasive, relational etc • How the message fits within the co-ordinated corporate communication mix: consistency, synergy
4	**Communication media and tools**	• Which media and tools will be used (with brief explanation/justification of each, if required): • Corporate advertising • Public Relations • Sponsorship • Corporate visual identity And so on...
5	**Timetable**	• Period over which communication will be required • Timescales for review and measurement
6	**Resource allocation**	• Estimated expenditure (or basis on which budget should be set)
7	**Monitoring and control**	• How progress and results will be monitored, reviewed and measured against objectives (see section 5 of this chapter)

Alternatively, you could merge sections 3 and 4 of this plan under the heading **Communication Action Plans** and either:

- Outline the use of each **selected communication tool** in turn, discussing the content and style of messages to be conveyed by each, or

- Outline **specific communication plans** based on the information needs of the stakeholder group(s) and your purposes for communicating. This is more flexible, whether or not your communication plan uses particular media. For example:

    - Customer communication scenario: TV advertising to convey message A (with a focus on image/awareness); print advertising to convey message B (giving more information); data capture and direct e-mail follow-up to convey message C (offer of added value through supportive behaviour).

    - Specific employee communication scenario: e-mail to all staff to notify of staff meeting; meeting to brief staff on changes; follow-up team briefings to enable more detailed discussion; phone or personal interviews with team leaders to gather feedback.

2 The corporate communication mix

The communication mix as it applies to **marketing communication** consists of a wide range of tools. The major components of the promotional (marketing communication) mix have traditionally been recognised as: advertising, personal selling, direct marketing, sales promotion and marketing-focused public relations. However, the range of tools is – as we will see in Chapter 8 – far more extensive, embracing: product packaging and design, corporate visual identity, product and corporate branding, exhibitions, web sites, internal marketing, sponsorship, field marketing, word-of-mouth promotion and so on.

The tools used for corporate-level or **organisational communication**, however, are typically more narrow in scope, because of the focus on corporate issues and corporate audiences. The tools specifically mentioned in the syllabus content include:

- Corporate advertising
- Sponsorships
- Public relations activity

We will discuss each of these here in general terms, and in more detail – as applied to specific stakeholder audiences – in Chapters 8 to 10.

2.1 Briefing a communication agency

You should have covered the selecting and briefing of advertising agencies in your earlier studies (eg for *Delivering Customer Value Through Marketing*), but it is worth noting that at the more strategic level of corporate communication, the desired contribution of an agency will be somewhat different.

In formulating a brief for an agency providing help with reputation research, corporation communication, corporate identity or branding, the organisation will need to address issues such as:

- The **focus of image/reputation and branding efforts**: product brands, strategic business units or the company as a whole?

- **Key stakeholder audiences**: which stakeholder groups are a priority, for their influence on the continuing success of the organisation?

- **Benchmark standards**: which competitor, industry leader or other excellent organisation does the organisation want to measure itself against?

- **Measurement methods**: which tools or standards of measurement will be used to measure the success of the communication or brand-building programme?

In addition, as with any other form of agency-designed communication campaign, creative specialists will have to be briefed with sufficient information to guide their thinking. A creative brief may consist of:

- The **communication objective**: what the organisation wants to achieve from the campaign (eg changes of knowledge/awareness, attitude and/or behaviour in target audiences) and how these will be measured.

- The **strategic and competitive context** of the campaign: the organisation's general and communication strategies to compete in its market.

- A description of the **desired identity** which is to be projected by the communication campaign, including (Hamel & Prahalad, 1996; Ind, 2007)):

    - Corporate mission and purpose

    - Core values

    - Core (distinctive, value-adding) competences

    - How the organisation and its employees 'live the brand': proven commitment to principles, values that shape corporate identity.

- A description of the **stakeholder audience**(s) to be targeted by the campaign: their interest and influence in the organisation; their defining characteristics, information needs and current perceptions of the organisation (where known).

- A description of **core themes and messages** to be conveyed by the campaign. If the organisation has already developed reputational platforms (starting points) and stories, this information may be ready to hand. It may already have articulated a PPT framework for the corporate story: core Promises, Proof points and Tone of Voice. (See section 5 of Chapter 4 if this doesn't ring a bell.)

- A description of **symbols** (visual and verbal) currently used in the organisation, where relevant, so that the agency can give thought to the consistency, coherence and synergy of its creative concept and use of symbols in the communication campaign: harmonisation with current corporate logos, visual images, music, tag lines and so on.

ACTIVITY 2

application

Using a commercial organisation of your choice as a model for the required information, and the above bullet points as a rough guide, draft a briefing for a corporate communication agency for an advertising campaign designed to reassure investors of the organisation's continued commitment to shareholder value and corporate social responsibility through the global financial downturn.

For a fascinating insight into the creative strategies and briefing processes used by various top advertising agencies (based on work done for Apple Computers), see the 'Strategy Seminar' posted at:

Link: http://www.adbuzz.com/OLD/Strategy.pdf

2.2 Corporate advertising

KEY CONCEPT

concept

Advertising is 'any **paid** form of **non-personal** presentation and promotion of ideas, goods or services by an **identifiable** sponsor.' (American Marketing Association)

Advertising can be effective for a range of purposes in product/service marketing, but corporate advertising is intended primarily to create an image of the organisation in the minds of target audiences; to raise awareness of corporate identity and/or brands; and by not-for-profit and public sector organisations to promote their programmes (eg to persuade audiences not to drink and drive, to support education, to give to a charitable cause and so on).

Advertising is often classed under one of three purpose-based headings:

- **Informative**: conveying information and raising awareness. For a first-time corporate campaign, or a re-branding or re-positioning campaign, the focus will be on information and reach: raising awareness and creating familiarity with the new or revised corporate identity or brand.

- **Persuasive**: stimulating change in target audience's attitudes or organisation-supporting behaviours, with campaigns more directly targeted to specific audiences with specific messages. This is often used once basic corporate brand awareness and familiarity have been established, especially in competitive settings.

- **Reminding**: maintaining awareness of the corporate identity or brand in the mind of audiences; reinforcing the engagement of current and potential customers/investors/employees, and confirming existing supporters in their decision (to invest, purchase etc).

Advertising occupies an ambiguous role in corporate brand-building, however. As we noted in Chapter 4, Core Brand's Brand Power analysis claims that advertising investment is the most significant driver of higher brand power. However, Davies *et al.* (*op cit*, p. 90–93) argue that:

- Several successful brands have grown **without significant advertising**, focusing instead on creating image-building experiences for customers and other stakeholders, encouraging word-of-mouth and so on.

- It is **counterproductive**, in reputation and brand building terms, to advertise experiences that are not delivered in practice by the organisation (eg being turned down for a loan by 'the bank that likes to say yes'): this attracts not only stakeholder disappointment, but negative media attention.

- The role of advertising is different in creating a **brand image for a service company** or a **corporate reputation** for any company, than it is for product branding. 'Advertising cannot generally be used to create an image in such circumstances. However, if the company has created a different experience for the customer, then this can be communicated using advertising.' The main role of advertising in the context of corporate branding is therefore providing factual information.

MARKETING AT WORK

application

Doughnut retailer **Krispy Kreme** (Australia) is an interesting example of a brand that relies (successfully) on buzz marketing and word-of-mouth as its main communications strategy.

'After a fire, Krispy Kreme staff send doughnuts to the firemen. On Mothers Day, they send doughnuts to the new mothers' wards at hospitals. And when they open a store, they don't advertise its location. 'Word-of-mouth has been integral to what we've achieved... Krispy Kreme is very much owned by the consumer... Seeding small amounts of information allows consumers to **tell their own stories** and ask their own questions about a brand.'

Ad News, 21/04/06

The **Body Shop International** is a classic example of a brand with a distinctive reputation platform and corporate story, based on ethics, social responsibility and sustainability values. It has been particularly adept in using stakeholder marketing to:

- Generate positive public relations and referrals from existing customers, to the point where it uses no advertising

- Gain extensive media coverage (without having to pay for formal advertising), by developing relationships with a wide range of media

- Develop relationships with local communities, by having each shop involved in a local community project

- Develop mutually-supportive relationships with a range of environmental pressure groups, including Greenpeace and Friends of the Earth

Link: http://www.thebodyshop.com (follow the link to 'values and campaigns')

ACTIVITY 3

application

If you haven't already done so, start collecting a file of corporate advertisements from the business, trade and quality press – including any advertising by any organisation that may form the focus of your assessment. Evaluate such advertisement for their purpose and effectiveness. Select benchmark advertisers, whose style and credibility you would want your organisation's advertising to emulate.

2.2.1 Advertising media

The choice of which media to use to convey corporate communication is extremely important. The majority of any communication budget is likely to be spent on media buying – as opposed to campaign design, production and evaluation.

Major advertising media include television, cinema, radio, newspapers, magazines and outdoor media (poster sites, bus stops, buildings etc). In addition, opportunities have emerged in a wide range of interactive digital media such as the internet, Direct Response Television, mobile phone applications, enhanced CD and CD-ROM, web sites and so on.

Media are generally selected according to:

- The size of the audience exposed to the medium (**range**), the number of exposures per audience member (**frequency**) and the time span over which exposures occur (**continuity**). Mass media such as TV, radio and national press, have large exposure. Reader/viewer/listener numbers (newspaper circulation, programme ratings) are closely monitored, helping media planners to assess the reach of the campaign.

- The type of people who form the audience of the medium (**targeting**). There is often a trade-off between the size and relevance of the available audience. Segmentation (for example, placing an ad in special-interest sections of a newspaper) or targeting (in local or regional media, specialist magazines and so on) may be possible where relevant.

- The suitability of the medium for the audience (**credibility**): the extent to which the content and style of the medium is congenial, authoritative and relevant to the target audience's motives and interests.

- The suitability of the medium for the message (**impact**). Print ads, for example, allow high volumes of information to be taken in and kept, with response mechanisms (eg coupons) if desired. Television, cinema and online video-streaming have a high impact on awareness and retention because of the potential for creativity, and sound/moving image combinations. Radio has a highly personal quality, but as a sound-only medium has limited potential for information retention.

- The medium's demonstrated/tested ability to yield results (**performance**): for example, measured audience response speed or volume, or response as a percentage of audience reached.

- The cost of the medium in relation to all the above (**budget**). Cinema and TV have very high space and production costs. Newspapers and magazines cost by circulation, which or may not be relevant to the target audience of the advertiser.

The following table shows a comparison of some of the key features of major above-the-line media.

Medium	Advantages	Disadvantages
Newspapers (Daily, metropolitan, national)	• Mass medium: large audience in single exposure • Targeted sections • Reader navigation: seeking news, information • Short lead time for production • Flexibility of ad size • Multiple readers/users • Allows detailed information allows (still) images and symbols • Allows response mechanisms	• Circulation does not equal meaningful exposures • Print/image reproduction of variable quality • No exclusivity: ad may be next to competitors or negative-association editorial • Costs loaded for preferred positions • Short life-span of news
Newspapers (Local, free)	• Low cost • Geographical/community targeting • High community readership	• Circulation not always audited • Variable editorial content • Subject to junk mail perception
Magazines	• High circulation (major titles) • Targeted audiences (special interest) • High quality reproduction • Potential high prestige • Reader motivation/identification • Long shelf life and multiple exposures	• High costs of production • Hyper-segmentation (by interest) • Long lead times

Medium	Advantages	Disadvantages
Television	• Mass medium, high penetration • Detailed monitoring of reach, exposure, viewing habits • Allows for high creativity • Impact of multimedia • Flexible, targeted scheduling • Synergy by association with programmes	• High media and production costs • Lack of targeting (except via programmes) • Long lead times for buying and production • Passive, unmotivated audience (eg 'zapping' by video fast-forward and remote control)
Radio	• Mass medium • Audience targeting • Opportunity: use in transit etc • Function: high usage for morning news, background etc • Personal (potential for dialogue) • Competitive air-time, production cost • Can be backed by promo, content	• May be passive 'background' noise: low attention, retention • May be 'cluttered' • Sound only: no tangibility (pressure on retention), no shelf-life or 'pass on' circulation, limited information capacity
Outdoor media	• Flexible sites, leases • Comparatively low cost • Opportunity: exposure to commuters, shoppers	• Difficulty verifying exposure and response • Subject to weather • Opportunity: site specific • Little audience targeting
Cinema	• Glamorous • High impact • Captive audience • Community audience	• High cost • Opportunity: site/time specific • Poor verification of response • Limited reach per exposure

Media planning, buying and scheduling, and the origination and production of highly designed and technically demanding advertising formats, are generally undertaken by specialist agencies, which form a multi-billion dollar global industry. The main tasks of the communication manager in the client organisation will be to brief the agency and liaise with account executives to monitor, co-ordinate and approve plans at each stage of the process.

ACTIVITY 4

application

Which media are used for corporate advertising by your own organisation (if any) and why?

If you can, get hold of copies of media plans and schedules. What kinds of decisions have been made in allocated communication budgets?

2.2.2 Developing the creative concept and advertising message

The appeal of a corporate reputation platform and story depends heavily on the creative concept used to convey them. 'The creative concept brings the story to life… Practically speaking, a robust creative concept should provide a frame of reference for all of the company's communications – a distinct format and context through which all corporate messages can be filtered and that typifies the company behind the product brands.' (van Riel & Fombrun, *op cit*, p. 172–3)

Elements of compelling creative concepts include:

- The core **values and themes** to be conveyed by the campaign

- The **story**, **tone and style** elements which will be used to convey the core values and themes (metaphors, narratives, tone of voice, images, layouts, visuals, logos, music etc)

- The key functional, psychological or social **benefits** offered to the targeted audience (the brand promise)

- The specific **attributes** or benefits that are to be communicated verbally or visually in relation to the brand.

Each of these elements should complement and reinforce one another. The total creative concept should be **consistent** with the corporate branding strategy; **targeted** to the information needs and characteristics of the target audience; simple, direct and **distinctive** enough to foster recognition and recall; **versatile** enough to be applied across different media; and with a sufficiently long **shelf-life** to build recognition and engagement over time (ie not too quickly dated by brand changes or environmental trends).

MARKETING AT WORK

application

The following press release was posted on the press site of the Coca Cola UK web site (www.coca-cola.co.uk) on May 8 2009.

COCA-COLA launches new summer campaign under the 'Open Happiness' umbrella

Summer is set to shine with integrated communications platform and exclusive bottle design

Open Happiness

Coca-Cola Great Britain's summer campaign is centred around inspiring people to say yes to the opportunities that summer brings and is set to hit screens with the new ad creative, 'Yeah Yeah Yeah, La La La'. The ad, created by Mother London features an exclusive track commissioned by Coca-Cola, which has been written and produced by electro superstar Calvin Harris.

The new 30 and 60 second spots go live in the UK on Friday 31 May. The story unfolds as one summer morning, a mysterious man pushes a large box into a park and up to the top of a hill. The man opens the box and it turns into a magical, summery organ with curious little creatures inside. He fits a chilled bottle of 'Coke' to a plug on the side of the musical machine and hits a key on the keyboard as a drop falls into the creature's mouths. With each drop, the creatures are refreshed with ice cold Coca-Cola and begin to sing 'yeah yeah yeah' and 'la la la' as a crowd of young people gathers in a surreal and summery scene.

'Yeah Yeah Yeah, La La La' is the first execution of the new Open Happiness platform in GB and with its happy, upbeat and vibrant soundtrack, should become an infectious and vibrant tune this summer. Open Happiness marks a continuation of the brand's iconic and award winning 'Coke Side of Life' brand communication and inspires the brand's point of view of optimism, positivity, refreshment and pleasure.

'Selfridges Centenary' Original Glass Bottle

'Coca-Cola' is celebrating Selfridges' 100th birthday with the exclusive *Selfridges Centenary Bottle*, an eye-catching limited edition original glass bottle that shines in the store's signature shade of yellow. The bottle sees the coming together of instantly recognisable icons: the coveted Selfridges' yellow shopping bag, the classic contoured original glass bottle and classic red 'Coca-Cola' script, creating a distinctive and bright bottle wrap.

The brands have a longstanding history, with 'Coca-Cola' being first poured in the UK in Selfridges in 1926. Over 80 years on, both brands are as relevant now as they ever were.

For reflection: what are the (a) brand platform, (b) corporate story and (c) creative concept elements of this integrated campaign?

2.3 Public relations

Public relations is the 'planned and sustained effort to establish and maintain goodwill and mutual understanding between an organisation and its publics' (Institute of Public Relations). The related discipline of publicity is defined as any form of non-paid, non-personal communication.

This is an important discipline for corporate communication, because although it may not directly stimulate sales, stakeholder goodwill is – as we have seen – an important factor in whether an organisation attracts and retains employees, whether consumers buy its products/services, whether the community supports or resists its presence and activities, whether the media reports positively on its operations, and whether pressure and interest groups attack or support it.

We summarised the various communication activities previously described under the umbrella of PR – and now referred to as corporate communication – in Chapter 6, and they will be explored in more detail in Chapter 8.

2.3.1 Publicity

Media coverage in editorial articles, blogs, product/service reviews and news items is an important source of low-cost communication and perceived third-party endorsement. It can be stimulated by:

- Building up a network of media contacts (or using a PR or media relations agency)
- Sending media/press releases and/or photos to relevant journalists/editors, or holding photo calls and press conferences (if something genuinely newsworthy can be revealed: wasting busy journalists' time is not good media relations!)
- Sending product samples for trial and review (often with added incentives such as supporting competitions or product give-aways, offering added value to the publication/programme's audience)
- Arranging publicity 'stunts' and events to which journalists/editors are invited, or which achieve coverage by being attached to covered events (such as sporting fixtures)
- Offering relevant spokespeople and experts for interview, comment, consultation or authorship (eg of technical articles for trade journals).

In a bid to counter the negative effect of its bird flu outbreak, **Thailand's Commerce Ministry** set up a task force charged with establishing exhibition exposure for the country's export industries. The task force was instructed to find at least 1,000 strategic exhibition opportunities over five years to promote Thai output. The thrust of the campaign was directed at department stores in targeted export markets, presenting Thailand as a market place for goods and services, with Thai produce itself also on display. Exhibits were set up in China, India, the Middle East and Russia among other countries in Eastern Europe, Africa and South America. Allied to the campaign, the Thai government organised an 'export rally' to solidify support among Thai exporters in targeting international events. (Kaenwong, 2004)

Brainstorm some items of corporate news, relevant to your own organisation, that the media might consider **newsworthy**: interesting (relevant to audiences); local (relevant to the area/region with which audiences identify); topical (happening now, has just happened, or is about to happen); important (will make a difference or impact on audiences); new or surprising. You might gather some ideas from actual news articles in the press which identify corporations by name.

Why do you think the launch of a Harry Potter book can attract worldwide media attention – including the cover of *Time* Magazine?

2.3.2 Evaluating PR effectiveness

The advantages and disadvantages of Public Relations as a corporate communication tool can be summarised as follows.

Advantages	Disadvantages
Raises awareness of a wider audience (including word-of-mouth promotion, media coverage, pressure group support)	Uncontrollability of media coverage: can't control content or guarantee coverage when desired
Supports 'competitive architecture, through positive relationships with stakeholders (eg labour, supply chains)	Media and other stakeholders have their own agendas (circulation/ratings, public information) which may not coincide with positive publicity
Relatively low cost (compared to media)	Risk of poor publicity and word-of-mouth
Perceived legitimacy (implies endorsement or recommendation by third parties)	Results/outcomes of public relations activity are not easy to monitor and measure
Supports corporate advertising, sponsorship and other corporate branding tools	

Media coverage can be easily monitored using cuttings or media monitoring agencies, where this is a measure of effectiveness. However, where possible, the achievement of specific objectives should be the criterion because PR is often perceived as 'free' and its results as intangible 'goodwill', it is too easy for costs to escalate without detailed justification.

MARKETING AT WORK

application

Gillette (USA)

Gillette is a strong independent subsidiary brand (not heavily endorsed by parent company Proctor & Gamble) with its 'The Best a Man Can Get' platform and its 'champions' creative concept, associating the brand with major sporting heroes (see www.gillette.com)

In 2004, however, Gillette spent more than US $1 million on a sponsorship package that included having samples of its razors added to the 'goodie bag' of delegates at the US Democratic National Convention. Unfortunately, hundreds of attendees were stopped when attempting to pass through security checks – and were not happy...

Nokia (Germany)

Attempting to invite its customers to a festive gathering at an industry trade show, cell-phone maker Nokia naturally used text-messaging as its medium. Unfortunately, the signal instantly disabled hundreds of phones, damaging them so badly that they had to be taken to Nokia service centres for repair.

Is there really 'no such thing as bad publicity'?

(Business 2.0, Jan/Feb 2005)

Some useful measures include:

- Defining the **key messages** that will fulfil the specific objective of the programme and use media monitoring, feedback, audience research and communication audits to establish whether the programme (a) reaches the target audience and (b) correctly conveys the messages, resulting in the desired attitudes, perceptions and awareness.

- Monitoring appropriate **performance measures** for specific communication objectives: fall in employee turnover following an internal communication campaign, for example; focus group awareness raised after a publicity campaign; sales recovery following crisis communication. Expect to see some results!

We will discuss these issues in more detail in the final section of this chapter.

2.4 Sponsorships

KEY CONCEPT

concept

Sponsorship involves supporting an event, activity or entity by providing money (or something else of value, such as product prizes for a competition), usually in return for naming rights, advertising or acknowledgement.

Corporate sponsorship is often actively sought for sporting and artistic bodies and events, educational initiatives, and charity/community events and initiatives. Organisations may sponsor local area or school groups and events – all the way up to national and international sporting and cultural events and entities. Sponsorship has been particularly useful in offering marketing communication avenues to organisations which are restricted in their advertising (such as alcohol and tobacco companies) or which wish to widen their awareness base among various target audiences.

The objectives of the sponsor may be:

- Awareness creation in the target audience of the sponsored event (where it coincides with the target audience of the sponsor)

- Media coverage generated by the sponsored events

- Opportunities for corporate hospitality (another tool of public relations) at sponsored events

- Association with prestigious or popular events, particular values or causes (for affinity and causal marketing benefits)

- Creation of a positive image among employees and/or the wider community by association with worthy causes or community events

- Securing potential employees (for example, by sponsoring vocational or tertiary education)

- Cost-effective achievement of the above (compared to, say, TV advertising).

Sponsorship activities must be fully integrated with other areas of marketing communications in order to capitalise on their potential value.

Sponsorship is often seen as part of a company's socially responsible and community-friendly public relations profile – and has causal and affinity marketing benefits of positive associations with the sponsored cause, entity or event. The profile gained (for example, in the case of television coverage of a sponsored sporting event) can be cost-effective compared to advertising. There may also be opportunities for corporate hospitality arising from sponsorship of cultural and sporting events: corporate hospitality offering a further tool of public relations.

However, as a communication tool, sponsorship relies heavily on awareness and association: unless additional advertising space or 'air time' is part of the deal, not much information may be conveyed. It is also possible that association with an entity or event may attach negative values to the corporate image in some circumstances (eg sports-related violence).

MARKETING AT WORK

concept

Australian banks **National Australia Bank** and **St George Bank** are examples of a balanced and targeted corporate sponsorship portfolio.

NAB's deal as a lead sponsor of the Australian Ballet – second only to [national telecom provider] Telstra – includes sponsorship of the ballet's education program, a grass roots element that aims to strengthen the bank's involvement in the community. St George has become presenting partner for the Sydney Symphony's Mozart in the City series.

The two banks, however, do not restrict themselves to arts sponsorships. NAB was also a major sponsor of the 2006 Commonwealth Games, while St George is a major sponsor of ruby league team Illawara Dragons [also known as 'St George'].

'We look at sponsorships that are going to complement our target segments,' St George sponsorship manager Pamela Chalmers said. 'Our customers have a wide range of interests. With all sponsorships, we look at how they will help us build our brand, build business, allow our staff to be involved and how they will support the St George Foundation, our non-profit philanthropic arm.'

Similarly for NAB, the sponsorship evaluation process considers how the event or property fits with the bank's brand, 'what it stands for and where it should be heading', said NAB head of sponsorship Maria McCarthy. And again, a sponsorship the bank's staff can be proud of and become involved in is another key consideration.

('Banks expand sponsorship deals', *AdNews*, 25 March 2005)

ACTIVITY 6

application

Next time you are at an event of any kind, look at the list of sponsors in the programme.

- What kind of sponsors support and identify themselves with different kinds of event – and why? (What synergies are their between the audiences or images of the event and the sponsor?)

- What amounts of sponsorship are cited – and what benefits (in terms of naming rights, advertising, visual branding, use of facilities) are given to sponsors in return?

2.5 Web sites

Web sites are now a key channel of corporate communication: every major organisation in any field will now have some form of web presence. Web sites are used for a number of communication purposes:

- **Corporate advertising and information**. Web sites can be used simply as a medium for advertising, plus stakeholder access to corporate information (often targeted specifically to public, customer, investor, media, employee and prospective employee audiences).

- **Interface with key stakeholders** (eg e-commerce, customer service/technical support, media relations, employee intranet), through posted information, FAQs, e-mail contact and so on.

- **Gathering stakeholder information and feedback**: eg via online surveys, site/purchase tracking, online community message boards; and so on.

- **Media/press relations**: via online media/press kits, e-mailed media releases, 'about us' and 'contact' pages, technical briefings and articles on key issues.

- **Public relations**: via 'about us' and FAW features; news bulletins (eg for issues or crisis management); public/information about sponsorships, exhibitions and events; sponsorship of popular/useful information sites.

- **Grass roots and viral marketing**: generating word of mouth among site users, via online chat or message board forums, 'introduce a friend' schemes, and viral communication tools (eg e-cards and links 'send this page to a friend').

- **E-mail**: direct mail communication as an alternative to postal direct mail, used to send corporate newsletters, press-releases and so on (as appropriate to target audiences) on a permission basis.

- **Corporate identity projection**: web design and content designed to create an integrated and coherent identity/branding message alongside all other corporate identity messages.

The general benefits of web communication may be described as follows (Rich, 2001):

'If you create an entire web site specifically to promote your company and its products and services, you're not limited by ad space (as you would be using a traditional print ad in a magazine, for example). You're also not forced to convey your message in 15, 40 or 60 seconds as you are when using TV or radio advertising. As long as you're offering the web surfer information (s)he wants or needs, your web site can potentially capture that person's attention and keep it for seconds, minutes or even hours as you convey your messages... This is something a TV ad, print ad or radio ad can't do.' The following (Figure 7.2) is an example of a web site (leading corporate brand Diageo's home page), showing the potential for corporate branding and addressing different stakeholder audiences.

Figure 7.2: The Diageo web site home page (www.diageo.com)

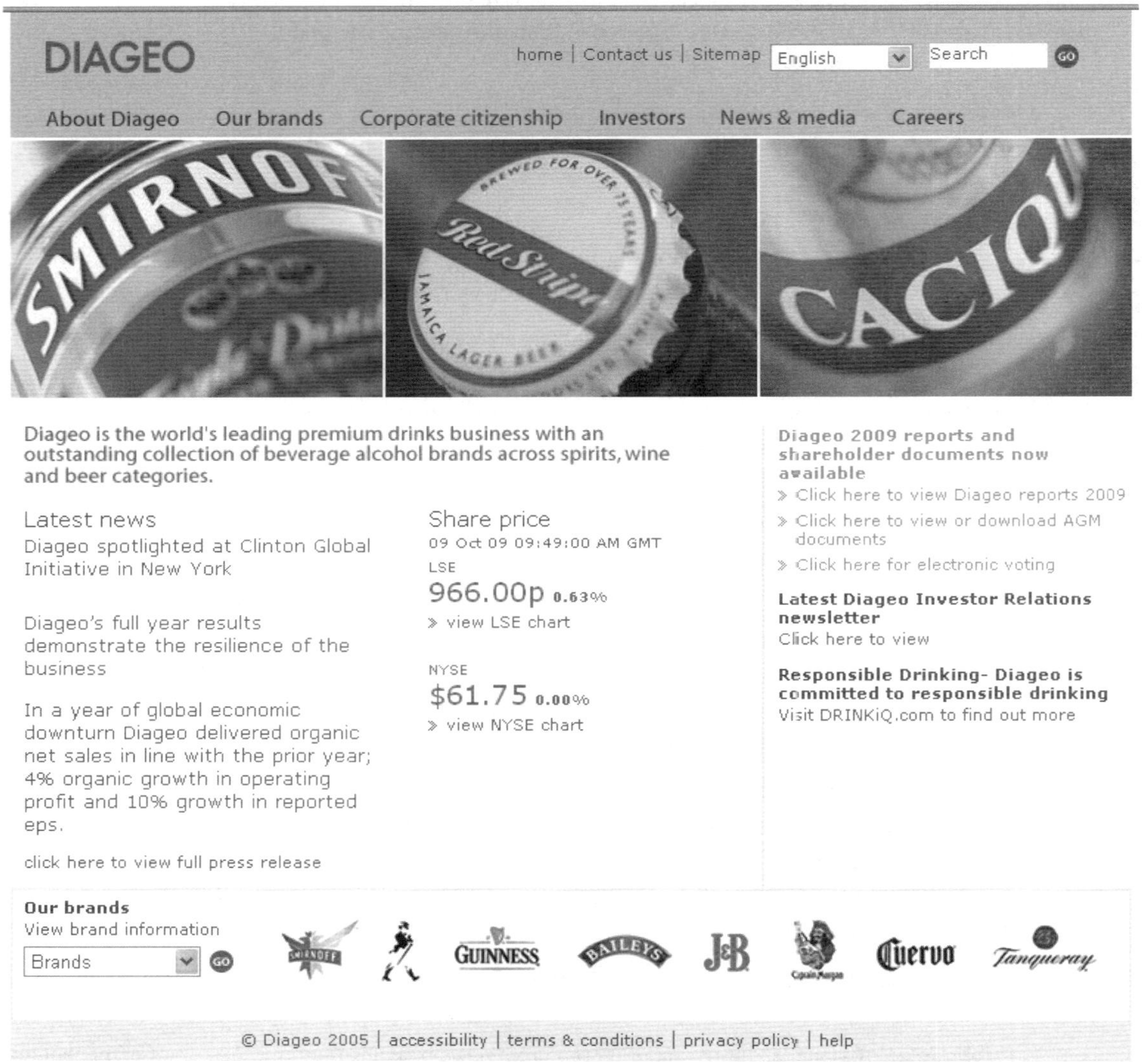

ACTIVITY 7

evaluation

Compare the consumer and corporate home pages of the following organisations.

- Adidas (www.adidas.com versus www.adidas-group.com)
- Marks and Spencer (www.marksandspencer.com versus http://corporate.marksandspencer.com)
- Disney (www.disney.com versus http://corporate.disney.go.com)

Also check out some major parent company web sites:

- Proctor & Gamble (www.pg.com)
- Unilever (www.unilever.com)

What are the distinguishing features of corporate web communication, compared to consumer web marketing?

2.6 Co-ordinating the mix

Choosing the correct mix of media and tools for corporate communication is not easy – although new technology is making it somewhat more scientific: software suites can match databased stakeholder and media profiles to formulate an optimal mix, and communication budgets and strategies can be modelled on spreadsheets for a variety of different mixes.

The key aim of media and campaign planning is to:

- Create **integrated communication campaigns**, which present core themes and messages coherently and consistently across media

- Create **synergistic communication campaigns**, which leverage the strengths of each medium and the potential for each medium to build on others (through reinforcement, recognition and so on)

- Create **optimal communication campaigns**, which allow the weaknesses and strengths of media to compensate for or complement each other, for the best overall impact.

3 Symbolism

As we saw in Chapter 4, one of the dimensions of corporate identity is **visual identity**: the names, logos, 'house style', preferred colour palettes, images and other symbols that are adopted consistently through all external and internal corporate communications. Olins (1990) argues that it is critical to examine 'how the visual style of a company influences its place in the market, and how the company's goals are made visible in its design and behaviour'.

The aims of a corporate visual identity programme may be:

- To maintain a consistent style and standard of communications throughout the organisation and to all publics, a part of an integrated corporate communication approach

- To differentiate the organisation's communications and corporate brand from those of competitors for audiences' attention and awareness

- To build recognition of the organisation's communication style, so that:

    - Audiences will extend the goodwill and interest from current messages/products to new or further ones

    - Existing messages/brands can be identified and located among competing offerings

- To communicate the values and attributes of the organisation to internal and external stakeholders

- To encourage employees, investors and other stakeholder groups to identify with a strong organisational image and set of associations. 'House style' may be one of the major influences in forming, or changing, the organisation's perception of, and attitude to, itself.

3.1 Corporate nomenclature

'Nomenclature' is the umbrella term used for names and symbols (such as logos). van Riel & Fombrun (*op cit*, p. 132) argue that: 'nomenclature serves the same function as religious icons, heraldry, national flags and other symbols: they encapsulate collective feelings of belonging, and make them visible.'

Corporate names are a strong cue for corporate branding, as they are often the first point of contact with stakeholders. Brand names and the taglines or formulas attached to them are often selected to express corporate activity (eg industry sector or core business focus), location (if divisionalised by region), competences/abilities (eg innovation, value creation) and core values (eg responsibility, the environment, human rights). Depending on the branding strategy for endorsement (as discussed in Chapter 4), they may also reflect affiliations (eg association with a parent company or 'family of companies).

What's in a name?

- When Hutchinson Telecom adopted the **Orange** brand in 1994, corporate names in the sector were purely descriptive. 'Orange' was an instant point of differentiation – associated with a 'different' service offering. As a colour, it also offered instant visual associations, which could be used in creative advertising.

- When confectionary company **Mars** wanted to harmonise its use of names across its global markets, it decided to give the UK Marathon bar the name of its US equivalent: Snickers. The brand had to work hard against a number of negative connotations possible in English culture – but the strong brand values appear to have transferred successfully to the new name. What would you do if you had to market the French drink brand 'Pschitt' in English-speaking nations, or the Toyota model MR2 (pronounced 'merde' in French, similarly translated as 'excrement') in France...? (Jobber, 2007)

When officials in the Convention & Visitors Bureau of Greater Cleveland (USA) decided in 2006 that they wanted to do something to set their city's marketing arm apart from others, they didn't decide on the new name, **Positively Cleveland**, right away. Even more than creating a unique identity, said Dennis Roche, president of Positively Cleveland, it wanted a name that would convey the attitude and energy of the city. They considered other options – Travel Cleveland, Genuine Cleveland and Visit Cleveland – before settling on Positively Cleveland. 'We're trying to communicate a message that's hard to get across when you call yourself a bureau. We wanted a name change and researched it for a year.'

Cleveland isn't alone. Destination management organisations across the country and world are changing their names from the conventional designation (City Name Convention & Visitors Bureau) to ones with some more pizzazz. The bureau in New York City became NYC & Company; the Los Angeles bureau, LA Inc (adding The Los Angeles Convention & Visitors Bureau at the end, just to be safe); and others followed: Meet Minneapolis, Choose Chicago...

Cleveland polled visitors about the new moniker and tested it with more than 11,000 meeting planners before deciding Positively Cleveland truly represented the city. The CBV changed its web site to www.positivelycleveland.com – and saw a drop in web traffic during the first couple of months. 'Not unexpectedly, it takes a while to gain some traction. But the change for us has been really very helpful. As a marketing tool, it really sets us apart.'

(*Tradeshow Week*, 24/3/2008)

3.1.1 Logos and taglines

Distinctive brand symbols (logos) and name styles (logotypes) are often developed and protected by organisations, and may be adopted and used across the communication mix, in communications, product packaging, advertising, transport fleet, staff uniforms and so on. 'A logo is not only a way of presenting the company name attractively. It is probably a far more powerful way of **adding associations** than by spending time worrying about any intrinsic associations with the brand name itself. The typeface, colour and associated design will carry more powerful symbolic messages to the stakeholder than the name itself.' (Davies *et al.*, *op cit*, p. 86).

A logo may be designed to be:

- **Symbolic**: representing the activity, attributes or name of the organisation (eg the panda of the World Wildlife Fund, the National Trust oak tree, the Apple apple, or the Shell shell)

- **Expressive**: creating impressions and associations relevant to the organisation's desired image (eg the Nike 'swoosh' with its suggestion of speed and success, or the CIM's use of the coat of arms, reflecting its Royal Charter, as a 'dot' over its 'i').

- **Recognisable**: creating recognition, recall, differentiation and identification (eg the Coca Cola logotype or the McDonalds golden arches).

Logos may be distinctive due to their type style (eg Coca Cola or Johnson and Johnson); a symbol or image (eg the Apple apple); or colour (eg BP's green and yellow, Orange's orange) – or a combination of these (eg Mcdonalds' golden arches).

Davies *et al.* (*op cit*, p. 226) suggest the following basic 'rules' for designing effective logos.

- Be original: scan the marketplace for similar designs and use of colour, to avoid confusion
- Ensure flexibility: consider whether the logo will reproduce in colour and black and white, and in all media at all sizes
- Try for symbolism or positive associations
- Ensure the logo is not culture bound: will it work as well in international markets?
- Check for unexpected symbolism: what could the logo represent, if someone wanted to interpret it negatively?

Taglines are concise slogans, mottos or identifiers attached to company names and logos, encapsulating the brand promise or proposition: what the organisation does and/or what it stands for. For example:

- Philips (Sense and simplicity)
- Tesco (Every little helps)
- World Wildlife Fund (For a living planet)
- Hewlett Packard (Invent)
- Nokia (Connecting people)
- McDonalds (I'm Lovin' It)
- BP (Beyond Petroleum)
- Woolworths Australia (The Fresh Food People)
- Microsoft (Your Potential, Our Passion)
- Nike (Just do it)
- Gillette (The best a man can get)

In practice, a corporate brand generally consists of a logo plus a tagline, working together to encapsulate everything the brand stands for – and acting as a trigger to elicit associations in the audience's mind. The following (Figure 7.3) are some examples of logos, with and without names or taglines, as drawn from a range of organisational, brand and destination websites.

Figure 7.3: Nomenclature examples

What would you identify as the 'starting point' or identity platform behind each of the tag line examples given above?

How effective are each of the logo examples given above, and why? (Bear in mind that we have not been able to portray them in full colour...)

What do you think is the balance and synergy of expressiveness between the name, the tagline and the logo in these cases?

3.2 Other tools of visual and symbolic identity

Nomenclature is by no means the only medium for corporate visual identity messages. A wide range of visual and symbolic cues may be given through:

- Corporate signage

- Corporate uniforms (or dress codes) and liveries (eg for transport fleets)

- The location, space, size, architecture and décor of corporate premises (particularly public-facing areas, but these aspects are also important for internal identity)

- Artefacts expressing the corporate history, culture and self-image: examples include company museums and displays, books about the history of the organisation, recipe books published by restaurants

- Corporate merchandise (T-shirts, baseball caps, key-rings and so on)

- Music commissioned by the organisation and/or associated with the brand (often through use in advertising campaigns and corporate events), and use of music in corporate premises and at corporate events. (Think of the various songs associated with the Coca Cola brand over the years. Or the use of 'theme songs' at political conventions. Or even the choice of 'on-hold' music on corporate telephone systems...)

'**BMW** has put a soundtrack to its love affair with content, commissioning techno group The Presets to remix a song and create a music video to launch its new 1 Series. The luxury car brand is claiming an Australian first with the brand-funded content program, which will result in a remixed version of Are You The One? in the commercial... The BMW – integrated marketing program includes a new music video that will feature the 1 Series in it, while plans are under consideration for live activity, such as concerts... Since 1975, the company has commissioned famous artists to paint BMWs as part of its Art Cars program, while its www.bmwfilms.com campaign from 2001 comprised a series of short films shot by Hollywood directors, each of which featured a BMW. 'We've entered into a partnership with The Presets similar to Art Cars.'... The music program is designed to create more interest from a broader, younger audience. 'We'll be able to have the message and media that are integrated in places that we wouldn't normally be – like online music sites.' (Ian Sinclair, *The Australian*, April 24, 2008)

Corporate visual identity guidelines may therefore include any or all of the following design aspects.

- The use, form and hierarchy of nomenclature (reflecting brand endorsement strategies)
- The use of logo symbols, logotypes and corporate 'livery' (colour schemes)
- The style, size and position of various design elements in various formats (eg letter heads, press releases, and so on)
- The format and content of standard corporate 'stationery' (letterheads, e-mail)
- Circumstances in which uniforms will be worn (and/or corporate dress codes)
- Architecture, layout and décor of corporate premises.

Corporate visual identity, having been established, is not easy to change. A brand image may need updating, but if it is changed too much, too quickly, it will lose its recognition and familiarity: audiences may lose track of the brand, or may be confused as to its identity. Organisations will therefore often make a series of changes over time, each of which is barely noticeable, so that consumers are not aware that they are 'recognising' something different. Think of the logos of Shell or Coca Cola (and the designs of their petrol stations and drinks bottles), for example. They have gradually changed over the years to keep pace with design trends, and to combat habituation (people being so used to seeing something that they begin to ignore it): yet at each stage, the general public has found them entirely 'familiar'. On the other hand, organisations may wish to re-brand completely (as discussed in Chapter 4) and make a radical break with previous associations: this will require significant launch and awareness-building communication around the new logo and style.

4 Behaviour

As we have argued throughout this Study Text, organisations cannot *not* communicate. They communicate by what they are – what stakeholders see and experience of them in action at multiple touch points and interactions – as much as, or more than, by what they say about themselves in their verbal and symbolic expressions. The behaviour of an organisation has the power to undermine, and even render counterproductive, brand promises and claims: if the reality doesn't 'match up', stakeholders' evaluation may be worse (through disappointment and the perception of unreliability or dishonesty) than if the claim had never been made.

It is less easy to cover this aspect of corporate communication because it is so diverse in nature – and in application in different organisations. You will have to look at the specific behaviours of any organisation you select as the focus of your assessment. The following are just some general guidelines as to the kinds of areas to look at.

4.1 Employee behaviour

The behaviour of employees, and particularly customer – or other stakeholder-facing employees, is a crucial element in corporate communication, image and reputation.

- Employee behaviour conveys a powerful impression of what the organisation stands for, the value it attaches to its customers and other stakeholders, and how it selects, develops and manages its staff. This may be stakeholders' first impression of the organisation, which exerts a strong 'halo effect' over all subsequent impressions.

- Employee behaviour reflects the culture and personality of the organisation: literally, representing its human face to the world. The image of many corporate brands, particularly in service organisations, rests upon the 'types' of people it recruits and develops: part of the total 'experience' of dealing with the organisation. (Think of the significance of employing young people for the McDonalds brand; the use of extroverted staff for the Virgin or Starbucks brand; the influence of front office staff on any hotel or hospitality brand...)

- Direct personal experience of an organisation (or product or service) is the most influential component in stakeholder evaluation and decision-making.

MARKETING AT WORK

application

'In the 1980s in the UK, the leading banks spent between them about £1 billion a year on media advertising, with slogans such as 'the listening bank' or 'the bank that likes to say yes'. One television advertisement showed a customer explaining to another that his bank opened another counter if there was a queue. The media took great delight in publicising any example of a loan being turned down by banks claiming to listen or to say yes, or banks that claimed to open more counters when they were crowded but did not.'

(Davies *et al.*, *op cit*, p. 91)

4.1.1 The importance of service quality

Corporate image and reputation depends on an organisation's ability consistently to fulfil stakeholder expectations and to create a positive experience of doing business, at every encounter and touch point with the organisation. This applies crucially to service encounters with customers.

In many service industries, the service encounter lasts only a few seconds. Services encounters may be seen as **episodes**: 'specific interactions between customers and... employees that are especially satisfying or unsatisfying' (Bitner *et al.*, cited in

Egan, 2004, p. 111). Some episodes are merely routine. Others may be 'critical' (or **'moments of truth'**, Carlzon, 1989): that is, the continuation of a relationship depends on them, either positively (because they are particularly satisfying) or negatively (because they are particularly dissatisfying).

A single disappointing service encounter – and/or a firm's subsequent poor response to handling the problem – may be sufficient to reduce loyalty and make the customer more amenable to switching brands in response to competitor offers. Customers may tolerate **negative critical incidents** for the time being, but they are taken into account in the long-term evaluation of the supplier's performance. In the worst case scenario, a single disappointment (and related loss of trust) may be sufficient to induce the customer to take their business elsewhere – and to further damage relationship marketing by spreading negative word-of-mouth. On the positive side of this equation, **positive critical incidents** (unusually satisfying service encounters) are an important source of added value for customers, a part of the package of benefits that helps to attract and retain them, and potentially a key differentiating factor between the supplier and its competitors.

MARKETING AT WORK   application

'Five Star Service Recovery with Thomas Cook'

An example of how to handle the dreaded airport delay can be found in the case of Thomas Cook, the UK travel agency and tour operator. An electrical fault on an aircraft... meant that 220 passengers were delayed at Funchal airport for two hours... Towards the end of this period, passengers were directed to the cafeteria to receive a free drink and snack.

When it became clear that the flight would not take place that day, a Thomas Cook representative announced that all passengers would stay the night in a five-star hotel and would receive free dinner with drinks. After 30 minutes, passengers boarded coaches and were seamlessly transferred to the hotel. While at the hotel, passengers were kept fully informed of the situation and given the time to meet the following morning. Representatives were on hand to answer queries...

When passengers met to take the early-morning trip to the airport, they were served coffee and biscuits. Coaches were waiting outside the hotel ready for departure.

Despite the inconvenience of arriving a day late, passengers appreciated the smoothness of the service recovery operation. Clearly, Thomas Cook and its airport representative Serviceair had service processes in place.'

(Jobber, *op cit*, p. 905)

4.1.2 Service gaps

It is worth noting that – as with other aspects of corporate reputation – it is **perceptions** that count, and that **gaps** may arise between reality and perception, or between the perceptions of different stakeholders. Parasuraman, Zeithaml and Berry (1985) developed a widely applied model of service quality, via interviews with 14 executives in four service businesses and 12 customer focus groups. The findings highlighted five potential quality gaps: Figure 7.4

Figure 7.4: Service gaps

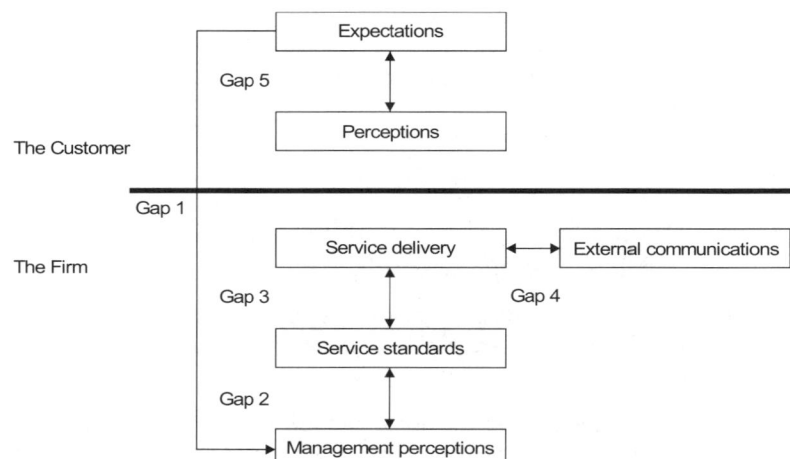

Gap 1 **Consumer expectations v management perceptions**	Managers' definition of value may not be the same as that of customers. They may not know what features connote high quality for customers, what features a service must have or what levels of performance are required by customers. **Action required**: • Market research programmes • Improvements based on customer comment and complaints • Strategies for service recovery • Improvements based on frontline staff experience and suggestion
Gap 2 **Management perceptions v service quality specification**	Resource constraints, market conditions and/or management indifference may lead to managers' understanding of required service quality not being translated into service level agreements or quality specifications. **Action required**: • New concepts of service rather than merely improving old ones • Attention to physical evidence of quality • Customer-focused activity goals
Gap 3 **Service quality specifications v service delivery**	Service level agreements and quality specifications may not translate into actual service levels. Employees may not be willing or able to perform to the specified standard, work may be poorly organised, supervised or resourced. **Action required**: • Define job roles and priorities clearly • Provide proper training • Build teams and team working • Empower frontline service staff • Improve technology • Recruit, train and reward for policy improvements
Gap 4 **Service delivery v external communications**	External communications may create exaggerated or uninformed expectations of service quality – setting customers up for disappointment. **Action required**: • Improve communications between internal staff • Educate customers as to what to expect from the service • Develop service rules – but do not over-promote to customers • Use marketing communications to emphasise what is actually delivered
Gap 5 **Expected service v perceived service**	What customers perceive they have received may fall short of what they expected: ie a shortfall in perceived service quality. **Action required**: • Research customer expectations • Measure service performance against expectations • Specify service quality/levels according to expectations • Manage and continuously improve service levels to match expectations

Parasuraman *et al.* (1995) developed the SERVQUAL questionnaire, which claims to be a global measure of service quality across all service organisations. It measures five generic criteria that consumers use in evaluating service quality.

• **Tangibles**: physical facilities, equipment, appearance of personnel
• **Reliability**: ability to perform the promised service dependably and accurately
• **Responsiveness**: willingness to help customers and provide prompt service
• **Assurance**: knowledge and courtesy of employees and their ability to convey trust and confidence
• **Empathy**: caring, individualised attention.

Respondents are asked first to give their expectations of the service on a seven-point scale, then to give their evaluation of the actual service on the same scale. Service quality is then calculated as the *difference* between perception and expectation, weighted for the importance of each item.

It is worth noting that customer perception of service quality can vary, even when a firm is getting the five generic dimensions 'right', due to intervening factors such as: product quality (where there is a physical element to service provision); price (ie perceived value for money); situational factors (such as the urgency of the customer's need); and personal factors (such as cultural, age or personality differences).

4.1.3 Managing service quality

Once a firm knows how it is performing on each of the dimensions of service quality, it can use a number of methods to improve its performance. There are many dimensions in service delivery, before and after the service encounter itself.

- The creation of a strong **corporate culture** which expresses and models desired values and behaviours (as part of the expression of corporate identity), and reinforces those values through its selection, appraisal and reward systems, and the messages it sends employees at every level.

- The creation of **service-supporting internal relationships and internal communication**: the recruitment of skilled stakeholder-facing people; the supply of appropriate training; the empowerment of staff to take decisions that will satisfy and retain stakeholders (and uphold communicated corporate identity values); and the reward and recognition of staff who deliver outstanding service.

- Gathering, analysing, communicating and acting on **stakeholder feedback**. Feedback and adjustment (addressing stakeholder concerns and complaints) are crucial in minimising dissatisfaction and demonstrating commitment to promise fulfilment.

- Establishing a **partnership approach** to network relationships in order to support high levels of service at all links in the value-delivery chain. This may help avoid reputational damage through the behaviour of suppliers and intermediaries which is inconsistent with the focal firm's desired identity.

- Ensuring **promise fulfilment** (Jobber, 2007, p. 902): Making realistic claims and promises (to manage stakeholder expectations); enabling staff and service systems to deliver on promises made; and keeping promises during all encounters and interactions with stakeholders.

- Offering **support services** to facilitate stakeholders in having satisfying and positive experiences with the organisation (eg using products safely, participating as shareholders), and supporting them through changes and difficulties.

The bottom line of service quality for reputation management is that people all over the organisation have direct influence over its image, value proposition and customer (and other stakeholder) retention. It is not possible to exercise direct control over all the 'marketing communications' represented by service encounters, but managers must be aware of them, appreciate their importance and do what they can to control – or at least influence – them indirectly.

This can partly be done through management of the **'extended (service) marketing mix'** elements:

- **Process** (the activities, information flows and supporting procedures and systems which create and deliver the service):

    - Setting-up policies, systems and procedures to govern interactions with key stakeholders, to ensure consistency.

    - Allowing adaptability and spontaneity, so that adherence to policy and procedure does not create barriers to service (eg dealing with unusual or urgent stakeholder needs).

    - Automating procedures where possible, to ensure consistency (although not in areas where stakeholders prefer to deal with human beings!)

    - Constantly monitoring and auditing performance and gathering stakeholder feedback.

    - Setting-up systems and procedures for service recovery: prompt action to address complaints and re-establish service provision.

- **People** (the employees and intermediaries who create and deliver the service):
    - Selecting, training and motivating people to give a high quality of service (and to deal with particular service challenges eg difficult and demanding customers).
    - Using internal marketing to promulgate the culture of service throughout the firm – and using internal communications to promulgate the core attributes and values that form part of the corporate brand promise.
    - Ensuring conformance with standards of behaviour, dress and appearance, procedures and modes of dealing with the public.
- **Physicals** (tangible evidences and physical factors in the service environment, which influence the experience of stakeholders at touch points with the organisation):
    - Designing physical expressions of the service that reflect and reinforce its quality goals: evidence of interaction (eg a receipt or voucher, or a bank statement); accessories (eg merchandise, concert programmes, destination booklets and merchandise).
    - Designing appropriate service brand identifiers (eg staff livery or uniforms, branded vehicles).
    - Designing appropriate service environments (eg showroom or service area décor, furnishing and ambience; web site design).

ACTIVITY 9

application

Summarise what you take to be the key roles of the corporate communication function in the development of service quality and the management of service gaps.

4.2 Managerial performance and communication

The conduct and performance of managerial level employees send strong communication cues to several key stakeholder groups.

For **employees**, management style, behaviour and communication:

- Are assumed to reflect the **attitude of their employer to its people**: the extent to which they are valued and trusted; the extent to which their views and concerns are listened to; whether they are likely to find opportunities for development and responsibility; and so on. This is likely to influence their morale, job satisfaction and commitment to the organisation and their work.
- Impact on how people are **motivated, equipped and empowered** to do their jobs: whether they are given sufficient information and resources; whether they are given discretion to respond to stakeholder needs; whether they understand their role in influencing corporate reputation; whether their suggestions and feedback are listened to; and so on.
- Influence **employee values and behaviours**, shaping corporate culture: which values and behaviours are expressed and practiced by managerial role models; which behaviours are incentivised, disciplined or rewarded; and so on.

Each of these managerial influences will have a knock-on effect on employee behaviour and identification – and, through them, on corporate image and reputation.

For **shareholders**, management performance (capabilities, vision, and track record in areas such as strategic decision-making, governance, financial management and risk management) and communications (eg managerial speeches and reports) will influence the **confidence** they have in the security, value and potential of their investment in the company, and the extent to which they are willing to support strategic initiatives.

Managerial decision-making and communication, at different levels, ultimately determines the experiences and attitudes of all stakeholder groups, since it reflects corporate strategy and its implementation. Managerial speeches and statements may create identity-consistent or –inconsistent messages for stakeholder audiences. Managerial decisions determine whether suppliers are treated ethically; what information is given to the media; how pressure groups are dealt with; how the organisation complies with, or seeks to influence, government policy and regulation; and so on.

4.3 The role of corporate leaders in brand building

Dowling (1993) among others has highlighted the role of founders and CEOs in determining the mission, vision and values of their organisations – and therefore their image and reputation. Strong, charismatic leadership by corporate figureheads can also shape the internal and projected personality of the organisation. Perhaps the most obvious example of this is the association of the Virgin brand with entrepreneurial founder Richard Branson, but many strong corporate identities can be traced to the stories, values and personalities of their founders: eg Laura and Bernard Ashley (Laura Ashley); the Marks family (Marks and Spencer); Ray Kroc (McDonalds); or Harlan Sanders (KFC).

MARKETING AT WORK
application

'The **Virgin** brand, a banner name for businesses ranging from entertainment and travel, to publishing and soft drinks, is well known by people everywhere. Richard Branson is the man behind the brand, the individual whose entrepreneurial values and strong leadership have been pivotal in establishing the Virgin identity...

Among the insights he offers, Branson stresses the need to 'Do the right things for the brand.' His desire to build and protect the Virgin brand is reflected in both his activities and his business style. In Branson's own words: 'If you get your face and your name out there enough, people will start to recognise you. Many people know the Virgin brand better than the names of the individual companies within the group' (www.virgin.com/uk/entertainment/richard-branson).

Branson has ensured that those within the corporation understand the role that identity plays in its success and about how this connects with the values around which the Virgin brand is based...

The role that Branson himself has played in establishing this image cannot be overstated. The company's web site cites Branson's personal reputation as a key success factor. This reputation extends far beyond pure business acumen, to include his passion for breaking records and high-profile, daredevil adventures... What is important for Virgin's identity is that these activities influence things that the company **does** and helps shape its image with stakeholders.'

Simões & Dibb (2008, pp. 77–78)

Link: http://www.virgin.com/AboutVirgin/RichardBranson

Introduced in typical Virgin style as: 'So who's the guy with the beard?', this gives access to online Branson video and written blogs (with audience comments: a great way of monitoring reputational effects!).

The role of the CEO as figurehead and representative of an organisation may also be particularly important in crisis communication. Media and online posted personal statements by CEOs are often used to establish visibility, and reassure stakeholders of leadership and accountability, in crisis scenarios. For example, when toy giant Mattel hit the headlines with its safety recall of millions of toys in 2007, due to the revelation that some of its Chinese manufacturers had used banned lead paints – at the same time as fears were raised over other hazards arising from the use of magnets and toxic substances in other products – the CEO Robert Eckhart immediately posted a video statement on the corporate web site:

- Taking personal, visible ownership of the need to communicate with key stakeholders

- Using rich communication media (video rather than a published statement) and value-laden language (promises and 'absolute commitments') to demonstrate empathy with the emotional dimensions of the crisis (logic being insufficient in issues surrounding child safety)

- Giving clear information, directions and targeted reassurances to ally stakeholders' anticipated concerns.

You might also like to consider, if relevant to your own organisation, the role of celebrities and/or politicians as the focus of country/destination image – or the role of celebrities, patrons and other figureheads in charity marketing.

5 Measuring the effectiveness of corporate communication

You should be familiar from your earlier studies (eg in *Stakeholder Marketing* or *Delivering Customer Value Through Marketing*) with a range of methods for monitoring and measuring the effectiveness of communications campaigns and processes.

- **Media exposure**: the amount, duration and frequency with which the organisation, brand or marketing message is featured across all communications media (or particular media segments): in other words, how much 'air time' the corporate message is getting. This may be measured by the organisation's media schedule and reach data, and/or the number of mentions in news and information media, the blogosphere and other forums (usually monitored by specialist media monitoring agencies).

- **Media monitoring**: organisations need to scan the press and other media continuously for references to them and feedback about them. This may be done by the communications function or other 'environment scanners' in the organisation, or it may employ a media monitoring agency to collect items relating to the organisation or industry. Monitoring should cover press and publicity (editorial and news articles, in all media), published industry/market reports, public statements and press releases (eg by government agencies, regulatory bodies or pressure groups) and the internet. Increasingly, shareholders share their views in virtual communities, via discussion boards, e-mail news groups, web logs (globs), user reviews (eg on Amazon.com or eBay) and content sharing (eg on YouTube and MySpace): organisations need to monitor this traffic to see what is being said about them.

- **Campaign measurement**: pre-campaign and post-campaign testing of stakeholder perceptions, the difference in which may be attributable to the campaign. Pre- and post-testing may use a variety of quantitative and qualitative techniques, including:

  - **Results**: increases in enquiries, responses, web site visits, sales (or donations, say), repeat sales or order values and so on.

  - **Survey questionnaires and/or depth (one-to-one) or focus group interviews**. These methods can direct questions to more complex information about the impact of the campaign on the target audience; awareness of the campaign/brand; recall and recognition of the campaign/brand; what messages were understood from the campaign; the congeniality (likeability) of the campaign/brand; perceptions and attitudes to the campaign/brand and so on.

- **Recall and recognition tests**

  - **Recall** tests are designed to measure how much of the content of corporate communications members of the target audience remember. They can be used to measure the 'memorability' of advertising, press/publicity, sponsorships and branding campaigns – both before the campaigns run (pre-testing, using mock-ups) and afterwards (post-testing). Survey or panel interviewees may be asked what advertisements and other communications they remember or have noticed. (This is called unprompted or unaided recall.) They may then be reminded of some details of the campaign, such as the theme of a series of advertisements or press articles, and asked what else they remember, or which ads/articles in the series they remember (prompted recall).

  - **Recognition** tests are similarly used to test the *penetration* of corporate communications: how much of the target audience have they reached? Survey or panel interviewees are asked to look through newspapers, magazines or journals they have already read, and to identity which marketing messages they remember.

- **Results-based measures** (addressing the behavioural 'domino' of the Knowledge-Attitude-Behaviour change domino effect):

  - **Response/enquiry measurement**: monitored via direct response advertising (with enquiry coupons, telephone lines or web address), web site traffic monitoring, and enquiry tests (comparing the number of enquiries generated by particular communication campaigns and/or media, and the 'cost per enquiry').

  - **Behavioural indicators:** such as rates of defection or retention of customers, employees or investors.

  - **Performance measures**: such as increased sales or sales value, improved conversion rates (how many responders, enquirers or prospects actually become customers), increased donations (for a charity), improved share price etc.

- **Stakeholder satisfaction, feedback and attitude surveys**: stakeholder perceptions can be systematically researched using a range of tools.

    - **Feedback forms** (such as the one at the back of this book) inviting stakeholders to rate and/or comment on the organisation, its performance (in areas relevant to the stakeholder) and the quality of its communication.

    - **Survey questionnaires** administered by post, telephone, personal interview or online. This method is often used for fairly large samples of stakeholders, as it gets answers to standard questions (so that results can be collated and compared) fairly cost-effectively.

    - **Attitude surveys** are often used in market and reputational research and also in employee relations (eg to gauge employee morale and attitudes to their work) and to monitor attitudes to particular planned changes). They are usually carried out by means of interview or questionnaire, using attitude scales which allow responses to be quantified.

    - **Depth interviews or group discussions (focus groups)** facilitated by trained interviewers, using open-ended conversation rather than a standardised questionnaire, to allow more complex feedback gathering. Interviews can be conducted online web conferencing, for greater convenience (and/or to reach widely dispersed and international stakeholders). The purpose of this kind of qualitative research is to understand stakeholder perceptions, expectations, drivers and attitudes in more depth.

MARKETING AT WORK   application

Vodafone's sponsorship deal with Manchester United cost Vodafone £30 million over a four-year period. Vodafone clearly had to evaluate the effectiveness of this partnership in terms of its own marketing objectives. It did so in four ways:

- *General awareness* was measured through consumer research. For example, consumers were asked questions such as: 'Did you know that Vodafone sponsors Manchester United?'

- The *impact* on the performance of Vodafone's phones and accessories was measured by charting ongoing improvements in sales.

- The success of *value-added services* such as ManUmobile was monitored in terms of the number of people registered and usage of the service.

- *Media evaluation:* Vodafone monitored TV and press coverage to measure the exposure of the Vodafone brand resulting from the sponsorship.

The syllabus focuses on specific tools for use in attitude survey, depth interviews and focus groups, which enable the organisation to measure the impact of not just communications, but the full corporate identity mix. (As in other areas of the syllabus, these appear to be drawn from the coverage in the core text by van Riel & Fombrun.) We will therefore look at these in a little more detail.

5.1 Kelly Repertory Grid

A Kelly Repertory Grid (KRG) is used to generate and evaluate stakeholder perceptions of organisational, product or campaign attributes in individual depth interviews or focus groups. It was originally used in the field of psychology, but was applied to the gathering of public opinion.

A repertory grid consists of four parts:

- A **topic** (eg a product category)

- A set of **elements**, which are examples or instances of the topic (eg a list of companies or brands)

- A set of **constructs**: the basic terms that people use to make sense of the elements, expressed as a contrast ('good versus poor'). These are derived by presenting respondents (using index cards) with three elements at a time, and asking them to specify in what way two of the elements are alike, but different from the third. (For example, Products A and B may be seen as similarly 'exciting', whereas Product C is different because it is 'dull'. This suggests that the respondent uses the construct 'exciting versus dull' when thinking about products.)

- A set of **ratings or rankings of elements on the basis of constructs**. Each element is rated on each of the relevant constructs, using a five- or seven-point rating scale system, or ranked (in order of the extent to which they possess the relevant constructs)

Key advantages of the repertory grid are:

- Ease of administration, and relatively low cost
- Effective at eliciting relatively sophisticated constructs, ratings and rankings relevant to corporate reputation
- Applicability to stakeholders regardless of their degree of familiarity or involvement with the subject
- Congeniality to stakeholders, since it does not take much time or knowledge

If you need to find out more about the Repertory Grid, a good starting point is the Wikipedia article on the topic and related links (including access to Repertory Grid software tools.

Link: http://en.wikipedia.org/wiki/Repertory_grid ▪

5.2 Natural Grouping

In the Natural Grouping method:

- Respondents are presented with a large set of company, product or brand names, and asked to sort them into two sub-sets.

- They are then asked to specify the criteria used to determine the grouping, and to describe the sub-sets in their own words – effectively setting up a 'construct' in the same way as in the Kelly Repertory Grid (eg 'quality brands' versus 'value-for-money brands').

- The process of subdivision is repeated until no further distinctions can be made.

The criteria given by respondents for grouping and sub-dividing (characteristics, evaluations, associations) are the attributes which stakeholders use to differentiate one company or brand from another.

The key advantages of natural grouping research are its ability to measure a wide range of associations, features and perceptions, and its relative congeniality for respondents. However:

- It is complex and costly to apply, requiring sophisticated data analysis and interpretation.

- The results are only valuable when respondents are relatively knowledgeable about the companies and industry.

5.3 Q-Sort

Q-Sort is a comparative rating method based on a personality assessment method developed by psychologists in the 1930s, and now used to assess stakeholder perceptions of a company or brand. Respondents:

- Are presented with a set of printed cards, each containing a statement about the company, drawn from organisational, marketing and stakeholder communications.

- Are asked to separate the cards/statements that they perceive to be applicable to the company from those that are not applicable.

- Are asked to sort the applicable cards/statements into a rank order, according to which statements they perceive as being most applicable to, or characteristic of, the company or brand, or which they most agree with. The same thing is then done with the non-applicable statements.

The result of a Q-Sort is thus a ranking of the perceived applicability of, or stakeholder agreement with, various statements (reflecting attributes of the company or brand): a detailed picture of positive and negative evaluations, which can be broken down by audience segments, for comparison, benchmarking and the targeting of communication strategies.

A major advantage of the Q-Sort method is that it can be applied using only a small number of respondents (25–30), if they are moderately sophisticated in their knowledge of a company (enabling them to rank the statements in a meaningful way). The ranking method forces respondents to discriminate: they cannot respond positively or negatively across the board. However, the method is complicated, time consuming and therefore not generally congenial to stakeholders. The complexity of the statistical analysis requires an advanced computer software package, and makes it difficult to present results in a user-friendly way.

5.4 Photo-Sort

Photo-sorting is another sorting method, developed (by advertising agency BBDO) as a proprietary projective research technique to increase creativity in advertising, also applied to the measurement of corporate reputation.

BBDO conceptualised corporate image as a combination of a 'Product' (Performance) image with a 'You' (User) image. 'People do not experience products or their performance directly through advertising. They experience images of the users – people the advertiser associates with the product.' The 'You' image is critical because: it creates emotional (not just rational) engagement with the product, company or brand; it adds value to performance claims; and it builds brand relevance and personality, which can help build brand loyalty. (http://www.adbuzz.com).

Photo-Sort is a projective technique designed to identify 'You' image perceptions and problems.

The researcher gives stakeholders a set of about 35 photos of people's faces, selected from a wider image bank during preliminary research as representative of major emotional categories or attributes potentially relevant to the company or brand. Respondents may then be asked to select a photo they believe typifies a company or brand, or asked: 'Of these people, which use this brand (or work for, or invest in, this organisation)?'

When the respondent has chosen a photograph, (s)he is asked:

- To give reasons for the selection (associating the attributes perceived in the photo with the perceived attributes of the company or brand)

- To describe the image the selected 'User' has of the brand or company.

This derives a rating based on the attributes associated with the brand (character expression) and the respondents' affinity with the person in the photograph (affinity score)

The advantage of a method such as this is that it gets to the emotional, sub-conscious layers of people's associations with a company or brand – without requiring respondents to be highly skilled at expressing themselves verbally: people attach complex significance to facial expressions in a relatively uninhibited way. The analysis is not fragmented into attributes, but is elicited in a holistic way (as stakeholders experience it), as a cluster of inter-related attributes which together form the brand or company image. The test is relatively quick and easy to administer, and is therefore relatively low-cost (once the necessary tools have been developed or accessed), although a relatively large sample size (at least 75 respondents per target group) is required.

5.5 Card sorting

The card sorting technique is based on the argument that reputation is, at heart, a process less of rational evaluation, based on reality, than one of 'associative reactions': imaginative and emotional connections between ideas and objects. (Hence some of the stereotyped associations that influence industry and country-of-origin image, for example.) Rating scales are effective in eliciting and measuring rational judgements, as appropriate to target audiences which have detailed factual knowledge of the company or brand – but are less effective in capturing the associations formed by respondents from less direct, factual information.

The card sorting technique was developed by the German Institut für Demoskopie, and refined by market research company NSS Market Research. Respondents are presented with a series of attributes (printed on cards, in face-to-face interviews, or read out in telephone interviews), and asked to say which ones fit or describe the company 'well' and 'not at all'.

The outputs from card sorting are:

- Profiling, based on the total number of choices made, and indicating the extent to which the described attributes are associated with the company. A high profile means that an attribute is an important element in the company's image or reputation.

- Relative reputation value, based on the attributes identified as high profile, indicates the quality of the company's image or reputation.

The advantages of this technique are its speed and simplicity. Respondents do not have to make choices, interpret and discriminate complex vocabulary, or make complex rankings or ratings. The information reflects the 'all or nothing' character of genuine reputations (van Westendorp & van der Herberg, 1984) better than fine discriminations and rankings.

5.6 Attitude surveys

van Riel & Fombrun (*op cit.*, p. 222) argue that 'when respondents are likely to have a moderate degree of elaboration [knowledge and opinion] about a company or brand, the reputation may be regarded as an attitude'.

KEY CONCEPT concept

An **attitude** is the aggregate of perceptions (cognition), feelings (affect) and intentions (conation) towards an object, and therefore has a strong influence on behaviour.

Measurement of attitude is thus as close as an organisation may get to predicting stakeholder behaviour towards it – short of measuring and projecting actual behaviour.

Attitude surveys are often used in market and reputational research and in employee relations (eg to gauge employee morale or to monitor attitudes to particular planned changes). They are usually carried out by means of interview or questionnaire, using attitude scales which allow responses to be quantified.

There are three main types of scale in common use:

- **Thurstone scales**. A number of statements are given, which cover a range of attitudes 'spaced out' at equal intervals from one extreme to another (eg 'My views are completely ignored by my supervisor' to 'My supervisor listens attentively and responds positively to my concerns and suggestions'). Respondents are asked to select the statement which most closely reflects their own attitude.

- **Likert scales**. For a given question, respondents are asked to select from a five- or seven-point series of possible responses (to allow for a neutral 'middle' response), reflecting a spectrum of answers (eg 'How far do you agree that....?' Scale: entirely disagree, slightly disagree, neither agree nor disagree, slightly agree, entirely agree).

- **Semantic differential scales**. These are based on extreme pairs of evaluations (strong-weak, good-bad, always-never), perhaps with intermediate attitudes as well. Respondents are asked to select the phrase that most closely corresponds to their evaluation of a given attribute.

In reputation surveys, for example, respondents may be asked to indicate (a) the extent to which they agree with statements about a group of companies, relating to attributes relevant to reputation and (b) the extent to which they feel each attribute is important. The reputational score for each company depends on how strongly it is identified with attributes which are perceived to be important (as discussed in section 1.1 of this chapter).

The advantage of attitude scales is that they enable quantitative measurement and comparative measurement (using the same attributes) of competitors' reputations for benchmarking purposes. The disadvantages are the difficulty of pre-establishing relevant attributes for measurement, and the necessity for lengthy questionnaires which may act as a disincentive to respondents.

MARKETING AT WORK application

Jobber (*op cit*, p. 539) offers the case study of charity **Christian Aid**, and its national 'Christian Aid Week' fundraising campaign in 2005. This shows the depth of information that can be gathered on the success of a particular campaign.

'Every year NOP carries out before (pre) and after (post) research on the effectiveness of Christian Aid Week using a UK representative sample and a street-based questionnaire...

Detailed results included:

- Significant shift in awareness of Christian Aid achieved by the 2005 campaign (pre-campaign compared to post-campaign): 8% increase in spontaneous awareness, 13% increase in total awareness

- Awareness of Christian Aid advertising in 2005 higher than in 2004: 13% increase in spontaneous awareness; 6% increase in total awareness

- The advertising in 2005 was seen as interesting and increased positive perceptions of Christian Aid: it made four out of ten respondents laugh; it wasn't the sort of advertising expected from Christian Aid; it was seen as different from other charity advertising.

- Recall of advertising content was very encouraging

- 70% of those who responded directly to Christian Aid Week advertising were new contacts

- The main messages were communicated well. Respondents understood the message as: giving a poor family a chicken is better than giving them an omelette (30%); Christian Aid invests in things that multiply (19%); Christian Aid helps people to help themselves (18%); Christian Aid helps people in the Third World stand on their own two feet (14%).

- Overall, Christian Aid Week donations were higher in 2005: the house-to-house envelope collection broke the £15 million (€21 million) for the first time and £100,000 (€140,000) was raised online.'

ACTIVITY 10

application

Find out, if you don't know, how your organisation measures the attitudes and perceptions of its key stakeholder groups, and the success of its corporate communication campaigns. Collect copies of any outputs from such measurements that are available (within confidentiality guidelines), for review.

You should read Chapter 9 of van Riel & Fombrun's Essentials of Corporate Communication, *the core text on which much of the syllabus content in this area is based. There is a particularly helpful table comparing the various measurement tools, on pages 226–227.*

In Melewar (ed) Facets of Corporate Identity, Communication and Reputation *(2008: Routledge) you might like to read Chapter 11 (An attitudinal measure of corporate reputation) by Albert Caruana.*

Learning objectives	Covered
1 Critically evaluate the different methods through which corporate communications can be delivered	☑ Planning corporate communications: image research; expressing the company (using the corporate story); outline communication plan
	☑ The corporate communication mix
	☑ Briefing a communication agency
	☑ Corporate advertising: advertising media; developing creative concepts; the role of advertising in corporate branding
	☑ Public relations and publicity: evaluating PR effectiveness
	☑ Sponsorship
	☑ Web sites
	☑ Symbolism: nomenclature (names and logos); and other tools of visual and symbolic identity
	☑ Behaviour: employee behaviour, managerial performance and managerial communication
2 Propose changes to enhance the systems, structure and processes necessary to support corporate communication	☑ The importance of service quality
	☑ Service quality gaps (Parasuraman *et al.*)
	☑ Using the service mix (people, process and physicals) for identity-consistent service quality
3 Propose methods of measuring the effectiveness of corporate communication	☑ Measures of communication/campaign success
	☑ Techniques for eliciting audience perceptions and constructs about the organisation: the Kelly Repertory Grid; natural grouping; Q-Sort; Photo-Sort; card sorting; and attitude surveys

1 Outline a process for implementing corporate communication.

2 What matters will be addressed in an agency brief for a corporate communication agency?

3 What criteria are used in the selection of advertising media?

4 How can an organisation stimulate positive publicity?

5 What are the objectives of corporate sponsorship?

6 What is 'nomenclature'? Give three examples of other features of visual identity.

7 Explain the five service gaps identified by Parasuraman *et al.*

8 How can the extended marketing mix be used to support corporate reputation?

9 How are audience 'constructs' elicited using a Kelly Repertory Grid?

10 What are the key advantages of (a) photo-sort and (b) card sorting techniques?

1   Just as an example of the sort of thing you might have drafted:

- Changes to terms and conditions = necessary. But HOW COMMUNICATED TO CUSTOMERS keeps or loses customers!

- State changes clearly: don't be perceived as 'sneaky'

  - Highlight and refer customers to important information strongly
  - Don't 'hide' information in small print

- Don't underestimate customer awareness of promotional communication

  - Don't claim 'benefits' if they are really costs: customers see through this!

- See things from the customer's point of view

  - The fact that you need to recoup costs is NOT THE CUSTOMER'S PROBLEM

2   Your own organisation's aims and attributes will form the core of your answer here, but note that (a) the audience is explicitly intended to be investors and (b) the core themes are intended to be shareholder value and CSR (in a recession context). Relevant parts of the corporate story will have to be tailored to the informational and emotional needs of investors (for security, reassurance) in this scenario. In any case, worth some practice at formulating answers in different formats – as you may well be required to do in your assessment.

3   Collecting benchmark examples is always a good idea for personal – and organisational – learning. One of the key characteristics of the Learning Organisation (Pedler, Burgoyne & Boydell) is learning from other organisations: sometimes known as SIS (Steal Ideas Shamelessly – within the bounds of law and ethics, of course!).

4   These kinds of activities should really go without saying: consider them a 'reminder' to set-up a filing system and start monitoring your communications environment.

5   Some examples of newsworthy items you might have identified: discovered a revolutionary new method/device that will impact audience's lives; recruited several hundred new workers in an area of high unemployment; won a large export order (good news for the country/region); signed up a major celebrity for a marketing campaign; restored a building of local/historic interest; raised money for a local/relevant charity or cause; started an environmental/CSR programme; produced the biggest/fastest/first 'whatever' in the country. (In the case of Harry Potter: broke pre-order sales records; revolutionised children's reading habits; stimulated unprecedented merchandising and brand recognition; created controversy.)

Your own organisation and research – although we have given some ideas in our brief coverage.

7   Corporate communication tends to be less high-impact (visual/emotive/interactive): not designed for 'stickiness' to the same extent. It tends to have more informational content. It tends to offer content focused on specific investor, media/press and career audiences. It tends to offer messages about financial performance, vision, mission, values and corporate social responsibility and/or environmental performance. It also tends to emphasise the 'brand family', where relevant, acting as a focal point or umbrella for a group of subsidiary or product brands.

8   This will partly depend on your own impressions and knowledge – which is the point of the exercise, since logos 'mean' whatever they 'mean' to audiences. But, for example: the starting point for the Philips tagline is technology; Tesco, service/value; WWF, ecology; HP, innovation; Nokia, networking; McDonalds, service; BP, future energy sources; Woolworths, fresh produce; Microsoft, passion; Nike, action; Gillette, potential; The Northern Territory (Australia), aboriginal culture.

In terms of the logos, some have obvious symbolic power (shell, flower/sun, halo – for 3i as finance 'angels' – peeled apple, endangered panda, Australian outback vignette). Others have distinctive logo type (hp, 3i, Johnson & Johnson).

9   Corporate communications functions have a key role in the development of service quality and the management of service gaps, through activities such as:

- Researching, analysing and reporting on customer expectations and perceptions (eg using critical incident analysis, feedback-gathering via complaints systems, customer research via surveys and focus groups), as the basis for service improvement planning

- Establishing systems facilitating customer complaint and feedback

- Internal and management communication: informing, motivating, equipping and empowering internal staff to develop and maintain a customer-focused approach to service quality

- Managing customer expectations and perceptions, through marketing communications aimed at: (a) image management; (b) accurate description of services and service levels; and (c) realistic quality promises and pricing

- Developing relationship marketing, in order to enhance stakeholder loyalty, lessening the potential impact of single negative service encounters, and facilitating the restoration of goodwill (eg by emphasising two-way dialogue, maintaining contact, using loyalty rewards and so on).

10   Your own organisation.

1   See Figure 7.1 for the process.

2   An agency brief will address: the focus of efforts (product, SBU or corporate level); key stakeholder audiences; benchmark standards; and measurement methods.

3   Criteria for evaluating media include: range, frequency and continuity of exposure; targeting; credibility; impact; performance (and measurability); and budget.

4   See section 2.3.1 for a list of points.

5   See section 2.4 for a list of points.

6   Nomenclature is the collective term for names and associated symbols and taglines. Other elements of visual identity include: signage, uniforms (or dress codes), livery, premises, artefacts, merchandise and music.

7   See the table in section 4.1.2 for a full explanation.

8   See section 4.1.3 for a full discussion.

9   Audience constructs are elicited by presenting respondents (using index cards) with three elements at a time, and asking them to specify in what way two of the elements are alike, but different from the third.

10   (a)   The key advantage of photo-sort is that it gets to the emotional, sub-conscious layers of people's associations with a company or brand – without requiring respondents to be highly skilled at expressing themselves verbally. In addition, the analysis is elicited in a holistic way (as stakeholders experience the organisation) as a cluster of interrelated attributes.

(b)   The key advantage of card sorting is its speed and simplicity. Respondents do not have to make choices, interpret vocabulary or make complex rankings or ratings, so the method is congenial to them. The information also reflects the holistic 'all or nothing' nature of reputations.

References

Cooper, A (1999) 'What's in a name?' in *Admap*, Vol 34 (6) pp 30-32

Carlzon, J (1989) *Moments of Truth*. Collins Business

Caruana, A (2008) 'An attitudinal measure of corporate reputation' in Melewar T C (ed.) *Facets of Corporate Identity, Communication and Reputation*. Abingdon, Oxon: Routledge

Cornelissen, J (2008) *Corporate Communication: A guide to theory and practice* (2nd ed). London: Sage

Davies G, Chun R, Da Silva R V & Roper S (2003) *Corporate Reputation and Competitiveness*. Abingdon, Oxon: Routledge

Dowling, G R (1993) 'Developing your company image into a corporate asset' in *Long Range Planning*. 26 (2) pp 101-109

Egan, J (2004) *Relationship Marketing: Exploring Relational Strategies in Marketing*. (2nd ed). Harlow, Essex: Pearson Education

Fill, C (2002) *Marketing Communications: Contexts, Strategies and Applications* (3rd ed). Harlow, Essex: Pearson Education Limited

Hamel, G & Prahalad, C K (1994) *Competing for the Future*. Boston: Harvard Business School Press

Ind, N (2007) *The Living Brand* (3rd ed). London: Kogan Page

Jobber, D (2007) *Principles & Practice of Marketing* (5th ed) Maidenhead: McGraw Hill

Kaenwong, K (2004) 'Thai taskforce to widen exhibition exposure worldwide', posted at http://www.tdc.trade.com.imn (5/2/04)

Markwick, N (1993) 'Corporate image as an aid to strategic development'. Unpublished MBA project, University of Portsmouth.

Olins, W (1990) *The Wolff Olins Guide to Corporate Identity*. London: The Design Council

Parasuraman A, Zeithaml V A & Berry (1988) 'SERVQUAL: A multiple-item scale for measuring customer perceptions of service quality' in *Journal of Retailing*. Spring, pp 12-40

Rich, J R (2001) *Unofficial Guide to Marketing your Business On-Line*. Foster City, CA: IDG Books.

Riel, C B M van & Fombrun, C J (2007) *Essentials of Corporate Communication: Implementing Practices for Effective Reputation Management*. Abingdon, Oxon: Routledge

Simões, C and Dibb, S (2008) 'Illustrations of the internal management of corporate identity' in Melewar T C (ed.) *Facets of Corporate Identity, Communication and Reputation*. Abingdon, Oxon: Routledge

Chapter 8

Customer, public and media relations

Topic list

Introduction

Earlier in the Study Text, we introduced the concept of corporate communication: what it consists of, what its aims are, when it is used, and how it is planned, managed and evaluated. We briefly introduced some of the core activities of corporate communication (marketing communication, public relations, investor relations, public affairs and internal communication) and the elements of the communication mix (advertising, public relations, sponsorship).

In this chapter, we explore in more detail approaches to corporate communication which are focused on particular target audiences. This coverage is designed to support you in formulating communication plans – or agency briefs – which appropriately address the communication preferences and information needs of each stakeholder group, and the messages required to build, maintain and defend the organisation's reputation with each group. The syllabus guidance notes that there may be opportunities for students to develop specific depth of knowledge and skills here (eg if they have particular interest in financial or internal communications areas, say) but that all students will be expected to have an understanding of investor, employee, government and customer communications.

The focus of this chapter is broadly on marketing communications and public relations. You should have covered this area in some detail in your earlier marketing studies (eg *Delivering Customer Value Through Marketing* at Level 6), as a key part of the marketing mix. We will recap some key issues in sections 1–4, with a more strategic focus on corporate (rather than product) communication programmes and campaigns.

In section 5, we broaden our scope to consider public relations, since the 'general public', local community or society in general are also a key target stakeholder audience.

Finally, in section 6, we explore media relations, since the media are (by definition) a key medium by which many corporate communications are delivered to other stakeholder audiences. Media relations are not explicitly mentioned in the syllabus content, but they are strongly implied by the other activities of corporate communication

Syllabus-linked learning objectives

By the end of the chapter you will be able to:

Learning objectives	Syllabus link
1 Understand the nature of marketing and public relations programmes	1.2.2
2 Formulate approaches to corporate communications that are customer focused and contextually determined	3.2.3
3 Formulate effective approaches to media relations	3.2.3

1   Marketing communications

As the final unit within the CIM suite of qualifications, you should be fully familiar with the topic of marketing communications. Here the topic is covered in the corporate context – looking at the marketing communications strategy perspective.

KEY CONCEPT

concept

Fill (2003, p 284) defines marketing communications strategy as follows:

'A marketing communications strategy refers to an organisation's preferred orientation and emphasis of its communication with customers and stakeholders, in the light of its business and marketing strategies. A marketing communications plan is concerned with the development and managerial processes involved in the articulation of an organisation's marketing communications strategy.'

1.1 The 3P's of promotional strategy

Fill (2003 p. 284) refers to the 3 Ps of promotional strategy. These are summarised in the table below, but in essence are explained as follows.

Push and **pull** refers to the actual direction of the communication to the marketing channel. If communications are pushed down the marketing channel they are considered a **push strategy**; if consumers or buyers are pulled via retailers as a result of communication – this is a **pull strategy**. Not that they do not relate to the intensity of the communication *per se*.

The third promotional strategy **profile** is different in that it relates to all stakeholders and in terms of the communications focus refers to the organisation as a whole. The communication goal is in fact to build reputation. This is the kind of promotional strategy that is most relevant to us when studying corporate reputation.

1.2 Profile strategy

Strategy	Target audience	Communication focus	Communication goal
Pull	Consumers	Product/service	Purchase
	End-user B2B customers	Product/service	Purchase
Push	Channel intermediaries	Product/service	Developing relationships and distribution network
Profile	All relevant stakeholders	The organisation	Building reputation and lasting relationships

Adapted from Fill (2003)

'There is a whole range of (other) stakeholders, many of whom need to know about and understand the organisation rather than actually purchase its products and services. This group of stakeholders may include financial analysts, trade unions, government bodies, employees or the local community. It should be easy to understand that these different stakeholder groups can influence the organisation in different ways and in doing so need to receive (and respond to) different types of messages. So, the financial analysts need to know about financial and trading performances and expectations, and the local community may be interested in employment and the impact of the organisation *on the local environment, whereas the government may be interested in the way that the organisation applies health and safety regulations...*'

What is significant in a profile strategy is that the direction for the communications is two-way and that all communications are two-way in nature. There is a two-way communication between an organisation and:

- Distributors
- Retailers
- Regulators
- Customers
- Finance markets
- Wholesalers
- Employees
- Local communities

Fill (2003) summarises: 'Traditionally these organisationally-orientated activities have been referred to as corporate communications, as they deal more or less exclusively with the corporate entity of the organisation. Products, services and other offerings are not normally the particular focus of these communications. It is the organisations and its role in the context of the particular stakeholder's activities that is important. However, it should be noted that as more corporate brands appear, the distraction between corporate and marketing communications begins to become much less clear. Indeed, when considered in light of the development and interest in internal marketing (and communication), it may be a greater advantage to consider corporate communications as part of an organisation's overall marketing communications activities....The awareness, perception and attitudes held by stakeholders towards an organisations need to be understood, shaped and acted upon'.

1.3 Issues for consideration when developing marketing communications

When developing a marketing communications plan, it is useful to take stock of what the main issues are. Fill, (2003, p. 298) notes the issues to be considered as tabled below.

Elements	Issue
Target audiences	Which type of audience do we need to reach and why?
Channel strategies	How do we make our products/services available – direct or indirect?
Objectives	What do we need to achieve, what are our goals?
Positioning	How do we want to be perceived and understood?
Branding	How strong and what values and associations do stakeholders make with our brands?
Integration	How consistent are our communications internally and externally?
Competitors	How do our communications compare with those of our key competitors?
Resources	What resources do we have and which do we need to secure?

The following diagram shows the marketing communications planning framework (Fill, 2003, p. 300). It contextualises the various goals – marketing, communications and corporate and the three different promotional strategies – and how these 'fit' with the various elements of the marketing communications planning process.

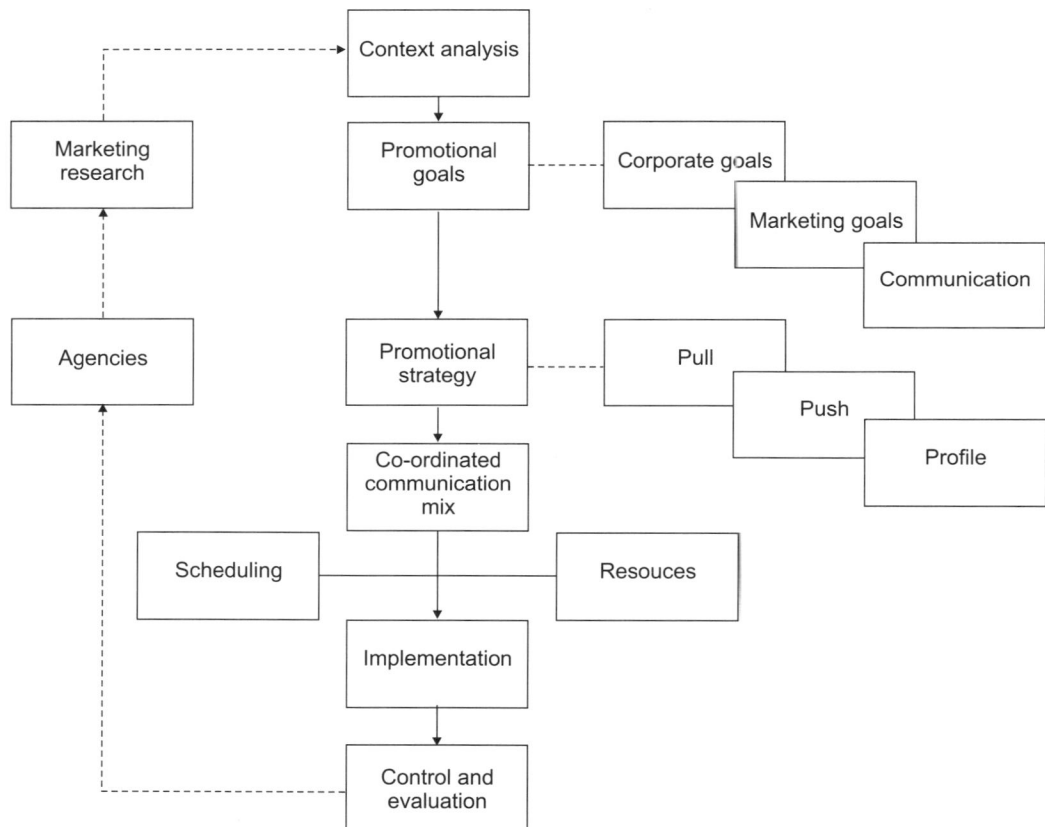

It is important to emphasise here that it is critical that the **communication strategy should be customer- and not method- or media-oriented**. Hence the communication strategy will need to adapt depending on the type of customer targeted. So for example, the strategy for one business segment (a distributor, say) will be different to that for another segment.

2 Public relations in context

2.1 Introduction

In Chapter 7, you were introduced to the concept of public relations (PR) and a definition explaining what it means. In essence, PR is about effective two-way communications with an organisation's wide range of stakeholders through building relationships.

KEY CONCEPT

concept

The Chief Examiner, Fill (2003, p.619), describes PR:

'Public relations is a management activity that attempts to shape the attitudes and opinions held by an organisation's stakeholders. Through dialogue with these stakeholders the organisation may adjust its own position and strategy. Therefore there is an attempt to identify with, and adjust an organisation's policies to, the interest of its stakeholders. To do this it formulates and executes a programme of action to develop mutual goodwill and understanding.'

Later Fill describes one of the characteristics of PR:

'While the credibility may be high, the amount of control that management is able to bring to the transmission of the public relations message is very low'.

In Chapter 6, you have read about identifying and prioritising key stakeholders and considering the communication needs of each. It is important to consider the perspectives of each stakeholder group, their interests and motivations. Seeing things from their viewpoint will help with developing appropriate and relevant communications is also significant. The range and number of stakeholders, where they are located and how they are connected with the organisation. Also, as communication planners, what is our ultimate motivation? Do we want to gain support, change attitudes or create interest? Consider the following examples.

MARKETING AT WORK

application

Here are three examples of PR campaigns which demonstrate, that PR can help gain support, change attitudes and change interest.

Example of PR gaining support: taking Pride in the Isle of Wight (Profile Extra, July 2009)

This campaign which won a CIPR Pride Award in 2007, aimed to improve the quality of life on the Isle of Wight.

'The 'One Island' programme had a simple but ambitious goal – to unite the island with a shared vision and improve residents' quality of life by developing mutual respect, local pride and value-for-money services. The programme also aimed to improve the reputation of the Council as an authority that listens to the needs of the residents and acts and delivers its promises. The programme, created after extensive consultation with Island residents, comprised 24 individual initiatives, with actions to address the Island's needs and priorities.

The main objective was to build awareness of the programme and to show how different projects can improve the quality of life of the residents. There was a considerable consultation programme with local residents which formed a major part of the PR planning, and one that responded directly to the needs of the residents during the year. This was followed by telephone interviews in order to ensure that the team were aware of the most pertinent issues to residents. There were three clear themes from this research for the programme as follows:

- **Respect** – Problems such as crime and anti-social behaviour, and building strong communities.

- **Pride** – Issues affecting the environment. Ensuring people live in cleaner, safer streets and dealing swiftly with rubbish, vandalism, and graffiti.

- **Value** – Focusing on value-for-money and the quality of services, such as roads and amenities. Also driving the longer-term vision of a progressive island built on economic success, high standards, and aspirations.

The campaign strategy combined communication methods to ensure that the Council's reputation for delivering its promises was made very clear to all audiences. An initial residents' survey was followed by an advertising campaign launched to feedback the results and encourage residents to explain what issues were significant to them. There was an eye-catching diamond-shaped leaflet which was circulated to residents inviting participation in a series of workshops. The media relations launched during February 2007 involved a proactive media strategy involving press releases, interviews around each major programme, local press advertisements and a four-page colour feature in the Council's One *Island magazine*. Schedules had respective programmes of actions, responsibilities and timings and informed residents of progress being made. Internal communications to staff involved regular updates in the staff magazine One Council and weekly briefings and weekly e-communications.

The results of the annual survey revealed that 1,200 residents were involved in the shaping and developing One Island. Nearly half of all residents – 47% were aware of the campaign two months after its launch. In addition, residents' satisfaction with the Council had risen from 9% to 26% in less than nine months. In terms of staff engagement, there was evidence that this had significantly improved as the number of staff who were critical of the Council fell 32% two months after the Council launched the campaign. Finally, in terms of the Council's overall reputation, over one-third of residents reported that Council services had improved over the 12-month period and up to 41% of residents were confident that services would improve in 2007–08.

Example of PR changing attitude

Liverpool Primary Care Trust – Liverpool's Challenge – reducing obesity (adapted from CIPR Member website 2009 Excellence Award)

Liverpool has seen a significant rise in obesity over the past 20 years, with an estimated 40% of the adult population overweight and 20% obese. The NHS in Liverpool spends £5m a year on treating obesity-related problems such as diabetes and heart disease, which cost the city's wider economy an additional £15m pa. To tackle the problem, the Primary Care Trust launched its *Healthy Weight: Healthy Liverpool* strategy in 2008, with the objective of stopping the rise in obesity by 2010 and reducing the level of obesity in the city from 2010. Liverpool's Challenge is a strand of that long-term strategy.

Research showed that people had 'good' intentions but struggled to change their habits. Insights were that people felt isolated and that the sense of being part of a community would be motivational. One strong theme was a need for a campaign that provided information in a non-judgemental and non-preaching way. People wanted a campaign that felt unique to Liverpool and that would foster the same sense of community as had the Capital of Culture. There was strong support for a rally-cry call to action. The PR campaign goals were:

- To challenge to people in Liverpool to collectively pledge to lose weight
- To use experiential 'million pound tanker' vehicle with live events
- To provide access to health professionals, information and local support
- To offer ongoing encouragement throughout relationship marketing techniques

The aim was to generate a sense of something 'big' happening in the city. A sense of community would be fostered and a feeling of ownership, which would be more effective than being preached at by 'the authorities'. It was felt that the campaign had to be PR- rather than advertising-led for it to have credibility and get public buy-in. Once people had signed up they would be motivated by ongoing media coverage and regular supportive messages. The media presence would keep the Challenge high on the agenda as the media were supplied with a succession of strong local stories – showing people 'just like me', celebrity photo calls, the tanker tour, Boots offering sign-up sessions, images of community food workers doing on-street cookery demonstrations.

The campaign's main aim was simple – to get people in Liverpool to lose weight. Specifically the aims were (by the end of February 2009):

- To get half a million pounds (of weight loss) pledged
- To generate unprompted public awareness of the campaign of 10%
- To generate prompted public awareness of 40%
- To get 50% of the public exercising more
- To get 50% of the public eating more healthily

A pre-launch teaser campaign aimed to generate curiosity and a sense that something big was happening. A city-wide ATL campaign using the strapline 'Liverpool has a million pounds to lose', was used to stimulate debate in the local media, including the two media partners, the Liverpool Echo and Radio City/City Talk, chosen because of their extensive reach and fit with the target audience.

In September the campaign was revealed and the launch event saw 'the million pound tanker', providing a focus for public and the media. The tanker has been the mainstay of the campaign, providing a hook and visual feature for the media and a way of reaching the public as it toured communities throughout January and February 2009. Inside the tanker visitors have a friendly and confidential consultation with an adviser, while outside community food workers and fitness advisers give cookery and exercise demonstrations.

Media coverage has been extensive. The Liverpool Echo ran ten full pages featuring campaign events and two front page features. Radio City/City Talk provided sponsorship of its Drive Time programme, with frequent mentions and celebrity endorsements. There was a weekly mention on the 'diary' feature, regular 30-second trailers, interviews, live broadcasts which saw presenters pledging and a day-long focus on the Challenge. The radio partnership also extended online, with banners, features and a sign-up button.

Celebrity supporters, chosen for their approachability, included Jamie Carragher from Liverpool FC; Beth Tweddle, Team GB gymnast; actress Claire Sweeney and comedian Johnny Vegas.

All this was backed by an advertising campaign designed to maximise PR coverage and contribute to the general buzz. This included an outdoor campaign using 6- and 48-sheets; press advertising; and 'community advertising' in Boots stores, GPs' surgeries, pharmacies, cafes and community centres. A strong online presence supported the campaign, with a web site on which people could view documentaries of pledgers and record their own progress. However, it was the adoption of the campaign by the local media that added the real credibility – from features expressing shock: '13,000 of our kids are obese' to editorials: 'This is the weigh to go' and 'Let's get together to fight the fat'.

Example of PR gaining interest or support

Prescription Charges Campaign (adapted from CIPR member web site, CIPR Excellence Awards, 2009)

This Prescription Charges Campaign entered by Macmillan Cancer Support, won a CIPR Excellence Award in 2009. The main aim was for government to abolish prescription charges for cancer patients in England and Northern Ireland. The facts were that most people with cancer under 60 have to pay for their prescriptions and calls to Macmillan helplines said that cancer patients were struggling to pay for them. The prescription charges exemption system had not been reformed in 40 years and did not take into account that cancer is now a long-term condition. The Department of Health said in July 2007 they would hold a public review for England but this was continually delayed. The subsequent announcement that any changes had to be cost-neutral was disappointing. It was clear that securing an exemption for cancer patients as a specific group was unlikely in the climate of shrinking budgets. The Northern Ireland Health Minister announced a review in May 2007 but no further announcement had been made.

A three-pronged approach was used to place direct and very public pressure on the governments in England and Northern Ireland: public relations, public campaigning, and public affairs. The objective was: to increase active public campaigners by 25%, generate 100 pieces of press and broadcast coverage, meet with 20 key political influencers and secure 80 EDM signatures, to influence the reviews in 2008 and exempt cancer patients from prescription charges.

An online survey took place using cancer patients to provide supporting campaign-evidence. The research showed that:

(a) A third of cancer patients were choosing not to get a prescribed treatment because they couldn't afford to pay the prescription charge.

(b) Nearly half of cancer patients were being forced to cut back on basic needs, such as food or heating, in order to pay for their prescriptions.

The campaign used the following approaches:

- **Media** – survey results together with emotive case studies were used to get widespread media coverage. Every media opportunity was explored and coverage gained in major broadcast outlets and hundreds of local papers. All of this placed added pressure on the governments in Westminster and Stormont. In Northern Ireland the campaign was the main driver for a major daily newspaper, the Belfast Telegraph, establishing its own campaign.

- **Public Affairs** – In Westminster written and oral Parliamentary Questions and an EDM to keep the pressure on Ministers were orchestrated. In Northern Ireland the support of several key MLAs and all political parties was secured. In both nations several face-to-face meetings with key Ministers took place and raised the issue repeatedly at public meetings where Ministers and officials were present.

- **Public campaigning** – Campaigners were asked to send a template letter to local MPs asking them to write to the Public Health Minister. They also sent a template letter to their local papers. More campaigners were recruited through the media, health professionals, support groups and relationships with corporate partners, for example Royal Mail highlighted the campaign and how to support it in their staff newsletter.

- **Marketing** – Posters and flyers were used to recruit new campaigners and promote the campaign.

- **Evaluation** was carried out through monthly evaluation meetings measuring progress against the objectives and changing tactics as and when necessary. In September 2008, free prescriptions for cancer patients announced in England and the abolition of prescription charges announced in Northern Ireland. The Department of Health said in its Q&A circulated the day after the decision in England that Macmillan's campaign convinced them to act immediately to help cancer patients. The Northern Ireland Health Minister referred specifically to Macmillan in his announcement that prescription charges would be phased out and asked Macmillan's Northern Ireland General Manager to join him for a photo call.

There were a number of specific ways that the campaign success was measured.

- 995 campaigners wrote to their MP.

- 4,100 local newspapers were sent a letter from a campaigner.

- 125 MPs signed the early day motion.

- There were 474 pieces of media coverage in England and Northern Ireland.

The results were measured against the set objectives and it was demonstrated that in the course of the campaign:

- The number of active public campaigners doubled (from 500 to nearly 1000), exceeding the target
- Over 474 pieces of media coverage were secured , over-achieving the target almost five times
- 125 MPs signed the EDM, a third more than target
- 28 meetings were held with political influencers

The vast local campaigning, media coverage and political lobbying made what looked like an impossible aim, achievable. Free prescriptions for cancer patients in England came into effect from 1 April 2009. In Northern Ireland, charges are being phased out and will be abolished completely in April 2010.

It is interesting to note that all work for this campaign was handled in-house and that the only direct costs were marketing materials costing less than £1,000.

The above examples show that, public relations (PR) can be used and applied in a number of different contexts – different types of organisations and in different specialisms – and that it has a significant role to play in the management of reputation.

2.2 What PR involves

PR is a planned activity which encompasses a wide range of different events (Fill, 2003, p. 621).

'Public relations does not require the purchase of airtime or space in media vehicles such as television or magazines. The decision on whether an organisation's public relations messages are transmitted or not rests with those charged with managing the media resource, not the message sponsor. Those that are selected are believed to be endorsements or the views of parties other than management. The outcome is that these message usually carry greater perceived credibility than those messages transmitted through paid media, such as advertising'. Fill (2003, p. 621)

Fill (2003, p621) suggests that one of the main characteristics of PR is that is can provide a very inexpensive way of communicating messages with maximum credibility but minimal cost.

PR campaigns can have numerous objectives and aims but generally speaking focus on achieving one or more of three different kinds of objectives:

- Knowledge or awareness related – raises awareness levels of a brand, an issue, a product or service.

- Attitude or motivation related – try to change or from a particular attitude.

- Behavioural – wanting to change behaviour in some way.

Further objectives can be applied at either a strategic or a more practical level. The table below taken from Gregory, 2000) contextualises strategic and tactical level objectives.

Issue	Strategic objective	Tactical objective
Company seen as backward	Position as company produces innovative products	Promote this product as innovative
Company not seen as contributor to community	Position as company that takes public responsibility seriously	Promote company-sponsored recycling scheme in community
Company not seen as caring employer	Position as company committed to employees	Promote women-returners scheme

(Gregory, 2000)

2.3 Appreciate the differing perspectives of PR

It is important to note that PR is viewed in a number of different ways by management and personnel within organisations. Public relations (PR) is very often viewed as a tactical or practical element of the marketing communications mix – specifically support product PR. Whereas corporate PR – or corporate communications as it is described most recently in this text – is a critical element of all organisations communications and forms part of an organisation's corporate strategy. Strong corporate communications help develop a strong corporate reputation. In short, irrespective of how the function of PR is viewed it is important to note the significance of communications at the corporate level to the well-being of an organisation.

MARKETING AT WORK

application

'Save a tree, plant a tree: new billing technology from it'

The following case received a CIPR Excellence Award 2009 in the corporate and business communications category.

In 2008, e-billing was recognised as legitimate and legal documentation in Turkey. Turk Telekom (TT) pioneered e-billing technology and was one of the first companies to issue e-bills. Consumer acceptance of online billing was critical to the campaign. It was important to ascertain what would motivate people to use online billing. enhance Save a Tree, Plant a Tree' was developed to improve TT's reputation and build business by which paper savings would be converted into ecological benefits.

The main approach was to expand awareness about environmental protection in the minds of the Turkish people. As an additional goal, was to reinforce the perception of TT as an environmentally sensitive institution. The focus was to save paper and to plant trees as an incentive to motivate people to make the switch. A massive campaign informed the general public about the impact of paper statements on their communities.

The objectives of the campaign were to convert 500,000 (roughly 8.25%) of the of the company's six million ADSL users paper bills to e-bills within one year. There was a goal to plant a tree for every 1,000 accounts that converted to e-billing.

As it begun, TT transferred its own archives from paper to electronic, saving 1,500 tonnes of paper each year, worth 24,000 trees. A reputation-building approach was then launched.

- A communications campaign blitz offering ten minutes of free calls every month for a year to those customers who chose e-billing was in virtually every newspaper in Turkey.

- Flyers were created as statement stuffers, other versions of the flyer were distributed in taxi cabs in major cities, Istanbul and Ankara.

- There were public service announcements placed on public and private television statements, and the topic was covered in talk shows.

- At the International Brand Conference, TT gave away cordless telephones (ie a sales promotion) to customers who then and there transferred their billing from paper to electronic statements.

- At the CEBIT fair, the largest IT expo in Turkey, TT created a special stand just for the introduction of the e-billing system.

The potential problem was the attitude about the environment. Given the diversity among the 80 plus regions in the country, it was not clear how attractive an environmental initiative would be. So a quantitative research study ascertained attitudes about the environment and investigated how TT was perceived as a responsible corporate citizen. This research helped TT redefine the top target audience as highly educated customers living in the rural areas. In addition, TT learned that, while it scored second as being environmentally sensitive, the percentage was not so large, and therefore it had a big job to do to reinforce its image as an environmentally friendly and responsible company.

Just before the 'Save a Tree, Plant a Tree' program began, TT was printing 23.5 million billing statements per month, using 350 tonnes of offset paper, 125 tonnes of company archive materials, 125 tonnes in customer copies and 100 tons in envelopes.

The campaign results actually doubled the objectives, converting 1,000,000 TT customer statements in the first year alone, saving more than 4,200 tonnes of paper on an annual basis. Also, TT is well underway towards planting some 100,000 trees in 2009. The multiplier effect of engaging customers at the local level has boosted consumer concern about the environment, substantiated by post-research of customer attitudes about TT's role as an environmentally responsible corporate citizen.

Adapted from the CIPR Pride Awards (2009)

MARKETING AT WORK

application

Fight to save the British honey bee

The following case study featured in PR Week in April 2009. Rowse Honey approached their PR consultancy IncediBull in January 2008 with the suggestion that they wanted to use PR rather than advertising to generate sales. They wanted to increase their market share which was then 35% of the sweet spread market in a recessive market. Simultaneously the global honey production was under threat as there was a virus destroying colonies of bees. The objectives of the PR campaign which ran between January 2009 and January 2009 were simply to increase sale and market share; to position Rowse as the leader in tackling the honey bee crisis through investment in research and to focus on the properties of honey in relation to health, the home and the natural environment.

The theme of 'save the honey bee' ran through all communications which cleverly appealed to both environmentally and health conscious consumer segments in addition to industry-type stakeholders. The theme of honey bee declines featured in headlines and media coverage and linked in to the use of celebrity Charlie Dimmock and her recommendations for keeping bees in the garden. The consultancy IncrediBull highlighted the health benefits of honey with honey tastings and celebrity endorsements such as that made by opera singer Katherine Jenkins who mentioned the use of Rowse Manuka Honey in her performance warm-ups. There were also a series of announcements to both trade and national media around the decline of the honey bee population and the impact of this decline on global agriculture. In addition there was a CSR initiative started which was called a 'Bee School' which was aimed at primary school children with the aim of putting more honey on UK dinner tables.

The success of the campaign can be shown in a variety of different ways. For example, there were 233 pieces of quality, positive coverage across a combination of national, regional, local, trade, broadcast and online media. There were in total an amazing 422 million opportunities or more to see the campaign (using the advertising equivalent to measure the success).

During the length of the media tour Rowse met 28 journalists for tutored honey tastings and slots on saving the honey bee appeared on Sky News, BBC News, BBC Radio 4's Today, Farming Today and You and Yours programmes. There were within four months of going live 30,000 downloads of the Bee School educational packs and *half of the web sites visitors said they were there as a result of the media coverage the campaign had gained. An MP Ed Vaizey supported the campaign and was taken to visit the Oxford-based factory of Rowse. In January 2009, the Department for the Environment, Food and Rural Affairs announced an investment of $4,3m over a five-year period into honey bee research. At this time, the Rowse market share was 40% and exceeded competitors and research showed that 750,000 more households bought honey in 2008 compared with 2007. Piggy backing on the save a honey bee theme was a clever move for Rowse and proved a very successful way of driving consumer sales through consumer PR.*

In an example of tactical PR in practice, typically key performance indicators would usually be linked to campaigns and sales and customer actions.

2.4 The relationship/dynamics between PR and marketing

PR can be viewed in a number of different ways in relation to marketing and very often the value given to PR related to the way that the PR function is organised within an organisation and the level of understanding awarded to the contribution PR makes to business. There has been a reasonable amount of literature written about this very thing. However, for the purpose of your studies, it is useful to be aware of these kinds of dynamics between overlapping disciplines and how this relates to the bigger picture as far as corporate communications goes.

The following model from Gregory (2000, p.15) explains the interrelationship between PR and marketing. It suggests that most marketing-related activity is largely one-way communication, whereas most PR-type activity is largely two-way communications.

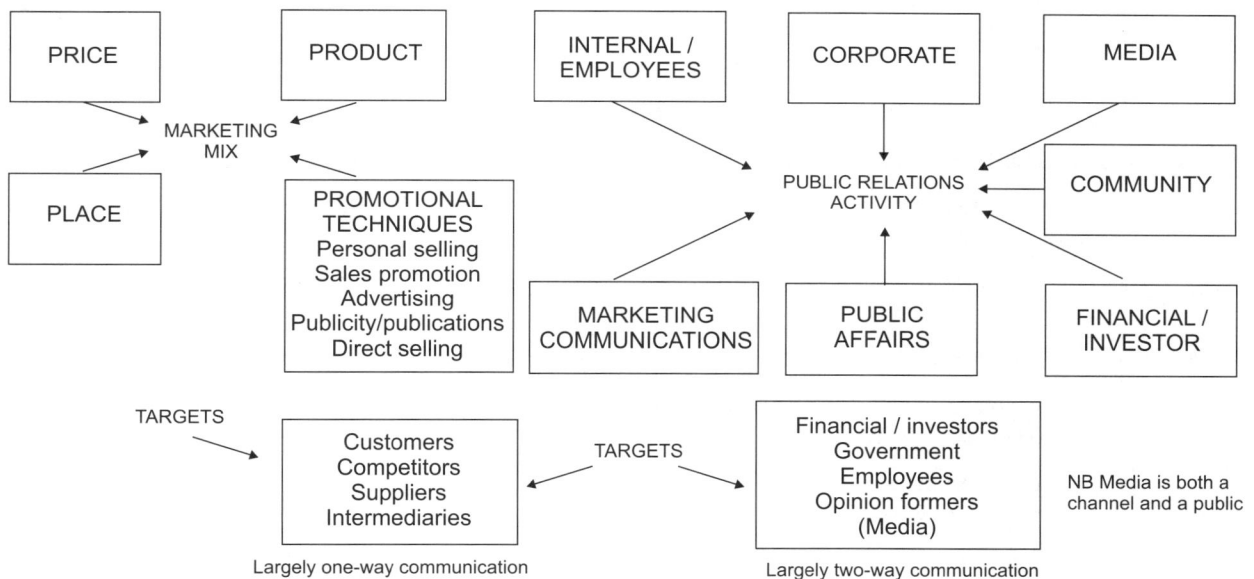

(Gregory, 2000)

2.5 The role of PR in context of corporate communications

KEY CONCEPT   concept

Yeoman and Tench (2009, p. 48) citing Fawkes, (2008) usefully summarise corporate communications as PR activity that is 'Communicating on behalf of the whole organisation, not at goods and services'. Examples of corporate communications include annual reports, newsletters, conferences and ethical or CSR statements.

3 Public and community relations

The public are an important stakeholder group for organisations because even if they are not customers themselves, collectively they harness significant vocal power. They are therefore likely to be strong opinion influencers in many scenarios.

3.1 Introducing community relations

Local people have a considerable influence over an organisation by their very closeness to the organisation. It is possible to keep local people informed and run community relations programmes which facilitate relationship building with the local people, they may identify better and build a stronger focus on the organisation itself. (Fill, 2003, p. 623).

'Community relations is not just about being good or being 'nice to people'. Although this may be one of its results. Instead the concept is based on sound commercial principles which can be summarised as: research, corporate vision, strategic objectives, tactical programme, measurement and evaluation and dissemination (Yeoman and Tench, 2009, p. 354).

Doorley and Garcia (2007, p. 184) suggest that:

'Community relations is the strategic development of mutually beneficial relationships with targeted communities toward the long-term objective of building reputation and trust'. Doorley and Garcia (2007, p.185) go on to suggest Hardy's Relationship as Building Principles summarised below.

(a)   Be involved. Be committed.
(b)   Building reputation, one relationship at a time is good business.
(c)   Choose the right projects. Be strategic.
(d)   Keep moving ahead.
(d)   Embrace diversity.
(e)   When things go wrong, make them as fast as you can.
(f)   Community relationships are based on trust.

3.2 Objectives of community programmes

Yeoman and Tench (2009) suggests there are typical objectives for a community programme:

* To create and develop a positive view of the company as a socially responsible, good corporate citizen among its key stakeholders.

* To capitalise on this positive perception in terms of employee motivation, recruitment of new personnel, supplier development and community goodwill.

* To support other initiatives aimed at creating an understanding of the company's aims and policies.

* To develop opportunities which encourage employee participation in the community through increased communication initiatives.

* To support the needs of the local community with innovative, role model initiatives, which position the company as a centre of excellence for community involvement.

* To brand the (community) programme clearly so that it is easily recognised and remembered.

3.3 Elements of successful community relations programmes

For a community involvement programme to be developed and be successful, it must include support from three interlinking areas as illustrated in the following diagram adapted from Yeoman and Tench (2009).

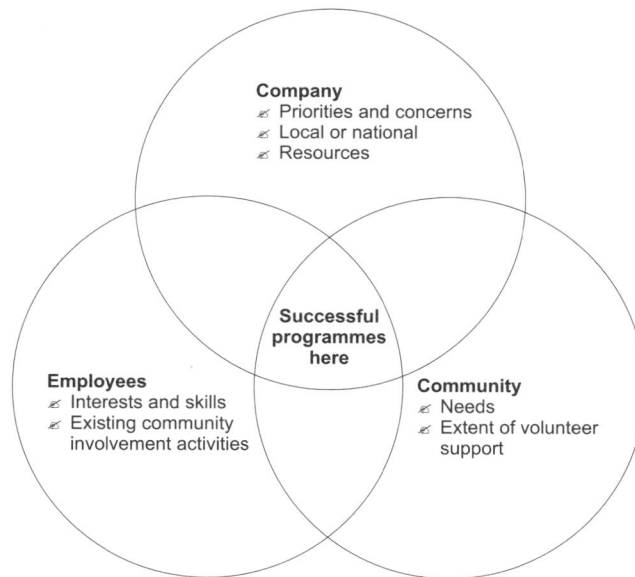

ACTIVITY 1

evaluation

Consider a new restaurant opening in your local area. Think for a moment about the range of local people that might have an interest (or a 'stake') in the restaurant and why? Once you have analysed the range of stakeholders consider what kind of community relations programme you could plan to involve the local stakeholders and their various interests, concerns or motivations in the restaurant.

You may question what is achievable from community relations programmes? Generally, they can create a fair amount of publicity for an organisation. Schemes involving much employee participation may well generate employee feedback; schemes may be quite creative and offer considerable value-for-money.

MARKETING AT WORK

application

Housing Review – Better Housing for Rhondda Cynon Taf Council

The following case received the Gold Award for the CIPR Cymru Wales Pride Awards in 2007 and the except is adapted from the CIPR Pride Awards web pages.

Rhondda Cynon Taf Council faced a major challenge to improve social housing for thousands of tenants in one of the UK's most deprived communities. With social housing across Wales in poor condition, the Welsh Assembly Government has introduced a new Welsh Housing Quality Standard (WHQS) to make sure it's improved. The standard gives minimum criteria for facilities in the home and must be met by all Welsh Councils by 2012. While Rhondda Cynon Taf Council agreed it is essential to meet the Welsh Housing Quality Standard and deliver better quality homes for tenants and significant local regeneration, the amount of money it needed (£170 million over the first five years) to reach the Standard far outweighed the money available (£50 million).

So it was agreed that the only way to meet the Standard in a way to give tenants control over their homes, safeguarding jobs for staff and providing local investment was to undertake a full transfer of the housing stock to a new Community Mutual Housing Organisation called RCT Homes, which the Council would help to set-up.

This would be a huge change for everyone involved and a very sensitive subject that would need to be communicated to a range of stakeholders. Most importantly, it was only with the support of tenants that a transfer could go ahead. Tenants would have to vote 'yes' at an independent ballot.

The campaign objectives included:

(a)   To encourage tenant and staff involvement and 'localise' the project.
(b)   To educate on reasons for, and benefits of, change.
(c)   To involve stakeholders in decision-making.
(d)   To encourage tenants to use their vote.

The project was two years in the making with communications making its mark between the Summer and the November 2006 ballot. An internal communications team – including a communications officer, senior housing professional and two administrative officers – was established. Nevertheless, the communications structure was far reaching. The Council supported the tenants to employ an Independent Tenants Advisor, who would be available to guide them through the process and offer help and free, impartial advice. There was also an Independent Staff Advisor who could provide the same service for staff. Both of these had freephone information lines, produced newsletters and held countless meetings. The Communications Team would feed into tenants groups to update on progress and get qualitative feedback. Importantly, in-house resources were used as much as possible including the design service and housing staff.

Overall, the key was to involve local people as much as possible and to be open and transparent. The project was about people being confident that a transfer would benefit local people and keep decision-making local.

The implementation included using an integrated campaign consisting of the following:

(a)   **Tenants**:

–   Five 'Your Home' newsletters posted to all tenants.

–   200 public meetings, estate and town centre roadshows (including a trailer with access to the dedicated – web site).

–   Web site (www.rctbetterhomes.co.uk).

–   DVD (explanatory).

–   Pocket guides.

–   Information cards.

–   Offer Document and easy guide to the tenants offer (which the tenants voted on).

–   Freephone helpline.

–   Four community show homes.

–   Call to action advertising campaign during ballot including – press and radio advertising, posters, advertising trailer, sms text to landline.

–   Independent Tenants Advisor – with newsletters, freephone line, conference and community event.

(b)   **Staff**:

–   Independent Staff Advisor – with newsletters, freephone line and staff advisory groups.

–   Payslip inserts.

–   Intranet.

–   Staff advisory group.

–   Staff newsletters.

–   Media briefings with local daily and weekly papers to give facts and figures, plus fortnightly press release over a 1 ½ year period.

Independent market research was carried out at regular intervals to ensure key messages were getting across and communications tools were being positively received. Consultation questionnaires issued to all tenants, to ask their future needs for the housing service received 4,500 returns. Unison 'vote no' newsletter sent to all tenant's home. Reacted with fact sheet, information from the ITA and signpost to factual information. All communications were given in Welsh and English language.

The creativity was really in giving things the local touch (key for a true community relations campaign). Tenants and staff were involved as much as possible:

- A DVD posted to all 10,500 homes that featured tenants and local presenters Roy Noble and Lucy Owen (which also gave celebrity endorsement).

- A Service Level Agreement with a community radio station (GTFM 107.9) to have weekly interviews with housing staff and tenants to give the personal touch. All participants supported and briefed as many were going into a studio for the first time.

- A door knocking exercise so that every tenant received a personal visit to check they had received and understood all the information they'd been given.

In November 2006, the tenants gave the go ahead. An independent ballot saw a turnout of 55% of an estimated 11,000 tenants. In total, 58% voted yes to the transfer proposals with 42% against. **The borough will now see its biggest sustained investment programme since the industrial revolution**.

- The reality for current and future tenants is improvements in the first five years after transfer and will include:
- 5000 new modern kitchens with new units.
- 4000 new modern bathrooms and showers.
- 6000 new modern energy efficient central heating boilers.
- More than £4million invested in things like fences, gates and paths.

The Council's result was a momentous success situated in one of the UK's most deprived areas, with high unemployment and a high reliance on State welfare. This is the largest local authority transfer result in the Principality to date. Ultimately, it was the communications with all stakeholders, particularly tenants, which led to a successful conclusion. Communications and good community relations continues to date with new tenant empowerment plans being put together.

Note: This is a good example of an award winning campaign which focuses not only on community relations but gave a good example of internal relations in practice (see Chapter 10 Employee Communications).

3.4 The general public as a target audience

We have discussed elsewhere in this chapter the main characteristics of community relations programmes and the elements of successful community relations have been explored. The general public is a very broad and non-specific term which is used to describe what could be considered as a whole range of different people with different stakes in an organisation. Consider the following statement made by van Riel and Fombrun (2007, p. 200) as a stakeholder group:

'The general public is probably the most diffuse stakeholder group that companies address. For one, the public seldom speaks directly to companies. The public largely voices its concerns either through the mouthpiece of politicians claiming to represent the public interest, or through the active initiatives of non-governmental organisations (NGOS) who claim to act on behalf of *the public*. In fact, the public consists of a large and diverse set of interests. After all, everyone is a member of *the public* – consumers, investors, employees, regulators, politicians – we are all part and parcel of the amorphous mass of people whose voice seldom rises above a whisper, and whose interests are only ever partially defended. The role of the public relations (PR) specialist, in many ways, is to communicate with the general public in ways that serve the interests of the company. PR therefore consists of numerous speciality areas that convey information about the company to the public, including sponsorships, events, media relations, and issues management.'

ACTIVITY 2
application

Consider for a moment the full range of stakeholders for a local primary school. List as many of them as you can. Pay particular attention to the range of local community or, as described in your Text, general public. How many stakeholders have you listed? What interests and motivations might they have in relation to the primary school?

4 Public relations programmes

Cutlip, *et al* (2000) suggest four stages for the planning of PR programmes:

1. Delivering the PR problem
2. Planning and programming
3. Taking action and communicating
4. Evaluating the programme

KEY CONCEPT

concept

A **public relations programme** is the planned schedule of activity for a planned course of practical PR. It will involve the following kinds of areas (Gregory 2000).

- Research and Analysis
- Objectives
- Publics
- Messages
- Strategy
- Tactics
- Timescales
- Resources
- Evaluation
- Review

In order to plan PR successfully, it is important that a number of key steps are followed. These, summarised from the planning framework above start with research and analysis. It is critical that there is a familiarity with the business environment and key current issues that an organisation faces, plus specific communications issues it has, followed by a familiarity with the competitive business environment. Once research and analysis has taken place, it is then possible to set PR objectives, building on the results of the research. The process could also involve a detailed stakeholder analysis in order to understand the various audiences and their motivations and interests in the organisation you are planning PR for. If you understand the stakeholders, have a clear idea of the issues and have some clear objectives that need to be met, it is possible to devise an appropriate PR strategy – an overall approach to planning your PR. The practical PR activity – the tactics – stems from the PR strategy and concerns the day-to-day detail of the PR itself and may include for example, events, media relations, production of literature, blogs, networking. Timescales for PR activity involve adding timings to what you plan week by week – month by month; resources involves allocating resources – such as people to activities that need to be completed. Evaluation involves measuring the PR that has been undertaken to evaluate the effectiveness of it.

MARKETING AT WORK

application

Application – Example of PR programme: Play O Digital PR Campaign – Things that make you go O!

(Adapted from CIPR Excellence Awards, 2009 where this campaign won an award)

The issue of living a happy sex life is generally discussed more online and in particular, in social media, than anywhere else. Therefore, set against the client's project objectives of 15–20 digital pieces of Play O coverage within the ten-week time-frame, McCann (the consultancy, acting on behalf of Durex, the client) created a social media campaign that would:

- Give Durex a presence in social media
- Start conversations between people and the brand
- Give Durex and Play O in particular, a human feel
- Ultimately help increase sales of Play O

With social media, it is vital that a brand listens first and then engages with people in conversations. Also, as sex is such a sensitive area, it was important to approach the campaign with discretion.

McCann came up with the theme of 'Things that Make you go O!' – all those things that give you knee trembling excitement such as a Marc Jacobs handbag or Jonny Depp. The idea being to associate Play O with these Things That Make You Go O! And start people talking about Play O in the content of knee trembling pleasure.

The campaign had four main stages:

(a) **Social media landscape mapping**

McCann analysed the conversations around sex, sex lives, relationships and sexual health across all forms of social media. From this, it was decided that a Facebook campaign and a blogger relationship-building campaign would best achieve the objectives.

(b) **Blogger engagement**

McCann identified the most influential bloggers on the subjects of sexual health; sex and relationships and the more risqué subject of having good sex. McCann contacted the bloggers individually and discussed what kind of information they look out for, explained a bit about the product and offered a sample for review. For those that wanted information, but not a sample, we sent a social media news release – a multimedia alert on the product with videos, photos and audio files that bloggers could easily use.

(c) **Facebook campaign**

McCann created a dedicated Page around 'The Things that Make You Go Oh!' and encouraged people to upload photos and descriptions of the 'Things that make them go Oh'. The best one would win a romantic weekend away with a 'Things that make you go Oh!' hamper of decadence [including the product]. The Page was supported with a one week Engagement Ad that directed people to fan the Page. McCann ran the content programme for the Page regularly posting about things they had found that made them go Oh!, commenting on people's posts and inviting other people to fan the Page.

(d) **Forum conversations**

McCann monitored conversations that were going on in forums about improving sex lives. Then, with permission from the moderators, McCann joined in the conversations on behalf of Play O and chatted to forum members about ways you can improve your sex life and when requested, provided information on the Play O product.

Over 700 Facebook fans were encouraged to upload their own ideas of 'Things that make you go O'. Engaging with the online Play O community was at the centre of the campaign, facebookers were then rewarded for their uploads with the chance of winning a decadent weekend away in a boutique Mr & Mrs Hotel.

This successful campaign awarded a CIPR Excellence Award (2009) resulted in 32 pieces of digital coverage from blogs, forums and web sites and over 216 'generated discussions' around the blog and forum posts, 35 Facebook uploads and 41 Facebook comments and 70,000 conversations in Facebook. The campaign included a competition and there were as a result 1,251 competition entries across Facebook, Body Confidential web site and Silicone Stilettos blog. There was a reported 34% increase in weekly sales and a 10% increase in online sales.

It is important to note that what was achieved in this campaign was far beyond the client's original objective of 15–20 online pieces of coverage over the designated three-month period.

It is also an example of how various forms of media work together in an integrated way – advertising (engagement advert to support Facebook part of campaign) was used and a competition (sales promotion) was also used as an integral part of the campaign to raise awareness and motivate participation.

4.1 Messages of public relations

By now, it will be becoming clearer how complex communicating with stakeholders can be, based on the types of stakeholders involved, their interests, expectations, needs and power and the importance of these stakeholders to the PR activity concerned – in other words are they priority stakeholders?

Other factors come in to play here too. For example, whether the audience that you are trying to communicate with are active, passive or aware (Grunig and Hunt 1984 cited in Yeoman and Tench, 2009, p. 229). Grunig and Hunt's situational theory, shown below, explains the differentiation between these types of stakeholder.

Latent publics	Groups that face a particular problem as a result of an organisation's action, but fail to recognise it.
Aware publics	Groups that recognise that a problem exists.
Active publics	Groups that organise to discuss and do something about the problem.

In essence, in addition to the complexity one faces in analysing the stakeholders in any given communications scenario, different types of messages will be appropriate to use to suit different kinds of objectives.

MARKETING AT WORK

application

A PR campaign run by the Department of Health in the UK had the primary objective of educating people about the latest issues associated with swine flu and preventing panic. In PR Week in April, 2009, the Department of Health's communications chief said *'We have been preparing for this type of situation for years. Our key messages are reassurance for the public that we have enough antivirals for half of the population. We are also promoting simple steps that the public can take concerning hygiene'.*

The messages here are of both a practical nature in an attempt to reassure and offer practical guidance to prevent spread of the illness.

4.2 Issues management and crisis communication

Issues management and crisis communication are a major part of PR and reputation management. Managing an organisation's reputation is a critical part of corporate communications. This area is covered in detail in Chapter 11. However, consider the following example of a crisis which occurred as this text was written.

MARKETING AT WORK

application

A Disney World monorail driver was killed in a collision between trains carrying tourists in the Florida resort. (adapted from the Telegraph Online, July 5, 2009)

The telegraph reported the following story.

The crash between the futuristic elevated trains occurred at around 2am on Sunday morning near to the entrance to the Magic Kingdom theme park, where the system's three routes interconnect.

The other train operator was not injured but was taken to a hospital because he was emotionally shaken. Five park guests were treated at the scene.

It was not immediately clear what caused the crash at the park, part of the largest and most visited recreational resort in the world.

The crash happened at the ticket and transportation centre near the Magic Kingdom's car park. About a dozen guards wearing blue Disney security uniforms guarded the monorail station on Sunday and stopped visitors from approaching the area. Disney World, part of the Walt Disney empire, closed the monorail system, which is used to carry tourists to parks and hotels in the 25,000-acre resort. The Magic Kingdom, which includes the famous Cinderella Castle, alone receives 17 million visitors a year, including many from Britain. Some tourists were clearly shaken by the accident. *'You would think it would be so safe. You don't expect it on holiday, do you?,'* said Lauren Shoebottom, a 20-year-old visitor from London. 'It's a bit shocking. Disney seems so perfect,' said Danielle Williams, 22, also from London. Ethan Meus, 17, said he and his family took the monorail to dinner at a resort hotel on Saturday night. He said he watched the Magic Kingdom fireworks from the monorail on the way back to his hotel and did not notice any problems with the train.

Mike Griffin, Walt Disney World's vice president of public affairs, offered condolences to the dead employee's family. Two monorail trains collided near the Magic Kingdom station in 1974 when one was unable to stop and hit the departing train in front. No guests were hurt but a driver was seriously injured. In 2006, a woman tourist died after riding on Disney World's 'Mission:Space' attraction.

Consider what would be required if you were handling crisis communications for Disney in this situation. A multinational organisation like Disney would have a clear crisis management procedure and protocol to follow, which would include informing the family of the member of staff who died, protecting the safety of all Disney customers and staff and keeping the media briefed on the incident and measures taken after the incident occurred. The reputation of Disney would depend on the effective and efficient handling of such incidents. Sometimes this is known as damage limitation. Note how the *Telegraph Online* also reminded the readers of another two accidents including a fatality incident in 2006.

5 Media relations

5.1 Introducing media relations

Many students muddle and are unable to distinguish between advertising and public relations when they commence their education. However understanding this is significant – in understanding the difference between editorial and advertising help understand the challenges faced in PR. In essence, the advertiser controls the message (by paying for it) and PR practitioner seeks to persuade other people ('third parties' to convey the message for them in a supportive way ('endorsement'). (Yeoman and Tench, 2009, p. 296).

5.2 Define media relations

When liaising with press Bland (1996) discusses the true purpose for the organisation as:

'The purpose of press relations is not to issue press releases or handle enquiries from journalists, or even to generate a massive pile of press cuttings. The true purpose of press relations is to enhance the reputation of an organisation and its products, and to influence and inform the target audience'.

KEY CONCEPT   concept

This is a fundamental point that needs to be understood. **Media relations** is critically about enhancing the reputation for an organisation and achieving this through effective and efficient handling of relations with the media – both proactively (researching and contacting media to attend a product launch, for example) and reactively (responding to a crisis such as food tampering or product recalls).

5.3 Understanding the media

An important element of understanding media relations is making sense of the perspective of the media – or very often the journalist – behind the media. It is useful to understand what motivates *the media* – as opposed to what motivates PR. This distinction is an important one.

What motivates the media

'Journalism is market-driven. The media respond to audience interest and strive to sell stories. These stories may range from industry-wide expose to CEO profiles – the reporter's interest may be salacious or high minded but all stories share one common denominator: they must attract 'eyes' or the media will go out of business. ...The media aren't there simply to sell your products or services or just to reprint your press releases. They have a job to do too.' (Schlenkler and Herrling, 2004, p. 8)

- They want to gain their audience's interest – seeking information from the media
- They may want to entertain their audience – which is often underestimated.

What news stories do they write?

Typically news stories fit broadly into three categories which include breaking news, feature stories and commentary. It is useful to understand what these three areas might entail so that you carrying out media relations can understand where your information might be able to fit – or where answers sought from you by a journalist might 'fit'. (Schlenkler and Herrling, 2004, p. 9)

What media do they use?

It is useful to understand the range of media that journalists work with and operate within then one can understand the parameters that they work within and the deadlines they might entail. As you know doubt know these include daily papers, weekly publications, broadcast television, radio and internet news sites.

How do they approach their task?

Finally, here it is important to appreciate how journalists might approach their tasks. Think of an 'inverted pyramid' in which all reporters, editors and news reporters are competing for an audience's attention and therefore they need to capture this immediately in the headline or first sentence of what is written. In the inverted pyramid then, the 'big idea' must go first, followed (probably) by some important fact, a quote and the context. The supporting information would follow at the end in a place where it could be easily removed if not time or space to cover this amount of detail.

'It is important to be aware of how journalists can 'spin' stories. There is some supplementary reading on an example of this looking at a case study of Marks and Spencer in Davies et al. (2003) ' p. 122–134 where you will learn how the media can have a significant impact upon the reputation of an organisation.

Bland *et al.* (2000) suggest that effective media (press) relations starts with effective targeting. *'There is no point in sending a technical story to a general newspaper, or a photograph of a victorious football team to a periodical which only carries product news, A local weekly newspaper might be interested in the latter story, and the periodical might find the former interesting.'*

Bland *et al.* (2000) continues to explain that there are four fundamental steps to media (press) relations as follows.

- **What is the function of the organisation**? – this will affect its media exposure.

- **What audiences are essential to its success**? – these are whom we try to reach via the media.

- **What messages does it wish to convey**? – as discussed earlier in the chapter, there will be diverse audiences requiring different tailored messages.

- **Which media are available for this**? – messages will be tailored to a wide variety of media but being clear about the audience.

Yeoman and Tench (2009, p. 302) also suggest some rules for effective media relations as follows.

- **Act as a service to the media**: answer questions. Return calls before deadlines, provide information and context.
- **Accept the independence of the media**: do not offer payment; do not ask for copy approval.
- **Disclose your interest** (ie let the journalist know who you are representing).
- **Be available to the media** when the news is bad as when you have good news to promote.

5.4 Tools of media relations

The area of media relations is one that is constantly changing and evolving – and also one that is very competitive. A strategy that has emerged is the idea of a media partnership. Which means that organisations and media are contractually bound in joint editorial, advertising and marketing relationships from which both parties can benefit.

5.5 Advantages and disadvantages of media

One of the advantages of media relations is said to be the cost involved – in that any editorial coverage that is gained is free. There is of course cost, because it is resource – or timely – to research, write and undertake media relations. However, editorial coverage cannot be guaranteed because if something more newsworthy breaks your item will be dropped. This can be very frustrating when, for example, you have worked very hard with a media contact and provided lots of relevant information, in anticipation of gaining editorial and it ultimately fails to happen.

5.6 The media in changing times

ACTIVITY 3

evaluation

Think carefully about how communication has changed. How specifically do you think technology has impacted upon PR and media communications?

5.7 Digital/new media

KEY CONCEPTS

'Digital media enable companies to introduce and market products in more targeted and personalised ways'.

Doorley and Garcia (2007, p. 105)

'The internet ushered in the new media era. It completely changed the dynamics of communication and rewrote the book on public relations. But the change did not happen overnight'.

Doorley and Garcia (2007, p. 106)

Briefly it is worth reminding ourselves of what we mean by new media and new media technology. Generally speaking, developments in technology have influenced print media in that new printing processes alongside the direct input of journalists have facilitated the quicker and more efficient printing of newspapers. Printing processes have also improved the speed at which colour magazines can be printed which traditionally would have taken several weeks to prepare. Broadcast and online media offer the most major developments.

Radio has also changed considerably over the last few years. Commercial radio stations have increased and community stations are growing in numbers. Integrated Services Digital Network (ISDN) enabling broadcast-quality audio has made possible more direct access to programming. The development of digital audio broadcasting has made it possible for a wider range of services to be offered through the same bandwidth.

New media terms include:

- Website Design
- Intranet/Extranets
- Blogs
- Really Simple Syndication (RSS)
- Search Engines
- Rich Media
- Email
- Database management
- Webinars
- Mobile phones and text
- Messaging

Satellite and cable television have also developed considerably since they first existed in the 1980s (Bland *et al.*, 2000). Digital broadcasting has created an increasing number of channels and a demand for more material to fill programme space and opportunities for PR-led stories. (Bland *et al.,* 2000)

5.8 The range of traditional media

There are a number of traditional media that continue to be used in media relations. This includes broadcast media such as radio, television – terrestrial, satellite and cable – plus non-broadcast media such as print. Print includes a plethora of different media from daily national newspapers to weekly local newspapers plus monthly specialist magazines and trade press, to name but a few examples.

The secret to is to understand the range of media available for you to work with and to use them in the most appropriate way possible. Bland *et al.*, (2000, pp. 64–65) suggest that there is clear approach that works well to achieve effective use of the media duplicated here:

- Use specialised media for the sector to announce developments and air matters of interest.

- Use academic or technical publications to enhance the reputation of staff and to discover if research is being supplicated elsewhere which would lead to collaboration.

- Use other specialised media to interest distributors, such as travel agents or retailers.

- Use the national press to announce major investments, new products if these are of sufficient interest (which in the case of many industrial and consumer products, is very rare), and company results if quoted on the Stock Exchange. Research, campaigns, events and crisis management are other areas to utilise the nationals. Major orders will also interest the nationals – but in this context 'major' means a value of tens of millions of pounds.

- Regional newspapers will often only be interested if they can be given the regional angle.

- Local newspapers will be interested in the activities of companies in their areas, not least because it affects the prosperity of the neighbourhood...

ACTIVITY 4

evaluation

What do you see as the advantages of using social media for PR rather than more traditional media ?

How do you think the way we communicate has changed in line with technology? What challenges do communicators face in trying to communicate with stakeholders or customers? How can they overcome these challenges?.

MARKETING AT WORK

application

Trunki UK Media Launch

An example of good media relations in practice is the Trunki media launch.

Sixteen months ago travel brand Trunki attempted to launch the world's first ride-on suitcase for globe trotting toddlers. Despite having a visibly unique product, the lengthy route to market, lack of retail presence, limited resources and disastrous early appearance on BBC Dragon's Den had impacted negatively on sales and brand recognition.

Outsourced PR expertise was sought to overcome these issues and drive a multi-layered campaign. The restoration of trust and credibility was paramount, along with swift sales conversion. Dangling Carrot PR prepared the following objectives, to be delivered, measured and evaluated over a 12-month period.

- Build visibility with consumers as 'the world's first ride-on suitcase for toddlers' in target media
- Engage new retail channels and drive UK sales
- Strengthen the brand position and curb damage caused by early TV appearance

PR was the only tool utilised to engage consumers and drive sales, which totalled £2,071,575 (139,500 units) on the back of 100 pieces of on-target coverage. Circulation totalled 70,758,031 with an average monthly hit of over five million, while audience reach totalled 89,328,032. Broadcast exposure totalling 2hrs 6mins blended heavyweight coverage such as BBC Radio 4 with entertainment programmes including Richard & Judy and BBC Radio 2 Drivetime. Despite being a Dragon's Den 'loser', the campaign delivered preferential placement in follow-up episodes and related newspaper features. Broadcast coverage contributed to 31% of the campaign reach and the client has since hosted an episode of CBBC Beat the Boss – a children's business programme that only works with market leaders.

Nineteen newspaper credits included five with the Daily Mail, four Telegraph, four Express and three with the Independent. Magazine highlights included interviews, product placements and tips across 38 leading travel, family and lifestyle publications. 68% of coverage featured new Trunki imagery, 59% featured a 'pack, pull and ride' message and trials had a 100% conversion rate.

The campaign helped re-establish credibility and open distribution channels – UK retailers totalled 520 in 2008 and included Mothercare, JLP and Harrods. Twelve national awards were secured, including Design Week, Mother & Baby, Nickelodeon Junior and Creative Britain.

A total campaign of £482,706 worth was delivered on a retainer budget of £18,900. The results met all client objectives.

(CIPR, 2008)

6 Customer communications

From a PR perspective, customer relations need to be managed and recognised as one of a number of shareholders to bear in mind.

6.1 Customer relations

Customer relations involves building two-way communications with customers enabling them the opportunity to offer feedback on the products and services that they buy and build a relationship with the brand. This element of communication is a critical one in order to try and build longevity in customer relations and build and maintain customer loyalty.

6.1.1 Marketing communication for reputation

Marketing communication to be valued as authentic needs to link closely into the organisations' overall communications so that marketing communications reflect and is integral with the organisation's reputation and corporate communication.

6.1.2 The customer communication mix

Although the 'corporate communication mix' (advertising, PR, sponsorship) was introduced in Chapter 7 as applied to corporate communications generally ie the broad purposes/nature of advertising, PR activity and sponsorship. The focus in this chapter is on strategic or reputational communications to customers (such as, for example, the use of advertising to position an organisation on 'green', 'fair trade', 'CSR' as key messages to customer audiences).

MARKETING AT WORK   application

Windows to the world (Corporate Comms, 2009)

An example of marketing communications being used in the context of corporate communications.

When learning disabilities charity Mencap decided to modernise its web site, its ultimate aim was to increase mainstream awareness of its cause. This it achieved when Channel 4 made the decision to make a documentary about learning disabilities having taking their inspiration from Mencap's new web site.

Mencap spent over 18 months developing the new web site and in doing so placed a greater emphasis on the use of video which was their most accessible form of content for people with learning difficulties. The strapline which was used was the voice of learning disability but they put on video people with learning difficulties showing they have the same aspirations as everyone else.

Four main audiences were identified including families and carers, professionals and supporters including campaigners, donors and volunteers. Mencap realised that once people were engaged although they were discerning supporters they would not only donate money but also volunteer or lobby on the charity's behalf.

Importantly, the web site gave access to support families and carers through the introduction of chat forums and in doing so gave people a voice. Visitor traffic has increased by an amazing 62% since March 2009 when the web site went live. The Mencap new web site is an example of a corporate website which offers a vital shop window for Mencap as indeed it has for many other organisations. Mencap said: *'The web site has really unified all of our communication. It is a great vehicle for bringing everyone together. The web site has become the starting point for all our messages.'*

Take a look at Mencap's site and see what you think http://www.mencap.org.uk/ ■

6.2 Customer communication tools

Broadly speaking, the main customer communication tools are those of *marketing* communications to which a large part of the communications budget is allocated. This includes advertising, personal selling and marketing public relations (van Riel and Fombrun, 2007, p. 194).

6.2.1 Advertising

KEY CONCEPT

concept

'Advertising can influence audiences by informing or reminding them of the existence of a brand, or alternatively by persuading or helping them differentiate a product or organisation from others on the market' (Fill, 2002, p.486).

'The main roles of advertising are to build awareness, induce a dialogue (if only on an internal basis) and to position brands, by changing either perceptions or attitudes' (Fill, 2002, p. 487).

Corporate advertising defined by Schlenker and Herrling (2003):

'Corporate advertising is the paid use of media to support a company's position and image (as opposed to conventional advertising that promote products and services). Usually a full-page printed statement such as ads are frequently couched as 'An Open Letter to' in which the intended recipient is one or another stakeholder group. Corporate advertising allows you to get your message across without any media filter. It is often employed during crises to communicate the company's position to all interested parties'.

6.2.2 Traditional media

There are many forms of media including:

Class	Type	Vehicles
Broadcast	Television	TV shoes, eg Friends, Coronation Street
	Radio	Virgin 1215, Classic FM
Print	Newspapers	The Times, The Sun
	Magazines	
	Consumer	Cosmopolitan, FHM, Woman
	Business	The Grocer, Plumbing News
Outdoor	Billboards	96 and 48 sheet
	Street furniture	Adshel, bus shelters
	Transit	London Underground, taxis, hot-air balloons

New media	Internet	Websites, e-mail, intranet
	Digital television	Freeview
	Teletext	SkyText, Ceefax
	CD-ROM	Various: music, educational, entertainment
Instore	Point of purchase	Bins, signs and displays
	Packaging	The Coca Cola contour bottle
Other	Cinema	Pearl and Dean
	Exhibitions	Ideal Home, The Motor Show
	Product placement	FedEx in Castaway, Galaxy in Bridget Jones's Diary
	Ambient	Litter bins, golf tees, petrol pumps
	Guerrilla	Flyposting

6.2.3 Digital/online media

Fill (2003 p.538) suggests:

'Media decisions have become significantly more important and certainly more visible areas attracting management attention in the late 1990s and early millennium. For example Beech 919990 reports that companies such as Scottish Courage need to make choices about the split between the internet, mass media, digital TV and consumer press. Companies such as BT, Ikea and ScottishPower need to use media strategically in order that they reach the right audience in the right context at the right time and at an acceptable cost. To help organisations achieve these goals a variety of approaches have been adopted. For example, New PHD is retained by BT to advise about strategic (media) planning and budget allocation.'

The point of significance here is the use of media strategically rather than practically.

KEY CONCEPT

concept

'Media' in terms of marketing communications *per se* is seen as a channel of communications and a means by which communications messages are sent to target audiences. But it is also useful to remember that the term 'media' is also in the context of PR and corporate communications a key stakeholder group, in that it provides a means of communicating PR messages to a variety of different stakeholders through editorial coverage in the media. Refer to the section later in this chapter on 'Media Relations'.

6.2.4 Sales promotion

KEY CONCEPT

concept

The classification of sales promotion

Yeshin (2006, p. 10) describes a classification of sales promotion which suggests that it can operate on three different levels:

(a) They communicate. They can direct a customer's attention to the point of purchase by providing additional information that may be relevant to the purchasing decision.

(b) They provide incentive. Sales promotion offers some form of direct inducement, either immediate or delayed, which changes the perceptual base of the purchasing decision.

(c) They advance the purchasing decision. They invite the consumer to engage in an immediate transaction.

Yeshin (2006, p.11) goes on to suggest that promotions have one of three possible forms of impact on a consumer.

(a)   Economic – monetary or non-monetary depending on the nature of the promotional offer.

(b)   Informational – in that it communicates information to a customer in regard to a brand that is previously unknown by the consumer.

(c)   Emotional – the feelings/emotions aroused by exposure to the promotional offer.

6.2.5 Strategic verses tactical use of sales promotion (SP)

Historically sales promotion has been considered merely a short term incentive to increase sales or appeal (Institute of Sales Promotion, 2004; Kotler *et al.*, 1999). However, more modern day thinking appreciates the fact that sales promotion contributes considerably to the brand strategically, very often being used to reinforce brand values (Gay 1997, cited in Yeshin, 2006).

One of the benefits of sales promotions is their flexibility. Sales promotion costs are variable with volume and this then enables smaller businesses to compete against larger businesses with larger budgets. Many sales promotions are easy to instigate and require minimal work in order to implement them and this means that they can be put in place in store quickly and taken off or changed just as quickly.

What then, do sale promotions achieve? Sales promotions, according to Peattie and Peattie (1994) cited by Yeshin (2006) are shown to achieve:

- Re-timed purchasing
- Brand switching
- Increased volume of purchase
- Product type substitutions
- Store substitutions.

6.2.6 Uses of sales promotions

Reach new customers	Trial of new products can be encouraged – for example brand switching.
Reduce distributor risk	Distributors risk can be kept to a minimum in stocking the new brand.
Reward behaviour	Reward loyalty or purchasing by customers previously – for example, money off next purchase.
Retention	Interest and attraction can lead to further communication and possible retention of customers.
Add value	Customers can be perceived to be receiving more value for their money – for example more of the product for the same price – 50% extra free product.
Induce action	Incentivising purchasing is a powerful tool – you want to change behaviour and encourage immediate purchase.
Preserve cash flow	Sales promotion can be implemented on a 'pay-as-you-go' basis and are fairly low cost and therefore a reasonable option for smaller regional brands who cannot compete with large brands with big advertising programmes.
Improve efficiency	Sales promotions allow manufacturers to use idle capacity and adjust demand and supply imbalances while maintaining the same list prices.
Integration	Can offer a means of integrating sales promotion with other elements of the marketing communications mix.
Assist segmentation	Sales promotions allow there to be discrimination in pricing amongst various consumer segments depending on price sensitivity.

Adapted from Fill (2003, p.558)

Go into the supermarket or shopping in your nearest retail outlet and observe how many different sales promotions you can see. Record which types of promotions are used for which promoters'. What might their objectives be in each instance? How effective do you think the sales promotion might be?

6.2.7 Personal selling

The following except about personal selling is taken from Egan (2007, p. 320)

'Personal selling is important in situations where other communication tools are weak, particularly where instant response and complex explanations are needed and where relationship-building and maintenance are major factors in the business. Where negotiation is the norm (largely but not exclusively in business-to-business situations) salesmanship is also an important factor in finalising the sale. It is also logical to assume that the smaller the number of customers and, consequentially, the greater percentage contribution these customers make to turnover, the more likely the requirement for a relationship-based, personal sales operation.

The value and salience of a product or service also appears to be important. Whereas 80% of car purchases involve buyers searching for information and only 5% of actual sales take place using this medium. Buyers still apparently want some form of human intervention (and the possibility of negotiation) that is not necessarily available through technological mediums... On the downside, personal selling has a number of distinct weaknesses notably: cost, reach and frequency and control'.

Egan (2007, pp. 321–322) goes on to describe a process known as the 7P's of selling used by sales personnel in an effort to manage the costs of personal selling.

- Prospecting: looking for prospective customers
- Preparation: customer research, objective setting, etc
- Presentation: demonstration and discussion
- Possible problems: foreseeing and handling objections
- Please give me the order: closing the sale and getting the order
- Pen-to-paper: recording details accurately
- Post-sales service: developing the relationship

One of the problems of controlling messages within a diverse sales force is a definite disadvantage of personal selling and, clearly poor inconsistent and inaccurate communications would be detrimental to a company's reputation.

6.2.8 PR in context of the marketing communications mix

Public relations in the context of the marketing mix is seen as a more tactical element of marketing communications and a marketing tool, However, throughout this chapter you have been exposed to examples of PR in practice which demonstrates the alternative role PR plays as a critical element of corporate communications and reputation management.

6.2.9 Co-ordinating the mix

Consider the following example of a non-advertising model such as The Body Shop as an example of maximising the stakeholder communications.

The **Body Shop International** is a classic example of an ethics-driven brand, focused on a range of social responsibility and sustainability values: avoidance of harmful stereotypes of female beauty, use of natural ingredients, opposition to animal testing, support for micro-suppliers in Third World countries, fair trading and community involvement. It has been particularly adept in using stakeholder relationship marketing to:

- Generate positive public relations and referrals from existing customers, to the point where it uses no advertising

- Gain extensive media coverage (without having to pay for formal advertising), by developing relationships with a wide range of media

- Develop relationships with local communities, by having each shop involved in a local community project

- Develop relationships with a range of environmental pressure groups, including Greenpeace and Friends of the Earth

- Link: http://www.thebodyshopinternational.com (follow the link to 'values and campaigns')

6.2.10 Messages of customer communication

Informational and emotional engagement

'The contacts we have with an organisation are a mixture of tangible and intangible, the rational and the emotional. We can read and study an article about an organisation. We can use or consume its products. We can visit its premises and meet its staff. All of these are tangibles, all capable of rational assessment. At the same time, we receive more ethereal communication, the tone of the press article, our subjective judgement of the newspaper as a reliable source. When we meet a company's employees we can judge them objectively by their height, weight, apparent age, product knowledge, the time they spend with us. Or we can judge them subjectively by the look in their eyes, the colour of their hair, or whether they have any. We can stereotype them from our experiences of previous contacts with the myriad of other people we have met. In so doing we risk forming a totally inaccurate impression of them and potentially of the company that employs them... Unfortunately, the typical customer will form an impression within the first 20 seconds of a customer facing employee.'

(Davies *et al.*, 2003, p. 64)

6.2.11 Experience marketing

'In many industries, the only source of differentiation for a company consists of the way its products and services are experienced by customers. The growing interest in 'experience marketing', for instance, recognises the value of creating a coherent corporate experience for customers of companies, particularly those who operate in the services sector. The explosive growth of coffee retailer Starbucks, for instance, can be traced to a combination of factors that consumers link to its corporate brand, namely: the product (premium coffee beans, the roasting process, quality snack foods), the environment (lounge chairs, a social atmosphere), and the symbols (a specialised language for ordering coffee). In similar ways, large casinos in Las Vegas such as Caesar's, Paris, Bellagio, Harrah's, have all become heavy investors in building a consistent and differentiating experience for their patrons in order to build customer loyalty and get repeat business, particularly from the high-stakes players they court assiduously. They cultivate their corporate brands systematically.'

(van Riel & Fombrun, 2007, p. 107)

According to van Riel & Fombrun (2007, pp. 193–194), marketing communications has been criticised for its lack of authenticity in building lasting gain for companies because of the lack of perceived authenticity and lack of connection and consistency with the reputation platform and the organisation communication.

Experience marketing: is an approach to marketing that is based on getting potential customers to 'experience' not only the product they could be buying but the entire organisation behind the product. Personalising the experience increases the likelihood that the customer will confer to a sense of 'authenticity' on the company's communications – thereby creating a bond between customer and organisation that will increase loyalty and create an emotional involvement by potential customers.

MARKETING AT WORK

application

One example of a company which builds its communications around reputation platform of 'creativity' is Danish Toy Company Lego. It has the slogan ' The Power to create' is clear in the way that the company presents itself in stores, in theme parks and in DVD games and on the internet. It demonstrate the kind of strong links that can be established between marketing communication and corporate communication and how it can be leveraged to build upon the reputation and value of the company as a whole rather than the Lego products alone.   (van Riel and Fombrun, (2007, pp. 194–195)

Learning objectives	Covered
1 Understand the nature of marketing and public relations programmes	☑ Compared marketing and PR
	☑ Demonstrated what PR programmes involve and the features and benefits PR practice brings corporately
2 Formulate approaches to corporate communications that are customer focused and contextually determined	☑ Contextualised PR practice
	☑ Highlighted the complexity of communications with diverse stakeholder groups
	☑ Explored PR practice in detail looking at media, community and consumer specific types of campaigns
3 Formulate effective approaches to media relations	☑ Contextualised media relations – what it is, what it means and what is involved, how the media are motivated
	☑ Traditional and online types of media
	☑ Considered the challenges faced in communications in current times

1 What do you understand by the term 'PR'?

2 Why is PR important to the reputation of an organisation?

3 Give two examples of activity that might be described as PR.

4 What are the different ways that PR might be viewed by an organisation?

5 How might PR be used to aid reputation management?

6 What is a corporate communication programme and what might it involve?

7 Why is it important to understand the full range of stakeholders for an organisation, rather than just its customers?

8 How does PR differ from other elements of the marketing communications mix?

9 Why is it useful to understand the power and influence different stakeholders might have?

10 Give an example of a PR campaign or PR in practice?

1 New restaurant opening

There are many people who might have an interest in a new local restaurant. You may have thought to compile a stakeholder map here which would summarise all of the stakeholders who might be considered. You should have included some of the following types of examples.

– Local residents – interest may be two-fold. Local customers when the restaurant opens and concern for noise and possible problems associated with a new business opening locally, eg building work, deliveries, etc

– Local people – interest in local employment, so potential employees – a new business will offer new employment opportunities for waiting staff, cook, cleaner, manager etc.

– Suppliers of food and non-food products – restaurant needs to buy-in food, stationery, cleaning products etc

– Local media – local radio, local newspapers – interest in a new business opening locally and the economic benefits that brings plus the new service being offered to local people

2 Stakeholders for a local primary school

Your list may include some of the following types of stakeholders. Note the diversity of their interests and motivations.

Stakeholders	Interest and motivations
People living in close proximity to school, ie local residents	Activities at school as part of local community, changes to the school that will affect local traffic, noise levels, etc.
Potential employees	People living in locality may be interested in employment within the school of a professional or more manual type of work – as a teacher, teacher's assistant or administrator or cleaner.
Local media	Local newspapers and local radio stations will be interested in what goes on at the school and anything that is newsworthy or of interest for their readers and listeners.
Other local businesses	Will be interested in supplying the school with products and services and see the school as a potential customer, but also as a possible ally and fellow local business/local organisation.
Local authority	If state school then it will be funded by the state and local authority and they have a 'stake' in how the school is run.
Parents	Parents of children who go to the school have a key 'stake' in how the school performs and how their children progress at school educationally and socially.
Teachers, teacher's assistants, headmaster/headmistress Cleaners, administrators, cooks, catering assistants	All employees have an interest in the school as their employer.
Children	Lastly, the children, of course, have an interest in the school as it is their place of education. Potential pupils attending school in the future will also be a stakeholder group.

3   **Media in changing times**

There are many things that might be relevant here but to give a broad outline, you may have considered the following:

-    Technology has changed considerably the way that we communicate – hence there are a whole new range of media opportunities through the growth of commercial radio, satellite, and cable television, in addition to the opportunities opened up by the internet.

-    The fragmentation of media has meant that there are many more ways of communicating with people – but this in itself means that people receive many more messages and it is more and more challenging to get your message heard above the 'noise'.

-    Technology has improved printing processes which has resulted in turnaround times for colour printing being far quicker than ever before.

-    The growth of the internet has created a 24/7 environment, a place where the media never sleeps, and this provides a challenging climate for media relations specialists.

4   **Advantages of using social media**

One of the advantages of social media is that information is made available almost immediately – for example, no long lead-up times to gaining editorial that one might experience with a trade publication or magazine. However, this can also be a disadvantage as it is part of the 24/7 media environment which is relentless and difficult to respond to with the speed and immediacy required.

How communication has changed with technology

You could have included a number of different points here – but communication has drastically been changed by technology. Even traditional media such as newspapers have online versions – and newspaper readership is dropping. Improved printing processes has meant quicker production times and a much wider range of specialist magazines and titles – more and more avenues to communicate with people! Technology-driven communications environment is a challenging one in which to practice PR.

5   **Sales promotions**

You will no doubt be bombarded with sales promotions and incentives when you visit the supermarket – although some supermarkets are more 'reserved' about promotions – Waitrose for example. You may well see extra volume offers for example, 25% extra free, or multi-purchase savings – or two products for £5. You may also see competitions, free prize draws, in, on or with pack promotions (cereal aisle is a popular location for these types of offers as is the newsagent section). There are, of course, a number of different objectives that these promotions aim to meet. Very often when multi-purchase is involved the perceived benefit to the consumer if the better price they are paying for the products when the value to the promoter is the saved storage space in warehousing the product before it is purchased. Sometimes new products are introduced with established brands, this offers an opportunity to encourage trial through association with the established brand. There are many examples that you could have included here. You might have also seen money-off vouchers or coupons.

1   Public relations is about building relationships with the wide range of stakeholders of an organisation and about informing and educating them to make informed choices. This is achieved through planned communications.

2   PR is important to the reputation of the organisation – because the reputation depends on how an organisation is perceived corporately – how good an employer it is; how good it is in a crisis; how it is performing financially; what coverage it gets in the media and what is said.

3   Examples of PR activity – there are numerous things you could include here – for example, events, exhibitions, media interviews, writing press releases, writing copy for a brochure or web site.

4   PR may be viewed differently as either part of marketing communications and a supportive strand of marketing or as a critical element of the organisation which says so much about the brand and what is stands for.

5   PR can be used to aid reputation management by damage limitation – for example in a crisis – or in a proactive way to build better relationships with the media; It can be used to form better relationships with employees and offer them opportunities to participate in decision making when change takes place.

6   A corporate communications programme is the communications that takes place on part of the organisation as a whole and concerns the holistic view of the organisation. Who they are. What they do. How they operate and carry out business. What they are like as an employer. For example, Dove is a product but the corporate brand is Unilever – corporate communications would focus on Unilever and not Dove.

7   There are many more important stakeholders other than customers who have an important *stake* in the organisation – for example, an organisation is nothing without its employees.

8   PR differs from other elements of the marketing mix in that it deals with a wider range of people rather than just customers – it informs people to make decisions based on information offered and is often educational in nature.

9   If one understands the amount of power and influence a stakeholder has one can prioritise the communication planned to the most important stakeholder groups based on that information.

10 Many examples could have been included here depending on your own reading and research. You could have also included a number of different examples cited in this chapter of the Study Text.

Bland, M., Theaker, A. And Wragg, D., (1996) <u>Effective Media Relations</u> (1st Ed.) CIPR Series, Kogan Page Limited

Bland, M., Theaker, A. And Wragg, D., (2000) <u>Effective Media Relations</u> (2nd Ed.) CIPR Series, Kogan Page Limited

BITC (Business in The Community) (2005) '<u>Annual Report</u>'. www.bitc.org.uk accessed 18 September 2008

Christensen, LT, Morsing, M & Cheney, G (2008) <u>Corporate Communications: Conventions, Complexity and Critique</u>. London: Sage Publications Ltd

CIPR Cymru Wales PRide Awards Gold Award (2007), <u>Better Housing for Rhondda Cynon Taf</u> http://www.cipr.co.uk/member_area/info/case_studies/new/Sorted/PRide_07/index.htm, [accessed 03/07/09]

CIPR Member Website (2009) CIPR Excellence Awardshttp://www.cipr.co.uk/member_area/info/index.asp [date accessed 9/07/09]

CIPR Pride Awards Wessex (2008) <u>Proclear 1 Day Partnership</u> http://www.cipr.co.uk/prideawards/regions/wessex/case/5g.html [accessed 070709]

Corp Comms (June 2009), <u>Windows to the world</u>, Issue 38, www.corpcommsmagazine.co.uk

Cutlip, S M, Center, A H and Broom, G N (2000), <u>Effective Public Relations</u> (8th Ed), Prentice-Hall International, Upper Saddle River, New Jersey

Davies G, Chun R, Da Silva RV & Roper S (2003) <u>Corporate Reputation and Competitiveness</u>. Abingdon, Oxon: Routledge

Disney World Monorail Crash Kills Driver (July5 2009), http://www.telegraph.co.uk/news/worldnews/northamerica/usa/5752356/Disney-World-monorail-crash-kills-driver.html

[accessed 12 July 2009]

Doorley, J & Garcia, HF (2007) <u>Reputation Management: The Key to Successful Public Relations and Corporate Communications</u> New York: Routledge

Egan, J. (2007), Marketing Communications, London: Thomson Learning

Fawkes, J. (2008), What is public relations? In <u>Handbook of Public Relations</u> (3rd Ed) A. Theaker (ed). London: Routledge

Fill, C (2002) <u>Marketing Communications: Contexts, Strategies and Applications</u> (3rd Ed). Harlow, Essex: Pearson Education Limited

Franklin, B., Hogan, M.Quentin, Langley, Q., Modsell, N. And Pill, E., (2009) <u>Key Concepts in Public Relations</u>, London, Sage Publications Limited

Gay, S. (1997), <u>Promotional challenge</u>, Marketing Week, 11 September

Gregory, A (2000), Planning and managing Public Relations Campaign (2nd Ed.), London, Kogan Page CIPR Series

Grunig J and Hunt T (1984) <u>Managing Public Relations</u>, New York, Holt, Rinehart and Winston

How do you know where you're going (July 2009), www.cipr-profile.co.uk, profile 67, [accessed 07.07.09]

Heath, R. (2001), <u>Handbook of Public Relations</u>, United States, Sake Publications Inc.

Institute of Sales Promotion www.isp.org [accessed 07.07.09]

Kelsey, R., (July 2009), <u>Corporate banks have a strong message</u>, www.profile-extra.co.uk , Profile 67[accessed 07.07.09]

Kotler, P., Armstrong, G., Saunders, j. And Wong, V. (1999), Principles of marketing, 2nd European Ed., Prentice Hall

Peattie S and Peattie, K. (1994). <u>Promoting financial services with glittering prizes</u>, International Journal of Bank marketing, 12 (6)

Profile Extra (July 2009), www.profile-extra.co.uk ,Issue 67

Riel, CBM Van & Fombrun, CJ (2007) <u>Essentials of Corporate Communication: Implementing Practices for Effective Reputation Management</u>. Abingdon, Oxon: Routledge

Schenkler, I. And Herrling, T., Guide to Media Relations, New Jersey, USA, Pearson Prentice Hall

Taking Pride in the Isle of Wight, www.cipr-profile.co.uk, profile 67, [accessed 07.07.09]

Tench, R & Yeomans, L (2006) Exploring Public Relations. Harlow, Essex: Pearson Education Limited

Tench, R & Yeomans, L (2009) Exploring Public Relations. Harlow, Essex: Pearson Education Limited

Wallace, C., (April 3, 2009) Fight to save the British honey bee, PR Week

WRAP Battery recycling campaign

http://www.utalkmarketing.com/Pages/Article.aspx?ArticleID=4677&Title=WRAP_Battery_recycling_PR_campaign [accessed 07.07.09]

Yeshin, T, (2006), Sales Promotion, London, Thompson Learning

Chapter 9

Investor and government relations

Topic list

1 Financial public relations
2 Investor relations
3 Media and messages for financial PR
4 Government relations
5 Public affairs programmes
6 Lobbying

Introduction

In Chapter 8, we began to explore communication to (or with) specific target audiences highlighted by the syllabus. In this chapter, we continue by focusing specifically on financial, investor and government audiences. These areas are much less likely to have been covered in detail in your previous studies, although the broad concepts were introduced in the *Stakeholder Marketing* module. It is also important to bear in mind that you will be expected to have an understanding of these 'specialist' areas – whether or not they are directly relevant to your current job role or the organisation you choose for your assessment.

In sections 1–2, we introduce the scope, roles and aims of financial and investor relations. These are the only areas covered by the specified syllabus content, but we go on in section 3 to consider various media and messages relevant to shareholder audiences.

In section 4, we introduce the field broadly known as 'public affairs' by highlighting the range of government stakeholders, and the breadth of communication that may, therefore, be required. Note that we do this within a UK setting: if you are studying outside the UK, you will need to be aware of the various government bodies, agencies and representatives that apply in your own national context.

Section 5 we explore the nature of public affairs and public affairs communication. Finally, in section 6, we focus more specifically on the activity of 'lobbying' or attempting to influence government policy.

Syllabus-linked learning objectives

By the end of the chapter you will be able to:

Learning objectives	Syllabus link
1 Understand the nature of public affairs and investor relations programmes	1.2.2
2 Formulate approaches to corporate communications that are investor-focused and contextually determined	3.2.2
3 Formulate approaches to corporate communications that are government-focused and contextually determined	3.2.5

1 Financial public relations

Before discussing investor relations, it is important to introduce the wider context within which investor relations fits and that is financial PR. Financial markets, similar to other markets have basically always been based on the flow of facts and knowledge, bringing buyers and sellers to an exchange of goods and services. The difference with modern financial markets is the importance and intensity of that flow of facts and knowledge – or information flow. The scale and complexity combined with their richness and actual reach means they have become what could be called a 'global media sphere' (Lewis, 2008). Financial networks, which span the globe and are, without doubt, a vital means of economic activity and are also strong media networks which contain numerous intermediaries. When you consider how financial markets have dominated the social agenda and political news in recent years, it is possible to see the extent of power and influence exerted by the 'global media sphere'.

1.1 Financial PR defined

KEY CONCEPT

concept

Financial PR is the **management of communication between a listed company and its financial audiences**.

Financial audiences include:

- Existing and potential investors
- City commentators such as the financial and investment media and analysts (Theaker, 2008).

Financial PR is employed to ensure the share price of a company adequately reflects its value and to help the liquidity of its shares. It does this by using communication to manage the relationship between the listed company and its financial audience, creating and maintaining awareness and understanding of the company. Theaker (2008) describes the role of PR practitioners:

'The financial PR practitioner is concerned with the presentation and management of communications with, and feedback from, all the financial audiences'. (Theaker, 2008, p. 275)

Financial PR's increasing importance is reflected in the following statement made in The Economist:

'To keep share price up, it is no longer enough merely to have a strategy. The strategy also needs to be articulated smartly – as any manager at BT, Ford or Marconi will tell you'. (The Economist, 2001, p. 75)

Communication with financial communities about an organisation's position and future strategy is essential to the development of a good financial reputation, which contributes to the overall reputation of an organisation.' (Yeoman and Tench, 2009, p465).

1.2 Financial stakeholders explained

Below is a diagram from Theaker (2008, p. 277) which illustrates how information flows amongst financial audiences and helps us to understand the likely dynamics of communications between theses specialist stakeholder groups.

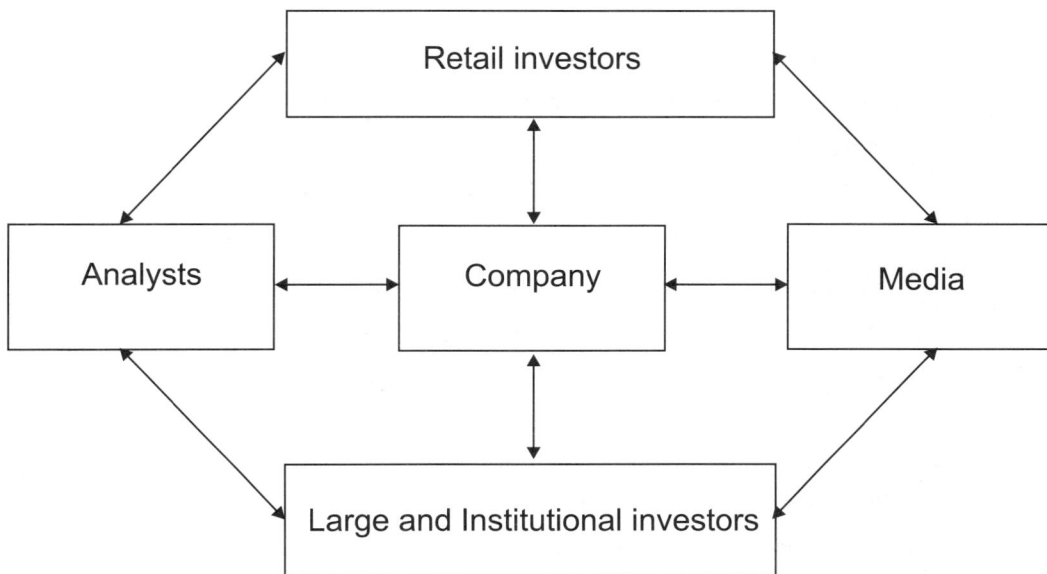

(a) **Institutional investors**

Institutional investors would include for example, existing shareholders, potential shareholders or past shareholders. In quoted companies the main institutional investors are insurance companies, investment banks and pension funds. Large institutions are influential investors as they may well have a significant financial stake in an individual company (for example, up to 20% of shares). Although a company's relationship with its institutional investors is normally and actively managed by the broker, it is important to understand that institutions will be significantly influenced by independent comment in the media by analysts and by regulatory company communications.

(b) **Analysts**

An analyst is a key opinion former who would, as part of their role, identify trends and irregularities and generate ideas of investment. Analysts are either what is known as a 'buy-side' analyst who would work to provide information for fund managers working for large funds or independent fund managers. A 'sell-side' analyst works for the brokers who look after the listed companies. All analysts provide information on how a company works and identifies what its prospects might be for the purposes of investment. Theaker (2008, p. 277) says: ' It is the unique responsibility of financial PR to encourage and maintain the relationship between a company and the financial analyst.'

(c)   **Private client stockbrokers**

A private stockbroker acts for private individuals who are in a position to invest their money and buys and sells shares on their behalf. They can provide advice on what companies to invest money in. What a stockbroker thinks will be influenced by the information that they have access to such as what is available through analysts' research or what is in the press. The role of financial PR is to manage the information between stockbroker and company for example at times when information is given such as during financial reporting.

(d)   **Retail investors**

Retail investor is the name given to private individuals who invest in the stock market. Theaker (2008, p. 278) suggests that over the last ten years that small retail investors have become more powerful and sophisticated. Retail investors not only have access to the internet for company and share information, but now also have access to discussion forums and financial blogs to gain information rather than the more traditional reliance on print media for financial information. For the PR person, this makes the use of the media to spread information a more complicated process.

(e)   **The media**

It is important to appreciate that the financial media is both the means of communicating to a range of different financial stakeholders, and a key stakeholder in their own right. In terms of financial PR this relates to the following types of media:

- Financial Times – www.ft.com

- Business sections of Sunday papers

- Investment journals, eg Investors Chronicle – http://investorschronicle.co.uk

- Shares Magazine – www.sharesmagazine.co.uk

- Growth Company Investor – www.growthcompany.co.uk

- Investor web sites – for example Money AM – www.moneyam.com

- Broadcast media – ie television and radio for example BBC news

- http://news.bbc.co.uk/1/hi/business/default.stm

- Specialist TV channels, for example Bloomberg – *www.bloomberg.com*

- Trade press – may be relevant for financial analysts who are following a particular industry or sector

- Wire services – Reuters, AFX News – fastest ways to spread information http://uk.reuters.com, http://www.aboutus.org/Afxnews.com

- Internet news services – Citywire, Money AM – www.citywire.co.uk, http://www.moneyam.com/

ACTIVITY 1

application

Browse through some of the web sites detailed above and familiarise yourself with the financial media. Get yourself in the 'mindset' of the financial media. Can you recall six examples of financial media?

Bowd and Harris (2003) have an interesting way of describing the City and its range of players as follows.

'The City, with its range of players (stakeholders) and international differences can be likened to a metro or tube system which sees money (equity) travel through various stations on rail lines. Different factors can influence the journey of movements of the equity each and every day of the year.'

1.3 What is communicated, when and how

Raising awareness of a company's activities and business strategy and profiling its management via PR can impact how the City judges a company by its financial performance and its growth potential. These communication also involves managing the City's expectations of the company. The City and investors will use the available information about a company and try to predict how it will perform in the future. ...Disappointment may lead to investors selling their shares and may discourage other investors from buying, which would bring the share price down. Analysts rely on companies to provide clear information that allows them to make realistic predictions about a company's future performance...' (Theaker, 2008, p. 280)

Financial communications take place when there are changes in financial circumstances (such as during a merger, acquisition or take-over) or as part of routine financial reporting as part of the financial calendar. Both of these instances are discussed further in the following section.

Financial PR concentrates on developing relationships and encouraging the flow of information through communications with key stakeholders and through financial networks. With developments in information communication technology, social media such as financial blogs and web sites are becoming increasingly important.

1.4 Instances when financial communications take place

It is important to understand instances when financial communications would routinely take place and in addition to understand when financial communications (or financial reporting) might take place within the financial calendar. The main examples are mergers and acquisitions, flotations and hostile takeovers.

1.4.1 Mergers and acquisitions

Mostly, mergers and acquisitions are carried out with the recommendations of the target company's board of directors. Under this friendly manner of execution, the risk of failure is lessened, therefore the cost of which one can raise capital to buy a company is lower. When 'friendly' deals take place, there is no need to offer a premium to the market and the advisor's bills will be less than if the situation were more complicated, The City expects most listed companies to engage in a merger-type scenario as part of their strategic plan at some point in their history (Yeoman and Tench, 2009, p. 475).

MARKETING AT WORK

application

M & A Mania (adapted from October/November 2005, Corp Comms)

Mergers and acquisitions can literally make or break a company; about two-thirds of takeovers fail to deliver value for shareholders. But before deals have a chance to succeed, they have to be taken safely from announcement to completion.

Communicating well plays a crucial role in ensuring the success of takeovers. Communication professionals need to support their executives in explaining deals to investors and analysts. Then they have to deal with the business media who love takeover stories as much as sports reporters revel in football transfers.

When rival offers, investor backlashes or financial setbacks occur, it's the corporate communications team that has to deal with resulting crises. According to Shane O'Riordain, Corporate Communications Director at banking group HBOS, it's very important to decide right from the start what the communications principles are. You have to be absolutely clear about how you are going to communicate and the style and tone you are going to adopt. You must have a communications plan that takes you to a point six-to-twelve months after the merger's completion.

O'Riordain was working for Halifax when it merged with Bank of Scotland to form HBOS in 2001. Bank of Scotland's talks with Abbey National (Now Abbey) had come unstuck because of management disagreements over which organisation would run the combined group and where it would be based. Halifax was determined not to repeat the mistake. It also needed regulatory consent.

The article quotes Riordain:

'*We agreed the communications plan, had it in place four months before the completion date and right from the start we decided – and communicated – who would be the top 50 managers in the combined company*'.

At Abbey, mergers were more complicated. The former head of Media Relations is quoted '*We had five unsolicited takeover approaches in four years*'. '*They came from Bank of Ireland, National Australia Bank, Lloyds TSB, Bank of Scotland and Spanish Bank Santander central Hispano, with which we merged last year. All got leaked and then there had to be formal communications*'.

1.4.2 Flotations

Basically, floatation is the process by which an organisation floats on an exchange in order that the public equity market is 'tapped' for funds. Companies that have been previously owned by private individuals, private equity companies or governments sell a stake in themselves on to a stock exchange of their choosing which then brings, in turn, an injection of equity known as the proceeds of the offer. This would typically be used to restructure debt or pay existing shareholders. Other incentives include the heightened profile and ability to use quoted shares as currency. (Yeoman and Tench, 2009, p. 474)

1.4.3 Hostile take-overs

Hostile takeovers occur when the company seeking to buy another either has an offer rejected by the board of the company they wish to purchase and still try to proceed with the transaction or they bypass the board in the first instance.

Though financial PR practitioners perform many tasks for the institution they work for, perhaps their role and importance is brought most firmly into focus during a company takeover. This is when the press s most interested in a company and where the messages, and in particular the sentiment can really make a difference to everybody's 'bottom line' (profitability). Financial institutions are well aware of this phenomenon and will pay a lot of money for professional media advice during this period.

An 'unsolicited' bid for a company is where financial PR gets more interesting. Here the bidder has not asked the directors of the target company for their support. They just go ahead and try to buy the company. Examples of this include Malcolm Glazer's bid for Manchester United plc, or Philip Green's attempt to buy Marks and Spencer. In both these situations the target company did not put itself up for sale – it become a target without wishing to do so. In both situations, however, the bidding parties wished to enter into negotiations with the target. In the Marks and Spencer case no formal offer was made for the company but there was significant media speculation surrounding the bid; handling this situation is the job of the financial PR practitioner.

1.5 Communications and the financial calendar

The following events (financial reporting) take place during the financial calendar (Gummer, 1995).

1.5.1 Interim results

Interim results offer what is sometimes referred to as a 'health check'; on the financial state of an organisation's results to that point in the year (half year in the UK) and provide insight into expectations for the next six months (Yeoman and Tench, 2009, p. 470).

1.5.2 Prelim results

A reporting for the City on a company's results and future prospects. The results are the City's first opportunity to see and judge whether or not the strategy of an organisation's management has been successful or not against their expectations. If it is felt an organisation is unlikely to meet the expectations for its financial stakeholders a 'profits warning statement' is issued via the regulatory wired services. This in essence will minimise the impact of the City in terms of loss of confidence and can include the lowering of share price or loss of financial reputation (Yeoman and Tench, 2009, p. 470).

1.5.3 Annual report and accounts

Annual reports and accounts are issued by the company to their shareholders and other interested stakeholders to detail the company's activities over the last year. Historically, annual reports have generally been regarded as a 'glossy' marketing tool through which a strong public relations message can be told. Potential investors will pay close attention to company annual reports and many financial decisions will be based upon the messages within the report.

As a vital communications tool, there are specialist annual report design agencies who focus on communication of key financial messages. Look at the following web site for an example of such an agency. There is also a page providing useful design tips when constructing an annual report.

http://www.d-t-c-corporate.com/#/useful-tips/4526327866 ■

1.5.4 Annual general meeting (AGM)

The annual general meeting gives an opportunity for all types of investors to meet and ask questions of an organisation's management. This is also the time when they can vote people on or off the board of directors as well as new company articles (or regulations). Both verbal and non-verbal messages must be carefully managed at this time in order to project an appropriate impression of the company.

2 Investor relations

2.1 Investors as a stakeholder audience

The following diagram taken from van Riel and Fombrun (2007, p. 185), breaks down and demonstrates the range of financial stakeholders and their relationships with the company as a whole and with the business environment.

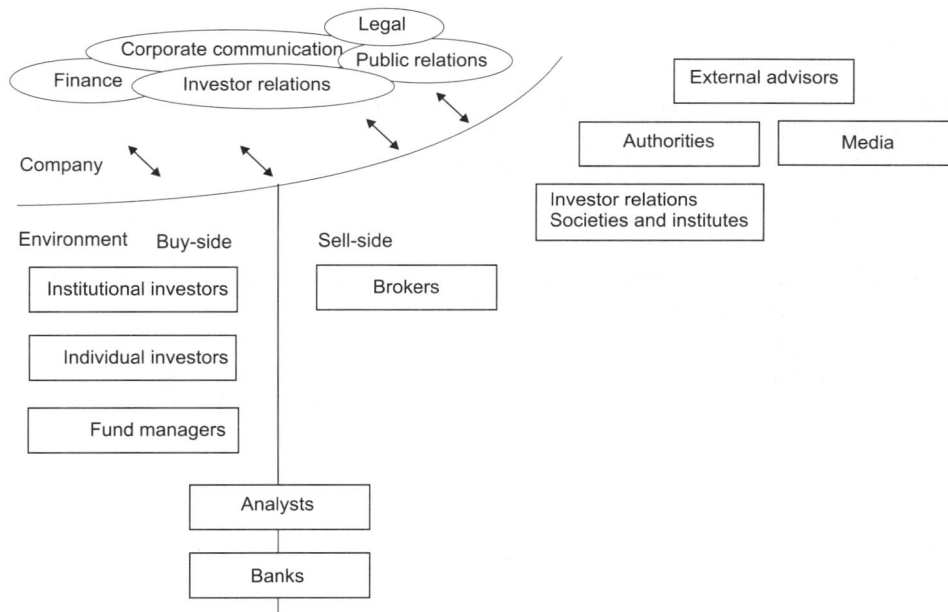

Financial stakeholders can be regarded as either internal or external.

Internal stakeholders include:

- Financial department
- Corporate communications department
- Legal department or representatives

The chief executive officer and the head of finance or chief financial officer are the persons responsible for ensuring that financial relations messages are not only created and practiced but also confirmed and carried out. This data forms a critical part of the company's corporate reputation platform and how the corporate story gets articulated outside the company to external stakeholders (van Riel and Fombrun, 2007).

External stakeholder communications include:

- Investor presentations
- Analyst discussions
- Company visits
- Webcasts
- Routine investor and analyst meetings

A variety of different ways of presenting the company to investors and analysts should be used to create a positive image about the company. Future prospects should also be considered in order that they might regard the company as an attractive and sound investment.

2.2 Roles of investor relations

There is, as Yeoman and Tench (2009, pp. 463–465) explain, differences in perspectives with relation to financial PR in the United States and in the UK. This is significant because many of the texts to which students refer are American and the view on financial PR is quite different:

'...*The fundamental difference is that American financial PR (IR) is focused on the shareholder whereas in the UK, financial PR is focused on raising awareness and building understanding amongst primarily the City's (financial exchanges) opinion-formers who influence investors and potential investors or stakeholders*' (Middleton, 2002, p. 160).

Important note: For the purpose of this Study Text and the study of corporate communications in the UK, your studies address the broader context of financial PR as interpreted in the UK. Bear in mind when reading American texts, they will refer to Investor Relations rather than Financial Relations.

2.2.1 Compliance

Whatever financial markets one is working with, it is important to understand that companies have to comply with financial regulations which means that there is certain information that they must provide their investors with at intervals throughout the year and during extraordinary occurrences (such as mergers or takeovers).

2.2.2 Relationships

Consider the following diagram taken from van Riel & Fombrun (2007, p. 186), which demonstrates how relationships and inter-relationships exist with stakeholders in financial or investor relations.

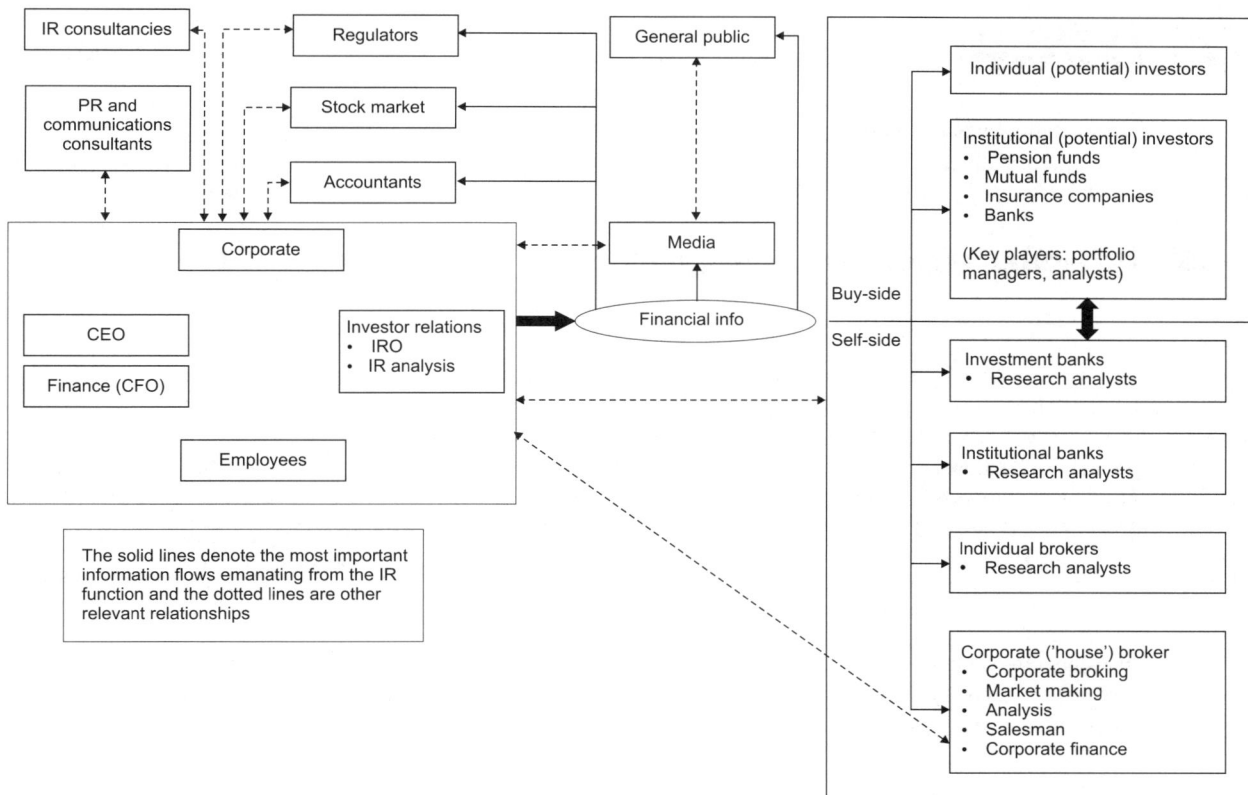

```
IR consultancies  - - →  Regulators  ←- - - - -  General public
                                                        ↑
PR and              - - - →  Stock market  ←- - - -    ↓
communications                                   ←
consultants         - - - →  Accountants  ←- - - -
                                                        Media
         Corporate                        ←- - - →
                                                        ↓
CEO              Investor relations  ═══→  (Financial info)   Buy-side
                 •  IRO
Finance (CFO)    •  IR analysis                         Self-side
                           - - - - - - - - - - - - - - - - - -
         Employees     - - - - - -
```

Individual (potential) investors

Institutional (potential) investors
• Pension funds
• Mutual funds
• Insurance companies
• Banks

(Key players: portfolio managers, analysts)

Investment banks
• Research analysts

Institutional banks
• Research analysts

Individual brokers
• Research analysts

Corporate ('house') broker
• Corporate broking
• Market making
• Analysis
• Salesman
• Corporate finance

The solid lines denote the most important information flows emanating from the IR function and the dotted lines are other relevant relationships

2.2.3 Reputation building

Government relations specialists convey information to key government agents and they are in a position to introduce and personalise the company to a wide range of powerful stakeholders. The company's reputation platform and corporate story is crucial. Skilled government relations specialists will know that they need to create a sensible interpretation that rationalises the company and what it stands for and then communicate its credibility, authenticity and responsiveness (van Riel and Fombrun, 2007, p. 199).

2.3 Aims of investor relations (IR)

Corporate communications as a function plays an important role for any modern listed business. There are a number of different aims of investor relations, summarised as follows.

Financial PR (IR) is used to create and maintain a demand for shares. To keep share price up, it is no longer enough to merely have a strategy. The strategy needs to be articulated smartly – as any manager at BT, Ford or Marconi will tell you. (The Economist, 2001, cited in Yeoman & Tench, 2009, p. 465)

'Communication with financial communities about organisations' position and future strategy is essential to the development of a good financial reputation, which in turn contributes to the overall reputation of an organisation.' (Yeoman and Tench, 2009, p. 465). Financial PR is important both in terms of building reputation as well as protecting an organisation's share price.

Financial PR when managed properly can have a significant impact on **reducing churn** – that is the loss or defection of a company's customers. Financial PR is used to present information on past performance of a company and additionally predict future performance based on the financial data available. Analysts provide the kind of data that can be used in these circumstances. Perceptions of a company must be managed in the financial arena and this means that a company's securities must be fairly and fully valued in the marketplace and this means that its stocks and bonds need to reflect both the past and present value of the company. (Doorley & Garcia, 2007, p. 212)

What are the benefits of financial PR? Try to put this into context for your own organisation.

3   Media and messages for financial PR

3.1 Financial media

The financial news media has declined in importance as a medium for directly conveying price-sensitive information and influencing investment decision-making. However, it also continues to be treated with caution by companies and is keenly followed by the investment community. It remains a core part of the 'culture' of the City. Journalists exchange ideas with all parties involved. News triggers and reinforces opinions even when it is not the main information source for decision-making. At times of company or market crisis it pushed trading activity to extremes. For all those reasons it continues to be targeted and managed by companies, and consumed studiously by professional investors.' (Davis, 2006).

3.2 Share market intermediaries

Investors often depend on the advice of specialist professionals known as analysts in order to inform investment decisions. Analysts are experts in specific sectors, industries or trends. Examples of instances where advice might be given would be asset allocation, promising industry opportunities and recommendations on specific companies. (Doorley and Garcia, 2007, p. 220)

3.3 Information needs of investor audiences

Stock exchanges and national regulatory bodies decide on most of what can be financially reported – that is the information that companies are under obligation to provide its investors. This is referred to as transparency. Many companies can actually release much more information than is absolutely necessary.

The internet has played a significant role in conveying information quickly and reliably to the financial markets, thereby increasing their perceived transparency and responsiveness. As a result the amount of influence of investor relations departments over market valuations has also increased (van Riel and Fombrun, 2007).

3.4 Methods used in financial relations

Doorley and Garcia (2007) describe a range of tools and techniques used for financial relations. These have been summarised below:

- **Press or news release** – posted in full on a company's web site and can be read directly by the public, employees, market researchers, competitors and other audiences. It is meant in other words for direct consumption by all.

- **Internet and text messaging** – companies sign up for e-mail alerts when company news is released, these would be distributed following important announcements and financial changes.

- **Conference calls** – can be arranged for investors and others to listen to teleconferences via webcasts and transcripts from these conversations can be posted on company web sites for others to read afterwards.

- **Web site** – not only used to post press releases but also executive biographies, ethics and corporate social responsibility guidelines, environmental policies, analysts' coverage and news coverage.

- **Mass release for material news** – in order to follow regulatory requirements regarding disclosure, companies follow exact procedures for releasing material news to ensure that all parties have the information at the same time. One would typically use third parties for distribution of press releases.

- **Corporate communications material** – many standard materials are used for this purpose such as factsheets, background documents, executive biographies, photographs, information on products and facilities, etc.

- **Investment conferences** – this involves opportunities for management speaking which involve senior executives and questions and answer periods and offer an opportunity for companies to market themselves directly to investors and meet with current and prospective investors directly and build relationships.

- **Limited use of advertising** – except during mergers and out of the ordinary events. However, some organisations advertise on business news channels in order to advertise directly with the investment community.

Comments on financial journalism

Consider the following excerpt taken from a journal article by Gillian Doyle (2006), which introduces a different perceptive on financial media – looking at things from the journalist's perceptive.

'Financial journalism is sometimes stereotyped as involving a poor-corporate bias, as though choices made about the content and framing of financial news are governed by a deliberate wish to portray corporations and their activities in a positive light. The conception is flawed. In covering corporate news, financial reporters tend to be extremely sceptical in their approach to how reliably companies account for themselves. Indeed, some journalists see corporate patronage as problem to favour negative over positive news – a point which reinforces findings highlighted in earlier research work (Thumber, 1993). Stories of competent management and stable performance, because they are unexceptional, are likely to be underplayed whereas much attention is focused on instances of corporate crisis or perceived failure.'

4 Government relations

If one thinks of government relations, who is it exactly that we are referring to in terms of stakeholders? van Riel & Fombrun (2007) suggest that government relations 'involves the network of regulators, legislators, elected officials, and appointed representatives that constrain, control, tax, review, delay, authorise, punish, and otherwise maintain oversight of the activities of the private sector. Government relations describes the set of professionals who have specialised in this area in recent years, a field that is often referred to as 'public affairs' because of its implicit focus on topics of widespread public interest'.

Harris and Moss (2001) cited by van Riel and Fombrun (2007) describe government relations as 'the management of the often complex external relations between the organisation and an array of governmental and non-governmental stakeholder groups'.

KEY CONCEPT

concept

*'**Government relations** is a broader term that includes all forms of lobbying and non-lobbying activity that have the ultimate goal of influencing public policy'*. Doorley & Garcia (2007, p. 162).

4.1 Government as a stakeholder audience

The government is quite a complicated audience to analyse as a stakeholder. It includes local government and central government and includes a variety of different level personnel including MPs, MEPs, Prime Minister, government officers and officials etc. Who representing the government you need to communicate with will very much depend on which department and focus your communication might take. For example, if one were wanting to develop a plan for lobbying local government for changes to road 'safety', transport representatives would be appropriate both locally and centrally.

4.1.1 Scope of the government audience

Gregory (2004) suggests pressure points in terms of key audiences who can influence decision-making in government relations. These include civil servants, specialist advisers, press and media and parliamentarians.

Civil servants have a strong influence over ministers and the decisions they make. The way to influence civil servants is through a form of argument. This should be through logical, unemotive, and carefully prepared briefs that can withhold scrutiny.

Special advisers are political animals that support general policies and serve ministers with advice, with speeches, and handle the media and act in a protective type of role to ministers in the political arena. They are often a best first point of call when seeking to sound out a minister.

Ministers pay much attention to the media in addition to their ministries and civil servants. The media without doubt influence the way in which ministers think and act (Gregory, 2004, p. 94). The popularity or lack of it can be gauged by ministers in the press and media.

Parliamentary colleagues are a significant influence on ministers in particular those mainly (but not totally) from their own political party. It is of course in Parliament (both Chambers and Committees) where the pitched battles often take place (Gregory, 2004).

5 Public affairs programmes

5.1 Defining public affairs

'Public affairs is a crucial and demanding specialism inside the broader field of public relations. It can claim this status because it involves influencing governments and therefore affects the quality of a country's democracy. In liberal democracies which are market-oriented and capitalist, external public relations for an organisation or group can be divided into two parts: dealing with markets; dealing with government, businesses, interest, and pressure groups. Marketing public relations communicates with the purchasers of goods and services, whether they are individual consumers or other businesses, public affairs communicates with government and other external stakeholders affecting a company or an organisation on matters of public policy (Yeoman & Tench, 2009).

Public affairs does not just involve corporate talking to government about big issues connected with public policy but it also involves businesses trying to work together before approaching government about an issue. There are also consumer-facing organisations that carry out public affairs. The Body Shop is a well-established campaigner to stop testing on animals. There are organisations that are not commercially-oriented that undertake public affairs too. For example, universities speaking to government about tuition fees for students (Yeoman & Tench, 2009).

KEY CONCEPT   concept

Public affairs is a public relations specialism that seeks to influence public policy-making via lobbying and/or through the media (Yeoman and Tench, 2009, p. 448).

Regulatory affairs, parliamentary liaison and lobbying tend to be subsumed under the broader term *public affairs*. Public affairs activities are generally those that involve a dialogue with government for the purposes of public policy-making, legislation and regulation (Baines *et al.,* (2004, p. 17).

MARKETING AT WORK   application

Here is an example of a public affairs programme, taken from www.connectpa.co.uk.

British Association for Adoption and Fostering

Communicating through the media was a key component of Connect's award-winning public affairs campaign with the British Association for Adoption and Fostering (BAAF). It won the Institute for Public Relations' prestigious 'Best Public Affairs Campaign' award in 2003.

The award recognises a campaign that promotes relationships between national and local government, government agencies, opinion-formers and the public. The campaign successfully secured an amendment to the Adoption and Children's Bill, allowing unmarried couples to adopt children.

Connect developed a communications strategy to position adoption by unmarried couples as an issue of children's rights and welfare and to distance it from any controversy surrounding gay rights and the relevance of the institution of marriage.

Through building contacts with key journalists and communicating our messages effectively, we ensured favourable front-page media coverage, to turn the campaign in favour of our client.

Connect helped BAAF to focus attention on the central issue at stake in the Bill: increasing the number of potential adopters to the benefit of children in foster care. This sensitive media campaign, alongside the briefing of Ministers and officials, shored up support among MPs, identified and developed Parliamentary champions and, importantly, secured a cross-party amendment allowing a free vote on the issue.

The initial success in the Commons was overturned by the Lords. BAAF successfully won support from the government to return the issue to the Upper House for a second vote. Close work with Peers and an eleventh-hour press conference contributed to a well-attended House of Lords vote and, on this occasion, the clause on adoption by unmarried couples was not thrown out. Connect Public Affairs and Connect Media took the issue, which the government was initially against, and secured its successful progress through both Houses of Parliament. The Bill now has royal assent and this new provision will benefit a large number of children and will have important implications for the legal rights of unmarried and gay couples. [http://www.connectpa.co.uk/casestudies.html, accessed 02.08.09]

ACTIVITY 3

application

Research some specialist public affairs consultancies such as the following and familiarise yourself with some examples of public affairs (and for Finsbury PR public affairs *and* financial) campaigns.

www.insightpa.com/video.html?gclid=CJ_7hL6xh5wCFV8B4wodMHSW_w

www.whitehouseconsulting.co.uk/?gclid=CJGUutKxh5wCFc0B4wod9Q8f-Q

www.finsbury.com

5.2 Media and messages of public affairs

As the various case studies in this chapter demonstrate, the range of audiences in public affairs are very complex and wide-ranging as are the messages. Communications more generally relate to trying to influence changes in public policies through a variety of different tools and techniques.

6 Lobbying

KEY CONCEPT

concept

Lobbying is defined by Theaker (2008, p. 129) citing Cutlip *et al.,* (1985) as involving:

'*direct attempts to influence legislative and regulatory decisions in government*' and public affairs is the specialised public relations effort designed to build and maintain community and governmental relations.'

Yeoman & Tench define lobbying as:

'the influence of public policy-making through the private means of meeting MP's, ministers, civil servants, councillors or local government officials'.

Doorley & Garcia (2007, p. 160) define lobbying as:
'*the practice of advocating one's policy position to government officials with the hopes of influencing legislation, regulation, or other government action*'.

Theaker suggests that the terms lobbying and public affairs are often used interchangeably although she argues that public affairs has a wider remit.

6.1 Uses of lobbying

6.1.1 Lobbying government

Theaker (2008, p. 130) states that lobbying has actually been used increasingly by organisations in order to present their case to government and groups of stakeholders. Lobbying is said to be either defensive (in that it is designed to get rid of or amend existing law) or offensive (geared towards pressurising the authorities to develop a law). One of the most important aspects of lobbying is to be very familiar with the legislative process in the country (or countries) within which the lobbying is taking place. For example, in the UK how the different national assemblies operate within the European Union. And, of course, it is increasingly important to take wide-ranging cultural and legislative practices into account as a result of competition on an international scale.

The following checklist on how to lobby government is taken from Yeoman & Tench (2006, p. 457)

- Define the matter to be lobbied
- Define success and failure
- Network with allies
- Monitor opponents
- Establish who the decision-makers are
- Decide whether to influence privately, publicly or both
- Lobby before policy is decided
- Write your case on one sheet of A4 paper
- Gain access

6.2 Public lobbying

Practical examples of public lobbying include – lobbying for changes to road safety or traffic measures to reduce traffic speed. The following summary taken from Yeoman & Tench (2006) considers the main points for consideration with regard to whether public lobbying is a suitable communications strategy.

An organisation or group would first ask itself:

- Is there easy access to councillors, MPs, senior civil servants and ministers?
- Is our policy position on the mainstream political agenda?

If the answers are 'no', you are halfway to doing a citizens' lobby. A citizen lobby involves a discreet group of specific stakeholders, eg a group of residents, parents within a school etc.

At the next stage two more questions would be asked:

- Have we got many people who would support us publicly?
- Can we get media coverage?

If the answer is 'yes', a public lobbying strategy would be more effective. Public lobbying would involve a much larger range of stakeholders than the citizen lobby would.

6.3 Private lobbying

Moloney (2006b) says that lobbying can take place in a private or public sphere, depending on whether an organisation has access to the decision-makers or not. He suggests that private lobbying could be carried out by using social networks to gain the attention of policy-makers. Professional lobbyists might be used in this kind of circumstance as they are more likely to know of the most appropriate skills to use.

Friends of the Earth's climate change campaign: The Big Ask (excerpt taken and adapted from CIPR Excellence Awards 2007)

Objectives

To gather public and political support for Friends of the Earth's proposed new Climate Change Bill. The Bill would commit the government to make at least 3% cuts in carbon dioxide (CO_2) emissions every year – ensuring that the UK plays a leading role in tackling climate change and sets an example to the rest of the world.

To empower people to press their MPs into representing their concerns about climate change – and specifically to support calls for a new Climate Change Bill.

To get at least 30,000 members of the public calling for a Climate Change Bill in the Queen's Speech of Autumn 2007 (constituting a pledge by the government to publish a Bill to tackle climate change).

Target audience: 'Eco-worriers' not 'eco-warriors'

To achieve our objectives we needed to reach beyond our traditional activist audiences to create a popular and political mandate for the Bill. Market research directed us to focus on the environmentally concerned but currently unsure as to how to act – the 'eco-worrier' – encouraging them to ask the big questions, of themselves and others, including what their MP is doing to address climate change.

An outreach strategy and targeted resources were developed. These included:

- A national media launch by Radiohead's Thom Yorke
- A 60-second cinema advertisement, 'Thinking'
- A campaign web site (www.thebigask.com)
- Viral advertisements
- Local activist toolkit containing: posters, postcards, leaflets, bookmarks, beermats and badges
- Direct marketing appeals
- Public meetings across the country
- The Big Ask Live – a series of music gigs culminating in flagship London gig with celebrity guests and public
- Presence at music festivals
- The Co-operative Bank partnership and research – followed up by online and newspaper advert

Our audience was encouraged to take action by postcard, e-mail, letter and SMS message.

The success of over 130,000 actions generated by these four methods, and a database of over 40,000 people, led us to launch The Big Ask Big Month Big Lobby in September 2006. This activity represented the groundswell of popular pressure for action on climate change. It encouraged our audience to lobby their MP to ask for a Climate Change Bill in the 2006 Queen's Speech (a year ahead of our original target date).

The Big Ask was publicised in:

- Friends of the Earth's supporter magazine 'Earthmatters' (reaching 100,000 people)
- Via our web site www.foe.co.uk
- Our youth and education materials
- Razorlight's 2006 and 2007 tours, with on-stage visuals, action postcards available at all venues and ads on the band's web site.
- Regular updates on Radiohead's Thom Yorke's web site
- Several TV shows

The Big Ask campaign has generated some of the highest levels of public interest on any single issue that Friends of the Earth has ever seen.

- Over 130,000 actions from postcards, letters, e-mails and texts.

- Cinema advertisement 'Thinking' reached an estimated half-a-million cinema-goers thanks to the pro bono support of over 50 independent cinemas in the UK.

- Radiohead singer Thom Yorke is a high-profile advocate of the campaign. Other celebrity supporters include Razorlight frontman Johnny Borrell, artist Kurt Jackson, musicians Gruff Rhys (Super Furry Animals) and Kate Rusby and designer Wayne Hemmingway.

- The Big Ask Live – a series of live gigs promoting the campaign including:

    - A benefit gig in May 06 at London's KOKO club featuring an exclusive performance by Radiohead's Thom Yorke. The gig sold out within minutes (1000 tickets). 3,000 new people signed up to the campaign following the gig's announcement.

    - Attendance at several music festivals in the UK in 2005/6 resulting in almost 13,000 people taking action.

- Viral advertising – 'Sticky Question' released in January 2006 had over 150,000 viewings.

- Climate change solutions postcards were distributed by our Local Groups network and used by MTV Europe in a programme featuring An Inconvenient Truth.

- Big Ask Big Month Big Lobby (12 Sept –11 Oct 06) – Constituents across the UK pledged to visit their MP on the need for a Climate Change Bill in the Queen's Speech. 1,300 pledges were received from 613 constituencies. That's 95% of the UK's constituencies.

- Appeals to 37,000 supporters to support our Big Ask work generated £144,000 of extra regular support.

- The heat is rising Sept 06 – A cash appeal to 55,000 people to contribute to the Big Ask Big Month Big Lobby. It cost £28,000 and generated £137,108.

6.4 Relationships

van Riel & Fombrun (2007, p. 198) suggest that developed and sustained personal relationships are an essential requirement for effective functioning between government relations specialists and the regulators, politicians and staff who work on specific issues. Personal and frequent contact is the best means of making contact with these influential decisions-makers – and build trust on which the relationship can develop.

6.5 Timing

The regulatory processes are quite complicated and they have long empty periods and a number of overlapping and interdependent cycles in which legislation is introduced and debated and regulations are voted on and passed. The government relations role is to make sure that decision-makers have the information that they need in a timely and appropriate manner.

There are, as one might imagine a number of variable factors that come into play when considering influencing policy-making. It is very difficult to anticipate when change will take place or whether there has been success or failure and to what actions success or behaviour can be attributed. It is important to appreciate that the desired objective will only happen – if it does happen after much planned and sustained and persuasive effort ensuring that there is a pre-defined goal plus a distinctive launch, middle and end (Yeoman & Tench, 2006, p. 455).

6.6 Expected behaviour of lobbyists

There is a certain expectation or standards of behaviour that are expected of professional and citizen lobbyists. All holders of public office should, according to the Nolan Committee Principles, cited by Yeoman & Tench (2006) expect to behave with:

- Selflessness
- Integrity
- Objectivity
- Accountability
- Openness
- Honesty
- Leadership

Note that public affairs can be a contentious activity and it should be given careful consideration before implementation. It touches on the quality of democracy by influencing government representatives and officials. It is part of wide public or community life and should be conducted to the high standards, detailed above, as established by the Nolan Committee.

Learning objectives	Covered
1 Understand the nature of public affairs and investor relations programmes	☑ Introduction to governmental PR (public affairs) and financial PR and what these types of communications programmes might involve in practice
	☑ Familiarisation with the range of specialist stakeholders within the financial PR and public affairs PR contexts
2 Formulate approaches to corporate communications that are investor-focused and contextually determined	☑ Identification of the information needs, likely messages and motivations of different stakeholder groups in financial PR contexts
	☑ Introduction to practical examples of financial PR campaigns
3 Formulate approaches to corporate communications that are government-focused and contextually determined	☑ Identification of the information needs, likely messages and motivations of different stakeholder groups in governmental PR contexts
	☑ Introduction to practical examples of public affairs and lobbying campaigns

1   List four financial stakeholders.

2   Why have retail investors become more powerful and sophisticated?

3   What kinds of financial communication takes place within the financial calendar?

4   What is a hostile takeover?

5   Name two financial media.

6   In what kinds of business situations might financial PR communications be particularly important?

7   What is the main measure of success in financial communications?

8   What is the difference between financial and investor relations?

9   Name two kinds of communication techniques used in investor relations.

10   Name an example of some information that might be portrayed on the company web site offering information for investors.

11   What is lobbying?

12   What kinds of organisations get involved in lobbying?

1　This is an activity of recall, wanting you to be able to remind yourself of the range of financial media. To remind yourself if you are unsure, look at section 1 in this chapter.

2　The benefits of financial PR include the following:

  −　Financial PR assists in maintaining the share price.
  −　Financial PR assists in developing the corporate reputation of a company.
  −　Overall, financial PR will lead to a better performance and profitability.

3　The intention here is for you to read more widely and research several specialist public affairs and financial PR specialists and understand more fully the types of work that they might do. Read through their case studies and past client sections to understand this as fully as you can.

1　Analysts, private investors, institutional investors, stockbrokers, financial media.

2　Retail investors have become more powerful and sophisticated because of the accessibility of information. They are no longer reliant on the printed media but have access to internet, financial discussion forums and financial blogs for their information.

3　Interim results, Prelim results, Annual Report and Accounts, AGM.

4　A hostile takeover is when the bidder has not sought the directors support and goes ahead and tries to buy the company hence the word 'hostile'.

5　You could include a number of different examples here within the broad areas of wire and news wire services, broadcast and print media. Note print media have far less significance here than in the past.

6　Financial communications will be important during takeovers and mergers and acquisitions, etc.

7　The main measure of success is the share price.

8　The difference between financial and investor relations is one of perspectives between countries for example, the UK and the US.

9　This could have included press releases, investor relations conferences, etc.

10　Executive biographies, analysts reports, news releases.

11　Lobbying involves direct attempts to influence legislation and regulation decisions in government.

12　All kinds of organisations can get involved in lobbying including pressure groups, small businesses and charities as well as large corporations.

Baines, P., Egan, J. And Jefkins, F. (2004) Public Relations: Contemporary Issues and Techniques, Elsevier, Oxford.

Bowman, P and Bing, R. (1993), Financial Public Relations, Butterworth-Heinmann Ltd., Oxford.

Bowd, R. And Harris, P. (2003), CSR – A Schools Approach to an Inclusive Definition: setting the scene for future Public Relations and communications research Conference paper BledCom 2003; 10th International Public Relations Research Symposium, Slovenia

Christensen, LT, Morsing, M & Cheney, G (2008) Corporate Communications: Conventions, Complexity and Critique. London: Sage Publications Ltd

CIPR Excellence Pride Awards, Scotland (2002), Building the Profile of Glasgow's International Financial Service District www.cipr.co.uk/member_area/infro/case_studies/pride_05

CIPR Excellence Awards (2007), Friends of the Earth's climate change campaign: the Big Ask www.cipr.co.uk/member_area/info/case_studies/excellence07/cat09.asp

Cave, A, (October/November 2005), M & A Mania, Corp Comms, Issue 3, Cross Border Ltd., London

CIPR PR Excellence Awards (2007) Standard Life: Corporate Image Transformation through PR Excellence

(Financial and Investor relations category), http://www.cipr.co.uk/member_area/info/index.asp

Cutlip, S.M., Center, A.H. and Broom, G.M. (1985), Effective Public relations (6th Ed.), Prentice Hall

Davies G, Chun R, Da Silva RV & Roper S (2003) Corporate Reputation and Competitiveness. Abingdon, Oxon: Routledge

Davis, A., (2006) The role of the mass media in investor relations, Journal of Communication Management, Vol.10, No.1, pp7-17

Doorley, J & Garcia, HF (2007) Reputation Management: The Key to Successful Public Relations and Corporate Communications New York: Routledge

Doyle, G. (2006), Financial new journalism: a post-Enron analysis of approaches towards economic and financial news production in the UK, Vol.7 (4) pp 433-452

Fill, C (2002) Marketing Communications: Contexts, Strategies and Applications (3rd ed). Harlow, Essex: Pearson Education Limited

Gregory, A. (2004) Public Relations in Practice (2nd Ed.) IPR Series, Kogan Page, London

Gummer, P. (1995), 'Financial Public Relations' in Strategic Public Relations. N. Hart (ed) Basingstoke: Macmillan Press

Harris, P. And Moss, D. (2001), Understanding public affairs, Journal of Public Affairs, 1 (1): 6-8

Lewis, R (2008), Cultural Studies London, Sage Publications

Linning, R., [accessed July 2009], Top Tips on Public Affairs http://www.cipr.co.uk/member_area/info/guides/publicaffairs.asp

Middleton, K. (2002), 'An introduction to financial public relations' in The Public Relations Handbook. A Theaker (ed.), London, Routledge

Moloney, K. (2006b), 'Public affairs' in R. Tench and L. Yeomans, Exploring Public Relations, FT Prentice Hall, pp 433-462

Riel, CBM van & Fombrun, CJ (2007) Essentials of Corporate Communication: Implementing Practices for Effective Reputation Management. Abingdon, Oxon: Routledge, Oxon

Tench, R & Yeoman, L (2003) Exploring Public Relations. Harlow, Essex: Pearson Education Limited

Tench, R & Yeoman, L (2006) Exploring Public Relations. Harlow, Essex: Pearson Education Limited

The Economist (2001), The Spin Doctor Gets Serious 14 July 2001360 (8230) pp74-75

Theaker, A.(2008), The Public Relations Handbook, (3rd Ed.), Routledge, Oxon.

Chapter 10
Internal communications

Topic list

Introduction

Why is internal communications so important? Why is it that communicating through internal communications is so critical in present business climates? Is internal communications as important as external communications and if so, why? What is the role of internal communications and who does it involve? What impact has technology had on delivery of internal communications? How might internal communications work effectively within organisations and how does internal communications 'sit' in the context of corporate communications? These are some of the issues this chapter will address.

Syllabus-linked learning objectives

By the end of the chapter you will be able to:

Learning objectives	Syllabus link
1 Understand the nature of internal communications programmes	1.2.2
2 Formulate approaches to corporate communications that are employee-focused and contextually determined.	3.2.4

1 Internal communications

1.1 Employees as a stakeholder audience

Current economic climates are uncertain. At the time of writing this Study Text, the UK economy is in the depths of a deep recession. Interest rates are at an all time low, businesses of all sizes are really struggling and redundancies are becoming frequent news. For example at the time of writing, there have been a number of recent redundancies announced in the UK. These have included BT to shed a further 15,000 jobs most of which will be in the UK with a reported annual loss of £134m, The Royal Bank of Scotland to cut a further 9,000 jobs and half of those to be lost in the UK and Nortel Networks UK going into administration resulting in more than 220 staff being made redundant without notice. Let's take a closer look for a moment at BT and consider the various perspectives and issues that theses redundancies raise for business and for the people involved.

MARKETING AT WORK

application

British Telecommunications (BT) plc

BT have made significant losses this year and in order to save costs has made a decision to cut jobs. BT reports itself as being a *Corporate Citizen* and 'BT is proud of its record as a world class employer...'

BT has strong corporate communications and will have given this announcement considerable thought and planning. Before the announcements were made to the media, there would have been considerable planned communications 'behind the scenes'. BT would have worked closely with senior staff across business functions, globally, in order to plan how communications would take place. Although most of the job losses were reported to take place in the UK, as BT operates in 170 countries with four main principle lines of business: BT Global Services, Openreach, BT Retail and BT Wholesale, it therefore needs to communicate to its internal audiences working in each area of business, globally about the redundancies. This in itself is complicated for a global organisation such as BT. The Human Resource (HR) team and the unions (such as Communication Workers Union) would need to explore the details, procedures and protocols of the redundancies. Procedure would have been to seek voluntary redundancies first and other job savings through natural wastage such as staff due to retire, for example. All staff would have been communicated through various communication methods and offered the opportunity to air their concerns about the job loss announcement so that they were aware of the situation before it was announced to the media. Personnel that the announcement would directly affect (those being made redundant) or indirectly (those whose work would be affected by staff changes) would also be made aware of the situation in addition to the wider range of employees. Staff would also be offered the opportunity to discuss their concerns and worries further and mechanisms would set up to ensure that this took place.

As you can see from looking at this example, there are many differing perspectives that need to be considered when planning the announcement of redundancies. Employees are arguably the most important audience and asset to an organisation because they communicate directly with the customers and, therefore, need to be nurtured, respected and well informed. Staff that are invested in will, as a result, offer far more than labour and will be motivated and committed in their day-to-day work. Equally, from the corporate perspective, organisations as employers need to be seen to be honourable employers that look after their staff. This will have a direct impact on their reputation at a corporate level.

The executive search firm Watson Helby made the following statement with regard to the Future of Internal Communications as reported by PR Week.

'The increasing pace of corporate change and the need to win employees' commitment, not just their labour, means corporations are working much harder at and investing much more in internal communication. And in the current volatile operating environment CEOs want and need an IC team that can share a fast-moving corporate story rapidly and engagingly; help senior leaders communicate to employees on the frontline; improve the delivery of redundancy programmes, restructurings and reorganisations and engage employees behind new business strategies and priorities'.

This statement usefully summarises some of the key points we need to consider with regard to internal communications in current economic climates. Change is taking place within organisations at a corporate level at a very rapid pace and as a result, that internal communications has become a **corporate** rather than more **functional** level activity. Maintaining employees' as your workforce is not enough. Organisations need the loyalty of a committed workforce and are recognising the need to work much harder in order to achieve that.

Fast moving changes need to be communicated effectively and rapidly and senior personnel need to be supported in their communications with employees who work at more junior levels. Where the inevitable redundancies, restructuring and reorganisations take place it is essential that these changes are implemented and communicated effectively and efficiently. Above all it is important that employees through effective internal communications remain engaged in the organisation's business however the business changes.

Doorley and Garcia (2007) describe employee communications:

*'To align the hearts, minds and hands of the employee constituency through **dialogue** and **engagement**'. They continue to describe employee communications today as **managing meaning** inside the organisation in a way that supports leadership and business objectives.*

You will have considered the range of stakeholders earlier in your studies. It is important to reiterate the importance of employees to an organisation as an audience. Quirke (2008, p xii) says that **people are our voice**. They are advocates and are truly influential and able to tell a story and argue its case. Consider the following exercise and answer the questions that follow.

ACTIVITY 1

evaluation

Consider the business activity relating to a well known retailer such as Marks and Spencer. You might want to revisit some of Marks and Spencer's websites – such as the examples listed below – and their core areas of business. In addition familiarise yourself with their corporate objectives, corporate communications, CSR, communications with customers, and so forth.

http://corporate.marksandspencer.com/mscareers

http://corporate.marksandspencer.com/howwedobusiness

http://corporate.marksandspencer.com/howwedobusiness/our_policies/our_people

- What are Marks and Spencer's corporate objectives and core values?
- How are these communicated?
- Who is it who deals directly with customers in stores?
- Who is it who deals with customers on the phone or online?
- What is likely to happen if the customer experience is not so good?
- Who is it who is able to offer feedback on customers' viewpoints?

If internal communications is part of an organisation's strategic communication function, then employees are a vital stakeholder group within the context of communications. *The behaviour of employees contribute towards the corporate identity and project it to the external stakeholders*, (Yeoman and Tench (2006). The following quotation is taken directly from Yeoman and Tench (2006):

'*The strategic purpose of internal communication can perhaps best be summarised as one that is concerned with building two-way, involving relationships with internal publics, with the goal of improving organisational effectiveness*'.

1.2 The role and importance of internal communication

It is important to note that the role of internal communications has changed significantly and it is now considered to be an important part of strategic communications at a corporate level. Historically, internal communications was not viewed in this way and this is a significant shift of mindset. It has been recognised that internal communications contributes towards the bottom line and directly impacts upon the reputation of the organisation. As a result, then of the significance of internal communications, it is critical not only to provide information but to provide a context for that information as well.

Doorley and Garcia (2007) citing a director of employee communications Barry Mike, describes eight business trends that have helped set the scene for an improved employee communication function:

1   **Growing cynicism** – as a result of greedy CEOs and an enlightened attitude towards employee communications.

2   **Organisations have dramatically flattened** – decreasing bureaucracy and bringing decision-making closer to the 'front line' employees.

3   **The rate of change is increasing** – 'by the book mentality is no longer valid. Emphasis is now on *flexibility* and *elasticity*.

4   **Speed has become a differentiator** – because of information technology – rather than just price and quality differentiating products.

5   **Lifetime employment is dead** – there is no longer the prospect of life long employment in return for loyalty, hence all employees can be offered is the prospect of expanding into new roles.

6   **Human capital** – that is the people becoming the key competitive differentiator.

7   **The desire for purpose** – employee communications can help employees feel part of 'something bigger'.

8   **Service sector rise** – resulted in internal branding being more important – as employee communications has become a vital extension of marketing and strategic planning in ensuring the delivery of brand promise.

Krone *et al.* (2001) suggests that there are four roles which internal communications should fulfil:

*   Efficiency
*   Shared meaning
*   Connectivity
*   Satisfaction

Each of these areas will now be addressed in turn.

1.2.1 Efficiency

Internal communications is fundamentally used to communicate and disseminate information about the corporate activities of the organisation. As an important stakeholder group, employees need to be fully informed, whatever the communication.

Efficiency means functioning effectively with little wasted effort (Collins, 2006, p88). Efficiency in terms of internal communications means that communications amongst employees is effective and efforts are not wasted, resources being used carefully and thoughtfully, without waste. The efficiency of internal communications can be measured to evaluate how efficient it has been.

Lyn Smith in her book *Internal Communications* reports on the CIPR 2002 Excellence Award winner, Seeboard. Seeboard was highlighted for conducting an evaluation at every stage of its branding project, using questionnaires, surveys, intranet surveys and mystery shopper-type surveys where performance was tested without the employees being aware of the process. An example of the evaluation was the first phase survey which showed that 99% of the staff understood the new customer vision. In addition, the twice annually staff survey recorded an 83% response rate. Seeboard was reported in this survey as being:

- A good place to work 88%
- Felt proud to work for Seeboard 92%
- An amazing 92% said they knew the priorities of their team.

Smith suggests that it is useful to look backward as well as onward in terms of measuring and planning for efficiency.

1.2.2 Shared meaning

The focus of internal communications has changed from addressing events and people to sharing corporate goals (Smith, 2009). Internal communications can now be used as a vehicle for building a shared understanding with employees about corporate aims and goals.

KEY CONCEPT
concept

The role of communication. Quirke (2008, p. 25) suggests that 'Communication is about the transfer of meaning from person to person, not simply the passing on of messages. The more chaotic, new or interconnected change becomes, the more employees are forced to make choices and prioritise. Helping them find their way through the maze of change depends on making information meaningful and highlighting its point. In other words, companies who want to create understanding need to make meaning and not messages.'

It is also important to consider different perspectives and what it is like to be on the receiving end. What are the staff perceptions, for example?

The John Lewis Partnership example, discussed later in this chapter, is a good example of a pioneering and very successful business making the shred meaning of its stakeholders in its business activity a core part of its functionality. They are putting measures in place to ensure that in the longer-term it is able to empower employees (or *partners* as it describe them) in the decision-making of the business. Its approach is an attempt to truly gain shared meaning between an organisation and its employees.

1.2.3 Connectivity

In order to achieve the high level of performance so many companies seek, it is necessary to show the connection between the company's success and the success of its employees. All need to understand what needs to be achieved whatever role they play in that process in order that they understand the 'bigger picture' (Quirke, 2008)

The following diagram provides a summary of a 'virtuous circle of communication' (Smith, 2009). Applying this model to internal communications it stresses the important points. Having researched, committed and owned the message, tailored your communication and tested it. The message is sent. However adding the opportunity to engage and express opinion opens up a virtuous circle of communication. Ideas and suggestions are fed back into the system with the intention of keeping communications flowing and 'connecting'. Note the point in the centre of the model. **More than 50% of communication is listening**. One needs to ensure that listening is taking place or otherwise even the best designed and developed communication will be worthless.

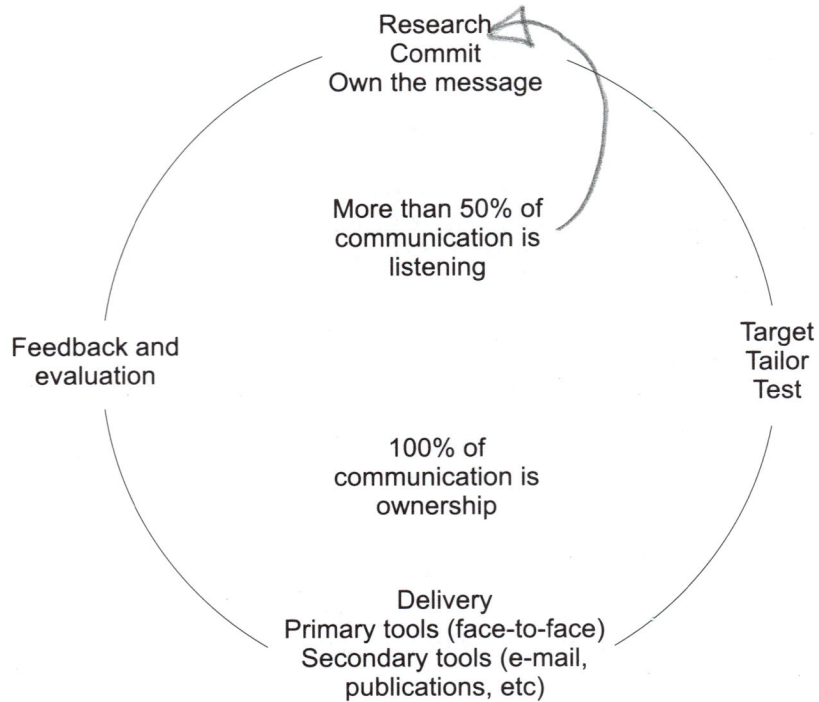

Research
Commit
Own the message

More than 50% of
communication is
listening

Feedback and
evaluation

Target
Tailor
Test

100% of
communication is
ownership

Delivery
Primary tools (face-to-face)
Secondary tools (e-mail,
publications, etc)

[Mounter, 2004]

1.2.4 Satisfaction

Internal communications is also used to improve job fulfilment throughout the organisation. If employees are satisfied, they perform better and are more motivated. Happy employees create a pleasant working environment.

ASSESSMENT TIP

application

Patterns of employment are often a 'tell tale' sign that all is not well amongst the employees. If employee turnover is high or there are difficulties recruiting personnel, this can often be linked back to internal communications and problems associated with an organisation's reputation. Think about staff turnover and the impact within your own organisation while preparing your assignment.

MARKETING AT WORK

application

JL Partnership

Consider the John Lewis Partnership one of the leading UK retailers and its approach to doing business and the role that its employees play in the way that they do business. Watch the following video available online which describes the Partnership Spirit ethos of John Lewis.

http://www.johnlewispartnership.co.uk/Display.aspx?MasterId=a82778d2-c27a-4da8-aa6d-e5be4eace0f8&NavigationId=860

The John Lewis Partnership operate a 'Partnership Spirit' which is really core to the way that it does business. As you may have followed in the video, the Partnership Spirit is built around four principles:

'Ensuring the happiness of Partners is at the centre of everything we do Building a sustainable business through profit and growth Serving our customers to the very best of our ability Caring about our communities and our environment'

At the John Lewis Partnership, employees are Partners, which means we are all owners of the business and share in its success. Our founder, John Spedan Lewis, had an ambitious vision of employee co-ownership with the happiness of Partners as the ultimate purpose, and his vision lives on in the modern Partnership of today.

Key elements of the Partnership include:

- Ensuring the happiness of Partners is at the centre of everything we do
- Owners of the business working together, self-responsibility, collective responsibility
- Job satisfaction, enjoyment and fun
- Open information and dialogue
- Shared profits
- Care of Partners when working and in retirement

All staff are referred to as partners. There are 69,000 partners in the John Lewis Partnership across the three main areas of business – Waitrose, John Lewis and Greenbee, The partnership is a democratic one and every partner has a share and voice in the business that they co-own. Partners are dedicated to serving their customers with flair and fairness. All partners share in the success of John Lewis and profit-sharing takes place. There are many aspects of the John Lewis Partnership, however, the six elements of Partnership behaviour that together make up Powered by our Principles are:

- Be honest
- Give respect
- ‘ Recognise others
- Show enterprise
- Work together
- Achieve more.

Here is the definition taken from the John Lewis Partnership web site about the Partnership Spirit:

'*The Partnership Spirit defines what is truly important to the John Lewis Partnership. It does not change from time to time, situation to situation or person to person; it transcends our growth ambitions*'.

It continues: '*Partners feel that the John Lewis Partnership is an exciting company to be part of and a very special place to work. Our distinctive culture – our spirit – lies behind this feeling and sense of belonging and enables Partners to serve customers to the best of their ability*'.

John Lewis Partnership provides an excellent example of internal communications working well. The whole ethos of the partners. After John Lewis and the way that it empowers employees to contribute to and be an integral part of its business is very forward thinking. Its approach demonstrates efficiency in the way that it does business and in how to get the best from its staff, shared meaning in that the employees and the business share the same goals. It connects with its employees and ultimately has staff who work well and have job satisfaction while keeping customers happy and doing business with them.

At the time of writing this chapter, there was an article in the Sunday Times (14 June, p. 7) about the John Lewis Partnership. The article focused on Patrick Lewis as a family member of the John Lewis Partnership – founded by his great uncle in 1929 – and the significance of his new role now working within the business. The article adds substance to the discussions so far about internal communications. It was reported as being a surprise in February when Patrick Lewis joined the board as a 'partnership counsellor'. His role was to ensure that the turned over £6.9 billion last year is being run for the benefit of the 69,000 partners. They shared £125.5m between them in 2008.

Sceptics have suggested the role could turn Lewis into a management stooge who bears bad news from the boardroom to the partners. He believes he can be a partners' champion with the staff having a direct line to him. 'There is an element of the independent director in my role', he said. 'So when the execs are building up a plan there is someone there to be independent on behalf of the partners. After all, they are our shareholders.

Lewis was reported to want to create a culture where the staff feel comfortable challenging what the business is doing. He said 'I am building on what we have done in the past. It doesn't need to be revolution, but there is big untapped potential here'. Lewis goes on to suggest that he needs to have a long run at this role:

'.. Success for me in five years would be for our partners to feel that they have a much stronger influence over the day-to-day working life.....what I really like about this business is that the partners don't think like that.' ■

It is important to note that the approach that John Lewis take towards internal communications and the ethos of employee ownership that forms that backbone of its internal communications strategy is significant and offers competitive differentiation in the market place.

MARKETING AT WORK

application

Northern Rail using internal communications effectively (excerpt taken from the HR Excellence Awards 2009)

In a particularly strong category, Northern Rail stood out for its comprehensive, practical and multi-dimensional approach to internal communications.

Northern Rail is a complex rail franchise formed in December 2004. It operates 2,600 trains a day, more than any other train operator, and manages 471 stations – 20% of the national rail network. It has 4,600 employees and its clear vision for communication is to be 'recognised as the UK business leader in the effectiveness, quality and range of its internal communications'.

It measures success through discernible improvements to internal communications processes. The strategy has nine themes, including relevance and creating a centre of communication excellence. Among the strategies admired was 'Tell Heidi' – a channel where employees send rumours they have heard to the managing director Heidi Mottram. This was developed after discovering that rumours were part of everyday life but a barrier to effective communication, potentially destroying morale. Heidi responds to each rumour through a monthly newsletter or replies personally. The company took the concept on the road with 'Tell Heidi' Live, involving Mottram or the engineering director in drop-in Q&A sessions. As well as giving people an outlet to discuss issues, they have also used it to mention ideas, resulting in improvements in business performance.

The 2007 employee survey achieved an 85% increase in response, while the measure 'being kept up-to-date with regular information and news' rose from 59% to 82%.

Judges agreed the firm had revolutionised communication in an industry where it is typically top-down. 'A strategic approach with a human face and a good way of capturing what was on the grapevine,' they said.

ACTIVITY 2

evaluation

For an organisation with which you are familiar, analyse its internal communications. Speak to various people in different roles and levels within the organisation and use the following questions as prompts for your analysis.

How happy were the people you spoke to about where they work? Why did they feel the way they felt?

Does the staff view of the organisation marry up to the corporate reputation the organisation portrays externally? If not, why not?

How are staff communicated with – what tools and channels are used? Is there an opportunity for staff feedback? How is this initiated and how does it work in practice?

What kind of change has gone on recently and how do staff feel about how change was communicated?

2 Communication systems and communication climate

2.1 The communication process

Communication can be depicted as a **'radio signal'** model. The sender codes the message and transmits it through a medium to the receiver who decodes it into information.

The process of communication can be shown as follows.

The communication process

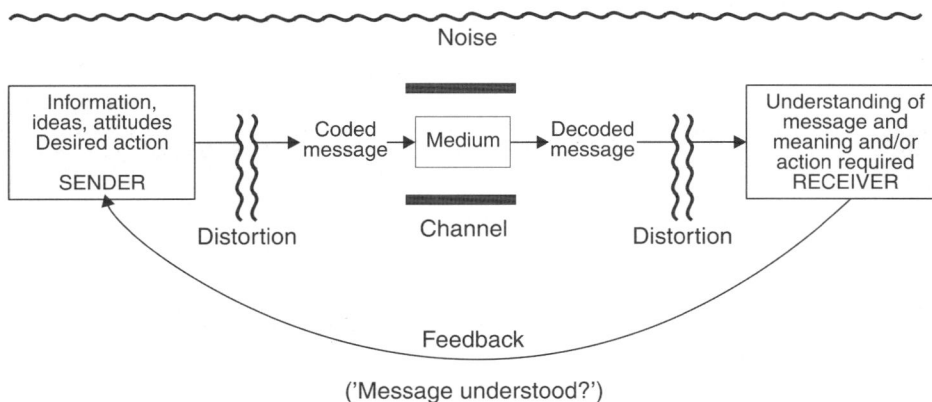

('Message understood?')

Element	Comment
Coding and decoding	The code or 'language' of a message may be verbal (spoken or written) or non-verbal (pictures, diagrams, numbers or body language). The needs and abilities of the target recipient of the message must be taken into account: not all codes (eg technical jargon or unlabelled diagrams) will be accessible to others.
Media and channels	The choice of medium (letter, memo, e-mail, report, presentation, telephone call) and channel of delivery (telecom system, notice board, postal system, World Wide Web) depends on a number of factors. • **Urgency**: the speed of transmission (eg phone or e-mail as opposed to post) • **Permanency**: the need for a written record for legal evidence, confirmation of a transaction or future reference • **Complexity**: eg the need for graphic illustration to explain concepts • **Sensitivity/confidentiality**: (eg a private letter) • **Ease of dissemination**: wide audience (eg a notice board) • **Cost effectiveness**: (taking into account all the above)
Feedback	The process by which the sender checks – and recipient signals – that the message has been received and understood. This is vital, as it makes communication a two-way – and much more reliable – process. Feedback may include: • Verbal messages ('I'd like to clarify...', 'What does that mean?') • Non-verbal cues (eg nodding and making encouraging noises, or looking perplexed) • Appropriate action (eg doing as requested by the message)
Distortion	A process through which the meaning of a message is lost in the coding or decoding stages. Misunderstandings may arise from technical or ambiguous language, misinterpretation of symbols or tones of voice and so on.

Element	Comment
Noise	Interference in the environment of communication which prevents the message getting through clearly. This may be:
	• Physical noise (eg passing traffic)
	• Technical noise (eg a bad internet connection)
	• Social noise (eg differences in the personalities, status or education of the parties)
	• Psychological noise (eg anger or prejudice distorting what is heard)

It is also worth including some PR theory here of relevance – the four models of communications. The diagram below cited in Yeoman and Tench (2006) is adapted from Grunig and Hunt (1984). What is significant here is that for internal communications to be two-way and symmetrical in the way that communications are carried out, that mutual understanding shows result. So much employee communications is actually one-way rather than two-way or does not offer sufficient feedback mechanisms.

| Characteristics | Model | | | |
	Press agency/publicity	Public information	Two-way asymmetric	Two-way symmetric
Purpose	Propaganda	Dissemination of information	Scientific persuasion	Mutual understanding
Nature of communication	One-way; complete truth not essential	One-way; truth important	Two-way; imbalanced effects	Two-way; balanced effects
Communication model	Source to receiver	Source to receiver	Source to receiver and feedback	Group to group and feedback
Nature of research	Little; 'counting house'	Little; readability, readership	Formative; evaluative of attitudes	Formative; evaluative of understanding

2.2 Formal communication channels

Formal communication channels are those which exist within the organisational structure. How complex these communication structures are depends very much on the complexity of the origination concerned in terms of how bureaucratic it is (in terms of process, policy and procedure for many things but certainly for communications). How hierarchical it is (how many layers there are of people within the organisational structure) or how flat the organisation is. How an organisation is structured has a significant impact upon how communication flows.

Quirke (2008) argues that communication channels need to be better managed:

'...to target information, reduce interruptions by irrelevant messages, and liberate employee's time and 'brain space'. Organisations need the right mix of communication channels and to be able to use the right channel for the right type of information. Equally, organisations need to target their audiences more closely and tailor messages more relevantly to address their peoples' interests and concerns.' (Quirke, 2008 p. 26).

2.3 Informal communication

Informal communication occurs within the informal organisation - an informal organisation always exists alongside the formal one. This was covered in detail in Chapter 3. Unlike the formal organisation, the informal organisation is loosely structured, flexible and spontaneous. It embraces such mechanisms as:

- **Social relationships and groupings** (eg cliques) within – or across – formal structures

- The '**grapevine**' or informal communication which by-passes the formal reporting channels and routes

- **Behavioural norms** and ways of doing things, both social and work-related, which may circumvent formal procedures and systems (for good or ill)

- **Power/influence structures**, irrespective of organisational authority: informal leaders are those who are trusted and looked to for advice.

concept

It is important to remember that the **grapevine** can be used strategically – as part of the internal communications planning – so that communications can be distributed using the informal network as opposed to just relying on the formal communication mechanisms.

2.4 Internal information flows

2.4.1 Direction of communication flows

Communication in an organisation **flows** downwards, upwards, sideways and diagonally.

Formal channels of communication in an organisation may run in three main directions.

(a) **Vertical**: ie up and down the scalar chain.

    (i) **Downward** communication is very common, and takes the form of instructions, briefings, rules and policies, announcement of plans and so on, from superior to subordinate.

    (ii) **Upward** communication is rarer – but very important for the organisation. It takes the form of reporting back, feedback, suggestions and so on. Managers need to encourage upward communication to take advantage of employees' experience and know-how, and to be able to understand their problems and needs in order to manage better.

(b) **Horizontal or lateral**: between people of the same rank, in the same section or department, or in different sections or departments. Horizontal communication between 'peer groups' is usually easier and more direct then vertical communication, being less inhibited by considerations of rank.

    (i) **Formally**: to co-ordinate the work of several people, and perhaps departments, who have to co-operate to carry out a certain operation

    (ii) **Informally**: to furnish emotional and social support to an individual

(c) **Diagonal**: this is interdepartmental communication by people of different ranks. Departments in the technostructure which serve the organisation in general, such as Human Resources or Information Systems, have no clear 'line authority' linking them to managers in other departments who need their involvement. Diagonal communication aids co-ordination, and also innovation and problem-solving, since it puts together the ideas and information of people in different functions and levels. It also helps to by-pass longer, less direct channels, avoiding blockages and speeding up decision-making.

2.4.2 Effective communication

Effective communication means: the right person receives the right information in the right way at the right time. The focus here is on effective *internal* communications.

What does 'good communication' look like? It is perhaps easiest to identify *poor* or ineffective communication, where information is not given; is given too late to be used; is too much to take in; is inaccurate or incomplete; is hard to understand. To recap here, then, **effective communication** is:

(a) **Directed to appropriate people**: this may be defined by the reporting structure of the organisation, but it may also be a matter of discretion, trust and so on.

(b) **Relevant to their needs**: not excessive in volume (causing overload); focused on relevant topics; communicated in a format, style and language that they can understand.

(c) **Accurate and complete** (within the recipient's needs): information should be 'accurate' in the sense of 'factually correct', but need not be minutely detailed: in business contexts, summaries and approximations are often used.

(d) **Timely**: information must be made available within the time period when it will be relevant (as input to a decision, say).

(e) **Flexible**: suited in style and structure to the needs of the parties and situation. Assertive, persuasive, supportive and informative communication styles have different applications.

(f) **Effective in conveying meaning**: style, format, language, and media all contribute to the other person's understanding or lack of understanding. If the other person doesn't understand the message, or misinterprets it, communication has not been effective.

(g) **Cost-effective**: in business organisations, all the above must be achieved, as far as possible, at reasonable cost.

2.5 Effective employee relations: linking structure, flow, content and climate

The following diagram taken from van Riel & Fombrun (2007), contextualises the elements of an effective internal communications function by illustrating the four main components and their effects on the organisation's identification. It is more and more the case that internal communications specialists must grasp the broader context of the organisation, its reputation platform and look for ways to enhance the company's consistency and distinctiveness by infusing key elements of the reputation platform into the internal communications channels of the company. Hence internal communications involves not only expressing core values but impressing those core values on new employees through the corporate stores that are told both formally and informally to them through training videos, company programming and through the grapevine.

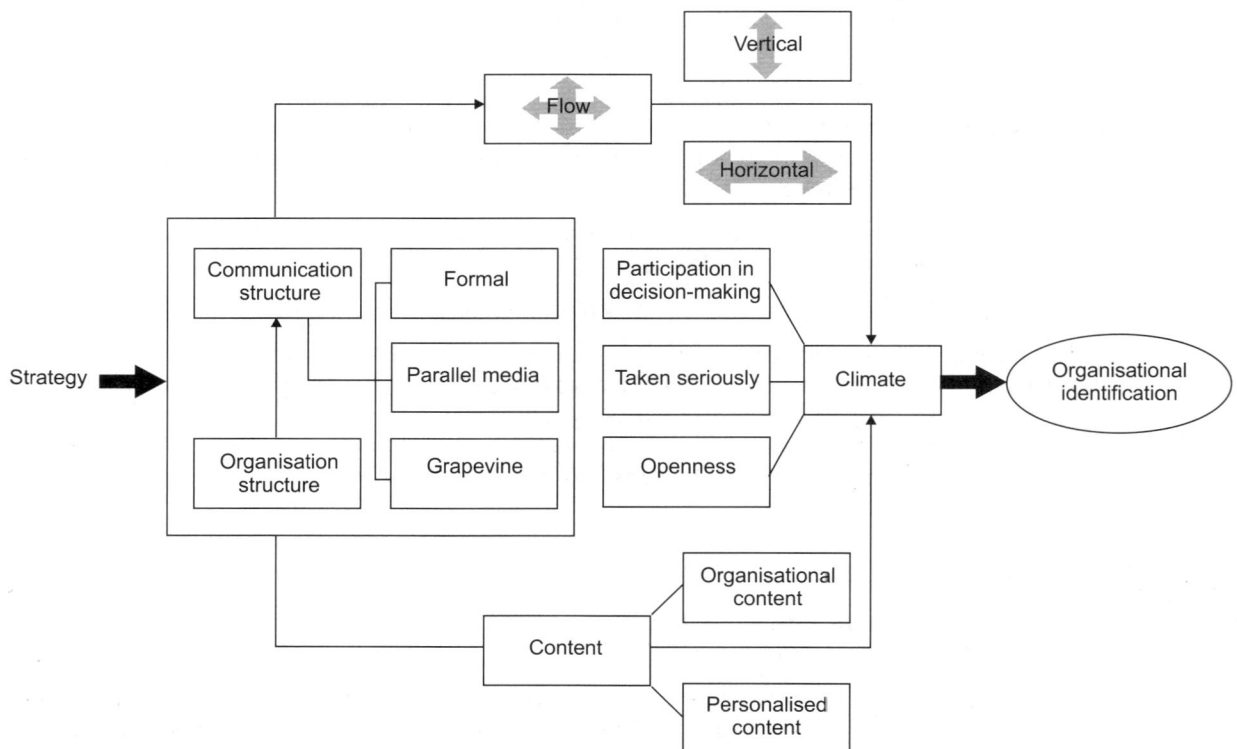

2.6 Tools of internal communication

A couple of important points before we discuss the plethora of tools available to the internal communications. First, communicators must be skilled at selecting exactly the *right* media to gain the greatest possible amount of message penetration across the target audience. What are your audiences' communication preferences – how do they want to be communicated with? Second, that despite all advances in technology, that face-to-face communication is still the preferred medium by most employees, so surveys tells us (Smith, 2009, p. 136).

Here follows some guidance points on internal communications (adapted from Smith 2009, pp. 79–92)

- Focus on the message before thinking about the channels.
- Think – how can I segment the audiences and what are their preferences – in terms of media.
- Consider a 'pick and mix' approach to media not choosing one but a selection.
- Employees rate face-to-face highest on their list – keep message short and simple.
- Use support materials in group face to face meetings.
- Remember to build in two-way feedback mechanisms into the communications.
- Remember that print is easily portable and is a medium of record.
- Keep a balance of news and features in print.
- Use the moving image to engage people.
- Remember that DVDs offer the opportunity for participation.
- Audio cassettes are still good for mobile audiences.
- E-mail and intranet can be 'hard on the eyes'.
- Adapt material for screen-based media.
- Flashes and alerts can be communicated well by text.
- Some quirky gimmicks like board games can engage people.
- Corporate Social Responsibility (CSR) can motivate the workforce.

ACTIVITY 3
application

Go and read pages 154 to 156 of your recommended text Doorley and Garcia. This section is an article by Sharyn Bearse of Bearse Communications offering a comprehensive list of tools of internal communications and the pros and cons of each activity. When you have read it, consider again an organisation with which you are familiar. How many of those tools are used there and how effective are they? What alternatives could be used instead?

The following exert, taken from Quirke (2007, p. 281) is an example of an organisation's channel guide.

ACTIVITY 4
evaluation

For an organisation that you know well, prepare to the best of your ability a channel guide for that organisation. Create a table similar to the one above for the channel guide example and have a go at completing all of the detail for that guide. What have you learnt as a result of this process?

It is critical in current climates to ensure that investment is being made in communication channels which demonstrate a clear return on investment. So often communications teams operate a range of channels which in practice actually duplicate effort and coverage and don't always use relevant content. It is also critical to understand what communications channels are used for what types of information and where, so it is clear where one's effort should be focused.

Channel	Description	Objectives	Audience	Frequency	Type of info	Strengths	Weaknesses
One World	Company-wide internal magazine.	'To inform and entertain' To make people feel part of the corporate family.	All staff	Bi-monthly	Business strategies and direction, product and performance news.	Well liked by audience, doesn't have a 'head office publication' feel to it.	Can't guarantee it will be read. Very little interaction from audience.
Info cards	Briefing sheets, principally for stores, displayed in staffroom in plastic holders.	To create awareness of issues and initiatives affecting day-to-day work.	All stores (main audience). Also HQ and regional offices.	Fortnightly	Minimum text and focus on graphics. Messenger must have a clear relevance to all store staff.	Popular channel. Good way to grab attention of audience and cross refer to more detailed communication elsewhere.	Not good for detail. Must be punchy or won't catch attention. Can't guarantee it will be read.
Management update	Management newsletter	To help managers understand the broader business context.	All managers	Monthly	A management overview combining progress/news about vision, strategy and the 5 year plan and how things fit in.	Opportunity to communicate to a more focused audience on management issues.	Content doesn't always link clearly to strategy/vision. No guarantee will be read.
Management forum	Strategy conference.	To communicate the strategy to management, and allow them to challenge and gain ownership of it.	All management from store manger and above.	Quarterly	Strategy and plans. May discuss results if the timing is right. Also recognising achievements.	Face-to-face delivery. Chance to reinforce strategy and key challenges for the year.	Large group of people and can be very one way – must work to keep it interactive.
Team briefs	Store team meetings.	To brief local teams about priorities for the week/day and to stimulate discussion and create involvement in better customer service.	Local store teams	Varies – up to three times a week.	Currently at manager's discretion.	Face-to-face channel. Easy to check understanding and raise issues.	No central feed into the process. No feedback process. Reliant on line manager for success.

2.7 Communication climate

The communications climate has been addressed earlier in Chapter 3 covered as part of section 4.4 addressing Organisation Culture. As a reminder, the communications climate is a sub-set of the broader organisational climate (culture), embracing the context of internal communications within the organisation and employee perceptions about their nature. The culture of an organisation may support or hinder communication. *John Lewis*, as discussed earlier in the chapter, provide a culture which encourages staff to feel comfortable with challenging what the business is doing.

3 Barriers to internal communication

3.1 Communication barriers

Barriers to communication include 'noise' (from the environment), poorly constructed or coded/decoded messages (distortion) and failures in understanding caused by the relative positions of senders and receivers.

General problems which can occur in the communication process include:

- Distortion and noise factors (described above)
- Misunderstanding due to lack of clarity or technical jargon
- Non-verbal signs (gesture, facial expression) contradicting the verbal message
- Failure to give or to seek feedback
- 'Overload' – a person being given too much information to digest in the time available
- Perceptual selection: people hearing only what they want to hear in a message
- Differences in social, racial or educational background
- Poor communication skills on the part of sender or recipient

Additional difficulties may arise from the **work context**, including:

(a) **Status** (of the sender and receiver of information)

(i) A senior manager's words are listened to closely and a colleague's perhaps discounted.

(ii) A subordinate might mistrust his or her superior's intentions and might look for 'hidden meanings' in a message.

(b) **Jargon**. People from different job or specialist backgrounds (eg accountants, HR managers, IT experts) can have difficulty in talking on a non-specialist's wavelength.

(c) **Priorities**. People or departments may have different priorities or perspectives so that one person places more or less emphasis on a situation than another.

(d) **Selective reporting**. Subordinates may give superiors incorrect or incomplete information (eg to protect a colleague, to avoid 'bothering' the superior). A senior manager may, however only be able to handle edited information because he does not have time to sift through details.

(e) **Use**. Managers may be prepared to make decisions on a 'hunch' without proper regard to the communications they may or may not have received.

(f) **Timing**. Information which has no immediate use tends to be forgotten.

(g) **Opportunity**. Mechanisms, formal or informal, for people to say what they think may be lacking, especially for upward communication.

(h) **Conflict**. Where there is conflict between individuals or departments, communications will be withdrawn and information withheld.

(i) **Cultural values** about communication. For example:

(i) **Secrecy**. Information might be given on a need-to-know basis, rather than be considered as a potential resource for everyone to use.

(ii) **Can't handle bad news**. The culture of some organisations may prevent the communication of certain messages. Organisations with a 'can-do' philosophy may not want to hear that certain tasks are impossible, for example.

(iii) **Religion**. Religion can block messages or change how messages are interpreted.

Smith (2009) in her book *Internal Communications*, summarises some typical blocks to internal communication as follows.

- Age
- Gender
- Disability
- Culture (religion)
- Channel distortion
- Overactive grapevine
- Previous history of organisation
- Distrust in management
- Too much of the same thing
- Regional differences

[handwritten note: Problems between Scotland, England and Wales]

3.2 Improving downward communication

Depending on the problem, measures to improve communication may be as follows.

(a) **Encourage, facilitate and reward** communication. Status and functional barriers (particularly to upward and inter-functional communication) can be minimised by improving opportunities for formal and informal networking and feedback.

(b) **Give training and guidance** in communication skills, including consideration of recipients, listening, giving feedback and so on.

(c) **Minimise the potential for misunderstanding** by making people aware of the difficulties arising from differences in culture and perception, and teach them to consider others' viewpoints.

(d) **Adapt technology, systems and procedures** to facilitate communication: making it more effective (clear mobile phone reception), faster (laptops for e-mailing instructions), more consistent (regular reporting routines) and more efficient (reporting by exception).

(e) **Manage conflict and politics** in the organisation, so that no basic unwillingness exists between units.

(f) **Establish communication channels and mechanisms** in all directions: regular staff or briefing meetings, house journal or intranet, quality circles and so on. Upward communication should particularly be encouraged, using mechanisms such as inter-unit meetings, suggestion schemes, 'open door' access to managers and regular performance management feedback sessions.

Communication between superiors and subordinates will be improved when **interpersonal trust** exists. Exactly how this is achieved will depend on the management style of the manager, the attitudes and personality of the individuals involved, and other environmental variables. *Peters and Waterman* advocate 'management by walking around' (MBWA), and **informality in superior/subordinate relationships** as a means of establishing closer links.

3.3 Improving upward communication

Consultation is particularly important, as a mechanism for upward communication.

Consultation is, basically, a process of gathering information and views from another party before making a decision.

(a) **Formal consultation** is required in some business contexts. Employers must consult with elected employee representatives on issues of concern to them and their work, including re-structuring and proposed redundancies.

(b) **Informal consultation** is a managerial style in which the manager invites team members to contribute their views and input to decisions.

3.4 Improving lateral communication

In addition to addressing upward and downward communication between employees and managers, it is also important to improve communications laterally – that is between employees working at similar levels.

The best practices in employee communications are summarised here taken from Doorley & Garcia (2007).

- The best stick to classic PR process: research, planning, communication and evaluation.
- Lead employee communicator has direct access to the senior leadership team.
- Employee communicators are senior by leadership as trusted advisors.
- Communicators articulate a communications strategy that is directly linked to business objectives.
- The communicators inventory, profile and prioritise their employee audiences.

'Further text links and wider reading

*http://www.crainc.com/commlog. **A web log dedicated to the communications strategy and practice inside organisations.***

Quirke, B (2008) Making the Connections: Using Internal Communication to Turn Strategy into Action'
p. 2 ■

4 Identity and identification

4.1 Identity and identification

Identity covered in Chapter 3 (in the sense of the term used by Davies *et al.*: contrasting 'identity' as the perception of the organisation held by *internal* stakeholders, and 'image' as the perception of the organisation held by *external* stakeholders).

van Riel and Fombrun (pp75-77, 2007)suggest that a company's identity matters because it creates identification. Employees who identify strongly with their organisations are more likely to have a supportive attitude towards them (Ashforth and Mael 1989, cited in van Riel and Fombrun, 2007).

It is possible to measure organisational identification using the Rotterdam Organisational Identification Test (ROIT). The ROIT test measures antecedents such **as employee communication**, **perceived organisational prestige**, **job satisfaction**, **goals and values** and **corporate culture**. The instrument measures the impact of these antecedents on employee identification with the company scale. The complete instrument consists of 225 statements respondents are asked to respond on a seven-point Likert scale. A ROIT survey as such facilitates the development of indicators to the degree to which employees identify with the organisation as a whole and provides information on how to improve employee identification by targeting key antecedents at corporate or business unit levels. Empirical research using the ROIT test instrument suggests that employee satisfaction is strongly influenced by two key predictors – employee perceptions of the company's reputation – and by employee's own **job satisfaction**. (van Riel and Fombrun, p. 95, 2007)

As we discussed in Chapter 1 a strong corporate identity is more likely to create i**dentification** on the part of employees, which is in turn likely to:

- Foster a supportive attitude toward the company

- Result in behaviour and decisions by employees that are consistent with the company's objectives

- Encourage a unity of purpose between the company's leaders and its employees (vertical alignment)

- Encourage unity, consistency and coherence between different units of the organisation (horizontal alignment)

- Create an 'authenticity' of values and performance which is projected to stakeholders, potentially resulting in stakeholder identification and alignment.

Identification can vary tremendously across different types of organisations. Religious or ideological organisations have traditionally generated higher degrees of identification than commercial ones. Individuals then making sense of the world through the organisations with which they identify. It is possible for employees who are motivated by the sense-giving initiatives to satisfy a psychological need for self categorisation. That is they can associate themselves with being a valued person as they work for an organisation that they identify with (van Riel and Fombrun, 2007).

Chapter 1 of this Study Text also covered the related issues of loyalty, and image. Refer back to the Corporate Reputation Chain Model and Reicheld's loyalty based cycle of growth. ▮

5 Messages of internal communication

5.1 Informational and emotional dimensions of engagement

Doorley and Garcia (2007) citing Hardaker and Fill (1995) suggest two types of engagement exist. Engagement can be emotional or intellectual and that employee communications function must nurture both of these to be effective. Doorley and Garcia summarise:

'The intellectual engagement initiatives (are) informational and could be considered one-way communication, whereas the emotional engagement initiatives (are) intended to produce dialogue and ambassadorial enthusiasm on the part of employees'.

It is important to recognise that engagement is necessary in order that employees feel and are perceived as part of the corporate brand.

Engaging with employees at both emotional and intellectual levels provides the opportunity for real connectivity between employees and the organisation, thus facilitating the connectiveness between the people and the activities.

5.2 The context of internal communications

There are some other aspects of internal communications that one needs to consider. For example, it is important to have some familiarity with what people actually want to hear and what subjects interest them. The following table, taken from Smith (2008) summarises subjects that are of interest to employees and rates them on a scale of 1–10.

SUBJECTS OF INTEREST TO EMPLOYEES		
Rank	Subject	Scale 1–10
1	Organisational plans for the future	8
2	Job advancement opportunities	7
3	Job-related how-to information	7
4	Productivity improvements	6
5	Personal policies and practices	6
6	How we're doing vs the competition	6
7	How my job fits into the organisation	6
8	How external events affect job	5
9	How profits are used	5
10	Financial results	4

One other useful point here is the four-step process of a conversation, according to Quirke (2008, p177) which includes:

- Content – keep messages simple so that the meaning is clear.

- Context – provide a context within which the communication takes place – so that they can relate to what is being said.

- Conversation – interaction, skills and dialogue are essential to the conversation process.

- Feedback – what feedback is required – something that needs due consideration. Receipt of messages, such as satisfaction or ideas for improvements?

It is also worth considering the breadth of internal communications that takes place. Smith (2008) cites a spectrum of internal communication, originally developed by Russell Grossman, then Head of Internal Communications for the BBC.

(a) **Internal communication spectrum**

    (i) **Day to day communication**

- Organisation news
- Awards, etc
- Housekeeping – pay, appraisals, appointments, operational, etc
- Interpreting external media coverage
- Listening and responding to worries, etc

    (ii) **Change communication**

- Explaining vision, purpose and values
- Helping leaders talk with their teams
- Sharing knowledge and best practice
- Embedding change initiatives
- Listening for reactions
- Understanding responses to change
- Celebrating team success
- Industry and other 'bigger picture' news

    (iii) **Marketing communication**

- Creating passion about product
- Internal marketing activity
- Inviting critique and discussion
- Marketing programmes
- Visual environment (building etc)

5.3 Internal communications and strategic alignment

It is important to understand what it meant by strategic alignment and to understand that **one measure of success is indeed the ability to draw internal support from employees for the company's strategic objectives**. Gagnon and Michael (2003) state that strategic alignment means when employees understand, buy into and are able to enact an organisations' strategic objectives.

'Creating strategic alignment is vital because companies depend on their employees to successfully implement their strategic objectives. Research shows that when employees are supportive towards a company's strategic objectives, they are more likely to make decisions that are consistent with those objectives'.

Strategic alignment is influenced by:

- A company's own internal control systems (citing Strahle *et al.,* 1996)
- The perceive fairness of the process of change (citing Caldwell *et al.,* 2004)
- The employee communication (citing Farmer *et al.,* 1998)

Gagnon & Michael (2003) also identify stimulators of dialogue and empowerment and related indicators of employee support as summarised in the table below. The outcome of these factors is strategic alignment and support for strategic initiatives.

Stimulators of dialogue and empowerment	Indicators of employee support
Management communication	Awareness of strategic initiatives
Internal media	Understanding of strategic initiatives
Cross-departmental communication	Attitude towards strategic initiative
Individual messaging	Capabilities from implementing strategic initiatives
Corporate messaging	
Communication climate	

5.4 Internal marketing

What do we mean by internal marketing? Consider the following definitions:

- Yeoman and Tench (2006) suggest that internal marketing is 'branding from the inside out'.

KEY CONCEPT

concept

Internal marketing involves the marketing to employees and in particular to customer-facing employees. These kind of employees can be referred to as **brand ambassadors** (Davies *et al.,* (2003, p. 199) Customer-facing employees in the service sector need to be familiar with:

- A strong sense of values
- Able to provide consistent standards as expected by customers, meeting the customers' ideal.

In challenging climates of 2009, many different types of organisations including the public sector (such as the NHS) and local councils for example, defined brand values that consumers can emotionally identify with. In order to do this, it is necessary for there to be employee commitment and understanding. Communications of course plays a crucial role in encouraging 'brand champions'. (Yeoman and Tench, (2006, p. 337). In lots of businesses it is possible to identify a number of stages in the customer experience and actually set standards for each of those. Think for example of McDonalds in the US where it would be totally unacceptable to be standing in a queue and waiting to place an order for five minutes. In addition to customer satisfactions, it is also important to consider staff satisfactions and both of these link back to compare image and identity. (Davies *et al.,* 2003, p. 200)

MARKETING AT WORK

application

Action for Children

The following press release was taken from the Action for Children web site, (July 2009) where it describes Action for Children in-house team winning the Internal Communications award for their approach to engaging internal audiences for the charity's re-brand. This was one of the largest re-branding exercises for the voluntary sector and therefore an example of significance.

'Children's charity recognised for award winning internal communications

Children's charity, Action for Children were winners at last night's (Tuesday 7 July) prestigious CIPR Excellence Awards, taking away the Internal Communications Award in recognition of their engagement with internal audiences for the charity's re-brand, from NCH to Action for Children. The charity fought off strong competition from the likes of Coca-Cola Europe and Surrey Police.

The charity's in-house team were tasked with engaging with 7,000 staff and volunteers, many of whom are based in nearly 420 projects throughout the UK, so they would champion the new brand when it launched in September 2008.

The internal campaign, based on an understanding that children are at the heart of the organisation, was built on sound segmentation of the charity's internal audiences and the critical role senior leaders had to play. Interactive tactics were employed for various departments of the vast organisation, including road show workshops across the UK, a live intranet forum with the Director responsible for the re-brand and a 'Switchover Day hotline'.

Rebecca Crosby, Internal Communications Manager, says: 'People make or break brands; therefore it was vital that all internal audiences were fully engaged as NCH became Action for Children. The size of the organisation made this no small task, but by making sure our communications were tailored to different audiences we were able to get people not just understanding the new brand, but really shouting about it! It's really great that our internal communications have been recognised in this way.'

CIPR President Kevin Taylor said: 'From over 900 entries and 145 finalists emerge 26 winners. This just goes to show what a remarkable achievement it is to win one of our rigorously judged CIPR Excellence Awards. The winners have proven themselves to be amongst the best in their industry and have highlighted just what excellent PR work can achieve. The new business, enhanced staff morale, and increased budgets they will surely enjoy are well deserved.'

The award was judged against the criteria of communication with, or involvement of, employees designed to promote corporate objectives in the public or private sector. Competition in the category included Coca- Cola Europe, CPP Group, Eisai Europe, Karian and Box, London Borough of Camden, London Borough of Hillingdon and Surrey Police.

6 Employee relations

6.1 The management of employee relations

Employee relations is the process of communicating within the organisation with employees. Very often in larger organisations this is handled by an internal communications function – or sometimes all or part of the function can also be outsourced to an internal communications agency.

ACTIVITY 5   concept

Look up the following internal communications agencies and read through some examples of their campaigns and understand the types of projects and clients they have and the types of issues they deal with.

http://www.theblueballroom.com

http://www.gatehousegroup.co.uk/about-us.php

Also look at the following blog on internal communications.

http://www.internalcommunications.co.uk/blog.php.

It is important to appreciate that all companies whether they are proactive or not communicate with their employees.

' An effective employee relations function is one that manages internal communications within and between groups in the organisation by systematically addressing structure, flow, content and climate with a view to improving the implementation of the organisations' strategic goals. (van Riel and Fombrun (2007). **Effective and efficient employee relations builds organisational identification and performance.**

6.2 Employee involvement

Earlier in this chapter we have discussed the idea of **shared meaning** and the need for employees to share an organisation's corporate goals to facilitate success. **Staff need to understand a context for communication they receive** – it is not enough to provide information without the means of people being able to 'make sense' of what is being said and relate back to it. Messages can be received but if what is seen in practice is contradictory to that staff will be confused and would have received mixed messages. Earlier on in this chapter, a detailed example of the John Lewis Partnership was discussed as a good example of the involvement of John Lewis staff known as partners in the integral running of the business. Employee involvement forms part of their ethos and way of being and gives the staff not only a voice but a sense of **ownership and an empowerment**.

6.3 Employee voice

Mechanisms have to be built into internal communications in order that feedback can be received and that employees do have a voice. Smith (2009, p. 103) ascertains **that feedback is one of the most important features which need to be built into a communications methods for the organisation and vehicle itself**.

MARKETING AT WORK

application

Involvement is key

One organisation which clearly understands the real power of its hierarchical organisation chart is not at the pinnacle of the triangle but in its base is the Church of England. Alexander Nicoll was the first Head of Internal Communications appointed by the Church's version of the Cabinet Office, the Archbishop's Council.

The Church came to internal communications as an identifiable function rather later, having taken a decision in council in 1998 that it was needed. Attempting the megaphone' approach to communication was felt unlikely to work. Parishes on the ground act rather like regional or local branches of some organisations; they can take it or leave it – a whatever it is.

'The way to describe the role is to imagine us in a maze. You cannot easily re-route the maze but you can trim the hedges so that those in the maze can be more aware of each other. Operational and other benefits accrue to all wherever we work for the Church as a result'. (Smith and Mounter, 2008, p. 103).

Learning objectives	Covered
1 Understand the nature of internal communication programmes	☑ Internal communications programmes in practice
	☑ The significance of employees as a stakeholder audience
	☑ The importance of internal communications and what it might involve – efficiency, shared meaning-connectivity and satisfaction
	☑ The communications process and communications climate under which internal communications takes place
	☑ Consider the various ways that communications can take place – the channels and the nature of those channels and the flow of communications – upward, downward and laterally
2 Formulate approaches to corporate communications that are employee-focused and contextually determined	☑ Consider different approaches to internal communications and what makes it effective
	☑ Consider what effective internal communication might involve
	☑ Contextualise employee communications – think about it from different perspectives
	☑ Familiarisation with barriers to communication and solutions for working with these barriers

1   In what ways has the role of internal communications changed?

2   What considerations should one make when considering communications channels?

3   How do employees prefer to be communicated with?

4   Why is it significant to aim for shared values and shared meaning amongst an organisation and its employees?

5   Why might e-mail and the intranet not be such good choices for communicating with employees?

6   Is it true that internal communications happens irrespective to whether you plan for it or not?

7   What is meant by the term 'grapevine'?

8   What kinds of issues involving organisational change might need to be communicated to employees?

9   Why is it that employees are such an important stakeholder group?

10   What four roles should communications fulfil?

1   **Marks and Spencer**

Marks and Spencer's corporate objectives are detailed below. They are communicated in many different ways for example through their publications such as their How we do business report, the following excerpt is taken from the 2009 report

'For 125 years M&S has been trusted by its customers to offer high quality, great value products. We are 'Your M&S' having grown from a Penny Bazaar stall to become the UK's leading retailer of quality clothing, food and home products. With over 21 million UK customers we are also an expanding international force, now in 43 territories. A team of 78,000 people and over 2,000 suppliers form the bedrock of our business, ensuring our brand will continue to offer Quality, Value, Service, Innovation and Trust'.

M&S communicate through its web site presence, and primarily through its employees. This excerpt succinctly describes its core values and its stance on corporate social responsibility (CSR) building on its core values is communicated through all of business functionality by its staff. In answer to the questions raised by the activity, it is of course the staff who communicate directly with the customers, the staff who are responsible for providing a high standard of customer service and it is the staff on whom M&S are dependent to ensure that customers are happy with the products they buy and the services that they receive so that they become repeat and ultimately loyal customers. Employees then play a critical role in doing business and staying in business. Arguably, the staff are the M&S brand.

2   **Analysis of internal communications**

The analysis of internal communications – your answer here will- of course- vary depending on the organisation and the issues faced at that particular time. For example, your work may relate to major changes going on in the organisation or reflect on the management of a crisis that has occurred and how communications were managed. Or, it may reflect on regular ongoing communications. Have you found the staff to be satisfied and happy? What is the staff view of the organisation and how does that marry up to the corporate view? What type of media are used to communicate with staff – and what proportion of traditional versus social media?

3   **Channels of internal communications**

Your answer here will be very individual and reflective in nature. You should become familiar with the various channels and be critical of the organisation that you are looking at. How much thought has been given to the channels used – what others could be incorporated into the internal communications planning?

4   **Examples of internal communications campaigns and issues**

You will have become more familiar with the wide range of projects and campaigns specialist agencies you might deal with and the broad range of issues internal communications actually involve.

1   The role of internal communications has changed significantly as internal communication is now seen as a strategic business function and part of the corporate reputation for the company. Employees are a company's voice and reputation is dependent on it. Gone are the times of internal communications being simply about communicating information. Employees need a context to the information they are given so it can be understood and meaning is gained from it.

2   When considering communications channels it is first important to consider the message that one is trying to get across and then consider the ways in which the target audiences can be segmented. It is also important to identify what employees preferences are in terms of communication.

3   Employees prefer face-to-face communication over all other communication methods.

4   If employees shared values and share meaning with the organisation they work for they then make meaning from what information they have been given as they can contextualise it.

5   E-mail and the intranet would not be such good choices for communicating with employees because they are much more 'cut and dry' and would not for example, be a good choice for communicating bad news (such as elements of change, redundancies, profit loss and cost savings, etc).

6   Yes, this is true. Communications within an organisation will take place irrespective of whether you plan for it or not. The internal grapevine – the informal means of communicating information can be used to one's advantage.

7   Informal communications often takes place through the 'grapevine' or informal network.

8   The main types of issues that relate to change and might need discussing with employees includes redundancies, restructuring, reorganisation, new business strategy or new business priorities.

9   Employees are an important stakeholder group because they are the main point of contact with customers and are an organisation's ambassadors.

10   Internal communications should fulfil the following roles: efficiency, shared meaning, connectivity and satisfaction.

Ashforth. B.E> and Mael, F. (1989) Social identity and the organisation, Academy or Management Review, 14 (1) 20-39

BT Group company profile (accessed 11 June 2009) http://www.btplc.com/Thegroup/Ourcompany/Companyprofile/index.htm

Caldwell, S.D., Herold, D.M., and Fedor, D.B. (2004) Towards an understanding of the relationships between organisational change, individual differences and changes in person-environment fit: a cross-level study, Journal of Applied Psychology, 89: 868-882

Christensen, LT, Morsing, M & Cheney, G (2008) Corporate Communications: Conventions, Complexity and Critique. London: Sage Publications Ltd

Collins English Dictionary (2006), HarperCollins Publishers

Davies G, Chun R, Da Silva RV & Roper S (2003) Corporate Reputation and Competitiveness. Abingdon, Oxon: Routledge

Doorley, J & Garcia, HF (2007) Reputation Management: The Key to Successful Public Relations and Corporate Communications New York: Routledge

Farmer, B.A., Slater, J.W. and Wright, K.S. (1998) The role of communications in achieving shared vision under new organisational leadership, Journal of Public Relations Research, 10 (4): 219-235

Fill, C (2002) Marketing Communications: Contexts, Strategies and Applications (3rd Ed). Harlow, Essex: Pearson Education Limited

Gagnon, M and Michael, J. (2003) Employee strategic alignment at a wood manufacturer: an exploratory analysis using lean manufacturing, Forest Products Journal, 53 (10), 24-29

Gouge, P (2006) Employee Research: How to Increase Employee Involvement Through Consultation. London: Market Research in Practice Series, Kogan Page Limited

Hardaker,S. & Fill, C. (Winter 1995) Corporate Reputation Review

HR Excellence Awards(2009), Most Effective Use of Internal Communications, www.hrmagazine.co.uk/news/916270/-Excellence-Awards-2009

John Lewis Partnership (accessed 13 June 2009) The Partnership Spirit http://www.johnlewispartnership.co.uk/Display.aspx?&MasterId=f7a66235-2266-45d0-92dd-5b61e878eb31&NavigationId=595

Live BBC News Channel (11 February 2009) Bank says UK in 'deep recession' http://news.bbc.co.uk/1/hi/business/7883255.stm

Live BBC News Channel (14 May 2009) BT to shed a further 15,000 jobs http://news.bbc.co.uk/1/hi/business/8049276.stm

Live BBC News Channel (7 April 2009) RBS to cut a further 9,000 jobs http://news.bbc.co.uk/1/hi/scotland/7987659.stm

Live BBC News Channel (29 May 2009) Ex-Nortel staff protest over cuts http://news.bbc.co.uk/1/hi/england/8074472.stm

Mounter, P. In Gregory, A. (2004) Public Relations in Practice, Kogan Page Ltd

PR Week (28 April 2009), The Future of Internal Communications , http://www.prweek.com/uk/news/901700/future-internal-communications

Quirke, B. (2008) Making the Connections: Using Internal Communication to Turn Strategy into Action (2nd Ed) Aldershot, Hampshire: Gower Publishing Limited

Riel, CBM Van & Fombrun, CJ (2007) Essentials of Corporate Communication: Implementing Practices for Effective Reputation Management. Abingdon, Oxon: Routledge

Smith, L. (2008) Effective Internal Communication (2nd Ed) London : CIPR Practice Series, Kogan Page Limited

Strahle, W.M., Spiro, R. L. And Acito, F. (1996) Marketing and sales: strategic alignment and functional implementation, Journal of Personal Selling and Sales Management, 16 (winter): 1-20

Tench, R & Yeomans, L (2006) Exploring Public Relations. Harlow, Essex: Pearson Education Limited

Theaker, A (2009) The Public Relations Handbook (3rd Ed) Canada and USA : Routledge

The Sunday Times Section 3 Business (14 June 2009) Me and my 69,000 partners: page 7

The BT Story (12 March 2009) http://www.btplc.com/Thegroup/Ourcompany/Companyprofile/TheBTstory/BTStory120309.pdf

Your M & S (2009) How we do business report: Doing the Right Thing http://corporate.marksandspencer.com/file.axd?pointerid=f3ccae91d1d348ff8f523ab8afe9d8a8&versionid=fbb46819901a428ca70ecf5a44aa8ddc (accessed 13 June 2009)

http://news.bbc.co.uk/1/hi/business/7883255.stm

http://news.bbc.co.uk/1/hi/business/8049276.stm

http://news.bbc.co.uk/1/hi/scotland/7987659.stm

http://news.bbc.co.uk/1/hi/england/8074472.stm

http://www.btplc.com/Thegroup/Ourcompany/Companyprofile/TheBTstory/BTStory120309.pdf

http://www.btplc.com/Thegroup/Ourcompany/Companyprofile/index.htm

PR Week (28 April 2009), The Future of Internal Communications , http://www.prweek.com/uk/news/901700/future-internl-communications/

http://www.johnlewispartnership.co.uk/Display.aspx?&MasterId=869aa67c-f6e6-42b4-98ca-0a1b16d906bb&NavigationId=547

Chapter 11
Defending reputation

Topic list

1   Reputational risk
2   Issues management
3   Managing pressure groups
4   Crisis communication

Introduction

In all the preceding chapters, we have dealt mainly with the means by which organisations can create and develop positive reputations with their stakeholder audiences. In this chapter, we recognise the value of the old sayings: that reputations are hard to win and easy to lose; and that they are built in a year and lost in a moment. The maintenance and defence of reputation is a form of risk management – because loss or damage to reputation is a significant risk event (with significant costs) for an organisation.

In section 1, we give an overview of reputation management as risk management, and appraise the nature of reputational risk.

In section 2, we explore the nature and processes of issues management, by which an organisation can proactively plan to manage the perceptions of stakeholders on identified issues of concern and potential reputational risk. As a related area, we look in section 3 at how the organisation can manage its relationship and communication with pressure, interest and advocacy groups who may have a particular interest (and influence) in relation to certain issues.

Issues management seeks to identify and resolve potential stakeholder concerns before they become 'crises': events with the power to significantly damage corporate image and reputation. Inevitably, however, crises happen – and it is vitally important for the organisation to have communication plans in place to handle them. Experience suggests that reputational damage only escalates if 'no-one is available to comment', or if unprepared or inconsistent messages are given out. In section 4, we discuss the key elements of effective crisis communication, and how crisis communication plans can be evaluated.

Syllabus-linked learning objectives

By the end of the chapter you will be able to:

Learning objectives	Syllabus link
1 Evaluate reputational risk	3.2.6
2 Explain the principles and practice of issues management	3.2.6
3 Explain the nature, role and processes of crisis management and associated communication	3.2.6

1 Reputational risk

Corporate reputations, once established, are constantly in danger of being eroded, undermined, damaged or destroyed. Regester & Larkin (2008, p. 2) argue that: 'Threats to reputation – whether real or perceived – can destroy, literally in hours or days, an image or brand developed and invested in over decades. These threats need to be anticipated, understood and planned for.'

KEY CONCEPT

concept

Risk may be defined as the probability of an unwanted outcome happening. Risk is normally assessed as a combination of the probability of the event (the likeliness of its happening) and the severity of any foreseeable adverse consequences or outcomes arising from it. A **risk event** is the actual occurrence of an envisaged risk.

The recognition of reputational risk has been one of the main drivers behind the growth in importance of **risk management** as a discipline. In the last two decades, the value of intangible assets (including brand assets and reputational capital) has grown in recognition and importance. As we saw in Chapter 5, the market value of organisations can significantly exceed their book value, based on the long-term earning potential of their brand names and reputations. Meanwhile, as products and services have become less differentiated, reputation is recognised as a key source of competitive advantage. The value of reputational assets – like any other assets of an organisation – must be protected. In fact, a recent survey on risk management by the Economic Intelligence Unit placed reputational risk (52%) above regulatory risk (41%) and human capital risk (41%) as a corporate risk management priority (www.theregister.co.uk).

1.1 Sources of reputational risk

Risks to reputation may arise from many sources, both internal and external:

- Loss of financial performance and profitability; collapse in share price; downward revision of profits or dividends; or downward restatements of the company's financial position

- Corporate governance and quality of management; allegations of fraud (eg misrepresentation of the company's financial position) or mismanagement

- Social, ethical and environmental performance (by the organisation and by its business partners and allies)

- Employees and corporate culture (corporate behaviour)

- Failure to comply with legislation and regulation (compliance risk)

- Product/service failures leading to reputational erosion or crisis (eg product recalls)

- Poor handling of crises (poor service recovery; lack of communication, transparency or accountability)

- Negative uncontrolled communications (media coverage, internet discussion, internal grapevine, external rumour mill)

- Association with other entities (industry, country of origin, individuals, supply and distribution partners, co-branded allies) whose reputations are affected by any of the above.

ACTIVITY 1

application

Just as a thought-starter: what could 'go wrong' in your organisation that might damage its image and reputation? What critical incidents highlight potential risks? What incidents have caused reputational damage to your organisation – and other similar organisations – in the past?

1.2 Risk management

concept

Risk management is 'the process whereby organisations methodically address the risks attaching to their activities with the goal of achieving sustained benefit within each activity and across the portfolio of all activities'

(Institute of Risk Management)

The process of risk management (Sadgrove, 2005) is often portrayed as a cycle.

The risk management cycle

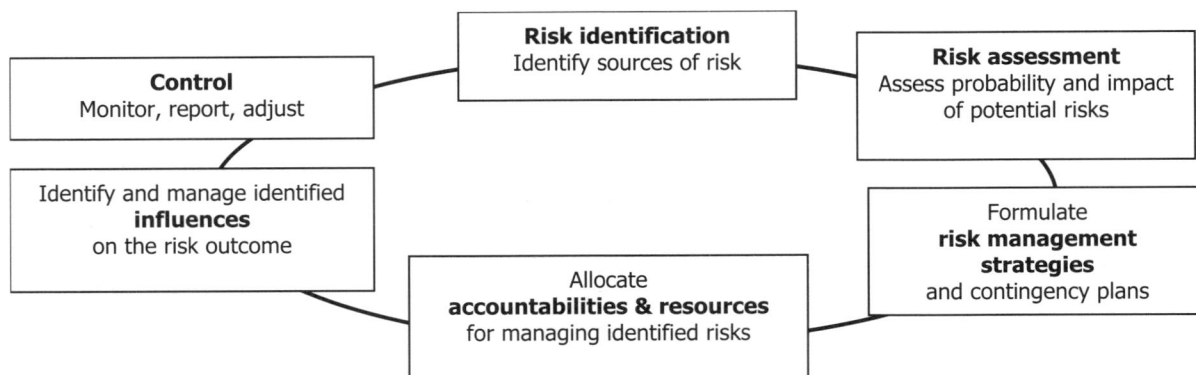

Control
Monitor, report, adjust

Risk identification
Identify sources of risk

Risk assessment
Assess probability and impact of potential risks

Identify and manage identified **influences** on the risk outcome

Allocate **accountabilities & resources** for managing identified risks

Formulate **risk management strategies** and contingency plans

1.2.1 Risk identification

Risk identification is the process of seeking to identify potential problems or areas of uncertainty: in other words, asking **'what could go wrong**?'.

This may be done by environmental scanning and corporate appraisal (PESTEL and SWOT analysis); formal risk assessments; monitoring risk events in benchmark organisations; critical incident investigations and process audits; monitoring stakeholder feedback and perceptions (brainstorming, surveys, workshops etc).

This should be an ongoing process, as the organisation's risk profile may continually change, presenting new risks or turning slight risks into potential crises.

1.2.2 Risk assessment

Risk assessment (or evaluation) is the appraisal of the probability and significance of identified potential risk events, as a basis for formulating strategies to accept, avoid or mitigate the risk: in other words, asking **'how likely is it and how bad could it be**?'

Risk can be quantified using the formula: Risk = Likelihood x Impact

- **Risk likelihood** is the probability of occurrence, given the nature of the risk and current risk management practices. This may be expressed as a number between 0 (no chance) and 1 (certainty) or as a percentage (100% = certainty) or as a score (1–10) or rating (Low–Medium–High). A low likelihood rating means that the risk event is unlikely to occur, given its nature – and the current risk management practices in place. A high likelihood rating means that the risk is likely to occur – *despite* any risk management practices that are in place.

  The more likely the risk event is to occur, the higher the overall level of risk, and the higher priority risk management will be.

- **Risk impact/consequence** is the likely loss/cost to the organisation or the likely level of impact on the organisation's ability to fulfil its objectives. The severity and tolerability of impacts may be quantified as estimated cost or loss in time, money or other resources; scored (1–10), or rated as Low–Medium–High (or Insignificant, Minor, Serious or Catastrophic: Sadgrove, 2005).

The costs of reputational crises will be discussed below, but downside risk impacts may include: loss of revenue, increase in costs, fall in share price, loss of market share, lost productivity (from poor staff morale), legal costs/penalties for non-compliance, disruption to stakeholder relations, and so on – quite apart from the operational and human costs of underlying risk events such as accident, fire or other disasters.

Even if assessed as improbable, high-impact events should be the subject of detailed contingency and recovery planning (including crisis communication planning), so that the organisation can respond to the event – if it occurs – in an informed manner.

Quantifying the risk allows the organisation to prioritise risk management resources to meet the most severe risks, and to set defined risk thresholds at which risk mitigation (eg issues management) action will be triggered. Risk assessment is therefore a foundation for determining appropriate risk management strategies.

Risk assessment grid

	Significant	Contingency planning	Manage and monitor risks	Risk management priority
Impact	Moderate	Risk may be accepted: monitor	Management effort worthwhile	Management effort required
	Minor	Risk may be accepted	Accept risk: monitor	Manage and monitor risk
		Low	*Medium*	*High*
			Likelihood	

ACTIVITY 2   application   [30%]

Select any one of the risks you identified in Activity 1 and attempt to quantify (a) its likelihood and (b) its impact and therefore (c) its overall risk. You may brainstorm your ideas, or gather input from others. If you have access to existing risk assessments prepared by your organisation, refer to them: how up-to-date and accurate are they, in your estimation?

1.2.3 Risk mitigation strategies

Risk management strategies (the answer to the question '**what can we do about it**?') are often classified as the Four Ts:

- **Tolerate** (or accept) the risk: if the assessed likelihood or impact of the risk (before or after mitigating action) is negligible.

- **Transfer** or spread the risk: eg by taking out insurance cover (not generally an adequate response in itself to reputational risk, but a necessary cover for operational and financial damage) or not putting all strategic/investment/reputational eggs in one basket.

- **Terminate** (or avoid) the risk: if the risk associated with a particular activity is too great, and cannot be reduced, the activity should not be undertaken.

- **Treat** (or mitigate) the risk: take active steps to manage the risk in such a way as to reduce or minimise its likelihood or potential impact, or both.

Risks may be mitigated (Sadgrove, 2005) using:

- **Preventive controls**: designed to limit the possibility of a negative outcome (eg safety procedures, maintenance schedules, internal financial controls, monitoring of supplier ethics)

- **Directive controls**: designed to ensure that a particular positive outcome is achieved (eg health and safety regulations, codes of conduct, media relations protocols)

- **Detective controls**: designed to identify and evaluate risk events, for mitigation planning (eg accident reporting, supplier monitoring, critical incident reporting and analysis, gathering stakeholder feedback, media monitoring, issues management planning)

- **Corrective controls**: designed to correct undesirable outcomes (eg contingency plans, crisis management and communication plans, business recovery plans).

In any case, the organisation will need to make **contingency plans** with regard to high-impact risks: alternative courses of action, workarounds and fallback positions (**'What will we do if**...?'). This is a key component of crisis management, as we shall see later in the chapter.

1.2.4 Risk monitoring, reporting and review

The monitoring and reporting of risks – and risk events – is an important part of the risk management process, in order to:

- Ascertain whether the organisation's risk profile and exposure is changing, and identify newly emerging or escalating risks

- Gain assurance that the organisation's risk management processes are effective, by demonstrating effective avoidance or mitigation of risks

- Indicate how the organisation's risk management processes need adjustment, by highlighting shortcomings such as: failure to identify risks, failure to assess the risk accurately, failure to mitigate the risk, failure of contingency plans/responses and so on.

Risk reporting is the process whereby the organisation reports and analyses risk events: in other words, **'What happened, and what can we learn**?'. This is important to gather feedback for process improvement and future risk identification and assessment.

MARKETING AT WORK   application

Coca-Cola South Pacific was recently forced by the Australian Competition and Consumer Commission to take out the following full-page advertisement in the Australian national press, following complaints about a major advertising campaign.

Coca-Cola: Setting the Record Straight.

We recently published some 'myth busting' advertisements featuring [Australian celebrity] Kerry Armstrong for Coca-Cola. The feedback we received from the Australian Competition and Consumer Commission and others is that the overall impression we created by those ads may have been misleading. What we meant to convey is that there can be a place for Coca-Cola in a balanced, sensible diet and active lifestyle.

We certainly did not intend our messages to be misleading or to convey an impression that Coca-Cola cannot contribute to weight or to cavities and other dental problems. We have listened to the feedback we received and want to set the record straight.

We said it was a 'myth' that Coca-Cola 'makes you fat.' The fact is: all kilojoules count. We did not mean to suggest that Coca-Cola does not contribute kilojoules to your diet. People consume many different foods and beverages, so no one single food or beverage alone is responsible for obesity or people being overweight. But all kilojoules count, whatever food or beverage they come from, including kilojoules from Coca-Cola... If you would like to read more about nutrition, balance, moderation and the importance of an active lifestyle, see the Australian Government's Healthy Weight web site: www.healthyactive.gov.au and click on 'healthy weight'.

We said it was a 'myth' that Coca-Cola 'rots your teeth'. The fact is: All products containing sugar and food acid have the potential to contribute to the risk of tooth decay and erosion. Coca-Cola contains sugar and food acid as do other foods and beverages, such as juices and juice beverages... All foods and beverages containing food acid have the potential to contribute to the risk of dental erosion. However, through good dental hygiene and other health practices, you can help reduce the risk of tooth decay and erosion. You may also want to read some of the recommendations of the Australian Dental Association posted in articles on www.dentalhealthweek.com.au/parents.htm.

We said that these two 'myths' about Coca-Cola were 'busted'. The fact is: we realise we should have been clearer. This process has reinforced in our minds that, even where advertising messages are well-intentioned, it is important to consider the overall impression that the messages may convey.

Finally, we said that 250ml of Diet Coca-Cola contains half the amount of caffeine as in 250ml of tea. We made an error – 250ml of Diet Coca-Cola contains about 2/3 the amount of caffeine as in the same amount of tea brewed from leaf or tea bag. If you would like to read more about levels of caffeine in our Cola drinks and that in tea and coffee, go to www.makeeverydropmatter.com.au

(This ad has been paid for and placed by Coca-Cola South Pacific as part of a court enforceable undertaking given to the Australian Competition and Consumer Commission.)

For reflection: How damaging might this incident have been to Coca-Cola's reputation, and why? How, and how effectively, does it attempt to minimise and repair the damage through the above advertisement? What might Coca-Cola learn from this incident?

1.3 Managing reputational risk

Reputational risk management therefore requires a clear focus on a wide range of issues.

- Clear corporate vision, values and principles ('what we stand for and are prepared to be held responsible for'). Augustine (2000) argues that: 'Organisations that have thought through what they stand for well in advance of a crisis are those that manage crises best. When all seems to be crashing down around them, they have principles to fall back on.' Clearly expressed values and principles also act as directive controls, making it more likely that employees will behave in reputation-consistent ways.

- Sound risk management practices, with consistent enforcement of controls on governance, business and legal compliance (eg internal controls, codes of conduct, policies clearly stating the organisation's expectations of employee and supply chain members).

- Proactive communication with all stakeholder groups, in order to understand their expectations, information requirements, sensitivities to particular issues and perceptions of the organisation. (We discuss this process as 'issues management' in the following section of this chapter.)

- A robust and dynamic risk management system, with continuous monitoring and assessment of reputational threats, and early warning of developing issues.

- An open and trusting organisation culture and communication climate, facilitating the flow of risk/problem information to decision-makers (without fear of 'shooting the messenger'), minimising the risk of potentially damaging 'cover-ups', and supporting organisational learning from mistakes.

- An organisation culture which values character, caring and competence – and is therefore less likely to respond with indifference or arrogance to stakeholder concerns (often the point at which issues turn into crises...)

- Ensuring that corporate social responsibility values, in particular, are communicated, implemented and monitored both within the organisation and in its supply, distribution and alliance networks.

- Establishing and regularly updating crisis management plans, defining specific decision-making and communication responsibilities.

- This should be part of an integrated approach to risk management throughout the organisation. Reputation may be regarded as a source of risk in its own right – but it is also a consequence of other risk events occurring (such as technology failure, fraud, sabotage, natural disaster, human error and so on). The critical point is to ensure that all major risks are systematically identified, monitored and assessed, and that appropriate action is taken to manage them.

It is also worth noting that risk perception is an important factor in reputation management not just for the organisation, but also for its *stakeholders*. '**Public perception of risk** has become a constant and recurring threat to reputation... In many Western societies today, we are living in an environment of unprecedented risk aversion and perceived lack of trust....

Understanding and communicating effectively around risk perception can help to reduce conflict and gain support and trust – critical attributes in securing and maintaining customer, investor and employee loyalty.' (Regester & Larkin, 2008, p. 2)

✏️ ACTIVITY 3 ··········· evaluation 🂡

Appraise the risk management processes of your own organisation.

- Do they include the identification, assessment and management of reputational risk?
- To whom do they allocate responsibility for monitoring and managing reputational risk?
- Does the organisation take steps to learn from risk incidents, to improve its risk management processes?

Review the risk register kept by your organisation (if any).

---

2 Issues management

2.1 What is an issue?

🔑 KEY CONCEPT ··········· concept 🂡

An **issue** may be defined as:

- Something arising 'as a consequence of some action taken, or proposed to be taken, by one or more parties which may result in private negotiation and adjustment, civil or criminal litigation, or it can become a matter of public policy through legislative or regulatory action'. (Hainsworth & Meng, 1988)

- 'An unsettled matter which is ready for decision.' (Jones & Chase, 1979)

- 'A condition or event, either internal or external to the organisation, that if it continues will have a significant effect on the functioning or performance of the organisation or on its future interests.' (Regester & Larkin, 2008)

Broadly speaking, an issue is a potential point of conflict between an organisation and one or more of its stakeholders. Some examples of issues which might trigger issues management processes in an organisation include: proposals for new legislation, a competitor initiative, facts, opinions or claims published in the media or other channels, which potentially cast the organisation or its activities in a bad light, and the performance or behaviour of the organisation (or groups to which it is linked) which runs counter to prevailing or emerging social values.

A range of *publics* 'make' issues: employees, the general public, government, media and pressure/interest groups. As we have argued throughout this Study Text, reputations are in the eye of the beholder. Organisations must be sensitive to the sensitivities of their stakeholders: anticipating what they perceive to be issues of concern or to be potential problems.

- According to ongoing consumer attitude monitoring by research firm Populus (www.populuslimited.com), three-quarters of the UK population claims to weigh up a company's reputation before buying its products or services, and nearly three in five say they actively avoid purchasing from certain companies because of questions they have about their social, environmental or ethical track record.

- Increasingly sophisticated awareness campaigns from a wide range of pressure and advocacy groups have contributed to heightened public sensitivity to a range of environmental and social issues, particularly targeting corporate activities.

- ICT-supported social networking (eg via internet sites such as FaceBook and MySpace) and content-sharing (eg via Wikipedia and YouTube) have had a significant effect on how 'issues' are defined and disseminated.

The effect of these developments has been to shift the power of 'voice' in the formation of corporate reputations away from companies themselves and towards their stakeholders... As new opinion leaders emerge via the internet, reducing the share of voice of corporations, reputation risk management is becoming defined increasingly to be external stakeholder perceptions of what they believe corporations should say and do, rather than by what a company says and does (Griffin, 2007).

KEY CONCEPT

concept

Issues management is a proactive process of monitoring potential controversies or public relations problems in relation to the business, and initiating communication programmes to manage public perceptions about them. It has been defined as:

- 'A tool which companies can use to identify, analyse and manage emerging issues (in a populist society experiencing discontinuous change) and respond to them before they become public knowledge.' (Jones and Chase, 1979)

- 'A management activity intended to bring some control to the impact caused by the discontinuity of the environment.' (Hainsworth & Meng, 1988)

- The 'set of organisational procedures, routines, personnel and processes devoted to perceiving, analysing and responding to strategic issues'. (Dutton & Ottensmeyer, 1987).

Ancient Chinese sage Lao Tzu wrote: 'Plan for what is difficult when it is most easy; do what is great while it is small'. This could be the motto for issues management.

Issues management endeavours not just to identify and fight public perception 'fires' as they arise, but to: proactively initiate dialogue with the public and pressure/interest groups to identify potential sensitivities and issues of concern; express the organisation's general responsibility and openness, educate stakeholders in the organisation's position and efforts on issues, and establish networks of goodwill and support (a 'reservoir of goodwill' which may be drawn on when an issue or crisis arises). Issues management is thus more proactive than crisis management.

ACTIVITY 4

application

What would you anticipate to be the benefits for an organisation of implementing effective issues management processes and techniques?

2.2 The issue life cycle (Hainsworth & Meng)

An issue originates as an idea that has potential impact on an organisation or public and may result in action that brings about increased awareness and/or reaction on the part of other organisations or publics (Hainsworth, 1990). In a model developed by Hainsworth & Meng (1988), this process can be described as the 'life cycle' of an issue. An issue can fail (or be resolved) at any point in the process, but issues that continue to mature appear to evolve consistently through four basic stages.

Stage	Status of the issue	Stage description	Implications
Origin	**Potential** issue: a condition or event which may turn into something of importance, but has not yet attracted significant expert or public attention. *Example:* preliminary research findings suggesting that smoking is damaging to health.	Issues emerge from developing political, economic or social trends, which give significance to problems, situations or events, and arouse concern in stakeholder groups. They only begin to gain definition when an organisation or group becomes aware of a problem, and plans to do something that potentially impacts on another organisation or group	Organisations must scan the environment for early identification of trends and potential points of conflict: this is the optimal opportunity to influence them – by creating misconceptions, promoting the organisation's position, heading off media coverage,

Stage	Status of the issue	Stage description	Implications
		(Grunig & Hunt, 1984): at this point, positions begin to form, and the potential for conflict emerges.	or eliminating the problem – before they attract significant attention.
Mediation and amplification	**Emerging** issue *Example:* consumer and medical groups promoting the adverse health effects of smoking, and attracting media attention.	Increasing **awareness** of the issue, as affected stakeholders network and seek support. The issue first gets coverage in relevant specialist media – and then attracts the attention of the mass media: from this point, momentum builds, and the issue is amplified into a public issue (Hainsworth, 1990). Increasing **pressure** on the organisation to accept and respond to the issue, usually as a result of one or more stakeholder groups trying to push or legitimise the issue (Meng, 1992).	There is still an opportunity for the organisation proactively to intervene to prevent the issue from developing further (if negative) and to shape the media coverage and interpretation of the issue, via intentional media relations and communications.
Organisation	**Current** issue: the various parties recognise its full importance and become actively involved. *Example:* the organisation of groups to lobby for anti-smoking legislation. **Crisis** issue: significant impact on the organisation's reputation and/or operations. *Example:* class action lawsuits against tobacco companies, or restriction of tobacco advertising.	Mediation has solidified positions: both sides seek to resolve the problem, often uniting to do something about it. As groups seek to communicate their positions, conflict becomes publicly visible, which may push the issue into the realm of public policy (Hainsworth, *op cit*) and motivate influential leaders to join the debate. Current issues can swiftly escalate into crisis, where some form of intervention is made to resolve the situation which significantly damages the organisation's operations or reputation.	Once the issue has reached current – and, even more, crisis – stage, the organisation's options and potential to influence the progress of the issue are severely limited, due to strong pressure and the need to 'fight fires' on multiple fronts
Resolution	**Dormant** issue: the issue is resolved. *Example:* pervasive anti-smoking legislation	Eventually, there is maximum pressure on the organisation to accept stakeholder demands, or to resolve the problem in some explicit way. Formal constraints (eg legal decision, regulation or legislation, or negotiated settlement) may be imposed. The conflict is resolved, media and pressure group focus falls away, and the issue becomes 'dormant'.	

The Hainsworth-Meng model can thus be depicted as follows.

The issue lifecycle (Hainsworth & Meng, 1988)

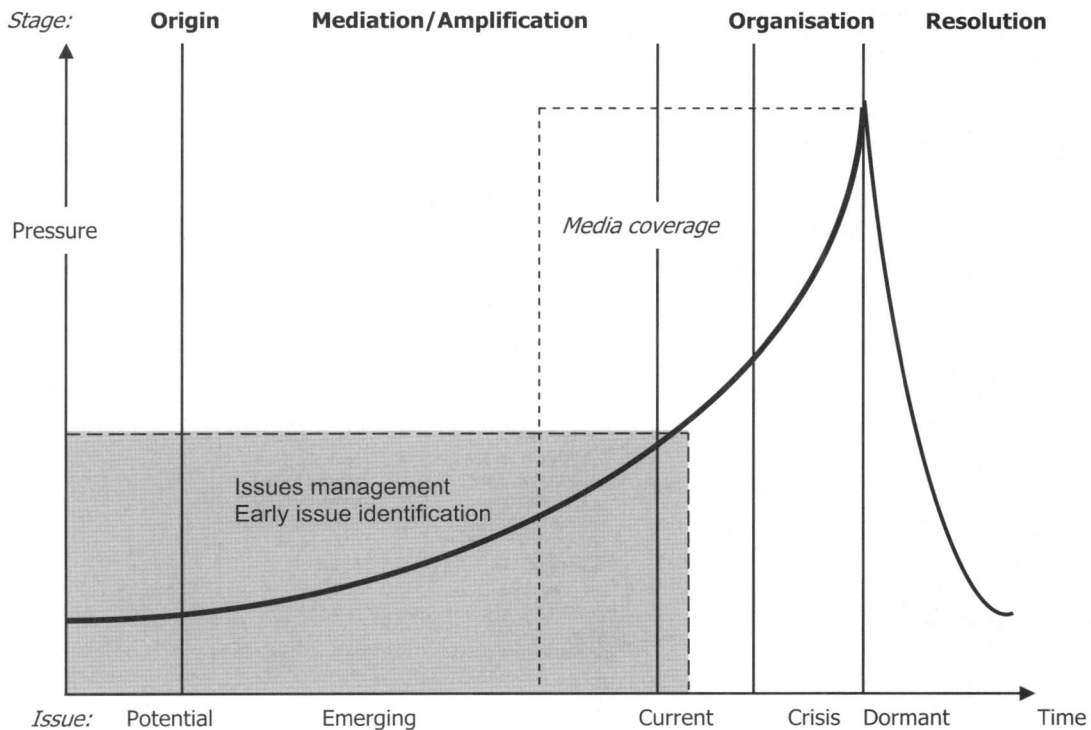

| *Stage:* | **Origin** | **Mediation/Amplification** | | **Organisation** | **Resolution** |

Pressure

Media coverage

Issues management
Early issue identification

| *Issue:* | Potential | Emerging | Current | Crisis | Dormant | Time |

MARKETING AT WORK

application

In the four years up to 1995, **Shell UK** evaluated a number of options to dispose of one of its floating storage/loading buoys, the Brent Spar, located off the north-east coast of Scotland. Numerous independent environmental and risk assessment studies (the principal findings of which were released for public consultation) had convinced the company that the best means of scrapping the vessel was to sink it in the deep waters of the Atlantic Ocean. It had also convinced the British government – and scrupulously observed all national and international legal and regulatory requirements.

However, environmental pressure group **Greenpeace** disagreed, seeing Brent Spar as a test case for environmental pollution. Activists boarded the vessel and occupied it, televising the dramatic confrontation as Shell attempted to 'recapture' the vessel. Despite Shell's logical and scientifically-supported counter-arguments that its solution was in fact the most environmentally sound, the pressure group captured the media agenda and public emotion – partly (as it later admitted) by knowingly exaggerating the environmental risks. Shell later admitted that it had underestimated the emotional dimension of public opinion.

The issue escalated into public demonstrations, consumer boycotts, diplomatic protests (many of the activists were from Germany) and even attacks on Shell petrol stations. Shell UK came under pressure from its European colleagues to abandon its plans – and did so.

Davies *et al.* (2003) summarise the lessons as follows: 'Pressure groups are powerful. They specialise in emphasising the emotional aspects of an issue, leaving company management floundering with their more factual platform. Firms have learnt that it is sometimes better to listen to activist groups and to keep them informed on controversial issues. At least managers will know what the arguments are that will be used against them. It is even possible that a compromise solution can be worked out to ensure that media coverage is less controversial.'

Regester & Larkin (2008, p. 105) illustrate the event, as an issue lifecycle, as follows:

The Brent Spar issue lifecycle

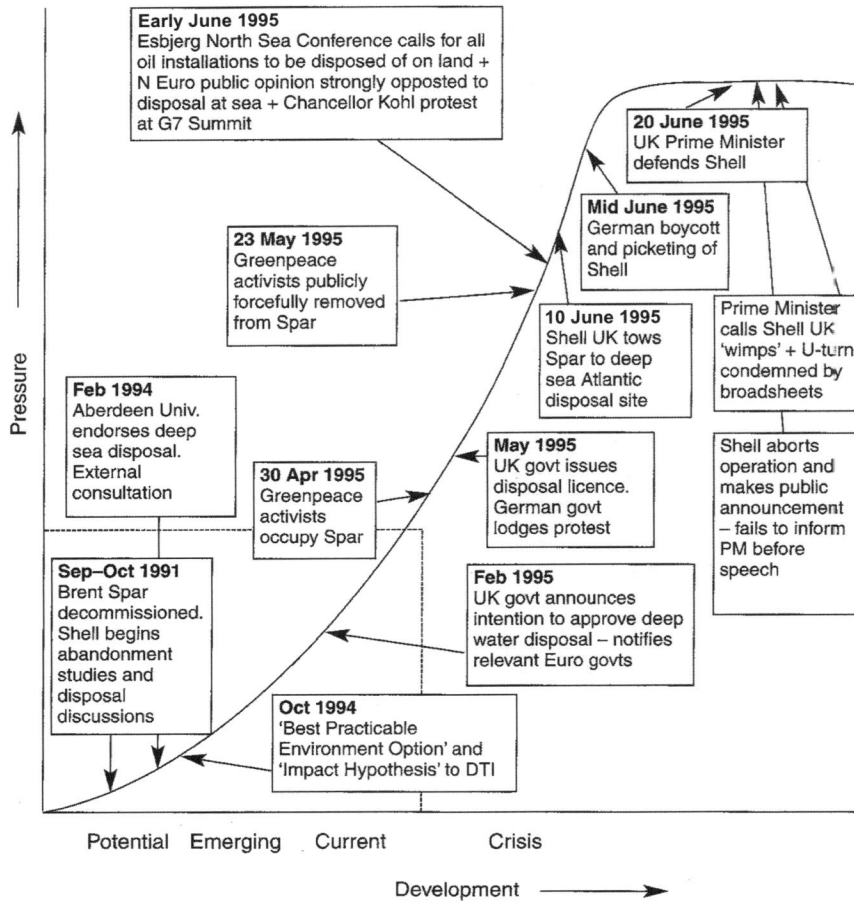

The Brent Spar issue lifecycle diagram. Vertical axis: Pressure. Horizontal axis: Development — Potential, Emerging, Current, Crisis.

Early June 1995
Esbjerg North Sea Conference calls for all oil installations to be disposed of on land + N Euro public opinion strongly opposed to disposal at sea + Chancellor Kohl protest at G7 Summit

20 June 1995
UK Prime Minister defends Shell

Mid June 1995
German boycott and picketing of Shell

23 May 1995
Greenpeace activists publicly forcefully removed from Spar

10 June 1995
Shell UK tows Spar to deep sea Atlantic disposal site

Prime Minister calls Shell UK 'wimps' + U-turn condemned by broadsheets

Feb 1994
Aberdeen Univ. endorses deep sea disposal. External consultation

30 Apr 1995
Greenpeace activists occupy Spar

May 1995
UK govt issues disposal licence. German govt lodges protest

Shell aborts operation and makes public announcement – fails to inform PM before speech

Sep–Oct 1991
Brent Spar decommissioned. Shell begins abandonment studies and disposal discussions

Feb 1995
UK govt announces intention to approve deep water disposal – notifies relevant Euro govts

Oct 1994
'Best Practicable Environment Option' and 'Impact Hypothesis' to DTI

✏️ **ACTIVITY 5**   format 🂡 10%

Select an issue or crisis faced by your own organisation (or a detailed case study you have come across in your reading), and see if you can plot the issues evolution using a lifecycle graph such as the one above. Include the dotted-line box in the bottom left-hand corner of the diagram, illustrating the window of opportunity for early detection and issues management, and reflect on the point at which the issue escalated beyond that opportunity into crisis. What (if anything) could the organisation have done to prevent or mitigate the crisis stage?

📚 *For a series of short case studies illustrating the issues life cycle – including the cases of Merck's Vioxx drug, Monsanto's attempted introduction of genetically modified foods, and Dell's massive laptop recall in 2006 – see:*

• *Regester & Larkin:* **Risk Issues and Crisis Management in Public Relations** *(2008, Kogan Page):* *Chapter 3 'Planning an issues management programme – an issues management model'.* ∎

2.3 Issues management models

2.3.1 van Riel & Fombrun

The syllabus terminology refers to the model briefly proposed by *van Riel & Fombrun (2007, p. 203)*, suggesting that issues management consists of three principal activities:

- **Detection** of issues that can potentially become a threat to the organisation. The earlier an organisation identifies issues which pose significant risk, the more able it will be to limit potential reputational damage, by dealing with events before they escalate to crisis. We will look at 'early warning systems' below.

- **Marshalling** of internal resources and forces to understand and prepare to address the issue.

- **Strategy**: the development of an issues management strategy, enabling the organisation to respond to the issue if and when it becomes necessary to do so. For each issue that is identified and prioritised (as a significant risk), the issues management team will develop a plan to (a) analyse the issue, (b) allocate resources to lessening its likelihood or impact, and (c) engage stakeholder support. There are various models for developing such strategies, and we will discuss these below.

Mitroff (1988, cited in Davies *et al.*, 2003, p .102) adds a fourth activity: **learning from the experience**, so that the organisation can be better prepared for the next issue or crisis. Mitroff's version of the model can therefore be depicted as follows.

Phases in issues/crisis management (Mitroff)

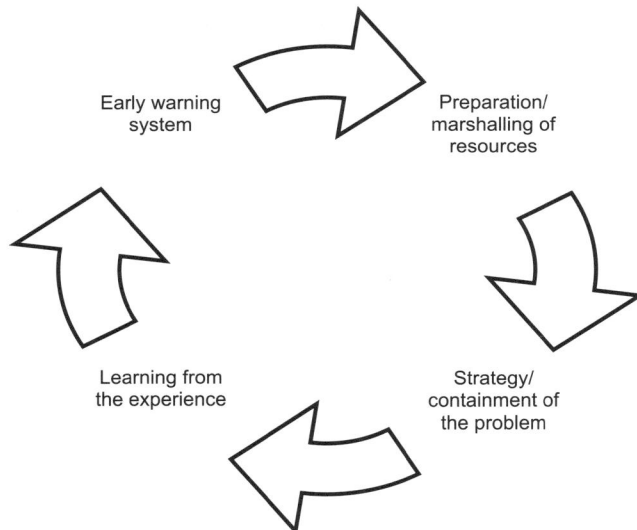

2.3.2 Issues Management Process Model

Jones & Chase (1979) suggest an Issues Management Process Model with four basic phases.

- **Issue identification and prioritisation**: monitoring the environment to identify trends from which issues might emerge, and stakeholder cues signalling potential issues, and prioritising issues on the basis of risk assessment.

- **Issue analysis**: determining the origin of the issue and its likely future evolution. This may involve a survey of existing qualitative and quantitative research and organisational knowledge networks and/or new applied research about the issue and its relevance to the organisation, targeted towards opinion leaders and media gatekeepers (what are potential influencers saying about the issue?) It may also involve an audit of the company's present position (if any) with regard to the issue, and its strengths and weaknesses in positioning itself on the issue.

- **Issue change strategy options**: making basic decisions about what the organisation's response to the issue should be.

- **Issue action programming**: policy formation and co-ordination of resources to support response objectives. Issues management may be the responsibility of the corporate communication department, but it may also be headed by the legal, government relations or risk management functions. In any case, it usually involves the input of a cross-functional (multi-disciplinary) team which meets regularly and at need, to examine issues from multiple corporate perspectives.

MARKETING AT WORK

application

The **Concerned Consumer Index** is a monthly measurement of consumer attitudes, conducted by research organisation Populus, in association with Good Business and *The Times*. According to the Populus web site (www.populuslimited.com):

The survey shows that nine out of ten people feel that companies have a wider responsibility than just delivering goods at the lowest possible price. As we noted in section 2.1, the Populus survey also shows that three-quarters of the population claim to weigh-up a company's reputation before buying its products or services, and nearly three in five people say they actively avoid purchasing from certain companies because of questions they have about their social, environmental or ethical track record.

What marks out the 'Concerned Consumer' is that they do all these things. They belong to that half of the adult population that not only cares about social, environmental and ethical issues but actually does so enough to change their purchasing behaviour. They make decisions based on values as well as value. They are prepared to reward companies that they feel care about more than just selling to them as cheaply as possible.

Concerned Consumers are prepared to act. 50% seek out information about companies before buying from them on a regular basis. They are also ready to urge others to follow their lead. Two in five of them say they recommend goods and services to others on a frequent basis, nearly half as many again as the rest of the population. They are also more likely to pick up on stories both good and bad about the way businesses conduct themselves, to register these and to translate them into future buying decisions.

For reflection: What do these research findings imply for the kinds of 'sensitivities' of stakeholder audiences that organisations will need to take into account, and the kinds of messages they will need to convey in their corporate communications?

Link: http://www.populuslimited.com/case-studies

The Populus surveys provide some interesting short case studies on how stakeholder attitude research can be used to identify potential issues, and plan communication campaigns.

2.3.3 Seven steps to issues management

Regester & Larkin (2008, pp. 123–131) recommend a seven-step practical implementation model summarised in a helpful checklist, which we have adapted here.

Step 1   **Monitoring**

☐   Analyse the business environment

☐   Monitor what is being said, written and done by the public, media, pressure/interest groups, government and other opinion leaders

☐   Constantly monitor new research findings, specialist media, competitor/regulatory activity and benchmark organisations for early warning signals

☐   Consider which issues and actions related to them may impact on the company or its strategic business units

Step 2   Issue identification

- [ ] Assess which elements of the business environment are important

- [ ] Look for trends and patterns which are potentially significant

- [ ] Identify the issues that impact on the company and are (or are likely to) gain widespread support

- [ ] Analyse the type of issue and where it is in its life cycle

Step 3   Issue prioritisation

- [ ] Assess how far-reaching an issue's impact is likely to be: product, sector, company, industry?

- [ ] Assess what is at stake: profit, reputation, freedom of action? (This will help to present a business case for allocation of resources to issues management.)

- [ ] Assess the likelihood of occurrence

- [ ] Assess the immediacy of the issue, or time available for response

Step 4   Issue analysis and preparation

- [ ] Analyse priority issues in more detail

- [ ] Assign each issue to an appropriately experienced individual within the organisation, who will act as 'issue champion': an authoritative, up-to-date source of information on the issue to assist task forces and managers in planning issue-related activities.

- [ ] Determine the probable impact on the organisation as precisely as possible

- [ ] Establish issue management/support teams if appropriate

- [ ] Identify and prioritise/rank stakeholders or issue owners (as supporters and opponents)

- [ ] Identify opinion leaders and influencers who might be co-opted to support or advance the organisation's position, or proactively build relationships (eg via consultation, sponsorship of research/publications)

- [ ] Build equity early, by developing and managing influential relationships with supportive academic and other opinion leaders, informed journalists, regulatory authorities, industry and employee associations, policy units, political groups, pressure and interest groups

- [ ] Set up an appropriately experienced/resourced task force to define and manage issue response strategies

Step 5   Strategy decision

- [ ] Evaluate strategic options

- [ ] Identify target audience groups

- [ ] Formulate a strategic response and define the content of the message

- [ ] Determine what resources are needed, and what specific actions should be taken, by whom and when (action planning)

Step 6 Implementation

☐ Implement the policies and programmes approved by management: information/education programmes, lobbying, regulatory affairs, media management and so on (as discussed in Chapters 8 to 10)

☐ Prepare background briefing materials (key messages, background information, presentation kits, FAQ sheets etc) for media/public contacts

☐ Communicate the response effectively with each target group in a credible form

☐ Advocate the company position, to prevent negative impacts and encourage supportive behaviours

Step 7 Evaluation

☐ Evaluate the success of policies and programmes to determine future strategies

☐ Capture learnings from failures and successes.

ACTIVITY 6   evaluation

Review the issues management processes of your own organisation, or any organisation that may form the focus of your assessment, obtaining (where possible) copies of any documentation.

Evaluate these issues management processes, using the above checklist as a general guide to good practice. What omissions can you identify (if any), that you might want to recommend?

2.4 Early warning systems

In the early stages of an issue, there will probably be limited public visibility: comment (if any) will be from 'overly concerned' internal or external stakeholders, pressure or interest groups, or specialist media. Once the issue escalates into a crisis (because the risk event has happened, or the hidden problem has come to light), the level of media comment typically rises exponentially. At this point, the issue can become unmanageable, with the company unable to take initiative because of the need to defend against multiple points of attack on the issue. It is therefore vitally important for an organisation to have early warning systems in place to pick up the first signals of a problem, in order either to solve the problem or to gain proactive control over how it is communicated.

An early warning system may involve:

- Establishing mechanisms (eg regular issues management team meetings, ongoing research, periodic feedback-seeking from key stakeholders) to gather information on potential issues

- Environmental scanning for potential issues. These may include possible legislative or regulatory activity, or law suits affecting the business, changes in the business climate, changes in social trends that may make policies or practices unacceptable, competitor activity, business partner/ally activity (because of the risk of damage by association), product quality and safety issues and pressure group activity

- Internal systems and performance monitoring (as part of ongoing risk management), to identify potential issues arising from factors such as poor internal controls, poor health and safety procedures, or the need to amend profit forecasts

- Identifying the 'sensitivities' of key stakeholder groups, areas in which they will be susceptible to risk perception and bad news

- Monitoring customer feedback, employee concerns, critical incident reports and specialist media comment, being alert for perceptions of risk

- Defining criteria for selecting and prioritising issues or 'topics' which need to be formally monitored and managed

- Risks analysis of highlighted incidents, issues and trends, to determine whether the issue needs to be taken seriously and become the subject of contingency planning

Issues will generally be prioritised using risk analysis (as described in section 1 above): how **likely** is it that the issue will cause a negative impact for the organisation – and how **significant** is the likely impact?

MARKETING AT WORK

application

Insurance giant **Swiss Re** has developed a systematic approach to proactive issues management, intended to:

- Meet the increasing demands of more critical stakeholders
- Manage emerging gaps between corporate action and stakeholder expectations
- Implement a global 'one voice' approach to communication on key topics

It starts by defining the '**sensitivities**' of its key stakeholder groups. For clients, these are identified as capital strength, expertise, and payment of claims; for investors, profitability, capital management and transparency; for regulators, capital adequacy and transparency; and for the general public, reliability, corporate governance and restructuring.

The company has defined criteria for selecting and prioritising '**Top Topics**' which need to be monitored and managed. These are defined by: potentially significant impact on corporate value, need for interaction with external stakeholders and need for action in terms of formulating and communicating a corporate position.

Swiss Re then utilises a five-stage process for **Top Topic issues management**:

- Topic identification: monitoring industry trends, product threats, regulatory issues and internal processes

- Topic analysis: by in-house experts

- Options development: should the organisation react, adapt or pro-actively shape the issue?

- Action: contingency planning and external and internal communication, co-ordinated by a Topic Manager (the top in-house expert on the topic)

- Process evaluation: effectiveness of communication, evolution of the topic

2.5 Issues management strategies

Jones & Chase (1979) propose three basic strategic options for issues management:

- **Reactive change** strategy (based on reluctance to change) attempts to find ways to continue existing behaviour eg by lobbying to maintain the *status quo* of public policy, or promoting the organisation's position on issues to gain or maintain public acceptance.

- **Adaptive change** strategy (based on openness to change and learning) seeks proactively to anticipate pressure for change and initiative constructive dialogue with stakeholders to find mutually acceptable compromise positions.

- **Dynamic response** strategy (based on a desire for change leadership) anticipates and attempts to shape the direction of public opinion and public policy, by setting the agenda and proactively determining how, when and where the dialogue over the issue will be carried out. In effect, the organisation becomes an advocate or agent of change.

Heugens *et al.* (2002, cited in van Riel & Fombrun, 2007) also offer a menu of strategic responses, depending on (a) the degree of public activism or resistance around the issue and (b) the time available for response.

Four issues management strategies

		Low	High
Allowed	*Long*	Silence	Dialogue with owners of the issue
response time	*Short*	Advocacy/ persuasion	Crisis communication

Public awareness and activism

- If awareness and organised activism are low, and there is little time pressure, the organisation may maintain **silence** on the issue, in order to enable it to implement changes, or marshal arguments, before the issue 'breaks'.

- If awareness and organised activism are low, but time is short before the issue escalates, the organisation may seek to pre-empt negative media coverage or stakeholder intervention, by 'getting in first' with its position (**advocacy**), and persuading potential opponents to take a less public or negative position.

- If awareness and activism are high, but there is little time pressure, the organisation can seek to enter into genuine two-way communication (**dialogue**) with the owners of the issue (groups directly affected and/or pressure and advocacy groups who claim to represent them), in order to secure understanding, support or mutually acceptable compromise agreements.

- If awareness and activism are high and time is short before the issue escalates out of control, there is a need for **crisis communication** to defuse or otherwise deal with the issue as a matter of urgency. We will discuss this activity in detail in section 4 of this chapter.

2.6 The issues management plan

An issues management and communication plan should consist of two key sections (Doorley & Garcia, 2007, p. 305).

- **Analysis**: identifying the issue, event or potential crisis; assessing the scope and likelihood of operational or reputational damage; and identifying the stakeholders likely to be affected.

- **Action plan**: the steps to take to protect the company from operational harm and to protect or restore the company's reputation.

ASSESSMENT TIP

format

Doorley & Garcia (*op cit*, p. 306) offer the following template for an Issues Management Plan, which you may like to use if asked to produce one in your assessment.

ISSUE ANALYSIS

☐ **Threat assessment**: identified issue, why it requires management, likelihood of occurrence, likely impact on the company and its stakeholders, likelihood that the company can minimise or prevent the harm (or make matters worse)

☐ **Magnitude analysis**: relative magnitude of the threat's impact on the company's reputation and operations (across several alternative scenarios, if relevant)

☐ **Likelihood analysis**: relative probability that the event will take place and will cause operational or reputational damage (taking account of different scenarios)

☐ **Affected constituencies**: inventory of stakeholders likely to be affected by the issue, and their likely attitudes or behaviours as a result

☐ **Additional information required**: additional specific information that needs to be obtained in order to fully assess the threat or develop the response plan

ISSUES MANAGEMENT PLAN

☐ **Business objectives**: business goals that the actions and communications will accomplish, formulated as desired outcomes (eg maintain market share despite a product recall, sustain productivity during a restructuring, preserve the ability to raise capital in the wake of financial scandal)

☐ **Issues management strategies**: how the business objectives will be achieved (in terms of conceptual frameworks, policies and processes, eg investigation, silence, advocacy or dialogue)

☐ **Actions to take (tactics)**: specific business decisions that need to be made, tactics to implement in response to, or in anticipation of, an issue (eg changes to an operating process, convening of a response team, steps to communication with stakeholders). This may be a menu of possible actions to be considered under various scenarios. It should include a timetable of expected events and actions.

☐ **Staffing**: designated team(s) who will work on issues day-to-day, frequency of core team meetings/contacts, internal and external resources who may be co-opted to the core team at need (eg legal counsel, crisis communication agency, or functional experts who can contribute depending on the nature of the crisis)

☐ **Logistics/budget**: forecast of the physical and financial resources required (if information is available) to manage the issue. (In general terms, issues management should not be driven by a budget, and certainly should not be held up while a budget is being developed and approved.)

COMMUNICATIONS PLAN

☐ **Communication objectives**: desired outcomes from communication (eg change in knowledge, awareness, support, feelings; steps the audience should take; neutralise negative messages)

☐ **Communication strategies**: how objectives will be achieved, in overview (eg keep stakeholders aware of progress being made to solve problems)

☐ **Target audience(s)**: to whom messages will be directed, in order of priority

☐ **Messages**: core themes to be reinforced, core 'take home' messages for stakeholders

☐ **Tactics**: detailed actions to take (eg prepare press releases, post CEO message on web site, advertisements, employee e-mails, key shareholder conference calls)

☐ **Documents**: specific pieces of communication to be drafted (press releases, media FAQs, employee FAQs, call centre FAQs/scripts, employee e-mails, ad agency briefs)

3 Managing pressure groups

3.1 Pressure and interest groups

KEY CONCEPT   concept

A **pressure group** is a group of people who have got together to promote a particular cause or issue (a causal pressure group or promotional group) or to promote the interests of a particular constituency (a sectional pressure group or interest group).

Individual stakeholders may be unable to exercise influence over an organisation, whether as consumers, employees or members of the public at large, in relation to a particular issue or infringement of their rights. In these circumstances, they may seek to enhance their power by joining or supporting a pressure group. These groups are an increasingly vocal and energetic movement, tackling a wide range of issues from climate change and animal welfare to trading standards, workplace discrimination, litter, noise, urban renewal – and so on. There are now more than 2,000 single-issue campaign groups in the UK alone, ranging from major multi-national organisations like Greenpeace or Amnesty International to specialist groups such as Surfers Against Sewage.

With internet and mobile phone technologies at their disposal, members of these groups do not have to meet to transmit information, opinions and direct action calls. This mass communication networking has significantly increased the potential power of pressure groups.

MARKETING AT WORK

application

In 1986, a small UK group called London Greenpeace (not linked to the Greenpeace environmental organisation) implemented a leaflet campaign – 'What's wrong with **McDonalds**?' – alleging that fast food giant McDonalds was guilty of environmental damage, unethical marketing to children, contribution to poor health and nutrition, and poor human relations policies. In 1989, McDonalds countered with 'McFact Cards' countering some of the allegations, but in 1990, in the face of continuing allegations, they served writs on identified leaders of the group for libel.

Known popularly as the 'McLibel' case, the trial began in 1994. McDonalds issued media releases arguing that the action was about 'the right to stop people telling lies' – against a widespread popular perception that this was a freedom of speech issue. The defendants were David to the McDonalds Goliath: nevertheless, they scored significant points on issues of health and nutrition. Meanwhile, understandably, the case attracted widespread media attention.

The case dragged on until 1996: the longest running case of its kind. McDonalds finally won the case – but lost the publicity war. The total cost to the corporation was estimated at around £10 million. They had arguably publicised their opponents' case more widely than any small-group leafleting campaign could have achieved – although the case may also have deterred other potential pressure group opponents (Davies *et al.*, 2005, p. 119). McDonalds were also forced (or persuaded) to change their strategy, particularly in the area of health and nutrition, implementing new 'healthy choices' options under the 'I'm Lovin' It' global re-positioning campaign.

Meanwhile, the **McSpotlight** web site (www.mcspotlight.org) was launched, with the mission statement: 'McDonalds spends over $2 billion a year broadcasting their glossy image to the world. This is a small space for alternatives to be heard.' The site had the tagline: 'McLibel, McDonalds, Multinationals. Judge for yourself.' It is worth visiting the site for yourself, to find out more about the **McLibel** case – as an example of how activists can use the internet to counter corporations' corporate communications and force corporations to defend their reputations (with litigation as a last resort!)...

Link: http://www.mcspotlight.org

ACTIVITY 7

application/format

List the specific causal and sectional pressure groups which are relevant to the sector and activity of your work organisation, or other selected organisation. Highlight those with which it has (or has had) direct dealings, relationships or problems.

Select one causal and one sectional pressure group from your list which has (or may have) an impact on, or involvement with, your organisation, and research:

- Its membership, size and budget
- Its aims and objectives
- The nature of its potential impact (positive or negative) on your organisation
- The nature of your organisation's relationship with the group (if any).

Format your findings appropriately for use in an Appendix to an issues management report.

3.2 Pressure group influence

Pressure group influence is based on the idea of banding together to form a coalition. Collective power both enlarges and leverages influence: it creates a larger presence or 'voice'; potentially attracts or co-opts influential members; and generates increasing networks, ideas and resources – which can be used for further promotion and growth in membership.

Methods used by pressure groups to wield influence include:

- Attempting to **influence government policy** (eg by employing lobbyists, making politicians directors of the group, providing members for government committees and consultative bodies, or donating funds to political parties)

- **Raising awareness and influencing public opinion** (and therefore exerting indirect influence on government or organisational policy) by advertising, public relations and publicity, and 'direct action' (eg volunteers confronting loggers or whaling fleets, boycotting brands with poor environmental or ethical records and so on).

- **Using their legitimate power to influence organisational decisions**. Recognised trade unions, for example, have formal power to negotiate on behalf of their members, and to use the threat of legitimate industrial action (eg official strike action) to reinforce their position. They have legal rights to be consulted on matters of significant interest or concern to their members (such as changes to working conditions, health and safety risks and any threat of redundancies).

- **Offering information and advice**, to influence their decision-making and policy formation. This may take the form of:

    - Raising awareness of an issue, and highlighting its potential impact on the business and its stakeholders

    - Providing research, statistics or other supporting information (eg signed petitions demonstrating public concern) to shape the organisation's thinking

    - Providing policy guidelines and benchmarks for best practice in relation to the issue

    - Using case studies, conferences or business networking to demonstrate the practice of (and benefits to) organisations who are leading the way on the issue

    - Offering incentives and rewards for the organisation to change its policy and practice on the issue (eg endorsement of its products, publicised awards, or co-promotions to sell the brand to the pressure group's membership and supporters).

- Offering the **opportunity to gain CSR or environmental credentials** through association with the group, or through showing support for the issue. Many organisations actively pursue relationships with pressure groups in order to enhance their image and reputation.

ACTIVITY 8

concept

It is important to realise that the organisation may regard pressure group influence not just as a potential nuisance, source of poor press and public relations, or constraint on decision-making but as a positive resource! Explain three ways in which pressure groups could represent a positive resource for the organisation.

An organisation may choose proactively to **ally or associate itself** with pressure groups which reflect its own corporate values, or those of its customers, in order to:

- **Support the aims of group, which further its own purposes**. For example, a bus or train company may ally with anti-pollution groups: their interests coincide, in that getting more people to use public transport reduces traffic emissions – and promoting reduced traffic emissions encourages more people to use public transport!

- **Form an association in people's minds**, so that supporters of the pressure group or cause will be disposed to support the brand (affinity or cause-related marketing). This may be practically reinforced by promotions in which, for example, a percentage of profits from sales of a product are donated to a charity.

- **Demonstrate its ethical and social responsibility credentials**, by promoting the fact that it is contributing to good causes (or causes supported by its customer base). Supermarkets, banks and other organisations that rely on a local customer base often have charitable fundraising and donation as part of their community involvement programmes, for example.

3.3 Managing pressure groups

It should be obvious that the corporate communication function has a specific role in the management of pressure groups, and the mitigation or exploitation of their impacts on the organisation.

- **Planned corporate communications** to encourage interaction and dialogue with relevant pressure groups. For key pressure groups, this may involve establishing direct contacts, with a view to discussing issues and potential for co-operation or sponsorship. There may be opportunities for contact at issues-based or industry conferences. More generally, the communications mix will include advertising, corporate reports and brochures, and public and media relations activity: stating the organisation's position on issues, demonstrating its commitment to social responsibility and ethics, and (where appropriate) highlighting its willingness to partner with pressure groups. These messages will be directed both at members of pressure groups and at the wider audiences who might be influenced by them.

- **Developing relationship, collaboration or association strategies**, such as sponsorship deals, co-branding or co-promotions, or cause-related sales promotions (eg motivating extra purchases by offering to denote a percentage of the sales price to a cause or charity).

- **Developing marketing approaches** such as societal, cause-related, fair trade, green and internal marketing (discussed earlier), to pre-empt, address – and if possible exploit opportunities arising from – pressure group activity.

- **Developing specific corporate branding and positioning messages** derived from interactions with pressure groups, in order to maximise their benefit for sales, brand positioning and corporate reputation.

- **Issues and crisis management**: proactive approaches to managing the effects of unplanned and uncontrollable messages such as news stories, reviews, opinion articles or blogs (web logs) which could put the organisation in a bad – or positive – light.

From the recommended reading list, you should read through:

- *Davies, Chun, da Silva & Roper,* **Corporate Reputation & Competitiveness** *(2003), 'Defending a reputation'.*

- *Doorley & Garcia,* **Reputation Management: The key to successful public relations and corporate communication**, *(2007) Chapters 11 'Issues Management' and 12 'Crisis Communication'.* ■

4 Crisis communication

KEY CONCEPT

concept

Crisis communication is the issuing of 'emergency' communications to inform stakeholders in a crisis and/or to minimise or counter the negative PR effects of crises. A crisis might include: the recall of a product due to safety defects; an ecological disaster such as an oil spill; or revelations of unethical behaviour by the organisation or its suppliers.

Despite the best issues and risk management effort, any organisation is potentially at risk of an event that causes significant operational and/or reputational damage. Crisis PR, many practitioners believe, has one defining characteristic: it will happen to you (Franklin *et al.*, 2009).

'Whether a company survives a crisis with its reputation, operations, and financial condition intact is determined less by the severity of the crisis – the underlying event – than by the timeliness and quality of its response to the crisis... Effective crisis response – including both what a company does and what it says – provides companies with a competitive advantage and can even enhance reputation. Ineffective crisis response can cause significant harm to a company's operations, reputation and competitive position.' (Doorley & Garcia, 2007, p. 327)

Effective crisis communication requires very careful management: recognising and responding to the likely level of concern; telling the organisation's side of the story without appearing to excuse or 'cover up'; demonstrating care and concern about the impact of the event on the target audience; and demonstrating action to solve the problem. Positive pre-established stakeholder relationships will be helpful in mobilising support (eg from journalists willing to give the organisation the benefit of the doubt, or from an independent, credible 'champion' who can vouch for the organisation and its steps to resolve the problem).

MARKETING AT WORK
application

'THIS just in – more bad news for **Coca-Cola**'s Dasani bottled water brand, which we learnt this week is merely filtered from the stuff that pours from taps in Sidcup, southeast London...

In my local newsagents, there's a sign next to the 500ml Dasani bottles, all unsold. It read: 'Buy one for 69p, get one free'.

Oh dear. The lady behind the counter says it's coming off sale this week – and is currently being given free to the paperboys and papergirls, who clearly don't read the papers they deliver. If they did, they would know that Coca-Cola has got itself into one of the worst **product crises management** scenarios for years – one which could cost the Atlanta-based giant up to $2 billion.

How Coca-Cola ever thought they could get away with this does smack of 1970s style American arrogance. Almost everything they have done since being found out has made matters worse. The company tried to calm Fleet Street [the British press] by saying that the Sidcup plant had been 'uniquely designed for the UK market'. To worsen this insult they assured analysts in the City that in France, where Dasani is to be rolled out, the water would come from a genuine mineral source.'

Does Coke think this is going to go down well in the average newspaper newsroom? As Del Boy might have said: *Quelle plonkeurs!* Coca-Cola's communications got worse when they allowed the line 'perfected by NASA' to be used by their briefers. It is true to say that the industrial process used in Sidcup and in America by Dasani was originally invented to serve the space agency. But in this country you don't mix NASA and water. People think you're taking the p***, which is, in more senses than one, exactly what the great Coca-Cola Company has been doing this week.'

Times Online (Yelland, 2004)

Identify the stakeholders in this situation. How were they impacted by the issue – and by Coke's communications about it? What did Coke get wrong here – and what alternative approaches might have worked better?

4.1 What is a 'crisis'?

KEY CONCEPT
concept

A **crisis** may be defined as any event or series of events that can imminently and significantly damage a company's reputation.

Doorley & Garcia (2007, p. 328) emphasise that a crisis is not necessarily a catastrophic event (although it may be), but rather an event that, left to usual business processes, causes significant reputational, operational or financial harm. Fink (1986, p. 15) suggests that: 'From a practical, business-oriented point of view, a crisis (a turning point) is any... situation that runs the risk of:

- Escalating in intensity
- Falling under close media or government scrutiny
- Interfering with the normal operations of business

- Jeopardising the positive public image presently enjoyed by a company or its officers
- Damaging a company's bottom line in any way.'

Some examples of crises therefore include: sabotage or extortion (attempts to extort money from companies by product tampering or contamination); the discovery of fraud or mismanagement; product safety recalls; consumer boycotts; a significant restatement of a company's financial position or profit forecasts; industrial accidents; technical failure or human error causing service/delivery failure or disasters (eg factory explosions or fires).

MARKETING AT WORK

application

The 'best practice' example of turning around an emotionally charged crisis, often quoted in the literature, is **Johnson & Johnson's** handling of the situation in 1982 and again in 1986 when its top-selling analgesic brand (Tylenol) had to be recalled, following a number of deaths from cyanide adulteration of a few capsules by an unknown extortionist.

The CEO at the time, Jim Burke, considered that immediate and forceful measures were needed: first, to ensure public safety and second, to restore trust in the company and the product.

The company recalled 31 million capsules from shops – and homes – across the US, using full-page newspaper advertisements and television spots to announce the move. Johnson & Johnson redesigned the packaging to make it tamper proof – and swiftly regained 95% of its pre-crisis market share. After the first incident, the company put a formal crisis plan in place to handle any similar event.

Johnson & Johnson was regarded as demonstrating both concern for its customers and commitment to its own corporate ethical standards: its reputation was enhanced, rather than damaged, by the crisis – and it continually features near the top of Most Admired Companies rankings.

According to Murray and Shohen (1992), the company's resilience in the face of crisis was supported by: a strong and positive reputation before the crises; being open with the media at the time of each crisis and afterwards; and clear, public leadership by the CEO at the time. The company has also said that 'its actions had been pre-ordained by its widely heralded corporate credo [ethical values]; no other response could even have been contemplated.' (Augustine, 2000).

4.1.1 Phases of crisis

Hainsworth & Meng (1988) identify the following phases through which most crises pass:

- **Scanning**: the organisation scans the environment to pick up signals that might herald a disaster (as for issues management, discussed earlier) and devises contingency plans, recovery plans and communication plans for identified risks.
- **Pre-impact**: the organisation prepares a specific crisis management plan, deploys the crisis team and informs key stakeholders of the impending crisis
- **Impact**: the crisis management plan is implemented, and close contact is maintained with the media and key stakeholder groups. The aim is to neutralise and localise (contain) the crisis, without hiding or diminishing its significance to stakeholders.
- **Readjustment**: the organisation implements strategies for reputational repair, and remains consistent, positive and concerned through investigations, compensation claims (where relevant) and other post-crisis tasks.

4.1.2 Costs and consequences of crisis

The financial and reputational costs of crises can be very high. Examples (Jolly, 2001, p. 93) include:

- Exxon ('Valdez' oil tanker spill): $13 billion
- PanAm (Lockerbie air crash): $652 million
- P & O Ferries (Zeebrugge sinking): $70 million
- Union Carbide (Bhopal) $527 million
- Perrier (benzene contamination incident): $263 million
- Occidental Oil (Piper Alpha oil rig explosion): $1.4 million
- Barings Bank (collapse): $900 million

Identify, from some of the case examples mentioned in this chapter and your wider reading, some of the possible *consequences* of crises for an organisation.

Fombrun & van Riel (2004, p. 34) argue that crisis costs are one way to estimate reputational capital. 'Over time, some companies recover dissipated value quickly and the crisis fizzles. Others experience more extended damage. Research suggests that the enduring difference may well lie in how the crisis is handled and what the reputation of the company was beforehand.'

4.2 A simple model for crisis communication

As a broad overview, Augustine (2000) sets out the following practical model of 'six stages of crisis management'.

Stage	Comments
Stage 1: **Avoid the crisis**	• 'Amazingly, [prevention] is usually skipped altogether, even though it is the least costly and the simplest way to control a potential crisis.'
	• Risk analysis: make a list of everything that could attract troubles to the business, consider the likelihood and possible consequences, and estimate the cost of prevention.
	• Some of the items on the list may be beyond the organisation's control – but it can still plan a contingency *response* to them.
	• Preventative measures may include: preventive maintenance of facilities, improving planning and controls, maintaining confidentiality (eg in regard to sensitive negotiations), and setting clear rules and expectations for employee behaviour.
Stage 2: **Prepare to manage the crisis**	• Make contingency plans to deal with a variety of risk events ('Noah started building the ark *before* it began to rain'): action plans, communication plans, back-up computer systems.
	• Put in place essential relationships: 'the midst of a disaster is the poorest possible time to establish new relationships and to introduce yourself to new organisations.'
	• Establish a crisis centre, pre-select a crisis team, set-up ready and redundant communication mechanisms.
	• Practise/test plans eg crisis simulations, fire and evacuation drills.
Stage 3: **Recognise the crisis**	• Recognise that a crisis event has, in fact, occurred: understand how others will perceive an issue and challenge your own assumptions.
	• Don't react to a 'technical' problem when you really have a perception or public relations problem. You may be 'right' – but if you ignore concerns or handle them badly, you become 'wrong'.
	• Monitor internal and external stakeholders' criticisms, concerns and questions: ignoring first signs of crisis allows escalation.
	• Use independent investigators, as well as outsiders, to assist in understanding the situation. ('Asking the people who were responsible for preventing a problem whether or not there is a problem is like delivering lettuce by rabbit.')

Stage	Comments
Stage 4: **Contain the crisis**	• Take tough decisions fast and decisively (eg don't wait for more information if employee or consumer lives may be at risk.) • Legal advisors may lobby for 'tell 'em nothing and tell 'em slow', but it is preferable to err on the side of disclosure, to avoid an information vacuum and build credibility. 'No comment' is no longer an acceptable answer. • 'Organisations that have thought through what they stand for well in advance of crisis are those that manage crisis best... They have principles to fall back on.' • Have a dedicated group of individuals working full-time to contain the crisis (crisis management team). • Identify a single individual as the company spokesperson, who makes all public comment. • Don't leave stakeholders to get their information from the media.
Stage 5: **Resolving the crisis**	• Speed is of the essence: act fast. • Take the facts direct to the public: promptly, backed by independent corroborators or champions. • Demonstrate responsibility, willingness and transparency in investigating the problem and putting it right. • Promote resolutions and improvements, and add incentives to retain or win back stakeholders (if necessary).
Stage 6: **Profiting from the crisis**	• 'Make lemonade from the abundance of available lemons'. • Reap the benefits of enhanced stakeholder trust as a result of positive, ethical, considerate handling of the crisis. • Learn from mistakes for enhanced risk/crisis management in future.

This accessible article ('Managing the Crisis You Tried to Prevent' by Norman R Augustine) is worth reading in full if you can get hold of it, in a back copy of the Harvard Business Review (November/December 1995). It is also available in the book-form compilation: Harvard Business Review on Crisis Management (2000: Harvard Business Review).

There are many interesting articles and resources available free on the internet. You could do worse than start with the Wikipedia article on 'Crisis Communication' and follow the links.

We particularly recommend The Institute for Public Relations 'Essential Knowledge Project' article on Crisis Management and Communications, posted at:

http://www.instituteforpr.org/essential_knowledge/detail/crisis_management_and_communications

4.3 Elements of successful crisis communication

From the syllabus, and a survey of the literature, the following points can be identified as some of the key elements of successful crisis communication.

4.3.1 Preparation

As we have argued throughout this chapter, proactive planning and preparation are essential for effective risk management. Preparation for crisis (Coombs, 2006) includes:

• Creating a contingency or crisis management plan (CMP) and updating it at least annually

• Forming a designed, cross-functional crisis management team (see further below)

- Conducting simulated crisis exercises to test the plans and teams

- Pre-drafting some crisis messages, including:

    - Templates for statements by top management and news releases (Corporate Leadership Council, 2003), leaving blanks where information can be inserted when known.

    - Dark web sites: that is, pre-prepared web pages, to which access is blocked until the site is activated in the event of crisis.

    This allows the communications team to pre-draft messages, and the legal team to pre-approve them, saving time when the crisis occurs.

4.3.2 The crisis team

There is general consensus that crisis needs to be managed by a small, cross-functional, trained crisis management team, with defined roles. This ensures that it is clear – under pressure and when time is short – exactly who makes the key decisions, who decides what to say to stakeholders, who talks to the media: a clear lead is given within the organisation, and coherent, consistent messages are given out, as part of a co-ordinated response.

All communication about a crisis, both internal and external, should be channelled through the team, so that at no time will there be 'no-one available for comment': an absence of official response only creates an information vacuum – which the media will fill regardless.

Barton (2001) identifies typical members of the crisis team as public relations, legal, security, operations, finance, and human resources. However, membership will need to vary according to the nature of the crisis (eg including an IT expert in a computer-related crisis such as hacking, virus or systems failure). Team members must be trained and rehearsed/tested in crisis drills to make decisions in a crisis situation (Augustine, 2000).

4.3.3 Speed of response

Doorley & Garcia (2007, p. 331) identify speed of response as a critical factor in protecting reputation in a crisis. Time is an enemy in a crisis. 'The sooner a company is seen as taking the event seriously, acting responsibly and communicating clearly, the more likely it is that the company will emerge with its reputation and operations intact. *The Wall Street Journal's* Ronald Alsop states that: 'Crises aren't like fine wines; they don't improve with age.'

A delay in responding to a crisis can be perceived by those affected by it as indifference to the harm caused or as arrogance or evasion (confirming suspicion of guilt and eroding trust).

A swift response also avoids the creation of a **communications void** while the company decides what to say. 'A communications void is highly dangerous during a time of crisis. Silence gives critics time to gain the upper hand and reinforces the public's suspicion that a company must be guilty. Without information from the company, rumours and misinformation can proliferate fast'.

If in doubt as to when to respond in a crisis, the crisis team will need to take into account:

- Whether others are already aware of and talking about the issue

- Whether key stakeholders expect the organisation to do or say something (and how inaction or silence will be interpreted)

- Whether waiting will worsen the situation, or erode the organisation's ability to determine the outcome, compared to acting or communicating immediately.

MARKETING AT WORK application

When **Perrier** discovered that its mineral water was in danger of contamination, it immediately withdrew all supplies, suffering huge losses. By acting ethically and promptly, however, the company's reputation was protected.

Coca Cola, when faced with the same problem in Belgium, dithered (for fourteen days), played down the issue, denied liability – and suffered a huge blow to its image.

Similarly, the initial response by **Mercedes** when its then prototype vehicle the A-Class turned over, when driven by journalists, was to deny that there was a problem. The denial, which lasted eight days, turned into a crisis, as 3,000 orders were lost and the media – understandably – refused to let go of the problem. The reputation of Mercedes was dented for the first time in a long time, and only the acknowledgement of the problem, and a public statement about the actions the company was to take with regard to product and design, alleviated the pressure.

The 3Rs of crisis management: Respond, Recompense, Recover.

4.3.4 Crisis communication channels

As we suggested earlier, an organisation may pre-prepare a separate (dark) web site or section of its existing web site for a crisis. Taylor and Kent (2007) argue that more organisations should be using the internet, especially web sites, during a crisis: stakeholders, including the news media, often turn to the internet in such circumstances. Their findings on best practice for use of the internet during a crisis are as follows.

- Include all traditional media relations materials on the web site.

- Make use of interactive tools for crisis web content.

- Provide detailed and clear information on web sites in cases of product recall, to help consumers identify whether their product is part of the recall and how the recall is to be handled.

- Use the crisis web site to tell your side of the story, including statements from managers: this may be vital in steering how the story will be told.

- When necessary, create different web pages for different stakeholders, to target their interests in the crisis.

- Work with government agencies, including links to relevant agency web sites.

Of course, if the organisation has chosen a 'silence' strategy (because the crisis is small and stakeholders are unlikely to hear about it from other sources), information may deliberately be kept *off* the web site.

Intranet sites (with access confined to employees and/or selected suppliers or clients) can also be used during a crisis. Dowling (2003) noted the value of American Airlines' use of its intranet system as an effective way of keeping its employees informed (and offering access to employee assistance programmes) following the 9/11 tragedy.

A **mass notification system** may also be used to notify employees and other key stakeholders of a crisis. Target recipients' contact information is pre-programmed into a database. Crisis managers can then enter short messages into the system, at need, for transmission to specified recipient networks, via specified channels (eg phones, text messages, voice messages, and e-mail). The system also allows for response – which is important when managers need to verify that key target individuals have received the news.

4.3.5 Agenda setting

KEY CONCEPT

concept

The **'agenda'** of public and media discourse is what people see as important, and how issues are presented: how perceptions of an issue or crisis are shaped.

The news media has a significant role in deciding:

- **'What is news'**: that is, what events are considered newsworthy (and therefore are likely to be reported in the news media) and

- **How it is reported**: that is, what 'frame' will be put on the story, or how reporters and editors will perceive, conceptualise and present the story. Framing draws on journalists' judgement and understanding, but may also be influenced by the editorial policy of the newspaper or TV/radio station, and/or the desire to maximise audience share (and revenue) by sensationalising issues. The same event or issue can be portrayed in a positive, negative or neutral light.

However, one of the goals of crisis communication is for the organisation itself to take control of the communication agenda: to influence what aspects of the issue are talked about and how they are presented – and not allowing the media, adversaries or the rumour mill to define the situation (and stakeholder responses to it). According to Doorley & Garcia (2007, p. 336) this means:

- **Tell it all**: bundle everything that will inevitably be known into the smallest number of news cycles possible, rather than letting bad news 'drip' out one bit at a time. However, disclose only what you are legally permitted to say (eg under confidentiality or privacy laws) and only what you know (eg if causes or the extent of the damage are not fully known, say so, with the promise that information will be notified as soon as possible).

- **Tell it fast**: try and be the one who brings the news to stakeholders' attention, rather than reacting to someone else's account, and get your information to stakeholders before rumours reach them.

- **Tell them what you're doing about it**: outline, as early as possible, the steps that are underway to resolve the crisis its underlying causes (if only the launching of an investigation).

- **Tell them when it's over**: update stakeholders to let them know that the crisis has been solved.

- **Get back to work**: don't let the crisis distract attention from business continuity. Crisis communication roles are clearly assigned to or by the crisis team: people not directly involved, should maintain business as usual.

ACTIVITY 10

concept

From our coverage here and in Chapter 8 on public and media relations, give some examples of the kinds of communication mechanisms an organisation might use for crisis PR, in order to begin shaping the media agenda.

4.3.6 Rumour management

Rumours circulate very fast in and around organisations, particularly with the advent of the internet, where vast amounts of information and opinion are exchanged, with very little verification or accountability for accuracy. Rumours tend to be passed on unchecked, and once started, can spread like wildfire (and often, with increasing inaccuracy) among employees, customers, suppliers, investors and other stakeholder networks. Some damaging rumours may be deliberately planted by adversaries (such as terminated employees or suppliers, competitors, activists or investors wanting to manipulate the market). If rumours are picked up by the news media, or aired in other credible forums, they may be legitimised: audiences without access to the true facts (or who are already predisposed to distrust a corporation's version of events) may assume that the rumour is true or confirmed 'because it was in the paper'.

ACTIVITY 11

concept

From your own experience of the 'rumour mill' in an organisation, what would you anticipate to be the effects of leaving rumours unaddressed?

Rumours generally arise from an unsatisfied need for information in the face of uncertainty, change and crisis (Shibutani, 1966). If no authoritative or adequate information is supplied to help people make sense of events, they alleviate their anxiety by filling in the gaps themselves. Rumours arise and are believed when official information is lacking or is not believed.

If management does not take stakeholders' concerns seriously, they will find reassurance from those around them, by sharing and exaggerating rumours. 'When people – whether as employees facing corporate downsizing... or investors in a corporation under investigation – do not believe they know the worst, they look for the slightest scrap of information to validate their fears. But when they know what will happen next, what the worst case is likely to be, or that the worst is in fact over, they are less likely to be driven by rumours or look for hidden meanings.' (Doorley & Garcia, 2007, p. 343)

An important role of corporate communication in a crisis is therefore to minimise or neutralise rumour by supplying information. 'Paradoxically, telling more and telling it faster has the effect of eliminating a rumour... Just as backburning removes the fuel that would feed a fire, so timely and robust communication removes the fuel – uncertainty and fear – that feeds a rumour' (*ibid*, p. 339).

In order to control or eliminate rumours, the organisation can therefore:

- Provide fast, clear, direct, honest, accurate, substantial information about the crisis, its causes, consequences and how it is being handled, to affected and interested audiences.

- Pre-empt rumours by exploiting media relations. In the very early stages of a rumour, very few journalists will know about the rumour or be working on the story: if you can convince them not to pursue a story at this stage, the chances are high that it will simply disappear. Once the story breaks, many more journalists want to cover the story, and it becomes much more difficult to control.

- Pre-empt rumours by addressing counter-communications to suit the news cycle (daily, weekly, fortnightly press), so that you can disarm negative information before it gets 'picked up' by another set of media.

4.3.7 Acknowledging the emotional aspects of crisis

Davies *et al.* (2003) argue that the essence of a crisis is that logic is put to one side. When people consider any issue they do so along two dimensions: the rational (cognitive) dimension that evaluates facts and arrives at an objective perspective – and the emotional (affective) dimension where feelings are important.

'In any crisis, the emphasis must be on handling the emotional aspects of the crisis, not just the more rational and information-giving tasks' (*ibid*, p. 108). In the example of the 'mad cow disease' (BSE) crisis in the UK, authorities claimed that beef was safe to eat, but this was not believed: they ignored the emotional aspects of the crisis. It does not matter one iota what leading scientific opinion is on a matter as sensitive as what we eat. What the consumer fears to be the truth is more important. Once the crisis becomes one of confidence, then significant symbolic action is essential.'

One interesting way of analysing the effect of a company attempting to present rational arguments when the public is in a heightened emotional state is **transactional analysis**, *which examines the match or mismatch between the ego states of the parties in a communication transaction. If you are interested in pursuing this area, you might look at:*

- *Davies et al. (Corporate Reputation & Competitiveness) p. 113–114.*

- *Christopher Fill (Marketing Communications: Contexts, Strategies and Applications): Chapter 16, under the heading 'Network conflict'.* ∎

4.3.8 Repairing reputational damage in a crisis

A number of writers in public relations, communication, and marketing have researched potential methods of repairing the reputational damage suffered by an organisation in crisis situations (eg Benoit 1997). A range of the strategies proposed in the literature (Coombs, 2007) includes:

- **Attack the accuser**: the crisis manager confronts the person or group claiming a problem with the organisation.

- **Denial**: the crisis manager asserts that there is no crisis.

- **Scapegoat**: the crisis manager blames external persons or groups for the crisis.

- **Excuse**: the crisis manager minimises organisational responsibility by denying intent to harm or by claiming good intentions; and/or by claiming inability to control the events that triggered the crisis, eg due to accident (lack of control over events leading to the crisis situation), provocation (the crisis was a result of response to someone else's actions) or defeasibility (lack of information about events leading to the crisis situation).

- **Justification**: the crisis manager minimises the perceived damage caused by the crisis.

- **Reminder**: the crisis manager tells stakeholders about the past good works of the organisation, to highlight trust and goodwill.

- **Ingratiation**: the crisis manager praises stakeholders for their actions and responses.

- **Compensation**: the crisis manager offers money or other benefits to victims.

- **Apology**: the crisis manager indicates that the organisation takes full responsibility for the crisis, and asks stakeholders for their understanding and forgiveness.

Note that these strategies vary widely in how much they accommodate victims of this crisis – as opposed to addressing the organisation's own reputational concerns. They can be used in the crisis response phase, or it may be perceived as more ethical to wait until the post-crisis phase to address reputational concerns.

4.3.9 Post-crisis follow-up

We noted earlier that it is important for management to focus on maintaining business as usual, as soon as possible after (or, where possible, during) a crisis. However, there are still some important tasks in the post-crisis phase.

- Crisis managers may have promised to provide additional information after the worst of the crisis has passed – and they must deliver on those promises or risk losing trust (and attracting further media scrutiny).

- The organisation may need to release updates on the recovery process, corrective actions and/or investigations and reports on the crisis (to employees, victims and regulatory bodies, for example).

- The organisation needs to share information and feedback on the crisis, and the crisis management process, in order to learn from it.

4.4 Summary

The following helpful summary is given by Davies *et al.* (2003, p. 122) of the practical lessons learned from their survey of case studies in crisis management.

- All organisations should plan for possible reputational crisis.

- Conducting a risk analysis, focusing particularly on risks from fire, explosion and theft, can identity some potential crises.

- Some issues can be predicted by picking up early warnings, for example from what is being commented upon in the technical media.

- All organisations of any size should have a crisis plan which should include the nomination of a crisis management team.

- In a crisis, all communication must be via the crisis team.

- Don't allow a media vacuum to occur. If the cause of the crisis and its solution are still unclear, then release a holding statement.

- Crises are times of emotion. A purely rational response may not be enough to protect a reputation. Going what appears to be one step too far may be the only way to respond to emotive aspects of a crisis.

- The bigger the crisis, the more it is essential for the CEO to be seen to take responsibility.

- Large corporations are vulnerable to attack from pressure groups many of which do not share the capitalist view of business. One answer could be to consult with leading pressure groups on sensitive decisions.

- Crises are often expensive in the short-term but rarely appear to damage companies in the long-run if they handle them well.

ACTIVITY 12

evaluation

Evaluate your own organisation's crisis communication plans against all the elements discussed in this section.

If you want to read about the issue of reputation defence, we can recommend:

- **Risk Issues and Crisis Management in Public Relations: A casebook of best practice,** *by Michael Regester & Judy Larkin (4th ed, 2008, Kogan Page).*

- **Harvard Business Review on Crisis Management** *(2000: Harvard Business School Press), which contains essays about particular crises such as executive defection, product recalls, business failure, and international expansion. The essay, 'Managing the Crisis You Tried to Prevent' by Norman R Augustine is a particularly accessible account of crisis management in action.* ∎

Learning objectives		Covered	
1	Evaluate reputational risk	☑	Sources of reputational risk
		☑	The risk management cycle: risk identification and assessment; risk management strategies (transfer, tolerate, terminate, treat)
		☑	Managing reputational risk
2	Explain the principles and practice of issues management	☑	What is an issue?
		☑	The issue lifecycle (Hainsworth & Meng)
		☑	Issues management models: detection/marshalling/strategy; the Issues Management Process Model (Jones & Chase); Seven Steps of Issues Management (Regester & Larkin)
		☑	Early warning systems
		☑	Issues management strategies: silence, dialogue, advocacy, crisis
		☑	Issues management plans
		☑	Managing pressure and interest groups
3	Explain the nature, role and processes of crisis management and associated communication	☑	What is a crisis?; phases of crisis; costs of crisis
		☑	Six-stage model for crisis management (Augustine)
		☑	Elements of successful crisis management: preparation; crisis team; speed of response; use of communication channels; agenda setting; rumour management; acknowledgement of emotional aspects of crisis; repairing reputational damage; post-crisis follow-up

1   Give three examples of sources of reputational risk.

2   How can risks be quantitatively assessed?

3   What is an 'issue'?

4   Describe the life cycle of an issue, according to Hainsworth & Meng.

5   Outline four phases of issues management.

6   Suggest the elements of an early warning system for issues.

7   How do pressure groups exert influence on organisations?

8   What is crisis communication?

9   How can an organisation set the agenda in a crisis situation?

10   What can an organisation do to control or eliminate rumours?

1   Answers will be based on your own organisation. Note that learning from critical incidents, past experience and the experience of other organisation is a valid set of risk management tools.

2   Again, the answers will depend on your own research.

3   The answer will, again, depend on your own organisation and research.

4   Academic research and case study examples (Regester & Larkin, *op cit*, p. 43) suggest that effective use of issues management techniques can:

- Enhance and protect corporate reputation
- Increase market share
- Build important relationships
- Protect business continuity
- Avoid regulatory impacts (by voluntarily pre-empting restrictive measures)
- Save money (by avoiding costs of crisis, non-compliance, lost revenue through consumer boycott and so on).

5   Your answer will depend on your own organisation. For further examples, you might like to browse through Regester & Larkin (2008) who draw life cycle graphs for a range of high-profile crises. It is worth having a go at such activities, because 'Presentation' is part of the 'Format' element of the CIM's Magic Formula for assessment.

6   Your answer will depend on your own organisation. Note that the output from this activity could be useful preparation for your assessment.

7   Your answer will depend on your own research – but again, do have a go at the presentation asked for in the activity (whichever format you choose). Presentation (format) is a component in the CIM's Magic Formula.

8   Pressure groups may be a positive resource as:

- A useful **barometer** of government and consumer concerns. If a pressure group represents the views of a powerful section of the community, it may be possible for the organisation to use its resources for stakeholder research and feedback-gathering.

- A source of **helpful advice and consultancy** in the group's area of concern and expertise. If the organisation recognises and seeks to remedy an area of concern in its policy or practices (eg to reduce its environmental impacts or improve its labour relations record), there may be potential for genuine collaborative problem-solving.

- A potential source of **promotional and reputational advantage**. If the organisation is able to work with a pressure group to solve problems, it may receive its approval and endorsement: using the pressure group's profile and influence to its advantage. An example includes food products receiving the Heart Foundation 'Tick of approval', or cosmetic products being certified as involving no animal testing. Such endorsements are more persuasive than mere advertising claims to the same effect, since they are perceived as coming from a concerned and expert source.

9   The consequences of crises include: product/service boycott or abandonment (eg in the case of Merck's Vioxx drug brand); loss of competitive advantage (eg Monsanto's GM products in Europe); share price collapse (eg Perrier being taken over by Nestlé) and the imposition of new, restrictive legislation (eg anti-smoking legislation).

10   Immediate communication mechanisms for crisis PR (Franklin *et al.*, 2009, p. 65) may include: some kind of **response statement** released within the first hour of an incident, and a fuller **press release** as soon as practicable; press conferences; media briefings on or off the record; a press pack; and the activation of a '**dark web site**' (pre-prepared areas of the web site closed off from public access until the information is to be released).

11   If left unaddressed, rumours can escalate an issue into a crisis, and in a crisis can cause more damage to an organisation's reputation than the crisis event itself. Some damaging rumours, for example, may become 'self-fulfilling prophecies': if a firm is rumoured to be in financial difficulty, prospective employees, financiers and suppliers may be reluctant to deal with it – making it more likely to find itself in financial difficulty...

12   Your answer will be based on your own organisation. Again, the output from this activity may be useful preparation for your assessment.

1   See section 1.1 for a list of sources of risk.

2   Risk is quantified as likelihood of risk event occurring (quantified as a score or probability) x risk impact/consequences (quantified as score or cost).

3   An issue is a condition or event that, if it continues, will have a significant effect on the functioning or performance of the organisation or on its interests. It is a potential point of conflict between an organisation and one or more of its stakeholders.

4   See section 2.2 for a full explanation.

5   Either: early warning, preparation/marshalling of resources, strategy/containment, and learning (Mitroff). Or: Identification and prioritisation, analysis, change strategy options and action programming (Jones & Chase).

6   See section 2.4 for a list of points.

7   Pressure groups can exert influence by influencing government policy; raising awareness and influencing public opinion; using legitimate power to influence management; offering information and advice; and offering endorsement.

8   Crisis communication is the issuing of communication to inform stakeholders and/or to minimise or counter negative public relation effects of a crisis situation.

9   See section 4.3.5 for a list of points.

10   See section 4.3.6 for a list of points.

Augustine, N R (2000) 'Managing the crisis you tried to prevent' in *Harvard Business Review on Crisis Management,* pp 1-32. Boston, Mass: Harvard Business Review

Barton, L (2001). *Crisis in organizations II* (2nd ed.), College Divisions South-Western: Cincinnati OH

Benoit, W L (1997) 'Image repair discourse and crisis communication' in *Public Relations Review*, 23(2), pp 177-180

Coombs, W T (2006) *Code Red in the Boardroom: Crisis Management as Organisational DNA.* Praegers: Westport, C N

Coombs, W T (2007) *Ongoing Crisis Communication: Planning, Managing, and Responding* (2nd ed.) Sage: Los Angeles

Corporate Leadership Council (2003) 'Crisis management strategies'. Posted at: http://www.executiveboard.com/EXBD/Images/PDF/Crisis%20Management%20Strategies.pdf

Davies G, Chun R, Da Silva R V & Roper S (2003) *Corporate Reputation and Competitiveness.* Routledge: Abingdon, Oxon

Doorley, J & Garcia, H F (2007) *Reputation Management: The Key to Successful Public Relations and Corporate Communications.* Routledge: New York

Dowling, J R (2003). 'American Airlines' use of mediated employee channels after the 9/11 attacks' in *Public Relations Review*, 30, pp 37-48

Dutton, J and Ottensmeyer, E (1987) 'Strategic Issue Management Systems: Forms, Functions and Contexts' in *Academy of Management Review*, 12(2) pp 355-365

Fill, C (2002) *Marketing Communications: Contexts, Strategies and Applications* (3rd ed). Pearson Education Limited: Harlow, Essex

Fink, S (1986) *Crisis Management: Planning for the Inevitable.* American Management Association: New York

Fombrun, C J & Riel, Van C B M (2004) *Fame and Fortune: How Successful Companies Build Winning Reputations* N J: Pearson Education: Upper Saddle River

Franklin B, Hogan M, Langley Q, Mosdell N & Pill E (2009) *Key Concepts in Public Relations*. Sage: London

Griffin, A (2007) *New Strategies for Reputation Management: Gaining control of issues, crises and corporate social responsibility*. Kogan Page: London

Grunig, J E & Hunt, T (1984) *Managing Public Relations*. Holt, Rinehart & Winston: New York

Hainsworth, B E (1990) 'Issues management: an overview' in *Public Relations Review*, 16 (1)

Hainsworth, B E & Meng, M (1988) 'How corporations define issues management' in *Public Relations Review*, winter

Heugens P P M A R, Bosch Van den F A J & Van Riel, C B M (2002) 'Stakeholder integration: building mutually enforcing relationships' in *Business and Society* 41(1) pp 33-61

Jolly, A (2001) *Managing Corporate Reputations*. Kogan Page: London

Jones, B L & Chase, W H (1979) 'Managing public policy issues' in *Public Relations Review* 5 (2).

Meng, M B (1992) 'Early identification aids issues management' in *Public Relations Journal*, March

Murray, E & Shohen, S (1992) 'Lessons from the Tylenol tragedy: on surviving a corporate crisis', in *Medical Marketing and Media*, February pp 14-19

Mitroff, I I (1988) 'Crisis management: cutting through the confusion' in *Sloan Management Review*, Winter pp 15-20

Regester, M & Larkin, J (2008) *Risk Issues and Crisis Management in Public Relations: A Casebook of Best Practice*. Kogan Page: London

Reputation Management., Routledge: Abingdon Oxon

Sadgrove, K (2005) *The Complete Guide to Business Risk Management*. (2nd ed). Gower: Aldersgate

Shibutani, T (1966) *Improvised News: A sociological study of rumour*. Bobbs Merril: Indianapolis

Taylor, M & Kent, M L (2007) 'Taxonomy of mediated crisis responses' in *Public Relations Review*, 33, pp140-146

Van Riel, C B M & Fombrun, C J (2007) *Essentials of Corporate Communication: Implementing Practices for Effective*

Yelland, D (2004) 'Coke could do without this message in a bottle', posted at *Times Online*: *www.thetimes.co.uk*

Index

3M, 76, 123

Above the line, 165
AC²ID Test, 57
Accenture, 121
Accounting, 7
Acquisitions, 269
Actual identity, 57, 139
Advertising, 201
Advertising media, 203
Advocacy, 328
Affinity marketing, 48
Agenda setting, 338
Albert and Whetten, 10, 104
Alcopops, 26
Altria Group, 114, 121
America's Most Admired, 147
Analysts, 267
Annual General Meeting, 271
Annual report and accounts, 271
Apple, 42
Apple i-Pod, 49
Applied identity, 59
Association, 48
Attitude, 174
Attitude surveys, 222, 225
Augustine, 335

Balanced scorecard, 78
Behaviour, 105, 174
Behaviour audits, 146
Below the line, 165
Blogs, 42
BMW, 214
Body Shop International, 202
Body Shop, The, 41, 46, 51, 76
Boundaryless structures, 86
Brand architecture, 118
Brand Asset Valuator (BAV), 149
Brand assets, 110, 135
Brand awareness, 120
Brand elements, 110
brand endorsement, 50
Brand engagement, 16
Brand equity, 151
Brand fingerprint, 118
Brand heritage, 120
brand identity, 109
Brand personality, 120
Brand positioning, 16, 50, 119
Brand Power, 149
Brand promise, 118
brand re-positioning, 175
Brand strategy, 118
Brand values, 125

Branding process, 118
BrandZ, 151
Branson, Richard, 125, 164, 220
Brent Spar, 321
Briefing a communication agency, 200
Briefing materials, 326
Britain's Most Admired Companies, 148
BSE, 340
Bureaucracies, 85
Burns and Stalker, 85

Cadbury Schweppes, 178
Campaign measurement, 221
Card Sorting, 224
Cause-related marketing, 48, 188
CEO communications, 164
CEOs, 220
Change of name, 121
Charities, 174
Christian Aid, 225
Coca Cola, 76, 153, 205, 316, 333, 337
Collaborative strategies, 47
Commercial systems for measuring reputation, 147
Communicated identity, 57, 140
Communication, 105
Communication attitude surveys, 92
Communication audit, 141
Communication audit survey instruments, 143
Communication channels, 83
Communication climate, 53, 317
Communication difficulties, 299
Communication plan, 199
Communication system, 5
Community based factors, 46
Competitive advantage, 6, 74
Competitive architecture, 16
Competitive strategies, 47
Competitiveness, 18
Compliance, 272
Comprehensive Reputation Management, 60
Conceived identity, 57, 140
Concerned Consumer Index, 324
Consensus profile, 71
Consensus profiling, 141
Consignia, 121
Consistency, 14
Consumer marketing, 8
Contingency plans, 316
Core competences, 52
Corporate, 52
Corporate advertising, 201, 209
Corporate brand, 13
Corporate branding, 105
Corporate communication, 5, 166
Corporate communication mix, 200
Corporate communication strategies, 53
Corporate communications, 171, 332
Corporate culture, 37